JC Smith's The Law of Contract

Paul S Davies

OXFORD
UNIVERSITY PRESS

OXFORD

UNIVERSITY PRESS

Great Clarendon Street, Oxford, OX2 6DP,
United Kingdom

Oxford University Press is a department of the University of Oxford.
It furthers the University's objective of excellence in research, scholarship,
and education by publishing worldwide. Oxford is a registered trade mark of
Oxford University Press in the UK and in certain other countries

Published in the United States of America by Oxford University Press
198 Madison Avenue, New York, NY 10016, United States of America

British Library Cataloguing in Publication Data

Data available

Library of Congress Control Number: 2015957950

ISBN 978–0–19–873353–9

Printed in Great Britain by
Bell & Bain Ltd., Glasgow

To Emma

Outline Contents

Detailed Contents

Preface and Acknowledgements

Professor Sir John Cyril Smith CBE QC FBA published the fourth edition of *The Law of Contract* in 2002. It was an excellent book: short and concise, but detailed and well suited to undergraduate contract law courses. His book provided a superb overview of the subject, suitable both for those approaching contract law for the first time, and for those revising the subject. This was facilitated by a large number of short chapters, each broken down under numerous headings. Moreover, JC Smith never wrote in a purely explanatory fashion, but his work was full of opinions and critical analysis. The aims of this book are the same as the last edition of *The Law of Contract*: to provide a pithy discussion of the key areas of contract law. The law is not simplified and the analysis is not misleading. But nor is the law presented in an unnecessarily detailed or confusing way. The focus is firmly placed on the leading cases. There is no other way of understanding contract law than by understanding the major cases. Contract law is still, fundamentally, a 'black-letter law' subject, which has been developed by judges through their reasoned decisions. Students are very much encouraged to read the cases in order to appreciate fully the boundaries and conceptual underpinnings of the subject. It is hoped that this book will help readers to appreciate how those cases fit together, and some of the crucial issues on which students might want to focus.

This book owes a great deal to Downing College, Cambridge. JC Smith was a student and subsequently an Honorary Fellow of Downing. Nearly 60 years after JC Smith, I also studied law at Downing. My first supervisors in the college were Cherry and John Hopkins. Before I began reading law, John had told me that *The Law of Contract* was all I would need for the subject. Cherry then taught me contract law, and *The Law of Contract* always guided me well. I owe both Cherry and John a great deal, and this book would simply not have been written without their support. I am also grateful to JC Smith's children—Amanda, Andrew, and Mark (himself another Downing lawyer)—for entrusting me with their father's work.

As my work on this book has progressed, I have been very fortunate to be able to call on Sarah Green and Nick McBride for their help and advice. I am also grateful to Sam Williams, and especially Martin Dickson, for their research assistance. The book has been supported by a large number of people at OUP, but I am particularly thankful to Nicola Hartley for her support and assistance, Joy Ruskin-Tompkins for such efficient copy-editing, Wendy Telfer for proofreading, and Sarah Stephenson for seeing the book through production. I would also like to thank my students for their feedback on draft chapters, and the reviewers (some of whom are listed below, and some remain anonymous) who have reviewed (at least aspects of) the book at various stages. Their comments have been very helpful as the book has evolved and sought to meet the demands of various undergraduate courses. Lecturers obviously approach the subject in very different and contrasting ways, and it would be impossible to produce a book that mirrors every undergraduate course. However, the short chapters hopefully enable lecturers easily to choose the order in which topics are tackled, and the basic doctrinal questions are fundamental to any contract law course. On a note of style, the masculine pronoun has tended to be preferred throughout the book (so 'he' and not 'he or she'). This is purely in order to keep the text short and concise. There is no magic in being male or female.

I am also grateful to my family for their love and support. My parents and sister have continued to encourage and support my writing, and Marine has put up with my working on this when I should have been spending time with her. Our daughter, Emma, arrived mid-way through this project, and helps to keep everything in perspective. This book is dedicated to her.

The text was completed in October 2015, but it has been possible to incorporate some more recent developments (and substantially to rewrite Chapter 27 in response to the decision of the Supreme Court in *Makdessi v Cavendish Square Holdings BV* [2015] UKSC 67, [2015] 3 WLR 1373).

Paul S Davies
Oxford
12 November 2015

The author and publisher would like sincerely to thank all those people who gave their time and expertise to review draft chapters throughout the writing process. Your help was invaluable.

Lana Ashby, Durham University
Mark Campbell, University of Bristol
David Collins, City University London
Stephen Dnes, University of Dundee
Charlotte Ellis, Northumbria University
Paula Giliker, University of Bristol
Jane Henderson, King's College London
Rob Jago, Royal Holloway, University of London
Cliona Kelly, University College Dublin
Katherine Reece Thomas, City University London
Stephen Truxal, City University London
Leonardo Valladares, Anglia Ruskin University
Eliza Varney, Keele University
Faye Wang, Brunel University, London

Guided Tour of the Online Resource Centre

www.oxfordtextbooks.co.uk/orc/davies/

For students

Guidance on answering the questions in the book

Questions posed at the end of each chapter in the book are accompanied by answer guidance, written by the author. This will help you understand what each question requires and how to go about answering them. This tailored guidance should be an extremely helpful revision tool.

Essay attempts from real students with author commentary

There are a number of genuine essay attempts from real students hosted on the Online Resource Centre. These essays have been 'marked' by the author to give you an insight into how an examiner might approach your work. The author also provides an estimated grade for each essay so you can identify what makes an essay first-class!

Question 1

In which of the following situations would B be entitled to the reward given in the offer of the contract on completion of the required act?

- a) B reads a poster on a lamppost for a reward of £50 for finding a lost cat, 'Lucky'. B later finds the cat and returns it to its owner.
- b) B finds a lost dog and takes it to a pet rescue centre where it is reunited with its owner. B later finds an advertisement in a newspaper of a £100 reward for the return the dog.
- c) B finds a lost dog and takes it to the police where she expects a reward for finding

MCQS

Interactive, multiple-choice questions for every chapter give you instant feedback, as well as page references, to help you focus on the areas that need further study.

Links to key cases

Esso Petroleum v Customs & Excise [1976] 1 WLR 1
http://www.bailii.org/uk/cases/UKHL/1975/4.html

Chappell & Co Ltd v Nestlé Co Ltd [1960] AC 87
http://www.bailii.org/uk/cases/UKHL/1959/1.html

Links to key cases

Arranged by chapter, these links will take you directly to the full text of each key case. Follow these links to read around the cases and enhance your understanding.

For lecturers

In Carlill v Carbolic Smoke Ball Co, which factors led the court to the conclusion that a unilateral contract formed?

- a. Mrs Carlill used the ball for two weeks, as requested in the advertisement.
- b. The advertisement stated that £1000 had been deposited with a bank.
- c. The offer was made to the public.
- d. All of the answers are correct.

General Feedback

Test bank

For adopting lecturers, this book provides a test bank of multiple-choice questions that are useful for quick class testing.

Guided Tour of the Book

Key Points

- The intentions of the parties are generally and their 'objective' meaning. This is know
- The 'subjective test' involves ascertaining
- The 'objective test' is generally used in co certainty in the law of contract.

Key points

Clear, concise key points begin each chapter and outline the main concepts and ideas covered. These provide a helpful signpost to what you can expect to learn, and a list of topics to aid your revision.

Further Reading

R Calnan, 'Construction of Commercial Co E Peel (eds), *Contract Terms* (OUP, 2007 Argues that *ICS* has caused much uncertain a compromise solution under which the ma nature and purpose of the transaction, and

Further reading

Selected recommendations are provided at the end of each chapter to guide you if you wish to take your learning further, or consider a topic from a different perspective. This feature provides a useful list of resources to consider in preparation for an essay or examination.

Questions

1. Piper offers to sell to Chapman her car f £8,400 for your car.' Piper suspects that £4,800, but nevertheless replies straigl Chapman quickly points out her mistal for the car.

Questions

Each chapter ends with either an essay or problem-based question(s). These questions are often based upon set examination or assignment questions and are designed to help you practice your exam/essay technique. The author has also written guidance on how to answer these questions; these are hosted on the book's Online Resource Centre.

Glossary

Ab initio 'from the beginning'.

Administrator/administratrix a court-appointed personal representative who manages a deceased's estate. To be distinguished from an **executor/executrix** who is chosen by the deceased to manage his estate. Administrator may refer to a male or female, whereas an administratrix is always female.

A fortiori 'all the more so', or 'for even greater reason'.'

Ancillary orders/relief an order subsidiary to and

Bankruptcy/bankrupt where the individual's assets else. A person usually enters exceed the value of his assets insolvency that is inapplicab

Bill of lading a document issued by a carrier to a shipp contain or evidence the part under a contract of carriage, dence that goods have been be transferred when the

Legal glossary

Key legal terms are highlighted where they first appear in the chapter and are collated into a glossary at the end of the book. This offers you an easy and practical way to revise and check your understanding of key definitions.

Table of Cases

Table of Legislation

Germany

Italy

Statutory Instruments

Table of European Directives

International Instruments

1 Introduction: contractual rights and duties

We all make contracts every day. Each time we buy anything—a train ticket, a pair of shoes, a meal—we make a contract. Many of us spend most of our lives performing contractual obligations owed to our employers. We may be conscious of contracting only when we enter into some important transaction, like buying a house or a new car. But the law of contract is always there, to be invoked when something goes wrong. If there is an accident on the railway, the shoes prove defective, or the meal causes food poisoning, a claim for breach of contract may succeed.

The same general principles govern commercial contracts as the everyday transactions mentioned. A case concerning the employment of an opera singer may be an important precedent in a dispute about the hiring of a ship. An advertiser's promises concerning the therapeutic qualities of his smoke ball may be governed by the same principles as the promises of a shipper of goods to the **stevedore** who will load them. These general principles are almost all principles of the **common law**. They are not to be found in any code or statute but are derived from precedent. Consequently, any study of the law of contract must be, to a large extent, a study of the cases which made it. However, there are some important statutory modifications of the common law principles which are examined in this book.[1]

In addition, there is a vast amount of legislation relating to particular types of contract. For example, the contract of employment is now heavily regulated by statute. Such contracts are necessarily the subject of specialised works, and it may be that the law is shifting towards recognising a law of contracts (plural) rather than a law of contract (singular), since particular types of contract have generated a particular body of jurisprudence. However, legislation generally assumes the existence of the principles of the common law which continue to apply, except insofar as the statute expressly or impliedly modifies them. An understanding of these principles is therefore essential to an understanding of the specialised law, and a sound appreciation of the principles underpinning the general law of contract remains helpful.

---

[1] Especially the Law Reform (Frustrated Contracts) Act 1943, the Misrepresentation Act 1967, the Unfair Contract Terms Act 1977, the Contracts (Rights of Third Parties) Act 1999, and the Consumer Rights Act 2015.

Moreover, questions under almost any other branch of the law may depend on the law of contract. A petrol company's offer to supply a 'World Cup Coin' of minute value to a motorist buying four gallons of petrol is unlikely to give rise to an action for breach of contract; but the effect of the offer in the law of contract determined whether the company was liable for a very large sum in purchase tax.[2] It would hardly be worth suing a chocolate company for its failure to fulfil its promise to supply a record of 'Rockin' Shoes' for a small sum of money and three chocolate wrappers; but the rights to substantial sums by way of royalties on the record depended on the answer to the question of whether the wrappers were part of the contractual price.[3]

The outcome of many actions in the law of tort turns on issues of contract. Even in the criminal law, many cases relating to property offences can be properly understood only in the light of contractual principles. The law of contract is a basic subject which must be grasped by anyone who aspires to understand or apply the law.

This introductory chapter will give a brief overview of the fundamental elements of what constitutes a contract. These will all be considered in greater depth in subsequent chapters. This chapter will then conclude by examining some general themes in contract law to which reference will be made throughout the book. The outline provided in this chapter is necessarily brief, and it is to be expected that some of the themes may seem a little difficult in the abstract. That should not trouble any student approaching this subject for the first time; the concepts will become familiar and more easily understood through concrete examples provided in later chapters.

1 Undertakings or promises

The distinguishing feature of contractual obligations is that they are not imposed by the law but undertaken by the contracting parties. The name of the old common law form of action was *assumpsit*—'he undertook'. The claimant alleged that the defendant undertook to do something and did not do it, or did it badly. Or the claimant alleged that the defendant undertook that something was so and it was not so (for example, the claimant undertook that the car was in good working order and it was not). Whereas contractual duties are voluntarily undertaken, many duties are imposed on us by the law whether we like it or not. If I drive my car on the road I owe an inescapable duty of care to all other road users. If, in breach of that duty, I negligently cause injury to one of them, he may sue me in the tort of negligence. The duty of care is imposed by the general law. By contrast, the only reason why I am bound to go to work in the morning is that I have given an undertaking to my employer to do so; and his undertaking to me is the only reason why I am entitled to my pay at the end of the month.

Contractual and tortious duties frequently overlap, especially where negligence is concerned. A carrier of passengers in a vehicle on the road will of course owe those passengers the duty which he owes to all other road users in tort. But if he is carrying them under a contract, it will be an implied term of the contract that he will exercise due care. The

---

[2] *Esso Petroleum v Customs & Excise* [1976] 1 WLR 1, see Chapter 8, Section 2.
[3] *Chappell & Co Ltd v Nestlé Co Ltd* [1960] AC 87, see Chapter 7, Section 1(a).

content of the two duties will be the same, so that free riders will be no worse off than those riding under a contract. But contractual duties are often stricter. If the diners in a restaurant are poisoned by the food, notwithstanding the fact that the restaurateur and his staff exercised all proper care, those who have contracted to buy the food have a remedy because the restaurateur has impliedly undertaken that the food is reasonably fit for eating. But any guests who are not parties to a contract have no claim except in the tort of negligence and the restaurateur has not been negligent.

Admittedly, the distinction between contractual and tortious duties is less clear-cut than it may so far have been made to appear. This is because, by statute, some contractual duties are now inescapable as well.[4] So, just as the motorist who drives on the road cannot evade the obligation to exercise reasonable care as regards other road users, the restaurateur who invites the public to buy food in his restaurant cannot evade the obligation to supply food fit for eating. But the former is a duty in tort and the latter remains a duty in contract.

The law of contract is about undertakings or promises. It determines which promises are, and which promises are not, binding in law. And it prescribes the remedies available to a person who complains that a binding promise has been broken. The word, 'promise', is generally used in ordinary speech to refer to acts to be done in the future and most contracts contemplate future performance by one or more of the parties. However, in the law of contract, 'promise' is used in a wider sense to include undertakings about existing facts, such as where the seller of a car promises that it is roadworthy or the occupier of premises promises that he has taken reasonable steps to make them safe. In many contracts, the only, or the only significant, promises relate to a matter of fact, such as where goods are bought in a shop for cash. The acts which the seller and buyer perform—delivery of the goods and payment of the price—are, for all practical purposes, coincident with the formation of the contract and the only promises likely to be relied on in a dispute between the parties are those of the seller relating to the quality of the goods.

2 Deeds

It would be impracticable to make all promises binding in law and therefore English law, like all other systems, has rules to define the promises which are binding. A promise is not binding unless it is made in 'a deed' or given 'for consideration'.[5] A person may make any lawful promise binding in law by executing a deed. At common law, a deed was a document which was 'signed, sealed, and delivered' but now section 1 of the Law of Property (Miscellaneous Provisions) Act 1989 provides that the execution of a deed by an individual (as distinct from a corporation) no longer requires a seal. It is sufficient that the document:

(a) makes it clear on its face that it is intended to be a deed, by describing itself as a deed or expressing itself to be **executed** and signed as a deed, or otherwise; and

---

[4] See Chapter 15.
[5] See Chapter 7.

(b) it is signed (and 'signed' includes making one's mark) either (i) by the maker in the presence of a witness who attests the signature or (ii) at the maker's direction and in his presence and the presence of two witnesses who each attest the signature; and

(c) it is 'delivered' as a deed by the maker or his agent. 'Delivery' is widely defined to include any act by the maker which indicates that he considers the deed to be binding.

3 Written and oral promises

The 1989 Act has simplified the making of a deed but the great majority of promises have never been made in this formal way. If the promise is not in a deed, it is binding only if it is given for consideration. Usually, it makes no difference whether the promise is oral or in a document which does not amount to a deed. Contracts of the greatest importance—the sale of diamonds worth a million pounds—may be made by word of mouth or any other conduct signifying an intention to contract. The only question is whether the promise was made for consideration. However, there are exceptional cases where statute provides (a) that a contract is not valid unless it is *made* in writing or (b) it is not enforceable in a court of law unless it is *evidenced* in writing. These are considered in Chapter 9.

4 Bargains

The 'doctrine' of consideration is considered in detail in Chapter 7 but it is so fundamental that it must be outlined immediately.

The general idea is that a promise to make a **gift** is not binding but a bargain is binding. A promise is given for consideration when the **promisor** asks for something in return for his promise and gets what he asks for. The promise is binding because the promisee has 'bought' it by giving 'the price' asked. 'I promise that I will give you my car' is a promise which may be seriously intended and may impose a moral obligation on the promisor but it is not capable of becoming a contractual promise as the promisor has asked for nothing in return. A prompt 'acceptance' by the promisee makes no difference. 'I promise that I will give you my car for your motorbike,' on the other hand, is an offer capable of becoming a contract. The promisor has specified what he wants in return for his promise and, when the promisee accepts the offer by giving it to him, a contract is made.

An offer to make a contract is a promise with a price tag.

5 Bilateral and unilateral contracts

Sometimes what the promisor wants is a promise from the other party. When he gets what he wants—in this case, the other party's promise—his own promise is binding. So too is that of the other party. O promises A that he will employ him from 1 January next year at a salary of £20,000 a year. On 1 October, A accepts the offer. He is, of course, thereby promising to perform the duties specified in the job description. Both parties are now bound. O has received consideration in the form of A's promise to do the work specified. A has received consideration in the form of *O*'s promise to pay his salary and fulfil all the other duties of an employer. This is called a 'bilateral' contract because each of the two parties has made contractual promises.

Sometimes, in return for his own promise, the **offeror** asks not for a promise but for an act. The typical example is the offer of a reward. '£10 to anyone who returns my lost dog.' The offeror is not seeking promises, but action. If *A* finds the dog and returns it to *O* he is entitled to the reward. He has paid the required price for the promise. This is called a 'unilateral' contract, because only one side has made a promise. *A* has not promised to do anything, and is not under any obligation to perform. The contract is only concluded when *A* returns the dog. Of course, there are two parties to a unilateral contract, but only one promisor.

6 Fundamental themes in contract law

The approach of this book is fundamentally doctrinal. Its aim is to provide a clear, succinct analysis of the English law of contract. Reference to further and more theoretical discussion of aspects of the law can be found in the sections entitled 'Further reading' at the end of every chapter. However, any principled understanding of the current law must rest upon a sound appreciation of the underlying basis of the law. This section will briefly introduce some of the major ideas that are thought to inform the development of contractual principles. Each will be considered further in subsequent chapters.

(a) **Freedom of contract**

Courts often refer to a principle of 'freedom of contract'. For example, in *Printing and Numerical Registering Co v Sampson*, Sir George Jessel MR said:[6]

> if there is one thing which more than another public policy requires it is that men of full age and competent understanding shall have the utmost liberty of contracting, and that their contracts when entered into freely and voluntarily shall be held sacred and shall be enforced by Courts of justice. Therefore, you have this paramount public policy to consider—that you are not lightly to interfere with this freedom of contract.

Freedom of contract is obviously an important principle. Binding contractual obligations arise because of the parties' consent, and parties are correspondingly free to agree upon what terms they are willing to be bound. Equally, freedom of contract suggests a freedom not to enter into a contract: contracts should not be forced upon unwilling parties.

It is clear that parties can, to a large extent, set the terms of the contract. It is also clear that courts do not have a general power to improve the bargain made by the parties.[7] Nevertheless, the parties' freedom to contract is not absolute, and there are some overarching restrictions on this freedom. For instance, the parties may not be able to exclude certain

---

[6] (1874–75) LR 19 Eq 462, 465.
[7] See eg *Prime Sight Ltd v Lavarello* [2013] UKPC 22, [2014] AC 436 [47] (Lord Toulson).

types of liability,[8] or contract in a manner which is contrary to public policy.[9] But such limitations are exceptions to the general principle of freedom of contract, which continues to be taken seriously by the courts.

(b) Will theory

The classical explanation for the basis of the law of contract is the 'will theory'. This is often linked to the principle of freedom of contract. It has been famously developed by Professor Fried, who argues that contractual obligations arise because of the promise itself.[10] This theory emphasises the autonomy of the parties to mould their obligations to one another, and is consistent with the traditional, liberal approach to contract law.

The promise-based model has been attacked. It has sometimes been seen as too individualistic, and contrary to the view that the law should be concerned with promoting the redistribution of wealth. Doctrinally, it might be thought that since the promisor is often not required to fulfil his promise,[11] the theory is undermined. Alternatives have therefore been proposed, such as the theory that obligations really only arise because one party has detrimentally relied upon the promise of the other party.[12] However, it is suggested that the will theory continues to provide a good explanation for large swathes of the law of contract, and lies at the heart of the traditional approach of the common law.

(c) Economic efficiency

A major challenge to the moral basis of the will theory, which is grounded in the importance of a party's promise, comes from those who favour a law and economics approach to contract law. This school of thought argues that the law should strive to be economically efficient. Indeed, Oliver Wendell Holmes, a judge in the US Supreme Court, notably said that 'The duty to keep a contract at common law means a prediction that you must pay damages if you do not keep it—and nothing else.'[13] This seems to go too far. It is clear that a party does not simply have a choice whether to pay damages or to perform his obligations. Indeed, in some circumstances a court will order **specific performance**, and thereby force a party to perform rather than pay damages. Parties contract in order to secure performance of a promise, and this should not be overlooked.

On a slightly different tack, but in a similar vein, Judge Richard Posner has written:[14]

> Suppose I sign a contract to deliver 100,000 custom-ground widgets at $.10 apiece to A, for use in his boiler factory. After I have delivered 10,000, B comes to me, explains that he desperately needs 25,000 custom-ground widgets at once since otherwise he will be forced to close his pianola factory at great cost, and offers me $.15 apiece for 25,000 widgets. I sell him the widgets and as a result do not complete timely delivery to A, who sustains $1000 in damages from

---

[8]　See Chapter 15.
[9]　See Chapter 22.
[10]　C Fried, *Contract as Promise: A Theory of Contractual Obligation* (2nd edn, OUP, 2015).
[11]　See the restrictions on specific performance discussed in Chapter 28, Section 7.
[12]　P Atiyah, *The Rise and Fall of Freedom of Contract* (OUP, 1979).
[13]　OW Holmes, 'The Path of the Law' (1897) 10 Harvard Law Review 457.
[14]　R Posner, *Economic Analysis of the Law* (8th edn, Aspen, 2011) 151.

my breach. Having obtained an additional profit of $1250 on the sale to B, I am better off even after reimbursing A for his loss. Society is also better off. Since B was willing to pay me $.15 per widget, it must mean that each widget was worth at least $.15 to him. But it was worth only $.14 to A—$.10, what he paid, plus $.04 ($1000 divided by 25,000), his expected profit. Thus the breach resulted in a transfer of the 25,000 widgets from a lower valued to a higher valued use.

This famously highlights the idea of 'efficient breach'. The person who values the goods the most (B) obtains the goods. A suffers no loss because he is adequately compensated. And I make a profit. As a result, there seems to be no 'losers' in this scenario, and everybody is a 'winner'. Indeed, in a capitalist society this sort of reasoning may be considered to be important for wealth creation.

However, care should be taken before endorsing wholeheartedly a view of contract law that rests squarely upon the principles of law and economics. Although it is possible that commercial parties may often desire an efficient outcome when dealing with generic goods in a liquid market, and considerations of efficiency may underpin doctrines such as mitigation,[15] many contract doctrines seem unconcerned with efficiency.[16] And non-commercial parties dealing with particular goods or services may not be aware of considerations of efficiency at all. More fundamentally, it is not always clear whether any breach of contract really is efficient. This is because there are often (sometimes hidden) costs associated with breach. As Macneil has put it, '"Talking after a breach" may be one of the most expensive forms of conversation to be found, involving, as it so often does, engaging high-price lawyers, and gambits like starting litigation, engaging in discovery, and even trying and appealing cases.'[17] There are therefore 'negotiation costs', 'litigation costs', and 'assessment costs' in quantifying damages in complicated scenarios. All these might make a breach of contract an expensive rather than efficient proposition. As a result, it is suggested that even though the approach in the basic example given by Posner is useful in a very simple case, and might help to explain why compensatory damages are generally thought to be sufficient, too much emphasis should not be placed on 'efficient breach'. After all, a breach of contract is an unlawful act and should not therefore be encouraged.

(d) Objectivity in contract law

It is a fundamental, general principle of contract law that a party's words and conduct must be interpreted objectively. The key question concerns what a reasonable person would understand that party to mean, rather than asking what that party actually meant. As Lord Reid put it in *McCutcheon v David MacBrayne Ltd*, 'The judicial task is not to discover the actual intentions of each party; it is to decide what each was reasonably entitled to conclude from the attitude of the other.'[18] The emphasis on 'objective' rather than 'subjective' intentions is so important that it is the subject of further examination in Chapter 2, before considering its significance to various substantive doctrines throughout the book.

---

[15] See Chapter 26, Section 2(c).
[16] See eg the discussion in Chapter 25, Section 4 and in Chapter 28, Section 2.
[17] I Macneil, 'Efficient Breach of Contract: Circles in the Sky' (1982) 68 Virginia Law Review 947, 968–9.
[18] [1964] 1 WLR 125, 128, HL (citing *Gloag on Contract* (2nd edn) p 7.

(e) Common law and equity

Equity has certain characteristics that distinguish it from the common law. These derive from the historical origins of the equitable jurisdiction.[19] From medieval times, the common law was a formalistic body of rules which were interpreted strictly. Where the common law did not provide a remedy or where the result reached by the common law was harsh, it was possible to petition the King, and later the Lord Chancellor, to provide a remedy through the exercise of his discretion. Eventually, so many petitions came to the Chancellor that it was necessary to establish a separate court, known as the Court of Chancery, to deal with them. The law that was applied in this court became known as equity.

In the *Earl of Oxford's case*,[20] Lord Chancellor Ellesmere recognised that equity's function was 'to soften and mollify the extremity of the law', and where there is a conflict between equity and the common law, equity should prevail. Since equitable relief depended upon the Chancellor's discretion, results could be unpredictable; for some time it was thought that 'Equity varies with the length of the Chancellor's foot.'[21] However, this no longer reflects the current state of the law. Equity has become more rule-based and principled, mainly because the equity jurisdiction was transferred from the Chancellor to judges, whose decisions had value as precedent for future decisions so that like cases could be treated alike. Moreover, it is no longer necessary to seek relief from the common law courts and then petition the Chancery courts.[22] The Judicature Acts of 1873 and 1875 abolished the common law and Chancery courts and replaced them with a single High Court. The effect of this legislation was to fuse the administration of common law and equity. The Judicature Acts emphasised that equity, as a body of law, could be applied in any court.[23] It is important to appreciate that although the common law and equity have been fused as a matter of *procedure*, the *substantive* body of law produced in the Chancery courts remains vital, and the *function* of equity remains the same. Principles of equity, just like principles of common law, are developed by judges in a principled, incremental manner. Equity is crucial to understanding fundamental aspects of common law systems.

In the contractual realm, equity plays a significant role, particularly as regards remedies.[24] It is important to appreciate that equitable doctrines only apply where the application of the common law rules would be too harsh. As a matter of technique, it is therefore crucial to apply the common law before considering equitable relief. So, for example, the common law of interpretation should be analysed before the equitable doctrine of rectification,[25] and the common law of consideration should be applied before considering promissory **estoppel**.[26]

---

[19] See J Baker, *Introduction to Legal History* (4th edn, OUP, 2002) 97–116.

[20] (1615) 1 Ch Rep 1.

[21] F Pollock (ed), *Table Talk of John Selden* (Selden Society, 1927) 43.

[22] This was a time-consuming, expensive, and inefficient way of conducting litigation; for literary criticism, see Charles Dickens, *Bleak House* (1853) commenting on the fictional case of *Jarndyce v Jarndyce*.

[23] See now the Senior Courts Act 1981, s 49.

[24] See eg Chapter 14 (rectification) and Chapter 28, Section 7 (specific performance).

[25] Chapter 24.

[26] Chapter 7.

(f) **Contract law within private law**

Contract law is only one area within the private law of obligations.[27] It has already been seen in Section 1 that contract should be distinguished from tort law, although contractual and tortious duties may arise concurrently. Contract law should also be distinguished from unjust enrichment. Claims in unjust enrichment are not based on a civil wrong. For example, if *A* transfers to *B* £100 by mistake, then we might think (without any further facts) that it would be unjust for *B* not to pay back £100 to *A*. *A* can therefore sue *B* for restitution of an unjust enrichment. Yet neither *A* nor *B* may be at fault at all. Moreover, the remedy in unjust enrichment is the reversal of the enrichment transferred to *B*; unjust enrichment is concerned with reversing gains. This is different from contract law, which generally awards compensation for loss, and views a breach of contract as a wrong.

It is important to appreciate that contract law does not exist in a vacuum in private law. The boundaries of contract law might be influenced by how broad an approach to tort and, in particular, unjust enrichment is considered appropriate. Unjust enrichment is generally thought to be subsidiary to contract,[28] and this has led to some tension about whether unjust enrichment is an appropriate remedy in situations where a contract has 'failed to materialise' and has not come into existence,[29] or where a contract has been terminated for **repudiatory** breach,[30] for instance.

(g) **International influences on contract law**

English law is subject to international influences, and these will be noted throughout the book. Most significantly, English law is subject to various Directives and Regulations from the European Union, especially as regards consumer protection, and these have had a considerable impact upon the common law. But other 'soft law codes', which can be adopted by parties if they choose, have also developed,[31] and this increases the choice of legal regimes available to (generally commercial) parties. There is a powerful view that contract law is ripe for a degree of harmonisation, and perhaps even codification, across national boundaries; after all, this could make international transactions easier because all parties would understand that the same principles apply regardless of location. On balance, however, it is suggested that this view should be resisted. Parties can choose which law governs their agreement, and it might be thought beneficial for parties to have a choice between different legal systems. Indeed, English law has proven to be particularly popular amongst commercial parties all over the world. This is because the common law of contract has proven itself to be (relatively) predictable, certain, and responsive to the needs of reasonable businessmen. The attractiveness of English law has brought a great deal of money and business to the City of London. Such advantages should not readily be discarded.

---

[27] See generally A Burrows, *Understanding the Law of Obligations: Essays on Contract, Tort and Restitution* (Hart, 1998).

[28] Chapter 28, Section 4.

[29] Chapter 5.

[30] Chapter 24.

[31] See eg UNIDROIT's *Principles of International Commercial Contracts* (2010) and, more locally, the *Principles of European Contract Law* (see O Lando and H Beale (eds), *Principles of European Contract Law* (Kluwer, 2000)).

Further Reading

P Atiyah, *The Rise and Fall of Freedom of Contract* (OUP, 1979).
Atiyah charts the development and subsequent decline (in his view) of freedom of contract, and discusses the broader implications of this.

S Whittaker, 'A Framework of Principle for European Contract Law?' (2009) 125 LQR 616.
Discusses the draft Common Frame of Reference, composed by the Study Group on a Civil Code and the Research Group on Existing EC Private Law. Considers the merits and nature of a codified European contract law.

C Fried, *Contract as Promise: A Theory of Contractual Obligation* (2nd edn, OUP, 2015).
Analyses the philosophical foundations of contract law and argues in favour of a moral basis grounded in the parties' promises.

2   Objectivity in contract law

🔑 Key Points

- The intentions of the parties are generally judged by their words and conduct and their 'objective' meaning. This is known as the 'objective test'.
- The 'subjective test' involves ascertaining a person's real state of mind.
- The 'objective test' is generally used in contract law. This helps to enhance certainty in the law of contract.
- Exceptions to a strictly objective interpretation of a contractual document can arise where *A* knows, or ought to know, that *O*'s real intention was different from his apparent intention, and where the objective facts are ambiguous.
- Motive is irrelevant to contract formation. However, if *A* knows that *O* is mistaken as to the *terms* of the contract, but concludes the contract on those terms anyway, *A* cannot enforce the objective meaning of those terms against *O*.
- The contents of a contract are determined objectively. The best evidence that a term has been incorporated into a contract and that a contract is binding is through the parties' signatures, although entirely oral contracts are equally possible.
- Contractual communications, whether oral or written, are generally to be understood in the way that a reasonable person in the position of the recipient would have understood them.

Sometimes a person's actual intention differs from how his intention is perceived by others (his apparent intention). He may in fact make a particular promise when his intention is to make a promise of a different kind or, perhaps, not to make a promise at all. In such a case, he will be bound by the promise he in fact made if it has become part of a bargain. If *O* makes an offer which can reasonably bear only one meaning and *A* accepts, *O* cannot escape liability by saying that he intended it to mean something else. *O*'s protests that this was not his real intention will be in vain.

In contract law, the intentions of the parties are generally judged by their words and conduct and their 'objective' meaning. This is known as the 'objective test'. Where the inquiry is directed to ascertaining a person's real state of mind, the test applied is 'subjective'. It is sometimes necessary to determine a person's real state of mind for the purposes of the law of contract,[1] but in most circumstances the law applies an objective test.[2] If any other

---

[1] See eg Chapter 14 and below.
[2] *RTS Flexible Systems Ltd v Molkerei Alois Müller GmbH* [2010] UKSC 14, [2010] 1 WLR 753 [45] (Lord Clarke).

approach were adopted, no one could ever act safely on a contract which he reasonably believed he had made. After all, there is always the possibility that the other party might be under some undisclosed, undiscoverable misapprehension as to the existence or nature or effect of the contract. But if he is, that is his misfortune.

The objective approach underpins much of the law of contract, and it is important to appreciate its significance at the outset. The theme of objectivity will be returned to throughout this book, but this chapter aims to provide an overview of this crucial concept through some illustrative examples. More detail will be provided in subsequent chapters.

1 The general rule: subjective intentions irrelevant

If any reasonable observer of the **promisor**'s conduct would have supposed that the promisor was making a particular promise X, and the **promisee** did suppose that the promisor was making promise X, then the promisor will be bound by promise X if it is included in a bargain with the promisee. In *Tamplin v James*,[3] the defendant attended an auction to buy 'The Ship' inn which was put up for sale as 'Lot 1'. The auctioneer drew bidders' attention to the particulars of sale and the plan, which made absolutely clear the extent of the property. Lot 1 was not sold at the auction. However, immediately after the auction, the defendant made an offer for it which was accepted. Later, it emerged that the defendant made the offer under the mistaken belief that Lot 1 included two adjacent plots of land. He had known the property from when he was a boy and had observed that these adjacent plots had always been occupied by the occupier of the inn. The defendant was set upon acquiring these adjacent plots, so declined to complete unless these two plots were also conveyed to him. The court held that the defendant was not entitled to these two plots, but was bound by his contract to buy Lot 1. Indeed, the court granted an order of **specific performance** that required the defendant to carry out that contract. Clearly, there was no actual *consensus ad idem* or 'meeting of minds'—a notion to which the older cases pay much lip service—between the vendor and purchaser. After all, the defendant intended to buy the inn and the two plots, and the claimant intended to sell only the inn. Nevertheless, there was a contract.

Conversely, imagine that the owner of adjacent properties, X and Y, decided to sell only X but invited offers on the basis of a plan and description which, by an error, included both properties. The owner would be bound by a contract to sell both properties to an **offeror** who made his offer on the reasonable supposition that both were for sale and whose offer was accepted.

2 Where A knows, or ought to know, that O's offer does not represent his real intention

In *Tamplin v James*, the vendor reasonably believed that the purchaser meant what he said. It is otherwise if A knows, or ought to know, that O's real intention is different. In *Hartog*

---

[3] (1880) 15 ChD 215, affirmed 15 ChD 219, CA.

v Colin and Shields,[4] the defendants offered to sell 30,000 Argentinian hare skins to the claimant at prices per pound. The previous negotiations had been carried on by reference to the price per piece. It was customary in the trade to refer to the price per piece. The value of a piece was about one-third that of a pound. The price stated was therefore absurdly low, and was snapped up by the claimant. The defendants argued that they had obviously made a mistake in writing 'pound' rather than 'piece' and that they were not obliged to sell the skins to the claimant at a price per pound. Singleton J held that the claimant could not enforce any contract. The judge observed that 'The **plaintiff** could not reasonably have supposed that the offer contained the offeror's real intention.' The claimant knew, or ought to have known, that the defendant did not really mean to say what he had in fact said. The claimant cannot 'snap up' an offer that is obviously made by mistake, since the claimant cannot in good faith say that he thought the defendant intended to be bound by that offer. However, the result in the *Hartog* case would have been different if the claimant had reasonably believed the defendant was mistaken only as to the value of the skins. If that had been his only mistake, the law would not preclude the buyer from taking advantage of the mistake which he knew the seller was making.[5]

3 Where the objective facts are ambiguous

In *Tamplin v James*, the objective facts were unambiguous. The reasonable observer who was aware of all the objective facts could have been in no doubt that the parties were contracting about Lot 1 as described. The only missing information was the defendant's secret thoughts, which are irrelevant to the objective exercise. However, if the objective facts are ambiguous then a different analysis must be adopted. Significantly, the party responsible for the ambiguity cannot enforce the contract in the sense in which he intended it, if the other party intended it in the other sense. In *Falck v Williams*,[6] the claimant, Falck, sent an offer in code by telegram. Because he did not use enough words, the offer was ambiguous: the offer might have been taken to refer to one or other of two contemplated transactions. Falck intended a contract for the carriage of copra from Fiji to the UK. Williams accepted, intending to contract for the carriage of coal from Sydney to Barcelona. Both were plausible, objective interpretations of the offer. Falck's action to enforce the contract in the sense in which he understood it failed. Falck had created the ambiguity, and could not subsequently enforce the interpretation of the offer which he preferred.

Lord Macnaghten said, *obiter*, that if Williams had sought to enforce the contract in accordance with his interpretation, Williams would equally have failed. It is difficult to be sure whether this approach is satisfactory. After all, Williams did not create the ambiguity. Imagine that Williams had taken expensive action in reliance on the contract he believed he had made, and was in no doubt that the telegram bore the meaning that he attributed to it. Should Falck, who was at fault in creating the ambiguity, be allowed to resist any claim by Williams by saying, 'You ought to have spotted it'? This seems doubtful.

---

[4] [1939] 2 All ER 566, QB.
[5] See Chapter 7, Section 1(c): English law will not examine the adequacy of the consideration.
[6] [1900] AC 176, PC.

However, where the ambiguity is the fault of neither party and each understands the contract in different senses, it is clear that there is no contract. In *Raffles v Wichelhaus*,[7] there was a written agreement for the sale by the claimants to the defendants of 125 bales of cotton, 'to arrive *ex Peerless* from Bombay'. Unknown to the parties, there were two ships called *Peerless*, one leaving Bombay in October and the other leaving Bombay in December. The seller's cotton was on the December *Peerless* but the buyer thought it was on the October *Peerless*. The buyer refused to accept the cargo of the December ship and the seller sued him. The court rejected the seller's argument that it did not matter whether the goods came from the December *Peerless* or the October *Peerless*. It was reasonable for the buyer to insist that it was important for him to know when he could expect delivery. After all, the contract was, or purported to be, a contract for the sale of a specific cargo, not simply a contract for the sale of 125 bales of cotton of a particular description. If the contract had been of the latter type, it was clear that the seller was ready and willing to perform it and so he would have been entitled to his damages. But, as it was intended to be the sale of a specific cargo, it was essential to determine which cargo was the subject of the contract. That was impossible, because each cargo fitted the contract description equally well. It was not clear that the ambiguity was the responsibility of one party rather than the other, so neither side could enforce their own interpretation of any 'agreement'.

If both parties had interpreted the telegram in *Falck v Williams* in the same sense, and if both parties in *Raffles v Wichelhaus* had had the same *Peerless* in mind, it seems that there would have been a valid contract, notwithstanding the objective ambiguity. In such cases, therefore, it may be necessary to determine the actual state of mind of the parties—to apply the subjective as well as the objective test. In *Raffles v Wichelhaus*, the seller admitted that the buyer was thinking of the other ship, so there was no need to prove it by evidence.

4 Where *A* knows that *O* is mistaken as to the terms of the contract

We have already noticed that *A* is not precluded from enforcing the contract because he knew that *O* was making a grave mistake as to the *value* of the subject matter of the contract. The same is true where *A* knows that *O* is making other material mistakes of fact which are not terms of the contract. Motive is irrelevant to contract formation. However, it is different if *A* knows that *O* is mistaken as to the *terms* of the contract. If, for example, *A* knows that *O* thinks the contract contains term *X*, but the contract in fact contains not term *X* but term *Y*, it is clear that *A* cannot then enforce the contract in the sense of *Y*, even though it undoubtedly says '*Y*'. In fact, *A* can probably enforce the contract against *O* in the sense of *X*, although this is less clear-cut.[8]

All these propositions are illustrated by *Smith v Hughes*.[9] The claimant sued the defendant on a contract for the sale of a specific parcel of oats. The defendant said that he had contracted for old oats. However, the claimant provided oats which were new and useless

---

[7] (1864) 2 H & C 906.
[8] See Chapter 14.
[9] (1871) LR 6 QB 597.

to the defendant. The defendant consequently refused to pay the contract price. The verdict reached by a jury was in favour of the defendant. The case is somewhat unsatisfactory and difficult because there were unresolved questions of fact, so it is necessary to consider the case on three hypotheses.

(a) *The word 'old' was used in the discussion leading to the oral contract of sale.* If this was the case, then the jury's verdict was right because it was a contract for the sale of old oats. The seller could not perform it by delivering new oats.

(b) *The word 'old' was not used but the seller knew that the buyer believed that the oats were in fact old.* If that was the case, the verdict was wrong. So long as he did nothing to induce or encourage it,[10] the law allowed the seller to take advantage of the buyer's mistake of fact. 'The passive acquiescence of the seller in the self-deception of the buyer,' said Cockburn CJ, did not 'entitle the latter to avoid the contract'. The question was not 'what a man of scrupulous morality or nice honour would do under such circumstances'. This would be a practical application of the important principle of English law known by the Latin words *caveat emptor*—roughly translated as 'buyer beware' or 'let the buyer look out for himself'.

(c) *The word 'old' was not used but the seller knew that the buyer believed that the seller was contracting that the oats were old.* In that case, the verdict was right.

The difference between (b) and (c) is that in (c) the seller knows that the buyer is making a mistake as to the *terms* of the contract, not merely a mistake as to fact or motive. The seller cannot then enforce the contract in a sense different from that which he knew the buyer intended at the time of contracting.

There is, however, one question left open by the decision in *Smith v Hughes*. That is, whether the seller's claim failed because the contract was void, or because there was a contract for the sale of old oats which the seller could not perform. It was not necessary for the court to decide this point.

Support for the contention that there was a contract which the seller could not perform may be found in *Roberts v Leicestershire County Council*.[11] The claimants were building contractors. They signed a contract in which they undertook to build a school in a period of 30 months. They had not read the contract and believed that the relevant period was 18 months, which would have been advantageous for them. Eighteen months was the period proposed in their original **tender** but that had been changed during the negotiations. The officers of the council knew that the claimants were labouring under this misapprehension about the contents of the contract when the council sealed the contract. Pennycuick J held that the contract should be rectified by substituting '18 months' for '30 months'. Rectification is considered in detail in Chapter 14. But it is important to note that a court will only order rectification of a written contract when it is satisfied by evidence which is impossible to refute that the written words do not represent the true contract between the parties.[12] This was an 18-month contract because the defendants knew at the time of

---

[10] See Chapter 16.
[11] [1961] Ch 555.
[12] See Chapter 14.

contracting that the claimants believed it was an 18-month contract—just as (in hypothesis (c)) the seller in *Smith v Hughes* knew that the buyer believed it was a contract for old oats.

However, there is also authority in favour of the view that the contract should be considered to be void. In *Statoil ASA v Louis Dreyfus Energy Services LP*,[13] Aikens J thought that, since there was no consensus between the parties concerning the relevant terms, there was no true agreement concerning the terms and thus 'there was never a contract at all'. Despite the difficulties surrounding the proper analysis of whether there was a contract in hypothesis (c), the authority of *Smith v Hughes* is clear on what it decided, and mistakes as to terms need to be distinguished from mistakes as to motives. In *Statoil*, the judge emphasised that 'the correctness of that decision [of *Smith v Hughes*] and the analysis in it has never been doubted'.

5 Objectivism and written signed contracts

'When a document containing contractual terms is signed, then, in the absence of fraud, or … misrepresentation, the party signing it is bound and it is wholly immaterial whether he has read the document or not.' The law was thus stated by Scrutton LJ in *L'Estrange v Graucob*.[14] The party is bound even though in his mind he does not really assent to the particular terms in the document because he does not actually know what they are. In *L'Estrange*, the claimant signed a contract for the purchase of a slot machine for selling cigarettes without reading it. The defendants knew that the claimant had not read the agreement, but were nonetheless entitled to enforce the agreement. The party who signs the document expresses his assent to the terms in it, whatever they may be and regardless of whether those terms have been read and understood.

The 'rule' in *L'Estrange v Graucob* is sometimes criticised as being unfair. Indeed, the successful counsel in the case was Alfred Denning (later Lord Denning) whose reputation grew after this victory. But Denning later confessed to being uncomfortable with the result,[15] and in the decision of the House of Lords in *McCutcheon v David MacBrayne Ltd*[16] Lord Denning said that signed writing 'should make no difference whatever. This sort of document is not meant to be read, still less to be understood. Its signature is in truth about as significant as a handshake that marks the formal conclusion of a bargain.' Such comments may have some traction in the consumer context, where legislation allows for the regulation of the substantive terms of an agreement, and this will be examined further in Chapter 11.[17] But there is little doubt that *L'Estrange v Graucob* remains a bedrock of English law; in *Peekay Intermark Ltd and another v Australia and New Zealand Banking*

---

[13] [2008] EWHC 2257 (Comm), [2009] 1 All ER (Comm) 1035.

[14] [1934] 2 KB 394, CA. See Chapter 11.

[15] Lord Denning later wrote: 'In those days I wasn't concerned so much with the rightness of the cause. I was concerned only, as a member of the Bar, to win it if I could' (Lord Denning, *The Family Story* (Butterworths, 1981) 99).

[16] [1964] 1 WLR 125.

[17] See Chapter 11, Section 2(a). The Ontario Court of Appeal in Canada has marked a slight shift away from a strict approach to *L'Estrange* in *Tilden Rent-A-Car Co v Clendenning* (1978) 83 DLR (3d) 400, which concerned a consumer hiring a car, by requiring that it be reasonable to believe that the signor accepted the relevant terms.

Group Ltd,[18] Moore-Bick LJ described it as 'an important principle of English law which underpins the whole of commercial life; any erosion of it would have serious repercussions far beyond the business community'.

6 Objectivism and written unsigned contracts

Signing a written contract is one method by which the parties can declare their willingness to be bound by the written terms. But the parties may also declare their willingness to be bound in other ways. Evidence that the parties agreed orally that the document should be the contract is just as effective as signature. And delivery by O to A of a paper containing the terms, or some of the terms, on which O is willing to contract can have the same effect, if it is made quite clear to A that these are O's terms. A's acceptance concludes a contract on those terms. However, if the paper contains a particularly onerous or unusual term, that term will not be part of the contract unless A has taken objectively reasonable steps to make clear that it is.[19]

7 The objective meaning of the contract

A contract will be enforced in its objective sense at the **suit** of either party unless there has been misrepresentation[20] or there are grounds for rectification.[21] The principles and materials relevant to interpreting the express terms of an agreement will be considered in detail in Chapter 12. But it is useful now to highlight that there is some debate about how 'objectivity' is to be understood. It seems clear that we are not trying to assess a party's words and conduct by reference to a reasonable person in that party's own position, but should we understand such words and conduct by reference to a reasonable person in the addressee's position or a reasonable person who is entirely detached from proceedings? The latter approach was apparently favoured in *Upton on Severn UDC v Powell*.[22] Powell called for Upton on Severn's fire service. Both parties thought that Powell was within the area for Upton on Severn's fire service and therefore entitled to the fire services for free. However, both parties were mistaken: Powell was outside the area for Upton on Severn's localised fire service. Neither party (seemingly reasonably) intended there to be a contract, but the court held that Powell was under a contractual obligation to pay for the services rendered. This seems to be an odd result. It is suggested that the obligation to pay would now be better analysed as arising not in contract but rather in unjust enrichment.[23] The preferable view, which has been put forward above, is that objectivity is generally assessed from the position of the recipient. In *Destiny 1 Ltd v Lloyds TSB Bank Plc*,[24] Moore-Bick LJ emphasised that

---

[18] [2006] EWCA Civ 386, [2006] 2 Lloyd's Rep 511.

[19] *Interfoto Picture Library Ltd v Stiletto Visual Programmes Ltd* [1988] 1 All ER 348, CA. This case is discussed in detail in Chapter 11.

[20] Chapter 16.

[21] Chapter 14.

[22] [1942] 1 All ER 220.

[23] See Chapter 28, Section 4.

[24] [2011] EWCA Civ 831.

'communications, whether oral or written, are to be understood in the way that a reasonable person in the position of the recipient would have understood them.' This approach is best-equipped to protect the expectations of a party which relies in good faith upon an objectively reasonable interpretation of the other party's words and conduct.

8 Estoppel

It is sometimes said that the basis of the objective approach to the meaning of a contract lies in the doctrine of **estoppel**.[25] Estoppel takes a variety of forms and is encountered on several issues in the law of contract.[26] Estoppel in its simplest and most common form arises where one person (the **representor**) makes a statement of fact to another (the **representee**) in reliance on which the representee reasonably supposes he is intended to, and does, act to his detriment. In any litigation which later takes place between them, the representor will not be allowed to say that his representation was untrue, even if it is certain that it was in fact untrue. In other words, the representor will be estopped from going back on his representation. In applying the objective test to promises, judges sometimes use similar language. In *Tamplin v James*,[27] Baggallay LJ said 'I think [the defendant] is not entitled to say to any effectual purpose that he was under a mistake.'

It is clear, however, that the basis of the objective test to promises is not estoppel because the objective test applies even though there has been no action by the other party in reliance on any 'representation' of intention to contract on certain terms. In one case a person who had signed a contract to sell a two-acre plot of land was held to be bound by the contract even though he tore up the agreement within minutes of signing it.[28] He believed that the contract related to only half an acre of the plot, but his belief was not induced by fraud or misrepresentation, and was irrelevant under the objective test. It was irrelevant that the other party had not relied upon the contract: it was binding from the point of formation. The only act which the party relying on the objective test need have done is to enter into the contract, and this may be very far from an act to his detriment.[29]

🅸🅽 Further Reading

J Spencer, 'The Rule in *L'Estrange v Graucob*' (1973) 32 CLJ 104.
Critical of the rule in *L'Estrange v Graucob*, favouring instead a robust application of the rule in *Smith v Hughes*.

---

[25] See generally P Atiyah, *The Rise and Fall of the Freedom of Contract* (Clarendon Press, 1979).
[26] See eg Chapter 7, Section 2 and Chapter 16, Section 7.
[27] Section 1.
[28] *Hasham v Zenab* [1960] AC 316, PC.
[29] *Centrovincial Estates plc v Merchant Investors Assurance Co Ltd* [1983] Com LR 158, CA.

W Howarth, 'The Meaning of Objectivity in Contract' (1984) 100 LQR 265.
J Vorster, 'A Comment on the Meaning of Objectivity in Contract' (1987) 103 LQR 274.
W Howarth, 'A Note on the Objective of Objectivity in Contract' (1987) 103 LQR 527.

These articles debate how notions such as 'detached objectivity', 'promisor objectivity', and 'promisee objectivity' fit with English contract law; compare the more recent criticisms of Chen-Wishart.

T Endicott, 'Objectivity, Subjectivity and Incomplete Agreements' in J Horder (ed), *Oxford Essays in Jurisprudence: Fourth Series* (OUP, 2000).

Argues that the existence and content of voluntary obligations must necessarily be determined by objective tests.

M Chen-Wishart, 'Objectivity and Mistake: The Oxymoron of *Smith v Hughes*' in J Neyers, R Bronough, and SGA Pitel (eds), *Exploring Contract Law* (Hart, 2009).

Re-examines *Smith v Hughes* and advocates a context-specific view of objectivity, which leaves no room for a resort to subjectivity.

? Questions

1. Piper offers to sell to Chapman her car for £5,000. Chapman replies by email: 'I am prepared to pay £8,400 for your car.' Piper suspects that Chapman had made a mistake in writing £8,400 instead of £4,800, but nevertheless replies straight away: 'Contract concluded. The car is yours for £8,400.' Chapman quickly points out her mistake to Piper, and writes that she is now happy to pay £5,000 for the car.

   Advise Chapman.

2. Laura sold an English bulldog to Alex for £2,000. Laura knew that Alex believed she was buying a French bulldog. The English bulldog was only worth £1,200.

   Advise Alex. Are there any other facts you would need to know in order to be confident with your advice?

3 Formation of bilateral contracts

🔑 Key Points

- Bilateral contracts are formed by an exchange of promises. Both the offeror (O) and acceptor (A) promise something.
- An offer must objectively show an intention to be bound by the terms of the offer.
- O is free to stipulate what A must do in order to accept the offer.
- The general rule is that A must communicate his acceptance to O.
- An important exception to this general rule arises where A posts his acceptance. In such circumstances, the contract is concluded on the moment of posting. This 'postal rule' has been narrowly construed and will not apply where it has been excluded by O or will lead to manifest absurdity.
- Offers may lapse after a reasonable amount of time.
- A counter-offer will terminate the original offer, in the same way as a rejection of the offer. However, a mere inquiry for further information will leave the original offer intact.
- O can revoke his offer at any point before it has been accepted: one party should not be bound without the other. However, the revocation must be communicated to A.

1 Offer and acceptance

As explained in the previous chapter, contracts are bargains. The natural way to make a bargain is for one side to propose the terms and the other to agree to them. So contracts are almost invariably made by a process of offer and acceptance. The law looks for an offer and acceptance, not because of some technical legal requirement, but because this is the way in which contracts are generally made.

However, it should be noted that the lack of offer and acceptance does not necessarily preclude the existence of a contract, if a bargain can be discerned from the facts in some other way. Suppose that a yacht club invites its members to take part in a race on the terms that 'Each competitor agrees with every other competitor that he will be liable for all damage caused by him through any breach of the rules in the course of the race.' When the race begins, there is a series of contracts between each competitor and every other competitor, even though it is impossible to say that one rather than the other is the **offeror** or the acceptor. This hypothetical example is based on *Clarke v Dunraven*.[1] In that case, each competitor made a written agreement with the club when he entered the race. Each competitor had certainly made a contract with the club that he would pay an injured competitor for damage he caused in breach of the rules. However, it was not the club which sued the defaulting yacht-owner, but the injured competitor.[2] The action succeeded. One possible explanation is that, on entering the race, each person made an offer to any subsequent entrants and accepted the offer already made by any previous entrants. As will be seen in this chapter, it is sometimes possible to discern an offer and acceptance in rather unpromising material; but this would not be possible in the case put above. The parties have simply agreed, 'I will be bound by the rules if you will'; there is a bargain, but no offer and acceptance.

This chapter will analyse the key elements traditionally required for the formation of a bilateral contract. It will first be necessary to explain what constitutes an offer, and various common scenarios will be discussed. The requirements of acceptance will then be considered, since this is what is required for a contract to be concluded. But, obviously, not all offers will be accepted. An offer might be revoked by the offeror; or rejected by the **offeree**; or the offeree might ask for further information; or the offer might lapse. All these possibilities will be considered.

2 Offer and promise

The first requirement of an offer is that it should contain a promise by the offeror. If there is no promise, there is no offer. In *Gibson v Manchester City Council*,[3] a letter from the council stated, 'The corporation may be prepared to sell the house to you at the purchase price of £2,725 … If you would like to make a formal application to buy …' The House of Lords held that this was not an offer to sell the house, capable of acceptance by Gibson. No reasonable reader of the letter could suppose that the council was promising to sell the house. It did not indicate that present willingness to be bound which is essential to an offer. The council was instead inviting Gibson to offer to buy it. Their letter was what is commonly called 'an invitation to treat', which is an invitation to make an offer.

The use of the word 'offer' does not necessarily mean that an offer in the contractual sense is being made. In *Spencer v Harding*,[4] a circular issued by the defendants began, 'We are instructed to offer to the wholesale trade by **tender** the stock in trade …' and went on to state that payment must be made in cash, and the time when the tenders would be opened. The claimants made the highest tender but the defendants refused to let them have the goods. It was held that there was no contract. The question in such a case is whether the reasonable reader of the circular would have supposed that the defendants were promising

---

[1] [1897] AC 59.

[2] The club would presumably have been able to recover only nominal damages from a defaulting competitor, because the club had suffered no loss. The injured competitor could not, at that date, rely on the contract between the defaulting competitor and the club because of the doctrine of privity of contract. It might be different since the Contracts (Rights of Third Parties) Act 1999 came into force; see Chapter 10.

[3] [1979] 1 WLR 294.

[4] (1870) LR 5, CP 561, Common Pleas.

to sell to the highest bidder. Did they really intend to do so, however low that bid might be? The answer must be in the negative. It would be different, as Willes J said, 'If the circular had gone on, "and we undertake to sell to the highest bidder"' since then the defendants would not only have been inviting bids but also promising to sell to the highest bidder.

The test is not one of the actual intention of the alleged offeror but of his intention as it would have appeared to a reasonable person. If the reasonable person would have thought that the offeror was promising to be bound, then he is promising to be bound. If not, there is no offer to contract. This 'objective'[5] approach leads to something approximating to rules of law in particular common situations; but they are rules which give way to an expression of a contrary intention. For example, it is generally thought that an advertisement in a newspaper that goods are for sale is only an invitation to treat rather than an offer.[6] This is a sound general rule; after all, the advertiser should not be found to have entered into a contract with every person who replies to the advertisement with an 'acceptance'. However, this is only a general rule and can be displaced by the expression of a contrary intention. So, if the advertisement were to offer particular goods for sale at a particular price and go on to say 'First come, first served', then it is highly likely that the first person to accept the offer would have a binding contract with the seller.[7]

(a) Display of goods in a shop

The display of goods in a shop window or in a self-service shop is not an offer to sell the goods but an invitation to the customers to offer to buy them—unless the shopkeeper in some way makes it clear that he does intend the display to be an offer. In *Pharmaceutical Society of Great Britain v Boots*,[8] the question was whether the sale of certain drugs was taking place, as required by law, under the supervision of a registered pharmacist. The society contended that the display of the goods in a self-service shop was an offer to sell the goods which was accepted by the customer when he took an article off the shelves and put it in the wire basket provided. That argument was rejected. The customer offered to buy the goods at the cash point and the cashier, supervised by the pharmacist, could then accept or reject the offer as appropriate. The court was persuaded by the argument that, if the society was right, a customer who took an article from the shelves would have to pay for it, since a contract would already have been concluded. He would not be able to put it back and take something else instead. But no reasonable person would suppose he had bought the item as soon as he put it in the shopping basket. This was therefore sufficient to dismiss the society's case. However, it may be questioned whether this is a conclusive argument against holding the display to be an offer. The court might have held, as some American courts have done,[9] that the display is an offer which is accepted by presenting the goods to the cashier, and not until then. That, however, would have produced a different result in the *Boots* case. In

---

[5] See Chapter 2.

[6] *Partridge v Crittenden* [1968] 1 WLR 1204.

[7] cf *Lefkowitz v Great Minneapolis Surplus Stores Inc*, 86 NW 2d 689 (Minn, 1957). See too *Carlill v Carbolic Smoke Ball Co*, discussed in Chapter 4.

[8] [1953] 1 QB 401, CA.

[9] eg *Sancho-Lopez v Fedor Food Corp*, 211 NYS 2d 953 (1961).

any event, the law is now settled that the mere display of goods is not an offer—unless the shopkeeper clearly indicates that it is.

(b) **Auctions**

The law in respect of auction sales is also well settled. The auctioneer who 'offers' goods for sale is, in law, merely inviting the potential bidders to make offers to buy them, offers which he may or may not accept. Consequently, a bidder may retract his bid at any time before the auctioneer signifies his acceptance by the fall of the hammer, or in another customary manner.[10] But where the auctioneer advertises that the sale shall be without reserve, he is bound to sell to the person who attends and makes the highest bid. The advertisement is an offer by the auctioneer to the whole world, inviting people to attend and bid. The contract is made with a bidder when it is clear that no one is going to make a higher bid than his. This is not a contract of sale: if the auctioneer does not accept the bid, the contract of sale is never made. But in such an event the auctioneer will have broken his contract to sell to the highest bidder and be liable in damages.

In *Barry v Davies*,[11] the auctioneer, *D*, said that certain machines were worth £28,000. *B* made the only bid of £400. *D* refused to accept it, in breach of his promise to sell to the highest bidder. *B* was awarded damages of £26,000. The contract between *B* and *D* was described as 'collateral' to the contract of sale, even though the latter contract (which would have been made between the owner of the machines, through the agency of the auctioneer, and *B*) was never concluded. The advertisement that the sale is to be without reserve is an inducement to attend and bid. The auctioneer obviously wants to attract as many potential bidders as possible so attendance in response to the advertisement is consideration for the auctioneer's promise that the sale shall be without reserve. The decision in *Barry v Davies* finally confirms the fully considered but technically *obiter* opinions stated as long ago as 1859 in *Warlow v Harrison*.[12]

The auctioneer's implied promise is: '*If I put the goods up for sale*, the sale shall be without reserve.' He does not promise that they will be put up for sale. In *Harris v Nickerson*,[13] an auctioneer advertised items for sale at public auction, but the goods were not put up for sale at all. The claimant, who had travelled from London to Bury St Edmunds to bid for the goods, failed in an action for breach of contract to recover his expenses. The court thought that the advertisement was a mere declaration of intention to put the articles up for sale, not a promise to do so. After all, many people may attend the auction in response to the announcement that the goods are to be sold, but there can be only one highest bona fide bidder. It would be 'excessively inconvenient' if the auctioneer were liable to all of those attending, on the basis that they had all intended to bid for some item which had been withdrawn. Reasonable men would not suppose that the auctioneer intended to undertake any such liability and so such a promise should not be imputed to him.

---

[10] Sale of Goods Act 1979, s 57, codifying the **common law**.
[11] [2000] 1 WLR 1962, CA.
[12] (1859) 1 E & E 309 (Exch Chamber).
[13] (1873) LR 8 QB 286.

Taken together, the cases suggest that the auctioneer who advertises that he will sell goods without reserve is saying, in effect, 'I intend (but do not promise) to put these articles up for sale. If I do put these articles up for sale, I promise that the sale shall be without reserve—in other words, I will accept the highest bona fide bid.' Auctioneers might be a little surprised at the complexity of the matter.

(c) Tenders

Whether an invitation to tender amounts to an offer depends on the terms of the invitation, as *Spencer v Harding*[14] shows. If it asks for tenders (in other words, if it asks people to bid for a contract) for the supply of goods of a specified type 'such as we may think fit to order' for one year,[15] it is clearly not an offer because there is no promise to order anything. However, a tender stating the prices at which the tenderer will supply the goods is, in the absence of contrary words, an offer which may be accepted by the placing of an order. As the offer is to remain open for a year and may be accepted from time to time, it is known as a 'standing offer'. Each time an order is placed for goods, there is a new contract. However, a 'general acceptance', not ordering any goods, appears to be no more than an expression of satisfaction of the invitor with the prices proposed. It seems clear that the offeror may, at any time during the year, revoke the offer[16] (not, of course, so as to affect acceptances already made, but for the future). He has received no consideration for any promise to keep the offer open for the year—unless, by a general acceptance of his tender, he can be said to have been promised: 'If we order any goods (and we do not promise to do so) we promise to order them from you.'

On the other hand, if the invitation to tender states that the invitor *will require* certain goods and asks for tenders to supply them, then a tender will, **prima facie**, be an offer capable of a once-and-for-all acceptance by the invitor.

A tenderer may incur substantial expense in responding to an invitation to tender. If his tender is not accepted, this expenditure will be wasted. If the tender has been fairly considered and rejected, he has no complaint. That is the chance he takes. But what if the tender, though submitted before the deadline stipulated and complying in all respects with the invitation, is not even considered? If tenders have been solicited from selected persons known to the invitor and there is a prescribed procedure for submission, then he will have an action for breach of a contract to consider his tender. It seems that he is reasonably entitled to suppose (in the absence of any evidence to the contrary[17]) that the invitor was impliedly promising: 'If you will submit a tender in accordance with these **conditions**, I promise to consider it.' He accepts this offer of a unilateral contract by submitting a tender conforming with the conditions.[18] There are, however, difficulties about quantifying the amount of damages the tenderer should receive: how do we assess the value of the opportunity for

---

[14] n 4.
[15] cf *Great Northern Railway v Witham* (1873) LR 9 CP 16.
[16] cf Chapter 4, Section 2.
[17] cf *Pratt Contractors Ltd v Transit New Zealand* [2003] UKPC 83, [2004] BLR 143.
[18] *Blackpool and Fylde Aeroclub Ltd v Blackpool Borough Council* [1990] 1 WLR 1195.

consideration of the tender which may, or may not, have been accepted? This is a difficult issue, but one which the courts are not afraid to tackle head-on.[19]

3 Acceptance of an offer

Since bilateral contracts consist of an exchange of promises, there must be a strong presumption that communication of an acceptance is required. *O* makes promises to *A* in return for *A* making promises to *O* which *O* requests from *A*. Clearly, this normally requires *A* to communicate to *O* his willingness to promise. After all, to decide to accept an offer is not the same thing as to accept it. For instance, if a committee resolves to accept the offer of a candidate for employment, that resolution will not make a contract. The decision to accept the offer will have to be communicated, and intentionally communicated. If the candidate happened to be listening at the door and overheard the committee's resolution to appoint him, he could not successfully claim to have a contract. If the decision were communicated to him by an unauthorised person he would be no better off,[20] unless that person had 'ostensible authority' (in other words, he was a person whom *A* had led *O* to believe to have authority to speak on *A*'s behalf).

(a) Cross-offers

Much attention has been devoted to the problem of 'cross-offers'. This problem arises where *X* and *Y* each posts an offer in identical terms to the other. Is there a contract when both offers arrive? In the one case in which the matter has been considered,[21] five judges out of six thought, *obiter*, that there is not. Some of the judges seem to have thought offer and acceptance essential and, of course, there was no acceptance. Others stressed the practical inconvenience of holding that a contract had been concluded: parties in this situation would not be clear where they stood, so the right course was to say that there was no contract until one of them had accepted. Until then the transaction lacks the quality of a bargain.

(b) Referential bids

Where the invitation to tender is a firm offer, can it be accepted by a 'referential bid'? The answer given by the House of Lords in *Harvela Investments Ltd v Royal Trust Co of Canada Ltd*[22] is that it cannot. A referential bid is one which can be quantified by reference to other bids. For example, the bid may be: 'I will pay £1,000, or £10 more than any other bid, whichever is higher.' If everyone made referential bids, it would be impossible to determine which was the highest. If a referential bid were effective, a buyer who made only a fixed bid would be deprived of the chance of success; the invitor's object of obtaining the best price that

---

[19] See Chapter 26, Section 6.
[20] *Powell v Lee* (1908) 99 LT 284.
[21] *Tinn v Hoffman* (1873) 29 LT 271.
[22] [1986] AC 207, HL.

bidders were prepared to pay would be frustrated and other bizarre results might follow. In the *Harvela* case, the Royal Trust Company of Canada invited bids for **shares** in a company. Harvela Investments Ltd bid $2.175 million. Sir Leonard Outerbridge bid $2.1 million, or $101,000 in excess of the next highest bid. The Royal Trust Company wrongly thought that the referential bid was a valid acceptance and acted accordingly. But the court held that the company did not understand the nature of the offer it had in fact made. An 'objective' meaning is given to the offer. Because of the unhappy consequences which would result from allowing referential bids, we must take it that the reasonable offeree would say, 'He cannot be supposed to have intended referential bids to be acceptable.'

Yet if the invitor says, 'Referential bids welcome', then referential bids must surely be valid and he must take the consequences. It is for him, and not for any court, to determine the conditions of his offer to contract. But in *Harvela* Lord Templeman thought that each bidder would need to specify a maximum sum he was prepared to bid: for example, '$2.1 million, or $101,000 in excess of the next highest bid, *up to a maximum of $2.5 million*'. This makes clear that bidder's 'best bid', eliminating any danger of the bids escalating forever. Nor would other bidders be deprived of any chance of success: this might be achieved by simply bidding over $2.5 million.

(c) Acceptance through silence

The principle that the offeror can, if he chooses, dispense with communication from the acceptor applies even in the context of bilateral contracts. The offeror can prescribe the mode of acceptance and, if he chooses to prescribe something other than communication, then he is bound by that and there is a contract when that other thing is done. So if O says to A, 'I will sell you my car for £5,000 if you run around my house three times', then all A has to do to accept the offer is run around O's house three times.

However, it is clear that O cannot force a contract on A by writing, 'If I do not hear from you within ten days I will assume that you have agreed to my terms.' A may simply throw such a letter in the bin and ignore it. O cannot impose a contract upon A in such a manner—A should not be forced to take steps in order to *avoid* a contract. It would be the same if O said that he would assume that A agreed to his terms if A did some commonplace act, such as going to his usual place of work on Monday morning. O cannot restrict A's liberty to do such an act, and A should not feel compelled not to go to work for fear of finding himself bound by a contract.

That principle is straightforward to state: O cannot force a contract upon A by saying that silence will constitute acceptance. But what if A wishes to accept the offer through silence? What if A takes O at his word and, with the intention of accepting the offer, remains silent? If A later seeks to enforce the contract, O's defence would be, 'But you did not communicate your acceptance to me.' Surely A may then fairly reply, 'But that was because you told me I need not communicate.' Yet the famous case of *Felthouse v Bindley*[23] affords some authority against this view. An uncle wrote to his nephew, saying that there had been a misunderstanding about the price at which he was to buy the nephew's horse. The uncle

---

[23] (1862) 11 CB (NS) 869, affirmed 7 LT 835.

had thought it was £30, the nephew had thought that it was 30 guineas. The uncle offered to split the difference, writing, 'if I hear no more about him, I consider the horse mine at £30 15s'. The nephew, who was about to sell his farming stock at auction, decided to accept this offer. The nephew did not communicate with his uncle, but directed the auctioneer to keep this horse out of the sale, 'as it had already been sold'. The auctioneer, by mistake, put up the horse with the rest of the stock and sold it. The uncle sued the auctioneer in conversion, alleging that it was his horse that the auctioneer had wrongly sold.

The action in the Court of Common Pleas failed for two reasons. First, there was no contract for the sale of the horse to the uncle because the nephew had not communicated his acceptance. Secondly, even if there were such a contract, it was not enforceable on the day of the auction because it was a contract for the sale of goods at the price of more than £10 and, on that day, there was not in existence a written memorandum of the contract as required by the Statute of Frauds 1677.[24] The Court of Exchequer Chamber affirmed the judgment of the Common Pleas, but on the second ground. The Statute of Frauds had not been complied with and, for that reason, the ownership in the horse had not vested in the claimant. That particular provision of the Statute of Frauds was re-enacted in the Sale of Goods Act 1893 but was repealed by the Law Reform (Enforcement of Contracts) Act 1954.

If the case came before the courts today, it would therefore be necessary to decide whether the first ground given by the Common Pleas was right or wrong. It is suggested that it was wrong. If the horse had died after the nephew had directed the auctioneer to keep it out of the sale but before the time of that sale, surely the uncle could not have resisted his nephew's claim for the price on the ground that the nephew had never communicated his acceptance to him. The uncle had dispensed with his right to have acceptance communicated to him. It was clear that the nephew intended to accept because of his direction to the auctioneer.

The situation would be more difficult if A simply did nothing. If A denied that he intended to accept, it would probably be impossible to challenge that denial effectively. And if A asserted that he intended to accept, O would be in equal difficulty. It might be thought that the difficulties are all of O's own making: O did not need to forego the general requirement that the acceptance be communicated. It should, however, be noted that in a case[25] where a written offer provided that it should become binding only upon its being signed by A, Lord Denning said that there was no contract until A signed the document *and* notified the offeror. Otherwise, '[A] would be able to keep the form in the office unsigned, and then play fast and loose as [A] pleased. [O] would not know whether or not there was a contract binding them …' The other judges did not find it necessary to express an opinion on this point. Where the offer is ambiguous, these considerations raised by Lord Denning should weigh heavily in deciding whether the offer really does relieve A from the need to communicate; but, if O's expressed intention is clear, should he not have to live with the consequences?

Similarly, 'Where the *offeree* himself indicates that an offer is to be taken as accepted if he does not indicate to the contrary by an ascertainable time, he is undertaking to speak if he does not want a contract to be concluded.' This was the view of Peter Gibson LJ, *obiter*, in *Re Selectmove*.[26] His Lordship added that there was no reason in principle why in such a case

---

[24] See Chapter 9.
[25] *Robophone Facilities Ltd v Blank* [1966] 1 WLR 1428, 1432, CA.
[26] [1995] 2 All ER 531, 535–6, CA (emphasis added).

the offeree's silence should not be an acceptance. However, it seems that the better view might be that, in the case envisaged, the offeree might be taken by his 'indication' to have accepted the offer conditionally on his not speaking before the end of the ascertained time.

(d) Contracts made through the post

Where the parties are in each other's presence, it is usually easy to infer that at a particular moment they are in agreement in the same terms on the same subject matter. But it is different where the parties communicate through the post. There will inevitably be a substantial interval between any expression of willingness to be bound by one party and the concurrence of the other. The former may have changed his mind before the latter expresses his concurrence. To meet this difficulty, the courts in the nineteenth century developed a rule ('the rule in *Adams v Lindsell*'[27] or 'the postal rule') that acceptance is complete, and the contract is made, when *A* posts the letter of acceptance. The rule was carried to its logical conclusion in a case which decided that the contract is good even though the letter of acceptance is lost in the post and never arrives.[28] The courts justified this decision on the theoretical basis that the Post Office was *O*'s agent to receive the acceptance. This is obviously a fiction. A pillar box is no more an agent than a hollow tree. And the Post Office's duty is simply to transmit the letter unread. The 'postal rule' is in fact simply one of business convenience. The law might equally have hit upon the moment of delivery of the acceptance as the moment of the formation of contract, but it would have been necessary to decide whether that moment was when the letter was delivered to the premises or when it was read—or, perhaps, ought to have been read in the normal course of business. Such difficulties are avoided by the postal rule, which is at least precise and relatively easy to prove. It is likely that the judges who developed the postal rule in the mid-nineteenth century were also aware that the rule that acceptance occurred upon posting had the benefit of encouraging businesses to use and rely upon the Royal Mail, which was considered to be advantageous. Indeed, the moment of the posting of the acceptance is the earliest moment at which it is possible to hold that a contract is in existence, thus making for expedition in business transactions.

It is, however, important to note the narrow limits of the rule in *Adams v Lindsell*. It is strictly confined to the acceptance of offers. It has no application to the making, or revocation, of offers, or to any other element in negotiations for a contract. This demonstrates the fictional nature of the agency theory. The Post Office is not deemed an agent to receive any of these other communications. As a result, most of the hypothetical cases put by Bramwell LJ in his dissent in *Household Fire Insurance Co v Grant* to demonstrate the absurdity of the postal rule laid down by the majority are simply not relevant.

If I am a **tenant** farmer and write to my **landlord**, offering to sell him some hay, and he replies accepting my offer and in the same letter (ungratefully!) gives me **notice to quit**, it is important to distinguish between the acceptance of my offer and his notice to quit. The contract of sale is concluded when the letter is posted, since the postal rule applies to the

---

[27] The rule is conveniently described in this way since *Adams v Lindsell* (1818) 1 B & Ald 681 is the case in which it first appeared.

[28] *Household Fire Insurance Co v Grant* (1879) 4 ExD 216, CA.

acceptance. But the notice to quit is not valid unless and until it arrives, since the postal rule applies to acceptances *only* and the notice to quit is not an acceptance. Some judges have sometimes fallen into the same trap as Bramwell LJ in their attempts to ridicule the postal rule by failing to distinguish acceptances from all other elements of communication. For instance, Lawton LJ has asked: 'Is a stockbroker who is holding shares to the order of his client liable in damages because he did not sell in a falling market in accordance with the instructions in a letter which was posted but never received?'[29] But the answer to this question is entirely straightforward. Of course he is not liable. The client's letter is not a letter accepting an offer of a contract. The rule in *Adams v Lindsell* simply does not apply.

The operation of the rule can always be excluded by *O* if he wishes. If he indicates, expressly or impliedly, that acceptance must actually be communicated, then the contract is not complete on posting but only when the acceptance arrives. Where an option to purchase **freehold** property (which is an offer) provided that it was exercisable (ie could be accepted) 'by notice in writing to [*O*]', it was held that the phrase, 'notice ... to' required actual communication.[30] The postal rule therefore did not apply. The case reveals some judicial unhappiness with the rule in *Adams v Lindsell*, and the opinion that 'it probably does not operate if its application would produce manifest inconvenience and absurdity'.[31] The courts may therefore now be more easily persuaded that the circumstances of the case are such that *A*, as a reasonable man, would have known that *O* did not intend the postal rule to apply. General principles would suggest that the test ought to be, 'Would the reasonable man who received the offer realise that the offeror required actual communication?' However, this approach is difficult to apply in this context because, unlike most of the principles governing the formation of contract, we are here dealing with an arbitrary and artificial rule which the ordinary person who has never studied law is probably unaware of. It may therefore be that the postal rule should be abolished. In any event, however, in commercial transactions the postal rule rarely applies because it is invariably excluded by the parties. Indeed, where *O* sets a deadline for acceptance, this is likely impliedly to exclude the rule in *Adams v Lindsell*. What is the point of setting a deadline if not actually to receive the acceptance before the specified time?

The application of the rule in *Adams v Lindsell* has not been confined to the case where the *offer* is made through the post. It has been said that it applies 'Where the circumstances are such that it must have been within the contemplation of the parties that, according to the ordinary usages of mankind, the post might be used as the means of communicating the acceptance of an offer ...'[32] The rule was therefore held to apply when *A*, who lived in Birkenhead, was handed the offer in *O*'s office in Liverpool and took it away with him. A contract was made when the acceptance was posted in Birkenhead. *O* must have contemplated that *A* might send his acceptance by post.[33] However, it should be noted that the above **dictum** was uttered when there was probably more enthusiasm for the rule in *Adams*

---

[29] *Holwell Securities Ltd v Hughes* [1974] 1 WLR 155, 161 (Lawton LJ).
[30] Ibid.
[31] Ibid, 161 (Lawton LJ).
[32] *Henthorn v Fraser* [1892] 2 Ch 27, 33 (Lord Herschell).
[33] Ibid.

v Lindsell than there is today. It is possible that the rule would now be less readily applied in similar circumstances.

It is worth emphasising that the postal rule is an exception to the general principle that an acceptance needs to be communicated to the offeror, and should therefore be interpreted narrowly: it only applies to letters sent via the Royal Mail and only to acceptances. It follows that the rule in *Adams v Lindsell* has no application to the revocation of an offer. If *O* has made an offer to *A* through the post and he wishes to revoke it, he must actually communicate his revocation to *A*. This was settled in the case of *Byrne v Van Tienhoven*,[34] where Lindley J held that the principle that the Post Office is an agent did not apply to the withdrawal of an offer. As the rule in *Adams v Lindsell* was by then well settled, it would have made no practical sense to hold that a revocation was effective on posting. One of the virtues of the postal rule is that *A*, once he has posted his letter, can act in absolute confidence that he has made a binding contract. But if a revocation were effective on posting, *A* could never know whether or not there was a letter revoking the offer in the post. *A* would not know how he stood, and nor would *O*, because when *O* posted his revocation he could not be sure whether an acceptance had already been posted. Under the law as it stands, at least *A* can be confident of his position, even though *O* cannot. However, if *A* has wrongly addressed his letter of acceptance, then it seems that the rule in *Adams v Lindsell* does not apply and the acceptance will only take effect, if at all, when it is received by *O*.[35] This is sensible: *A* is in a position to know when the contract is made by complying with the postal rule, but if he is at fault in increasing further the delay in communication of the letter by writing the wrong address, the consequence should be that *A* **forfeits** the protection afforded by the rule in *Adams v Lindsell*.

One difficult question which seems to arise more in theory than in practice concerns what should happen if *A* accepts an offer by post but then changes his mind and rings up *O* to tell him that he rejects the offer. This might be important where the contract is for the sale of goods in a fluctuating market. Imagine that *O* offers for sale to *A* 1,000 shares in a company for £1,000. *A* thinks this is a good deal and posts his acceptance. The next day, the stock market crashes such that the shares are now only worth £500. *A* realises that he has made a bad deal so rings up *O* to reject the offer. Of course, the first communication that *O* actually receives is the telephone call, so it might be thought that *O* is not prejudiced if *A* is allowed to escape any deal. This appears to have been the view, *obiter*, of Bramwell LJ in *Household Fire Insurance Co v Grant*. However, it is suggested that it is unsatisfactory to allow *A* to speculate in this way. The postal rule should be strictly applied: the contract was concluded at the moment of posting, and *A* cannot 'revoke' an acceptance—that would simply be a breach of contract.[36] Of course, if *O* acted upon the telephone call by selling the shares to a third party, then *A* should not later be able to change his mind again and argue that he is entitled to the shares because the postal rule applies. That would clearly be unfair.

---

[34] (1880) 5 CPD 344.

[35] *Korbetis v Transgrain Shipping BV* [2005] EWHC 1345 (QB) [15] (Toulson J).

[36] This was the view of Lord Craigie, dissenting, in *Countess of Dunmore v Alexander* (1830) 9 S 190 (Scotland).

(e) **Instantaneous means of communication**

As has already been observed, the reason for the rule in *Adams v Lindsell* was the substantial delay which necessarily occurs in expressions of intention through the post. There is no reason to apply the rule to instantaneous communications and it has been decided that it does not apply. In the case of communications through **telex** or fax or email which are, and are intended to be, virtually instantaneous, the general rule that acceptance must be communicated applies. So, when O in London made an offer by telex to A in the Netherlands, and A's acceptance was received on O's telex machine in London, the contract was held to be made in London, because it was made when and where the acceptance was received.[37] When A posts a letter, he is adopting a means of communication which does not usually fail but he has no means of knowing whether the letter will arrive or, later, whether it has arrived. But the same is not true when A sends a telex or fax or email message to O during O's business hours, since A will usually either receive an immediate acknowledgement or a bounce-back message if something has gone wrong. As a result, A should be able to ascertain whether or not the acceptance has been communicated. If A receives such a bounce-back message, he cannot reasonably act on the assumption that his acceptance has arrived or will arrive. He must try to get through again, since there will be no contract unless and until the acceptance is actually received. In *Entores Ltd v Miles Far East Corp*, Denning LJ famously gave a string of similar examples, such as where in the course of acceptance over the telephone the line goes dead, or, more dramatically, whilst shouting an acceptance over a ravine an aircraft flies overhead and drowns out A's words. In such situations, A cannot assume that an acceptance has been communicated so A must try again. The only exception would be where O leads A to suppose that the acceptance has been received when it has not. O would then be **estopped** from denying that there was a contract.

This is the position when the communication is, and is intended to be, instantaneous. But a telex, fax, or email communication may be neither instantaneous nor intended to be so. It may be sent or received through third parties. Lord Wilberforce has said that[38] 'No universal rule can cover all such cases; they must be resolved by reference to the intentions of the parties, by sound business practice and in some cases by a judgment where the risks should lie.' So, if A sends an acceptance to O at an hour when he knows O's office is closed and that the message will not be read for some time, the position is not entirely settled. It is suggested that the acceptance should be held to have been communicated only when O's office reopens for business.[39] For example, if A sends an acceptance at midnight on Friday evening, knowing that O's business is shut until 9 am on Monday morning, the acceptance will only be considered to have been communicated soon after 9 am on Monday morning.

(f) **Parties become bound when they intend to do so**

'[P]arties become bound by contract when, and in the manner in which, they intend and contemplate becoming bound.'[40] This is a fundamental principle. The offeror may dictate

---

[37] *Entores Ltd v Miles Far East Corp* [1955] 2 QB 327, CA.
[38] *Brinkibon Ltd v Stahag Stahl* [1983] 2 AC 34, 42.
[39] See *The Brimnes* [1975] QB 929, CA.
[40] Lord Greene MR in *Eccles v Bryant* [1948] Ch 93.

the terms on which he is prepared to be bound. If both parties have proceeded on the basis that the contract shall be concluded at a particular time and in a particular manner, then the contract can be made only at that time and in that manner.

O may therefore lay down his own rules as to how his offer may be accepted. If he chooses to stipulate some eccentric act as the only manner in which his offer may be accepted, that is effective. *O* may require *A* to place his letter of acceptance in the hollow tree before midnight if he so wishes. But *A* must comply with the form of acceptance demanded by *O*. So, if *O* stipulates that acceptance must be by notice in writing to himself, *O*, then a notice given to *O*'s solicitor is ineffective.[41] However, unless *O* makes it quite clear that only the specified method of acceptance will suffice, the court is likely to interpret the offer to mean that any other method of acceptance which is no less advantageous to *O* will conclude the contract. Thus, if an offer is made through the post, it would generally be possible to accept that offer over the telephone or by email rather than by letter. Once again, the test should presumably be: how would a reasonable person interpret the offer?

(g) **Conveyancing transactions**

There is a well-established practice among solicitors that contracts for the sale of land become binding only when the two copies of the contract, signed by the vendor and by the purchaser respectively, are exchanged. Even though each party to the contract has already signed a contractual document in identical terms, the contract is not concluded until the two documents are exchanged. This is because the parties, through their solicitors, do not intend it to be binding until the documents are exchanged. In *Eccles v Bryant*,[42] both parties had signed a copy of the contract. The purchaser had posted his part and it had been received by the vendor, but the vendor declined to deliver his part and **repudiated** the agreement. There was therefore no contract. Lord Greene thought that the earliest time at which a contract could come into existence is when the later of the two documents is actually put into the post. This is the rule in the Law Society's *Conditions of Sale*, 2.1.1[43] in accordance with which solicitors commonly act.

It follows from the broad principle stated in *Eccles v Bryant* that the 'exchange rule' does not apply if the conduct of the parties indicates that they do not intend it to apply. In other words, the 'default approach' can be modified by the parties' intentions. In *Storer v Manchester City Council*,[44] the council wrote to the claimant, a council house tenant, as follows: 'I understand you wish to purchase your council house and enclose the Agreement for Sale. If you will sign the agreement and return it to me I will send the agreement signed on behalf of [the Council] in exchange.' The claimant signed and sent back the agreement but, before the town clerk returned it, Labour gained control of the council from the Conservatives and declined to proceed with the sale. The Court of Appeal held that there was a specifically enforceable contract between the claimant and the council. The council had made a firm offer to sell which the claimant had accepted by signing and returning the agreement as requested. It was immaterial that the town clerk did not subjectively intend

---

41 *Holwell Securities Ltd v Hughes* [1974] 1 WLR 155.
42 [1948] Ch 93.
43 Law Society, *Conditions of Sale* (5th edn, 2011).
44 [1974] 1 WLR 1403, CA.

to be bound, except on exchange. As assessed objectively by a reasonable observer, he had not evinced that intention. On the contrary, he had expressed a willingness to be bound before exchange.

The usual 'exchange principle' is a valuable one because it ensures that neither party is bound until he has a document of **title** in his hands. However, it has sometimes caused particular difficulties where there is a chain of contracts for the sale and purchase of houses. For example, it is very common for X and Y to have agreed, subject to contract, on the sale of Y's house to X; but X cannot afford to bind himself to buy until he has a contract for the sale of his own house to W; and Y may be unwilling to bind himself to sell the house to X until he has secured a firm contract with Z to buy Z's house. The chain of contracts contemplated may be represented as follows:

$$W \leftrightarrow X \leftrightarrow Y \leftrightarrow Z$$

If the procedure envisaged in *Eccles v Bryant* is followed and each contract is concluded only when an exchange through the post is complete, there is a grave risk that X may find that he has committed himself to buy Y's house, but that W has changed his mind and refuses to buy X's house, with the result that X has two houses on his hands. And Y may find that he has committed himself to sell to X, but that Z has changed his mind, meaning that Y is left without a house at all. The risks are inevitable because of the delay involved in the process of exchange. If the solicitors of all four parties could meet together and exchange the signed parts of the contracts virtually simultaneously, all risk could be eliminated; but it will usually be impracticable for them to meet. A solution has been found in a system of 'exchange' by telephone. If all the contracts have been signed and all the parties are ready to proceed, W's solicitor may agree to hold the contract signed by W to the order of X's solicitor who in turn will agree to hold X's signed contract to sell to W to the order of W's solicitor. X's solicitor will also agree to hold X's signed contract to buy from Y to the order of Y's solicitor—and so on down the chain. Some of the contracts may have been physically delivered in advance and held to the order of the delivering solicitor until the time agreed for the 'constructive' (or notional) transfer. But it seems that there need be no physical delivery at all. In the leading case of *Domb v Isoz*[45] Buckley LJ said: 'Exchange of a written contract for sale is in my judgment effected as soon as each part of the contract signed by the vendor or the purchaser as the case may be, is in the actual or constructive possession of the other party or of his solicitor.' When W's solicitor agreed to hold the contract signed by W to the order of X's solicitor, that document, though physically held by W's solicitor, was in the 'constructive' possession of X's solicitor. This, in Buckley LJ's words,[46] satisfies 'the essential characteristic of exchange of contracts' since 'each party shall have a document signed by the other party in his possession or control so that, at his own need, he can have the document available for his own use.' The assumption is that a client is no worse off when a document is held on his behalf by someone else's solicitor than when it is held by his own solicitor. The system therefore assumes the integrity of solicitors. When a solicitor is instructed by a vendor or purchaser, he has, in the absence of instructions to the contrary, authority to carry the transaction through in accordance with the custom and practice of

---

[45] [1980] Ch 548, 557.
[46] Ibid, 557.

the profession, including the procedure of exchange and now the procedure of exchange by telephone. The Law Society's *Conditions of Sale*, 2.1.2 provide:[47]

> If the parties' solicitors agree to treat exchange as taking place before duplicate copies are actually exchanged, the contract is made as so agreed.

4 The duration of an offer

An offer continues in existence for so long as the offeror intends it to continue. If he states, 'This offer is to remain open until noon on 1 April', it remains open until that moment and then ceases to exist. It may be that the offeror specifies no time for the termination of the offer but it is highly improbable that he intended it to last for ever, and the reasonable person would not suppose that he did. The offer therefore comes to an end after the lapse of a reasonable time. The most obvious explanation for this is that there is an implied term to that effect in the offer itself: any reasonable observer would assume that this is what the offeror in fact intended, even though he did not actually say so. But in one case Buckley J suggested a different explanation; namely, that the failure to accept within a reasonable time amounts to an implied rejection of the offer, which also brings the offer to an end.[48] The practical difference was thought to be that the implied term theory involves an inquiry into what the parties as reasonable men would have thought to be a reasonable time *when the offer was made*; whereas the implied rejection theory required the court to take into account events occurring after the offer was made, enabling it to make an objective assessment of the facts and to decide whether, in fairness to both parties, the offeree should be regarded as having refused the offer. As Buckley J wanted to take into account events occurring after the offer was made, he preferred the latter theory.

5 Rejection, counter-offers, and mere inquiries

An offer comes to an end when the offeree rejects it. This is because, on receipt of the rejection, the offeror will naturally regard himself as free to make inconsistent offers to others, free from the liability to become bound to the first offeree; and the offeree, as a reasonable person, must know this. A counter-offer has the same effect as a rejection. For example, imagine that *O* offers to sell his farm to *A* for £1,000. *A* replies, offering to buy the farm for £950. *O* refuses this counter-offer. *A* then 'accepts' the offer to sell for £1,000. But *A* is too late. *O*'s offer terminated when *O* received the counter-offer.[49] Again, the reason would appear to be that, on receipt of the counter-offer, *O* was entitled to suppose that *A* was not interested in the offer to sell for £1,000 and to regard himself as free to offer the property elsewhere. Whether he in fact offers it elsewhere is immaterial.

---

[47] Law Society, *Conditions of Sale* (5th edn, 2011).

[48] *Manchester Diocesan Council for Education v Commercial and General Investments Ltd* [1970] 1 WLR 241.

[49] *Hyde v Wrench* (1840) 3 Beav 334.

It is necessary to distinguish between a counter-offer and a mere inquiry. A mere inquiry is not an offer nor a rejection; the making of a mere inquiry leaves the original offer standing. In *Stevenson, Jaques & Co v McLean*, O offered to sell A some iron for 40 shillings, and specified no time for delivery. A replied: 'Please wire whether you would accept 40 for delivery over two months, or if not, longest time you would give.' It was held that A's reply left the offer intact, and therefore a subsequent acceptance of it was valid.[50] It is important to note that A was not offering to buy at 40 shillings for delivery over two months and that his message did not contradict any express term in the offer.

It follows logically from these principles that all the terms of the contract must be contained, expressly or impliedly, in the offer. An acceptance which purports to add something to the terms is, by definition, a counter-offer and does not create a contract unless and until it is accepted. Attention should, however, be drawn to 'The Uniform Law on the Formation of Contracts for the International Sale of Goods' in Schedule 2 to the Uniform Laws on International Sales Act 1967. This provides (Article 7.2) that:

> a reply to an offer which purports to be an acceptance but which contains additional or different terms which do not materially alter the terms of the offer shall constitute an acceptance unless the offeror promptly objects to the discrepancy; if he does not so object, the terms of the contract shall be the terms of the offer with the modifications contained in the acceptance.

While this is the law of England where the parties choose the Uniform Law of Sales as the law of the contract, it does not necessarily follow that it is the law for any other type of contract governed by English law. When O has made an offer on particular terms, he should not have different or additional terms forced upon him. It is for him, not for the court, to say whether any modification is 'material' or not. To impose on O the obligation promptly to object if he does not wish to be bound seems to be contrary to the principle of *Felthouse v Bindley*.[51] If, however, O proceeds to act on the proposed contract after receiving A's modified acceptance, then he might properly be held to have agreed to the modification proposed; that would simply be an acceptance by conduct of A's counter-offer.

(a) Battle of the forms

This problem is of practical importance in what has become known as 'the battle of the forms'. Two businesses each have standard forms of agreement, but they are not the same as one another. Each business is anxious that the proposed contract shall be governed by its standard terms and not the other side's. X makes an offer on his form. Y replies purporting to accept, but on his form. Clearly, X cannot preclude Y from offering different terms by including in his offer a statement that his terms are to prevail over any terms in Y's reply.

If Y does reply, offering different terms and X then accepts—either expressly or by conduct—the contract is made on Y's terms. In the leading case, *Butler Machine Tool Co Ltd v Ex-Cell-O Corp (England) Ltd*,[52] X signed and returned a tear-off slip on Y's form that

---

[50] (1880) 5 QBD 346.
[51] See Section 3(c).
[52] [1979] 1 WLR 401.

stated: 'We accept your order on the terms and conditions stated thereon'. Although they added, referring back to their own form, 'Your official order ... is being entered in accordance with our revised quotation on 23rd May', the return of the slip made it clear that the contract was made on *Y*'s terms. *Y* had fired the 'last shot' in offering to contract on *Y*'s standard terms, and *X* had accepted this. The majority of the Court of Appeal thought that this conclusion was in accordance with standard principles of offer and acceptance and, indeed, Lord Denning himself appears to have applied these principles too. However, Lord Denning (but not the majority) thought that this was a somewhat arbitrary and rigid approach, commenting that 'In many of these cases our traditional analysis of offer, counter-offer, rejection, acceptance and so forth is out-of-date.' Lord Denning preferred an approach that gave the courts the flexibility to find agreement on material terms and decide which terms constituted the agreement. This clearly gives judges a more active role in contract formation than has traditionally been recognised, and seems inappropriate. Indeed, in *Tekdata Interconnections Ltd v Amphenol*,[53] the Court of Appeal insisted upon the general application of offer and acceptance principles and declined to follow Lord Denning's favoured approach. Thus, where a 'last shot' is accepted, the terms of the last shot will be the terms of the contract. Where such a last shot cannot be discerned, and there genuinely is no offer and acceptance, the preferable view may well be that there is no contract and a remedy should be sought in unjust enrichment.[54] So, if *X* refuses to accept *Y*'s last shot and makes it clear that acceptance is only on *X*'s terms, and *Y* disputes this, then there is no last shot that is accepted and therefore no correspondence of offer and acceptance. In such circumstances, the better conclusion is arguably that no contract has been concluded, and if *Y* has already supplied goods to *X*, *Y* should be able to recover the reasonable value of those goods from *X* through a claim in unjust enrichment.[55]

6 Revocation of offers

A promise to keep an offer open for a specified period, like promises in English law generally, is enforceable only if it is in a deed or given for consideration. If *O* offers to sell property to *A* and says that he will keep the offer open for six weeks, *O* may, at any time within the six weeks, revoke the offer by giving notice to *A*.[56] The rationale is that *A* is not bound in any way, so why should *O* be bound? The rule has been criticised and may perhaps give rise to injustice where *A* acts in reliance on the offer. For instance, *A* might enter into other contracts on the assumption that he can call on *O* to perform the contract he has offered to make, which *A* will obviously not be able to do if the offer has been revoked. Nevertheless, the principle that *O* remains able to revoke his offer is clear and well entrenched in English law.

However, if *O* accepts consideration from *A* in return for a promise to keep the offer open, then *A* will have an effective remedy against *O* if *O* tries to revoke the offer. In

---

[53] [2009] EWCA Civ 1209, [2010] 1 Lloyd's Rep 357.

[54] *British Steel Corp v Cleveland Bridge & Engineering Co Ltd* [1984] 1 All ER 504.

[55] See Chapter 28, Section 4.

[56] *Routledge v Grant* (1828) 4 Bing 653.

Mountford v Scott,[57] *O*, in consideration of the payment of £1, granted in writing an option to *A* to purchase *O*'s house for £10,000, exercisable within six months. Within the six months and before the option was exercised, *O* purported to withdraw his offer. *A* then exercised the option. The Court of Appeal held that *A* was entitled to **specific performance** of a contract for the sale of the house. Even though the Court of Appeal held that the trial judge had wrongly concentrated on the question of whether the option agreement was specifically enforceable, the decision seems, in effect, to be that the option agreement *was* specifically enforceable. The offer continued in existence notwithstanding *O*'s purported revocation of it. *A* was not restricted to damages for breach of the option agreement.

Where the offer is made to a particular person or persons, the offer can be revoked by communicating with that person or persons. But where the offer is made to the public at large, communication of a revocation to everyone individually is impracticable. The question of the revocation of such an offer does not seem to have arisen in England. In the United States, the solution is that the offer may be revoked by giving the same notoriety to the revocation as was given to the offer.[58] If that is done, the offer is revoked. It is immaterial that *A*, who thereafter purports to accept, was unaware of the revocation. On the assumption that it ought to be possible for a person who has made an offer to the public to be able to revoke it, this seems to be the only practicable solution. Yet it is not free from difficulty. If the offer has been made by a full-page advertisement in *The Times*, then it can be revoked by a full-page advertisement in *The Times*, but when is the revocation effective? Perhaps the answer is when ordinary readers of *The Times* might reasonably have been expected to see it.

O revokes his offer by making it clear to *A* that he is no longer willing to be bound on the terms specified in the offer. If he does this, it is immaterial that his communication is not explicitly in terms of the revocation of an offer. In one case, *O* was wrongly under the impression that his offer to buy a car had been accepted, but he did not wish to go through with the supposed contract, and he returned the car offering to forfeit his deposit. In fact, his offer to buy had not been accepted. The court held that what *O* did was sufficient to revoke the offer. Even though *O* thought he was offering to **rescind** what he believed to be a binding contract, he had in fact made it clear that he did not wish to be bound by his offer. As that offer was still unaccepted, what *O* did was enough to revoke it.[59]

If *O* does something inconsistent with the continued existence of his offer and *A* has notice of this, *A* can no longer accept. In effect, the offer is revoked. If *O* offers to sell property to *A*, and then sells it to *B*, or enters into a binding contract to sell it to *B*, then *A* cannot subsequently accept *O*'s offer if *A* has already received notice of this fact from a trustworthy source. This was the decision in *Dickinson v Dodds*.[60] In an unguarded example, Mellish LJ appeared to suggest that the mere sale of the property by *O* to *B* was sufficient to revoke his offer to *A*. However, this is clearly not so, and it is certain that Mellish LJ did not intend to

---

[57] [1975] 2 WLR 114.
[58] *Shuey v United States*, 92 US 73 (1875).
[59] *Financings Ltd v Stimson* [1962] 1 WLR 1184.
[60] (1876) 2 ChD 463.

say so. If *A* were to accept within the time specified in the offer to him, in ignorance of the fact that *O* had already sold to *B*, *O* would be bound to both *A* and *B* and would necessarily be forced to break his contract with one of them.

7 Express or implied terms terminating offer

If *O* states that his offer is to terminate on the occurrence of a specified event and that event occurs, the offer is at an end. *A* can no longer accept, regardless of whether or not he is aware of the occurrence of the event. An offer may be subject to implied as well as express conditions. An actual contract may be terminated by the occurrence of certain events under the doctrine of frustration.[61]

It is obvious that any event which would frustrate the proposed contract, had it been entered into, must also terminate the offer when the event occurs before the offer is accepted. For example, imagine *O* offers to let his theatre to *A* for a performance on 1 April; but on 1 February, before *A* has accepted, the theatre is burnt down.[62] Or suppose *O* offers to let rooms to *A* to view a procession on 1 May but on 10 April, before *A* has accepted, the procession is cancelled.[63] In such cases the offer must be terminated because, even if it had been accepted, the contract would have been frustrated.

The question is whether an offer might be 'frustrated' in circumstances in which the contemplated contract, had it been made, would not. In *Financings Ltd v Stimson*,[64] *O* offered to buy *A*'s car. In the interval between *O*'s offering to buy the car and *A*'s acceptance of that offer, the car was stolen and badly damaged. It was held that the acceptance was not effective. The offer had come to an end. There was an express provision in the offer that the buyer had examined the car and satisfied himself that it was in good order and condition. The court held that the offer was impliedly conditional on the car remaining in substantially the same condition until the moment of acceptance. If the contract had been concluded, it is not clear that the damage to the car, after the contract was made but before delivery, would have amounted to frustration.

Suppose *O* offers to buy *A*'s garage business for £100,000. The offer is to remain open for seven days. Two days later, plans are announced for a by-pass which will divert the bulk of the traffic away from the garage. Realising that *O* will no longer want the garage, or at least that *O* will not want to pay so large a sum for it, *A* immediately posts a letter of acceptance. If the contract had been made, the announcement would not have frustrated it, but there seem to be good grounds for arguing that the offer should no longer be regarded as open. If *A* must, as a reasonable person, have realised that *O* would no longer wish his offer to stand in the changed circumstances, it is arguable that the offer should be regarded as at an end.

---

[61] See Chapter 23.
[62] cf *Taylor v Caldwell* (1863) 3 B & S 826, QB.
[63] cf *Krell v Henry* [1903] 2 KB 740, CA.
[64] [1962] 1 WLR 1184.

(a) **Death of the offeror**

The effect on the offer of O's death depends on the nature of the offer. If it is to render personal services of some kind, the offer terminates upon O's death. If O, having written to A offering to write a book, dies after posting the letter, A cannot then accept and sue O's **personal representatives** for damages when the book fails to materialise. The offer died with O and it is quite immaterial whether A knew of O's death when he purported to accept. However, where the contract is not one for personal services and remains capable of performance notwithstanding O's death, then A may accept so long as he is unaware of O's death. This may be possible where the obligation merely involves the payment of money. In *Bradbury v Morgan*,[65] O asked A to extend credit from time to time to X and promised to guarantee payment of the balance of X's account. O died, but A, unaware of O's death, continued to extend credit to X. O had made a standing offer to A. Each time A gave credit to X, A accepted O's offer. It was held that A was entitled to claim the money from O's **executors** on O's guarantee. Bramwell B thought that the offer would not come to an end until the executor of the offeror gave notice; but later cases hold that such a guarantee comes to an end when the offeree has notice that the guarantor is dead. This amounts to notice of trusts which, if the guarantor has made a will may be, and if he has died intestate will be,[66] incompatible with the continuance of the guarantee.

These principles apply to the case of a simple offer. It may be different if the deceased has contracted to keep the offer open, for then that contract is binding on his personal representatives. In *Lloyd's v Harper*,[67] a father promised Lloyd's that, if they would admit his son as an underwriter, he would bear responsibility for all his son's engagements as an underwriter. That was an offer of a unilateral contract which was concluded when Lloyd's admitted the son. When, after the father's death, the son ran into financial difficulties, it was held that the contract was binding on his personal representatives. The guarantee, having been given for a once-and-for-all consideration, was irrevocable in the guarantor's lifetime and was not revoked by his death.[68]

These cases tend to concern unilateral contracts. Offers of bilateral contracts are less likely to survive the death of the offeror because the impossibility of performance on either side will nullify the offer. Moreover, the process of exchanging promises may well bring to the notice of the offeree the fact that the offeror is dead. But there seems no reason in principle why offers of contracts not requiring personal performance by the offeror should not survive his death.

---

[65] (1862) 1 H & C 249.

[66] *Re Whelan* [1897] 1 IR 575 (Chatterton V-C).

[67] (1880) 16 ChD 290.

[68] See too *Errington v Errington* [1952] 1 KB 290, considered in Chapter 4, Section 2: Denning LJ held that the father's offer to his son and daughter-in-law was not revoked by the father's death, even though, obviously, the offerees knew he had died. In that case, the father had contracted in his lifetime to keep the offer open and that contract was binding on his personal representative.

(b) **Death of the offeree**

If knowledge of the other party's death precludes the conclusion of a contract, it follows that the offeree's death will generally bring the offer to an end. Unlike cases such as *Bradbury v Morgan*, the act of acceptance cannot be done in ignorance of the death of the other party because it is to be done by the party who is dead. Moreover, any authority of an agent to conclude the contract on his behalf is revoked by his death.

Further Reading

A Hudson, 'Retractation of Letters of Acceptance' (1966) 82 LQR 169.
Considers the unclear point about whether A who has posted a letter of acceptance can 'retract' his acceptance by a speedier means of communication in order to avoid being bound.

C Miller, '*Felthouse v Bindley* Revisited' (1972) 35 MLR 489.
Critically analyses the decision in *Felthouse v Bindley*, arguing it was wrongly decided: positive conduct by A is unnecessary where O has waived the need for communication.

D Nolan, 'Offer and Acceptance in the Electronic Age' in A Burrows and E Peel (eds), *Contract Formation and Parties* (OUP, 2010).
Discusses contracts concluded by email, and argues that an email is received when it arrives on the server which manages the offeror's email, and that the contract should generally be concluded at that moment rather than a later point at which the email was read or ought reasonably to have been read.

Question

On Monday, Fitz wrote to Olivia and Cyrus as follows: 'I own Usain Bolt's running shoes, which he used in the 2012 Olympics. I am prepared to sell the shoes to the highest bidder. Please submit your best bid by 09:00 next Thursday.'

On Tuesday, Olivia sent Fitz a letter which said: 'I will pay £30,000 or £500 more than the highest fixed-price bid, subject to a maximum of £45,000.' This letter arrived the following day but was ignored by Fitz.

On Thursday at 08:55 (just before the deadline), Cyrus emailed Fitz: 'I can pay £40,000 by instalments over the next six months.' Fitz replied by email at 08:59: 'Let's keep it simple. I assume that you're bidding £40,000 for immediate payment.' Cyrus replied at 09.01: 'Agreed; I'll pay £40,000 in cash on delivery.'

On Thursday at 15:00, Fitz received a telephone call from Huck, who offered £50,000 for the shoes.

Advise Fitz.

4 Formation of unilateral contracts

🔑 Key Points

- A unilateral contract arises where O promises A something if A does a particular act which is not the making of a promise to O.
- A unilateral contract only imposes obligations on O. A is not obliged to do anything.
- A unilateral offer can be accepted by A regardless of A's motive for doing the required act. However, A must know of the offer in order for a contract to be formed.
- O may not be able to revoke the offer if A has embarked upon performance. This will depend upon whether or not O has made an implied promise not to revoke the offer.

O makes an offer of a unilateral contract to A when he promises A that he will do something (or that something is so) *if* A will do a specified act, other than the making of a promise to O. A may then accept the offer by doing that act. A standard example arises when O promises A £100 if A will walk to York. The promise becomes binding only when A reaches York. If A falls and breaks his leg five yards from the city boundary and completes the journey in an ambulance, he is entitled to nothing. Nor has A committed a breach of contract. He did not promise to do anything. He was entirely free not to start on the walk or to abandon it at any time.

When deciding whether an offer is an offer of a bilateral contract or of a unilateral contract the usual principles of interpretation must be applied.[1] Would a reasonable person in the position of A think he was being asked to promise to do the act, or being asked simply to go ahead and do it? For example, is A being asked to promise to walk to York (which could lead to a bilateral contract) or is A being asked simply to walk to York (which could lead to a unilateral contract)? If the latter, A cannot turn the offer of a unilateral contract into a bilateral contract by promising to walk to York. A's promise would be irrelevant. It would not be an acceptance. It is for O, and him alone, to prescribe the mode of acceptance. O is therefore free to prescribe that A must actually walk to York (rather than promise to walk to York) in order to accept the offer. Of course, A is free just to ignore the offer if he considers it unattractive.

---

[1] See Chapter 12.

The classic case on unilateral contracts is *Carlill v Carbolic Smoke Ball Co.*[2] The company advertised that it would pay a £100 'reward' to any person who caught influenza after having used the smoke ball three times daily for two weeks, according to the printed directions supplied with each smoke ball. Mrs Carlill used the ball as prescribed and then caught influenza. It was held by the Court of Appeal that she was entitled to the reward. The act requested, and therefore the consideration supplied by her, was the use of the ball for two weeks. As soon as she had completed that act she had a contract with the company which continued to exist at least as long as she persisted in using the smoke ball three times daily. Moreover, it was clear that the company had made an offer in their advertisement, rather than simply an invitation to treat,[3] and intended to be taken seriously. This was because the company explicitly stated that '£1000 is deposited with the Alliance Bank Regent Street, shewing our sincerity in the matter'. Thus, the reasonable reader would have understood the company to be making an offer of a binding unilateral contract.

It should be emphasised that the company was not obliged to do anything until Mrs Carlill caught flu. However, catching flu was a **condition** of the company's liability, not part of the consideration—clearly, catching flu was not something which the company asked people to do. So this was rather like a contract of insurance. The 'premium' was using the smoke ball three times daily for two weeks. Catching flu—far from being something that the **offeree** was asked to do—was 'the accident' in the event of which compensation was payable. The terms of the offer made it clear that the consideration to be provided by Mrs Carlill was the use of the smoke ball, not simply the purchase of it. So it made no difference whether Mrs Carlill had bought the ball or been given it as a present, or even whether she had borrowed it. Of course, the company was really interested in the sales of the smoke balls, but the balls could not be used unless they were first bought by someone.

The traditional examples of unilateral contracts are of a trivial domestic nature—walking to York, using the smoke ball, and so on—but the concept plays a large and useful part in commercial transactions. If a shipper of goods says to a firm of **stevedores**, 'If you will load my goods on to the ship, I promise you that your liability shall be limited to £500', and, in consequence, the stevedores do load the goods on the ship, it is clear that there is a unilateral contract and that the stevedores' liability is accordingly limited.[4]

1 Motive and ignorance

Where *A* is aware of the offer and does the act requested a contract is formed. This will be the case even if his motive in doing the act may have been something quite different from obtaining the consideration offered by *O*. In *Williams v Carwardine*,[5] a woman knew (or at least it was assumed that she knew) of the existence of an offer of a reward for information leading to the conviction of a murderer. The woman provided the relevant information, but she only did so because she thought she was going to die and wanted to ease her conscience.

---

[2] [1893] 1 QB 256, CA.
[3] See Chapter 3, Section 2.
[4] See Chapter 10, Section 5.
[5] (1833) 5 C & P 566.

She did not give the information in order to receive the reward. Nevertheless, it was held that she was entitled to the reward. Motive is irrelevant when considering whether or not a contract has been formed. Mrs Carlill would have been no less entitled to the reward if it had been proved that her sole reason for using the ball was to avoid catching flu.

However, motive should be distinguished from ignorance. Where *A* does the required act in ignorance of the offer, it seems that there is no contract. In an Australian case,[6] it was held that where *A* had once known of the offer but had forgotten its existence when he did the act requested, there was no contract. The court said that a contract could not be made in ignorance of the offer; and forgetting about the offer was apparently the same as never even hearing of it.

This analysis of the Australian courts might be criticised. There may be arguments of public policy in support of the view that, where an offer is made to the whole world, anyone who does the act requested should be entitled to recover the promised reward, whether or not that particular person has heard of the offer. For example, consider offers of rewards for information leading to the apprehension of criminals. The public-spirited citizen who gives the information as soon as it comes to his attention may be at a disadvantage compared to the selfish person who waits to see if a reward is offered. If knowledge of a reward is required, it would seem that only the selfish person, and not the public-spirited citizen, has a contractual right to claim the reward offered. At first glance, this might seem inappropriate. But, on balance, it is suggested that the law is satisfactory. It must be remembered that the **offeror** will usually have made the offer in order to induce people to provide information, and not simply out of a desire to reward a worthy citizen. Since the offeror should only have a liability imposed on him if he can properly be said to have undertaken it, the better view is that the offeror has not undertaken to reward those who provide information in ignorance of his offer. Admittedly, the law treats the person who knows of the offer as an acceptor even though he is not in fact induced by the offer because his motive is something else, but that is because of the more general principle that motive is normally irrelevant in the law of contract. It would seem wrong to go further and say that even ignorance of the offer made should be irrelevant.

Knowledge of the offer is therefore required. But when must the offeree know of the offer? *Gibbons v Proctor*[7] suggests that it is sufficient that the offeree knows at the moment before the act of acceptance is complete. *O* had offered a reward in return for information. *A* was a policeman who was unaware of the offer, but gave the relevant information to a fellow officer, *B*, who gave it to a superior, *C*, who gave it to *O*. When *C* gave the information to *O*, *A* knew of the offer. It was held that that was sufficient for there to be a contract between *O* and *A*. Even though *A* did not know of the offer when he passed the information on, acceptance of the offer was only complete when the information was communicated to *O*, and *A* did know by that point. It would follow that if *A* posted a letter to *O* containing information, being unaware that *O* had offered a reward for that information, *A* would be entitled to the reward if he learned of the offer before the letter arrived. Similarly, if Mrs Carlill had learned of the offer only when she had used the smoke ball three times daily

---

[6] *R v Clarke* (1927) 40 CLR 227.
[7] (1891) 55 JP 616.

for 13 days, there would still be a binding contract between her and the Carbolic Smoke Ball Company when she continued to use the smoke ball on the fourteenth day and then fell ill. Indeed, the same result would presumably follow had Mrs Carlill learned of the offer after the fourteenth day but before she caught flu, provided she was continuing to use the smoke ball in accordance with the directions.

2 Revocation of the offer of a unilateral contract

It is clear that O's offer becomes a binding contract only when A completely performs the act requested. At first sight, it therefore appears that O may revoke his offer at any moment before the act is complete. Clearly, A is free to abandon performance at any time and so it has been argued that O should be equally free to call the whole thing off. This may, however, seem very unfair where A has expended time, money, and effort in reliance on the promise. Does the law really allow O to drive by in his Rolls-Royce, as A toils along the last hundred yards into York, and call out, 'Offer revoked'? Could the Carbolic Smoke Ball Company really have revoked its offer when Mrs Carlill was embarking on the fourteenth day of sniffing?

The answer to these questions is not altogether straightforward. But it should be noted at the outset that if A has conferred a benefit on O before O revokes the offer, then A may recover the value of that benefit in an action in unjust enrichment.[8] So, if the request was to dig the whole of O's garden and O, without justification, told A to get out when the job was nearly done, A would be entitled to the value to O of the service rendered—which might be more or less than the reward offered. But this would be of no help in the walking to York or the Carbolic Smoke Ball case because no discernible benefit has been conferred on the offeror.

The most common, and most attractive, solution that has been proposed is that O is unable to revoke his offer after A has begun performance if O has also made a second, implied promise that O will not revoke the offer if A embarks upon performance. So, when O says to A, 'I will pay you £100 if you walk to York', he might be considered to be making two promises. First, the express promise to pay £100 when the walk is complete (and not before). Secondly, an implied 'collateral' promise not to revoke his offer if A sets out on the walk. By making a start, A accepts the second offer. He supplies consideration for the implied promise by starting to walk.

The courts will, however, imply a promise only when it is necessary to do so to give 'business efficacy' to the transaction (in other words, to make the contract work) or because the parties, as reasonable persons, must have intended such a promise (in other words, it was something that went without saying).[9] In the examples discussed above, such a promise might well be implied—what reasonable person would expect to embark, or expect another to embark, on some arduous endeavour to earn a reward on the basis that the offeror could, on a whim, call the whole thing off? But such a promise will not always be implied in

---

[8] *Morrison Shipping Co Ltd (in liquidation) v R* (1925) 20 Lloyd's List Law Reports 283 (Viscount Cave LC); see Chapter 28, Section 4.

[9] See Chapter 13.

the case of offers of unilateral contracts. In *Luxor (Eastbourne) Ltd v Cooper*,[10] O offered A £10,000 if A introduced to O a party who bought O's two cinemas. A introduced X to O. X agreed, subject to contract, to buy the cinemas. However, O ultimately declined to proceed with the sale, despite the fact that X remained ready and willing to buy. A argued that the consideration for O's promise was supplied when A introduced X to O, and that it therefore followed that the contract between O and A was made at that point. Although the sale of the cinemas was a condition of recovery of the commission (like the catching of flu in *Carlill*), this event was outside the control of A, and O had prevented that event from happening. Nevertheless, the courts rejected A's arguments. A's action for the commission failed because the commission was payable only on the completion of the sale of the cinemas, and this had never occurred. Furthermore, A's action for the breach of an alleged implied promise by O to do nothing to prevent the completion of the sale also failed. The House of Lords held that there was no room for the implication of such a promise. It was not necessary to imply such a promise to give business efficacy to the contract: A was taking a risk in the hope of substantial remuneration (the equivalent, the House of Lords observed, of the Lord Chancellor's salary for a year) for a comparatively small exertion (eight or nine days' work). The prospective bargain was a very reasonable one without the implication of any term that O would do nothing to prevent the completion of the sale. A reasonable person may well have been glad to take the chance of obtaining such a lucrative reward without any such implied term.

However, in many cases it will be necessary to imply a term that the offer will not be revoked once the other party begins to perform. The leading example of this is *Errington v Errington*.[11] A father bought a house in his own name for his son and daughter-in-law to live in. He paid part of the price in cash and borrowed the rest from a building society. He left the couple to pay the instalments and told them that the house would be theirs when all the instalments were paid. Denning LJ treated this as an offer of a unilateral contract, namely: 'If you will pay off the instalments, I will convey the house to you.' The couple were not bound to pay the instalments, since a unilateral contract was at issue. However, if the couple did pay all the instalments, they would be entitled to the house. The couple moved into the house and began to pay the instalments, but before the couple had paid all the instalments the father died and his widow claimed possession of the house. The Court of Appeal dismissed her claim. Denning LJ held that there was an implied promise by the father not to revoke his offer once the couple embarked upon performance by moving into the house and beginning to pay the instalments. The widow, as the **personal representative** of her late husband, could be in no better position than her husband. As a result, the couple were entitled to remain in possession. An arrangement which would have allowed the father to turn the couple out when they had paid almost all the instalments on his house was (it may well be thought) one which no reasonable couple would expect, or be expected, to agree to.

If this is the right approach, there is no universal rule as to the revocability of offers of unilateral contracts. Everything depends on the circumstances of the particular case. This

---

[10] [1941] AC 108.
[11] [1952] 1 KB 290.

has the disadvantage of uncertainty but the corresponding advantage of flexibility. It enables the court to reach a just solution when a rigid rule—either that such offers are always revocable or that they are always irrevocable—would not do so. This approach is consistent with the reasoning of Denning LJ in *Errington v Errington*, and has been supported, albeit *obiter*, by Goff LJ in *Daulia v Four Millbank Nominees Ltd*[12] and Longmore LJ in *Soulsbury v Soulsbury*.[13] However, it is worth noting that *Chitty on Contracts* takes a different view,[14] and suggests that A accepts O's offer by beginning to perform the contract, even though A cannot enforce O's promise before satisfying the stipulated conditions. This explanation was favoured by Waller LJ, dissenting, in *Schweppe v Harper*.[15] Yet it seems artificial to say that A has accepted O's offer to pay the price simply by beginning to perform, particularly since A cannot sue O for the price at that point, and it may be difficult to judge what constitutes sufficiently unequivocal conduct for acceptance. The flexibility afforded by an implied, collateral obligation on O not to revoke the offer once A begins to perform should be preferred.

But what is A's remedy if O does revoke the offer to pay £100 after A has started to walk to York? A should generally be able to treat the revocation as inoperative and proceed to earn the £100.[16] But if A requires the cooperation of a third party in order to fulfil all the conditions required for payment by O, then A may sue for damages for loss of a chance to earn the agreed sum.[17]

3 Communicating acceptance of offers of unilateral contracts

Whether communication of an acceptance is required depends on the terms of the offer. Communication is for the benefit of the offeror, so he can dispense with it if he wishes.[18] In the case of many offers of unilateral contracts, it is obvious from the nature of the offer that communication is not required. No reader of the Carbolic Smoke Ball Company's advertisement would have supposed that he was expected to write and tell the company that he was using the ball and accepting its offer of a reward in the event of his catching flu. The same will generally be true of offers made to the public. However, in the case of offers of rewards for information, the act of acceptance is obviously the communication of the information, albeit not necessarily to the offeror: communication to the police, for example, might constitute the acceptance. As always, the test must be: how would the reasonable reader of the offer understand it?

---

[12] [1978] Ch 231.
[13] [2007] EWCA Civ 969, [2008] Fam 1.
[14] H Beale (ed), *Chitty on Contracts* (31st edn, Sweet & Maxwell, 2012) para 2-079.
[15] [2008] EWCA Civ 442.
[16] *Mountford v Scott* [1975] 2 WLR 114, CA.
[17] *Schweppe v Harper* [2008] EWCA Civ 442 [51]–[54] (Waller LJ, dissenting on a different issue).
[18] *Attrill v Dresdner Kleinwort Ltd* [2013] EWCA Civ 394, [2013] 3 All ER 807 [98].

Further Reading

I Wormser, 'The True Conception of Unilateral Contract' (1916) 26 Yale LJ 136.
Discusses the example of '$100 to walk across the Brooklyn Bridge' and offers the view (contrary to that given here) that the offeror should be free to revoke his offer at any point up until the walk has been completed.

A Hudson, '*Gibbons v Proctor* Revisited' (1968) 84 LQR 503.
Considers the troublesome case of *Gibbons v Proctor* and whether a contract can be concluded in ignorance of an offer.

AWB Simpson, 'Quackery and Contract Law: *Carlill v. Carbolic Smoke Ball Company* (1893)' in AWB Simpson, *Leading Cases in the Common Law* (Clarendon Press, 1996).
Analyses the circumstances and context of *Carlill v Carbolic Smoke Ball Co* and how it came to be a leading case in the **common law**.

Question

On 1 April, Jack placed an advertisement in a national English newspaper which states that Jack will pay £50,000 to anybody who cycles from London to Zagreb in 30 days, leaving on 1 June. Many competitors set off on 1 June. Only Curtis, David, Edgar, and Tony reached Zagreb within 30 days.

On 10 May, Jack heard that Curtis—a famous cyclist—intended to take part in the challenge. Jack posted a letter to Curtis to inform him that he would not be eligible for the prize, but this letter was lost in the post and never read by Curtis. After the start of the race, Jack's financial situation took a turn for the worse, and on 15 June, Jack placed another advertisement in the same newspaper to withdraw his offer of a £50,000 prize. David only learned of this once he had reached Zagreb. Edgar was told of Jack's second advertisement by a journalist on 16 June, but Edgar did not believe the journalist. Tony only found out about both advertisements on arriving in Zagreb. Tony had decided to cycle from London to Zagreb in order to keep his friend, Edgar, company and to see if he could rise to the physical challenge.

Advise Jack. Would your answer be different if Jack's newspaper announcement had appeared on the morning before the start of the race?

5 Contract as an agreement

🔐 Key Points

- Until the parties have agreed on everything which they consider requires agreement, there is no contract.
- However, a failure explicitly to set out all the terms of the agreement is not necessarily fatal to there being a contract, since a court might be able to imply terms to fill in any gaps. But a court will be unable to do this if it would contradict the intentions of the parties.
- Parties may agree not to negotiate with anyone else for a specified period of time. But an agreement to negotiate with one another is not binding because it is insufficiently certain.
- An agreement may be made 'subject' to something or other. If so, the contract is not binding until that particular event occurs.

1 The need for a concluded bargain

To be a good contract there must be a concluded bargain and a concluded contract is one which settles everything that is necessary to be settled and leaves nothing to be settled by agreement between the parties.

Viscount Dunedin stated this fundamental principle in *May and Butcher v R*.[1] Until the parties have agreed on everything which they consider requires agreement, there is no contract. The parties are still in the course of negotiation. It is sometimes said that a contract is precluded only if there is some essential term yet to be agreed. But any term, however trivial it may appear to others, is 'essential' if the parties consider it requires agreement and they have not agreed on it. Indeed, the same must be true if only one of the parties considers that it requires agreement, provided that he has made this clear to the other party.

If an otherwise complete contract states that there is some matter yet to be agreed between the parties, that will preclude the conclusion of the contract (at least while it remains **executory**[2]). In *May and Butcher* the parties had entered into an elaborate arrangement for the sale of tentage but it provided that 'The price or prices to be paid, and the date or dates on which payment is to be made shall be agreed upon from time to time between [the sellers and the buyers].' This precluded a contract, for there was still no concluded bargain. The arrangement included a clause requiring all disputes to be submitted to arbitration but that did not help to solve the problem because, like the rest of the clauses in the proposed

---

[1] (1929) [1934] 2 KB 17n, HL.
[2] ie still to be carried out.

agreement, that arbitration clause would only become binding when the bargain was concluded, and that had never happened. The parties had never agreed on any price or date for payment.

It would probably have been different if the clauses had made no mention of the price or date. It is quite common for people to make contracts for the supply of goods or services without specifying the price to be paid. If they have done all the agreeing they intend to do, then there is an enforceable contract to pay a reasonable price. The law presumes that this is what the parties must have intended.[3] It is the same with many other terms. If no time is specified for delivery or other performance, then it must be done within a reasonable time. As a result, a court is entitled to find that a contract has been concluded between the parties, even if the contract is silent as to what may be important terms, provided that the silence can be filled through an implied term. However, if the parties are not simply silent as to a matter such as the time of delivery, but instead specify that 'time of delivery is to be agreed', then there is no room to imply a term that delivery should occur within a reasonable time. An implied term cannot contradict an express term.[4] In such circumstances the time of delivery must be agreed before the contract becomes effective. After all, one or other of the parties, or perhaps even both, might not have been willing to agree upon what a court would consider to be the reasonable time.

In *May and Butcher* the parties expressly left something to be agreed. As a result, there was no contract between the parties. Indeed, parties may impliedly leave something to be agreed, and that can be equally fatal to the existence of a contract. Although the courts can often fill in the gaps in a quite skeletal agreement through implying a term, there must be such a skeletal agreement in place. There is a certain minimum which is required for there to be a contract. If such a minimum is not in place, the court cannot say what the contract is or imply terms into the 'contract'. After all, if a court were to be called on to enforce an agreement which fell short of that minimum, the judges would not know what it was that they were supposed to enforce. This was highlighted in *Scammel (G) and Nephew Ltd v Ouston*.[5] O agreed to buy from S a new motor van but stipulated that 'this order is given on the understanding that the balance of the purchase price can be had on **hire-purchase** terms over a period of two years'. The House of Lords held that this sentence was 'so vaguely expressed that it cannot, standing by itself, be given a definite meaning—that is to say, it requires further agreement to be reached between the parties before there would be a complete *consensus ad idem*'. This is because hire-purchase agreements can take a wide variety of different forms and there were no means by which the court could determine what terms the parties intended to apply, or would have agreed to. It might have been different if there had been any well-known 'usual terms' in such a contract, since the court might then have assumed that the parties intended these to apply and implied such terms into the agreement.[6] But there were no such 'usual terms'. It is different in the context of a contract for the sale of land, for example: it is sufficient that the parties, the property, and the price

---

[3] Such a term may be implied at common law or as a result of legislation (see eg Sale of Goods Act 1979, s 8(2)). For implied terms generally, see Chapter 13.

[4] See Chapter 13, Section 5.

[5] [1941] AC 251, HL.

[6] See Chapter 13.

are specified. The parties will usually wish, and will usually be well advised, to reach agreement on many other matters, but, if they are content to leave the matter there and have demonstrated an intention to be bound without further agreement, the law will imply the other terms which are necessary for the transaction to be carried out. Of course, parties negotiating for the sale of land will usually agree to buy and sell at an agreed price 'subject to contract', the importance of which is considered further below.[7]

2 Executed and executory agreements

A distinction has to be made between an arrangement which is still wholly executory and one which is executed by one or both parties. An agreement is 'executory' when performance lies in the future, and nothing has been done to carry out the arrangement. This was the position in *May and Butcher*: the tentage had not been delivered. By contrast, an agreement is 'executed' when it has been performed by one party or the other. So, if there was an arrangement like that in *May and Butcher* but tentage is delivered and accepted (and perhaps resold) without any agreement as to the price, then the agreement would be 'executed'. In such circumstances, it would be outrageous if the buyer did not have to pay for the tentage because there was no contract. In such a case 'the law will say that there is necessarily implied, from the conduct of the parties, a contract that, in default of agreement, a reasonable sum is to be paid'. This proposition was stated by Denning J in *British Bank for Foreign Trade v Novinex*.[8] The claimants had a friend with access to large quantities of oilskin suits. The defendants, who wanted to acquire oilskins, wrote to the claimants to say (in effect) 'If you will put us in direct touch with your friend we undertake to pay you an agreed commission on any business transacted with him.' The claimants put the defendants in direct touch with their friend. The defendants later declined to pay any commission. The Court of Appeal (reversing Denning J, who had stated the principle accurately but failed properly to apply it) held that the claimants were entitled to a reasonable commission on transactions between the defendants and the claimants' friend. The commission had never been 'agreed' as the defendants' offer required, but it was an offer of a unilateral contract which was accepted and wholly performed by the claimants when they put the defendants in touch with the friend. It is important to remember that unilateral contracts, of course, are never 'wholly executory', because there is no contract until the offeree has done his part.

In *Foley v Classique Coaches*,[9] the contract was bilateral. The claimant agreed to sell some land to the defendants for a coach station in consideration of the defendants' agreeing to buy all their petrol from him. The agreement concerning the sale of the land and the agreement concerning the sale of the petrol were put into separate documents, the former stating that it was conditional on the defendants' entering into the latter and the latter stating that it was supplemental to the former. At issue was a single bargain and the two parts either stood or fell together. The petrol agreement provided that the petrol was to be sold 'at a price to be agreed by the parties in writing and from time to time'. It would

---

[7] See Section 5.
[8] [1949] 1 KB 623.
[9] [1934] 2 KB 1.

appear that when both documents were signed, there was no contract, since the case seems indistinguishable from *May and Butcher*. But the land was conveyed and petrol was bought and sold for three years. Only then did the defendants **repudiate** the petrol agreement. The court rejected the argument that the contract was not yet concluded, and held that it was binding. The principle stated by Denning J many years later was applicable. The agreement had been substantially executed on both sides and it would have been very remarkable indeed if, after all that, the court had held that there had never been a contract at all.

3 'Lock-out' agreements and agreements to negotiate

A 'lock-out' agreement is an agreement between *A* and *B* not to negotiate with anyone else for a specified period of time. For example, when negotiating a contract for the sale of a property, *B* might promise *A* (for consideration supplied by *A*) that, for a specified period of time, *B* will not negotiate with anyone except *A* for the sale of his (*B*'s) property. This is a good contract. *A* might consider such a lock-out agreement to be desirable where he is unable to assess what he is prepared to offer for *B*'s property without considerable expenditure. *A* may be unwilling to incur this expenditure unless he is assured that the property will not be disposed of before he is in a position to make an offer for it. As a result, *A* may be willing to pay for the security afforded by a lock-out agreement.

The leading case on lock-out agreements is *Walford v Miles*.[10] The House of Lords recognised the validity of such an agreement, provided that there was a term in the lock-out agreement which specified the duration of the agreement. Such a term is essential; a court would not be able to imply a term which limited the lock-out agreement to a reasonable time. However, this conclusion was not obvious, and there does not seem to be any reason in principle why a lock-out agreement should not be impliedly limited to the time necessary for *A* to make the proposed assessment of the property.

Walford v Miles decides that a valid lock-out agreement operates only as a negative agreement. In other words, the agreement can only operate as an agreement not to negotiate with anyone else. It is impossible to have a 'lock-in' agreement, under which *B* makes a positive agreement to negotiate with *A*. An express agreement to negotiate is not binding because, like an agreement to agree, it lacks the necessary certainty. The argument that *B* may fall under an obligation to negotiate 'in good faith' was rejected by the House of Lords in *Walford v Miles* as being repugnant to the adversarial nature of negotiation: a negotiator must be free to threaten to withdraw if he is not offered terms better than those on the table. A 'good faith' restriction would be unworkable because neither the negotiator nor the court could know when it operated. On the other hand, an agreement by *B* in a contract with *A* to 'use all reasonable endeavours to obtain [for *A*] the right of first negotiation' from a third party is enforceable. That agreement is not an agreement to negotiate and it is clear what *B* is obliged to do.[11] However, the boundaries and content of 'good faith' are very controversial generally, and will be examined further in Chapter 19.

---

[10] [1992] 2 AC 128, HL.
[11] *Lambert v HTV Cymru (Wales) Ltd*, The Times, 17 March 1998.

4 Terms to be settled otherwise than by agreement of the parties

Leaving something to be settled by agreement between the parties precludes an executory contract but leaving it to be settled in some other way does not. An agreement that the price is to be fixed by the buyer (or the seller) is a valid, though perhaps rash, contract. No further agreement is required. An agreement that a lender of money may vary the interest rate at his discretion is valid at **common law** and under the Consumer Credit Act 1974,[12] although it may be subject to an implied term that the discretion will not be exercised for an improper purpose, dishonestly, capriciously, or as no reasonable lender would.[13] Since the parties do not need to do any further agreeing, there is a binding contract.

There is a principle of the common law which is applicable to contracts generally but has been encapsulated by statute in the particular context of the sale of goods by section 8(1) of the Sale of Goods Act 1979: 'The price ... may be left to be fixed in the manner thereby agreed, or may be determined by the course of dealing between the parties'; and section 9 recognises that the price may be fixed by the valuation of a third party. If the parties (A and B) agree that the price shall be fixed by X, that is a perfectly good contract. It does not require any further agreement between A and B. If X fixes the price in good faith, the parties are bound by the price he has fixed, no matter how unhappy either of them may be about that price and no matter how much the price chosen by X may depart from a reasonable price. The parties did not agree to buy and sell for a reasonable price, but for a price to be fixed by X. If X is being paid by the parties for this service, he owes both parties a duty to act with reasonable care and skill and, if he has not done so, the injured party may sue him for damages.[14] Of course, if there were fraud or collusion with one of the parties, the price will not be binding on the other party.

The proper interpretation of this situation seems to be that there is a contract as soon as the parties have agreed on all the matters which they consider require agreement, including the term that the price is to be fixed by X. Section 9(2) of the Sale of Goods Act 1979 provides that if one of the parties then prevents X from fixing the price, the other party may sue him for damages. This is also undoubtedly a principle of the common law, since the basis of it must be that there is necessarily implied an undertaking by each party that he will do nothing to prevent the price being fixed.[15] The contract would lack 'business efficacy' if either party were at liberty to prevent X from fixing the price. However, even if neither party prevents X from fixing the price, it may be that X does not fix the price for other reasons. According to section 9(1) of the Sale of Goods Act 1979, in such circumstances the contract is 'avoided'. The parties have made a contract for sale at a price to be fixed by X and such a contract is now, without the fault of either, impossible to perform. In effect, the contract is frustrated.[16]

---

[12] *Lombard Tricity Finance Ltd v Paton* [1984] 1 All ER 918, applying *May and Butcher v R* [1934] 2 KB 17, 21.
[13] *Paragon Finance plc v Nash* [2001] 2 All ER 1025 (Comm), CA. See Chapter 15, Section 2(c)(ii).
[14] *Campbell v Edwards* [1976] 1 WLR 403.
[15] See Chapter 13.
[16] See Chapter 23.

As we have seen, an agreement that the price shall be fixed by the parties precludes a contract, since the parties still have more agreeing to do. By contrast, if the parties agree that the price should be agreed by two valuers, one to be nominated by each of them, or, in default of such agreement by an umpire appointed by the valuers, then the contract between the parties can be binding. There is no more agreeing for the parties themselves to do. In *Sudbrook Trading Estate Ltd v Eggleton*,[17] the House of Lords held[18] that this was, in effect, a contract for sale at a fair and reasonable price. The parties had done no more than specify the machinery for ascertaining the fair and reasonable price. Lord Scarman asked, 'What was the object of their contract? A fair and reasonable price? Or a price reached only by the means specified?' He held that the former was the correct interpretation. It therefore followed that when one party refused to appoint a valuer, claiming that the contract was void for uncertainty, the court held that the contract (for the sale of land) could be specific-ally enforced, with the price to be fixed by a valuation ordered by the court.

Whilst an agreement to agree is unenforceable because no one can say what the parties would have agreed to if they have not agreed in fact, in some situations a contract to make a contract may be perfectly valid. The key factor is whether or not there is any more agreeing to be done between the parties. A contract to grant a **lease** is a common and obvious example of a contract to make a contract which can be binding. The lease itself is a contract, imposing obligations on the **tenant** to pay rent, on the **landlord** to keep the property in good repair, and so on. The point is that in this example of a contract to make a contract, all the terms of the second contract (whether express or implied) are to be found in the first contract. There is no further agreeing to be done.[19] The second contract merely puts into proper legal form and language terms which have already been agreed, even though they have perhaps not been expressed in words. Of course, in some situations at the borderline there may occasionally be some doubt about whether phrases used by the parties properly mean that there is further negotiation to be done (in which case there is no contract) or merely that the agreement which they have reached is to be reproduced in a formal document (in which case there is a contract). In *Branca v Cobarro*,[20] a written agreement for a lease of a mushroom farm was declared to be 'a provisional agreement until a fully legalised agreement, drawn up by a solicitor and embodying all the **conditions** herewith stated is signed'. At first instance, Denning J thought that this was an agreement to agree, but his decision was overturned by the Court of Appeal. That court held that there was an immediately binding contract: that was the effect of the word 'provisional'.

5 Agreements subject to …

It is very common for agreements to be made 'subject' to something or other. This indicates that all the terms of the contract are in place, but the contract is not to become binding until the occurrence of a particular event. Such contracts can become binding on the occurrence

---

[17] [1983] 1 AC 444.
[18] By a 4:1 majority; Lord Russell dissented.
[19] *Chillingworth v Esche* [1924] 1 Ch 97.
[20] [1947] KB 854.

of that event. It is helpful to distinguish between agreements which are expressed to be 'subject to contract'—where a final 'contract' is required, but this is often simply the signature of the parties—and agreements which are subject to a different term.

(a) Agreements subject to contract

It is not uncommon for negotiations to be expressed to be 'subject to contract'. Indeed, this is very normal in many situations. For example, when purchasing a house, if a vendor accepts a purchaser's offer then the property is often said to be 'Sold STC' or 'Sold Subject To Contract'. Even though the vendor and purchaser have agreed on the subject matter of the contract (the house) and the price, there are further terms to be negotiated and there is not yet any binding agreement. It is understood that there will only be a binding agreement when the formal, written contract has been concluded (generally upon exchange of contracts[21]).

'Subject to contract' is therefore often quite straightforward: there is no binding agreement until the formal contract is entered into. However, problems arise where one party begins to perform the work before the formal contract is entered into. If A performs work for B which B accepts, then B will have to pay for that work. It is possible to analyse this as a claim in unjust enrichment—B should have to pay for an enrichment transferred on a consideration which has totally failed[22]—but it is difficult to be sure that such a claim should be recognised because A's claim in unjust enrichment should fail if A has taken a risk of not being paid. After all, 'there is nothing unjust about being visited with the consequences of a risk which one has consciously run'.[23] If A performs services prior to the agreement being concluded, then it may be argued that A was taking a risk by 'jumping the gun' and performing without having reached an agreement with B.

It is suggested that if A is to obtain redress from B this should be in the law of contract. As the Supreme Court observed in *RTS Flexible Systems Ltd v Molkerei Alois Müller GmbH and Co KG (UK) Productions*, the better approach 'is to agree first and to start work later'.[24] But where A has done work for B prior to a formal, written contract being signed, it still needs to be established whether, objectively, it can be said that the 'subject to contract' bar has simply been waived and the negotiated agreement takes full effect, or whether instead a different, 'collateral' agreement to the 'main' contemplated agreement has been concluded through the parties' conduct. If the latter, then the court will imply a term that a reasonable sum be paid. If the former, then the negotiated rate (if any) will apply.

A possible example of a 'collateral' agreement arising is provided by the facts of *Whittle Movers Ltd v Hollywood Express Ltd*.[25] The parties were negotiating a long-term, written contract for the distribution and warehousing of food and drink products. During the negotiations, A began to perform the envisaged services, and B paid for them. After a relatively short period of time, B cancelled the arrangement. A argued that this was a breach of

---

[21] See Chapter 3, Section 3(g).
[22] See Chapter 28, Section 4.
[23] *Stephen Donald Architects Ltd v King* [2003] EWHC 1867 (TCC) [79] (HHJ Richard Seymour QC).
[24] [2010] UKSC 14, [2010] 1 WLR 753 [1].
[25] [2009] EWCA Civ 1189, [2009] 2 CLC 771.

contract. Both the trial judge and Court of Appeal agreed that no long-term agreement had been reached, since negotiations were still ongoing. But that did not preclude the claimant from contending that an interim, collateral contract had been concluded by the parties' conduct for the services actually rendered. This argument was attractive to the judge, and seems appropriate. After all, whether or not a contract is concluded by conduct is essentially a question of fact.[26] There may legitimately be some debate about what price should be paid under that contract,[27] but that should not distract the court from the important point that the parties were agreed that the services would be paid for, and that the consensual nature of the transaction means that the claim properly belongs within the law of contract.

In the Court of Appeal in *Whittle*, the judges seemed to favour an approach based on unjust enrichment.[28] But this sits uncomfortably with the subsequent decision of the Supreme Court in *RTS Flexible Systems Ltd v Molkerei Alois Müller GmbH and Co KG (UK) Productions* that the parties must agree first if they are to recover for work subsequently carried out. In that case, detailed negotiations took place and were said to be 'subject to contract'. Nevertheless, work began without a formal, signed, written contract in place. The Supreme Court held that even though the 'subject to contract' bar indicated that the detailed terms were not to take effect until the relevant documents were executed and signed,[29] the parties were still free to dictate when and how they enter into contractual obligations; as the Supreme Court pointed out, the intention not to be bound before signature could be 'waived'.[30] This must be right: the parties may initially intend to be bound by entering into a written contract, but this intention cannot be irrevocably binding upon them. If they change their minds and wish to enter into binding obligations through another route, then this must be possible. A 'subject to contract' clause is no more than an indication that, determined objectively, the parties do not intend to create legal relations until the contract is signed. But, in *Müller*, the Supreme Court held that the parties must have intended to create legal relations through their conduct, and no longer required an executed and signed contract. The Justices held that '[a]ny other conclusion makes no commercial sense', and that 'the reasonable, honest businessman … whether he was an RTS man or a Müller man … would have concluded that the work should be carried out for the agreed price on the agreed terms … without the necessity for a formal written agreement, which had been overtaken by events.'[31] Of course, it may be difficult to decide exactly when 'the die was cast'[32] and the requirement for a signed contract has been dispensed with, but this is a question to be decided on the facts of any particular case.

---

[26] *Dinkha Latchin v General Mediterranean Holdings SA* [2003] EWCA Civ 1786 [20]–[23].

[27] In *Whittle*, the trial judge accepted that the price of the interim contract was the same as that envisaged under the longer term contract, but it may have been more appropriate to imply a term that a reasonable price be paid in the context of the shorter term agreement, using the Supply of Goods and Services Act 1982, s 15. See Chapter 13, Section 3.

[28] See Chapter 28, Section 4.

[29] *RTS Flexible Systems Ltd v Molkerei Alois Müller GmbH and Co KG (UK) Productions* [2010] UKSC 14, [2010] 1 WLR 753 [31].

[30] Ibid, [86]–[88].

[31] Ibid, [86].

[32] Ibid, [87].

(b) Agreements subject to other terms

It is possible to state that an agreement is subject to an event other than the signing of a formal, written agreement. Agreements to buy land are often made 'subject to satisfactory survey', 'subject to the purchaser obtaining a satisfactory **mortgage**', or 'subject to planning permission being given'. Commercial contracts are often made 'subject to the opening of a credit by the purchaser' or 'subject to the obtaining of a **licence**' by one or other of the parties. These all present a different problem from the 'subject to contract' case because they do not contemplate any further agreeing between the parties. In each case, something must be done before the contract becomes operative, but that thing is not further agreement. There may be a binding contract provided that, on its true interpretation, the clause:

(i)   is sufficiently precise and definite for a court to be able to say when it is satisfied; and

(ii) does not leave either party with a discretion about whether to go on with the transaction.

Since the whole contract is subject to the event in question, the contract cannot be enforced unless the court is able to say whether the condition has been satisfied. Significantly, this condition is not like a meaningless term which the court can simply ignore and still find a complete contract. Whether the court can simply ignore the term is a matter of interpretation. In *Nicolene Ltd v Simmonds*,[33] a contract for the sale of steel included the words, 'We are in agreement that the usual conditions of acceptance apply.' However, there were no 'usual conditions of acceptance'. The Court of Appeal therefore treated this as a meaningless term in a contract, rather than a condition precedent to the existence or operation of the whole bargain. The term was severable from the rest of the contract in the sense that, if those words were struck out, a perfectly good contract for the sale of steel would remain. In that respect, *Nicolene Ltd v Simmonds* was unlike *Scammel v Ouston*,[34] since in the latter case the striking out of the meaningless words would have destroyed the substance of the intended bargain (which was some sort of hire-purchase contract).

If the meaning of the clause is that one of the parties has a complete discretion whether or not to go ahead with the transaction, that is incompatible with the existence of a contract. After all, the whole essence of a contract is that the parties bind themselves. It is important to remember that any phrase must be read in its context; as a result, the same phrase may have different meanings in two different contracts. For instance, it has been held in contracts for the sale of land and of ships that the phrase 'subject to satisfactory survey' generally means that the buyer reserves to himself the absolute right to say whether the surveyor's report is satisfactory to him. So, even if the surveyor's report is expressed in glowing, uniformly positive terms, the buyer is still at liberty to say he does not like the report and to refuse to proceed. In such circumstances, there is no contract. But in another case[35] it was held that very similar words meant that the buyer was under an obligation to have the property surveyed and to consider, bona fide, whether the survey was

---

[33] [1953] 1 QB 543, CA.

[34] See Section 1.

[35] *Graham and Scott (Southgate) Ltd v Oxlade* [1950] 2 KB 257, CA (land); *Astra Trust Ltd v Williams* [1969] 1 Lloyd's Rep 81 (Megaw J) (a yacht).

satisfactory or not.[36] This assumes that, in the last resort, the court is prepared to decide that the survey was satisfactory—that is, that it would satisfy any reasonable person and that the buyer's expression of dissatisfaction was immaterial.

Similarly, different interpretations have been put on the phrase, 'subject to the purchaser obtaining a satisfactory mortgage'.[37] Such differences may be explicable on the ground of the different contexts in which the words are used or it may be that the cases are simply irreconcilable. The principle, however, is plain enough. The problem is one of interpreting the words used and it is not surprising that judges should sometimes disagree as to the proper interpretation of words.[38]

If the parties agree that the arbiter of whether the survey (or other matter) shall be some third party, that clause does not preclude the existence of a contract. The parties have completed their agreement in the matter and neither has a discretion. A building society may have agreed to give the buyer a mortgage, subject to satisfactory survey. If the buyer then agrees to buy 'subject to the survey being satisfactory to the building society', the agreement is sufficiently precise and definite because the society either says that it is satisfied, in which case the contract is on, or it says that it is dissatisfied, in which case it is off; and neither party has a discretion, even if the building society does.

Where a clause of this nature is for the exclusive benefit of one party, he may waive it, whereupon the contract, if in other respects complete, will become immediately operative. A survey, for example, will usually be for the exclusive benefit of the buyer. In such a case, a buyer may simply inform the seller that he is not going to bother with a survey. There may have been no contract up to that point, because the clause gave the buyer a discretion. If so, the contract came into existence the moment he waived the condition. Such a clause then leaves the buyer in the position of an offeree. Unlike the 'subject to contract' case, no further agreement is required.

Where the parties have reached complete agreement and neither has reserved any discretion not to proceed, the better view is that there is a contract even though some condition must be satisfied before its major terms become operative. The matter has been confused by the leading case of *Pym v Campbell*.[39] The defendant had agreed in writing to buy a share of the claimant's invention. He then declined to do so. The agreement was quite unconditional but the defendant adduced evidence that when the parties met to inspect the invention he was prepared to buy it only if an engineer, Abernethie, approved of it; and Abernethie could not be found. As it would be troublesome to arrange another meeting between the parties, the defendant agreed to sign the document on the understanding that it would be the agreement if Abernethie approved of the invention. When Abernethie saw the invention, he did not approve of it. An important question in the case was whether, because of

---

[36] *Ee v Kakar* (1979) 124 SJ 327.

[37] *Lee-Parker v Izzet* [1971] 1 WLR 1688 (Goff J); *Lee-Parker v Izzet (No 2)* [1972] 1 WLR 775 (Goulding J). In *Graham v Pitkin* [1992] 2 All ER 235, 237, PC, Lord Templeman doubted Goulding J's holding that there was no contract, saying that 'the purchaser, if he had the money, could always have declared that a mortgage of £10 from his brother-in-law was "satisfactory"'. But this seems to confirm the view that the purchaser has an absolute discretion to declare anything, or nothing, 'satisfactory': ie an absolute discretion incompatible with the existence of a contract.

[38] See Chapter 12.

[39] (1856) 6 El & Bl 379.

the **parol evidence** rule,[40] oral evidence was admissible to qualify the effect of the written agreement. The court held that it was admissible because it showed that in fact there was 'never any agreement at all'. This was an inaccurate way of describing the situation. The parties had done all the agreeing they intended to do and there was no disagreement between them. The agreement was perfect—but subject to a condition: that Abernethie give his approval. In such a case it seems clear that there is a contract though its major terms are not yet operative. Surely the seller was bound to give Abernethie the opportunity to inspect the invention—just as the seller, at a price to be fixed by X, is bound to allow X the necessary facilities to fix the price.[41] The seller would have been in breach of contract if he had sold the invention to another before Abernethie had had an opportunity to inspect it; and the buyer could have waived the condition since it was clearly exclusively for his benefit.

Later cases confirm that these are good principles of law. In *Marten v Whale*,[42] the claimant agreed to buy a plot of land from Thacker in consideration of Thacker agreeing to buy the claimant's car. The sale of the land, and therefore the whole bargain, was 'subject to purchaser's solicitor's approval of **title** and restrictions'. The car was delivered to Thacker before the ownership passed to him and he wrongfully sold it to the defendant. The question whether Thacker had given a good title depended on whether he was a person who had 'agreed to buy' the car within section 25(2) of the Sale of Goods Act 1893 (1979 Act, s 25(1)). The Court of Appeal held that he was. The contract for the sale of the car was 'subject to "[the claimant's] solicitor's approval of title and restrictions" to the land'; but this did not give the claimant a mere option. There was an implied term that he would appoint a solicitor and consult him in good faith and that the solicitor would give his honest opinion. Clearly, there was a contract as soon as the documents were signed, even though the major terms of the contract were to become operative only if and when the solicitor gave his approval.

Further Reading

E McKendrick (ch 11) and S Hedley (ch 12) in W Cornish, R Nolan, J O'Sullivan, and G Virgo (eds), *Restitution: Past, Present and Future* (Hart, 1998).

These two chapters offer contrasting views regarding the appropriate analysis in situations where a party may be able to recover for work done when a 'contract fails to materialise': McKendrick argues that the claim will generally be in unjust enrichment, whereas Hedley argues that such claims will generally still lie within the law of contract.

P Davies, 'Anticipatory Contracts: Room for Agreement' (2010) 69 CLJ 467.

Considers recent cases such as *RTS Flexible Systems Ltd v Molkerei Alois Müller GmbH and Co KG (UK) Productions* and argues that the boundaries of contract law are sufficiently wide to cover work already done under an 'anticipatory contract'.

---

[40] See Chapter 11, Section 4.
[41] See Section 4.
[42] [1917] 2 KB 480.

? Question

Chuck seeks someone to supply his business with regular cleaning services. Morgan runs a cleaning company, and Chuck and Morgan enter into negotiations for a five-year agreement. They both promise to negotiate with each other for a six-month period, and not with anyone else.

After three months of negotiations, the agreement is concluded 'subject to contract'. Happy with the outcome, Morgan begins to supply Chuck with the required cleaning services. Two months later, Chuck refuses to sign the formal, written contract and tells Morgan his services are no longer required.

Advise Morgan.

6 Identity of offeror and offeree

🔑 Key Points

- If one party (*A*) makes an offer to another party (*B*) and to *B* alone, that offer cannot be accepted by a third party (*C*). Whether an offer is restricted to *B* alone is a question of interpretation.

- If *A* makes a mistake as to the other party's *identity*, no contract will be formed (or, as it is sometimes said, the contract will be void). If *A* makes a mistake as to the other party's *attributes* (such as his creditworthiness) then a contract will be formed. However, that contract may be voidable as a result of a misrepresentation.

- Whether a contract is void or voidable is particularly important where third parties have acquired rights in the subject matter of a contract. If *O* 'contracts' to sell a car to a rogue, *R*, who then sells the car to *C*, *O* might try to sue *C* in conversion. *O*'s claim will succeed if the 'contract' is void due to mistake of identity: *R* acquired no title to the car, so could give no title to *C*. But if the contract with *R* was only voidable due to *R*'s misrepresentation, then *R* would acquire a title to the car. As a result, if *R* sells the car to *C* before *O* rescinds his contract with *R*, *O*'s claim against *C* will fail: *C* is a bona fide purchaser for value without notice of *O*'s right to rescind the contract, so *C* will acquire good title.

- Where the contract is concluded by writing and the parties are not dealing face-to-face, the court is more likely to find that the identity of the party named in the written document is crucial.

- Where the contract is concluded face-to-face, there is a strong presumption that *O* intended to deal with the person present, such that the contract will not be void due to a unilateral mistake as to identity, but rather voidable due to a misrepresentation. It will be difficult to rebut this presumption.

The preceding chapters have focused on the situation where one party (*A*) makes an offer to another party (*B*) and the contract is concluded between them. This chapter is concerned with situations where it looks like a third party (*C*) purports to accept the offer made by *A*. The principle to be applied to these cases is clear enough. If *A* makes an offer to *B*, and only to *B*, *B* may accept that offer but no one else can. Any purported acceptance by *C* is obviously inoperative (Figure 6.1). Equally obviously, there is no contract where *A* makes an offer to *B* and *B* addresses an acceptance to *C* (Figure 6.2). Nevertheless, the cases to be considered in this chapter have given rise to difficulty and controversy for many years.

This is often because *C* is a rogue who obtains *A*'s property by fraudulent means, and then quickly sells that property on to another person (*X*) who buys that property in good faith. *C* then disappears, and *A* sues *X*. As a general rule, *A*'s claim will succeed if his offer was to *B* alone, meaning that *C* could not accept the offer. But *A*'s claim will fail if his offer was made to *B* and *C*.

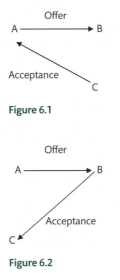

Figure 6.1

Figure 6.2

It may therefore be vitally important to ascertain to whom *A*'s offer was addressed. Was it addressed to *B* alone, or was *C* also an **offeree**? This question should be answered in accordance with the usual objective principles. An offer is made to the person or persons to whom it reasonably appears to be made.[1] A secret reservation in the mind of the **offeror**—such as 'I intended my offer only for *B*'—is irrelevant if the offer is expressed in a way that meant that *C* reasonably thought it was addressed to him.

A slightly difficult decision to explain is that of *Boulton v Jones*.[2] Jones sent an order for certain goods addressed to Brocklehurst at his shop. On the same day, unknown to Jones, Brocklehurst had sold his business and stock-in-trade to his foreman, Boulton, who delivered the goods ordered. Jones consumed the goods, unaware that they had been delivered by Boulton. When Boulton asked for the contract price, Jones refused to pay. The court held that Boulton was unable to sue for the price. This was because, in the court's view, Boulton was purporting to accept an offer which was addressed to Brocklehurst and to Brocklehurst alone.

However, on the facts of the case, this conclusion was not obviously straightforward. Of course, if the offer was properly regarded as addressed to Brocklehurst personally, and to

---

[1] Where there have been negotiations it may often be a matter of chance whether *A* or *B* is the offeror, but this point is unimportant for the analysis in this chapter. The result is the same in both cases: there is no contract.
[2] (1857) 2 H & N 564.

him alone, the decision is evidently right: *C* may not accept an offer made to *B* exclusively. But might not Boulton, as a reasonable man, have thought that the offer was addressed to the owner of the business for the time being? If so, the fact that Jones wrongly thought that his name was Brocklehurst was irrelevant. The court appears to have been persuaded not to adopt this approach because Jones had a running account with Brocklehurst and a 'set-off' against him. In other words, Brocklehurst was already indebted to Jones, and Jones intended to set off the amount of that debt against the price of the goods he had ordered. Jones could not do that against Boulton or anyone other than Brocklehurst. This appears to have convinced the court that Jones's offer was for Brocklehurst only. However, it is suggested that although this factor may have been excellent evidence that Jones *intended* to deal with Brocklehurst personally, it is not clear that it is relevant to the objective interpretation of the offer. If Boulton neither knew nor ought to have known of the set-off, then the set-off seems to be irrelevant. If the set-off were considered to be irrelevant, then it should follow that Boulton was entitled to suppose, as a reasonable man, that the offer made by Jones was an offer to the owner of the business, whoever he might be, and that a valid contract should have been recognised.

Even though the application of the legal principle to the particular facts of *Boulton v Jones* may be dubious, the principle itself is clear enough: if *A* makes an offer to *B*, *C* cannot accept that offer. But *B* may accept the offer and make a valid contract even if *A* was making some quite important mistakes when he made the offer. This raises the difficult distinction that exists between mistakes as to identity and mistakes as to attributes.

1 Mistakes as to identity and mistakes as to attributes

Most mistakes will not prevent *B* from accepting *A*'s offer. For instance, *A* might make an offer to contract to *B*, thinking that *B* is a wealthy man, an aristocrat, and the owner of a large mansion—essentially, a thoroughly creditworthy person. Unfortunately, *B* is none of these things. Nevertheless, *B* can accept *A*'s offer. This is because *A* has only made a mistake as to *B*'s attributes, rather than a mistake as to *B*'s identity. This is true even if *B* has dishonestly misled *A* about these attributes, since fraud makes a contract merely voidable, not void; in other words, there is a contract with all the effects of a perfect contract unless and until *A* takes steps to **rescind** it.[3] This drives us, inevitably, into making a distinction between *A*'s mistake as to *B*'s attributes and *A*'s mistake as to identity in confusing *B* with *C*.

The distinction between mistakes as to identity and mistakes as to attributes has been much criticised, most critically by pointing out that 'identity' is merely the sum of a person's 'attributes'. In the words of Lord Denning MR:

> A mistake as to identity, it is said, avoids a contract: whereas a mistake as to attributes does not. But this is a distinction without a difference. A man's very name is one of his attributes. It is also a key to his identity. If then, he gives a false name, is it a mistake as to his identity? or a mistake as to his attributes? These fine distinctions do no good to the law.[4]

---

[3] See further Chapter 16, Section 4.
[4] *Lewis v Averay* [1972] 1 QB 198.

Although it is clearly true that it may be extremely difficult in borderline cases to say whether a mistake is as to attribute or as to identity, it is suggested that the criticisms of Lord Denning MR go too far. Almost all legal distinctions run into similar problems at the borders, but this in no way invalidates the distinction being made. The focus of the cases has rightly been on deciding whether the mistake in any particular situation has been as to attribute or identity. In considering this issue, it is helpful to distinguish between contracts concluded in writing by parties at a distance one from the other (*inter absentes*), and contracts concluded face-to-face (*inter praesentes*). But first it is important to understand why it matters whether the contract is void because of a mistake of identity or voidable because of a (fraudulent) misrepresentation.

2 Void and voidable contracts and the passing of property

In *Boulton v Jones*, there was no question of any fraud or dishonesty, but that was an exceptional case. The problem posed in the cases considered in this chapter typically arises on the following fact-pattern. O, the owner of goods, encounters a rogue, R, who by fraud induces O to sell the goods. R gets possession of the goods but does not pay for them. He then resells and delivers the goods to a **bona fide purchaser** for value without notice of the fraud (a 'BFP'). The BFP is essentially a person who buys and pays for the goods in good faith, quite unaware of the dishonest way in which R has acquired those goods. R then usually disappears from the scene. He cannot be identified or found, or he is sent to prison. In any event, O will be unable to obtain satisfactory redress from R, which means that it is not worth suing R. But when O discovers that his property (as he believes) is in the possession of the BFP, O sues the BFP in the tort of **conversion**, claiming that the BFP is wrongly asserting **title** to his, O's, property. The BFP is naturally unwilling to part with the goods, since the BFP paid for the goods in good faith.

Should O's claim against the BFP succeed? It depends. There is a well-established general principle (though one subject to many exceptions) that one person cannot pass on to another person a better title to goods than he has himself. This principle has been recognised by statute[5] and is often expressed by the Latin phrase ***nemo dat quod non habet***, which can be translated as 'no one can give what he does not have'. So, if R had no title to the goods, he could not give good title to the goods to the BFP, which means that the goods still belong to O and O's action will succeed. But, if R did have a title to the goods, even a voidable one, he could pass this on (assuming O had not already rescinded his contract with R) and, as against the BFP, the principle is that the title to the property is no longer voidable.

A 'voidable' title is one which can be rescinded, or set aside. Rescission means that the whole transaction will be set aside and both parties restored to the position they were in before the contract was entered into. Title may be voidable due to a range of **vitiating factors**—such as misrepresentation, duress, and undue influence—and these will be

---

[5] Sale of Goods Act 1979, s 21(1).

examined in detail in subsequent chapters.[6] The nature and operation of rescission will be examined in detail in Chapter 16.[7] For present purposes, it is important to appreciate that when *R* lies to *O* in order to induce *O* to enter into a contract with *R*, then *R* has committed a fraudulent misrepresentation which entitles *O* to rescind the contract. However, because the contract is voidable and not void, this means that the contract between *R* and *O* is valid unless and until it is rescinded. As a result, *R* does get good title to the goods (prior to rescission) and, if he sells the goods to the *BFP* before *O* rescinds his contract with *R*, then rescission will be barred as against the *BFP*. *O* has lost his right to avoid the contract and his action against the *BFP* will fail. A *BFP* is sometimes as known as '**Equity**'s Darling', since such a purchaser will take title to the purchased property free from any equitable claims, including *O*'s right to rescind the original contract with *R*.[8]

However, if *O* rescinds his contract with *R* before *R* sells the goods to the *BFP*, then the act of rescission means that title to the goods was revested in *O* prior to the sale to the *BFP*, which means that *R* no longer had title to the goods at the time of the sale to the *BFP*. As a result, the *BFP* does not get title to the goods, since *R* cannot give good title to the goods to the *BFP* as a result of the *nemo dat* principle.[9] *O* will therefore be able to sue the *BFP* in the tort of conversion—this is a **common law** claim, not an equitable claim, and is not subject to the defence that *C* is a bona fide purchaser for value without notice.

To sum up, the result of the action *O v BFP* will therefore turn on whether there was a contract between *O* and *R*. If there was, it was at least voidable because of *R*'s fraud. But if it was merely voidable, the ownership in the goods passed to *R*. *R* therefore had a title to the goods, albeit a voidable one, and once the *BFP* had paid for the goods in good faith, the *BFP* had a title which was no longer voidable. However, imagine that *O*'s offer to sell the goods was not made to *R* but to *S*, and *R* had purported to accept. Clearly, that is not a contract (though it is often described as 'a void contract') and, even though *R* may get possession of the goods, he does not get ownership of them. Because *R* has no title to the goods, he can pass on no title to the *BFP* (*nemo dat quod non habet*), so *O*'s action will succeed. If, on the other hand, *R*'s fraud merely misled *O* as to *R*'s attributes so that *O*'s offer was made to *R*, then, notwithstanding his fraud, *R* could accept the offer so as to create a voidable contract and acquire the ownership of the property delivered to him.

3 Contracts made in writing

The leading case is still *Cundy v Lindsay*.[10] The rogue, Blenkarn, hired a room in 37 Wood Street, London, close to a well-known and reputable firm, Blenkiron & Sons, carrying on business at 123 Wood Street. Blenkarn wrote letters to Lindsay, the owner of a firm of linen manufacturers, ordering a large quantity of handkerchiefs and signing the letters 'A Blenkarn & Co.', but hoping that this would be read as 'A Blenkiron & Co.'. It was indeed read in this way by a member of Lindsay's firm who knew of Blenkiron & Sons as a

---

[6] See Chapters 16–19.
[7] See Chapter 16, Section 4.
[8] See further Chapter 16, Section 4(d)(iv).
[9] See Chapter 16, Section 4(d)(iv).
[10] (1878) 3 App Cas 459, HL.

reputable firm. Consequently, the handkerchiefs were despatched to 'Messrs Blenkiron & Co., 37 Wood Street', where they were received by Blenkarn and resold by him to the *BFP*, Cundy. Blenkarn received the price from Cundy. However, Blenkarn did not pay Lindsay. The fraud was discovered and Blenkarn was sent to prison. Lindsay sued Cundy for conversion of the handkerchiefs.

Was this the case of an offer made by *A* (Lindsay) to *B* (Blenkiron & Sons) which was 'accepted' by *C* (Blenkarn)? If so, Blenkarn obtained no title to the handkerchiefs and Lindsay's action deserved to succeed. Or, alternatively, was it a case of an offer made to *C* (Blenkarn) under a mistake as to *C*'s attributes? If so, *C* obtained a voidable title to the goods and passed on good title to the *BFP*, Cundy. The Queen's Bench Division took the latter view, holding that Lindsay intended to deal with the person carrying on business at 37 Wood Street—Blenkarn—and therefore there was a contract with him. But the Court of Appeal and the House of Lords held otherwise. Lindsay intended to deal with the well-known, reputable firm of Blenkiron & Sons (and Lindsay was well aware of the existence of Blenkiron & Sons) and not with Blenkarn (and Lindsay had never heard of Blenkarn). This was surely the right answer. Blenkarn intended Lindsay to think he was dealing with Blenkiron and that is what Lindsay did think. Lindsay mistakenly believed that the letter came from Blenkiron and that Blenkiron's address was 37 Wood Street. It is literally true to say that Lindsay intended to carry on business with the person at 37 Wood Street (who in fact was Blenkarn), but that is only because Lindsay thought that person was Blenkiron. The address, in itself, was of no significance. The identity of Blenkiron was crucial. Of course, the outcome of the case was hard for Cundy. Cundy had paid for the goods in good faith, and yet was bound to pay the value of the goods to Lindsay since Cundy had no title to the handkerchiefs. *Cundy v Lindsay* was therefore a case where the court had to decide which of two innocent persons should suffer because of the fraud of a third party.

It is useful to contrast *Cundy v Lindsay* with *King's Norton Metal Co Ltd v Edridge, Merrett & Co Ltd*.[11] The rogue in that case, Wallis, wrote a letter to King's Norton. The letter was written on headed notepaper purporting to be that of Hallam & Co, Soho Hackle, Pin and Wire Works, Sheffield. The letter suggested that the company had a large factory and made statements that Hallam & Co had depots in Belfast, Lille, and Ghent. An order was placed for goods, which King's Norton sent off to Hallam & Co's address. The goods were never paid for but were resold to the *BFP*, Edridge, Merrett & Co. Again, this was essentially a case where *O* sued the *BFP* and the question was whether there was a contract between *O* and *R*. At first sight, *King's Norton* looks just like *Cundy v Lindsay*. But there is a crucial difference. In *Cundy*, Blenkiron & Sons was a real, existing firm, known to Lindsay. In *King's Norton*, on the other hand, Hallam & Co, with its factory and depots, seems merely to have been a figment of *R*'s imagination. Nevertheless, even in *King's Norton*, *O* must have intended to deal with someone. The question is, who? There was only one possible candidate—the writer of the letter, which was *R*. Admittedly, *R* had made some pretty fundamental misrepresentations—that he was carrying on business under the name of Hallam and Co, that he owned a large factory, and so on—but these were representations as to his attributes. *R* had not represented himself to be some other real, existing person to *O*.

---

[11] (1897) 14 TLR 98, CA.

The court observed that, 'If it could have been shown that there was a separate entity called Hallam & Co. and another entity called Wallis, then the case might have come within *Cundy v. Lindsay*.' It was impossible for King's Norton to claim that the identity of the party it was dealing with was crucial, since Hallam & Co was entirely fictional. King's Norton was *only* concerned with the *attributes* of the other party. And the key attribute related to creditworthiness—namely, could the other party pay for the goods?

In *Shogun Finance Ltd v Hudson*,[12] R agreed with a dealer to buy a car on **hire-purchase**. R produced a stolen driving licence belonging to DP and forged DP's signature on the proposed hire-purchase agreement. R therefore committed a fraudulent misrepresentation in pretending to be DP. A finance company, O, made a credit search in respect of DP which was satisfactory. The finance company therefore indicated its willingness to proceed with the hire-purchase transaction, and to enter into a contract with DP. As a result, the dealer accepted a 10 per cent deposit from R, pursuant to an agreement which transferred the ownership in the car from the dealer to O and purported to let the car to the hirer named in the agreement, which was DP. R then sold the car to the BFP, and O subsequently sued the BFP in conversion.

Importantly, even though a person who has possession of a car under a hire-purchase agreement (called 'the **debtor**') is not the owner, section 27 of the Hire Purchase Act 1964 provides that a BFP who purchases that car from the debtor nevertheless acquires a good title. However, in the opinion of a bare majority of the House of Lords, R did not hold the car under a hire-purchase agreement and was not 'the debtor', because O intended to deal not with R, but only with DP. There had been a crucial mistake of identity: O made an offer to DP which was not open to R to accept. The BFP was therefore liable in conversion.

This decision is controversial.[13] However, the outcome is entirely consistent with *Cundy v Lindsay*. Lord Hobhouse offered strong support for the **parol evidence** rule,[14] such that where the contract is written down the identity of the parties to the contract is established from the written document and nothing else.[15] It was crucial for O to deal with DP, and the offer could therefore not be accepted by R. It is important to appreciate that the supposed contract in *Shogun Finance* was concluded in writing between parties who were not dealing face-to-face. This is because the supposed contract was between O, the finance company, and DP. Although R was in the presence of the dealer, the dealer was not the agent of the finance company. If the dealer had been authorised by the finance company to enter into the hire-purchase agreement, the face-to-face principle would have applied and the result would probably have been different[16]—but this was not the correct analysis on the facts of *Shogun Finance*. *Shogun Finance* is simply a modern application of *Cundy v Lindsay*, although instead of the sale of handkerchiefs the contract concerned the hire-purchase of a car. But in both instances the owners of the goods at issue thought that they were dealing with a particular person known to them who did in fact exist (Blenkiron and DP respectively) and the offer could only have been accepted by that particular person, and not by the rogue.

[12] [2003] UKHL 62, [2004] 1 AC 919.
[13] See further Section 6.
[14] See Chapter 11, Section 4.
[15] See too *Hector v Lyons* (1989) 58 P & CR 156, 158–9 (Sir Nicolas Browne-Wilkinson V-C).
[16] See Section 4.

4 Where the parties are face-to-face

In *Cundy v Lindsay*, where the contract was made through the post, it was not too difficult for the courts to conclude that Lindsay intended to deal with Blenkiron, and not with Blenkarn. When *O* and *R* are face-to-face it is less easy to conclude that *O* intended not to deal with *R*, the very person present, but with someone else. Nevertheless, problems can arise when *R* represents himself to be another existing person so that, like *Cundy v Lindsay* and *Shogun Finance* but unlike *King's Norton v Edridge*, there are two separate entities. It by no means follows that *Cundy v Lindsay* will be applied. Indeed, the opposite result will be likely.

In *Phillips v Brooks Ltd*,[17] the rogue, North, went to a jeweller's shop and selected pearls at the price of £2,550 and a ring at £450. Up to that point, North had not mentioned his name, so the jeweller was plainly dealing with the man in the shop, whoever he might be. It might even be suggested that the contract was made at this point and the ownership in the goods passed to North before he had made any misrepresentation. But a more likely interpretation of the facts is that the jeweller contemplated discussion of further terms, such as mode of payment and time of delivery. After all, the jeweller would hardly be expecting the buyer to produce this large sum in cash—especially in 1919—so the better view is that the contract was not yet formed. North produced a cheque book and wrote out a cheque for £3,000, saying that his name was Sir George Bullough and giving an address in St James's Square. This was a lie and at this point North obviously misrepresented himself to the jeweller. The jeweller had heard of Sir George and he checked in a directory that the address was correct. Satisfied by his checks, the jeweller asked North if he would like to take the goods with him. North said that the jeweller had better have the cheque cleared first. However, North also said that he would like to take the ring away with him as it was his wife's birthday the next day. The jeweller agreed, so North took the ring and promptly **pledged** it with the *BFP*, the defendant **pawnbrokers**. The cheque, of course, was **dishonoured** and the jeweller sued the *BFP* in conversion.

The jeweller argued that he intended to sell to Sir George, not to North. But Horridge J held that the jeweller simply intended to deal with the person present. There was therefore a contract between the jeweller and North. Although this contract was voidable for fraud, ownership passed to North under the contract and, since the contract had not been rescinded before he pledged the ring with the defendants, North gave a good title to the defendants. The jeweller was undoubtedly dealing with the man in the shop until he gave the false name and the judge's view was that what happened subsequently was not sufficient to displace that initial intention to sell to the person present in the shop. The jeweller was misled as to that person's attributes—he believed the man in the shop to be called Sir George Bullough, to be a baronet, to have an address in St James's Square, and to be an honest and creditworthy person—but nevertheless he was still dealing with the man in front of him. The jeweller's claim against the *BFP* therefore failed.

It is worth highlighting two subsequent Court of Appeal decisions with rather similar facts. In the first, *Ingram and Others v Little*,[18] it was held that there was no contract with

[17] [1919] 2 KB 243 (Horridge J).
[18] [1961] 1 QB 31.

the rogue, but the second, *Lewis v Averay*,[19] reached the same result as *Phillips v Brooks*. It is doubtful if the cases can be reconciled. *Ingram v Little* concerned three ladies selling a car. A rogue (who was never identified) calling himself Hutchinson offered to buy the car for £717. The ladies were prepared to accept this price. At this point, the ladies were undoubtedly dealing with the man in their drawing room. Nevertheless, when the man offered to pay by cheque, the ladies said that they would in no circumstances accept a cheque and the deal was off. This seems to be the only possible point of distinction from *Phillips v Brooks*. Up to this point, the identity of the man present had been unimportant to the sellers because they were anticipating a cash sale and one man's cash was as good as any other's. Yet the rogue was now opening negotiations for a sale on credit, where identity was vitally important. The rogue said that he was PGM Hutchinson of Stanstead House, Stanstead Road, Caterham. One of the ladies ascertained from a directory that there was such a person. And, eventually, the ladies were persuaded to take a cheque and let the rogue have the car. He went off with it and was never seen again. However, the car was later found in the possession of the defendant, the *BFP*.

Pearce LJ summarised the difficulty facing the court:

> It is not easy to decide whether the vendor was selling to the man in her drawing-room (fraudulently misrepresented as being a man of substance with the attributes of the real Hutchinson) or to P. G. M. Hutchinson of Stanstead House (fraudulently misrepresented as being the man in her drawing-room).[20]

The majority of the Court of Appeal was influenced by the fact that the trial judge had held that the ladies intended to sell to the real Hutchinson, and that this was a crucial mistake as to identity. The majority judges emphasised that an **appellate court** should not readily interfere with the opinion of the trial judge, who had heard the witnesses, on a question of intention. On the other hand, the dissenting judge, Devlin LJ, thought that the trial judge was no better equipped than the Court of Appeal to answer this question. Devlin LJ held that the presumption that a person is intending to contract with the person to whom he is actually addressing words of a contract is a very strong one and was not rebutted in this case.

The facts in the second case, *Lewis v Averay*,[21] were very similar. The rogue represented that he was Richard Greene, a famous actor, and persuaded the seller to take a cheque for his car. A differently constituted Court of Appeal applied the very strong presumption stated by Devlin LJ in *Ingram v Little* and held that it could not be rebutted on the facts. Lord Denning thought that *Phillips v Brooks* and *Ingram v Little* were irreconcilable and that *Phillips v Brooks* was right. This is probably the better view.

In *Ingram v Little*, Devlin LJ did recognise that there is at least one way in which the presumption of dealing with the party present can be rebutted. That is where the rogue dishonestly claims to be acting as agent for another party. There is no contract with that other party because the rogue has no authority of any kind to act as his agent. And there

---

[19] [1972] 1 QB 198.
[20] [1961] 1 QB 31, 59.
[21] Ibid.

is no contract with the rogue because the contract does not purport to be made with him. *Hardman v Booth*[22] is an illustration of this. The claimants went to the office of Gandell & Sons and encountered Edward Gandell, the rogue. He was not a member of the firm of Gandell & Sons and had no authority to act on the firm's behalf. Nevertheless, he gave the claimants an order in the firm's name, intercepted the goods when they arrived, and then delivered them to the defendant, the *BFP*. The claimants' action against the *BFP* succeeded. There was never any suggestion that the claimants were selling the goods to Edward Gandell personally, so there was no contract with him. And there was no contract with Gandell & Sons because Edward had no authority to bind the firm in any way.

This is not necessarily the only way by which the presumption that *O* intends to deal with the other person present is rebuttable. Suppose that *R* impersonates *O*'s established customer, *S*, so that from the start *O* believes that he is dealing with *S*. If the negotiations were conducted over the telephone, *R* imitating *S*'s well-known voice to perfection, there would surely be no contract if identity was important. Similarly, if *R* entered *O*'s shop with an equally effective disguise, so as to be greeted, 'Good morning, Mr *S*', it is difficult to see that there is any difference in principle.

The above analysis is consistent with what was said by the House of Lords in *Shogun Finance*. As explained in Section 3, that case did not concern face-to-face dealings but rather a written contract concluded by two parties who were not face-to-face. Nevertheless, some of their Lordships did discuss the cases raised in this section. The result in *Ingram v Little* was criticised, and two members of the House of Lords expressly said that it was incorrect.[23] However, there is no real need to overrule *Ingram*, since it can readily be sidelined to its own particular facts where the court thought that the presumption that *O* intended to deal with the person actually present was rebutted. The suggestion made in *Shogun Finance* that this presumption should be irrebuttable[24] should be rejected. In some circumstances, even where transactions are carried out face-to-face, the identity of a person will still be crucial.

5 Estoppel

In some circumstances, the *BFP* can invoke the doctrine of **estoppel**.[25] This might be possible where *O* has represented to the *BFP* that *R* is the owner of the goods, or has the power to dispose of them, and *O* knows, or ought to know, that the *BFP* will act on that statement. If the *BFP* does then rely on *O*'s statement by giving *R* value for the goods, *O* will be estopped from denying that *R* was the owner or had that power. The effect is that the *BFP* gets a good title to the goods. In *Henderson v Williams*,[26] Grey & Co owned a certain quantity of sugar lying in the defendant's warehouse. The rogue, Fletcher, pretended to be the agent of Robinson, a well-known customer of Grey, and fraudulently induced Grey to 'sell' him the

---

[22] (1863) 1 H & C 803.
[23] See eg [2003] UKHL 62, [2004] 1 AC 919 [185] (Lord Walker) and [110] (Lord Millett).
[24] See ibid, [67] (Lord Millett).
[25] See Chapter 2, Section 8.
[26] [1895] 1 QB 521.

sugar. It seems clear that the ownership of the goods passed neither to Fletcher (because there was no intention to contract with him) nor to Robinson (because Fletcher was not his agent and he knew nothing of the transaction) so the sugar still belonged to Grey. But Grey advised the defendant that Grey had sold the sugar and that the defendant was to hold it to Fletcher's order. Fletcher offered to sell the sugar to the claimant, the *BFP*. Before accepting this offer, the *BFP* asked the defendant whether the sugar was held to Fletcher's order. The defendant replied that it was and the claimant thereupon 'bought' the sugar from Fletcher. Grey, having discovered the fraud, induced the defendant to detain the sugar and indemnified him for doing so. In effect, Grey was therefore the real defendant when the claimant sued for the sugar. The court held that, even if there was no contract at all with Fletcher, Grey was estopped from setting up its title against the claimant who had acted on that representation, since Grey had (through the defendant) 'held out' Fletcher as having the power to dispose of the goods.

However, it must be noted that there is a vital difference between 'holding out' the rogue to be the owner and merely enabling the rogue to hold himself out as the owner. In the latter case there is no estoppel. After all, there is no representation which is intended to be relied upon. In *Cundy v Lindsay*, Lindsay enabled Blenkarn to hold himself out as owner since Lindsay put the goods into Blenkarn's possession. As the possessor, Blenkarn was able to present every appearance of being the owner. Nevertheless, there was no question of an estoppel. Otherwise everyone who entrusted his goods to another person would be estopped from asserting his title if that other person dishonestly disposed of them to a *BFP*.

6 Proposals for reform

Under the present law, someone (or in many cases someone's insurer) has to bear the whole loss. Either the owner bears the whole loss or the *BFP* does. The outcome depends on the nature of a transaction (the 'contract' between *O* and *R*) about which, by definition, the *BFP* knew nothing. This can seem somewhat arbitrary and harsh on the *BFP*. Devlin LJ, in his dissenting judgment in *Ingram v Little*,[27] suggested that the law should be reformed, as it has been in other areas, to allow an apportionment between *O* and the *BFP*. The loss would be borne equally unless there was fault or imprudence on one side or the other. If there was, the party at fault would bear such greater proportion of the loss as the court found to be just.

This suggestion of Devlin LJ was considered and rejected by the Law Reform Committee.[28] The Law Reform Committee envisaged great practical difficulties, particularly in cases where there has been more than one *BFP*. For example, some goods, such as cars, pass from hand to hand very rapidly. It may be that *R* has sold to *A* who has sold to *B* who has sold to *C*, all before *O* discovers the fraud. *O* then finds the goods in the hands of *C*, so it is *C* whom *O* sues in conversion. But in every contract of sale there is an implied promise by the seller

---

[27]   [1961] 1 QB 31.
[28]   Twelfth Report, *Transfer of Title to Chattels* (Cmnd 2958, 1966).

that he has a right to sell the goods. As a result, *C* will wish to join *B* in the action on the ground that, if he (*C*) is guilty of conversion of *O*'s goods, it is only because *B* is in breach of his contractual promise that he had a right to sell the goods. If the goods belonged to *O* all the time, *B* did not have a right to sell those goods. So *B* must indemnify *C* against any damages *C* has to pay *O* for conversion. And similarly *B* will wish to join in *A* on the same basis. Of course, sometimes the chain may be much longer. The Law Reform Committee thought that adopting an approach based upon apportionment might therefore require the courts to become involved in an inquiry into the degree of fault, if any, of each party in the chain. This would lead to so much complexity and uncertainty as to render the proposal undesirable.

The Law Reform Committee did recommend that, where goods are sold under a mistake as to the buyer's identity, the contract should be voidable and not void, at least so far as third parties are concerned. The effect of this recommendation would be, of course, that the *BFP* would get a good title and *Cundy v Lindsay* would be reversed. This proposal has not been implemented. It was, however, the favoured solution of the minority of the House of Lords in *Shogun Finance*. Such a solution would represent a significant shift for English law. At the moment, a mistake does not make a contract voidable. A contract can only be void (or, as it should preferably be expressed, does not come into existence) because of a mistake as to identity. What makes the contract voidable is the misrepresentation of the rogue.[29]

Admittedly, the current stance taken by the law does lead to the peculiar fact that *O* is better protected if he can establish his own mistake as to identity than if he relies upon the fraud of *R*. If *O* can establish his own mistake as to identity, *R* will not get title to the goods, so *O* will be able to sue a *BFP* in conversion. Yet if *O* depends upon *R*'s fraud, then *R* will acquire (voidable) title to the goods, so *O* will not be able to sue a *BFP* in conversion. This was one reason why the minority in *Shogun Finance* thought that a mistake of identity should only ever render a contract voidable.

The fact that in *Shogun Finance* a strong panel of judges in the House of Lords split 3:2 indicates that the arguments are finely balanced. The powerful dissents of Lord Millett and Lord Nicholls failed to convince the majority of Lord Hobhouse, Lord Phillips, and Lord Walker. The minority found that there was no convincing reason to distinguish between contracts concluded in writing *inter absentes* and contracts formed face-to-face; in the modern world, it may become increasingly difficult to differentiate between the two as contracts might be concluded by video-link and a number of different means of communication. Nevertheless, it is suggested that the decision of the majority is to be preferred. It is important to preserve the certainty and sanctity of written agreements: this is an important reason why English commercial law has been so successful and popular. The principle that an offer made by *A* to *B* (and to *B* alone) cannot be accepted by *C* should not be jettisoned.

As a matter of policy it might be thought that the result in *Shogun Finance* does little to encourage finance companies to take great care about thoroughly checking the persons they are dealing with. On the other hand, if *Shogun Finance* had been decided differently, it might have become much more difficult for finance companies to be prepared to enter into hire-purchase agreements, which could make it more burdensome or expensive for

---

[29] See Chapter 16.

legitimate customers to enter into such contracts. Following the strong and contrasting views expressed in *Shogun Finance*, the Law Commission again proposed to examine this area of law.[30] However, this proposal has since been dropped.[31] It is important to appreciate that *Cundy v Lindsay* remains good law and was supported by the majority in *Shogun Finance*. It therefore remains crucial to determine whether *O* has made a mistake as to the identity or an attribute of *R*. The former possibility is much more likely where the contract is made in writing, but highly unlikely where the contract is made face-to-face.

 Further Reading

Twelfth Report of the Law Reform Committee, *Transfer of Title to Chattels* (Cmnd 2958, 1966).
Considers the options for reforming the law, ultimately rejecting proportionate liability based on relative fault, but recommending that, so far as third parties are concerned, a mistake as to the buyer's identity should render the contract voidable not void.

C Macmillan, 'Rogues, Swindlers and Cheats: The Development of Mistake of Identity in English Contract Law' (2005) 64 CLJ 711.
Discusses the historical background to the early cases on mistake, and argues that the decision in *Cundy v Lindsay* was influenced by the approach of the criminal law at the time.

RH Stevens, 'Objectivity, Mistake and the Parol Evidence Rule' in A Burrows and E Peel, *Contract Terms* (OUP, 2007).
Examines the decision in *Shogun Finance* and concludes that the approach of Lord Hobhouse should be supported where a contract is concluded in writing.

? Questions

1. According to Lord Hobhouse in *Shogun Finance Ltd v Hudson* (2003), the principles of law concerning the effect of mistake of identity 'are clear and sound and need no revision'.
   Do you agree?

2. Neal works as a David Beckham lookalike. Neal learns that David has recently moved to Hertfordshire, and Neal decides to go to Hertfordshire to try to meet David. Whilst there, Neal enters a luxury car showroom. The owner of the showroom, Mozzie, mistakes Neal for David Beckham and tries to persuade him to buy a car. Neal takes the McLaren Spider, valued at £200,000, for a test drive. Neal tells Mozzie that he would very much like to buy it, but does not have the cash to do so at the moment. Mozzie is keen to be able to say that David Beckham is a customer of his, so asks what he could get in return for the McLaren Spider. Neal decides to pretend that he is David Beckham, and says that he can give Mozzie his Porsche 911 Turbo and five of his signed England football shirts in three days' time. Mozzie agrees, and allows Neal to drive the McLaren Spider away from the showroom.
   The following day, Neal drives the McLaren Spider to a nearby pub. Whilst in the pub, he meets David Beckham, and the two of them strike up a conversation about how similar they are in

---

[30] Law Commission, *Ninth Programme of Law Reform* (Law Com No 293, 2005), para 1.16.
[31] Law Commission, *Eleventh Programme of Law Reform* (Law Com No 330, 2011), paras 3.5–3.6.

appearance. Neal then offers to swap cars with David. David has arrived in his Porsche 911 Turbo, and tells Neal that it is not worth anywhere near as much as the McLaren Spider. Neal said that he does not care about that, and David agrees to the deal.

Three days later, Mozzie realises that he was talking to Neal and not David Beckham in his showroom. He tries to contact Neal, but Neal has now disappeared.

Advise Mozzie and David.

7 Consideration and promissory estoppel

🔑 Key Points

- Contracts will generally only be binding if supported by consideration. Consideration might be considered to be 'the price tag on the promise': a party must provide something in exchange for the promise in order to be able to enforce that promise. That 'something' is called 'consideration', and might itself be a promise.

- Consideration must be sufficient, but need not be adequate. The act which constitutes the consideration must not contravene public policy, but it does not matter whether the deal seems objectively reasonable for a contract to be formed.

- Difficulties arise where the consideration provided is in the form of doing, or promising to do, something that the party is already under a legal obligation to do. It is generally said that the promisee's performance of duties imposed by law is not a sufficient consideration, but the reverse is true where the consideration is the performance of a duty owed only to a third party.

- More problematic are situations where the promisor offers the promisee more money to perform obligations the promisee already owes: the promisee may provide good consideration for the extra money by performing his obligations if the promisor 'obtains in practice a benefit, or obviates a disbenefit'.

- However, part payment of a debt is not good consideration for the extinguishment of that debt. But the act of paying early, or otherwise changing the conditions of payment, may, if accepted as such by the creditor, constitute good consideration to extinguish the debt.

- The requirement of consideration is demanded by the common law. But, in some situations, equity will allow a promisee to enforce a promise, despite a lack of consideration, through the doctrine of promissory estoppel. Where the promisor makes a clear promise, intended to be binding, intended to be acted upon, and in fact acted upon, the courts will not allow the promisor to act inconsistently with that promise if to do so would be unconscionable. Promissory estoppel does not create a cause of action, and as a general rule can only be invoked as a defence after a binding contract has been formed.

1 The price tag on the promise

We have seen in Chapter 1 that an offer is not an offer to contract unless, expressly or impliedly, it asks for something in return. The element of consideration is fundamental to the idea of contract as a bargain. Acceptance of an offer consists of giving what is asked for, whether that be a promise or an act. That promise, or that act, is the consideration. An offer which asks for nothing in return is an offer to make a **gift** and is not enforceable. So, there is a very important difference between my offering to give you £50 next week, and my offering to give you £50 next week if you promise to come to my office. The former is an offer of a gift and is not enforceable. The latter asks for something in return (a promise to come to my office) and is therefore an offer to contract.

It is for this reason that in many of the seminal cases we find the court looking for a 'request' in the offer. An instructive example is *Shadwell v Shadwell*.[1]

An uncle wrote to his nephew:

> I am glad to hear of your intended marriage with Ellen Nicholl and, as I promised to assist you at starting, I am happy to tell you that I will pay to you one hundred and fifty pounds yearly during my life, and until your income derived from your profession of a Chancery barrister shall amount to six hundred guineas ...

The nephew married Ellen, and his income never reached 600 guineas. However, the uncle only paid 12 annual sums, and died leaving five unpaid. The nephew sued his uncle's **personal representative** for the unpaid instalments. One of the defences raised by the uncle's personal representative was that the marriage had been arranged before the alleged agreement, without any request from the uncle, and that there was no consideration for the uncle's promise to pay. Since an agreement in **consideration of marriage** was one of those contracts which the Statute of Frauds 1677 then required to be evidenced in writing,[2] the consideration had to be found in the uncle's letter or not at all.

The word 'request' appears repeatedly in the judgments of the majority, who decided in favour of the nephew, and of Byles J, who dissented. The majority, taking into account the relationship between the uncle and nephew, held that the letter was an inducement to the nephew to marry and therefore a request to marry. Byles J agreed that 'Marriage of the **plaintiff** at the **testator**'s express request would be, no doubt, an ample consideration; but marriage of the plaintiff without the testator's request is no consideration to the testator.' The difference between the judges was not on the principles of the law of contract, but only on the construction of the letter.[3] Byles J could find no request to marry in the letter, whereas the majority could. Over a hundred years later, Salmon LJ said that he would, without hesitation, have decided the case in accordance with the views of Byles J.[4] It is suggested that the majority judges took a very strained view of the letter. Was the uncle not simply offering a rather generous wedding present? If the relatives and friends of an

---

[1] (1860) 9 CB (NS) 159.
[2] Chapter 9.
[3] See Chapter 12.
[4] *Jones v Padavatton* [1969] 1 WLR 328, 333.

engaged couple promise them lavish wedding presents, this may indeed be an inducement to marry, but it would surely be very surprising if they were held to have contracted to give the presents.

However, suppose that the nephew had told his uncle that he intended to break off his engagement to Ellen, and the uncle had then written: 'I am disappointed to hear that you are thinking of breaking off your engagement. Ellen is a splendid girl. If you marry her, I will pay you …' Clearly, the uncle would then have been asking for something in return for his promise and presumably Byles J and Salmon LJ would agree that there was then a contract supported by consideration.[5]

It is sometimes difficult to distinguish between a conditional offer to make a gift and an offer to contract. If the offer is to pay money (or give some other benefit) upon the occurrence of a certain event, not being an act or promise by the **offeree**, that appears to be an offer to make a gift. The offeree is not asked to do anything. It is simply that the gift is conditional upon the occurrence of an event. So if I say: 'If you should be so unlucky as to catch flu, I will pay you £100', that is an offer of a conditional gift. But if I say: 'I will pay you £100 if you will use the smoke ball three times daily for two weeks and then have the misfortune to catch flu', that is an offer of a contract, since the use of the smoke ball constitutes the consideration requested.[6]

The problem is more difficult when the alleged **condition** is something to be done or, as the case may be, not done, by the offeree. In *Wyatt v Kreglinger and Fernau*,[7] the claimant, Wyatt, was a retiring employee who was not entitled to a pension. However, the defendant firm wrote to Wyatt to inform him that the firm had decided to pay him a pension of £200 per year, and that he was at liberty to enter into any business or employment, 'except in the wool trade'. After some years the defendant stopped the pension and Wyatt sued. All the judges in the Court of Appeal agreed that, if this was a contract, it was illegal as being in restraint of trade. But the judges split on the question of whether Wyatt would otherwise be contractually entitled to the pension of £200 per year. Scrutton LJ agreed with the trial judge that this was a voluntary gratuitous payment and that the words 'except in the wool trade' were merely an intimation to Wyatt that, if he did enter the wool trade, the pension would stop. However, Slesser and Greer LJJ thought that, but for the illegality, there would have been a good contract, the consideration being Wyatt's refraining from entering the wool trade. This again illustrates that whether or not there is a gift or a contract involves difficult questions of interpretation about which opinions can reasonably differ.[8]

In any event, it is surely the case that a person who makes a gift may make it clear that, if the donee behaves in a certain way, the gift will come to an end. This can be done without turning the gift into a binding contract. For example, if a man promises to pay his widowed daughter-in-law £5,000 a year, he should surely be able to withdraw that promise on finding himself in more difficult financial circumstances, or on falling out with her, or because she has married a wealthy man. But imagine that the man initially limits his promise to pay the allowance by the addition of the words, 'so long as you remain unmarried'. Are

---

[5] Subject to another difficulty: see the following discussion and Section 1(e)(ii).
[6] *Carlill v Carbolic Smoke Ball Co* [1893] 1 QB 256; see Chapter 4.
[7] [1933] 1 KB 793, CA.
[8] See Chapter 12.

those words merely used to define the extent of a gratuitous promise? Or is their effect that the man has now made an offer to contract, the consideration provided by his daughter-in-law being that she does not remarry? It is suggested that the former is the better view. Of course, it would be different if the man, because he was so distressed at hearing of his daughter-in-law's intention to remarry, were to say, 'Please do not remarry. I will pay you £5,000 a year so long as you remain unmarried.' Then he would clearly be asking a price for his promise. Similarly, in *Wyatt v Kreglinger*, the employer would have been asking a price for its promise if the employer had discovered, to its dismay, that its former employee was about to join its greatest rival and had only offered the former employee a pension to induce him to refrain from doing so.

Of course, there is no magic in the word 'request'. The question is one of substance rather than form. An objective assessment is required. Was the **promisor** asking a price for his promise? Was his promise a free gift or was he 'selling' it? Was it, in a word, a bargain?

(a) **Benefit and detriment**

It has been traditional to state that consideration must be a benefit to the promisor or a detriment to the **promisee**. For instance, in *Currie v Misa*, Lush J stated that 'A valuable consideration, in the sense of the law, may consist either in some right, interest, profit, or benefit accruing to one party, or some **forbearance**, detriment, loss or responsibility, given, suffered or undertaken by the other.'[9] Of course, it is almost always both. *O* asks for a 'price' because it is a benefit he wants to receive; and the giving of the price is, almost inevitably, a detriment of some kind to *A*. The language of benefit and detriment is often associated with the notion that consideration must be of some economic value.

However, the practice of the courts, as distinct from what they say, shows that the language of benefit and detriment has long been out of date and has no substantial meaning at the present day. It is true that there are some things which the law regards as incapable of amounting to consideration for reasons of policy,[10] but, subject to that, *anything* that the promisor asks for in return for his promise is consideration. If *O* makes a promise to *A* in consideration of *A*'s supplying him with three chocolate wrappers, there is a perfectly good contract provided that the promise was seriously intended.[11] It does not matter that the wrappers are quite useless and that *O* will instantly throw them away. The point is that *O* has got what he asked for and that is a sufficient 'benefit'. And *A* has parted with something he might have kept, so *A* has done something which he did not have to do, and that is a sufficient 'detriment'. The fact that the wrappers are of no value and that *A* is glad to be rid of them is simply immaterial.

The economic value of the consideration provided seems to be irrelevant. Judges have recognised (in a hypothetical but much quoted example[12]) that *O*'s promise to pay *A* £100 if *A* will walk to York can be a perfectly good contract, yet no one has ever demonstrated what economic value there is in walking to York. The same might be said of promises of a reward

[9] (1875) LR 10 Ex 153, 162.
[10] See Section 1(e); see too Chapter 22.
[11] *Chappell v Nestlé* [1960] AC 87.
[12] See Chapter 4.

for not smoking,[13] or promises by the father of an illegitimate child to pay the mother an allowance if she proves to him that the child is well looked after and happy.[14] The promisor may derive satisfaction and peace of mind from the fact that the promisee is not smoking or that the child is happy, but there is no economic value in it for him. But that does not matter. The promisor has got what he bargained for and that is consideration. On this basis, it is suggested that the decision in *White v Bluett*[15] may be doubted. A father lent his son some money. When the father died, his **executor** asked the son for the money back. The son argued that the father had promised not to ask for repayment of the money if the son stopped complaining about his situation compared to that of his brothers. Nevertheless, the court held that the son had to repay the money. It seems that the court thought that the son's promise not to bore his father could not amount to consideration. But it is difficult to accept this. After all, the father asked for his son to stop complaining, and his son was at liberty to complain, so the father did get what he asked for, and that should be consideration. It may be that the result in *White v Bluett* can be explained on other grounds—such as uncertainty[16] or a lack of intention to create legal relations[17]—but the analysis of consideration is unconvincing.

(b) 'Past consideration' is no consideration

An offer must ask for something in return if a binding contract is to be formed. One corollary of this is that a promise is not enforceable if it is only to pay for services already rendered, or for some other benefit already conferred. Promises must ask for something more to be binding. Imagine a man brings up an orphan and spends large sums of money on the orphan's maintenance and education. On growing up and achieving success in life, the orphan promises to repay the money spent. That promise is not enforceable.[18] The only possible consideration which could be found to support that promise would be the sums spent on the orphan's maintenance and education, but those acts had occurred in the past, before any promise or request had been made. 'Past consideration is no consideration.'[19]

However, 'past consideration' must be distinguished from the 'executed consideration' which is found in unilateral contracts, because there the act is done at the request of the promisor.[20] If an act is done pursuant to a request then the consideration cannot be 'past consideration'. Where there is no express promise to pay for a service requested, the court may imply a promise to pay a reasonable sum. This is particularly likely if the request is for an ordinary commercial service which everyone expects to pay for.[21] For instance, if I invite a passing window cleaner to clean the windows of my house, saying nothing

---

[13] *Hamer v Sidway*, 27 NE 256 (1881).
[14] *Ward v Byham* [1956] 1 WLR 496.
[15] (1853) 23 LJ Ex 36.
[16] See Chapter 5.
[17] See Chapter 8.
[18] *Eastwood v Kenyon* (1840) 11 Ad & El 438.
[19] *Latimer Management Consultants v Ellingham Investments Ltd* [2005] EWHC 1732 (Ch) [29].
[20] See Chapter 4.
[21] See Chapter 13.

about payment, there is clearly a contract to pay a reasonable sum when the windows have been cleaned.

In *Lampleigh v Brathwait*,[22] *B* had killed a man and he asked *L* to get him a pardon from the king. At considerable trouble and expense, *L* obtained the pardon and *B* then promised to pay him £100 for his efforts. It was held that the promise was enforceable, because the service provided by *L* was rendered at *B*'s request. The request to *L* to obtain a pardon contained an implied promise to pay him for his trouble. Though it looks very different from the window cleaner case, we must assume that the same principle applies: *B* would have been liable to pay a reasonable sum, even if he had never made the subsequent promise to pay £100. The court clearly distinguished an act done at the request of the promisor from 'a mere voluntary courtesy'. However, it might be wondered whether the promise to pay £100 corresponded exactly to the amount that the court might have awarded under an implied promise to pay a reasonable sum for the services rendered. In *Re Casey's Patents*, Bowen LJ suggested that the general principle is that where the parties, as reasonable persons, must have intended that the services provided should be paid for, but no price was stated and subsequently a promise is made to pay:

> that promise may be treated either as an admission which evidences or as a positive bargain which fixes the amount of that reasonable remuneration on the faith of which the service was originally rendered.[23]

Of course, 'evidence' of the reasonable sum is not the same as a positive bargain to 'fix' the price. The two need to be distinguished. Both rest upon the premise that, if *A* has rendered the service, a reasonable sum is due. If *O* then offers to pay a specified sum that is acceptable to *A*, that will be regarded as excellent evidence of what that reasonable sum is. But that only 'evidences' and does not 'fix'. Imagine *O* promised to pay £200 and *A* sues *O* for this amount. *O* may argue that his promise was an extravagant one, and that the reasonable sum is only, say, £100. As a result, his promise to pay £200 was made without any consideration for the additional £100. If *O* can establish that the reasonable sum was only £100, that is all he should have to pay. However, if there is a dispute about the reasonable price, pursuant to which *O* offers £100, *A* demands £300, and they finally agree on £200, then there will have been a 'positive bargain which fixes' the amount of the reasonable remuneration. There is here a new contract, with each party giving consideration by abandoning his claim in favour of the intermediate sum. It is thus not strictly true to say, as the Privy Council did in *Pao On v Lau Yiu Long*:

> An act done before the giving of a promise to make a payment or confer some other benefit can sometimes be consideration for the promise.[24]

The enforceable promise is either the implied promise to pay a reasonable sum which is made *before* the act is done, or the subsequent express promise to pay a particular sum, the consideration for which is the abandonment of the claim by the other party. *Lampleigh v*

---

[22] (1615) Hob 105.
[23] *Re Casey's Patents; Stewart v Casey* [1892] 1 Ch 104, 116.
[24] [1980] AC 614, PC.

Brathwait, as interpreted today, is therefore not an exception to the rule that past consideration is no consideration, because there was an implied promise to pay a reasonable sum which was made before the services were rendered.

As a practical matter, when deciding whether an act done by *A* can be regarded as consideration where the act was carried out before *O* made an express promise to pay *A*, it is often helpful to bear in mind the three requirements identified by Lord Scarman in *Pao On v Lau Yiu Long*. First, the act should have been done pursuant to the promisor's request. Secondly, the parties must have understood that the act was to be remunerated. Thirdly, the payment must have been legally enforceable had it been promised in advance. Of course, this third requirement is generally applicable to all promises, so the focus really lies on the first two requirements.

There is one minor exception to the rule that past consideration is no consideration under the Bills of Exchange Act 1882. Section 27(1) provides that 'Valuable consideration for a bill may be constituted by ... (b) An antecedent debt or liability.' So, if I owe you £100 and I give a cheque (a variety of bill of exchange) in payment, you may **sue me on the cheque**—as well as on the original debt. But this is a limited exception. If, owing you £100, I give you a cheque for £200, you can only recover £100 on the cheque. The promise to pay the other £100 is without consideration.[25] If I owe you £100 for work done and a third person, *X*, who is not acting as my agent, gives you his cheque in payment of my debt, you have no right of action against *X* if the cheque is **dishonoured**. *X* has received no consideration for the promise implied in the cheque.[26] Of course, as the usage of cheques diminishes this exception will become even less significant.

(c) **Consideration need not be adequate**

It is often said that the court will not inquire into the adequacy of the consideration.[27] In effect, this encapsulates the rule that if the promisor gets what he has asked for in return for his promise, the court is not concerned with the question of whether or not he was making a good bargain. It simply does not matter whether the satisfaction of having *A* walk to York was worth £100, or whether the goods or services were worth the price that the promisor agreed to pay for them. If a party has made a bad bargain, that is his own lookout and no concern of the courts.[28]

A leading case is the strange one of *Bainbridge v Firmstone*.[29] The admitted facts were that the defendant said to the claimant (in effect): 'If you will let me weigh your two valuable boilers, I promise you that I will return them to you in perfect condition.' The claimant then allowed the defendant to weigh the boilers. The defendant left the boilers in pieces and the claimant had great trouble putting them together again. The defendant contended that there was no consideration and therefore no contract, but that argument was rejected and

---

[25] *Thoni Gesellschaft GmbH & Co v RTP Equipment Ltd* [1979] 2 Lloyd's Rep 282, CA.

[26] *AEG (UK) Ltd v Lewis*, The Times, 29 December 1992, [1993] 2 Bank LR 119.

[27] The adequacy of the consideration may, however, be relevant in determining the extent of the other party's obligation: the less you pay, the less you may be entitled to expect—see the discussion of *Photo Productions v Securicor* [1980] 1 All ER 556 in Chapter 15, Section 1(c).

[28] cf Chapter 15.

[29] (1838) 1 P & D 2.

the claimant recovered damages for breach of contract. Even though it was not clear what benefit the defendant derived from his strange request, that was immaterial. The defendant got what he wanted in return for his promise. Given the facts admitted by the parties, it seems a perfectly clear case of a contract. A boiler-weighing fetishist must pay the price he promises to pay for the indulgence granted by a boiler owner.

(d) Consideration must be 'sufficient'

Although the court will not inquire into the adequacy of the consideration, there are certain acts and promises which, for reasons of policy, are deemed to be of no value in the law and which are therefore an 'insufficient' consideration. This is why it is often said that the consideration need not be adequate but it must be sufficient. A promise to do any act, or to refrain from doing any act, which the promisor might lawfully do, is generally a sufficient consideration; but there are some promises which the law regards as void, and if a promise is void—or a nullity—it is not sufficient consideration for a counter-promise. For instance, a wife's promise not to go to court to seek maintenance from her estranged husband was deemed to be void as contrary to public policy—the courts would not countenance the exclusion of their statutory jurisdiction to award maintenance—so it followed that her husband's promise to pay her money in consideration of her promise not to go to court was made without consideration and also void.[30] That particular case has now been altered by statute[31] but the principle of the **common law**—that a void promise is not consideration—is not affected.

A promise to refrain from suing, or actual forbearance from suing, is generally a sufficient consideration. If I claim £5,000 which I believe you owe me, and you promise me £2,500 if I will drop the claim, then you have made an offer to make a binding contract. It makes no difference whether I have started an action against you or not. My discontinuing, or not initiating, the action, or my promise to do so, is consideration for your promise to pay £2,500. In a sense, one of us may appear to be getting something for nothing. Either the action would have succeeded (in which case I have thrown away £2,500) or it would not (in which case you have thrown away £2,500). However, the outcome of legal proceedings is rarely, if ever, absolutely certain and the reality is that I have abandoned my claim that you owe me £5,000 in consideration of your abandoning your claim that nothing is due. This is well illustrated by *Cook v Wright*.[32] Commissioners responsible for executing a local Act wrongly believed the defendant to be liable to pay certain charges. The defendant denied liability but, being threatened with legal proceedings, agreed to pay a reduced sum in three instalments by **promissory notes**. Even though it was later admitted that he had never been liable to pay the charges, he was held liable on the notes which had been given

---

[30] *Gaisberg v Storr* [1950] 1 KB 107, CA.

[31] The Matrimonial Causes Act 1973, s 34 confirms that the wife's promise is void but provides that the husband's promise shall not be void or unenforceable, unless there is some other reason why it should be. This appears to be an example of a promise (that of the husband) which, by statute, is enforceable even though without consideration and not under seal (see Chapter 9).

[32] (1861) 1 B & S 559.

in consideration of the Commissioners' refraining from bringing the action which they thought to be a proper claim.

It is very important that such agreements should be binding because the great majority of legal disputes are settled by a compromise of this kind. However, the same analysis does not seem to apply where a claim is brought or threatened in bad faith. If I start, or threaten to start, legal proceedings against you, knowing that I have no cause of action, my forbearance to prosecute (in other words, my refraining from prosecuting) that claim which I know to be unfounded is not a sufficient consideration for any promise which you may make. You may in fact receive a substantial benefit in being saved the worry and expense of defending the action, and there is always a possibility that the claim might have succeeded, notwithstanding its invalidity, through perjury or error. But that does not matter: it would be contrary to policy to recognise that the abandonment of a claim, known by the claimant to be invalid, is of any value in the eyes of the law.[33]

Refraining from doing what one has no right to do cannot be a sufficient consideration. If I constantly trespass on your land, your promise to pay me money if I refrain from doing so is made without consideration. If, on the other hand, you are irritated by my lawful use of the highway past your house and offer me money if I will go another way, my refraining from exercising my liberty to use the highway is sufficient consideration.

It does not follow, however, that refraining from doing what one may lawfully do is always sufficient consideration. In some exceptional situations, the court will refuse to recognise a valid contract where the facts establish the existence of blackmail. If I know my neighbour is committing adultery, I am perfectly entitled to tell his wife. But if I say to my neighbour, 'I will refrain from telling your wife if you will pay me £1,000', that is clearly blackmail and therefore cannot be an offer of a valid contract. The borderline between a good contract and blackmail may be quite fine.[34]

It is suggested that, when deciding on what side of the borderline a case falls, it is important to determine whether the person has a legitimate (commercial) interest in doing that which he refrains from doing. If *A* has written his memoirs, which are true but contain information very damaging to *B*, there seems to be no reason why *A* should not make a contract with *B* that he will refrain from publishing if *B* will pay him the sum which he has been offered by a newspaper. Here *A* has something of commercial value which he may lawfully sell, and, if he can sell it to the newspaper, there is no reason why he should not sell it to *B* for what it is worth. But if he requests from *B* more than the commercial value of the memoirs, then he is taking advantage of *B*'s predicament, probably committing blackmail, and therefore not making a good contract. This is an unusual and limited type of case where the court will have regard to the value of the alleged consideration in determining whether it is sufficient.

---

[33] *Wade v Simeon* (1846) 2 CB 548. However, in *Pitt v PHH Asset Management Ltd* [1993] 4 All ER 961, 966, Peter Gibson LJ said that the claimant's refraining from seeking an **injunction**, although regarding a claim which was bound to fail and had only 'nuisance value', was a benefit to the defendant which amounted to an element in the consideration.

[34] See Chapter 17, Section 4(b); see too D Ormerod, *Smith & Hogan's Criminal Law* (13th edn, OUP, 2011) ch 25.

(e) **Performance of a legal duty as consideration**

The question here is whether *A*'s doing, or promising to do, something that he is already under a legal obligation to do constitutes a sufficient consideration in a contract with *B*. There are three types of duty to consider:

(a) a duty imposed upon A by the general law;

(b) a duty owed by *A* to *C* to do that thing for *B*—in other words, *A* has already contracted with *C* to do the relevant act for *B*;

(c) a duty owed by *A* to *B*, arising out of an existing contract, or the judgment of a court, or otherwise.

Each type of duty must now be examined in turn.

(i) **Duties imposed by law**

It has generally been stated that the performance of, or the promise to perform, a duty imposed by law is not a sufficient consideration. *A* is only doing, or promising to do, what he is already bound to do, and *B* is getting nothing more than that to which he is entitled under the general law, so he is receiving no consideration. Thus a promise to pay a fee to a witness who has been properly **subpoenaed** to attend a trial has been held to be made without consideration: *Collins v Godefroy*.[35] The witness had a public duty to attend.

Glasbrook Bros Ltd v Glamorgan County Council[36] is a leading case often invoked in support of the principle that the performance of a duty imposed by law is not a sufficient consideration, even though the principle is only to be found in *obiter dicta* and therefore cannot be said to be conclusively established from that case alone. The council, as the police authority, sued on a contract it had made with the owners of a colliery, contending that the owners had agreed to pay for a police garrison supplied to the colliery to protect the 'safety men' during a strike. The safety men were unwilling to go to work without police protection. If the safety men had not gone to work, the mine would have become flooded. The owners of the colliery argued that they did not have to pay the council, since there was no consideration for the promise because the police were already under a duty to protect persons and property. On the facts, the claim of the police succeeded. However, this was only on the ground that the police were doing more than was required by their public duty. In the judgment of the senior police officer, a garrison was unnecessary to preserve the peace; a mobile force would have been quite adequate. Yet on the insistence of the colliery manager, he agreed to provide the garrison in return for the promise to pay for it. The decision as to what measures were necessary to preserve the peace was for the senior police officer on the spot and, provided it was made reasonably and in good faith, the court could not interfere with it. So the police had done more than they were obliged to do and were entitled to be paid for such work. But if, as two dissenting judges in the House of Lords held, the police had done no more than their duty, their action would presumably have failed. There

---

[35] (1813) 1 B & Ald 950.
[36] [1925] AC 270.

are two possible explanations for this result. The first rests upon grounds of public policy. The second upon a lack of consideration.[37] In any event, if the facts of *Glasbrook Bros Ltd v Glamorgan County Council* were to arise today, the issue would not solely be determined by the common law: section 25(1) of the Police Act 1996 provides that 'The chief officer of police of a police force may provide, at the request of any person, special police services at any premises or in any locality in the police area for which the force is maintained, subject to the payment to the local policing body of charges on such scales as may be determined by that body.'

The 'rule' that the performance of a duty imposed by law is not a sufficient consideration was consistently disputed by Lord Denning. For example, in *Ward v Byham*[38] a man promised to pay the mother of his illegitimate child £1 per week if the mother ensured that the child was 'well looked after and happy'. Denning LJ thought that even if the mother was not promising to do anything more than her statutory duty to maintain the child, she was still providing consideration to support the man's promise since she was providing a benefit to the father of her child. This may now be described as a 'practical benefit' and therefore consideration.[39]

Indeed, some decisions are undoubtedly difficult to reconcile with the existence of any rule that the performance of a duty imposed by law is not a sufficient consideration. For example, there are numerous cases in the law reports concerning offers of rewards for information leading to the conviction of felons, and the validity of any resulting contracts to pay never seems to have been questioned.[40] However, in *Sykes v DPP*,[41] in 1961, it was decided that the concealment of, or failure to reveal, information about a felony known to have been committed was an offence, known as misprision of felony. Citizens had a legal duty to reveal felonies known to them. A person giving information leading to the conviction of a felon was doing no more than the criminal law required him to do. One of the arguments advanced in *Sykes* was that the reward cases showed that there was no such crime as misprision of felony; if there were, actions for rewards would all have failed on the ground that the informer was doing no more than his legal duty. The House of Lords decided there was such a crime but did not deal with this argument. That leaves two possibilities: either the reward cases were all wrongly decided (which seems very unlikely) or there is no general rule that the performance of a public duty is incapable of being consideration. It should be added that felonies, and therefore the offence of misprision of felony, were abolished by the Criminal Law Act 1967, so that particular problem does not arise today; but that in no way affects the validity of the above argument regarding the possibility that the performance of a duty imposed by the general law might constitute consideration to support a binding contract.

In most cases it would make no difference if the court proceeded on the basis that the matter was one for public policy rather than consideration. If, when Lord Denning was on the bench, he had been faced with witnesses demanding payment for appearing in response

---

[37] *Leeds United Football Club Ltd v Chief Constable of West Yorkshire* [2013] EWCA Civ 115, [2014] QB 168.
[38] *Ward v Byham* [1956] 1 WLR 496; see too eg *Williams v Williams* [1957] 1 WLR 148.
[39] See *Williams v Roffey Bros*, discussed in Section 1(e)(iii).
[40] cf *Williams v Carwardine* (1833) 4 B & Ad 621.
[41] [1962] AC 528, HL.

to subpoena and police officers claiming money promised to them in return for doing their plain duty, he would have given them short shrift on public policy grounds. That approach gives the court more flexibility (and Lord Denning was always in favour of that), but also allows for the opinion, perhaps, that there is nothing against public policy in rewards to encourage members of the public to betray felons, even if that was their duty.

(ii) Performance of a duty owed only to a third party

The law on this point is now settled. In deciding whether there is a contract between *A* and *B*, it is immaterial that the only consideration supplied by *A* is the performance, or the promise to perform, an obligation which he already owes to *C*. Here *B* clearly is getting something more than *he* is entitled to. *A*'s failure to perform his obligation to *C* would be a breach of contract with *C*, but it would not amount to any legal wrong against *B* if there is no contract between *A* and *B*.

In *Shadwell v Shadwell*,[42] Byles J, as well as taking the arguably good point that the uncle had made no request, also took a bad one, namely that the nephew was already engaged to Ellen Nicholl (which was then an enforceable contract) and so, in marrying her, he was only doing what he was legally bound to do. This was a bad point because the uncle had no right to demand that his nephew should marry Ellen just because there was a contract between the nephew and Ellen. Therefore the nephew's doing so, at the uncle's request, would in fact have been sufficient consideration. Modern cases in the Privy Council have established the point beyond doubt. So, where a **stevedore**, at the request of the shipper of goods, removed the goods from a ship, this was consideration for a promise by the shipper, even though the stevedore, in removing the goods, was only performing a contractual duty owed to the shipowner.[43]

Some situations which formerly fell within this category may, since the coming into force of the Contracts (Rights of Third Parties) Act 1999,[44] now fall into the next. Imagine that *X* contracts with *Y* to do something for the benefit of an identified person, *Z*. Before that Act, *X*'s performance was generally the fulfilment of a duty owed only to *Y*. But if the Act applies to the contract, the duty may now also be owed to *Z*. So, if *Z* promises *X* remuneration to perform the contractual obligation, he is now promising to pay for something to which *he* (and not only *Y*) is already legally entitled, and the analysis presented in the following section will apply.

(iii) Performance of a duty owed to the promisor

This is much more controversial and has become probably the most difficult aspect of the law on consideration. The nineteenth-century authorities, on the other hand, were clear. The performance by *A*, or *A*'s promise to perform, a duty which he already owed to *B*, was

---

[42] See Section 1.
[43] *New Zealand Shipping Co Ltd v AM Satterthwaite & Co Ltd* [1975] AC 154, PC; cf *Pao On v Lau Yiu Long* [1980] AC 614, PC. See further Chapter 10, Section 5.
[44] See Chapter 10, Section 10.

no consideration for a promise by *B*. Here *B* is getting nothing more than he is already entitled to. However, the law has since become much more complicated.

The traditional, orthodox approach derives from the famous (or notorious) rule in *Pinnel's* case, decided by Lord Coke in 1602, which provides:

> that payment of a lesser sum on the day [that a debt is due] cannot be any satisfaction for the whole because it appears to the judges that by no possibility a lesser sum can be satisfaction to the claimant for a greater sum …[45]

This passage has spawned the general rule that part payment of a debt is not good consideration for the extinguishment of that debt. The **creditor** is getting less than he is entitled to and that cannot be sufficient consideration for any promise he may have made to forego the balance owed. So even if he has made such a promise, he may still sue for, and recover, the balance of the debt.

But if the creditor asks the **debtor** to do, or the creditor accepts the debtor's offer to do, anything that the debtor is not already bound to do, and the debtor then does that thing, then that does constitute consideration and the court will not inquire into its adequacy. This is because the debtor is then doing something in addition to what he was already bound to do. So, where the debtor offers to pay a day before the debt is due, if the creditor will accept half the sum due in full satisfaction, he is offering consideration. The creditor who accepts such an offer may be making a bad bargain in **forfeiting** half his debt for the sake of getting payment a day earlier, but that is immaterial: the court will not examine the adequacy of the consideration.[46] Similarly, if the debt is payable at a particular place, payment at another place is a sufficient consideration if that is at the request of, and for the benefit of, the creditor. However, in *Vanbergen v St Edmund's Properties Ltd*,[47] a creditor's promise that he would not serve a **bankruptcy** notice if the whole debt was paid on the day due was held not to be binding (he was only getting what he was entitled to) even though the debt was due in London and payment was made in Eastbourne. By paying in Eastbourne, the debtor was doing something he was not bound to do, but the evidence showed that it was entirely for the convenience of the debtor that the variation in mode of payment was made. It was a concession by the creditor; the debtor was getting a benefit for himself, not giving a benefit to the creditor, by paying in Eastbourne rather than in London.

The court in *Pinnel's* case went on to say:

> but the gift of a horse, hawk or robe, etc., in satisfaction is good for it shall be intended that a horse, hawk or robe, etc., might be more beneficial to the claimant than money, in respect of some circumstance, or otherwise the claimant would not have accepted it in satisfaction.

In giving the horse, hawk, or robe, the debtor is doing something which he is not obliged to do; and the court will not inquire into the adequacy of the consideration if the creditor freely accepts that horse, hawk, or robe as full satisfaction for the extinguishing of the debt. In such a case, it is thought that the argument that the 'change in mode of payment'

---

[45] (1602) 5 Co Rep 117a.
[46] See Section 1(c).
[47] *Vanbergen v St Edmund's Properties Ltd* [1933] 2 KB 223.

is for the benefit of the debtor is not open. If I offer you my old car in full satisfaction of the debt of £10,000 which I owe you—'It's the best I can do—take it or leave it—but it is to be in full satisfaction'—and you then decide to take it, the debt is satisfied, no matter how grudging and grumbling your acceptance may be. That is so even if the old car is objectively worth only £100. Whilst it is impossible for anyone to say £100 is worth £10,000,[48] it is not impossible for a particular individual to value something that is not money—such as an old car—in a bizarre and idiosyncratic way. The courts will not then assess the adequacy of the consideration.

The rule in *Pinnel's* case was confirmed by the House of Lords in *Foakes v Beer* in 1884.[49] The House of Lords did not seem to like the rule very much, and said that it was only an *obiter dictum*, apparently never applied by the Court of Exchequer Chamber, let alone by the House of Lords itself. Nevertheless, their Lordships held that the rule in *Pinnel's* case had the authority of the great 'Lord' Coke and had been accepted as law by the profession ever since, so it was taken to be the law and that understanding of the law should not be disturbed. In *Foakes*, the written but unsealed agreement between the parties recited that Beer had obtained judgment against Foakes for £2,090 19s in the High Court and that, at Foakes's request, Beer had agreed to give him more time to pay. The agreement went on to provide that Beer (the creditor) agreed not to take any proceedings on the judgment against Foakes (the debtor) in consideration of (a) the debtor's paying £500 in part satisfaction of the debt (the receipt of which the creditor acknowledged) and (b) on condition of the debtor paying £150 on 1 July and 1 January every year until the whole of the sum of £2,090 19s had been paid.

The debtor duly paid off the whole capital sum by instalments as agreed. But, by law, interest is payable on a judgment debt from the day on which it becomes due. Beer demanded the interest which had accrued, Foakes refused to pay, and Beer brought an action on the judgment—the very thing she had promised not to do—for the interest. But what consideration had Foakes given for Beer's promise not to sue? The expressed consideration—the payment of £500—was only part of the larger sum already due and, even if the payment of the instalments were to be treated as part of the consideration, it only amounted to the fulfilment of an existing obligation. Foakes had not done or promised to do anything that he was not already obliged to do, and so he was held liable to pay the interest.

Lord Blackburn in particular was minded to dissent in *Foakes v Beer*, but ultimately was persuaded not to do so. His Lordship clearly felt sorry for Foakes, and thought that Beer may have gained some benefit, since actual performance may be more valuable than a theoretical right to performance. After all, 'a bird in the hand is worth two in the bush'. But before we shed too many tears over the plight of Foakes, it should be noted that Beer probably never intended to let Foakes not pay the interest anyway. The object of the agreement was most likely only to give Foakes time to pay whatever was due, not to forgive him anything. Indeed, two of the five judges—Lords Watson and Fitzgerald—held that this was the proper construction of the agreement and that Beer succeeded on that ground. So, if

---

[48] Or that a cheque for £100 is better than cash for £100 and therefore good consideration: *D and C Builders v Rees* [1965] 3 All ER 837.

[49] (1884) 9 App Cas 605.

the agreement had been under seal,[50] Lords Watson and Fitzgerald would nonetheless have reached the same conclusion, whilst the majority would have held that the action failed and that Beer, probably unwittingly, had forfeited her interest.[51]

The approach taken towards consideration by the House of Lords in *Foakes v Beer* appears also to have been adopted in *Stilk v Myrick*.[52] A crew of seamen had contracted to serve on a voyage at a specified rate. During the course of the voyage, two seamen deserted. The captain promised to divide the wages of the two seamen who had deserted amongst the remaining seamen. Upon returning to England, the captain refused to honour his promise and the remaining seamen sued the captain for breach of contract. The court held that the captain's promise was unenforceable. Lord Ellenborough held that the seamen had 'undertaken to do all that they could under all the emergencies of the voyage' and had sold the whole of their services for the voyage, so in continuing to sail the ship after the desertion of their two colleagues, they were doing nothing more than they were already obliged to do.

However, *Stilk v Myrick* may be distinguished where, in the course of a voyage, not just two but 17 of a 36-man crew deserted. The effect of this was to frustrate the contract of the remainder of the seamen.[53] Sailing the ship at little more than half strength was fundamentally different from the obligation that they had undertaken. Because their original agreement had been frustrated and therefore 'killed off' by the desertion of virtually half the crew, the remaining seamen were free to make a new bargain. As a result, the captain's promise to pay the remaining seamen additional wages if they continued with the voyage was enforceable: *Hartley v Ponsonby*.[54] It is crucial to appreciate that the remaining seamen and captain were able to enter into a new contract because the original agreement had been killed off by a frustrating event. A similar situation can arise where both parties to a contract mutually agree to **rescind** an existing agreement. The parties are then free to enter into a new contract on whatever terms they like. It should be noted that both the agreement to rescind and the new agreement will be supported by consideration. As regards the rescission, each party provides consideration by sacrificing their contractual rights. And the new agreement is then supported by consideration since neither party already owes any legal duties at the time of making the agreement. Of course, the practical effect of rescinding one contract to then enter into a new contract is very similar to simply varying the original contract, but in principle reflects a different intention of the parties.[55]

The above analysis of the law would have been relatively uncontroversial prior to 1990. However, the status of the principle of *Stilk v Myrick* is now in some doubt as a result of the decision of the Court of Appeal in *Williams v Roffey Bros*.[56] The defendants had contracted to refurbish a block of flats and had subcontracted the carpentry work to the claimant for a price of £20,000. The claimant had made a bad bargain. The price was, as the defendants

---

[50] See Chapter 9.

[51] Although if it could have been clearly proved that the document did not truly represent the agreement between the parties, it might have been rectified: see Chapter 14.

[52] (1809) 2 Camp 317.

[53] See Chapter 23.

[54] (1857) 7 El & Bl 872.

[55] *Compagnie Noga d'Importation et d'Exportation SA v Abacha (No 4)* [2003] EWCA Civ 1100, [2003] 2 All ER (Comm) 915.

[56] [1990] 2 WLR 1153, CA. Cf *Atlas Express Ltd v Kafco*, Chapter 17, Section 2.

acknowledged, unreasonably low and the claimant got into difficulties. The defendants were liable to a financial penalty if the work was not completed on time. In order to ensure that the claimant continued with the work and finished it on time, the defendants offered the claimant an additional £10,300 at the rate of £575 for each flat on which the carpentry work had been completed. The claimant then substantially completed the work. The defendants declined to pay the additional sum and the claimant sued. The Court of Appeal unanimously held that the claimant was entitled to recover the additional payment, even though he had done no more work than he had originally agreed to do. It was sufficient that the performance of the work amounted in practice to a benefit, or obviated a 'disbenefit' (in the inelegant terminology of the court), to the promisor.

The 'practical benefit' in *Williams v Roffey Bros* seems to lie in the defendant's avoiding liability to pay the financial penalty for late performance and avoiding the trouble and expense of obtaining a substitute subcontractor to do the carpentry work. Russell LJ placed some weight on the fact that the defendant promised an additional sum for each individual flat completed; this meant that the claimant should work on each flat in turn, rather than in the haphazard way which was allowed under the original agreement. If it is right that the claimants made a new promise to work in a different manner to that originally agreed then this would be new, 'fresh' consideration even on orthodox principles and thus sufficient to justify the result. However, since Russell LJ was the only judge to raise this issue it does not form part of the ***ratio*** of the decision and will not be discussed further.

All three judges in the Court of Appeal in *Williams v Roffey Bros* asserted that their decision was compatible with *Stilk v Myrick*, but it is difficult to understand how this can be so. Surely it was a great practical benefit (and the avoidance of a 'disbenefit') to the captain in *Stilk v Myrick* to have the crew sail the ship home rather than abandon him and the ship in a foreign port. Indeed, there must be few cases in which it will not be a benefit to a contracting party to have the other party perform rather than default; and in any case where he has agreed to pay more to secure performance, it is self-evident that he regarded performance as a significant benefit. Nevertheless, the Court of Appeal thought the true ground of decisions like *Stilk v Myrick* was public policy, the captain in those days being at the mercy of his crew on a long voyage.[57] Yet in the most authoritative report of *Stilk v Myrick*, given by Campbell,[58] the public policy ground is doubted by Lord Ellenborough who plainly put his decision on the ground that the agreement was void for lack of consideration. Admittedly, a different report of the case does place some weight upon factors of public policy, but this report is given by Espinasse, who was notoriously unreliable,[59] and is more dubious than that of Campbell.[60] But if *Williams v Roffey Bros* is correct to favour that report of Espinasse on this point, it appears necessary to explain *Stilk v Myrick* as an instance of duress, and to recognise that there was consideration for the promise to pay

---

[57] See too G Gilmore, *The Death of Contract* (Ohio State University Press, 1974) 22–8.

[58] (1809) 2 Camp 317.

[59] See eg *Small v Nairne* (1849) 13 QB 840, 844 (Lord Denman CJ): 'I am tempted to remark, for the benefit of the profession, that Espinasse's Reports, in days nearer their own time, when their want of accuracy was better known than it is now, were never quoted without doubt and hesitation; and a special reason was often given as an apology for citing that particular case.'

[60] 6 Esp 129. For duress generally, see Chapter 17.

more money for the performance which was already due because a 'practical benefit' was received in return for those promises. However, this explanation may fail to convince; after all, there is no indication in *Stilk v Myrick* of any evidence of a demand, still less of a threat by members of the crew, and a demand or threat is an essential element in a claim of duress.

If duress is able to distinguish *Stilk* from *Williams v Roffey Bros*, then it may be significant that in *Williams v Roffey Bros* the head-contractors approached the subcontractors and offered them more money: if the subcontractors had demanded more money, then perhaps that would have constituted illegitimate pressure sufficient to ground a claim in duress. This issue of duress is considered more fully in Chapter 17, but it is important to note that the pressure exercised by the subcontractors may have been latent even if not made explicit: the slow rate of work may well have made it obvious that extra money was required in order to finish on time, such that an overt request for more money was redundant. This could be problematic: a head-contractor may well choose to contract with a particular subcontractor because the price quoted seems to be the most reasonable, and yet end up having to pay much more than the agreed price if it later transpires that the subcontractor underestimated the amount of work involved.[61]

Williams v Roffey Bros was followed and *Stilk v Myrick* was again distinguished in *Anangel v IHI*,[62] where the claimants' agreement to take delivery of a ship on the date on which they were already contractually bound to take it was held to be consideration for promises made by the defendants. Performance by the claimants was seen by the defendants as being a very substantial benefit because it would encourage other reluctant customers to take delivery in accordance with their contracts. This factor was regarded as significant in the same way as the existence of the financial penalty clause in *Williams v Roffey Bros*. Yet neither factor was an element in the price to be paid by the respective promises, so it remains hard to see how it could be regarded as consideration.

The law is currently very complex and in many respects unsatisfactory. This is exacerbated by the fact that the same principle which underlies *Pinnel*'s case also seems to underpin the more reliable report of *Stilk v Myrick*, and yet, remarkably, neither *Pinnel*'s case nor *Foakes v Beer* were even mentioned in *Williams v Roffey Bros*. The cases are difficult to fit together. Most significantly, it is important to ask whether *Williams v Roffey Bros* and *Foakes v Beer* can both be right. In *Re Selectmove Ltd*,[63] the Court of Appeal was confronted by the conflict between these cases. The alleged consideration was an agreement to pay to the Revenue income tax which was due in law. The court pointed out that if the principle of *Williams v Roffey Bros* was extended to an obligation to pay money, it would leave the principle of *Foakes* with no application. That was not possible, since *Foakes* is a House of Lords decision which has not been departed from. So, on the facts of *Re Selectmove*, the court was bound to follow *Foakes*, since that was a decision of the House of Lords and *Williams v Roffey Bros* only a decision of the Court of Appeal. As a matter of precedent, the approach of the Court of Appeal in *Re Selectmove* must be right. However, the Court of Appeal did not hold that *Williams v Roffey Bros* was wrongly decided, and simply said that *Williams v Roffey Bros* may apply to obligations of a different nature. The result in *Re Selectmove* seems

---

[61] See Chapter 17, Section 2.
[62] [1990] 2 Lloyd's Rep 526 (Hirst J).
[63] [1995] 2 All ER 531.

to leave us with an utterly illogical distinction: the performance of an obligation to render services may be good consideration (*Williams v Roffey Bros*), but the performance of an obligation to pay money may not (*Foakes*).[64] As Peter Gibson LJ suggested in *Re Selectmove*, the law in this area deserves the attention of the House of Lords or of Parliament after consideration by the Law Commission.[65]

(f) Compositions with creditors

One of the matters that has worried the courts and commentators is the validity of **compositions** with creditors. This is a contract that arises not only between the debtor and creditors but also between the creditors themselves. An **insolvent** person meets his creditors and all the creditors agree to accept a **dividend**—a percentage of the debt due—in full satisfaction of the debt. One difficulty is whether the insolvent person has provided any consideration for the extinguishment of the debt. Of course, the rule in *Pinnel's* case could be satisfied by the debtor offering each creditor some **chattel** (in other words, physical thing) of trivial value in addition to his dividend, thus giving consideration; but as Sir George Jessel MR once caustically remarked, not every debtor had 'a stock of canary birds, or tomtits, or rubbish of that kind to add to his dividend'.[66] There is, however, no difficulty in finding consideration between the creditors. Each of them agrees to accept the dividend in full satisfaction, in consideration of every other creditor doing so; as a result, if one creditor goes back on the agreement and, to the detriment of the rest, sues for the full amount due to him, that is a breach of contract with every other creditor. The debtor, though perhaps a party to the agreement, is not a party to the contract since he gave no consideration; but, if he is sued by one of the creditors, he might be able to join other creditors and have the action **stayed** on the ground that it is brought in breach of contract with them. If, however, all the creditors who were parties to the composition unite to sue the debtor— as might happen, for example, where the debtor has unexpectedly come into a large sum of money—it would seem that at common law he would have no answer to the action. But since the composition apparently 'purports to confer a benefit' on the debtor, he might now enforce it 'in his own right' by virtue of the Contracts (Rights of Third Parties) Act 1999.[67] This is so whether he is sued by one or all of the creditors, provided he has assented to the composition or relied upon it.

A somewhat similar issue arises where a third party pays the creditor part of the debt in full satisfaction of that debt. If the creditor accepts the part payment, any action against the debtor would be a breach of contract with the third party and this will not be permitted. In *Hirachand Punamchand v Temple*,[68] a variety of reasons were given

---

[64] In *South Caribbean Trading Ltd v Trafigura Beheer BV* [2004] EWHC 2676 (Comm), [2005] 1 Lloyd's Rep 128 [108], Colman J said that he would not have followed *Williams v Roffey Bros* had it not been a decision of the Court of Appeal.

[65] See too *Adam Opel GmbH v Mitras Automotive (UK) Ltd* [2007] EWHC 3481 (QB) [41] (David Donaldson QC).

[66] *Couldery v Bartrum* (1881) 19 ChD 394, 400.

[67] See Chapter 10, Section 10.

[68] [1911] 2 KB 330, CA.

why the creditor's action must fail. The debtor had given the creditor a promissory note for the sum due. The creditor then accepted a lesser sum from a third party (the debtor's father) as full satisfaction of the debt. However, the creditor then sued the debtor on the promissory note for the remaining balance. Vaughan Williams LJ advanced three propositions in support of his conclusion that the creditor's action must fail. First, he thought that, when the creditor accepted the lesser sum from the third party, the note ceased to be a **negotiable instrument** just as if the debtor's signature had been erased. This is a remarkable proposition in the context of negotiable instruments, and one on which he understandably did not place great emphasis. His Lordship's second proposition was that the creditor now held the note on trust for the third party. In other words, the third party had bought the equitable interest in the note. The third proposition was that the action by the creditor against the debtor was a fraud on the third party which the court could not aid, so the debt was gone. The latter two propositions both have some merit. However, if the trust solution is correct, the benefit to the debtor is qualified, since the third party could potentially sue on the note and might be justified in doing so if, for example, the debtor came into money and refused to refund to the third party the amount paid out for his benefit.[69] It is suggested that the third proposition is the best explanation of the decision in *Temple*: the court should not allow the creditor to make an agreement with the third party which is clearly supported by consideration (the third party being under no prior obligations) and yet then permit the creditor to turn around, go back on his promise, and do the very thing he had promised not to do, namely sue the original debtor.

In any event, if the facts of the *Temple* case were to arise today, the outcome of the case may well be decided by the Contracts (Rights of Third Parties) Act 1999, which could provide the debtor with a defence in his own right.[70] This would avoid the complexities faced by the Court of Appeal in the *Temple* case itself.

(g) 'Gifts' of onerous property

Care must be taken when analysing situations where O offers to give A certain property, the ownership of which involves obligations. For example, O might offer to **assign** his **leasehold** property to A, or to give him his **shares** on which **calls** are due. If A accepts, he will have to pay the rent or the calls when they are made. O thereby manages to rid himself of his obligations and instead A undertakes to perform them. The value of the property transferred may greatly exceed the obligation but it seems that this is nevertheless regarded as a contract, not a gift.[71] A's agreement to take the obligations which attach to the property off O's shoulders onto his own is good consideration.

---

[69] See Chapter 10, Section 8.
[70] See Chapter 10, Section 10.
[71] *Cheale v Kenward* (1858) 27 LJ Ch 784 (shares); *Price v Jenkins* (1877) 5 ChD 619; *Johnsey Estates Ltd v Lewis & Manley Engineering Ltd* (1987) 54 P & CR 296, CA.

2 Promissory estoppel and the *High Trees* case

The rule in *Pinnel*'s case as applied in *Foakes v Beer* still undoubtedly represents the common law when considering whether part payment of a debt is good consideration for the extinguishment of that debt, but there is some question as to how far it is modified by an equitable principle known as promissory **estoppel**. The starting point for this discussion must be the decision of Denning J in *Central London Property Trust Ltd v High Trees House*.[72] The claimants granted the defendants a **lease** of a block of flats for 99 years from September 1937 at £2,500 a year. During the war the flats could not be fully let, so the defendants were in some difficulty about paying the rent. The claimants agreed that the rent should be reduced to £1,250. The defendants paid the reduced rent while the war was ongoing. However, even after the war ended in 1945 and all the flats were let again, the defendant continued to pay at the reduced rate. A **receiver** was appointed for the claimants and he claimed that **arrears** of £7,916 were due. To test the legal position, he brought an action to recover the difference between the reserved rent of £2,500 and the reduced rent of £1,250 for the two quarters ending 29 September and 25 December 1945.

Denning J held that the agreement to reduce the rent was intended to apply only while the wartime conditions prevailed. The agreement was clearly not intended to run for the full term of the lease. The war had come to an end before the two quarters in question so the claimant was entitled to recover the amount claimed. Denning J could have stopped there, but this would not really have answered the question that concerned the two companies, who did not know what the position was as regards the £1,250 per year which had not been paid whilst the war was ongoing. Moreover, Denning J was not the sort of man to pass over such a wonderful opportunity to express his views, so he went on to consider whether the wartime agreement was binding and decided that it was: the claimants were estopped from claiming the balance of the rent. However, it is helpful to remember that the *ratio* of the case concerns the rent payable *after* the war had ended, whilst Denning J's discussion of the balance of the rent that had not been paid *during* the war was *obiter dicta*.

In deciding that the claimants were unable to recover the £1,250 per year which had not been paid during the war, Denning J had to overcome two obstacles, either of which would have been sufficiently formidable to deter any ordinary judge. The first was the decision of the House of Lords in *Jordan v Money*,[73] which held that estoppel applies only to representations of fact. That was brushed aside rather summarily on the ground that the law had not been standing still and, anyway, *Jordan v Money* was distinguishable because the promisor in that case did not intend to be legally bound—a fact not discoverable easily, if at all, from the report.

The second obstacle, of course, was *Foakes v Beer*, since *High Trees* was similarly a case of a lesser sum being accepted in satisfaction of a greater sum. That received even more summary treatment. The principle to be applied in the present case was an equitable principle that was not considered in *Foakes v Beer*, which concerned only the common law of consideration. The equitable principle was that a clear promise, intended to be binding,

---

[72] [1947] 1 KB 130, KBD.
[73] (1854) 5 HLC 185.

intended to be acted on, and in fact acted on,[74] is binding in the sense that the courts will not allow the promisor to act inconsistently with it if to do so would be unconscionable. It was immaterial that there was no consideration. Denning J added, however, that the courts had not gone so far as to allow an action for damages for breach of such a promise: promissory estoppel is a defence to a cause of action but not a cause of action in itself.

(a) The credentials of the *High Trees* case

Denning J cited a series of decisions which, he said, were a natural result of the **fusion** of law and **equity** in 1873–5.[75] But do those decisions support the principle enunciated in *High Trees*? The most important case relied upon by Denning J is that of the House of Lords in *Hughes v Metropolitan Railway Co.*[76] A **landlord** gave his **tenant** six months' notice to repair the premises, the lease being forfeitable if the tenant failed to comply. During the six months, the parties entered into negotiations for the sale of the lease to the landlord and, with the landlord's concurrence, no repairs were done while the negotiations were in progress. The negotiations failed. On the expiry of six months from the original notice, the landlord claimed to treat the lease as forfeit. The House held that the tenant was entitled to relief in equity against forfeiture:[77] the six months allowed for repair should run from the date of the failure of the negotiations. This was a case where, in effect, A said to B: 'You need not fulfil your contractual duty to repair the premises within six months of the notice I have given you'; and then, when B took him at his word and did not carry out the repairs, A declared that B had broken his contract and that he was terminating it. It seems a very elementary principle of justice that a party who has agreed to the non-performance of a contract should not be allowed to treat that non-performance as a breach of contract. Since he has consented to it, no wrong is done to him—he has 'waived' his right to performance. There would be an exact analogy in a case like *High Trees* if the landlord, having accepted half-rent for, say, one year, were to say to the tenant, 'You have broken your contract by failing to pay the whole rent and I forfeit the lease.' But that is obviously not what happened in *High Trees*.

Most of the cases relied on in support of the *High Trees* decision are waivers of this kind. For example, in *Panoutsos v Raymond Hadley*,[78] a case frequently cited by Lord Denning, B, a buyer of goods, had a duty to open a confirmed credit. He opened an unconfirmed credit. A, the seller, led B to suppose that he was content with an unconfirmed credit. Then, without prior warning, A terminated the contract on the ground of B's breach in failing to open a confirmed credit. It was held that he could not do so—but he could insist that B open a confirmed credit within a reasonable time. If B did not do so, he would then be in breach of contract.

---

[74] Apparently not necessarily to that party's detriment: see eg *Alan v El Nasr* [1972] 2 QB 189 and *High Trees* itself, although it must of course be inequitable to go back on the promise.

[75] See further Chapter 1, Section 6(e).

[76] (1877) 2 App Cas 439.

[77] See Chapter 27, Section 2.

[78] [1917] 2 KB 473, CA.

The principle of these cases is that if *A* tells *B*, by words or conduct, that *B* need not perform a contractual obligation owed by *B* to *A*, and *B* takes *A* at his word and does not perform that obligation, *A* cannot treat the non-performance as a breach of contract, entitling him to damages or to terminate the contract.

The *High Trees* case was quite different. The landlord did not claim that the tenant had broken the contract—he was not asking for damages or claiming to be entitled to terminate the lease. He was saying only that the tenant must perform the contract by paying the stipulated rent. *Hughes* does not say that he cannot do this. The landlord could require performance of the contractual obligation to repair in the future. There could be no question of the obligation to repair being enforced retrospectively; it is impossible to comply with an obligation to do something by a specified date when that date has passed. But there was no such impossibility in the obligation to pay the full rent in *High Trees*. Moreover, *Foakes v Beer* says that the creditor may enforce the obligation retrospectively. There is no material difference between the interest on the judgment debt which had accrued from day to day in *Foakes v Beer*, and the rent payable under the lease which accrued from time to time in *High Trees*. Both were obligations which had arisen, but had been 'waived', before the claimant made the claim in issue.

Foakes v Beer (1884) was, of course, decided after the (procedural) fusion of law and equity (see Chapter 1, Section 6(e)) and indeed after *Hughes v Metropolitan Railway* (1877). *Hughes* was not cited in *Foakes*, despite the fact that Lords Selborne and Blackburn were in both cases. But, contrary to whatever Lord Denning may have thought, this is not at all surprising: the principle was simply not applicable. Any contention that the House of Lords in *Foakes* was unaware of equitable doctrine is impossible to support. *Hughes* certainly tends to show that the non-payment of rent in *High Trees* was not a breach of contract, but it says nothing on the question of whether the tenant could be required to perform his contract. *High Trees* was therefore a new and radical departure.

(b) The effect of *High Trees*

Assuming for the moment that the *High Trees* principle now represents the law, it is important to be clear about what is required for its satisfaction. First, a clear and unequivocal promise must have been made. An ambiguous statement cannot lie at the basis of promissory estoppel.[79] Secondly, the promisee must rely upon that promise. It would appear that such reliance does not need to be to the promisee's detriment.[80] Thirdly, it must be inequitable or unconscionable to go back on the promise. Thus, if the promisor seeks to go back on his promise after a short period of time, before the promisee can reasonably have relied upon the promise (at least to his detriment), a defence of promissory estoppel will not succeed.[81] However, a number of important questions still need to be considered.

---

[79] *Woodhouse AC Israel Cocoa SA v Nigerian Produce Marketing Co Ltd* [1972] AC 741.

[80] *WJ Alan & Co v El Nasr Export & Import Co* [1972] 2 QB 189; *Collier v P & MJ Wright (Holdings) Ltd* [2007] EWCA Civ 1329, [2008] 1 WLR 643 (discussed in Section 2(b)(ii)).

[81] *Société Italo-Belge pour le Commerce et L'Industrie SA v Palm and Vegetable Oils (Malaysia) Sdn Bhd (The Post Chaser)* [1982] 1 All ER 19. See too the discussion of *D & C Builders v Rees* [1966] 2 QB 617 in Section 2(b)(iii).

(i) Does it create a cause of action?

In *Combe v Combe*,[82] Denning LJ confirmed what he had said in *High Trees*: 'the principle never stands alone as giving a cause of action in itself' and 'it can never do away with the necessity of consideration when that is an essential part of the cause of action'. Birkett LJ said that the doctrine can be used as a shield but not a sword. In *Combe*, a husband had promised to pay his wife £100 a year after their divorce. Byrne J had held that this was a promise, intended to be binding, intended to be acted on, and in fact acted on as required by *High Trees*, such that the wife could sue on it. The Court of Appeal insisted that that was wrong. The promise to pay was not binding unless there was consideration for it.[83]

But the 'sword and shield' metaphor is misleading. Estoppel, of whatever kind, may be part of the armoury of the claimant no less than of the defendant. In itself, it is neither a cause of action nor a defence, but it may enable a party to establish the conditions necessary for either, since it prevents another from relying upon his rights. In *Robertson v Minister of Pensions*,[84] the War Office wrote to the claimant, 'Your disability has been accepted as attributable to military service.' On the faith of that assurance, he took no steps to obtain an independent medical opinion, which he would otherwise have done. Subsequently, a pensions appeal tribunal decided that his injury was not due to war service. Denning J, following the *High Trees* case, held that the Crown was estopped from denying that the injury was due to war service. Arguably, this was an ordinary estoppel, being a representation of fact.[85] But whatever its nature, it enabled the claimant to make out his cause of action which was based not on any promise, but on his statutory right to a pension.

There is an exception to the rule that estoppel does not in itself found a cause of action where *A* purports to give but does not effectively convey, or alternatively promises to give, land or an interest in land to *B*, knowing that *B* will expend money or otherwise act to his detriment in reliance on the supposed or promised gift. When *B* does indeed act to his detriment in reliance on *A*'s representation, this gives *B* an 'equity' to require *A* to complete the gift.[86] But, significantly, *B* will only be able to sue upon the promise if it relates to property: this explains why it is often said that *proprietary* estoppel, but not promissory estoppel, gives rise to a cause of action. Proprietary estoppel is covered in more detail in texts on land law and will only be dealt with briefly here.[87]

In *Crabb v Arun District Council*,[88] Lord Denning said: 'There are estoppels and estoppels. Some do give rise to a cause of action. Some do not. In the species of estoppel called proprietary estoppel, it does give rise to a cause of action.' The council had led Crabb to believe 'that he had, or would be granted, a right of access' at a certain point, and he took detrimental action in reliance on that assurance. If the assurance was that he *had* the

---

[82] [1951] 2 KB 215.

[83] However, in some other jurisdictions promissory estoppel can be a cause of action: see eg *Walton Stores v Maher* (1988) 62 ALJR 110, (1988) 164 CLR 387; *Commonwealth of Australia v Verwayen* (1990) 64 ALJR 540, (1990) 170 CLR 394.

[84] [1949] 1 KB 227.

[85] See further Chapter 2, Section 8.

[86] For further discussion of the remedies available for proprietary estoppel, see generally B McFarlane, *The Law of Proprietary Estoppel* (OUP, 2014) ch 9.

[87] See further K Gray & S Gray, *Land Law* (7th edn, OUP, 2011) 495–523.

[88] [1976] Ch 179.

right—that is, it had already been granted to him—it was a case of estoppel under established principles; but, if it was a case of 'would be granted', it was a promise which might be expected to be unenforceable in the absence of consideration or of the appropriate writing. Though the language of the court is ambiguous, Lord Denning's conclusion was that Crabb 'has a right of access ... and a right of way ... I would declare that he has an **easement** accordingly'. This was not to say that there was a promise which had to be performed, but that a proprietary interest had been granted.

Although proprietary estoppel is virtually always restricted to interests in land, in *Cobbe v Yeoman's Row Management Ltd*, Lord Scott said 'The estoppel becomes a "proprietary" estoppel—a sub-species of a "promissory" estoppel—if the right claimed is a proprietary right, usually a right to or over land but, in principle, equally available in relation to chattels or **choses in action**.'[89] That case suggests that it will be difficult for proprietary estoppel to succeed in a commercial environment in which the parties understood the risks they were running in operating without a contract. The situation might be different where an individual did not understand that the lack of consideration would mean that a promise was unenforceable, and nonetheless went on to rely upon a clear representation to his detriment. Thus, in *Thorner v Major* a nephew was able to enforce his deceased uncle's promise to leave him his land by relying upon proprietary estoppel.[90] Lord Walker said that the doctrine is based upon three main elements: (a) a representation or assurance made to the claimant; (b) reliance on the representation by the claimant; and (c) some detriment suffered by the claimant as a consequence of his reliance on the representation.

In other jurisdictions, promissory estoppel can found a cause of action even where the representation does not relate to property. This is well illustrated by the decision of the High Court of Australia in *Waltons Stores v Maher*.[91] The parties were negotiating for the claimants to demolish a building on the Mahers' land, and then construct a new building according to Waltons Stores' specifications which would be leased to Waltons Stores as retail premises. There was never any exchange of contracts, but everything seemed to be progressing satisfactorily, and, having been encouraged by Waltons Stores to do so, the Mahers commenced the planned work. Later, when about 40 per cent of the work had been completed, Waltons Stores told the Mahers that it would not enter into the lease. The High Court of Australia held that it would be unconscionable for Waltons Stores to resile from its promise, and that the Mahers could enforce the promise through promissory estoppel.

The decision in *Waltons Stores v Maher* brings together proprietary and promissory estoppel and says that both can found a cause of action. This has the merit of consistency if estoppel is considered to be based upon wrongdoing. But English law has consistently rejected such an approach, saying that property law—particularly concerning land—is special and can justify separate treatment.[92] The Supreme Court might, conceivably, change the law in this regard, but it is suggested that this is very unlikely. In any event, as a

---

[89] [2008] UKHL 55, [2008] 1 WLR 1752 [14]. Eg in *Thorner v Major* [2009] UKHL 18, [2009] 1 WLR 776, the claim in proprietary estoppel succeeded not only over a farm, but also over chattels, live and dead stock, and working capital standing to the credit of the farm account at a bank.

[90] [2009] UKHL 18, [2009] 1 WLR 776.

[91] (1988) 62 ALJR 110, (1988) 164 CLR 387.

[92] See too Chapter 28, Section 7.

matter of authority, the Court of Appeal has clearly rejected *Waltons Stores v Maher* in this jurisdiction. In *Baird Textiles Holdings Ltd v Marks & Spencer plc*,[93] the Court of Appeal rightly insisted that promissory estoppel does not provide a cause of action unless and until the Supreme Court or Parliament decides the contrary. Baird Textiles supplied Marks & Spencer for 30 years, but without the benefit of a long-term contract.[94] When Marks & Spencer gave notice that they would no longer purchase goods from Baird Textiles, the latter argued that Marks & Spencer was estopped from terminating the relationship by giving so short a notice period. The Court of Appeal rejected that argument: the cause of action must be breach of contract, and only then could promissory estoppel become relevant.

(ii) Does it suspend or extinguish rights?

There has been much controversy about this. It is suggested that the preferable view is that promissory estoppel can have an extinctive effect as regards existing obligations, but is suspensory as regards future obligations. Both these points emerge in the *Tool Metal* case.[95] Tool Metal had licensed Tungsten to deal in certain metals, for which Tool Metal owned the patents, in consideration of Tungsten paying a royalty of 10 per cent up to a certain amount and, thereafter, 30 per cent. During the war, Tool Metal agreed to waive their right to 30 per cent and to accept a flat rate of 10 per cent. After the war a dispute arose. Tool Metal claimed the waived 20 per cent in respect of material which had been used after 1 June 1945. In these respects, then, it was exactly like the *High Trees* case, except that the wartime agreement had not terminated. It was held by the Court of Appeal, following *Hughes v Metropolitan Railway*,[96] that the claim failed. As a result, the existing 'rights' under the contract were clearly extinguished—the extra 20 per cent was lost forever. But the contract to pay 30 per cent was still in existence (though waived) and the House of Lords held, on the assumption that the waiver was binding (as had been held by the Court of Appeal), that Tool Metal could resume their rights to the 30 per cent for the future, by giving reasonable notice that the waiver was at an end. Their future rights under the contract were only suspended until they had given proper notice that they wished to resume them. It seems to follow from this decision that in *High Trees*, if the landlord had given notice during the war that, from a reasonable time in the future (say, three months) he wanted the full rent again, he would have been entitled to it; but that, for the periods in the past, the balance of the rent was lost for ever. His 'rights' for the past rents were extinguished, whereas his 'rights' for the future rents merely suspended.

The extinctive effect of promissory estoppel appears also to have been recognised by the Court of Appeal in *Collier v Wright Holdings*.[97] The claimant was one of three partners who were jointly and severally liable for a considerable sum to the defendant. The defendant creditor could have sued any individual partner for the full amount, but the defendant

---

[93] [2001] EWCA Civ 274, [2002] 1 All ER (Comm) 737.

[94] See Chapter 8.

[95] *Tool Metal Manufacturing Co Ltd v Tungsten Electric Co Ltd* [1955] 1 WLR 761.

[96] The court did not refer to *High Trees*; yet as argued in Section 2(b), *Hughes* has nothing to say on this issue, while *High Trees* is directly in point.

[97] [2007] EWCA Civ 1329, [2008] 1 WLR 643.

promised the claimant that, if the claimant paid one-third of the amount due, the defendant would not pursue the matter with the claimant any further but pursue the other two partners instead. The claimant paid one-third of the amount due, but the defendant nonetheless sued the claimant for the balance. Clearly, following *Pinnel's* case and *Foakes v Beer*, there was no consideration to support the promise to accept part payment of a debt as good consideration for the extinguishment of the debt. However, Arden LJ was very critical of *Foakes v Beer* and lavished praise upon 'the brilliant obiter dictum of Denning J, as he was, in the *High Trees* case'.[98] Her Ladyship thought it arguable that the defendant should not be able to sue for the outstanding amount because it was estopped from doing so; she therefore held that the arguments concerning promissory estoppel should be heard at a full hearing rather than dismissed in a **summary judgment**. Arden LJ clearly thought that promissory estoppel could extinguish the debt. However, the decision in *Collier v Wright* should be treated with circumspection. It was only an application for summary judgment, so did not decide whether promissory estoppel was actually established, only that the defence was arguable. Moreover, Longmore LJ was much more cautious about the possibility of promissory estoppel ultimately providing a defence on the facts of the case. It is important to remember that, as a matter of precedent, *Foakes v Beer* remains the leading decision on part payment of a debt, and in that case the House of Lords did not think it unfair for a creditor to resile from a promise to accept part payment as full satisfaction of the debt.

(iii) Does *High Trees*, in effect, 'overrule' *Pinnel's* case and *Foakes v Beer*?

Of course, a judge of first instance has no power to overrule those cases in the strict sense, but if the effect of Denning J's judgment, as subsequently applied, destroys their effect, then the result is much the same. However, the answer to the question posed above must be in the negative. Lord Denning himself has recognised that *Foakes v Beer* still represents the common law and that the *High Trees* doctrine only operates (like other equitable doctrines) as a supplement or corrective to the common law, when the common law would otherwise do injustice. The *High Trees* principle should be applied only when it is equitable to apply it. That was not the case in *D & C Builders v Rees*.[99] The defendants owed the claimants £746. Payment was well overdue and the claimants were in desperate need of money. The defendant offered £300, insisting that it was to be in full satisfaction of the debt. Because of their financial plight, the claimants reluctantly accepted, saying, 'We have no choice.' Later they sued for the balance. The Court of Appeal held, following *Foakes v Beer*, that they were entitled to recover the balance of £446 plus interest. Lord Denning observed that 'The creditor is barred from his legal rights only when it would be *inequitable* for him to insist on them.' In this case it was not inequitable because the creditor had agreed to take a lesser sum only because of undue pressure by the debtor; the debtor was guilty of intimidation by threatening to break his contract to pay the full amount. So *Foakes v Beer* still represents the common law, and *High Trees* applies to qualify it only when it is fair that it should do so. If Lord Denning had been in *Foakes v Beer* he may have expressed the same reservations about the

---

[98] Ibid, [42].
[99] [1966] 2 QB 617, CA.

decision as did Lord Blackburn, but it may be that Lord Denning would have been happy to concur in the result on the ground that Beer did not intend to forgive the interest anyway, and that it was therefore not inequitable for her to insist on her statutory right to it.[100]

(c) The status of *High Trees*

Although the *High Trees* case has provoked an enormous amount of discussion, the principle in *High Trees* has not often been applied. In *High Trees* itself, the principle was not applied because the actual decision of Denning J was that the claimant's claim to recover the balance of the rent succeeded. In *Combe v Combe*, Denning LJ remarked on the excellence of the doctrine but agreed that it did not apply in the circumstances of that case. In *D & C Builders v Rees*, while again commending the virtues of the doctrine, Lord Denning held that it was inapplicable and *Foakes v Beer* ruled. In other cases where Lord Denning has given the doctrine an airing, the case could have been decided, or was decided by other judges, on some other well-established principle: common law estoppel in *Robertson v Minister of Pensions*[101] and *Lyle-Meller v Lewis*,[102] and a variation of the contract in *Alan v El Nasr*[103] and in *Brikom Investments Ltd v Carr & Others*.[104] One decision squarely on the point seems to be that of the Court of Appeal in the first action in the *Tool Metal* case. The decision of the House of Lords was in a second action in which the parties were estopped[105] by the decision in the first from denying that the principle operated. The House made it very clear that they were not deciding whether the first Court of Appeal was right or wrong. Given that a promissory estoppel was in operation, the only question for the judges was whether sufficient notice had been given to bring it to an end. They decided only that, *if* there is a doctrine of promissory estoppel which operates in these circumstances, its operation may be terminated by reasonable notice and, in the circumstances, reasonable notice had been given. Similarly, the more recent decision in *Collier v Wright* did not decide whether or not promissory estoppel was established on the facts of the case—only that a defence of promissory estoppel was arguable.

The problem of reconciling *Foakes v Beer* with the *High Trees* principle and its application by the Court of Appeal in the *Tool Metal* case remains. Denning J apparently took the view that they were irreconcilable, *Foakes v Beer* having been decided **per incuriam**, through overlooking a principle of equity. The irreconcilability may conceivably be accepted, but the opinion that all the Law Lords forgot about equity—especially when two of them had been involved in the leading case five years before—is harder to swallow and should be rejected. In any event, it is clear that 'consideration remains a fundamental principle of the law of contract and is not to be reduced out of existence by the law of estoppel'.[106]

---

[100] See Section 1(e)(iii).

[101] [1949] 1 KB 227.

[102] [1956] 1 WLR 29.

[103] [1972] 2 QB 189.

[104] [1979] QB 467.

[105] Estoppel by record (the record of the court)—an entirely different variety of estoppel from those discussed in this book.

[106] *Prime Sight Ltd v Lavarello* [2013] UKPC 22, [2014] AC 436 [30] (Lord Toulson).

3 The future of consideration

Some lawyers have suggested that the decision in *Williams v Roffey Bros* undermines the doctrine of consideration. This is not necessarily so. Even if the decision were regarded as overruling *Stilk v Myrick* and were to lead to the overruling of *Pinnel's* case and *Foakes v Beer*, the essence of the doctrine of consideration would remain intact. A person who agrees to pay an increased price in order to induce another to fulfil his contractual duty, or to take a lesser sum in full satisfaction in order to induce his debtor to pay something, is making a bargain. He asks for something in return for his promise to pay more, or not to sue for the balance, as the case may be, and gets what he asks for. To hold him bound, far from impairing the basic rule that bargains are binding, would be to abolish an exception to that rule. Lord Blackburn recognised this in *Foakes v Beer* but was dissuaded by his brethren from dissenting on that ground.

The bargain would not always be enforceable. The outcome would depend on whether the party surrendering his contractual rights did so under economic duress.[107] So the result in *D & C Builders v Rees*[108] would be unaffected as would that in *Atlas Express Ltd v Kafco Ltd*.[109] Indeed, further inquiry into the facts of *High Trees*—irrelevant, while the rule in *Foakes v Beer* prevails—might reveal a bargain ('We shall have to go into **liquidation** and be unable to pay you anything unless you can reduce the rent') which would be enforceable as a contract, unless it involved duress. The actual result in *Foakes v Beer* might be unaffected because there probably was no bargain and no intention to release any existing rights. Economic duress, which would assume greater importance, is a doctrine of uncertain extent—but so is the *High Trees* doctrine which, to some extent, it would replace.

All this is somewhat speculative until the courts face the fact that *Williams v Roffey Bros* is irreconcilable with *Stilk v Myrick* and therefore with *Foakes v Beer*. It would be preferable for *Williams v Roffey Bros* to be overruled. If it is to be maintained, then it may be that a distinction could evolve where consideration is required for the formation of contracts, but not for their variation.[110] However, even as regards contract formation, consideration is a controversial requirement and its abolition has been recommended.[111] If consideration were abolished, greater emphasis would be placed on whether the promise should seriously be intended as legally binding,[112] or whether there was a good reason for enforcing the promise such as the promisee's reliance on it.[113] But that might lead to the enforcement of gratuitous promises, which is contrary to long-standing orthodoxy: promises to make gifts are not contracts if not made by deed. Moreover, even if it were right that consideration

---

[107] See Chapter 17, Section 2.

[108] [1966] 2 QB 617, CA.

[109] See Chapter 17, Section 2.

[110] This appears to be consistent with the approach adopted in New Zealand: *Antons Trawling Co Ltd v Smith* [2003] 2 NZLR 23. See too *Adam Opel GmbH v Mitras Automotive (UK) Ltd* [2007] EWHC 3481 (QB) [42] (David Donaldson QC).

[111] See eg Law Revision Committee, *Sixth Interim Reports: Statute of Frauds and the Doctrine of Consideration* (1937).

[112] See Chapter 8.

[113] P Atiyah, 'Consideration in Contracts: A Fundamental Restatement' (Australian National University Press, 1971), reprinted as 'Consideration: A Restatement' in P Atiyah (ed), *Essays on Contract* (OUP, 1986). Cf G Treitel, 'Consideration: A Critical Analysis of Professor Atiyah's Fundamental Restatement' (1976) 50 ALJ 439.

only provides evidence of the parties' intentions to create legal relations, this may in itself be useful: as will be seen in Chapter 8, it is not always easy to ascertain whether the parties did intend to create legal relations, and consideration may be a more effective mechanism for demarcating the boundaries of contract law.

Further Reading

P Atiyah, 'Consideration: A Restatement' in P Atiyah, *Essays on Contract* (OUP, 1986).
Argues that the courts do not really look for 'consideration' as it is classically understood, but simply seek a 'good reason' why a promise should be enforced. Reliance on a promise might be a 'good reason' to enforce the promise.

G Treitel, 'Consideration: A Critical Analysis of Professor Atiyah's Fundamental Restatement' (1976) 50 ALJ 439.
Disagrees with Atiyah's analysis of the law, arguing that promissory estoppel should be kept within narrow confines given the broad definition of consideration.

J O'Sullivan, 'In Defence of *Foakes v Beer*' (1996) 55 CLJ 219.
Controversially suggests that a promise to pay more (as in *Williams v Roffey Bros*) can be legitimately distinguished from a promise to accept less (as in *Foakes v Beer*), but that if the two instances are irreconcilable, *Foakes v Beer* should be preferred.

R Halson, 'The Offensive Limits of Promissory Estoppel' [1999] LMCLQ 256.
Examines possible applications of the doctrine of promissory estoppel and argues that there are good reasons why promissory estoppel does not create a cause of action.

M Chen-Wishart, 'A Bird in the Hand: Consideration and Promissory Estoppel' in A Burrows and E Peel (eds), *Contract Formation and Parties* (OUP, 2010).
Considers the line of cases leading to *Williams v Roffey Bros*, and neatly explains that decision on the basis that the promisor is paying more for the performance of the pre-existing duty, rather than the promise to perform, and that a new unilateral contract between the parties is created. This is a different view from that presented in this chapter, and relies upon there being an important difference between the receipt of performance and the right to contractual performance. However, this might be thought to be a very fine distinction and not to reflect the intention of the parties.

Question

Phil agrees to rent woodland from Jay for £2,000 per month for five years to use for a paintballing business. After paying the agreed rent for four months, there is an accident on the site and an investigation into Phil's business practices. As a result, Phil has to cancel all bookings made and stop taking new bookings for paintballing activities. Jay feels sorry for Phil, so tells Phil that he only has to pay £1,200 per month while Phil's business is suffering. Phil is very grateful for Jay's offer, and agrees to pay the reduced rent.

Three months later, Phil inherits £500,000 under his uncle's will. Four months after that, the investigation clears Phil's business of any wrongdoing. Phil starts to accept bookings for his paintballing business again, and the business is quickly very successful.

Jay becomes aware of the success of Phil's business straight away, at which point he also learns of Phil's inheritance.

Advise Jay.

8 Intention to create legal relations

🔑 Key Points

- Intention to create legal relations is an essential and distinct element in the formation of a contract. This intention is assessed objectively.
- In a domestic or social context, there is a presumption that the parties do not intend to create legal relations.
- In a commercial context, however, the reverse applies and it is presumed that the parties do intend to create legal relations.
- No matter which presumption initially applies, that presumption may be rebutted by evidence to the contrary.

1 Domestic and social transactions

Imagine the following exchange. *A* says to *B*: 'I will host the book club and provide dinner on Wednesday if you will do so the following week.' *B* replies, 'I agree.' All the elements of a bargain that we have come across so far are present here, since there is an offer, acceptance, and consideration. But it is extremely improbable that this is a binding contract. In the unlikely event of the matter coming before a court, it would almost certainly be held that this exchange was only a social transaction and not a contract because there was no intention to create legal relations. The key point is that an intention to create legal relations is an essential and distinct element in the formation of a contract.

In a purely domestic or social transaction (like the arrangements for the book club), an objective approach to the parties' intentions might lead to the conclusion that there was no intention to create legal relations. In the leading case of *Balfour v Balfour*,[1] a man was returning to his employment abroad and leaving his wife in England. They agreed that he would pay her a monthly allowance. But the Court of Appeal, reversing the judge at first instance, held that the agreement was not intended by the parties to have legal consequences, even if the wife was giving consideration by accepting the agreed sum each month in lieu of the husband's obligation to maintain her. The parties had not explicitly said that they had no intention to create legal relations, but it was the court's inference from the circumstances that led to its decision.

---

[1] [1919] 2 KB 571, CA.

In another case, *Jones v Padavatton*,[2] a mother promised her daughter that, if the daughter gave up her job in America and read for the Bar in England, the mother would pay her $200 maintenance per month. The daughter complied with her side of the agreement, and the arrangement was then varied such that the mother bought a house in London for the daughter to live in, rather than pay maintenance. After some time, the daughter had still not successfully taken the Bar exams, and she fell out with her mother. The mother sought possession of the house, which was granted by the Court of Appeal. The court found that there was no valid contract between the mother and daughter since there was no intention to create legal relations.

Balfour v Balfour and *Jones v Padavatton* are leading examples of how domestic agreements are presumed not to be legally binding since the parties are presumed not to intend to create legal relations. There are obviously many domestic arrangements where it would be wholly inappropriate for the courts to intervene, such as the arrangements between spouses for keeping up with household chores and expenses. This is not only because such promises may be trivial, but also because domestic and social promises should not be subject to an intrusive legal process. Moreover, from a practical point of view, the court system simply could not withstand being swamped by the excessive litigation which might arise if purely domestic promises resulted in binding contracts.

However, even the leading decision of *Balfour v Balfour* is perhaps close to the borderline between situations where there is an intention to create legal relations and those where there is not. Spouses may, and often do, demonstrate an intention to create legal relations where property is concerned. Moreover, the presumption that legal relations are not intended does not apply where spouses are not living amicably but are separated or about to separate.[3] Following the decision of the Supreme Court in *Radmacher v Granatino*,[4] it is now clear that, when deciding whether to make ancillary financial orders on the breakdown of a marriage, a court should give effect to ante-nuptial or post-nuptial agreements if it is fair in all the circumstances to do so and the relevant agreement was freely entered into with a full appreciation of its implications. Admittedly, the court did not decide whether such agreements should be classified as contractual, but the majority did emphasise that 'It is, of course, important that each party should intend that the agreement should be effective.'[5]

This is an area where it is difficult to lay down precise rules. However, it appears that the significance and importance of the action to be taken by one party in reliance on the promise of the other may persuade the court that the promise must have been intended to be legally binding. For example, an agreement to share a house was held to be a contract when, as both parties knew, it was necessary for one of them to take the drastic and irrevocable step of disposing of his own residence in order to adopt the arrangement.[6] Similarly, an intention to create legal relations was found in *Simpkins v Pays* where there was an arrangement between *A*, *A*'s granddaughter, and *A*'s lodger to enter a Sunday newspaper fashion competition. Although the competition was entered into in *A*'s name, each

---

[2] [1969] 1 WLR 328, CA.
[3] *Merritt v Merritt* [1970] 1 WLR 1211.
[4] [2010] UKSC 42, [2011] 1 AC 534.
[5] Ibid, [70].
[6] *Parker v Clark* [1960] 1 WLR 286 (Devlin J).

party filled in one line of the entry, and a binding contract was formed between the parties such that, when *A* won the competition, the winnings were to be split equally between the three parties.[7] This decision is significant as it means that in the vast majority of cases the agreement between members of a lottery syndicate to split any winnings between them is contractually binding.

Binding contracts have also been recognised between spouses regarding 'the ownership or tenancy of the matrimonial home, bank accounts, savings or other assets'[8] and between brothers concerning the running of a family company.[9] In all these instances, the subject matter of the promise was clearly quite important. A promise by a husband to take the bins out if his wife does the washing-up is far less important, and remains unlikely to be legally binding.

2 Commercial transactions

Commercial transactions are considered in a different manner to domestic transactions by the courts. In ordinary business matters, there is a strong presumption that legal relations are intended.[10] Whilst the ordinary shopper in the high street does not have a conscious intention to create legal relations as he makes his various purchases, he is undoubtedly entering into a series of contracts for the sale of goods. For example, if he is poisoned by the fish purchased from the local fishmonger, he will have a cause of action on the terms implied into the contract by section 14 of the Sale of Goods Act 1979 or section 9 of the Consumer Rights Act 2015[11] that the fish is of satisfactory quality and reasonably fit for eating. The truthful shopper might admit under cross-examination that it had never crossed his mind that, when he bought the fish, he was making a contract; but that would not matter in the least. The matter would be judged objectively.[12] As Lord Clarke said in *RTS Flexible Systems Ltd v Molkerei Alois Müller GmbH and Co KG (UK) Productions*:[13]

> Whether there is a binding contract between the parties and, if so, upon what terms depends upon what they have agreed. It depends not upon their subjective state of mind, but upon a consideration of what was communicated between them by words or conduct, and whether that leads objectively to a conclusion that they intended to create legal relations and had agreed upon all the terms which they regarded or the law requires as essential for the formulation of legally binding relations.

---

[7] *Simpkins v Pays* [1955] 1 WLR 975 (Sellers J).

[8] *Radmacher v Granatino* [2010] UKSC 42, [2011] 1 AC 534 [142] (Lady Hale).

[9] *Snelling v John G Snelling Ltd* [1973] QB 87 (discussed further in Chapter 10, Section 6(c)).

[10] Although there must first be 'an agreement on essentials with sufficient certainty to be enforceable', per Mance LJ in *Baird Textiles Holdings Ltd v Marks & Spencer plc* [2001] EWCA Civ 274, [2002] 1 All ER (Comm) 737 [59], discussed in Chapter 7, Section 2(b)(i).

[11] See Chapter 13, Section 3.

[12] This might also explain the importance placed on the fact that the Carbolic Smoke Ball Co deposited £1,000 at the Alliance Bank in *Carlill v Carbolic Smoke Ball Co* [1893] 1 QB 256, discussed in Chapter 4.

[13] [2010] UKSC 14, [2010] 1 WLR 753 [45].

The presumption that legal relations are intended is not irrebuttable, but the burden of rebutting the presumption is placed upon the party who asserts that no legal effect was intended; 'the onus is a heavy one'.[14] One example of the courts finding it difficult to decide whether the presumption was rebutted on the facts is *Esso Petroleum Ltd v Commissioners of Customs and Excise*.[15] Esso displayed posters offering one 'World Cup Coin' with every four gallons of petrol. Each coin bore the head of one of the 30 members of the England squad for the 1970 World Cup. The Commissioners of Customs and Excise argued that the coins were 'produced in quantity for general sale', which meant that Esso was liable to pay purchase tax on these coins. Esso argued that there was no contract of sale of the coins, and that Esso was simply making an offer of free **gifts** of the coins. This issue was of great financial importance: if there was a contract of sale of the coins, then Esso would be liable to pay around £200,000 in purchase tax. Pennycuick J, and the majority of the House of Lords, held that there was a valid contract to supply the coins. But this was by no means an obvious conclusion. The Court of Appeal had thought that Esso was simply making an offer of free gifts of the coins, and the two dissenting judges in the House of Lords (Viscount Dilhorne and Lord Russell) agreed, saying that there was no intention to enter into legal relations as regards the coins. It was, of course, extremely improbable that anyone would ever have sued on a contract to supply one of these coins of minute intrinsic value, but that did not deter the majority from holding that there was a binding contract. Although Viscount Dilhorne thought the offer of a 'free' coin was not properly regarded as a business matter, Lord Simon, in the majority, stressed that the advertising was for commercial advantage and that the transaction took place in a setting of business relations.

However, even in a commercial transaction, the parties may expressly exclude any intention to enter into legal relations. In *Rose and Frank Co v JR Crompton and Brothers Ltd*,[16] the parties entered into an agency arrangement for the sale of tissues, which was clearly a commercial transaction. The following provision was included in the agency arrangement:

> This arrangement is not entered into, nor is this memorandum written, as a formal or legal agreement, and shall not be subject to legal jurisdiction in the Law Courts either of the United States or England, but it is only a definite expression and record of the purpose and intention of the three parties concerned, to which they each honourably **pledge** themselves . . .

Because of this 'honourable pledge clause', as it was called, it was held that the arrangement was not a binding contract. But that conclusion applied only to the arrangement to which it was expressly stated the clause should apply. The presumption that legal relations were intended came into effect again when subsequent orders were given and accepted, without any such 'honourable pledge' clause, and so binding contracts were formed.

It should be noted that there is a rule of public policy that an agreement purporting to oust the jurisdiction of the courts is 'illegal' and void. How is this to be reconciled with *Rose and Frank*'s case? The answer seems to be that any attempt to set up another

---

[14] *Edwards v Skyways Ltd* [1964] 1 WLR 349, 355 (Megaw J); *Attrill v Dresdner Kleinwort Ltd* [2013] EWCA Civ 394, [2013] 3 All ER 607 [79]–[81] (Elias LJ).

[15] [1976] 1 WLR 1.

[16] [1925] AC 445.

contract-enforcing authority to the exclusion of the courts is void, but there is nothing contrary to public policy in an agreement that the transaction should not be enforceable at all,
by anyone. As Scrutton LJ said in the Court of Appeal in *Rose and Frank*'s case, the parties
may 'exclude all idea of settling disputes by any outside intervention . . .'[17] But, to avoid the
public policy ban, it is probably necessary that the agreement, like that in *Rose and Frank*,
should not be enforceable, even by the private sanctions of an association with which the
defaulting party has contracted.[18]

(a) Letters of comfort

A modern development is the use by businessmen of 'letters of comfort'. These appear usually to take the form of encouragement to a lender to advance money to a third party. They
are frequently, and perhaps deliberately, phrased in equivocal and ambiguous language,
and fall short of being a guarantee. In *Kleinwort Benson Ltd v Malaysia Mining Corp Bhd*,[19]
the claimants agreed to make a loan of £10 million to Metals Ltd, a wholly owned subsidiary of the defendants. The defendants had declined to guarantee repayment by Metals Ltd
but offered instead a letter of comfort to the claimant. In that letter, the defendants stated
that it was their 'policy to ensure' that Metals Ltd was at all times in a position to meet its
liabilities. Hirst J held that, in a commercial banking transaction, this amounted to an
undertaking, and therefore that there was a contract between the claimants and defendants. However, the Court of Appeal held that, on a proper interpretation of the document,
the defendants were at liberty to change their 'policy' at any time, and did not intend to be
contractually bound to keep that policy in place. As a result, the very serious consequences
of the **repudiation** by the defendants of any 'moral responsibility' was not a matter for
the court.

Clearly, whether or not there is a binding contract is a question for the courts to decide
on the particular facts of a case. This was recognised more recently in the Court of Appeal
by Maurice Kay LJ, who said: 'I regard a letter of comfort, properly so called, as one that
does not give rise to contractual liability. The label used by the parties is not necessarily
determinative. It is a matter of construction of the document as a whole.'[20]

(b) Letters of intent

Slightly different, perhaps, is a 'letter of intent'. Such letters envisage the possibility of
later entering into a contract, but may be expressly stated to be 'subject to contract', such
that there is as yet no binding agreement.[21] However, where the envisaged transaction has
then been performed on both sides, it will often be 'unrealistic' to argue that there was no
intention to enter into legal relations.[22] This has been confirmed by the Supreme Court in

---

[17] [1923] 2 KB 261.
[18] *Baker v Jones* [1954] 1 WLR 1005.
[19] [1989] 1 All ER 785.
[20] *Associated British Ports v Ferryways NV* [2009] EWCA Civ 189, [2009] 1 Lloyd's Rep 595 [24].
[21] For further consideration of agreements said to be 'subject to contract', see Chapter 5, Section 5.
[22] *G Percy Trentham Ltd v Archital Luxfer Ltd* [1993] 1 Lloyd's Rep 25, 27 (Steyn LJ).

RTS Flexible Systems Ltd v Molkerei Alois Müller GmbH & Co KG (UK Productions).[23] The claimant, RTS, was negotiating a contract for the construction and installation of equipment to be used by Müller. Detailed negotiations took place, and work began on the basis of a letter of intent. The letter of intent expired, but RTS continued to supply the goods and services to Müller, who paid some, but not all, of the envisaged contract price. Although the original negotiations were said to be 'subject to contract', the Supreme Court pointed out that any intention not to be bound before signature could be 'waived'.[24] A 'subject to contract' clause is no more than an indication that, determined objectively, the parties do not intend to create legal relations until the contract is signed. The Supreme Court held that the parties' own conduct indicated that they must have intended to create legal relations, and no longer required an **executed** and signed contract. The Supreme Court Justices found that '[a]ny other conclusion makes no commercial sense', and that 'the reasonable, honest businessman ... whether he was an RTS man or a Müller man ... would have concluded that the work should be carried out for the agreed price on the agreed terms ... without the necessity for a formal written agreement, which had been overtaken by events.'[25]

(c) **Trade unions**

One common exception to the principle that an intention to create legal relations is presumed in the context of commercial agreements involves trade unions. Collective agreements between trade unions and employers do not give rise to legal relations. This was recognised at **common law**,[26] and by statute it is now 'conclusively presumed' that this is the case, unless the agreement is in writing and states that the parties intend that the agreement should be a legally enforceable contract.[27]

3 The future of intention to create legal relations

The lack of unanimity in cases such as *Esso Petroleum Ltd v Commissioners of Customs and Excise* highlights that it will not always be easy to decide whether an arrangement is more 'social' than 'commercial'. And courts continue to be split on whether or not an intention to create legal relations is present in particular disputes. For example, in *Modahl v British Athletic Federation*,[28] Diane Modahl, an international 800-metre runner, successfully argued that there was a contract between her and the British Athletic Federation when Modahl accepted an invitation from the federation to run on its behalf. Nevertheless, there was a strong dissent from Jonathan Parker LJ in the Court of Appeal, who could not discern any intention to create legal relations. More recently, in *Preston v President of the Methodist Conference*,[29] Baroness Hale disagreed with the other Justices of the Supreme Court on

---

[23] [2010] UKSC 14, [2010] 1 WLR 753.
[24] Ibid, [86]–[88].
[25] Ibid, [86].
[26] *Ford Motor Co Ltd v AEF* [1969] 1 WLR 339.
[27] Trade Union and Labour Relations (Consolidation) Act 1992, s 179.
[28] [2001] EWCA Civ 1447, [2002] 1 WLR 1192.
[29] [2013] UKSC 29, [2013] 2 AC 163.

the question of whether there was an intention to create legal relations, and therefore a contract, between a Methodist priest and her church. The majority held that there was no intention to create legal relations. Lord Sumption, who gave the leading judgment, said that '[t]he question is whether the parties intended these benefits and burdens of the ministry to be the subject of a legally binding agreement between them', and that this required the court to 'examine the rules and practices of the particular church and any special arrangements made with the particular minister'.[30] This involves a very fact-specific inquiry into the nature of the particular relationship, with little help from any 'presumption' either way. Baroness Hale, on the other hand, thought that 'it would be very odd indeed if a minister who was not paid her stipend or was threatened with summary eviction from her manse could not rely upon the terms of her appointment either to enforce the payment or to resist a possession action'[31] and that therefore an intention to create legal relations should at least be presumed.

Such decisions highlight some of the difficulties that arise from the doctrine of intention to create legal relations. As a result, some have contended that it should be abolished in its entirety. This is highly unlikely to happen, and would only shift the same issue to the prior question of whether the offer or acceptance was intended to be legally binding, rendering that stage of analysis more uncertain. Indeed, it is perhaps more likely that intention to create legal relations takes on a larger role as a result of the loosening of the requirements of consideration,[32] although this would still leave the problem of how to deal with gratuitous promises. The current, orthodox approach is likely to prevail for some time to come. Both consideration and intention to create legal relations are required for a binding contract. The latter will essentially continue to keep contract law out of domestic arrangements, but make sure it applies to commercial agreements, unless an objective interpretation of the particular facts of a case suggests otherwise.

Further Reading

B Hepple, 'Intention to Create Legal Relations' (1970) 28 CLJ 122 (especially 127–37).
Argues that there is no need for a requirement of 'intention to create legal relations' and that where there is offer, acceptance, and consideration, some bargains are not enforceable for policy reasons. (NB: this article predates the Trade Union and Labour Relations (Consolidation) Act 1992, s 179.)

S Hedley, 'Keeping Contract in its Place – *Balfour v Balfour* and the Enforceability of Informal Agreements' (1985) 5 OJLS 391.
Criticises 'intention to create legal relations' as obscuring the true reasons for judges' decisions. Contends that the cases on 'intention to create legal relations' essentially mean that where the parties were dealing at arm's length, promises will generally be enforced; but in domestic contexts, contractual liability will be imposed only if the party seeking enforcement has already performed one side of the bargain and is simply seeking reciprocity.

---

[30] Ibid, [26].
[31] Ibid, [45].
[32] See Chapter 7, Section 1(e)(iii).

P Giliker, 'Taking Comfort in Certainty: To Enforce or Not to Enforce the Letter of Comfort' [2004] LMCLQ 219.
Argues that it is commercially desirable for letters of comfort not to be enforced, and that the different approach in France should not be followed.

 ## Question

In *Baird Textiles Holdings Ltd v Marks & Spencer plc*, Mance LJ said:

[59.] For a contract to come into existence, there must be both (a) an agreement on essentials with sufficient certainty to be enforceable and (b) an intention to create legal relations.

[60.] Both requirements are normally judged objectively. Absence of the former may involve or be explained by the latter. But this is not always so. A sufficiently certain agreement may be reached, but there may be either expressly (i.e. by express agreement) or impliedly (e.g. in some family situations) no intention to create legal relations.

Should an intention to create legal relations always be presumed? Is the law in need of reform?

9 Contracts requiring writing

Key Points

- In general, contracts may be made entirely orally. It is only in some circumstances that written formalities are required.

- Section 4 of the Statute of Frauds 1677 provides that contracts of guarantee are unenforceable if not evidenced in writing. This situation typically arises where *A* is, or may become, under a liability (whether in contract or in tort) to *B*. *C* then promises *B* (for consideration) that, if *A* does not discharge his liability, *C* will do so. *C*'s promise to *B* is not enforceable unless evidenced in writing.

- Section 2 of the Law of Property (Miscellaneous Provisions) Act 1989 provides that contracts for the sale, or other disposition, of an interest in land must be made in writing. If such a 'contract' is not made in writing then it is void (and not merely unenforceable).

As we have already seen in Chapter 1,[1] the general principle is that contracts may be made entirely orally, no matter how valuable or important the subject matter of the contract may be. However, there are some exceptions to the general rule that no written formalities are required, and this chapter will examine two classes of contract. The first encompasses particular categories of contract which must be in writing as a result of legislation. The second concerns certain types of contract which are not enforceable unless evidenced in writing. It should be noted straight away that there are important differences between the two classes. As regards the first, the 'contract' will be void if not in writing. But as regards the second class of contract, any contract will be valid but simply unenforceable if not evidenced in writing. This means that, where a contract is made orally, neither party can sue on it unless and until a party can produce the appropriate written evidence of it. Such evidence may come into existence after the contract has been made.

It may seem that insisting upon certain formalities is time-consuming and burdensome, making the process of contracting more onerous. However, it should be appreciated that formality requirements do serve useful purposes.[2] For example, they serve an 'evidentiary function', since the written document will serve as good evidence of the contract made. Formality requirements also serve a 'cautionary function': parties may be more inclined to check and make sure of their agreement if it is formally written down. There may also be a 'channelling function', in that the fulfilment of the requisite formalities provides a

---

[1] See Chapter 1, Section 3.
[2] The following analysis is based upon L Fuller, 'Consideration and Form' (1941) 41 Columbia Law Review 799, see especially 800–4.

simple, objective test of enforceability. However, even though requirements of formalities are not without merit, there is clearly a tension between giving effect to the formality rules and achieving what might be perceived to be a 'fair' result on the facts of a particular case. This tension may be particularly acute where the parties are unaware of the need to satisfy certain formalities, and insisting upon strict fulfilment of the formality requirements would allow a party to escape his agreement despite the apparent merits leading towards the opposite result.

1 Contracts unenforceable for lack of writing

The origin of the unenforceable contract is to be found in sections 4 and 17 of the Statute of Frauds 1677. The purpose of the statute was to prevent fraud by requiring written evidence of certain types of promise which were considered to be particularly vulnerable to dishonest claims. Throughout its history the statute has been heavily criticised both for its drafting and its substance, since it was often thought to assist rather than to prevent fraud! However, it was not until 1954 that the Law Reform (Enforcement of Contracts) Act repealed important parts of it. From 1677 to 1954 the statute applied to:

(a) a promise by an **executor** or **administrator** to pay damages out of his own property;

(b) a promise made in **consideration of marriage**. This referred not to the mutual promises of the engaged couple (which was an enforceable contract until the Law Reform (Miscellaneous Provisions) Act 1970, s 1(1)) but to marriage settlements and ancillary agreements, such as that alleged in *Shadwell v Shadwell*;[3]

(c) a promise not to be performed within one year of its making; and

(d) a contract for the sale of any goods of the value of £10 or more. (This provision was re-enacted in the Sale of Goods Act 1893, s 4.)

For contracts made after the 1954 Act came into force, these provisions are of no significance. However, it is useful to be aware of them in order to gain a proper understanding of cases such as *Shadwell v Shadwell, Jorden v Money*,[4] and *Felthouse v Bindley*[5] which, while affected by the repealed parts of the Statute of Frauds, remain authorities on general principles that are still applicable.

Significantly, the 1954 Act left unrepealed the requirement of writing in respect of two classes of contract. One was any contract for the sale or other **disposition** of an interest in land. Since 1989 these contracts have been governed by a new rule, which is examined in Section 2. The only survivor of the Statute of Frauds is now: a 'special promise to answer for the debt, default or miscarriage of another person'.

This antique language of section 4 of the 1677 Act is still in force but it has been heavily overlaid with case law. As interpreted, it applies only where three parties are involved. Invariably, *A* is, or may become, under a liability (whether in contract or in tort) to *B*. *C*

---

[3] Chapter 7, Section 1.
[4] Chapter 7, Section 2.
[5] Chapter 3, Section 3(c).

then promises B (for consideration) that, if A does not discharge his liability, he (C) will do so. C's promise to B is not enforceable unless evidenced in writing.

It is important to note that section 4 has been interpreted somewhat narrowly. So, a promise made by C to A (the person primarily answerable for the 'debt, default or miscarriage') is not within the statute and is enforceable (if given for consideration) without written evidence.[6] And the statute also does not apply where C promises B that he (C) will meet A's liability in any event, not only conditionally upon A's failing to do so. Such an unconditional promise is called 'an indemnity', and should be contrasted with the conditional promise, which is called 'a guarantee'. It is now clear that the statute applies only to guarantees. This can raise difficult questions of interpretation, where the court has to decide whether an indemnity or a guarantee is at issue. The usual objective test applies, and the fact that the parties use one term rather than the other is not conclusive; the key question is: what is the true meaning of the promise?[7]

These restrictions on the meaning of the statute are not easy to justify. But the restrictions on the ambit of section 4 do not end there. Even where C's promise is undoubtedly a guarantee it is held to be outside the statute if it is part of a wider transaction. Most notably, the statute does not apply to *del credere* agency. A *del credere* agent is an agent who guarantees that persons whom the agent introduces to his principal will perform their contracts. The main object of the contract is the introduction and the guarantee is incidental to it; as a result, the guarantee falls outside the scope of the Statute of Frauds 1677.[8] Nor does the statute apply where C gives the guarantee in order to secure the release by A of an **encumbrance** affecting C's proprietary rights. For instance, in *Fitzgerald v Dressler*,[9] A sold goods to B who resold the goods to C. A was still in possession of the goods and, since he had not been paid by B, A had a **lien** (or **charge**) on the goods. C was anxious to obtain possession of the goods quickly, so guaranteed payment by B if A would deliver directly to him. A did so and later sought to enforce C's guarantee. C tried to escape liability by relying on the statute, but this attempt failed and the guarantee was held to be valid despite the lack of writing.[10]

Such decisions are explicable only on the ground of the judges' understandable dislike of a statute, which has led them to restrict the scope of the statute as much as they possibly can. After all, if the statute applies, then a party is able to dishonour with impunity an obligation which he has clearly undertaken. Nevertheless, section 4 of the Statute of Frauds 1677 was retained in 1954 for the protection of the public against unscrupulous persons who might claim that guarantees had been given when they had not. However, it is doubtful whether this is a good reason for the retention of the strange and illogical law which has grown up around the words of the statute.

---

[6] *Eastwood v Kenyon* (1840) 11 Ad & E 438.

[7] *Mountstephen v Lakeman* (1874) LR 7 HL 17; *Guild v Conrad* [1894] 2 QB 885; *Pitts v Jones* [2007] EWCA Civ 1301, [2008] QB 706.

[8] *Couturier v Hastie* (1852) 8 Exch 40.

[9] (1859) 7 CB (NS) 374.

[10] C, having bought the goods, was the owner of them. Where C had no proprietary interest but only a personal interest to protect, *Fitzgerald v Dressler* was distinguished and the statute applied: *Harburg India Rubber Comb Co v Martin* [1902] 1 KB 778, CA.

(a) The requirement of writing

Section 4 of the 1677 Act provides that no action may be brought on the guarantee:

> unless the agreement ..., or some memorandum or note thereof, shall be in writing and signed by the party to be charged therewith or by some other person thereunto by him lawfully authorised.

The note or memorandum may take any form. For example, it might be a letter. However, the note or memorandum must identify the parties and include all the express terms of the contract (although it need not contain any terms which are implied by law). It is possible to form a complete memorandum by joining together several documents, even if each document would in itself be insufficient, provided that there is an express or even an implied reference in the signed document to the other documents. For instance, the courts have allowed a letter to be joined with an envelope proved orally to have enclosed it,[11] and an agreement to buy land to be joined with a receipt for the deposit signed by the vendor.[12]

A similarly lax approach has been taken to the requirement of 'signature': a manual, formal signature is not essential. Any representation of the defendant's name is sufficient if the court is satisfied that it is intended to authenticate the whole document. Indeed, it would seem that contracts made by email or by trading on a website will generally fulfil any requirement of writing that may exist by analogy with documents in hard copy.[13] After all, the European Electronic Commerce Directive requires Member States to ensure that contracts are not deprived of legal effectiveness by reason of their being made by electronic means.[14] It has even been held that a sequence of emails was sufficient to satisfy the requirement of writing under section 4.[15]

In *Pereira Fernandes SA v Mehta*, Judge Pelling QC sensibly observed that:[16]

> a party can sign a document for the purposes of section 4 by using his full name or his last name prefixed by some or all of his initials or using his initials, and possibly by using a pseudonym or a combination of letters and numbers ... providing always that whatever was used was inserted into the document in order to give, and with the intention of giving, authenticity to it...
>
> I have no doubt that if a party creates and sends an electronically created document then he will be treated as having signed it to the same extent that he would in law be treated as having signed a hard copy of the same document. The fact that the document is created electronically as opposed to as a hard copy can make no difference.

In that case, the judge found that the automatic insertion of an email address in an email did not mean that it was 'intended for signature'. The judge's conclusion would likely have been different if the insertion of an email address was carried out deliberately in order to provide authenticity.

---

[11] *Pearce v Gardner* [1897] 1 QB 688.
[12] *North v Loomes* [1919] 1 Ch 378.
[13] *Pereira Fernandes SA v Mehta* [2006] EWHC 813 (Ch), [2006] 1 WLR 1543.
[14] Directive 2000/31/EC.
[15] *Golden Ocean Group Ltd v Salgaocar Mining Industries Pvt Ltd* [2012] EWCA Civ 265, [2012] 1 WLR 3674.
[16] [2006] EWHC 813 (Ch), [2006] 1 WLR 1543 [27]–[29].

(b) **Effect of non-compliance**

For many years the courts held that the effect of non-compliance with the Statute of Frauds 1677 was to render the contract void. As late as 1862, in *Felthouse v Bindley*,[17] it was held that the lack of a memorandum at the date of the auction prevented the property in the horse passing from the nephew to his uncle even though there was a memorandum at the time the action was brought. Yet in 1852, in *Leroux v Brown*,[18] it had already been held that the effect of the statute was not substantive but procedural: a contract made in France and governed by French law was not enforceable in an English court without a memorandum because English procedural rules applied. This was confirmed by the House of Lords in *Maddison v Alderson* in 1883.[19] It is now clear that a failure to comply with the formalities of the Statute of Frauds 1677 does not render the contract void, but does make the contract unenforceable.

This means that the relevant oral contract is valid. That contract may be enforced against any party as soon as he has signed a sufficient memorandum. However, it may not be enforced against a party who has not signed such a memorandum. Even so, that does not mean that the contract is of no effect. Acts done in performance of the unenforceable contract are validly done. As a result, a party who has paid money under the contract cannot recover the money as he could if the contract were void. The payee may rely on the contract to justify his retention of the money, even though he could not sue on the contract, provided that he remains ready and willing to perform his own obligations.[20]

As the requirement of writing is procedural and not substantive, the defendant may waive it. But if he wishes to rely on the statute, he must plead it.

2 Contracts required to be in writing

The most important contract in this class is a contract for the sale, or other disposition, of an interest in land.[21] Until 1989, these contracts could be made orally but contracts made between 1677 and 29 September 1989 were, and remain, unenforceable unless evidenced in writing. The requirement was imposed by section 4 of the Statute of Frauds (analysed in the preceding section) which was re-enacted in more modern language by section 40 of the Law of Property Act 1925. But section 40 was repealed and replaced by section 2 of the Law of Property (Miscellaneous Provisions) Act 1989 which provides:

2.—(1) A contract for the sale or other disposition of an interest in land can only be made in writing and only by incorporating all the terms which the parties have expressly agreed in one document or, where contracts are exchanged, in each.

---

[17] (1862) 11 CB (NS) 869, affirmed 7 LT 835. See Chapter 3, Section 3(c).

[18] (1852) 12 CB 801.

[19] (1883) 8 App Cas 467, 488 (Lord Blackburn).

[20] *Thomas v Brown* (1876) 1 QBD 714.

[21] Other examples include consumer credit agreements (see Consumer Credit Act 1974, ss 60, 64) and contracts of marine insurance (Marine Insurance Act 1906, s 22).

(2) The terms may be incorporated in a document either by being set out in it or by reference to some other document.

(3) The document incorporating the terms or, where contracts are exchanged, one of the documents incorporating them (but not necessarily the same one) must be signed by or on behalf of each party to the contract.

If the parties wish to change a term in a contract they have made for the sale of land (for example, by changing the completion date) the contract as varied must satisfy the formalities of section 2. If it does not, the original contract remains valid.[22]

The section has caused difficulty in connection with the exercise of an option to buy land. In *Spiro v Glencrown Properties Ltd*,[23] the claimant (S) granted the first defendant (G) an option to buy land for £745,000. The agreement was in two parts, each signed by both parties and exchanged. The option was exercisable by notice in writing to S. G duly delivered a letter exercising the option. This letter was signed on behalf of G but not, of course, by S. G failed to complete the alleged contract for the sale of the land and S sued for damages. G's defence was that, applying section 2, there was no contract for the sale of the land since the letter concluding the contract was not signed by S. This was a formidable objection and one with grave consequences. If it were upheld, options to buy land would be invalid unless some new and cumbersome procedure were introduced. Hoffmann J thought that this could not have been intended by Parliament. He held that section 2 was intended to apply to the agreement which created the option and not to the notice by which it was exercised. The grant of the option was the *only* 'contract for the sale or other disposition of an interest in land' within the meaning of the section.

This decision no doubt produced a sensible result, but there are serious theoretical difficulties. It may well be fair to say that the option was a *contract to sell*; after all, S was conditionally bound, since his offer to sell was irrevocable. But it seems much more difficult to say that there was a contract to buy. This is because G was not bound to buy—whether G exercised the option was entirely at his discretion. Yet it was G's contract to buy which was enforced. If the grant of the option was the only contract for the sale of land, by what process did G become bound to buy? The answer to this question remains unclear.

In any event, it should be noted that a 'lock-out' agreement, whereby a prospective vendor agrees that for a specified period he will not deal with anyone other than a particular purchaser, is not covered by section 2: the vendor does not agree to sell to anyone, nor does the purchaser agree to buy.[24] Similarly, a term for the payment of a 'finder's fee' regarding the sale of property falls outside the scope of section 2 and, if it is not made in writing, does not invalidate the contract for sale itself.[25] As the Court of Appeal has pointed out, 'The expressly agreed term must, if it is required by section 2 to be included in the single document, be a term of the sale of the land, rather than a term of some simultaneous contract

---

[22] *McCausland v Duncan Lawrie Ltd* [1996] 4 All ER 995.
[23] [1991] 2 WLR 931, ChD.
[24] *Pitt v PHH Asset Management Ltd* [1993] 4 All ER 961.
[25] *North Eastern Properties Ltd v Coleman & Quinn Conveyancing* [2010] EWCA Civ 277, [2010] 1 WLR 2715.

(whether for the sale of a **chattel** or the provision of a service) which happens to take place at the same time as the land contract, and to form part of one commercial transaction.'[26]

It is worth emphasising that section 2 of the 1989 Act differs significantly from section 4 of the Statute of Frauds.[27] Section 2 requires that the contract be made in writing, and not merely evidenced in writing. As a result, a contract which is not made in writing is void—regardless of whether it is later evidenced in writing. This is clearly different from the Statute of Frauds.

3 Evading the formalities requirements

The long history of the Statute of Frauds shows that procedural requirements often stand in the way of just results and that courts will often strive to find a way around them. Sometimes this can be done without undue strain, as in the use of the collateral contract which has already proved its utility in relation to section 2.[28] In other circumstances, such as those in *Spiro*, it seems to involve distortions which are hard to justify. In any event, it is clear that a party cannot invoke **estoppel** in order to circumvent the operation of section 4 of the Statute of Frauds. In *Actionstrength Ltd v International Glass Engineering SpA*,[29] the defendant orally promised the claimant subcontractor that it would guarantee payments which were due to the claimant from the main contractor in consideration for the claimant not withdrawing its labour from the site. The claimant sought to enforce this guarantee, and the defendant contended that it was unenforceable under section 4 of the Statute of Frauds 1677 because it was not supported by a written note or memorandum. In response, the claimant argued that its reliance on the defendant's oral promise gave rise to an estoppel, but this was rejected by the House of Lords. Allowing a claim in estoppel to succeed would deprive section 4 of any real effect, and a claimant should not be able to succeed simply by 'relabelling' its claim. Nevertheless, the result in *Actionstrength* was harsh on the claimant, since it allowed the defendant simply to walk away from his promise.

However, it should be noted that section 2(5) of the 1989 Act expressly states that section 2 does not affect the creation or operation of resulting, implied, or constructive trusts. And it has further been held that section 2 does not preclude claims in proprietary estoppel. In *Thorner v Major*,[30] Lord Neuberger thought that section 2 does not have any impact on 'a straightforward estoppel claim without any contractual connection'. But although this allows some scope for estoppel to operate, it should be recognised that the potential field of operation of proprietary estoppel is very narrow.[31]

---

[26] Ibid, [46] (Briggs J).
[27] See eg *Firstpost Homes Ltd v Johnson* [1995] 1 WLR 1567, 1576 (Peter Gibson LJ).
[28] See *Record v Bell* [1991] 4 All ER 471, ChD, see Chapter 11, Section 3.
[29] [2003] UKHL 17, [2003] 2 AC 541.
[30] [2009] UKHL 18, [2009] 1 WLR 776 [99].
[31] See Chapter 7, Section 2(b)(i).

Further Reading

L Fuller, 'Consideration and Form' (1941) 41 Columbia Law Review 799.
Considers the role of formalities generally, with particular reference to consideration.

J Phillips, 'Guarantees: Protecting the Bankers' [2012] Journal of Business Law 248.
Discusses the law concerning guarantees, with particular reference to the Statute of Frauds in the first part of the article.

Question

'It may be questionable whether, in relation to contracts of guarantee, the mischief at which section 4 was originally aimed, is not now outweighed, at least in some classes of case, by the mischief to which it can give rise.' (Lord Bingham in *Actionstrength Ltd v International Glass Engineering SpA* [2003] UKHL 17, [2003] 2 AC 541)

Should the requirements for written formalities be entirely abolished?

10 Third parties

Key Points

- At common law, a contract between A and B cannot be enforced by a third party, C, even if the contract is for the benefit of C. Nor can a contract between A and B impose burdens on C.

- C will be a third party if he does not provide any consideration to A: consideration must move from the promisee.

- The general rule is that the promisee, B, is only able to recover damages for his own loss, rather than that of C. However, some exceptions have been recognised, such as where A contracts with B to erect buildings on C's land and the work is defective.

- Where A and B contract to confer a benefit on C, the courts have sometimes developed the common law to allow C to bring a claim against A. Various methods have been employed: courts may find that B held A's promise on trust for C, or that there was a collateral contract between A and C, or that the principles of negligence, bailment, or agency can apply such that C's claim can succeed.

- As well as these common law developments, there is now a major statutory exception to the principle that C acquires no rights under a contract between A and B as a result of the Contracts (Rights of Third Parties) Act 1999. This Act operates alongside the common law and does not replace it. The application of the 1999 Act can be excluded by the parties at the time of contracting.

- Under the 1999 Act, a third party might be able to enforce a term of the contract if the contract expressly provides that he may, or if the relevant term purports to confer a benefit on him.

1 Introduction

There are two principal questions to be considered in this chapter:

(a) May a person who is not a party to a contract acquire rights under it?
(b) Can a contract impose duties on a person who is not a party to it?

Subject to some exceptions, the **common law** gave the answer 'No' to both these questions. So, if A, for consideration supplied by B, promised to do something for the benefit of C, then C acquired no rights at common law. If A failed to carry out his promise, he should be liable for a breach of contract with B but C would not have any claim. The common law generally held, subject to some exceptions, that C has no remedy. Moreover, B might be able to recover only nominal damages because B suffered no loss.[1] However, the Contracts (Rights of Third Parties) Act 1999 now creates a major exception to any rule that third parties to a contract cannot acquire rights under that contract. It is important to appreciate that the 1999 Act only affects the answer to the first question posed above: the statute has no impact upon the question of whether or not a contract between A and B can impose duties on C. As is explained in Section 11 of this chapter, the traditional rule that a contract cannot burden third parties continues to be maintained and is subject to very limited exceptions only. The more interesting issues concern whether or not C can gain any rights under a contract between A and B.

Most judgments will now commence with an analysis of the Act as this represents the most likely avenue for C to obtain satisfactory redress (and answers to problem questions in an exam should normally adopt the same approach!). However, in this chapter we will first consider the common law in order to understand the difficulties that the common law experienced and why the Act was such an important piece of legislation. Moreover, the rules developed by the common law remain important because:

(a) the Act does not apply to some classes of contract;

(b) the parties can always exclude the Act's operation if they wish; and

(c) the Act does not affect rights or remedies otherwise available under the common law, so the common law remains relevant and continues to apply in parallel to the Act.

2 Acquisition of rights by third parties

It is usually said that there are two principles involved in the acquisition of rights by third parties. The first is illustrated in Figure 10.1. This principle is commonly called 'privity of contract': only a **promisee** can enforce the promise. Imagine that A promises B, for consideration supplied by B, that he will do something for the benefit of C. Only A and B are 'privy' to that contract. Because C is not a promisee, and therefore not 'privy' to the contract, he has no right to enforce the promise.

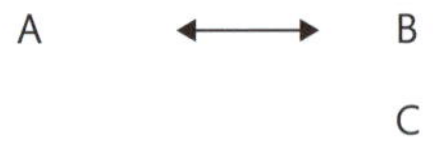

Figure 10.1

The second principle is illustrated in Figure 10.2. This principle provides that 'consideration must move from the promisee'. Imagine that A promises B *and* C, for consideration supplied by B, that he will do something for the benefit of C. C is a promisee but no consideration 'moved' from him, so C cannot enforce the promise. The arrows in Figure 10.2 illustrate the movement of consideration between A and B, but notice the one-way arrow between A and C: C provides no consideration to A.

---

[1] See Chapter 24.

Figure 10.2

C is no better off in the second case than the first. Since it is irrelevant whether he is a promisee or not, it is clear that the crucial principle is the second one: consideration must move from the promisee. Indeed, the first can scarcely be said to be a principle at all, since the operation of the second leaves no room for any independent application of the first. The rule of privity of contract is really no more than an application of the doctrine of consideration, which is why it is considered at this point. The leading cases support this theory. One that has been particularly influential is that of the Court of Queen's Bench in *Tweddle v Atkinson*.[2] After the claimant's marriage, his father (*B*) made a contract with the bride's father (*A*) under which each of them undertook to pay a sum of money to the claimant (*C*). It was a contract made by *A* and *B* for the benefit of *C*. *C* was not a promisee and he gave no consideration. *B* paid *C* as agreed, but *A* did not do so and later died. *A*'s failure to pay was, of course, a breach of contract with *B*. Although the agreement provided that *C* should have 'full power to sue' for the sums promised, *C*'s action against *A*'s **executor** failed. It failed not because *C* was not a promisee, but because *C* was, as Wightman J put it, 'a stranger to the consideration'. The judges appear to have thought it self-evident that *C* should have no right to sue *A* since consideration did not move from *C*. Crompton J thought that 'it would be a monstrous proposition to say that a person was a party to the contract for the purpose of suing upon it for his own advantage and not a party to it for the purpose of being sued'. This raises the question: why did *B* not sue? The answer possibly lies in the fact that *B* had suffered no loss (apart from losing the satisfaction of seeing a benefit accrue to his son) and so would have received only nominal damages.[3]

Of even greater importance is the decision of the House of Lords in *Dunlop Pneumatic Tyre Co Ltd v Selfridge*.[4] Dunlop sold its tyres to a wholesaler, Dew. In order to maintain the price of its tyres, Dunlop included a term in the contract of sale that required Dew to obtain an undertaking in writing from any trade customers to whom he resold the tyres. That undertaking provided that, in consideration of being allowed a discount off the list price of the tyres, the trade customers would observe the list price on any further resale to a consumer and would pay Dunlop £5 for every tyre sold in breach of that agreement. Dew sold a tyre to Selfridge and duly obtained the undertaking in favour of Dunlop from Selfridge. Selfridge sold the tyre in breach of this agreement and Dunlop sued for the £5. Figure 10.3 illustrates this.

Figure 10.3

---

[2] (1861) 1 B & S 393.
[3] This raises the difficult issue about whether *B* can recover for *C*'s loss: see Section 6(b) below.
[4] [1915] AC 847.

It seems clear that Dew was acting as agent for Dunlop in exacting from Selfridge the undertaking in Dunlop's favour, and five of the six judges in the House of Lords were prepared to accept this. So this might fairly be regarded as a case where the promise was made to *C* (Dunlop), as well as to *B* (Dew). But even so, this did not benefit Dunlop. Dunlop's action failed because Dunlop gave no consideration to Selfridge for the latter's promises to observe the list price and to pay Dunlop £5 if it failed to do so. A promise made to, and received by, one's agent is only as good as a promise made to oneself—and no better. Dunlop gave Selfridge no consideration for Selfridge's promises—and that was fatal.

It was argued that Dunlop gave consideration to Selfridge by allowing Selfridge to buy the tyres at a discount, since the tyres were sold below list price. But their Lordships had no difficulty in exposing the fallacy in that argument: the tyres belonged to Dew, and any reduction in the price charged to Selfridge came out of Dew's pocket, not Dunlop's.

The question in *Dunlop v Selfridge* could not arise in the same form today because resale price-maintenance agreements of that kind have been outlawed since the Resale Prices Act 1956, which has now been replaced by the Competition Act 1998; but this in no way impairs the authority of the case on the principles of the common law involved.

3 Is the rule that consideration must move from the promisee a myth?

It should, however, now be noted that it has been strenuously argued in recent years that, where there are joint promisees, one of them may sue even if the consideration was supplied exclusively by the other. If correct, this would mean that if the promise is made by *A* to both *B* and *C*, *C* may sue *A* even though only *B* supplied any consideration. This theory finds support in the *dicta* of four out of five judges of the High Court of Australia in *Coulls v Bagot's Executor and Trustee Co Ltd*,[5] and has also been favoured by distinguished academics[6] and, perhaps most importantly, by the Law Commission in its Report which led to the 1999 Act.[7] The Law Commission was clearly influenced by the fact that the rights of a promisee are more secure than third party rights under the 1999 Act.[8] This led the Law Commission to conclude that it would be absurd if a joint promisee were better off if he could argue that he was not a promisee and 'merely' a third party which could enjoy rights under the 1999 Act. If the Law Commission is right, then the rule that consideration must move from the promisee is a myth. But that is hard to believe. The 1999 Act will be analysed further below,[9] but on this issue of joint promisees it is important to note that, ultimately, the Law Commission left this matter for the common law to resolve. It remains to be seen whether the *dicta* in *Coulls* will be adopted in this jurisdiction.

---

[5] (1967) 119 CLR 460.

[6] eg P Atiyah, *Consideration in Contracts: A Fundamental Restatement* (Australian National University Press, 1971) 41–2; E Peel, *Treitel on the Law of Contract* (14th edn, Sweet & Maxwell, 2015) para 13-034. See *contra* B Coote, 'Consideration and Joint Promisees' (1978) 37 CLJ 300.

[7] Law Commission, *Privity of Contract: Contracts for the Benefit of Third Parties* (Law Com No 242, 1996), paras 6.9–6.12.

[8] See eg the Contracts (Rights of Third Parties) Act 1999, s 2, considered in Section 10(b).

[9] See Section 10.

4 Where consideration moves from both *B* and *C*

The previous section raised the issue of *A* making a promise to both *B* and *C*, but the consideration only moved from *B*. But it may be that, even if *A* is dealing exclusively with *B*, the consideration actually moves from both *B* and *C*. In such circumstances, *B* and *C* are both contracting parties. Where *B* deposits money in a bank account in the names of *B* and *C*, the consideration is given by both and either may sue the bank for failure to return the deposit or to pay the agreed amount of interest.[10] It is immaterial that the money deposited belongs to *B* alone, or, indeed to *C* alone. Who owns the money is simply none of the bank's business.

C is also a contracting party where *C* will be bound to supply the consideration if *B* does not, even though *A* might expect *B* to supply the consideration. For example, in *Lockett v Charles*, a woman was poisoned by a meal in a restaurant. Despite the fact that her husband had paid the bill and she had not, the woman successfully sued the restaurateur for breach of contract in supplying unfit food.[11] At the time of the case (1938), the restaurateur was no doubt looking to the husband for payment, but the source of the money was no more his business than the ownership of the deposit was that of the bank manager. If the husband had left without paying, it may confidently be expected that the restaurateur would have looked to the wife for payment. Even if she was undertaking only a contingent liability, that would be sufficient consideration.

5 A contract is not available to third parties as a defence

Dunlop v Selfridge and *Tweddle v Atkinson* concerned the question of whether *C* can sue *A* on a promise made by *A* in a contract with *B*. A related but slightly different question is: can *C* rely on that contract by way of a defence when he is sued by *A*? The answer is generally the same: *C*, having given no consideration to *A*, cannot rely on *A*'s promise by way of defence any more than he can use it to found a claim.

Since there is no contract between *A* and *C*, any cause of action *A* may have against *C* must be in tort. A duty of care may be imposed on *C* by the law of tort in relation to goods or other property belonging to *A*. If *C*, in breach of that duty of care, damages that property, *A* may sue *C* in the tort of negligence. For example, in the course of performing a contract between *A* and *B*, *A* may deliver goods to *B* who entrusts them to *C*. *C* then owes a duty to *A* to take reasonable care not to cause damage to the goods. Similarly, where *B*, in pursuance of his contract to do certain work on *A*'s premises, employs *C* as a subcontractor, *C* owes *A* a duty of care in respect of the premises. *C*'s duty of care in these examples is imposed by the general law (of tort) and not by the law of contract. The pertinent question is whether the existence of that duty, or the effect of a breach of it, can be affected by the contract between *A* and *B*.

---

[10] cf *McEvoy v Belfast Banking Corporation* [1935] AC 24, HL.
[11] *Lockett v Charles* [1938] 4 All ER 170, KBD. See too *Olley v Marlborough Court* [1949] 1 KB 532, CA (discussed further in Chapter 15) where a wife's action against a hotel succeeded even though the husband booked the accommodation and paid the bill.

The leading case remains *Scruttons Ltd v Midland Silicones Ltd.*[12] This decision of the House of Lords holds that, at common law, *C* cannot 'take advantage' of a contract between *A* and *B* by way of defence. This mirrors the principle that *C* cannot sue upon that contract either. *Scruttons* was a case about a contract for the carriage of goods by sea and, in order to understand the case properly, some special rules have to be explained. When a person (the shipper) sends goods, he receives a written document known as a **bill of lading**. The bill of lading is signed on behalf of the shipowner (or carrier), acknowledging receipt of the goods and undertaking to deliver them at the end of the voyage, subject to the **conditions** contained in the bill. There is some debate about whether the bill actually is the contract of carriage or only evidence of its terms, but that is not important for present purposes. The shipper delivers the bill of lading to the **consignee** and this enables the consignee to obtain possession of the goods at the end of the voyage. Not only does the delivery of the bill of lading transfer the ownership in the goods from the shipper to the consignee, it also transfers the contractual relationship with the carrier from shipper to consignee. Section 1 of the Bills of Lading Act 1855 provided that the consignee to whom the property passes 'shall have transferred to and vested in him all rights of **suit**, and be subject to the same liabilities in respect of such goods as if the contract contained in the bill of lading had been made with himself', and this language has been replicated in section 2(1) of the Carriage of Goods by Sea Act 1992. The consignee steps into the shipper's contractual shoes so that, in cases of the type considered here, the one is equated with the other. Of immediate importance are cases which also involve a second contract—one made by the carrier with a firm of **stevedores** to load or unload the goods on to or from the ship. The position may be represented as follows in Figure 10.4

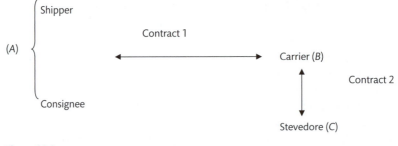

Figure 10.4

In *Scruttons*, the contract between the shipper and the carrier (contract 1) included a clause which limited the liability of the carrier to $500. The contract between the carrier and the stevedore (contract 2) also contained a clause limiting the liability of the stevedore to $500. In the course of performing its contractual obligations with the carrier, the stevedore negligently dropped the shipper's goods, which caused damage totalling $593. The stevedore owed a duty of care to the owners of the goods he was handling, so the shipper

---

[12] [1962] AC 446, HL.

sued him in the tort of negligence. The stevedore argued that his liability should be limited to $500 but his difficulty should be readily apparent. There were two contracts limiting liability but, on the face of it, no contract between the shipper and the stevedore and therefore no term as between the shipper and the stevedore which limited the latter's liability. The stevedore was therefore held liable for the full amount. The stevedore tried to rely upon contract 1, but that failed because the stevedore was not a party to that contract. He had not been asked for, and had not given, any consideration to the shipper.

Even Lord Denning, who dissented, agreed that the stevedore could not rely on contract 1. Unlike the rest of the House, however, Lord Denning thought that the stevedore would have been entitled to rely on that contract if it had stated clearly that the exclusion clause applied for the protection of the stevedore as well as the carrier. It did not. But in any event, even if it had done so, that would have made no difference for the majority, given the absence of consideration moving from stevedore to shipper.[13] Nevertheless, Lord Denning also invoked a different principle, which the majority did not say anything about. Lord Denning thought that the stevedore could rely on contract 2. The carrier is a **bailee** of the shipper's goods and it is a special feature of the law of **bailment** that the **bailor** is bound by any contract which he has expressly or impliedly authorised the bailee to make in relation to the goods. The shipper of goods may be presumed to know that the carrier will have to make contracts with stevedores for the loading and unloading of the goods, so he should be bound by the terms of any exclusion clause in such a contract.

This argument was not mentioned by the majority, but Lord Denning reiterated it in *Morris v Martin*[14] and it now has powerful support, having been applied by the Privy Council in *The Pioneer Container*[15] and approved in *The Mahkutai*.[16] In *The Pioneer Container*, the claimants (A) contracted with carriers (B) for the carriage of A's goods from Taiwan to Hong Kong by bills of lading which provided that B was entitled to subcontract 'on any terms' the whole or any part of the carriage. B subcontracted the carriage to the defendants (C) on bills of lading which provided that the contract was governed by Chinese law and any dispute was to be determined in Taiwan ('the exclusive jurisdiction clause'). The ship sank and the question was whether A could sue C in Hong Kong. It was accepted that there was no contract between A and C, but the Hong Kong Court of Appeal held that A was bound by the exclusive jurisdiction clause. The Privy Council, applying the principle stated by Lord Denning in *Morris v Martin*, dismissed A's appeal. C became a bailee of the goods for reward[17] and both A and B had, concurrently, the rights of a bailor against C. The obligation owed by C to A (as well as to B) was that of a bailee for reward, even though the reward was payable not by A but by B. It would be inconsistent to impose on the bailee two different standards of care in respect of the goods entrusted to him.

---

[13] Because the stevedore was not identified in contract 1, either individually or as a member of a class, he could not, as we shall see in Section 10(a), now rely on the 1999 Act; but, if he had been so identified, he would be able to do so.

[14] *Morris v CW Martin & Sons Ltd* [1966] 1 QB 716, CA (see Section 11).

[15] *The Pioneer Container* [1994] 2 AC 324, PC.

[16] *The Mahkutai* [1996] 3 All ER 502, PC.

[17] A bailee for reward (ie consideration) owes a higher obligation than a gratuitous bailee.

The reasoning in *The Pioneer Container* is compelling. It could, arguably, be suggested that the failure of the majority in *Scruttons* to consider the law of bailment means that that case was decided **per incuriam**. However, since decisions of the Privy Council are not binding on English courts, *Scruttons* does remain the law of this jurisdiction, pending any reconsideration by the Supreme Court or Parliament.

In the meantime, however, other decisions of the Privy Council have avoided the effect of *Scruttons* by taking a rather strained view of the facts. One example of this is *The Eurymedon*.[18] The facts were very similar to those in *Scruttons* with the important difference that the bill of lading stated that the exemptions contained in it should extend to protect agents of the carrier including independent contractors—like stevedores.[19] That would certainly have been enough for Lord Denning, but apparently not for the other judges in *Scruttons*, since there remained the vital question of consideration. The Privy Council overcame this difficulty by finding that the shipper was, in effect, saying to the stevedore, through the shipper's agent, the carrier, 'If you will load (or unload) my goods, I undertake that your liability will be limited ...' Now, if this really happened, the matter was in fact quite straightforward, since there was a third contract—a 'collateral contract'[20]—between shipper and stevedore. When sued, the stevedore was relying on that contract, to which he was in fact privy and not merely a third party. He had supplied consideration by doing the act requested, namely the loading or unloading of the ship. The difficulty, of course, is to conclude that this accords with the reality of the case. Viscount Dilhorne and Lord Simon of Glaisdale, dissenting, were unable to do so. The dissenting judges held that the clause in the bill of lading was not an offer to the stevedores but an agreement between the shipper and the carrier; there was in fact no request to the stevedore or any action by him in reliance on the promise. This seems to be the true view of the facts but it is nonetheless a minority view and it is the fiction which prevails.

The Eurymedon was followed by the Privy Council in *The New York Star*,[21] and, even though these decisions are not technically binding on English courts, it is likely that they will be followed. Indeed, this approach in *The Eurymedon* was approved by the House of Lords in *The Starsin*.[22] The cases were 'explained' in *The Mahkutai* on the basis that an agreement between the stevedores and the shippers, entered into through the agency of the shipowners, may, even though initially unsupported by consideration, later become enforceable by the consideration supplied by the stevedores actually performing their duties. The Privy Council indicated that the time may come when the courts take 'the final, and perhaps inevitable step in this development and recognise in these cases a fully fledged exception to the doctrine of privity of contract'.[23] This would be better than indulging the fictions relied upon by the majority in *The Eurymedon*. Nevertheless, it is important to note that, on their own terms, these fictions do not create any exceptions to the doctrine

---

[18] *New Zealand Shipping Co Ltd v AM Satterthwaite & Co Ltd, The Eurymedon* [1975] AC 154, PC.

[19] If this sufficiently identified the stevedore company as a member of a class, it could now rely on the 1999 Act, enjoying the double protection of contracts 1 and 3.

[20] See Chapter 11, Section 3.

[21] *Port Jackson Stevedoring Pty Ltd v Salmond & Spraggon Pty (Australia) Ltd, The New York Star* [1981] 1 WLR 138.

[22] *Homburg Houtimport BV v Agrosin Private Ltd, The Starsin* [2003] UKHL 12, [2004] 1 AC 715.

[23] [1996] 3 All ER 512.

of privity or the rule that consideration must move from the promisee. The stevedore is protected because he is held, however artificially, to be a party to a contract and to have given consideration. This is well illustrated by Figure 10.5. The better view now seems to be that there could be a unilateral contract between the shipper and the stevedore:[24] in effect, the shipper promises the stevedore that if the stevedore loads or unloads the goods, the stevedore's liability will be limited. The stevedore provides consideration to support the shipper's promise by actually loading or unloading the goods.

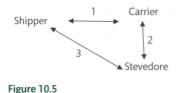

Figure 10.5

One case that is difficult to reconcile with the above analysis is *Norwich City Council v Harvey and others*.[25] *A* employed contractors, *B*, to extend a swimming pool. The contract, by clause 20, provided that the risk of damage by fire should lie with *A* and required *A* to maintain adequate insurance. *B* subcontracted roofing work to *C2*. The subcontract referred to clause 20 of the main contract and stated that it would apply. *C2*'s employee, *C1*, negligently set fire to the building. *A* sued both *C1* and *C2* in the tort of negligence. However, *A*'s claims failed. The justice of the result is obvious. Presumably *A* fulfilled its obligation to insure and was compensated by its insurers, whereas *C2*, reasonably relying on clause 20, may have thought it quite unnecessary to insure. The claim in the case was therefore really brought for the benefit of *A*'s insurers, and if the claim had succeeded it may have been disastrous for *C1* and *C2*. Indeed, the workman, *C1*, could not have been expected to know of the existence of clause 20; but he might reasonably have supposed that his employer would have taken adequate precautions regarding insurance. So the outcome of the case therefore seems satisfactory.

However, the Court of Appeal dismissed *A*'s claim on the ground that the defendants owed no duty of care to *A*, and that is much more difficult to accept. It is therefore easier to be satisfied of the justice of the result than of the legal principles or of how it is to be distinguished from the leading cases. Somewhat strangely, *Scruttons* was cited in argument in the *Norwich* case but not mentioned in the judgment. In the *Norwich* case, the contract between *A* and *B* established the defence to *C* which failed in *Scruttons*, and did so without resort to the artificial device of the third contract on which *C* succeeded in *The Eurymedon*. Why? One possible answer is that the *Norwich* case was wrongly decided. But it was so obviously just that a court might be reluctant to depart from the case so brusquely. One potential distinction is that, in the shipping cases, there was no question of the contract between *A* and *B* *negativing* *C*'s duty of care, because if the relevant clauses affected *C*'s liability at all, they merely limited it—in other words, in the shipping cases, they assumed

---

[24] See eg ibid, [196]–[197] (Lord Millett), [147]–[153] (Lord Hobhouse), [93] (Lord Hoffmann); cf [34] (Lord Bingham).
[25] [1989] 1 WLR 828, CA.

that *C did* owe a duty of care to *A* and that *C* was, indeed, in breach of it. This was not the same in the *Norwich* case. It would, however, be a strange law which allowed the contract to which *C* is not a party to negative his liability altogether, but not to limit it. The analogy of a principle governing the interpretation of exclusion clauses would in fact suggest the opposite result.[26] The decision in the *Norwich* case remains very difficult to explain satisfactorily.

6 Enforcement of the contract by a contracting party for the benefit of a third party

When *A* and *B* have made a contract under which *A*, for consideration supplied by *B*, has made some promise for the benefit of *C*, and *A* then withholds that benefit, *A* commits a breach of contract with *B*. What can *B* do to enforce the contract? There are three possibilities.

(a) *B* might obtain a decree of **specific performance**[27] against *A* and so compel him to confer the benefit on *C*.

(b) *B* might sue *A* for damages for breach of his contract to confer the benefit on *C*.

(c) Where *A* is taking action against *C* in breach of his contract with *B*, *B* might seek an **injunction** to restrain him from doing so.

Each of these possibilities will be considered in turn. It is important to emphasise at the outset that these options are available to *B* as a party to the contract; if *B* decides not to bring a claim against *A*, *C* cannot force *B* to do so.[28]

(a) **Specific performance**

The first possibility outlined refers to specific performance. If the contract between *A* and *B* belongs to that limited class of contracts for which specific performance is available,[29] *B* may, if he chooses, sue *A* and obtain an order from the court that compels *A* to perform the contract in favour of *C*. Once the order has been obtained, *C* is able to enforce it himself. The leading case is *Beswick v Beswick*.[30] Peter Beswick (*B*), entered into a contract with his nephew (*A*) under which he **assigned** to *A* his business of coal merchant in consideration of *A* employing him as a consultant for the rest of his life and paying an annuity to *B*'s widow, *C*, after his death. After *B*'s death, *A* declined to pay the annuity to *C*. *C* sued as the **administratrix** of her husband's, *B*'s, estate and obtained a decree of specific performance. Ignoring (as the courts did) the element of personal service (the 'consultancy'), the contract was one which was specifically enforceable by either *A* or *B* during *B*'s lifetime and it

---

[26] See Chapter 15, Section 1(b)(i).
[27] See Chapter 28, Section 7.
[28] Unless *B* is a trustee for *C*: see Section 8.
[29] See Chapter 28, Section 7.
[30] [1968] AC 58, HL.

continued to be specifically enforceable after his death. As *B*'s administratrix, *C* stood in *B*'s shoes for legal purposes, and was able to exercise all his legal rights. It was thus a case where the legal personalities of *B* and *C* were combined in the one person, *C*.

It is important, however, to appreciate the limitations of the decision in *Beswick v Beswick*. It applies only where the contract between *A* and *B* is of a kind which is specifically enforceable. If it had been a true contract for personal services it would not have been specifically enforceable and the action must have failed. For example, if *B*, a famous painter, contracts with *A* to paint *A*'s portrait in consideration of *A*'s undertaking to pay an annuity to *B*'s widow, *C*, then *C* will not be able to obtain specific performance, even as the deceased *B*'s **personal representative**. This is because *A* could not have obtained such a decree during *B*'s lifetime and so, the remedy being 'mutual', *B* could not have obtained specific performance either.[31] Importantly, *C* could be in no better position that *B* himself, so *C* would similarly be unable to compel *A* to perform the contract.

Most significantly, perhaps, it is crucial to note that *Beswick v Beswick* does not provide any remedy for *C* personally. From the widow's point of view, it was a happy accident that she was her late husband's personal representative and so able to enforce his rights. If the deceased *B* had appointed an executor who had declined to sue for *C*'s benefit, it seems that *C* would have had no redress. If (as was not the case) *B* had died **insolvent** and his **creditors** were pressing for payment, it is possible that it would have been the duty of *B*'s personal representative to compromise the contract with *A*—'I will release you from your obligation to pay the annuity to *C* in return for £100'—in order to provide more money to meet the legitimate claims of *B*'s creditors. After all, *B*, during his lifetime, could have **rescinded** the contract by agreement with *A*, so *B*'s personal representative should have been able to do so after *B*'s death. Indeed, it may even have been the personal representative's duty to do so. In any event, on the facts of *Beswick v Beswick*, *C* had no personal right to recover the annuity at common law, as she did not provide any consideration for *A*'s promise. However, *C* would now be able to enforce the contract in her own right under the 1999 Act.[32]

(b) **Recovery of damages**

The law regarding recovery of damages is more problematic than specific performance. There is no doubt, of course, that by failing to confer the promised benefit on *C*, *A* has broken his contract with *B*. It follows that *B* is entitled to damages. The question is, how much and for whose benefit? One view is that *B* is entitled only to nominal damages because *B* has suffered no loss. For example, in *West v Houghton*[33] the lessor of shooting rights (*B*) sought damages for breach of a **covenant** by the **lessee** (*A*) to keep down the rabbits so that no appreciable damage would be done on the estate. Damage had been done by the rabbits, to the detriment of *C*, the **tenant** of the land. *A* had committed a breach of his contract with *B*, but the Divisional Court held that *B* had suffered no loss and so was entitled only to nominal damages. However, the outcome would have been different if *B* had been under

[31] See Chapter 28, Section 7.
[32] See Section 10.
[33] (1879) 4 CPD 197, DC.

a duty to *C* to keep the rabbits down and that fact had been brought to the attention of *A* before he entered into the covenant.

To return to *Beswick v Beswick*, the question of damages was considered by the judges. In the Court of Appeal, Lord Denning was adamant that *A* could not escape from his obligation 'by such a shifty means' as an allegation that *B* had suffered only nominal damages. In Lord Denning's view, *B* should be able to recover the money which should have been paid to *C*, for *C*'s benefit. But this is doubtful, and was not supported in the House of Lords. However, Lord Pearce, agreeing with Windeyer J in the Australian case of *Coulls v Bagot's Executor*,[34] thought that the damages which *B* would suffer on *A*'s failure to pay a promised £500 to *C* would not be merely nominal; they might be less or more than £500.

Unlike Lord Denning, though, Lord Pearce was talking about the damages that *B* (not *C*) would suffer. It is difficult to see what the basis of assessment for *B*'s damages would be. Is it the loss of satisfaction which *B* would have derived from the benefit to *C*? That is not the kind of loss for which contractual damages are usually awarded, and it would be difficult to estimate realistically.[35] Or is it the value of the consideration which *B* has given to *A* in return for *A*'s promise to benefit *C*? As a result of this breach, that has become a wasted expenditure and damages are sometimes recoverable for wasted expenditure.[36] There is no certain answer to these questions, but in *Woodar Investments Development Ltd v Wimpey Construction UK Ltd*,[37] the House of Lords made clear its opinion that *B* cannot recover the loss sustained by *C*. *B* had agreed to sell land to *A* in consideration of *A* paying £750,000 to *B* and £150,000 to *C*. The Court of Appeal had held that *A* had breached this contract, and that *B* was entitled to recover damages not only for its own loss but also that of *C*. As it ultimately turned out, the House of Lords held that there had been no breach of contract by *A*; but, if there had been, *B* would not have been entitled to recover damages for the loss sustained by *C*. Whether *B* could recover any more than nominal damages was 'a question of great doubt and difficulty' according to Lord Wilberforce. It still awaits resolution.[38]

(i) Exceptions to any rule that *B* cannot recover for damage sustained by *C*

If there is a rule that *B* can recover only nominal damages where *A* has failed to perform a contract to benefit *C* and *B* has suffered no loss, the common law recognises some exceptions to it.

Where *B* and *C* each has an insurable interest in goods and *B* takes out a policy with *A* covering the insurable interests of both *B* and *C*, then *B* may sue on the policy for *C*'s loss (for which *B* must account to *C*) as well as his own loss. In *A Tomlinson (Hauliers) Ltd v Hepburn*,[39] *B* (the hauliers) contracted to carry two lorry-loads of cigarettes belonging to *C* (Hepburn) and to insure them comprehensively. Without any fault on *B*'s part, the cigarettes were stolen. *B*'s insurer, *A*, argued that the policy covered only such liability

---

[34] (1967) 40 ALJR 471, 486.
[35] See Chapter 26, Section 4.
[36] See Chapter 26, Section 7.
[37] [1980] 1 WLR 277, HL.
[38] See too Chapter 26, Section 8.
[39] [1966] AC 451.

as *B* might incur to *C*, and since *B* was not at fault, *B* had not incurred any liability to *C*. Nevertheless, the court held that *B* could recover the full value of the goods and had to account for them to *C*.

In a commercial contract, the parties, *A* and *B*, may well contemplate that the proprietary interest in goods might be transferred from *B* to *C* after the contract has been entered into. For instance, *A* may enter into a contract with *B* to transport specific goods, and both *A* and *B* expect that *B* will sell those goods to *C* before the contract is performed. If that happens, and *A* subsequently commits a breach of contract which causes loss or damage to goods now belonging to *C*, *B* may recover the loss sustained by *C*. This principle derives from the leading decision of the House of Lords in *The Albazero*.[40]

Where *A* contracts with *B* to erect buildings on *C*'s land and the work is defective, *B*, who has suffered no loss, may recover damages for the loss sustained by *C*.[41] Recognition of this principle was partly motivated by a desire to avoid a 'legal black hole' that might arise if *A* did not have to pay a substantial sum either to *B*, since *B* suffered no loss, or to *C*, since *C* had no right of action: it would be unsatisfactory for construction companies not to have to pay out when their breach of contract caused loss. However, where *A* had **executed** a deed in favour of *C* which gave *C* a direct remedy for *A*'s failure to exercise reasonable care, the principle allowing *B* to recover for *C*'s loss was excluded.[42]

Some eminent judges, however, would base these decisions on a broader ground: they are not exceptions but examples of a general principle that *B*, far from being limited to nominal damages, is entitled to compensation for loss of his bargain—*B* should be able to recover substantial damages for *B*'s own loss, not for any loss suffered by *C*. In *Linden Gardens*, Lord Griffiths put the case of a husband (*B*) who contracts with a builder (*A*) to repair the roof of the matrimonial home, which is owned by *B*'s wife. When the repair is botched, *B* has suffered financial loss 'because he has to spend money to give him the benefit of the bargain which the defendant had promised but failed to deliver'. This theory would cover not only the case where performance was defective, but also situations where *A* fails to perform at all and *B* has to pay a higher price to the second builder. Lords Goff and Millett favoured this 'broad ground' in *Panatown*. Lord Clyde, on the other hand, thought that, while a breach of contract may cause a loss, a breach of contract is not itself a loss in any meaningful sense. And if *B* were truly recovering damages for his own loss, he would be under no obligation to use the damages for the benefit of *C*. This has been referred to as the 'narrow ground'.

Lord Goff gave the example of a philanthropist (*B*) who undertakes to renovate the village hall, owned by **trustees**, at his own expense. He contracts with a builder (*A*) who does defective work. *B* recovers damages. In Lord Goff's opinion, *B* could not keep the damages for himself, leaving the hall in its defective state. It would be implicit in the **licence** to renovate the hall that, if the work was begun, he would take reasonable steps to procure its satisfactory completion. This somewhat blurs the distinction as to whether *B* recovers for *B*'s own loss or that suffered by the third party, *C*—in this example, the trustees of the

---

[40] *The Albazero* [1977] AC 774, HL.

[41] *Linden Gardens Trust Ltd v Lenesta Sludge Disposals Ltd* [1994] 1 AC 85.

[42] *Panatown Ltd v Alfred McAlpine Construction Ltd* [2000] 4 All ER 97, HL.

village hall. The controversy in this area remains unresolved, and is discussed further in Chapter 28: whether *B*'s loss of performance of the agreed bargain is a loss which can be valued, such that substantial damages are awarded, raises broader issues than those which concern third parties.[43] In *Panatown*, the 'broad ground' only received explicit support from Lord Goff and Lord Millett and therefore it cannot be said clearly to represent the law: Lord Browne-Wilkinson was ambiguous, and Lord Clyde and Lord Jauncey favoured the 'narrow ground' whereby *B* recovers on behalf of *C*. However, even if the 'broad ground' were to be accepted, it nevertheless seems important to avoid *A*'s having to compensate both *B* on the 'broad ground' approach and *C* on a separate basis. This perhaps explains the ultimate decision in *Panatown* that *B* could not recover where *C* could sue *A* under a separate contract, especially because where *C* has a direct claim against *A* there is no danger of damages disappearing down a 'legal black hole'. It may therefore be that the result in *Panatown* would have been the same if *C* had a direct claim against *A* not under a separate contract but rather under the 1999 Act, for instance.[44]

(ii) *B*'s damages affected by effect on *C*

Sometimes, however, when determining the amount of the loss sustained by *B* it may be proper to consider the effect of the breach of contract on *C*. In *Jackson v Horizon Holidays*,[45] the claimant (*B*) entered into a contract with the defendants (*A*) for a holiday for himself and his family (*C*). It was a disaster. Reversing the trial judge, the Court of Appeal held that the damages should include the distress to the claimant's wife and two small children, as well as to himself. Lord Denning took the view that *B* was recovering damages on their behalf. However, in *Woodar v Wimpey*, the House of Lords, while agreeing with the amount of damages awarded in *Jackson*, considered that they were damages for loss sustained by the husband, *B*. Lord Russell said, '[*B*] had bought and paid for a high class family holiday; he did not get it, and therefore he was entitled to substantial damages for the failure to supply *him* with one.'[46]

(c) **Injunction to restrain breach**

If *A*, for consideration supplied by *B*, has undertaken that, in certain circumstances, he will not sue *C* and, those circumstances having arisen, nevertheless proceeds to do so, *B* may be able to obtain an injunction to restrain *A* from breaking his contract.

In *Gore v Van der Lann*,[47] Liverpool Corporation (*B*) gave Gore, a 'retirement pensioner' (*A*), a 'free pass' for their buses in consideration of *A* agreeing (amongst other things) that neither the corporation nor its servants or agents should be liable to *A* for any injury, however caused. *A* was injured by (she alleged) the negligence of Van der Lann (*C*), a bus conductor employed by the corporation. *A* therefore sued *C*. The corporation applied for a **stay**

---

[43] See Chapter 28, Section 8.
[44] cf *Catline Estates v Carter Jonas* [2005] EWHC 2315 (TCC), [2006] PNLR 15 [302]–[304] (HHJ Toulmin QC).
[45] [1975] 1 WLR 1468, CA.
[46] Emphasis in original.
[47] [1967] 2 QB 31.

of the action on the ground that, by bringing her claim, the retirement pensioner, *A*, was defrauding the corporation, *B*. On the particular facts of the case, the corporation failed because the grant of the pass was 'a contract for the conveyance of a passenger in a public service vehicle' and section 151 of the Road Traffic Act 1960 (now the Public Passenger Vehicles Act 1981, s 29) renders void any term in such a contract which purports to exclude liability for bodily injury. *A* was therefore not acting in breach of her contract with *B* in bringing the action against *C*.

However, Willmer LJ gave two additional reasons why the action failed. First, although *A* had agreed with *B* that *C* should not be liable, there was no express promise by *A* not to sue *C*. Secondly, since it had not been proved that *B* was liable to indemnify *C* against any damages *C* might have to pay *A*, *B* had no sufficient interest entitling it to relief. This, however, was *obiter*, and does not seem to have been followed in *Snelling v John G Snelling Ltd*.[48] In that case, Ormrod J decided in favour of *B* even though there was no express promise by *A*. Three brothers, *A*, *B1*, and *B2*, had each loaned money to a company, Snelling Ltd (*C*). The brothers entered into a contract by which each brother promised that, if any one of them resigned his directorship of the company, he would **forfeit** the money owed to him by the company, and the remaining directors would use the money to pay off a loan made to the company by a separate finance company. *A* resigned and, in breach of that contract, sued *C* for repayment of his loan. Ormrod J held that *B1* and *B2* were entitled to a declaration that *A* was bound by the agreement. Although *C* was not a party to the agreement and was not entitled to rely on it, the judge held that a declaration should be granted that *A* was not entitled to call upon *C* to repay the loan. As a result, *A*'s action against *C* was dismissed. Ormrod J said that, notwithstanding *Gore*'s case, it was not essential that *A* should have expressly promised not to sue *C*. It is sufficient that such a promise is a necessary implication. That must surely be right. There is no material difference between *A*'s agreeing, as in *Gore*'s case, that *C* is 'not to be liable' to *A*, and *A*'s agreeing not to sue *C*. Once again, it should be noted that *C* has no personal right to rely on the contract between *A* and *B*: he is dependent on the willingness of *B* to intervene to protect him from action by *A*.[49]

7 The third party's right to receive and to retain a benefit

Although *C* has no right to recover the benefit which *A* and *B* have contracted to bestow on him, once *C* has received that benefit, it belongs to him. *B*, by giving consideration to *A*, has paid for the benefit, so it is a **gift** to *C*. Once a gift is completely constituted, it cannot be undone by the donor.[50]

Moreover, where the contract between *A* and *B* is that *A* shall confer a benefit on *C*, *B* has no right to prevent *A* from carrying out the contract and conferring the benefit. He may,

---

[48] [1973] QB 87.

[49] Comparison may, however, be made with *Hirachand Punamchand v Temple*, see Chapter 7, Section 1(f), where *C*, the **debtor**, was able to invoke the contract between *A*, the creditor, and *B*, on the ground that *A*'s action was a fraud on *B*, even though there was no intervention by *B*.

[50] Unless *A*'s intent has been vitiated due to a factor such as undue influence: see Chapter 18.

of course, invite *A* to rescind the contract and, if *A* agrees to do so, *C* will not receive the benefit and he has no redress.[51] But if *A* declines to rescind and insists on performing, any attempt by *B* to prevent *A* from carrying out the contract by conferring the benefit on *C* will be a breach of contract by *B* and perhaps a tort or even a crime.

These principles are stated in *Re Schebsmann*.[52] *B*, on his retirement from a company, *A*, entered into a contract with *A* by which *A* agreed to pay a sum of money to *B* by annual instalments for a given period of time and, if *B* died during that period, to make the payments to *B*'s widow, *C*. *B* died insolvent before all the instalments were paid. *B*'s trustee in **bankruptcy**, who inherited all *B*'s legal rights, sought a declaration that the money payable by *A* belonged to *B*'s estate and should therefore be available for *B*'s creditors. The action failed. *A* was entitled to perform the contract and pay *C*. During his lifetime, *B* could have rescinded the contract by agreement with *A*, but he had no right unilaterally to terminate or change it. *B*'s trustee in bankruptcy could be in no better position than *B* was in. The court rejected an argument that, because *B* had supplied the consideration for it, *C* held the money on a resulting trust for *B*'s estate. The contract was that the money should be paid by *A* to *C* for her own benefit and, if the court had prevented that from happening, it would have been assisting in a breach of contract, which was clearly inappropriate.

8　Privity and trusts of contractual obligations

If *A* transfers property to *B*, who agrees to hold that property on trust for *C*, *C* acquires an equitable interest in the property. *C* has given no consideration, but he has acquired enforceable rights under the trust. This is because he is not merely the recipient of a promise but has acquired a proprietary interest in the property as a beneficiary under a trust. In **equity**, the gift to him is complete, such that *C* might be called the 'equitable owner'. His rights are not dependent on someone doing what they have promised to do; they exist because of something already done. This *A*–*B*–*C* situation is quite similar to that already discussed in this chapter in relation to contracts which do not involve trusts. In fact, if we were able to say more generally that *B* was a trustee for *C*, such that *C* acquired enforceable rights under the trust, many perceived deficiencies in the law concerning privity of contract would be overcome (see Figure 10.6). However, it is only in very limited circumstances that the courts will find a trust to have been created in these sorts of cases.

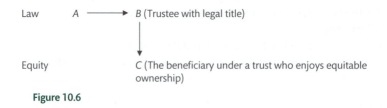

Law　　　　A ⟶ B (Trustee with legal title)

Equity　　　　C (The beneficiary under a trust who enjoys equitable ownership)

Figure 10.6

---

[51]　Subject now to section 2 of the 1999 Act: see Section 10(b).
[52]　[1944] Ch 83, CA.

In order to have a trust, we have to find some property which *B* holds on trust and in which *C* has an equitable interest. The most obvious possibility is the contractual right which *B* has against *A*: the right is a **chose in action**, or a 'thing in action', and therefore a type of intangible property which can be held on trust. If *B* does hold the contractual right on trust for *C*, then *B*, as trustee, is bound to exercise that contractual right for *C*'s benefit and to hold any property which accrues from it on trust for *C*. *C*, as the equitable owner, may insist on *B*'s doing so.

It is therefore possible to find that the contractual promise is the subject matter of the trust, and, in the past, the courts have been willing to utilise the trust device in this way. For example, in *Les Affréteurs Réunis Société Anonyme v Leopold Walford (London) Ltd*,[53] *A*, a shipowner, entered into a contract to **charter** a ship to *B* and undertook to pay a commission to a **broker**, *C*. *C* was not a party to the contract. Nevertheless, it was held that *C* was entitled to recover the commission from *A*. *B* had contracted as trustee for *C* and held on trust the contractual obligation owed by *A* to pay money to *C*. As trustee, *B* could have sued for the agreed sum. There would have been no question of his being limited to nominal damages because he would not have been claiming for any loss *he* had suffered. He would have been getting in the trust property. As *C* could have required *B* to take this action, it was held that *C* could proceed personally and recover the commission directly from *A*.

This decision might appear to suggest a readily available solution to what otherwise might be manifest injustice. However, in effect, this trust-based solution has largely been discarded by the courts since the decision of the Privy Council in *Vandepitte v Preferred Accident Insurance Corporation of New York*,[54] in which Lord Wright stated that 'the intention to constitute a trust must be affirmatively proved'. This is likely to be difficult because rarely will there be, in truth, any such intention. There will frequently be formidable reasons for saying that no trust was intended. Prominent among these is the fact that, if *A* and *B* have set up a trust for *C*, they have put it out of their power to rescind or vary their contract: *C* has vested equitable rights, and *A* and *B* cannot deprive *C* of such rights without *C*'s consent. In most cases, it is highly improbable that *A* and *B* intended to put it out of their power to rescind or vary their contract, and it therefore follows that they did *not* intend to set up a trust. In *Re Schebsmann*,[55] for example, an argument that there was a trust for *C* was rejected since *B* might have wished, during his lifetime, to vary the arrangement if his wife, *C*, had gone off with another man. Unless he intended to put it out of his power to do so, he did not intend to create a trust in favour of *C*. This point strongly influenced the court in its decision that there was no trust.

If the exact facts of *Walford*'s case were to recur today, *C* could probably invoke the 1999 Act. But, whether that is so or not, he could rely on his right as a beneficiary under a trust, so the utility of the trust concept in this area cannot be said to be entirely defunct.[56] Indeed, *C* might prefer to assert his rights as a beneficiary under a trust rather than under the 1999 Act since his rights under the 1999 Act may be lost if *A* and *B* decide to vary the contract,[57]

[53] [1919] AC 801, HL.
[54] [1933] AC 70.
[55] Discussed in Section 7.
[56] See eg *Nisshin Shipping Co Ltd v Cleaves & Co Ltd* [2003] EWHC 2602 (Comm), [2004] 1 Lloyd's Rep 38.
[57] See Section 10(b).

whereas this cannot occur if a trust has already been fully constituted. However, affirmative evidence that B was contracting as trustee for C is required. If B declared to C that he was so contracting, then no doubt a trust would arise on the conclusion of the contract.

9 Some exceptions

Some cases which are often treated as if they were exceptions to the rule of privity of contract are not true exceptions. *The Eurymedon* and *The New York Star*[58] do not create exceptions because the courts found, however deviously and improbably, that there was a separate contract between the shipper and the stevedore. This analysis also explains the cases on 'collateral contracts', such as *Shanklin v Detel Products*,[59] considered in Chapter 11. In all these cases, C is found to be a contracting party with A, and sues on that contract to which he is privy. Such decisions do not therefore allow C to sue as a third party to a contract between A and B. C is suing in a different capacity—as a party to a collateral contract with A.

Trust cases, such as *Walford*'s case, are sometimes regarded as true exceptions to the privity doctrine, but should be viewed as not relying upon principles of contract law but distinct principles of the law of trusts. The basis of *Walford*'s case is therefore not really contract law but trusts law. As a result, it might be thought that contract law doctrine is not much affected. Similarly, the fact that in some very unusual circumstances C might be able to sue A in the tort of negligence, despite the existence of a contract between A and B, need not be seen as an exception to the doctrine of privity of contract but as the application of a distinct body of law which relies upon its own rules and principles.[60]

Another commonly cited exception to the principle of privity of contract is the rule in the *Elder Dempster* case[61] that, in a contract of carriage between the shipper of goods, A, and the charterer of a ship, B, a clause in the bill of lading providing that 'the shipowners' should not be liable for any damage is effective to protect not only B (who is a 'shipowner' for this purpose) but also the actual shipowner, C, who chartered the ship to B. Lord Denning attempted to use this decision to undermine the whole doctrine of privity of contract. However, in *Scruttons*, the House of Lords rejected Lord Denning's manoeuvres: Lord Reid concluded that the case was 'an anomalous and unexplained exception to the general principle that a stranger cannot rely for his protection on provisions in a contract to which he is not a party'.[62] Other judges condemned the decision as 'a judicial nightmare'[63] and 'heavily comatosed, if not long interred',[64] but it appears now to have been rehabilitated and is regarded as properly decided on the ground that the shippers impliedly

---

[58] See Section 5.

[59] See Chapter 11, Section 3.

[60] See eg *Junior Books v Veitchi* [1983] 1 AC 520, HL, and *White v Jones* [1995] 2 AC 207, HL, discussed in S Hedley, *Tort* (7th edn, OUP, 2011) ch 5.

[61] *Elder Dempster & Co Ltd v Paterson, Zochonis & Co Ltd* [1924] AC 522, HL.

[62] [1962] AC 446, 479.

[63] *Johnson Matthey & Co v Constantine Terminals Ltd* [1976] 2 Lloyd's Rep 215, 219 (Donaldson J).

[64] *The Forum Craftsman* [1985] 1 Lloyd's Rep 291 (Ackner LJ).

agreed that the goods were received by the shipowners as bailees subject to the exceptions and limitations in the bill of lading.[65]

Statute has created numerous exceptions to the doctrine of privity, but it is impossible to consider all of these here.[66] However, the Contracts (Rights of Third Parties) Act 1999 creates a major exception to the principle that a third party cannot sue on a contract to which he is not a party, and this warrants further consideration.

10 The Contracts (Rights of Third Parties) Act 1999

It is important to consider the effect of the 1999 Act on the rule that consideration must move from the promisee, and any separate doctrine of privity that may exist. The Act came into force on 11 November 1999, and applies to contracts made on or after 11 May 2000, and any contracts made between those dates which expressly provide that it should apply.

The Law Commission, in its report *Privity of Contract: Contracts for the Benefit of Third Parties*[67] intended the Act to apply only to what was described as Case 1, depicted by Figure 10.1.[68] Clause 8 of its draft Bill expressly excluded Case 2, depicted by Figure 10.2. But clause 8 was not included in the Bill introduced in Parliament, nor does any such provision appear in the Act. The Law Commission acknowledged that it would be absurd if C were better off if he was not a promisee than if he was, but proposed to exclude the promisee for two reasons. First, it assumed that the *dicta* in *Coulls v Bagot's Executors*[69] are correct, which would mean that C had a right at common law to sue A, and the Law Commission thought that C should not be deprived of that right. After all, C's common law right as a promisee would be a more secure right than any right C would obtain under the Act because C would not have to satisfy the statutory test of enforceability in section 1. However, as we have seen, it is unclear whether *Coulls v Bagot's Executors* should be followed on this point. The second reason the Law Commission gave for excluding the promisee from the scope of its proposals was the need to ensure that the rules concerning joint creditors continued to apply, which are different from the new rules regarding third parties.[70]

The 1999 Act is, according to its preamble, 'An Act to make provision for the enforcement of contractual terms by third parties.' This is ambiguous. Does it mean third parties *to the contract*? Or third parties *to the promise*? If the former, C is a third party in both Case 1 and Case 2. If the latter, C is 'a third party' in Case 1, but not in Case 2. The answer should now be found through the construction of the Act. A third party is, according to section 1(1): 'a person who is not a party to a contract'. Is C in Case 2 'a party to a contract'? If he is (as the Law Commission thought), he cannot rely on the Act but must invoke his common law rights. If he is not, he may rely on the Act. C, when he is a promisee, would be well advised to make his claim in the alternative.

---

[65] *The Pioneer Container* [1994] 2 AC 324; *The Mahkutai* [1996] 3 All ER 502, PC.
[66] Further examples include the Road Traffic Act 1988, s 148(7) and the Law of Property Act 1925, s 56.
[67] Law Com No 242, 1996.
[68] Section 2.
[69] Section 3.
[70] cf Section 3.

(a) **The third party's right**

Section 1(1) provides that a person who is not a party to a contract:

> … may in his own right enforce a term of the contract, if—
>
> (a) the contract expressly provides that he may, or
>
> (b) the term purports to confer a benefit on him.

Section 1(1)(a) will only be satisfied in limited circumstances, since it requires a term of the contract expressly to state that C can enforce the contract. Where the contract is not so explicit, but the relevant term is for the benefit of C, C will have to rely upon section 1(1)(b). It is important properly to identify and interpret the particular term upon which C relies. Indeed, the term enforceable by C is intended to include implied terms. Suppose that B contracts to buy furniture from A as a wedding present for C, informing A that it is a present and instructing A to deliver the goods to C. If the furniture proves defective, C, in the opinion of the Law Commission, can sue A for breach of the implied term that the goods will be of satisfactory quality (Sale of Goods Act 1979, s 14, although now probably under Consumer Rights Act 2015, s 9). But if B does not advise A that the furniture is a gift until after the contract has been concluded, it would seem that C has no remedy. This approach is sensible, although it is admittedly difficult to see how an implied term itself can 'purport to confer a benefit' on C.

In any event, even if section 1(1)(b) is satisfied, C's right to enforce the term of the contract is subject to section 1(2), which provides that section 1(1)(b) does not apply if, on a proper construction of the contract, it appears that the parties did not intend the term to be enforceable by C. The Law Commission thought that section 1(1)(b) created a rebuttable presumption in favour of C, and the courts appear to have given effect to this: the onus is on A to prove that a proper construction of the entire contract under section 1(2) means that section 1(1)(b) should be disapplied.[71] The test of intention is objective, but it must be the intention of both parties. Moreover, for section 1(1)(b) to apply at all, it should be one of the purposes of the contract that C benefit; it is insufficient if the benefit to C is merely an incidental effect of the contract.[72]

Section 1(3) demands that C must be *expressly* identified in the contract by name, or as a member of a class, or as answering a particular description.[73] Thus, the Act would have been of no assistance to the stevedore in the *Scruttons* case,[74] but it might have assisted the stevedore in *The Eurymedon*[75] if he had not been a party to the contract supplying consideration.[76] C need not, however, be in existence at the time when the contract is made. For

---

[71] *Nisshin Shipping Co Ltd v Cleaves & Co Ltd* [2003] EWHC 2602 (Comm), [2004] 1 Lloyd's Rep 38; *The Laemthong Glory (No 2)* [2005] EWCA Civ 519, [2005] 1 Lloyd's Rep 688; *Dolphin Maritime & Aviation Services Ltd v Sveriges Angfartygs Assurans Forening* [2009] EWHC 716 (Comm), [2009] 2 Lloyd's Rep 123.

[72] *Dolphin Maritime & Aviation Services Ltd v Sveriges Angfartygs Assurans Forening* [2009] EWHC 716 (Comm), [2009] 2 Lloyd's Rep 123; Law Com No 242, paras 7.19ff.

[73] See too *Avraamides v Colwill* [2006] EWCA Civ 1533.

[74] Section 5.

[75] Section 5.

[76] A term of the contract may be used by a third party as a defence if s 1 is satisfied: see s 1(6).

example, an unborn child or a company not yet formed may acquire rights under a contract from the moment the child is born or the company comes into existence.

It is clear that, on the facts of *Tweddle v Atkinson*,[77] C (who was expressly identified and was not a party to the contract) would today be able to recover the specified sum from A. Similarly, but for the Competition Act 1998, in *Dunlop Pneumatic Tyre Co Ltd v Selfridge*, Dunlop (if not 'a party to a contract') would be able to recover £5 from Selfridge under the Act.[78]

When either section 1(1)(a) or section 1(1)(b) applies, section 1(5) provides that C has all the remedies that a party to the contract would have.

(b) Rescission or variation

If, immediately after making the contract for the benefit of C, A and B agree to rescind or vary it in any way, they are generally able to do so. However, according to section 2(1) they will lose this right when:

(a) C communicates his assent to the **promisor** (A) (and note that it is not good enough for C only to communicate his assent to the promisee (B)); or

(b) A is aware that C has relied on the term; or

(c) A can reasonably be expected to have foreseen that C would rely on the term and C has in fact relied on it.

Once one of these events has occurred, C's right may not be revoked without his consent, unless there is an express term in the contract allowing revocation. If A and B wish to obtain C's consent to rescind or vary the contract but C's whereabouts cannot reasonably be ascertained, or he is mentally incapable of giving his consent, section 2(4) provides that they may apply to a court or arbitral tribunal which may dispense with C's consent. The same applies where A and B satisfy the court or arbitral tribunal that it cannot reasonably be ascertained whether C has in fact relied on the term: section 2(5).

Overall, section 2 limits the ability of A and B to depart from their contract where this would disadvantage C, but it clearly does not entirely abolish their right to do so. For this reason, C may well continue to seek to argue that he is a beneficiary under a trust, or that C is a party to a collateral contract with A, since in those circumstances C's rights cannot be altered by a subsequent agreement between A and B.

(c) Defences available to A

It may be that if B had sued A for breach of his contract to benefit C, A would have been able to rely on some matter by way of defence or set-off. B may, for example, have induced the contract by misrepresentation, or be indebted to A in respect of some related transaction. If C sues A in reliance on the Act, the defence or set-off that would have been available to A in an action against him by B is available against C: section 3(2). In addition, the contract may expressly provide that a defence or set-off that would have been available against B

---

[77] Section 2.
[78] Section 2.

shall be available against *C*: section 3(3). Again, it may be that if *C* had been a party to the contract, *A* would have had a defence or set-off or counterclaim to an action brought by *C*. *C* might, for instance, have induced *A* to contract with *B* by a misrepresentation. If *C*, not being a party to the contract, sues *A* under the Act, such a defence, set-off, or counterclaim is available to *A*: section 3(4).

(d) Enforcement of the contract by B

B's common law right to enforce *A*'s promise to benefit *C* is expressly preserved under section 4.[79] But *A* is protected from double liability. Where *B* has recovered from *A* a sum representing the loss caused to *C* by *A*'s breach, or *B*'s expense in making good to *C* the default of *A*, then, in proceedings brought by *C*, the court 'shall reduce any award to [*C*] to such extent as it thinks appropriate to take account of the sum recovered by [*B*]': section 5. *A* should not have to pay twice for the same damage.

(e) Exceptions

Section 6 of the Act provides that section 1 confers no rights on a third party to: a contract on a bill of exchange, **promissory note**, or cheque; a contract binding on a company and its members under section 33 of the Companies Act 2006 (the contracts implied in the memorandum and articles of association); terms in contracts of employment; and contracts for the carriage of goods by sea, or by road, rail, or air which are subject to the appropriate international transport convention, with the important exception that a person may avail himself of an exclusion or limitation of liability in a contract: section 6(5).

11 Imposition of burdens on third parties

It would be surprising if a contract between *A* and *B* could impose an obligation on *C*, and the general principle is that it cannot do so. Of course, if *B* is *C*'s agent to enter into the contract with *A*, *C* does incur obligations as well as acquiring rights, but that is because *C* is a contracting party. A true exception, however, may be that relied on by Lord Denning in the *Scruttons* case—that a bailor of goods is bound by contracts made by the bailee in relation to the goods, to which the bailor has impliedly consented.[80] There, it will be recalled, Lord Denning held that a contract entered into by the carrier (the bailee), *B*, with the stevedore, *A*, which limited the stevedore's liability, was also binding upon *C*, the shipper of goods (the bailor).

Another case in which Lord Denning saw scope for the application of this principle is *Morris v CW Martin & Sons Ltd*.[81] *C* (the bailor) sent a mink stole to *B* (the bailee) to be cleaned. *B*, acting as principal and not as agent for *C*, made a contract with *A* for the

---

[79] Although the quantum of *B*'s claim where a loss is really suffered by *C* remains a difficult issue: see Section 6(b).

[80] See Section 5.

[81] [1966] 1 QB 716.

cleaning of the stole. *A* lost it and *C* sued him in tort. *A* relied on a clause in his contract with *B*, which he claimed excluded his liability to *C*. The Court of Appeal held that it did not do so. Lord Denning reached this conclusion only on the ground that the clause was not clearly expressed to exclude liability to *C*. If the clause had been clearly expressed to exclude liability to *C*, he thought it would have been effective, notwithstanding the fact that it was in a contract between *A* and *B* to which *C* was not a party. Salmon LJ was also strongly attracted by this view. Lord Denning said:

> Suppose the owner of a car lets it out on hire, and the hirer sends it for repair, and the repairer holds it for a **lien**. The owner is bound by the lien because he impliedly consented to the repairs being done, since they were reasonably incidental to the use of the car: see *Argus v. Tappenden* [1964] 2 Q.B. 815.

It may be argued, however, that this is a case going beyond simple contract because the repairer's lien is in the nature of a proprietary interest (sometimes called 'a special property') in the car. This is therefore yet another of Lord Denning's theories about which there is some degree of uncertainty.

A person who acquires property may find himself bound by obligations, contractual in origin, which are incidental to the property. Covenants in a **lease** are binding not only on the original parties but also on their successors in **title**. Covenants restricting the use of land are binding in equity not only on the original covenantor but also on subsequent purchasers of the land with notice of the covenant, provided that the covenantee has retained other land for the benefit of which the covenant was taken.[82] However, this principle is limited to covenants concerning land only. In *Taddy & Co v Sterious*,[83] Swinfen Eady J declined to apply a similar principle to a **chattel**. Taddy & Co sold a packet of cigarettes with a notice stating that it was sold on the express condition that retailers would not sell it below stipulated prices. The judge held that 'acceptance of the goods will be deemed to be a contract between the purchaser and Taddy & Co. that he will observe these stipulations'. However, the defendants, who had purchased the cigarettes through a wholesaler, were not bound by those stipulations even though they had notice of them.

It is also a tort knowingly to induce a breach of contract between two other parties.[84] Where *C* knows of a contract between *A* and *B*, but nevertheless enters into another contract, the performance of which will cause a breach of the contract between *A* and *B*, *C* may be restrained by injunction from enforcing his contractual rights in a manner which would cause such a breach. For instance, *C* may know that *B* has granted *A* a right of first refusal over certain land, but nevertheless enters into a contract to buy the land from *B*. *C* may be restrained from enforcing that contract.[85] Similarly, where *C* has acquired a proprietary interest, he may be restrained from exercising it in such a way as to cause a breach of a contract between *A* and *B* if he was aware of that contract when he acquired the proprietary interest. For example, *C* may know that *B* has chartered his ship to *A*, but *C* may

---

[82] *Tulk v Moxhay* (1848) 2 Ph 74. See further K Gray and S Gray, *Land Law* (7th edn, OUP, 2011) 131–40.
[83] [1904] 1 Ch 354.
[84] *Lumley v Gye* (1853) 2 E & B 216.
[85] *Manchester Ship Canal Co v Manchester Racecourse Co* [1901] 2 Ch 37.

nevertheless buy that ship from *B*. *C* may be restrained by injunction from using the ship inconsistently with *A*'s rights.[86] In all these instances, the courts are consistent in insisting that it is unlawful for *C* knowingly to induce a breach of contract. In a restrictive sense, therefore, *C* might be said to be bound by the terms of the contract between *A* and *B*, but it is important to note that *C* is not bound positively to do anything just because a contract has been concluded between *A* and *B*. Rather, *C* is merely bound not knowingly to induce or procure a breach of that contract.

Further Reading

B Coote, 'Consideration and the Joint Promisee' (1978) 37 CLJ 301.
Considers *Coulls v Bagot's Executor and Trustee Co Ltd* and is ultimately critical of it, arguing that a party must have provided consideration in order to be a party to the contract.

R Stevens, 'The Contracts (Rights of Third Parties) Act 1999' (2004) 120 LQR 292.
Argues that a third party has not provided consideration and therefore should not acquire any rights under the contract, and is critical of the 1999 Act and some of the problems which remain even after the implementation of legislation.

H Beale, 'A Review of the Contracts (Rights of Third Parties) Act 1999' in A Burrows and E Peel (eds), *Contract Formation and Parties* (OUP, 2010).
Analyses the impact and utility of the 1999 Act, and suggests that even greater use of the statutory regime would be welcome.

Questions

1. Francis and Clare are friends. They decide to play the National Lottery each week. Each is to con-tribute £3 and they will take it in turns to choose three sets of numbers. They agree that any win-nings are to be divided equally between the two of them and another friend, Doug. Doug learns of this agreement and tells Clare that he is very happy and grateful for it. In the sixth week, when Francis had chosen the numbers, one of the line of numbers chosen wins a prize of £250,000. Francis, in whose name the ticket was registered, wishes to keep the prize.

   Advise Francis as to his liability to Clare and to Doug.

2. Sissy hires Rayburn Ltd to transport her grand piano from Nottingham to Devon. She pays Rayburn Ltd £1,500 for this service. The contract includes the following two clauses:

   (a) Rayburn Ltd may employ independent contractors to perform any part of this service.

   (b) Liability for any damage to the piano during transportation will be limited to £5,000.

   Rayburn Ltd hires Eric to transport the piano. Unfortunately, the piano is damaged by the negli-gence of Eric during the transport, causing damage to the value of £12,000.

   Advise Sissy.

---

[86] *Lord Strathcona Steamship Co Ltd v Dominion Coal Co* [1926] AC 108, PC. Cf *Swiss Bank Corp v Lloyds Bank Ltd* [1979] 2 All ER 853 (Browne-Wilkinson J), reversed on other grounds, by the Court of Appeal and House of Lords [1982] AC 854.

11 Identifying the terms of a contract

🔐 Key Points

- A statement made in the course of negotiations may become a term if the parties intend it to be a term. This is an objective test. Important factors to take into account include the relative means of knowledge of the parties and the reliance placed on the statement when entering into the contract.

- Terms may be incorporated into a contract by signature. A person will be bound by terms in a document that he has signed.

- One exception to the 'signature rule' arises where the doctrine of *non est factum* (which can be translated as 'it is not my deed') applies. So, if A's signature has been procured by the fraud of B, and B's fraud was such as to lead A to believe that the contents of the document were fundamentally different from what they actually were, and A was not guilty of negligence in so signing, then the requirements of *non est factum* are satisfied and the document is void.

- Where a party has not signed the contract, then the other party seeking to rely upon a term must take reasonable steps to bring the term to the party's attention in order to incorporate that term into the contract. The more onerous the term, the more the other party must do in order to incorporate the term into the agreement.

- Terms may also be incorporated into a contract by a course of dealing that is consistent and regular.

- Terms may be contained in a contract which is 'collateral' to the 'main' contract. For a 'collateral contract' to be found, the usual requirements of contract formation must be satisfied, including offer and acceptance, and consideration.

- When the parties have formally recorded the whole of their agreement in writing, then there is a presumption that that document is the contract and the whole contract. The courts have long asserted that they will not admit evidence to add to, vary, or contradict the written agreement. This is known as the 'parol evidence rule'. However, this rule is riddled with exceptions.

It is important to understand how the terms of a contract are identified before discussing how the terms of a contract are understood[1] and, exceptionally, controlled.[2] In many cases, this will be a relatively straightforward exercise: the terms of the contract will be those

---

[1] See Chapters 12–14.
[2] See Chapter 15.

expressed in a written contract. But even then it will need to be established whether such terms have been properly incorporated in the contract, often by being brought to the notice of the other party at or before the time at which the contract was entered into.

This chapter will first examine the distinction between a 'term' and a 'representation', before considering how those terms can be incorporated into a contract. It is then appropriate to discuss the nature of the contract being examined—even if the relevant term is not to be found in the 'main' contract, it may be found in a 'collateral', or ancillary, contract. Finally, the 'parol evidence rule' will be addressed. Essentially, this rule states that where there is a written contract, extrinsic evidence cannot be used to establish other terms. This rule is riddled with exceptions and often dismissed, although it is suggested that it should not be entirely discarded.

1 Terms or representations?

During the course of the negotiations, statements about the proposed contract will frequently be made by one or both of the parties. These statements may or may not form part of the contract. Even if they are not terms of the contract, they may affect its enforceability: misrepresentation will be examined in Chapter 16.[3] The focus of the present inquiry will be upon whether or not a statement has become a term of the contract.

If the contract is concluded entirely orally, then its terms will probably be found in the negotiations. For example, the offer and acceptance in a contract for the sale of a car may consist simply of O saying to A: 'I offer you £1,000 for the car'; and A then replying: 'I accept.' But the buyer may have received various assurances from the seller in the course of the negotiations. For instance, the seller may have said that the car is a 2010 model, that the seller has owned it since it was new, that the mileage on the odometer is correct, and so on. Such assurances are very likely to have contributed to the buyer's decision to make his offer. The seller, as a reasonable man, must be taken to know this. The key question is therefore: was the buyer, as a reasonable man, entitled to believe that the seller was promising him that the car was a 2010 model, and that he was giving an undertaking to that effect? If the answer to that question is 'Yes', it is a term in the contract that the car is a 2010 model. If that term is breached (for example, because the car is in fact a 2009 model), the buyer can recover damages.

It has always been said by the courts that whether a statement is a term of the contract depends on whether the parties intended it to be a term. Significantly, the test of intention is objective.[4] In applying the objective test, the court will take into account all the relevant circumstances in the particular case but there are some matters which will commonly be influential, namely the relative means of knowledge of the parties and whether the parties relied on the statement at the time of contract. These will be examined in turn. However, it should first be noted that the focus here is on contracts concluded orally. If the contract is written down, and there is no mention of the fact that the car is a 2010 model, for example, it will be more difficult to establish that it is a term of the contract that the car is a 2010

---

[3] See Chapter 16.
[4] See Chapter 2.

model. When the parties have formally recorded the whole of their agreement in writing, then that document is, **prima facie**, the whole contract. This is the effect of the parol evidence rule.[5] But the buyer may still have a remedy if there is a collateral contract with the seller that the car is a 2010 model,[6] or in misrepresentation.[7]

(a) The relative means of knowledge of the parties

In *De Lassalle v Guildford*, AL Smith MR said in respect of a representation made prior to a contract of sale:

> In determining whether it is so intended [to be a term], a decisive test is whether the vendor assumes to assert a fact of which the buyer is ignorant or merely states an opinion or judgment upon a matter of which the vendor has no special knowledge, and on which the buyer may be expected also to have an opinion and to exercise his judgment.[8]

Because all the circumstances must be taken into account when deciding whether something is a term, it is dangerous to state as a general proposition that any one is 'decisive', and as a result this 'test' of AL Smith MR has been criticised.[9] Nevertheless, this particular factor is highly significant and may indeed often be decisive. Where both parties have the same means of knowledge and they are aware of this, it is very unlikely that a statement made by either of them will have the status of a term. This is because neither party will be relying on the other. Instead, each party will be relying on his own means of knowledge when entering into the contract.

In *Oscar Chess Ltd v Williams*,[10] the seller of a car stated that it was a 1948 model. In fact, it was a 1939 model and therefore worth significantly less. At first sight, this might look like a term of the contract. However, the relative means of knowledge of the parties was not the same. The buyer was in the motor trade, whilst the seller was a layman. It was obvious to any reasonable buyer that the seller had no actual knowledge of when the car was first registered. Indeed, the seller did not know anything more about this than the buyer. The buyer was in a much better position than the seller to check and find out the true date of manufacture of the car, since the buyer was in the motor trade and the seller was not. In fact, the buyer knew full well that the seller was simply repeating what he had read in the car's registration book. This had, at some stage, been forged to misstate the year of the car's manufacture and it showed five changes of ownership between 1948 and 1954. The book was produced by the seller to the buyer. As a result, the buyer was not entitled to believe that the seller was promising that the car was a 1948 model and undertaking responsibility for that fact. It was therefore not a term of the contract that the car was a 1948 model.

Oscar Chess Ltd v Williams can be contrasted with *Bentley (Dick) Productions Ltd and Another v Smith (Harold) (Motors) Ltd*.[11] In that case, a car dealer was instructed to find a

---

[5] See Section 4.
[6] See Section 3.
[7] See Chapter 16.
[8] *De Lassalle v Guildford* [1901] 2 KB 215, 221.
[9] See eg *Heilbut, Symons & Co v Buckleton* [1913] AC 30 (Lord Moulton).
[10] [1957] 1 WLR 370.
[11] *Bentley (Dick) Productions Ltd and Another v Smith (Harold) (Motors) Ltd* [1965] 1 WLR 623.

'well-vetted' Bentley car. The car dealer found a car which, he told the buyer, had done only 20,000 miles since being fitted with a replacement engine and gearbox. This was false: the true figure was around 100,000 miles. The buyer sued for breach of contract, and the Court of Appeal held that it was a term of the contract that the car had done only 20,000 miles since being fitted with a replacement engine. The buyer was a layman who was not in the trade, whilst the seller was in the motor trade. This is the opposite way around to the *Oscar Chess* case, and explains why the opposite result was reached. In the *Bentley* case, the buyer was entitled to suppose that the seller knew what he was talking about and was promising him that the car was as described.

Even where a party has done no more than express an opinion, his superior knowledge or means of knowledge may lead the court to infer that he was impliedly promising that he had reasonable grounds for the opinion expressed. In *Esso Petroleum Co Ltd v Mardon*,[12] Esso's experienced representative persuaded Mardon to enter into a tenancy of a new petrol filling station by telling him that Esso estimated that the throughput of petrol would reach 200,000 gallons in the third year of operation. Even with sound management, the site was not good enough to achieve anything like that throughput. There was clearly no promise by Esso that the throughput would reach the estimated figure—it was only an opinion—but there was an implied promise that the forecast was made with reasonable care and skill. That promise was broken, so Mardon was entitled to damages.

(b) Reliance at the time of contracting

Statements made by *A* to *B* during the course of negotiations will not become a term unless *B* reasonably relies on *A*'s statement and *A* knows, or ought to know, that *B* may be relying on that statement. The smaller the interval between the statement and the time of contracting, the more likely it is that *A* is relying on the statement and that *B* is aware of it. However, this is only a question of evidence, not a rule of law.

In *Schawel v Reade*,[13] the owner of a horse said to a potential buyer who was examining it: 'You need not look for anything: the horse is perfectly sound. If there was anything the matter with the horse I would tell you.' Having been told this, the buyer stopped examining the horse. Three weeks later, he bought the horse. He subsequently discovered that the horse had an eye disease and could not be used as a stud. The court held that the owner's statement that the horse was sound constituted a warranty and was a term of the contract.

Schawel v Reade must be distinguished from *Hopkins v Tanqueray*.[14] The material facts of both cases were the same except in one crucial respect: in *Hopkins v Tanqueray*, both parties knew at the time of the conversation that the horse was to be sold by auction at Tattersalls the following day, and it was at that sale that the claimant bought the horse. The well-known course of business at Tattersalls was that sales were without a warranty. The court therefore held that there was no warranty in the contract: there was no term of the contract that the horse was sound. The basis of the decision seems to be that, since both parties must be taken to have known of the well-known course of business at

---

[12] [1976] QB 801.
[13] [1913] 2 Ir Rep 81, HL.
[14] (1854) 15 CB 130.

Tattersalls, they could not have intended a warranty. After all, the parties could not have supposed that this bidder would be in a better position than other bidders at the sale, who would certainly have had no warranty. No doubt the buyer was in fact relying on what he had been told; but he had no right to take it to be a binding promise because he had no right to suppose that he was being promised more than other bidders.

2 Was the clause incorporated in the contract?

It is important to be sure that a statement has been properly incorporated into the contract. Many of the cases concern exclusion clauses contained in one party's standard terms. However, there are no special rules relating to the incorporation of exclusion clauses in contracts. The relevant principles apply to all terms generally. Nevertheless, courts have traditionally been particularly sensitive about holding that an exclusion clause has been incorporated into a contract because this might well enable a business to rely upon its own exclusion clause to escape liability when this would be unfair. But such reluctance to find that a clause is incorporated into a contract may no longer be as necessary as it once was, following the enactment of the Unfair Contract Terms Act 1977 and the Consumer Rights Act 2015. Under these 'new' legislative regimes—examined in Chapter 15—a court may find that some clauses are unenforceable if they are 'unfair', even if they have been incorporated into a contract. This was impossible at **common law**, and may explain why in some of the older cases it seems that courts were very willing to strain the relevant principles in order to avoid finding that an exclusion clause was incorporated into the agreement.

There are three main methods by which a clause can be incorporated into the agreement: signature, reasonable notice, and by a consistent course of dealing between the parties. Each will now be examined in turn.

(a) **Signature**

If the clause is included in a written and signed agreement, it is plainly part of the contract. As Scrutton LJ put it in *L'Estrange v Graucob*,[15] 'When a document containing contractual terms is signed, then, in the absence of fraud, or … misrepresentation, the party signing it is bound and it is wholly immaterial whether he has read the document or not.' The party is bound although he does not really in his mind assent to the particular terms in the document, because he does not know what they are. In *L'Estrange*, the claimant signed a contract for the purchase of a slot machine for selling cigarettes without reading it. The defendants knew that the claimant had not read the agreement, but were nonetheless entitled to enforce the agreement. The party who signs the document expresses his assent to the terms in it, whatever they may be and regardless of whether those terms have been read and understood.

The 'rule' in *L'Estrange v Graucob* is sometimes criticised as being unfair. Indeed, the successful counsel in the case was Alfred Denning, whose reputation grew after this victory.

---

[15] [1934] 2 KB 394, CA.

But Denning later confessed to being uncomfortable with the result,[16] and in the decision of the House of Lords in *McCutcheon v David MacBrayne Ltd*[17] Lord Denning said that signed writing 'should make no difference whatever. This sort of document is not meant to be read, still less to be understood. Its signature is in truth about as significant as a handshake that marks the formal conclusion of a bargain'. Nevertheless, there is little doubt that *L'Estrange v Graucob* remains a bedrock of English law;[18] in *Peekay Intermark Ltd and another v Australia and New Zealand Banking Group Ltd*,[19] Moore-Bick LJ described it as 'an important principle of English law which underpins the whole of commercial life; any erosion of it would have serious repercussions far beyond the business community'.

What is signed must be a contractual sort of document, in the sense that the party signing it must expect that the document will include contractual terms. This is illustrated by *Grogan v Robin Meredith Plant Hire*.[20] The defendant hired out a machine to another company. The contract was made orally, and at the end of the first week of hire an employee of the hirer signed a time sheet provided by the defendant. At the bottom of the time sheet there was the following clause: 'All hire undertaken under Contractors' Plant Association standard **conditions**, copy available on request.' Those standard conditions included a term that the hirer would indemnify the defendant against any liability to third parties that would be incurred due to the hire. Mr Grogan was injured in an accident involving the machine, and sued the defendant. The Court of Appeal, reversing the decision of the trial judge, held that the defendant could not rely upon the clause printed on the time sheet and seek an indemnity from the hirer. A reasonable person would not have expected the time sheet to contain contractual terms. The time sheet was essentially an administrative document, and the clause printed on it was not incorporated into the contract.

(i) *Non est factum*

There is a narrow but important exception to the principle that a person is bound by whatever he signs. This is encapsulated by the doctrine of *non est factum*, which can be translated as 'it is not my deed'. A person is able to deny that he should be bound by what he signed where *non est factum* applies since the signed document is void. However, it should be appreciated at the outset that claims of *non est factum* rarely succeed, and this is a very limited exception to the 'rule' in *L'Estrange v Graucob*.

Non est factum applies where:

(a) *A*'s signature has been procured by the fraud of *B*;

(b) *B*'s fraud was such as to lead *A* to believe that the contents of the document were fundamentally different from what they actually were; and

(c) *A* was not guilty of negligence in so signing.

---

[16] See Chapter 2, n 15.

[17] [1964] 1 WLR 125.

[18] The Ontario Court of Appeal in Canada has marked a slight shift away from a strict approach to *L'Estrange* in *Tilden Rent-A-Car Co v Clendenning* (1978) 83 DLR (3d) 400, which concerned a consumer hiring a car, by requiring that it be reasonable to believe that the signor accepted the relevant terms.

[19] [2006] EWCA Civ 386, [2006] 2 Lloyd's Rep 511.

[20] [1996] CLC 1127.

The doctrine originated in cases where illiterate or blind persons were induced to make deeds by another's fraud as to the nature of the document. The signer could then plead *non est factum* against both the fraudster and any innocent third party purchaser, because the signer never intended to sign any such deed. The doctrine thus arose in order to protect vulnerable parties labouring under some sort of 'disability', and grew from there. So, in the old case of *Foster v MacKinnon*,[21] an elderly man was induced to sign a bill of exchange by a fraudulent representation that it was a guarantee. An innocent third party subsequently gave value for the bill, relying on the elderly man's signature on the bill. It was held that the elderly man was entitled to plead *non est factum* and that that claim was good against the third party, provided that the elderly man was not guilty of any negligence in signing the document. (At the time, this issue of negligence was a question for the jury.) The document signed by the old man belonged to an entirely different class from what it was represented to be.

However, it is now clear that the document need not be in an entirely different class, provided that it is 'fundamentally' or 'radically' or 'totally' different from what the signer envisaged. So the doctrine might apply if B had told A that the document was a **promissory note** for £10 and it was in fact a promissory note for £10,000. Significantly, the difference must be one which is material to the signer. In other words, it must be the case that the signer would certainly not have signed the document had he known the truth. The leading case is *Gallie v Lee*.[22] Mrs Gallie was an elderly widow. She could not read the document in front of her because she had broken her spectacles, but nevertheless signed the document which she believed to be a deed of **gift** of her house to her nephew Parkin. Mrs Gallie was devoted to Parkin. Yet the document was not in fact a deed of gift but a deed of sale of the house to Lee for £3,000. Mrs Gallie acknowledged receipt of this money in the deed but she did not in fact receive anything. This certainly looks like an instance where there was a fundamental difference between what the signer thought the document was and what the document was in actual fact. But the House of Lords held that the document was not void for *non est factum*. Their Lordships insisted that it is important to consider the 'object of the exercise'. The document was put before Mrs Gallie by Lee in the presence of Parkin. Mrs Gallie knew that the transaction was intended to divest her of her interest in the house, in order to enable Lee and Parkin to pursue a joint project by raising money on the **security** of the house. As a result, the document did in fact carry out the object she intended it to carry out. *Non est factum* therefore did not apply. The case illustrates the reluctance of the courts to allow a person to avoid the effect of a document which she has in fact signed. This is particularly acute in a case such as *Gallie v Lee*, where an innocent third party—in that case, the building society which had advanced money in reliance on Mrs Gallie's signature on the deed—would be severely prejudiced by finding the document to be void.

The defence of *non est factum* is very narrowly construed. A person who has signed a document bears a heavy onus of proof when seeking to escape liability on a document that he has signed. If A grants a power of attorney to B, whom he knows or ought to know is incompetent, he cannot successfully plead *non est factum* when B, exercising the power

---

[21] *Foster v MacKinnon* (1869) LR 4 CP 704.
[22] [1971] AC 1004, HL (note that this case is also sometimes known by the name *Saunders v Anglia Building Society*).

of attorney, signs a document which she does not understand.[23] Similarly, a court will be slow to find that a person who makes a mistake in signing a document was not negligent, in the sense of being careless. In *Gallie v Lee*, Lord Pearson considered that a businessman who signs 'blind' a pile of letters put before him by his trusted secretary for signature may be 'exercising a wise economy of his time and energy'; but if the secretary has slipped in a guarantee of her overdraft, the signer should be liable to the bank which allows her to overdraw. The businessman takes the chance of a fraudulent substitution.

(b) Unsigned contracts: reasonable notice

If the contract has been reduced to writing but not signed, then clearly the rule in *L'Estrange v Graucob* cannot apply. It therefore has to be proved, by some means other than signature, that the party gave his assent to the written terms being the contract. The key requirement is that reasonable notice was given of the relevant terms such that they are incorporated into the contract. This is an objective test, and it does not matter whether or not a party actually read and understood the terms.

This principle was established in *Parker v South Eastern Railway*.[24] In that case, the claimant left a bag in the cloakroom at the defendant's railway station, and then received a ticket with a number, the date, and the words 'See back' on the front of it. On the back were printed several clauses, including 'The company will not be responsible for any package exceeding the value of £10.' The claimant did not read the ticket. Unfortunately, the claimant's bag, valued at £24 10s, was subsequently lost. It was held that, at trial, the judge had misdirected the jury, so a new trial was ordered in order to ensure that the jury could determine whether what the claimant did was reasonably sufficient to give the defendant notice of that term. This was a question of fact. If the notice given was reasonable, the term was part of the contract and the defendant's liability was limited. If the notice given was not reasonable, then the clause was totally ineffective.

All the relevant circumstances must be taken into account when deciding whether reasonable notice has been given. It is worth emphasising that what constitutes 'reasonable notice' must be assessed objectively. It has been said that the party giving notice is entitled to assume that those to whom the relevant term is addressed speak English and can read.[25] Indeed, individual handicaps, like illiteracy, which are not brought to the attention of the other party, may be treated as irrelevant to the issue of reasonable notice, even though they are plainly relevant to the question of whether the notice was actually read.

Mellish LJ, in his classic judgment in *Parker v The South Eastern Railway Co*,[26] distinguished between two types of paper on which exclusion clauses might be printed. On the one hand, there is the type of paper which an ordinary person would not expect to contain contractual terms, and on the other hand there is the type of paper which all reasonably well-informed persons would expect to contain such terms. As an example of the first type, Mellish LJ instanced a turnpike ticket (ie a ticket for a toll road) which (in 1877) the

---

[23] *Norwich and Peterborough Building Society v Steed (No 2)* [1993] Ch 116, CA.
[24] (1877) 2 CPD 416.
[25] *Thompson v London Midland & Southern Railway Co* [1930] 1 KB 41.
[26] (1877) 2 CPD 416.

reasonable recipient might well put in his pocket unread, assuming that it was merely something he might have to produce to show that he had paid the toll. In effect, the ticket was simply a receipt.[27] The example given by Mellish LJ of the second type was a **bill of lading** which invariably contains the terms of the contract of carriage. Mellish LJ thought that a shipper of goods who did not happen to know this and did not read the bill would have to 'bear the consequences of his own exceptional ignorance'. The shipper would almost certainly be bound by the terms in the bill of lading, but the holder of the unread turnpike ticket would probably not be bound by whatever was written on the ticket. The law is not stated more definitively simply because it is a question of fact (and at the time of the decision in *Parker* had to be left to a jury).

Even juries, however, did not have unlimited power to decide what was reasonable. Their decisions on questions of fact were always controlled by the judge in two ways. First, they were not allowed to find a fact proved unless there was sufficient evidence for a reasonable jury to be able to find that fact proved. Secondly, juries were required to find a fact proved if that was the only conclusion to which a reasonable jury could come on the evidence. This is well illustrated by the decision in *Thompson v London, Midland and Scottish Railway*.[28] In that case, a passenger (who could not read) purchased a ticket. On the face of the ticket the following words were printed: 'Excursion, for conditions see back.' On the back of the ticket, it was stated that the ticket was issued subject to the conditions in the company's timetables and excursion bills. Those conditions provided that excursion ticket holders should have no right of action against the company in respect of any injury, howsoever caused. The jury found that reasonable notice had not been given to the passenger. The judge held that was not a possible conclusion on the facts and overruled the jury. Moreover, the Court of Appeal upheld the judge's conclusion that a jury which said that reasonable notice was not given to the passenger should be held to be making a perverse decision. It is suggested that this decision in *Thompson* might reasonably be considered to be difficult. After all, the relevant conditions were not at all easy to dig out. In any event, it should be noted that such a clause would now be invalid under the Consumer Rights Act 2015,[29] but that does not affect the discussion of principle: *Thompson* remains an important authority on the objective nature of the test of reasonable notice.

(i) A stricter test of notice for more onerous terms

Later cases have taken a stricter view of the notice requirement than seems to have been favoured in *Thompson v London, Midland and Scottish Railway*. In *Thornton v Shoe Lane Parking Ltd*,[30] the Court of Appeal held that the more far-reaching the clause, the greater must be the clarity of the notice if the clause is to satisfy the requirement of reasonableness. That case concerned a car-parking contract, and the relevant clause purported to exclude liability for personal injury (which would now be invalid under the Unfair Contract Terms

---

[27] See similarly *Chapelton v Barry Urban District Council* [1940] 1 KB 532, discussed in Section 2(b)(ii).
[28] [1930] 1 KB 41, CA.
[29] See Chapter 15, Section 4.
[30] [1971] 2 QB 163. See too *J Spurling Ltd v Bradshaw* [1956] 1 WLR 461.

Act 1977[31]). Lord Denning thought that such a clause would 'need to be printed in red ink with a red hand pointing to it—or something equally startling'. This high threshold was not met on the facts of the case: the relevant clause was simply posted on a pillar opposite the ticket machine, and this was not sufficient to exclude liability for the personal injury which resulted from an accident. However, Lord Denning MR emphasised that personal injury was a severe sort of injury; a lesser sort of injury (such as property damage) may not require as extensive measures in order for a court to find that reasonable steps had been taken to bring an exclusion clause to the other party's attention.

Another good example of the courts being cautious about accepting that reasonable steps have been taken to bring an onerous clause to the other party's attention is *Interfoto Picture Library Ltd v Stiletto Visual Programmes Ltd*.[32] The claimants had a library of photographic transparencies. The defendants inquired about photographs of the 1950s. The claimants sent 47 transparencies with a delivery note, which was plainly a contractual document, containing the claimants' terms of business. A contract was made either when the defendants had the opportunity to read the terms or, at the latest, when they telephoned to say that some of the transparencies could be of interest and they would call back. But then this matter appears to have been forgotten about by the claimants and all the transparencies were retained for 28 days. The key term in the contract provided that all transparencies must be returned within 14 days of delivery, and that a holding fee of £5.00 plus VAT per day would be charged for each transparency retained beyond that time. Consequently, the defendants received a huge bill for £3,783.50, which the defendants refused to pay. The Court of Appeal held that insufficient notice had been given of this particularly onerous term and that it was not binding on the defendants.

If the holding fee had been 5p instead of £5, the clause would undoubtedly have been incorporated into the contract, even if it had been printed with no greater degree of prominence. But this is problematic. If the reasonable recipient of the delivery note would have known of the existence of the 5p clause, it is hard to see why he would not also have known of the £5 clause. It is suggested that the court strained the device of reasonable notice to exclude what the judges thought was an unfair term. This might be considered to be somewhat unsatisfactory.

Fortunately, the approach in *Interfoto* is now of reduced importance: if a term should not be enforced because it is unfair, then reliance should generally be placed on the Unfair Contract Terms Act 1977 or the Consumer Rights Act 2015; the common law rules on incorporation should be applied in a consistent manner regardless of whether the relevant term is fair.[33] However, the approach in *Interfoto* is not entirely without purpose, and cases have continued to arise which slip between the gaps in the statutory regimes. A good example is *O'Brien v MGN Ltd*,[34] which Hale LJ said 'would make an excellent question in an

---

[31] See Chapter 15, Section 2(c)(i).

[32] [1988] 1 All ER 348, CA.

[33] See eg the dissenting judgment of Hobhouse LJ in *AEG (UK) Ltd v Logic Resource Ltd* [1996] CLC 265, 277: 'If it is to be the policy of English law that in every case those clauses are to be gone through with, in effect, a toothcomb to see whether they were entirely usual and entirely desirable in the particular contract, then one is completely distorting the contractual relationship between the parties and the ordinary mechanisms of making contracts. It will introduce uncertainty into the law of contract.'

[34] [2001] EWCA Civ 1279, [2002] CLC 33.

undergraduate contract law seminar or examination'. The newspaper, the *Daily Mirror*, ran a scratchcard game. Mr O'Brien played the game, and the scratchcard which he purchased indicated to him that he had won £50,000. Unfortunately, another 1,472 people also won the same prize according to their own scratchcards. The *Daily Mirror* refused to pay the prize to Mr O'Brien. The newspaper argued that one of the rules of the game was that if more prizes were claimed than were available in any prize category for any reason, then a draw would take place for the prize. Mr O'Brien was not the lucky winner of this draw. Understandably disappointed, Mr O'Brien argued that the rules were not incorporated into his contract with the newspaper. This was because, although the rules were regularly printed in the newspaper, they had not been included in the newspaper on the particular day that Mr O'Brien bought his scratchcard. Nevertheless, the Court of Appeal, somewhat reluctantly, held that this sort of clause was a normal clause to include in this sort of contract, that the clause was not particularly onerous, and that the newspaper had taken reasonable steps to incorporate it into the contract. The judges appeared to think that there was an important difference between imposing an extra burden on the claimant (as in *Interfoto*) and depriving the claimant of a windfall (as in *O'Brien*). This may not be entirely convincing; as Evans LJ noted, 'The promise of significant riches, in my judgment, deserves more.'[35]

(ii) Timing

However clear the notice may be, it must be given before the contract is entered into. Once the contract has been made, neither side can alter its terms without the consent of the other. In *Chapelton v Barry Urban District Council*,[36] the council displayed a notice beside a pile of deckchairs, stating the charge and inviting the public to obtain tickets from an attendant. The claimant took a chair and sat in it. Later, the attendant came round and gave him a ticket which the claimant put in his pocket unread. The chair gave way and he was consequently injured. He claimed damages for negligence and the council relied on an exclusion clause on the ticket. The clause was held to be ineffective for two reasons. First, the ticket (like Mellish LJ's turnpike ticket[37]) was not one which a reasonable person would expect to contain contractual terms; it was simply a receipt for the money already paid. Secondly, the contract was made when the claimant took the chair and sat in it, thus incurring an obligation to pay the charge when the attendant came to collect it. The ticket therefore came too late: the contract had already been concluded.

Similarly, in *Olley v Marlborough Court Ltd*,[38] a notice displayed in a hotel bedroom was held to be ineffective when the contract had been made in the lobby of the hotel before the guest entered the bedroom. The notice said 'the proprieters will not hold themselves responsible for articles lost or stolen unless handed to the manageress for safe custody', but the proprietors were unable to rely upon this clause in order to escape liability after a thief had entered the guest's bedroom and stolen various items. The contract had already been made in the lobby, and could not be altered when the guest later entered the bedroom.

---

[35] Ibid, [27].
[36] [1940] 1 KB 532, CA.
[37] See Section 2(b).
[38] [1949] 1 KB 532, CA.

A more arguable point was that, in the course of an extended stay, the contract had been renewed from time to time after the guest had had ample opportunity to read the notice, but the court was unimpressed by this, taking the view that it was for the hotelier to prove that there had been a change in the terms of the contract which was made on arrival at the hotel.

(c) **Course of dealing**

If there has been a consistent 'course of dealing' between *A* and *B* of such a nature that any reasonable person would know that *A* invariably intends to contract only on certain terms, *B* will be bound by those terms even if he is in fact unaware of them. The leading case is *Hardwick Game Farm v Suffolk Agricultural Poultry Producers Association*.[39] A farmer ordered feeding stuff from a merchant. It came with a sold note which had an exclusion clause printed on the back. Clearly, that was not part of the contract. As in *Olley v Marlborough Court Ltd*,[40] notice was not given until after the contract had been made. But the farmer continued to order feeding stuff from the merchant three or four times a month, for three years. On each occasion a sold note, with the same term, came with the goods. Well over 100 sold notes were delivered. There was then one time when, as usual, the farmer's order was given and accepted orally, but the stuff delivered with the usual note proved to be poisonous and caused the farmer substantial loss. The merchant relied successfully on the exclusion clause. It was immaterial that the farmer had never in fact read it. He had, by now, ample notice that these were the terms on which the seller did business, and, if he telephoned an order, it was implicit in his offer that it was to be on those terms.

In order for a term to be incorporated into a contract through a course of dealing, that course of dealing must be consistent. In *McCutcheon v David MacBrayne Ltd*,[41] the shipper of a car on the carrier's ship was not bound by a clause in the carrier's 'risk note', even though he had shipped goods on the carrier's vessels on a number of occasions previously. The shipper had not always been asked to sign a risk note, probably because of chaotic conditions in the carrier's office. On the relevant occasion in the case itself, the shipper had not been asked to do so. The shipper was not in fact aware of the terms in the 'risk note' and was not bound by them. The carrier's course of dealing was inconsistent and did not incorporate the term into the contract.

Even if the same practice is followed on every occasion, those occasions must be sufficiently numerous and proximate in time to make it clear to the reasonable person that these are the terms on which the other party does business. In *Hollier v Rambler Motors (AMC) Ltd*,[42] it was held that three or four transactions over a period of five years was not such a 'course of dealing' as to attract the operation of this principle.

A similar principle may operate where both parties are 'in the trade' and it is, or should be, well known to both that a particular term is generally used in the trade. In *British Crane Hire Corp Ltd v Ipswich Plant Hire Ltd*,[43] both parties were in the business of hiring out

---

[39] [1969] 2 AC 31, HL.
[40] Section 2(b)(ii).
[41] [1964] 1 WLR 125, HL.
[42] [1972] 2 QB 71, CA.
[43] [1975] QB 303, CA.

heavy earth-moving equipment. The defendants, having an urgent need for a drag-line crane, hired one by telephone from the claimants. In accordance with the usual practice, the claimants sent the crane with a printed form to be signed by the defendants. Before the form was signed, the crane sank in marshy ground. It was held that the usual conditions (which were in the unsigned form) were incorporated into the contract. As reasonable persons in the trade, the defendants must have known that the claimants would not let out their crane except on some such terms.

3 Collateral contracts

It may be that a promise is contractually binding not in the 'main' contract, but in a contract which is 'collateral' to the 'main' contract. A good example is *De Lassalle v Guildford*.[44] *A* was a potential **tenant** of a house. He refused to sign the **lease** until the **landlord**, *B*, gave him an assurance that the drains were in good order. *B* gave such an assurance, but the lease said nothing about the drains. The court held that *B* had nevertheless contracted that the drains were in good order. In addition to the contract contained in the lease, there was also a 'collateral contract' between the parties. In consideration of *A*'s signing the lease, *B* was promising that the drains were in good order. This was a collateral, unilateral contract: *A* was not obliged to sign the lease, but if he did he could enforce *B*'s promise that the drains were in good order. Two contracts therefore came into existence at the same moment: the bilateral contract contained in the lease and the collateral, unilateral contract. Such a 'collateral' contract obviously achieves a fair result and implements the true intention of the parties. It is important to note that in no way is this collateral contract a fiction: there was a real bargain between the parties.

However, the courts have been discouraged from finding such collateral contracts by the speech of Lord Moulton in *Heilbut Symons & Co v Buckleton*.[45] Lord Moulton recognised that a contract which is collateral to the main contract has an independent existence and the full character and status of a contract, but thought that such contracts must, from their very nature, be rare. His Lordship thought that the more natural way of adding to the terms of the main contract was by an additional term, and that contracts adding to or varying the main contract were 'viewed with suspicion by the law'. Although Lord Moulton's remarks have been quoted with great respect, they are usually also distinguished. The device of the collateral contract has proved to be too useful to be lightly brushed aside.

Indeed, *Heilbut v Buckleton* itself was not a case where a collateral contract was likely to be found, so the comments of Lord Moulton were very much *obiter*. In that case, there was a written contract to take **shares** in a new company. The claimant argued that the defendant had promised that the company was 'a rubber company'. The written contract did not say anything on this point. The claimant argued that the collateral promise that the company was 'a rubber company' was given by the defendant in a telephone conversation. However, the evidence did not establish that the claimant was seeking an assurance that the company was 'a rubber company'. What the claimant really wanted to know was whether the

---

[44] [1901] 2 KB 215, CA.
[45] [1913] AC 30, HL.

company was 'all right'—in other words, whether the company was a sound company, likely to make good profits. Had the claimant said, 'I am not interested unless you can assure me that it is a rubber company', and the defendant then gave that assurance, then there may well have been a collateral contract and the claimant could have succeeded. But the defendant's representative might have declined to give any such assurance. On the true facts, it was not made clear to the defendant that such an assurance was being required; nor, probably, was it.

The inhibiting effect of Lord Moulton's comments seems, in practice, to have been slight. For instance, in *Webster v Higgin*,[46] a buyer was hesitating about signing a written agreement to buy a car. The seller of the car then said to the buyer: 'If you buy the Hillman 10, we will guarantee that it is in good condition.' As a result, the seller signed the contract. The car turned out to be 'a mass of second-hand and dilapidated ironmongery'. It was held that the buyer's signing the agreement was consideration for the seller's guarantee, and that the buyer could therefore sue on this collateral contract. The buyer's claim therefore succeeded even though the written contract contained far-reaching exclusion clauses.

A very strong and unusual illustration of collateral contracts can be found in the decision of Harman J in *City and Westminster Properties v Mudd*.[47] The main contract was a lease which contained a **covenant** not to use the premises for any purposes other than trade purposes. Under an earlier lease, the defendant had been in the habit of sleeping on the premises (even though this was contrary to the lease), and he declined to sign the new lease unless the claimants agreed to his sleeping there. The claimants were unwilling to include a clause permitting the defendant to sleep on the premises in the lease, because such a clause might have attracted the operation of the Rent Restriction Acts. However, the claimants orally assured the defendant that he could sleep there. The claimants brought an action against the defendant for **forfeiture** of the lease. The claimants relied upon the fact that the defendant was sleeping on the premises, in breach of the covenant to use the premises for trade purposes only. However, the claimants' action failed. Harman J held that there was a clear contract not to enforce the covenant. The defendant provided consideration for this contract by **executing** the lease in the form put before him. Whilst the result of the case seems just, since it gave effect to the true intention of the parties, it does mean that there were two simultaneous contracts at issue, one saying that the tenant may use the premises for trade purposes only, and the other saying that he may sleep there. It is difficult not to conclude that the collateral contract flatly contradicted the express terms of the main, written contract. By giving effect to the collateral contract, the parol evidence rule was greatly undermined.[48]

The same principle underpinning collateral contract applies where *A* makes a promise to *B* in consideration of *B*'s entering into a contract, or making some arrangement, with *C*. When *B* does so, he concludes a unilateral contract with *A* and can sue *A* on his promise. In *Shanklin Pier Ltd v Detel Products Ltd*,[49] the defendants (*A*) told the claimants (*B*) that if *B* would specify (as they were entitled to) that their contractors (*C*) should use *A*'s paint on

---

[46] [1948] 2 All ER 127, CA.
[47] [1959] Ch 129.
[48] See Section 4.
[49] [1951] 2 KB 854.

the pier, A could assure B that the paint would last seven years. B did as A asked. C therefore bought A's paint and used it on the pier. Unfortunately, the paint only lasted about three months. Although the contract of sale of the paint was between A and C, McNair J held that B could sue A on the collateral contract: B had given the consideration for A's promise that the paint was good for seven years by specifying that C should use that paint.

The principle was sometimes applied before the Sale of Goods Act 1979,[50] and is still capable of application, to the common situation in which a dealer (A) induces his customer (B) to enter into a credit-sale or **hire-purchase** contract not with A, but with a finance company (C), as a result of A's representations as to the quality of the goods. Such representations can be held to be promises given by A to B in consideration of B's entering into the contract with C. For instance, in *Andrews v Hopkinson*,[51] the car dealer (A) told the claimant (B) that 'It's a good little bus. I would stake my life on it.' The claimant was thereby induced to enter into a contract of hire-purchase with the finance company (C). The bus later proved to be unroadworthy, but B was nevertheless able to sue A on the promise which was 'collateral' to B's contract with C.

A remarkable application of this principle is found in *Wells (Merstham) Ltd v Buckland Sand and Silica Ltd*.[52] B, a chrysanthemum grower, visited A, a sand merchant. B was looking for sand suitable for growing chrysanthemums. A said that its 'BW sand' would be suitable and produced an analysis showing a low iron oxide content, which would have been suitable for B's purposes. Subsequently, B entered into a contract with C to buy BW sand from C which C had purchased from A. The BW sand was not suitable for growing chrysanthemums, and B's chrysanthemums therefore died. If B had bought the sand directly from A then there would clearly have been a contractual undertaking by A that the sand was suitable for the purpose. But B did not buy the sand from A but rather from C. Nevertheless, Edmund Davies J held that B had given consideration to A for A's promise that the BW sand was suitable for his purposes. The consideration provided by B consisted of buying the sand from C. This decision goes further than the other cases since there was no evidence that A requested B to enter into the contract with C, or even contemplated the possibility that he might do so. Yet Edmund Davies J held that it was sufficient that (a) A's promise was one that B might reasonably regard as being contractual in nature and (b) that B had bought the sand in reliance on that promise.

Although section 2 of the Law of Property (Miscellaneous Provisions) Act 1989 requires that, in a contract for the sale of land, all the terms expressly agreed by the parties must be incorporated in one document, it is still possible to find a collateral contract between the parties in some circumstances. For instance, in *Record v Bell*,[53] the court held that a letter by the vendor offering a warranty as to the **title** to the land, which was written in order to induce the purchaser to go ahead with the transaction, can provide the basis of a collateral contract when the purchaser accepts the vendor's offer of a warranty by going ahead with the transaction and exchanging contracts.

---

[50] See s 14(3).
[51] [1957] 1 QB 289 (McNair J).
[52] [1965] 2 QB 170 (Edmund Davies J).
[53] [1991] 4 All ER 471, ChD (Judge Baker).

4 The parol evidence rule

Finally, it is appropriate to consider the nature and scope of the parol evidence 'rule'. When the parties have formally recorded the whole of their agreement in writing, then there is a presumption that that document is the contract and the whole contract. The courts have long asserted that they will not admit evidence to add to, vary, or contradict the written agreement. This is known as the 'parol evidence rule'. In *Shogun Finance Ltd v Hudson*,[54] Lord Hobhouse offered strong support for the rule:

> The rule that other evidence may not be adduced to contradict the provisions of a contract contained in a written document is fundamental to the mercantile law of this country; the bargain is the document; the certainty of the contract depends on it. The relevant principle is well summarised in *Phipson on Evidence* 15th ed (2000), pp 1165–1166, paras 42-11 and 42-12:
>
>> 'when the parties have deliberately put their agreement into writing, it is conclusively presumed between themselves and their privies that they intend the writing to form a full and final statement of their intentions, and one which should be placed beyond the reach of future controversy, bad faith or treacherous memory.'
>
> ... This rule is one of the great strengths of English commercial law and is one of the main reasons for the international success of English law in preference to laxer systems which do not provide the same certainty.

The rule clearly purports to provide certainty since parties can proceed on the basis that they only have to concern themselves with the terms of the written document, rather than a range of other terms and considerations. Indeed, the notion that this is what parties—and particularly commercial parties—desire is perhaps supported by the increasing prevalence of entire agreement clauses, which may be welcome since they 'preclude a party to a written agreement from threshing through the undergrowth and finding in the course of negotiations some (chance) remark or statement (often long forgotten or difficult to recall or explain) on which to found a claim ... to the existence of a collateral warranty'.[55]

Entire agreement clauses are expressly chosen by the parties and are considered further in Chapter 16, since the major area of controversy surrounding such clauses is whether they purport to restrict any liability or remedy in misrepresentation.[56] However, it is worth pointing out that even an entire agreement clause does not prevent a party from introducing extrinsic evidence in a claim for rectification.[57] Similarly, there are numerous ways around the parol evidence rule. For example, extrinsic evidence can be introduced for the purposes of rectification, and to show that the contract is invalid or vitiated by reason of misrepresentation or duress. Furthermore, extrinsic evidence is admissible in order to establish the identity of the parties or to reveal the subject matter of the contract. And, as has been seen above,[58] the parol evidence rule does not prevent

---

[54] [2003] UKHL 62, [2004] 1 AC 919.

[55] *Inntrepreneur Pub Co Ltd v East Crown Ltd* [2000] 2 Lloyd's Rep 611, [2000] 3 EGLR 31 [7] (Lightman J),

[56] See Chapter 16, Section 7.

[57] See Chapter 14; *Surgicraft Ltd v Paradigm Biodevices Inc* [2010] EWHC 1291 (Ch).

[58] See eg *City and Westminster Properties v Mudd* [1959] Ch 129, discussed in Chapter 3.

the court from finding that collateral contracts have been formed. Of course, given that a collateral contract is a separate contract from the written contract under consideration, this is not formally inconsistent with the parol evidence rule, but nevertheless in practice undermines its utility.

The parol evidence rule is therefore riddled with exceptions. The logic of the rule is sound: there should be a strong presumption that a written contract represents the entirety of the parties' agreement. But this is only a starting point, and can be readily displaced by evidence of the parties' contrary intention. For this reason, the Law Commission thought that the 'rule' no longer served any real purpose,[59] and Lord Mance has said that 'the trouble with the parol evidence rule ... is one is liable to go round in a circle with [it]. If the court finds that ... all the terms of an agreement have not been reduced to the written document, of course the court is going to let in evidence of other terms'.[60] Nevertheless, the parol evidence rule has not been entirely discarded. Where the parties intend all the terms of the contract to be in the written contract, then extrinsic evidence cannot be adduced to vary or contradict that. This remains a sensible starting point.

Further Reading

J Stone, 'The Limits of *Non Est Factum* after *Gallie v Lee*' (1972) 88 LQR 190.
Examines the scope of *non est factum* after *Gallie v Lee*.

J Spencer, 'Signature, Consent, and the Rule in *L'Estrange v Graucob*' (1973) 32 CLJ 104.
Critical of the decision in *L'Estrange v Graucob*, and argues that a unilateral mistake was at issue in that case.

R Stevens, 'Objectivity, Mistake and the Parol Evidence Rule' in A Burrows and E Peel (eds),
    Contract Terms (OUP, 2007).
Offers a defence of the parol evidence rule, and support for the majority decision in *Shogun Finance Ltd v Hudson* (examined in Chapter 6).

Questions

1. Phoebe (who does not have a business of selling greyhounds) offers to sell her greyhound to Monica for £10,000. Monica asks whether the greyhound is in a good condition and likely to win races. Phoebe says: 'I give you my guarantee that the greyhound is sound, fit, and healthy in every respect.' Subsequently, the parties sign a written contract of sale which includes the following term: 'No warranty, condition, description, or representation is given or implied.' The greyhound turns out to be unhealthy, diseased, and unable to race.
    Advise Monica.

---

[59] Law Commission, *Law of Contract: The Parol Evidence Rule* (Law Com Report No 154, 1986).
[60] *Prince Jefri Bolkiah v State of Brunei Darussalam* [2007] UKPC 63.

2. Ross books a team-bonding experience for his company with Chandler Ltd. Ross pays for the experience by giving his card details over the telephone. Soon afterwards, Ross receives an email from Chandler Ltd. In the body of the email, it is stated that: 'Opening the attached terms and conditions means that you agreed to be bound by those terms.' Ross opens the attached terms and conditions, which include the following provisions:

(a) 'Under no circumstances will Chandler Ltd be liable for any loss whatsoever if the event is cancelled.'

(b) 'If you do not agree to these terms and conditions, and wish to obtain a refund, you must let us know within 14 days.'

Three weeks later, the event is cancelled due to a fire at Chandler Ltd which makes the event impossible.

Advise Ross.

12 Interpretation

Key Points

- Interpretation is the exercise by which the meaning of the contract is ascertained.
- The meaning of the contract is ascertained objectively.
- The traditional approach to interpretation focused upon the literal or plain meaning of the words used.
- The modern approach takes into account the 'matrix of fact' in which the contract is concluded, including the purpose of the contract.
- Under the modern approach, the courts may even be able to depart from clear and unambiguous language when interpreting a term.
- The modern approach has been praised for allowing judges greater flexibility in order to reach a fair result, but criticised for undermining commercial certainty, potentially prejudicing third parties, and intruding into the domain traditionally occupied by the doctrine of rectification.
- There is no real limit to what might conceivably be included in the 'matrix of fact', but the court should not have regard to pre-contractual negotiations or post-contractual conduct.

1 The meaning of interpretation

Interpretation is the exercise by which the meaning of the contract is ascertained. It is crucial to much commercial litigation: parties regularly dispute how a contract should be interpreted. The process of 'interpretation' is sometimes known as 'construction', but this language can be confusing in this context and so will largely be avoided. The 'construction' of a commercial contract has nothing to do with the formation, or bringing about, of a contract as the word might suggest. Rather, it is solely concerned with ascertaining the meaning of the contract entered into by the parties. A judge engaged in the exercise of construction has no jurisdiction to construct an agreement for the parties, or to improve the bargain made. The judge must simply give effect to the contract reached.

When interpreting a contract, a court seeks to give effect to the parties' intentions. As has been seen, an objective approach to the parties' intentions is taken;[1] the best objective evidence of the parties' intentions is the written contract itself. A well-drafted contract should have a clear, plain meaning that will be evident to the parties to the agreement, as well as to advisers and judges. However, the courts' approach to interpretation has evolved

---

[1] See Chapter 2.

over time. Under what might be called the 'traditional' approach to interpretation, where the contractual language chosen was clear and unambiguous, that language was simply given effect. This 'traditional' approach gained little academic attention: interpretation was a relatively straightforward matter of understanding the meaning of the words chosen by the parties, and there is little legal principle involved in such a process. By contrast, under what might be called the 'modern' approach to interpretation, a much broader range of factors can be taken into account, and courts now appear able to depart from the 'plain meaning' of a written document. There is no doubt that the law concerning interpretation has become very important indeed, and is central to many contractual disputes. It is therefore important to understand the key principles involved. However, it should be noted at the outset that the 'modern' approach is controversial, and future developments of the law in this area will be assessed at the end of this chapter.

2 The traditional approach to interpretation

The traditional approach to interpretation focused upon the plain meaning of the words used in a written document. Such meaning was given effect by the court. External considerations were only considered if the language itself was ambiguous.[2] There were many instances of such a 'literal' approach. For example, *In the Goods of Peel*,[3] the **testator** appointed as his **executor** 'Francis Courtnay Thorpe, of Hampton … Middlesex'. There were in fact two people called Francis Thorpe who lived in Hampton, Middlesex. Francis Courtnay Thorpe was 12 years old. Francis Corbet Thorpe was that boy's father and a friend of the testator. Lord Penzance insisted that even though it might be thought that the testator intended to appoint his friend as the executor, the written language was clear and unambiguous and should be given effect. As a result, the court held that the boy was an executor, although he was in fact one of three executors. It is, however, important to note that this is the outcome of the interpretative exercise: if a mistake had been made, this might have been corrected through the equitable remedy of rectification.[4]

3 The modern approach to interpretation

The most-cited modern decision on the interpretation of contracts is undoubtedly *Investors Compensation Scheme Ltd v West Bromwich Building Society*.[5] That case concerned a large number of elderly investors who entered into 'home income plans' with a building society on the advice of a firm of independent financial advisers. This involved the investors remortgaging their homes and investing the proceeds in **shares** or bonds. The investments failed and the advisers were **insolvent,** so the investors claimed compensation and **rescission** of the **mortgages** from the building society which had provided the mortgages. This

[2] *Shore v Wilson* (1842) 9 Cl & Fin 355, 365 (Tindal CJ).
[3] (1870) LR 2 P & D 46. This case concerned a will, but the same approach is employed as for contracts.
[4] See Chapter 14.
[5] [1998] 1 WLR 896.

claim against the building society was actually brought by the Investors Compensation Scheme (ICS), which had agreed to compensate the investors from its own funds in return for an **assignment** of the investors' causes of action. The building society argued that ICS was not entitled to bring a claim for damages because a term in the contract of assignment between the investors and ICS provided that the following claims would not be assigned, but rather retained by the investors:

> Any claim (whether sounding in rescission for undue influence or otherwise) that you [the investors] have or may have against the West Bromwich Building Society . . .

The 'natural meaning' of the clause was that ICS could not sue the building society for the damages suffered by the investors: the clause allowed the investors to retain *any claim* for damages they had against West Bromwich. Nevertheless, the majority of the House of Lords felt able to *interpret* the clause to mean: 'Any claim sounding in rescission (whether for undue influence or otherwise).'[6] This was because the background to the contract indicated that that must have been what the parties intended. Lord Hoffmann emphasised that the purpose of the agreement between ICS and the investors was that the investors were compensated and ICS would take over the investors' claims for damages; if the investors were able to sue the building society for damages they may be left over-compensated. The House of Lords therefore favoured a 'purposive' approach to interpretation.

In the course of his leading judgment, Lord Hoffmann laid down the following principles, which have proved to be extremely influential and deserve to be set out in full:

(1) Interpretation is the ascertainment of the meaning which the document would convey to a reasonable person having all the background knowledge which would reasonably have been available to the parties in the situation in which they were at the time of the contract.

(2) The background was famously referred to by Lord Wilberforce as the 'matrix of fact', but this phrase is, if anything, an understated description of what the background may include. Subject to the requirement that it should have been reasonably available to the parties and to the exception to be mentioned next, it includes absolutely anything which would have affected the way in which the language of the document would have been understood by a reasonable man.

(3) The law excludes from the admissible background the previous negotiations of the parties and their declarations of subjective intent. They are admissible only in an action for rectification. The law makes this distinction for reasons of practical policy and, in this respect only, legal interpretation differs from the way we would interpret utterances in ordinary life. The boundaries of this exception are in some respects unclear. But this is not the occasion on which to explore them.

(4) The meaning which a document (or any other utterance) would convey to a reasonable man is not the same thing as the meaning of its words. The meaning of words is a matter of dictionaries and grammars; the meaning of the document is what the parties using those words against the relevant background would reasonably have been understood to mean. The background may not merely enable the reasonable man to choose between the possible meanings of words which are ambiguous, but even (as occasionally happens in ordinary life) to conclude that the parties must, for whatever reason, have used the wrong words or

---

[6] Ibid, 912–13.

syntax (see *Mannai Investment Co Ltd v Eagle Star Life Assurance Co Ltd* [1997] 3 All ER 352, [1997] 2 WLR 945).

(5) The 'rule' that words should be given their 'natural and ordinary meaning' reflects the common sense proposition that we do not easily accept that people have made linguistic mistakes, particularly in formal documents. On the other hand, if one would nevertheless conclude from the background that something must have gone wrong with the language, the law does not require judges to attribute to the parties an intention which they plainly could not have had. Lord Diplock made this point more vigorously when he said in *Antaios Cia Naviera SA v Salen Rederierna AB, The Antaios* [1984] 3 All ER 229 at 233, [1985] AC 191 at 201:

> 'if detailed semantic and syntactical analysis of words in a commercial contract is going to lead to a conclusion that flouts business commonsense, it must be made to yield to business commonsense'.[7]

A leading treatise on the interpretation of contracts begins by citing this passage and then remarking that 'the lazy reader can stop here', such is the importance of these principles.[8] However, there is much more that needs to be analysed, and it is worth emphasising that the decision in *ICS* itself was controversial. The interpretation favoured by the majority does not correspond to the obvious meaning of the words used by the parties in the written contract, and for that reason had been rejected by the Court of Appeal. Lord Lloyd, dissenting in the House of Lords, said that:

> such a construction does violence to the language. I know of no principle of construction ... which would enable the court to take words from within the brackets, where they are clearly intended to underline the width of 'any claim,' and place them outside the brackets where they have the exact opposite effect. As Leggatt LJ said in the Court of Appeal, such a construction is simply not an available meaning of the words used; and it is, after all, from the words used that one must ascertain what the parties meant.[9]

4 The borderline between rectification and interpretation

In *ICS*, Lord Lloyd considered that if a mistake had been made then that should be corrected via the equitable doctrine of rectification rather than interpretation. Rectification will be considered in Chapter 14, and is focused on correcting mistakes. It is clear that the relationship between rectification and interpretation is 'close'.[10] It is suggested that the modern approach encapsulated in *ICS* blurs the boundary between interpretation and rectification, and that this is unfortunate. It would be preferable if mistakes were, at least as a general rule, only corrected by a doctrine which is designed for that task: that doctrine is rectification and not interpretation. An important aspect of interpretation should be that it is possible to ascertain the meaning of a contract in a straightforward and predictable

---

[7] *Investors Compensation Scheme Ltd v West Bromwich Building Society* [1998] 1 WLR 896, 912–13.

[8] Sir K Lewison, *The Interpretation of Contracts* (5th edn, Sweet & Maxwell, 2011) para 1.01.

[9] [1998] 1 WLR 896, 904. See too the decision of the Court of Appeal: [1997] CLC 348, 368.

[10] *Oceanbulk Shipping & Trading SA v TMT Asia* [2010] UKSC 44, [2011] 1 AC 662 [44].

manner. Commercial certainty might be undermined by departing from a more literal approach, and this is the result of being able to rely upon a wide range of background material beyond the four corners of the written document itself.[11]

5 The 'factual matrix'

In *ICS*, Lord Hoffmann referred to the 'matrix of fact', which derives from language previously used by Lord Wilberforce.[12] The important point is that Lord Hoffmann thought that judges should be able to take into account a range of factors beyond the words used in the contract when deciding what the contract means. This might be explained by the fact that language is never divorced from the context in which it is used. Lord Hoffmann insisted that it is important 'to assimilate the way in which [contractual] documents are interpreted by judges to the common sense principles by which any serious utterance would be interpreted in ordinary life'.[13]

The theoretical basis of Lord Hoffmann's approach in *ICS* can be readily understood: language is complicated and judges should be sensitive to this fact and the background to any particular contract. An analogy could be drawn with the everyday scenario where I put my hand on your back. I might be greeting you, or hitting you, or trying to save you from choking. But the reasonable observer would want to know the context of my actions in order to understand them accurately. Similarly, taking into account broader considerations of the 'factual matrix' might be welcomed when interpreting a contract as it is more likely to give effect to what the parties really intended (whilst still focusing on the objective intention of the parties rather than their actual intentions). The principles of *ICS* could therefore be considered to lead to a more flexible and fair approach. Consistent with this view, Lord Mance has remarked that the proper approach to interpretation is 'contextual and purposive'.[14] To give another everyday example, imagine that two people, *A* and *B*, are in a room with no windows, but one door. If *A* gestures to the door and says to *B*, 'Please shut the window, it's cold', then the words in isolation cannot be given effect: there is no window to shut. But it should be clear from the relevant background that what *A* intended was to ask *B* to shut the door.

However, broad references to the 'matrix of fact' and the perceived need to bring contract law into line with how language is interpreted in everyday situations have not been met with universal approval. For example, Sir Kim Lewison has observed that:

> in everyday life a listener may ask for clarification in cases of ambiguity; whereas it is precisely in those cases that the court is called upon to interpret a contract, with no possibility of seeking clarification. In addition, in everyday life a speaker whose words are interpreted in a way he did not intend may legitimately say that he has been misunderstood. It would be a churlish response to say that he has not, simply because his words conveyed a different meaning to a reasonable listener.[15]

---

[11] R Buxton, '"Construction" and Rectification after *Chartbrook*' (2010) 69 CLJ 253.
[12] *Prenn v Simmonds* [1971] 1 WLR 1381 (Lord Wilberforce); *Reardon Smith Lines Ltd v Hansen Tangan* [1976] 1 WLR 989.
[13] *ICS* 912.
[14] *Lloyds TSB Foundation for Scotland v Lloyds Banking Group plc* [2013] UKSC 3, [2013] 1 WLR 366 [21].
[15] Sir K Lewison, *The Interpretation of Contracts* (5th edn, Sweet & Maxwell, 2011) para 1.03.

The peculiar nature of commercial contracts has led to some desire to restrict recourse to the 'factual matrix'. After all, commercial certainty might be undermined if a wide array of background material can be introduced even where the written contract is clear. Indeed, the court may interpret the bargain in a way which is not even 'available' from the language of the document, as in *ICS*.[16] This should be a cause for concern: businessmen enter into a written contract in order to provide certainty as to the nature and extent of their rights and obligations, and do not wish to go through expensive litigation in order to ascertain the meaning of their contract. Commercial contracts are intended to be read by businessmen and, often, lawyers; the better view is that the particular context of commercial contracts should generally mean that recourse to background material and departure from clear contractual language should occur far less frequently than for everyday utterances. Linguistic purity needs to be coupled with commercial pragmatism; it is therefore suggested that the swift resolution of disputes requires a more restrained approach to contractual interpretation.

Indeed, the ability of parties to introduce a wide range of background material in support of a particular interpretation of a contract—even if it contradicts the natural and ordinary meaning of the words actually used by the parties—makes it very difficult for lawyers to give advice about the meaning of agreements.[17] Whereas it might be relatively quick and simple to advise on the meaning of the words chosen on the basis of a written document alone, it will generally be much more time-consuming and expensive to trawl through background material in order to ascertain the context within which the agreement was concluded. This is not conducive to the efficient resolution of disputes, and often such material may not be very helpful anyway. The introduction of a wide range of background material increases the costs of litigation and judicial time, and this has caused some consternation.[18] It is therefore important to consider the limits of the factual matrix, which might (at least partly) allay the concerns expressed with a liberal approach towards interpretation.

(a) The boundaries of the factual matrix

In *ICS*, Lord Hoffmann said that the admissible background to a contract 'includes absolutely anything which would have affected the way in which the language of the document would have been understood by a reasonable man'. Not long afterwards, there was further discussion about the scope of the factual matrix in the decision of the House of Lords in *Bank of Credit and Commerce International v Ali*.[19] Lord Hoffmann actually dissented on the application of his own principles enunciated in *ICS*, but clarified that when he said in *ICS* that the background 'includes absolutely anything', it was implicit that the material introduced must be relevant to the point of interpretation at issue. By itself, this seems to have done little to reduce the avalanche of material that is placed before the courts in

---

[16] Sir C Staughton, 'How Do the Courts Interpret Commercial Contracts?' (1999) 58 CLJ 303; J Spigelman, 'From Text to Context: Contemporary Contractual Interpretation' (2007) 81 ALJ 322.

[17] A Berg, 'Thrashing through the Undergrowth' (2006) 122 LQR 354.

[18] See eg *Scottish Power Plc v Britoil (Exploration) Ltd* [1997] EWCA Civ 2752 (Staughton LJ).

[19] [2001] UKHL 8, [2002] 1 AC 251.

disputes concerning contractual interpretation. More significant restrictions of the scope of the matrix of fact can be found in the rules that neither pre-contractual negotiations nor post-contractual conduct is admissible in the interpretative exercise. The role of 'business common sense' in the factual matrix must also be discussed, and there is also some suggestion that the scope of the 'factual matrix' might be more limited where the contract is unambiguous, and where third parties might be affected by a particular interpretation of the contract. These factors will all be considered in this section in turn.

(i) Pre-contractual negotiations

The most significant restriction upon the factual matrix is that pre-contractual negotiations are excluded from the interpretative exercise. Lord Hoffmann recognised this in *ICS* and observed that the 'boundaries of this exception are in some respects unclear'.[20] In *Prenn v Simmonds*, Lord Wilberforce had expressed the view that such material was 'unhelpful',[21] but others have emphasised that if the pre-contractual negotiations were objectively known to both sides, then they may help to cast light on the meaning of the contract later concluded.[22] Many commentators thought that the outright exclusion of pre-contractual negotiations would not survive the push towards the liberalisation of background material by ICS.[23]

However, in *Chartbrook Ltd v Persimmon Homes Ltd*,[24] Lord Hoffmann accepted the pragmatic basis for excluding prior communications: there may be an abundance of material which the court would have to consider, and the majority of statements presented would be 'drenched in subjectivity'.[25] Lord Hoffmann said that a system which ignores pre-contractual negotiations, even where helpful, might be 'justified in the more general interest of economy and predictability in obtaining advice and adjudicating disputes'.[26] In *Chartbrook*, Chartbrook Ltd contracted with Persimmon Homes Ltd for the development of land owned by Chartbrook Ltd. The parties disagreed on the interpretation of a particular clause about how much money Persimmon would have to pay Chartbrook. Ultimately, the House of Lords disagreed with the Court of Appeal below, and held that it was not necessary to refer to pre-contractual negotiations in order to ascertain the true meaning of the contract. But their Lordships were clear that pre-contractual negotiations should not be admissible in the interpretative exercise in any event. *Chartbrook* therefore firmly shuts the door, in the short term at least, on the possibility of parties relying upon pre-contractual negotiations in order to support a particular interpretation of the contract.

---

[20] *ICS* 912–13: see Principle 3.

[21] [1971] 1 WLR 1381, 1384.

[22] eg *Proforce Recruit Ltd v The Rugby Group Ltd* [2006] EWCA Civ 69 (Arden LJ) (though see, subsequently, [2007] EWHC 1621 (QB), [2008] 1 All ER (Comm) 569).

[23] Lord Nicholls, 'My Kingdom for a Horse: The Meaning of Words' (2005) 121 LQR 577; G McMeel, 'Prior Negotiations and Subsequent Conduct—The Next Step Forward for Contractual Interpretation?' (2003) 119 LQR 272.

[24] [2009] UKHL 38, [2009] 1 AC 1101.

[25] *Chartbrook* [38]. Lord Hoffmann was also suspicious of arguments in favour of admissibility drawn from continental legal systems (see [39]).

[26] Ibid, [41].

Indeed, Lord Hoffmann also noted other reasons in favour of the exclusionary rule, such as a possible adverse effect on third parties[27] and the danger of encouraging parties to lay a paper trail of self-serving documents.[28] These are powerful reasons for restricting the scope of background material. But such reasoning might apply equally to other material commonly introduced by the parties and is not limited to prior negotiations. It may be that a more limited approach to the range of admissible evidence should be adopted for commercial contracts generally.

In any event, this is not to say that pre-contractual negotiations serve no utility at all, since they may be relevant to the equitable doctrine of rectification.[29] Although it may sometimes be difficult to do in practice, interpretation and rectification should be considered separately; it is important that courts are not influenced by evidence of pre-contractual negotiations, which are admissible for the question of rectification, when deciding issues of interpretation.[30] However, pre-contractual negotiations are still sometimes used in the process of interpretation when establishing the 'genesis' and the objective 'aim' of the transaction.[31] Yet it is difficult to decide whether evidence of pre-contractual negotiations is being introduced to prove a fact which is known to the parties or to establish what the contract means. Only the former is admissible as part of the relevant background used in the interpretative exercise. Flaux J has observed that the dividing line between admissibility and inadmissibility regarding pre-contractual negotiations is 'so fine it almost vanishes',[32] and in *Oceanbulk Shipping & Trading SA v TMT Asia Ltd*,[33] Lord Clarke acknowledged that it may not be easy to distinguish between the two. Given such practical difficulties, it may be preferable simply not to admit pre-contractual negotiations into the interpretative process at all. After all, '[s]tatements made in the course of negotiations are often no more than statements of a negotiating stance at that point in time, thus shedding more heat than light on issues as to interpretation of the final deal.'[34]

(ii) Post-contractual conduct

Even though pre-contractual negotiations remain excluded, the general drive to widen the scope of the 'factual matrix' may suggest that the parties' conduct *after* concluding the contract should be taken into account when ascertaining the objective meaning of the contract.[35] The New Zealand courts have recognised the utility of such evidence,[36] but the traditional approach of English law is to exclude such evidence; as Lord Reid commented in *James Miller Partners Ltd v Whitworth Street Estates (Manchester) Ltd*, 'otherwise one

---

[27] Ibid, [40].

[28] Ibid, [38].

[29] See Chapter 14.

[30] *Tartsinis v Navona Management Co* [2015] EWHC 57 (Comm) [8]–[13] (Leggatt J).

[31] *Prenn* 1385 (Lord Wilberforce).

[32] *Excelsior Group Productions Ltd v Yorkshire Television Ltd* [2009] EWHC 1751 (Comm) [25].

[33] *Oceanbulk* (see n 54).

[34] *Scottish Widows Fund and Life Assurance Society v BGC International* [2012] EWCA Civ 607 [34] (Arden LJ).

[35] Lord Bingham, 'A New Thing Under the Sun: The Interpretation of Contract and the *ICS* Decision' (2008) 12 Edinburgh Law Review 374, 389–90.

[36] *Wholesale Distributors Ltd v Gibbons Holdings Ltd* [2007] NZSC 37.

might have the result that a contract meant one thing the day it was signed, but by reason of subsequent events meant something different a month or a year later'.[37] This would clearly be unsatisfactory. Demands for commercial certainty may support the maintenance of a rule excluding post-contractual conduct in the same manner as pre-contractual negotiations. Moreover, 'subsequent conduct is equally referable to what the parties meant to say as to the meaning of what they said'.[38]

However, post-contractual conduct might be relevant to **estoppel**. Suppose that one of the parties, X, misunderstands the agreement and misleads the other, Y, as to its meaning. If Y acts to his detriment in reliance on that misinterpretation, X will be estopped from denying that this is the true construction of the contract. The meaning of the contract will have been effectively changed.[39] Furthermore, even where there is no misrepresentation but the parties have mutually agreed that the contract bears a particular meaning (which is not the true, objective meaning), and they act on that assumption, both will be estopped from denying that it has the meaning assumed. This is known as 'estoppel by convention'. This was what occurred in *Amalgamated Investment and Property Co v Texas Commerce*.[40] A guaranteed a loan made by T to a subsidiary of A. The wording of the guarantee only covered loans made by T, but this particular loan was actually made by P, a subsidiary of T. A went into **liquidation**, and A's liquidators sought a declaration that A was not liable on this guarantee, since the loan had not been made by T as agreed, but by T's subsidiary. The Court of Appeal held that A was estopped from denying that it had guaranteed the loan, since all the parties had acted on the understanding that A was guaranteeing this particular loan, and it would be unfair for A now to depart from that promise to the detriment of T and P. However, while the doctrine of estoppel applies to a mistaken interpretation of a contract, it cannot operate so as to defeat a rule of law. For example, where the parties to an agreement for a **lease** intended it to have retrospective effect, the **landlord** cannot be estopped from denying that it had that effect. It is a rule of law that a grant of land cannot take effect retrospectively.[41]

(iii) 'Business common sense'

The *ICS* principles also draw upon a notion of 'business common sense' as being relevant to the interpretation of the contract. This is a somewhat vague notion and judges clearly differ as to how it should be applied. The warning of Neuberger LJ in *Skanska Rashleigh Weatherfoil Ltd v Somerfield Stores Ltd* should be heeded:[42]

> the court must be careful before departing from the natural meaning of the provision in the contract merely because it may conflict with its notions of commercial common sense of what

---

[37] *James Miller Partners Ltd v Whitworth Street Estates (Manchester) Ltd* [1970] AC 583, 603.

[38] *L Schuler AG v Wickman Machine Tool Sales Ltd* [1974] AC 235, 269 (Lord Simon).

[39] *Sarat Chunder Dey v Gopal Chunder Lala* (1892) 19 Ind App 203, PC, and *Calgary Milling Co Ltd v American Surety Co of New York* [1919] 3 WWR 98, PC, both relied on by Robert Goff J in *Amalgamated Investment and Property Co v Texas Commerce* [1981] 1 All ER 923, affirmed [1982] QB 84.

[40] [1981] 1 All ER 923, affirmed [1982] QB 84.

[41] *Keen v Holland* [1984] 1 WLR 251, CA.

[42] *Skanska Rashleigh Weatherfoil Ltd v Somerfield Stores Ltd* [2006] EWCA Civ 1732, [2007] CILL 2449 [22].

the parties may, must or should have thought or intended. Judges are not always the most commercially-minded, let alone the most commercially experienced, of people, and should, I think, avoid arrogating to themselves overconfidently the role of arbiter of commercial reasonableness or likelihood.

Disputes regarding the 'commerciality' of a particular interpretation are common; but the weight that should be given to this notion, and its content, remain unclear.[43] As Arden LJ observed in *Re Golden Key*: 'The line between giving weight to the commerciality of a provision and writing a provision into an agreement can become a fine one.'[44] Judges often disagree about whether or not a particular interpretation complies with 'business common sense'; as Ward LJ amusingly said, 'the higher you go [in the judiciary], the less the essential oxygen of common sense is available to you'.[45]

The distinction between holding that an agreement makes no commercial common sense and concluding that one of the parties simply made a bad bargain may be very fine indeed. There was even a split about whether or not the plain meaning of the contract made 'business common sense' in the leading case of *ICS*. Lord Hoffmann thought it made no sense for ICS to compensate the elderly investors and then not be entitled to recover damages. His Lordship also thought that there was no satisfactory explanation why the parenthesis in the relevant clause only referred to rescission on the basis of undue influence, rather than on other grounds as well (such as misrepresentation). Lord Hoffmann concluded that the literal meaning of the contract made little commercial sense, which in turn indicated that something had gone wrong with the language chosen. On the other hand, the dissenting judge, Lord Lloyd, thought that the language used was perfectly clear, intelligible, and not necessarily contrary to business common sense. His Lordship relied upon the fact that the investors certainly did retain some rights against the building society, and there was no obvious reason why those rights would not include a right to damages. After all, there were other parties ICS might sue in order to recover damages (such as firms of solicitors) and it was not up to the court to improve the bargain that ICS, the larger commercial entity, had made. Given the need for certainty in commercial contracts, it is suggested that it might be better only to depart from the clear language of a written contract on the basis of 'business common sense' or 'commerciality' where the conventional meaning of the contract would lead to 'manifest absurdity'.[46] This is a high threshold.

The Supreme Court has recently also urged caution about invoking 'commercial common sense' when interpreting a contract. *Arnold v Britton*[47] concerned the interpretation of a service charge clause in leases of holiday chalets. The clause differed slightly (but

---

[43] In a different context, Lord Phillips has observed that there is no universal meaning of 'common sense': *Moore Stephens (A Firm) v Stone Rolls Ltd (in liquidation)* [2009] UKHL 39, [2009] 3 WLR 455 [5].

[44] *Re Golden Key* [2009] EWCA Civ 636 [29].

[45] *Oceanbulk Shipping & Trading SA v TMT Asia Ltd* [2010] EWCA Civ 79, [2010] 1 WLR 1803 [41], but see subsequently [2010] UKSC 44, [2011] 1 AC 662.

[46] This was perhaps the 'traditional' approach to interpretation: *River Wear Commissioners v Adamson* (1877) 2 App Cas 743, 764–5 (Lord Blackburn): 'an absurdity or inconvenience so great as to convince the Court that the intention could not have been to use in their ordinary signification'.

[47] [2015] UKSC 36, [2015] AC 1619.

immaterially for our present purposes) in different leases, but a typical clause provided that the landlords were:

> To pay to the **Lessors** without any deductions in addition to the said rent a proportionate part of the expenses and outgoings incurred by the Lessors in the repair maintenance and renewal of the facilities of the Estate and the provision of services thereafter set out the year sum of Ninety Pounds and value added tax (if any) for the first year of the term hereby granted increasing thereafter by Ten Pounds per Hundred for every subsequent year thereof.

The plain and natural meaning of this clause was that the charge was £90 in the first year, rising by 10 per cent each year thereafter. The Supreme Court, by a majority, gave effect to the unambiguous contractual language. This was despite Lord Carnwath, dissenting, pointing out that the charge would significantly exceed the cost of providing the services, and made no commercial sense. Lord Hodge, in the majority, recognised the force of Lord Carnwath's dissent; Lord Hodge expressly acknowledged that the result was 'highly unsatisfactory' and that Parliament might wish to intervene in this area.[48] However, Lord Hodge also insisted that it was illegitimate to rewrite the contract 'in the name of commercial good sense'.[49] After all, the parties might simply have made a bad bargain; there was no other interpretation of the contract that had the requisite basis in the words used and factual matrix.

Lord Neuberger, with whom Lord Sumption and Lord Hughes agreed, was equally forthright. His Lordship emphasised that 'commercial common sense … should not be invoked to undervalue the importance of the language in the provision which is to be construed'.[50] This was particularly important since 'unlike commercial common sense and the surrounding circumstances, the parties have control over the language they use in a contract'.[51] Moreover, 'commercial common sense is not to be invoked retrospectively',[52] so the fact that a contract has turned out badly for one party is not a reason to depart from the contractual language shown. In the same vein, 'a court should be very slow to reject the natural meaning of a provision as correct simply because it appears to be a very imprudent term for one of the parties to have agreed, even ignoring the benefit of wisdom of hindsight'.[53] The court must not rescue a contract from a bad bargain by rewriting a contract simply because it fails to accord with a vague notion of 'commercial common sense'.

(iv) The role of ambiguity

In *Oceanbulk Shipping & Trading SA v TMT Asia Ltd*, Lord Clarke cited with approval a previous speech of Lord Steyn, in which he said of *ICS* that 'Lord Hoffmann made crystal clear that an ambiguity need not be established before the surrounding circumstances

---

[48] Ibid, [66].
[49] Ibid, [77].
[50] Ibid, [17].
[51] Ibid.
[52] Ibid, [19].
[53] Ibid, [20].

may be taken into account'.[54] Indeed, in *Chartbrook*, Lord Hoffmann said that 'there is not, so to speak, a limit to the amount of red ink or verbal rearrangement or correction which the court is allowed'.[55] This highlights that judges may effectively rewrite a particular term of a contract in order for it to reflect what they think a reasonable observer, informed of the matrix of fact within which the contract was made, would understand the contract to mean, even if the written term is clear and unambiguous. This reduces the importance placed on the terms chosen by the parties in their final, written agreement. It is unclear whether this is a welcome development.

A good example of this phenomenon is *Mannai Investment Co Ltd v Eagle Star Life Assurance Co Ltd*.[56] The contract at issue was a lease of an office in Jermyn Street, London, for ten years from 13 January 1992. There was a break clause which could only be exercised by serving, in writing, not less than six months' notice on the landlord to expire 'on the third anniversary of the term commencement date'. The office rental market crashed, so the **tenant** wanted to exercise the break clause and take advantage of lower rents. Unfortunately, the tenant sent a notice purporting to terminate the lease on 12 January 1995. This was a mistake: the correct date for the termination was 13 January 1995. Nevertheless the House of Lords felt able to *interpret* '12 January' as *objectively* meaning '13 January', without relying upon rectification on the basis of mistake. The result in *Mannai* was only reached by a bare majority of the House of Lords, and is a good example of the ability of judges now to correct mistakes through the interpretative process.

Although all language might in some sense be said to be ambiguous without being put in its proper context, clearly some terms will have an ordinarily accepted plain meaning. Lord Mustill's helpful reminder in *Charter Reinsurance Co Ltd v Fagan* must not be forgotten:[57]

> There comes a point at which the court should remind itself that the task is to discover what the parties meant from what they have said, and that to force upon the words a meaning which they cannot fairly bear is to substitute for the bargain actually made one which the court believes could better have been made. This is an illegitimate role for a court. Particularly in the field of commerce, where the parties need to know what they must do and what they can insist on not doing, it is essential for them to be confident that they can rely on the court to enforce their contract according to its terms.

It seems unsatisfactory for the courts to undermine unambiguous language which has been deliberately chosen by the parties. The plain meaning of the contractual language agreed by the parties should be the starting point for the interpretative exercise, and it is arguable that where the language is clear and unambiguous, the issue of interpretation should not require further resort to other factors. Parties strive—or should be encouraged to strive—for clear contractual language which should be straightforward to interpret, and this should be afforded the utmost respect.

---

[54] *Oceanbulk Shipping & Trading SA v TMT Asia Ltd* [2010] UKSC 44, [2011] 1 AC 662 [36], approving *R (Westminster City Council) v National Asylum Support Service* [2002] UKHL 38, [2002] 1 WLR 2956 [5]. Compare the situation in Australia: eg *Codelfa Construction Pty Ltd v State Rail Authority of NSW* (1982) 149 CLR 337; *Western Export Services Inc v Jireh International Pty Ltd* [2011] HCA 45, (2011) 86 ALJR 1.

[55] *Chartbrook* [25].

[56] [1997] 3 All ER 352.

[57] [1997] AC 313.

It may be possible to discern a recent trend in this direction. Thus in *Rainy Sky SA v Kookmin Bank*, Lord Clarke stated that: 'Where the parties have used unambiguous language, the court must apply it.'[58] Similarly, in *Multi-Link Leisure Developments Ltd v North Lanarkshire Council*, concerning the interpretation of a lease, Lord Hope held that 'words … should not be changed, taken out or moved … until it has become clear that the language the parties actually used creates an ambiguity which cannot be solved otherwise'.[59] Similar comments were recently made by the Supreme Court in *Arnold v Britton*, in which Lord Neuberger emphasised that a court should not try to construct an ambiguity, and should instead focus on the plain meaning of the relevant words.[60] A requirement of ambiguity may be welcomed by the lower courts, since it renders the task of a judge more straightforward where there is a clear, plain meaning of a contract; this would force a claimant to seek rectification if that meaning is to be altered.[61] Of course, where the term itself is ambiguous, recourse to the factual matrix is understandable, as the courts must choose between competing interpretations and have to look beyond the contract itself in order to do so.[62]

(v) The impact on third parties

Lord Hoffmann himself recognised that in some circumstances the scope of the factual matrix may be limited.[63] This idea has been developed in subsequent cases and may pose significant brakes upon any wholesale shift 'from text to context' in the interpretative exercise.[64] In *Re Sigma*, a complicated commercial trust deed included a clause about how assets were to be distributed.[65] The Supreme Court excluded from the admissible background circumstances which would not have been known to **creditors** since third parties who were unaware of 'surrounding circumstances' known only to the signatories of the contract should not be unfairly prejudiced.

A similar concern to protect third parties was shown by the majority of the Court of Appeal in *Cherry Tree Ltd v Landmain Ltd*.[66] In that case, Dancastle Associates Ltd had a registered **charge** over land owned by Landmain Ltd. The legal charge itself contained no indication that the statutory power of sale under section 101(3) of the Law of Property Act 1925[67] might have been varied, but Dancastle and Landmain also entered into a parallel 'facility agreement', **executed** on the same date as the registered charge in July 2010,

---

[58] [2011] UKSC 50, [2001] 1 WLR 2900 [23].

[59] [2010] UKSC 47, [2011] 1 All ER 175 [11].

[60] *Arnold v Britton* [2015] UKSC 36, [2015] AC 1619 [18].

[61] *William Hare Ltd v Shepherd Construction Ltd* [2010] EWCA Civ 283, [2010] BLR 358; *Swallowfalls Ltd v Monaco Yachting and Technologies SAM* [2014] EWCA Civ 186.

[62] Indeed, an ambiguous term may generally be interpreted against the person relying upon it due to the principle of *contra proferentem*: see Chapter 15, Section 1(b).

[63] *Mannai* 779: 'There are documents in which the need for certainty is paramount and which admissible background is restricted to avoid the possibility that the same document may have different meanings for different people according to their knowledge of the background.'

[64] J Spigelman, 'From Text to Context: Contemporary Contractual Interpretation' (2007) 81 ALJ 322.

[65] *Re Sigma Finance Corp (in administration)* [2009] UKSC 2, [2010] 1 All ER 571.

[66] *Cherry Tree Ltd v Landmain Ltd* [2012] EWCA Civ 736, [2013] Ch 305.

[67] This provides that there is a power to sell the charged property which can be exercised when the mortgage money has become due.

which stated that the charge was immediately enforceable, even if there was no default in repayment. In December 2010, Dancastle exercised its extended power of sale and sold the property to Cherry Tree Ltd. Cherry Tree sought to become the registered proprietor of the property. However, Landmain was not in default and argued that, since there was nothing in the charge itself to extend the statutory power of sale, Dancastle was not authorised to enforce the legal charge. Cherry Tree therefore needed to be able to introduce the 'facility agreement' as part of the factual matrix in order to interpret the charge in a manner consistent with its becoming the registered proprietor of the property.

Only Arden LJ, dissenting, favoured this outcome. Her Ladyship took a broad approach to the *ICS* principles, which she preferred as 'more likely to achieve the meaning which the parties would themselves have intended'.[68] By contrast, the majority insisted that the task of the court is 'not ... to ascertain "what the parties intended to agree" but what the instrument means'.[69] The former question should be better dealt with through the doctrine of rectification.[70] The majority emphasised that the Land Register is meant to be conclusive and complete;[71] only the charge was open to inspection on the register. Third parties who looked at the register would not be aware of the parallel facility agreement. As a result, the facility agreement should not form part of the admissible background.

The robust approach of the majority in *Cherry Tree* represents a significant inroad into the wide-ranging applicability of the *ICS* principles. Lewison LJ thought that a similarly restrictive approach to background material was required when considering 'negotiable and registrable contracts or public documents' generally, including planning permissions, companies' articles of association, **injunctions**, and receivership orders.[72] As Lewison LJ explained, 'the justification for the restrictive approach is that third parties might (not will) need to rely on the terms of the instrument under consideration without access to extraneous material'.[73]

The decision of the majority in *Cherry Tree* is sensible. But it does not sit entirely comfortably with the general tenor of the modern approach to interpretation encapsulated in *ICS*. After all, 'ordinary' commercial contracts may be assigned or charged, and their meaning should be equally clear to third parties. This has troubled some judges who, as a result, have adopted a conservative approach to contract interpretation.[74] A former Chief Justice of New South Wales has remarked, extra-judicially, that 'the impact on, and the import to third parties is, in my opinion, significantly understated in this analysis' of Lord Hoffmann in *ICS*; that the background should, in the former Chief Justice's view, be significantly restricted in a substantial range of commercial contracts, including derivatives, represents 'a significant defect in Lord Hoffmann's schema'.[75]

---

[68] *Cherry Tree Ltd* [37]. See too M Barber and R Thomas, 'Contractual Interpretation, Registered Documents and Third Party Effects' (2014) 77 MLR 597.

[69] *Cherry Tree Ltd* [99] (Lewison LJ).

[70] See Chapter 14.

[71] See eg Land Registration Act 2002, ss 120(2), 58.

[72] *Cherry Tree Ltd* [124]–[125].

[73] Ibid, [125].

[74] eg *National Bank of Sharjah v Dellborg*, unreported, 9 July 1997 (Saville LJ).

[75] Spigelman (n 64) 334.

However, in *Chartbrook*, Lord Hoffmann explicitly considered this issue concerning the protection of third parties. Having recognised that the impact upon third parties was a further pragmatic reason for excluding evidence of prior negotiations from the process of interpretation, his Lordship acknowledged that:

> The law has sometimes to compromise between protecting the interests of the contracting parties and those of third parties. But an extension of the admissible background will, at any rate in theory, increase the risk that a third party will find that the contract does not mean what he thought. How often this is likely to be a practical problem is hard to say.[76]

It has been suggested that the risk of prejudicing third parties may be sufficiently accommodated by the possibility of contractual estoppel: for example, if an assignee has acted to his detriment in reliance on the 'conventional' meaning of the written document which does not correspond to a more 'liberal' interpretation of the contract, the assignee might be protected by estoppel. But it nevertheless seems unsatisfactory for there to be a different meaning of a contract if the claimant is the original contracting party or an assignee.

In *Chartbrook*, Lord Hoffmann said that 'an assignee must either inquire as to any relevant background or take his chance on how that might affect the meaning a court will give to the document'.[77] This seems to represent the current law, but may be considered to place an excessive burden on the assignee. The robust, pragmatic approach of *Cherry Tree* might be preferred. On the facts of *Cherry Tree*, the third party would not actually have been unfairly prejudiced by taking into account the background information. Nevertheless, the Court of Appeal held that the mere *risk* of prejudice, and the requirement for there to be a single, consistent interpretation of the contract, meant that the relevant background needed to be restricted.

6 Interpretation: the future

The consistent flow of cases up to the highest level indicates, at the very least, that interpretation is not easy. This is emphasised by the fact that decisions at the highest level are rarely reached unanimously. But this might also indicate that the relevant principles are difficult to apply and, perhaps, need to be refined. The purposive approach to interpretation affords the court greater flexibility in determining what the parties meant, but increases the risk of the court rewriting the parties' contract. It is important to remember what Lord Simon said in *Schuler*:[78]

> There is one general principle of law which is ... most pungently expressed in *Norton on Deeds* (1906), p. 43, though it applies to all written instruments:

---

[76] *Chartbrook* [40].
[77] Ibid, [40].
[78] *Schuler* [1974] AC 235, 263.

'... the question to be answered always is, "What is the meaning of what the parties have said?" not, "What did the parties mean to say?" ... it being a presumption *juris et de jure* ... that the parties intended to say that which they have said.'

Particularly in the commercial context, where written contracts are generally at issue, correcting mistakes is best left to rectification.[79] At the very least, it is suggested that the courts should be more cautious about deciding that something has gone wrong with the language used by the parties or that it fails to accord with business common sense: the sanctity of the document freely signed by commercial parties should be greatly respected. This appears to have been recognised by the Supreme Court in *Arnold v Britton* and should be endorsed. Perhaps a compromise position between the 'traditional' and 'modern' approach will ultimately be adopted along the lines proposed by Calnan. Calnan has suggested that, when interpreting commercial contracts, the matrix of fact be limited to the identity of the parties, the nature and purpose of the transaction, and the market in which the transaction took place.[80] Such contextual factors will invariably be well known to both the contracting parties and third party observers without the need for any extensive trawl through extrinsic material. This restrictive approach to background material represents a much more conservative approach to the surrounding circumstances than that suggested by Lord Hoffmann, but it might increase parties' control over how their agreements will be interpreted, and make it easier to give advice on the meaning of a contract.

Further Reading

R Calnan, 'Construction of Commercial Contracts: A Practitioner's Perspective' in A Burrows and E Peel (eds), *Contract Terms* (OUP, 2007).
Argues that *ICS* has caused much uncertainty when drafting commercial contracts, and favours a compromise solution under which the matrix of fact is limited to the identity of the parties, the nature and purpose of the transaction, and the market in which the transaction took place.

PS Davies, 'The Meaning of Commercial Contracts' in PS Davies and J Pila (eds), *The Jurisprudence of Lord Hoffmann* (Hart, 2015).
Discusses the impact of Lord Hoffmann's principles in *ICS* and suggests that the courts may now be rowing back slightly from the very liberal approach favoured by Lord Hoffmann.

D McLauchlan, 'The Lingering Confusion and Uncertainty in the Law of Contract Interpretation' [2015] LMCLQ 406.
Analyses recent developments in the law of interpretation and argues in favour of maintaining the 'commercial interpretation' approach advocated by Lord Hoffmann.

---

[79] See Chapter 14.
[80] R Calnan, *Principles of Contractual Interpretation* (OUP, 2013) 66.

? Question

'What is clear from these cases is that there is not, so to speak, a limit to the amount of red ink or verbal rearrangement or correction which the court is allowed. All that is required is that it should be clear that something has gone wrong with the language and that it should be clear what a reasonable person would have understood the parties to have meant.' (Lord Hoffmann in *Chartbrook Ltd v Persimmon Homes Ltd*)

What limits, if any, should be placed on the interpretative exercise?

13 Implication

🔑 Key Points

- A term can be implied into a particular contract because it is necessary to give effect to the parties' intentions. This is known as 'implication in fact'.
- Whether a term should be implied 'in fact' has traditionally depended upon whether the term was so obvious to both parties that it went without saying, or whether the term was necessary to give 'business efficacy' to the contract.
- A more recent trend has sought to equate implication in fact with the modern approach to interpretation. This is controversial. There may be a significant difference between interpreting express terms and implying a term to fill a gap in the written contract.
- Terms may also be implied because they are customary in a particular trade.
- A term might be implied 'in law' into all contracts of a particular type. Such terms might be implied as a result of statute or judicial decisions.
- Where a judge decides that a term should be implied 'in law', courts can take into account policy reasons when deciding whether an implied term is necessary for the type of contract at issue. This sort of implied term does not depend upon the parties' intentions.
- A court should not imply a term if to do so would be inconsistent with an express term of the contract.

In Chapter 12 the focus was upon ascertaining the meaning of the words chosen by the parties—the process of interpretation. In the present chapter, the question is whether a term should be imported into the contract although it was never expressed in words; should the term be implied? The actual words used by the parties, even when these are set down in a formal, written contract, do not always—indeed, they hardly ever—represent the full extent of the agreement. The parties may omit mention of some matter for the very reason that it is so obvious that 'it goes without saying'. For example, we have already seen that if A agrees to sell his car to B at a price to be fixed by C, if either party prevents C from fixing the price, he is liable in damages to the other.[1] A did not expressly promise B that he would allow C to have access to the car in order to estimate its value. He is nevertheless in breach of contract if he refuses access to C. The contract simply cannot work if C cannot examine the car, and it must be taken that both parties intended their contract to work. The reasonable seller would, no doubt, be surprised if he was asked to make such a promise in express terms.

---

[1] See Chapter 5, Section 4.

1 Terms implied 'in fact'

(a) The traditional tests: necessary to make the contract work

The court will find that the contract includes such implied terms as are necessary to make it work—to give it 'business efficacy', in the traditional terminology of the law. The theory is that the court is not making a contract for the parties but is implementing their intentions because this is something that they *must* have intended. As MacKinnon LJ put it in *Shirlaw v Southern Foundries Ltd*:[2]

> **Prima facie** that which in any contract is left to be implied and need not be expressed is something so obvious that it goes without saying; so that, if, while the parties were making their bargain, an officious bystander were to suggest some express provision for it in their agreement, they would testily suppress him with a common, 'Oh, of course!'...

This 'officious bystander' test is a strict one. The court must be satisfied that both parties would actually have responded 'Oh, of course!'[3] A good example of the test in operation is *Spring v National Amalgamated Stevedores and Dockers Society*.[4] That case concerned a trade union dispute; it was argued that there was an implied term that members would act in conformity with the Bridlington Agreement.[5] However, the claimant, who became a union member, was completely unaware of the Bridlington Agreement. As a result, had he been asked by an officious bystander whether it was a term of the contract that he act in accordance with that agreement, he would not have replied, 'Oh, of course!' but rather, 'What is that?' The judge therefore rightly refused to imply such a term into the agreement.

The business efficacy principle is sometimes called the doctrine of *The Moorcock*, after the leading case.[6] A shipowner contracted with the owner of a wharf to moor his ship at the owner's jetty on the Thames. Both parties knew that the ship would settle on the river bed at low water. When it did so, the centre of the vessel settled on a hard ridge beneath mud and sustained damage. The shipowner recovered damages in contract for breach of an implied term that the owner of the wharf had taken reasonable care to find out whether the berth was safe. If he had taken such care, he would have found out that it was unsafe and, it must be presumed, would not have invited ships to tie up there. In determining whether a term should be implied, the relative knowledge or means of knowledge of the parties is of no less importance than in determining whether an express statement is intended to be a contractual term.[7] A crucial fact here was that 'with regard to the safety of the ground outside the jetty the shipowner could know nothing at all, and the jetty owner might with reasonable care know everything'.[8] The reasonable shipowner was entitled to suppose that

---

[2] [1939] 2 KB 206, 227.

[3] Or at least that the reasonable people in the position of the parties would have so responded: see *Marks & Spencer plc v BNP Paribas Securities Services Trust Co (Jersey) Ltd* [2015] UKSC 72.

[4] [1956] 1 WLR 585 (Sir Leonard Stone V-C).

[5] The Bridlington Agreement between trade unions prohibited each trade union from poaching the members of other trade unions.

[6] (1889) 14 PD 64, CA.

[7] See Chapter 6, Section 1(a).

[8] (1889) 14 PD 64, 68.

the wharf owner had at least taken reasonable care to find out whether the berth was safe before inviting ships to moor there—otherwise the shipowner was simply 'buying an opportunity of danger'.[9] The term was necessary to give the contract business efficacy.[10] Note that the court went no further than was necessary to give the claimant redress. It did not hold that the wharf owner had guaranteed that the berth was safe, nor even that the wharf owner had taken reasonable steps to make it safe. The berth outside the jetty was under the control of the river authority, not the wharf owner, and the court indicated an unwillingness to imply a promise to do something (make the berth safe) which it was not within the alleged **promisor**'s power to do.

The 'officious bystander' and 'business efficacy' tests operate alongside one another and often overlap: what is necessary to make the contract work will generally go without saying. It is crucial to note that the touchstone of implication is always necessity, not reasonableness, and the courts will adopt a strict approach. So, where a firm of solicitors made an unconditional offer of articles (which would now be called a training contract) to a student, not drawing his attention to their standard terms, including a term that the offer was subject to the student's having passed (or be waiting the results of) the Solicitor's Final Examination (now the Legal Practice Course), it was held that no term to that effect should be implied. The term was not necessary; it could not be said that the contract would make no sense without it, nor that it was so obvious that it was unnecessary to make it explicit. This was not something that 'goes without saying'.[11] In *Errington v Errington*,[12] it will be recalled that Lord Denning, applying the orthodox test, held that it was necessary to imply a term into the father's offer that he would not revoke it, once the children had embarked on performance; but the House of Lords could detect no such necessity in *Luxor v Cooper*.[13] In the latter case, the offer made was an attractive one, which a reasonable business man might well have been happy to act on, without the argued-for implied term. The express terms did not lack business efficacy.

(b) A broader, interpretative approach?

The officious bystander and business efficacy tests ensure that the courts only add terms to the parties' contract where it is necessary to do so. Any loss suffered which is not covered by the agreement should simply lie where it falls. However, it may be thought that a broader test for implication was suggested by Lord Hoffmann in the Privy Council decision of *Attorney General of Belize v Belize Telecom Ltd*:[14]

> It follows that in every case in which it is said that some provision ought to be implied in an instrument, the question for the court is whether such a provision would spell out in express words what the instrument, read against the relevant background, would reasonably be

---

[9] Ibid.

[10] In *Reigate v Union Manufacturing Co (Ramsbottom) Ltd* [1918] 1 KB 592, 605, Scrutton LJ said that '[a] term can only be implied if it is necessary in the business sense to give efficacy to the contract'.

[11] *Stubbes v Trower* [1987] IRLR 321, CA.

[12] [1952] 1 KB 290.

[13] [1941] AC 108; see generally Chapter 3, Section 2.

[14] [2009] UKPC 10, [2009] 2 All ER (Comm) 1 [21]. Although the facts of the case concerned the articles of association of a company, Lord Hoffmann's speech makes it clear that the principles are equally applicable in the law of contract generally.

understood to mean … There is only one question: is that what the instrument, read as a whole against the relevant background, would reasonably be understood to mean?

This approach would appear to assimilate implication within the broad approach to interpretation of written contracts examined in Chapter 12.[15] This is consistent with Lord Hoffmann's approach to interpretation generally: if there really is no limit to the amount of red ink that can be spilled in the interpretative process,[16] then existing words might be altered and new terms added under the umbrella of interpretation. However, there is an important difference between, on the one hand, what the parties choose to express, and, on the other hand, silence. If the parties have clearly chosen certain words, such language should be given the utmost respect and interpretation should, generally, be straightforward. Silence, by contrast, is inherently ambiguous; there should be no interpretation of silence. Moreover, it is particularly important that courts do not imply a term simply because it would be reasonable to do so.[17] That would intrude far too greatly into the parties' bargain. Whilst a reasonable interpretation of words actually chosen by the parties may be acceptable, the courts should only add terms implied in fact where that is necessary. The difference between implication and interpretation was clearly recognised by Sir Thomas Bingham MR in *Philips Electronique Grand Public SA v British Sky Broadcasting Ltd*, who went on to say that:[18]

the court comes to the task of implication with the benefit of hindsight, and it is tempting for the court then to fashion a term which will reflect the merits of the situation as they then appear. Tempting, but wrong.

The decision in *Belize* has been regularly cited by courts, and was quickly accepted as representing English law.[19] But judges have rightly remained unwilling to imply a term simply because it would be reasonable to do so. Different parts of Lord Hoffmann's judgment in *Belize* have been relied upon to maintain the test of necessity developed through decisions such as *Shirlaw* and *The Moorcock*. For example, in *The Reborn*,[20] Sir Anthony Clarke MR placed great weight on the default position being that no term should be implied,[21] and took care to 'stress the importance of the test of necessity'.[22]

---

[15] cf *Equitable Life Assurance Society v Hyman* [2002] 1 AC 408, [2000] 3 WLR 529, HL.

[16] See *Chartbrook Ltd v Persimmon Homes Ltd* [2009] UKHL 38, [2009] 1 AC 1101 [25], discussed at Chapter 12, Section 5(a)(iv).

[17] For a broader approach to implied terms which led to the court implying a term that the contract would be performed in good faith, see *Yam Seng Pte Ltd (A company registered in Singapore) v International Trade Corp Ltd* [2013] EWHC 111 (QB), [2013] 1 All ER (Comm) 1321 [123]–[153] (Leggatt J); cf *Mid Essex Hospital Services NHS Trust v Compass Group UK and Ireland Ltd (t/a Medirest)* [2013] EWCA Civ 200, [2013] BLR 265 [77]–[92] (Jackson LJ). For further discussion of implied terms of good faith, see Chapter 19.

[18] [1995] EMLR 472, 482. This passage has recently been endorsed by the Supreme Court: see *Zurich Insurance PLC UK Branch (Appellant) v International Energy Group Limited* [2015] UKSC 33 [149] (Lord Sumption, with whom Lord Neuberger and Lord Reed agreed).

[19] eg *Mediterranean Salvage & Towage Ltd v Seamar Trading & Commerce Inc* [2009] EWCA Civ 531, [2010] 1 All ER (Comm) 1, CA.

[20] Ibid.

[21] Ibid, [10]–[11].

[22] Ibid, [17]. See too eg [48] (Rix LJ) and [63] (Carnwath LJ).

Indeed, the Supreme Court has continued to refer to the traditional tests of implication. For example, the officious bystander test and business efficacy doctrine were invoked by Lord Clarke in *Aberdeen City Council v Stewart Milne Group Ltd*,[23] which made no reference to *Belize*. And although *Belize* was noted in the decision of the Supreme Court in *Geys v Société Générale, London Branch*, Baroness Hale immediately followed the citation of *Belize* with the comment that 'terms are only implied where it is necessary to give business efficacy to the particular contract in question'.[24]

More recently, in *Marks & Spencer plc v BNP Paribas Securities Services Trust Co (Jersey) Ltd*,[25] the Supreme Court insisted that the traditional tests must be maintained, and that the decision of the Privy Council in *Belize* did not change the law. Marks & Spencer had paid to its landlord, BNP Paribas, the rent for a quarter of the year in advance. Marks & Spencer also validly exercised a break clause which terminated the lease before that quarter was over. Marks & Spencer argued that it was entitled to a refund of the rent paid for the period after the lease had been terminated, since a term should be implied to that effect. Even if such a term was reasonable on the facts, the Supreme Court was clear that no such term should be implied. In a detailed commercial contract, a term would only be implied if that was necessary. Lord Neuberger, with whom Lord Sumption and Lord Hodge agreed,[26] thought that '[i]t is necessary to emphasise that there has been no dilution of the requirements which have to be satisfied before a term will be implied'[27] after the decision in *Belize*. Indeed, the Supreme Court held that 'the law governing the circumstances in which a term will be implied into a contract remains unchanged following *Belize Telecom*'.[28] Lord Neuberger sensibly pointed out that the express terms of a contract must be interpreted before there can be any question of interpretation,[29] and effectively sidelined the decision in *Belize*. In fact, Lord Neuberger even said that 'those observations [of Lord Hoffmann in *Belize*] should henceforth be treated as a characteristically inspired discussion rather than authoritative guidance on the law of implied terms'.[30]

The decision in the *Marks and Spencer* case will no doubt provoke much debate. Lord Carnwath alone offered support for the thrust of Lord Hoffmann's approach in *Belize*, but it seems that Lord Hoffmann's broad approach to both interpretation and implication is at odds with the current majority view of the Supreme Court.[31] This will no doubt disappoint some commentators,[32] but should nevertheless be welcomed. In the context of implication,

---

[23] [2011] UKSC 56 [38].

[24] [2012] UKSC 63, [2013] 1 AC 523 [55].

[25] [2015] UKSC 72. See too *Trump International Golf Club Scotland Ltd v The Scottish Ministers* [2015] UKSC 74, [33]–[35] Lord Hodge; cf [41]–[44] (Lord Mance).

[26] Lord Clarke also agreed with the reasons given by Lord Neuberger: ibid, [75].

[27] [24].

[28] [24]. See similarly the approach of the Singapore Court of Appeal: eg *Foo Jong Peng v Phua Kiah Mai* [2012] SGCA 55; *Sembcorp Marine Ltd v PPL Holdings Pte Ltd* [2013] SGCA 43.

[29] [28].

[30] [31].

[31] See too *Arnold v Britton* [2015] UKSC 36, discussed in Chapter 12, where again Lord Carnwath dissented from the majority view expressed by Lord Neuberger.

[32] See eg A Kramer, 'Implication in Fact as an Instance of Contractual Interpretation' (2004) 63 CLJ 384; R Hooley, 'Implied Terms after *Belize Telecom*' (2014) 73 CLJ 315.

it is important to emphasise that the touchstone for implication is necessity and not reasonableness, and that any contrary suggestion contained within *Belize* should be allowed to fade away. Implication and interpretation should remain distinct. An implied term still, strictly, needs to be interpreted.

2 Customary terms

Terms may also be implied because they are 'customary' in a particular trade or profession, or in certain types of contract in a particular locality. Once again, the theory is that the court is implementing the intention of the parties, on the assumption that they intended to contract with reference to the known usages of the trade, profession, or locality to which both parties belong. The court must, of course, be satisfied that there is such a custom as is alleged, but once it is so satisfied, the term will be imported unless there is something to show that the parties did not intend it to apply. Customary terms must be certain, well-known, and recognised as binding.[33] An express exclusion of the custom will obviously be effective as will any express term which is inconsistent with the alleged implied term. In *Hutton v Warren*,[34] the **tenant** of a farm, on quitting in accordance with notice given by the **landlord**, was held entitled to a fair allowance for the seeds and labour which he had expended on the arable land and of which the landlord would now reap the benefit. There was nothing in the terms of the **lease** to entitle the tenant to the allowance but it was proved that there was a custom of the country to that effect and there was nothing in the express terms of the contract which was inconsistent with the existence of the customary term.

3 Terms implied 'in law'

These terms are similar in principle to customary terms, but they are not confined to any particular trade, profession, or locality. Over the years, the courts have established that some terms are so generally implicit in contracts of a particular type that it can be asserted that those terms will be implied unless the parties have, in some way, indicated an intention that they should not apply. It is not necessary to examine the particular context of the parties' individual agreement in order to decide whether it is necessary to imply a term in order to give effect to the intentions of the parties. Rather, terms implied into all contracts of a particular type might be considered to be necessary in order to make that type of contract 'work'.

The most obvious example is the contract for the sale of goods. The seller of goods will hardly ever say, 'And I have a right to sell these goods, you know.' If he did, the buyer's suspicions might well be aroused. It is surely something that should be taken to go without saying; and so it became established that this term would always be implied in a contract for the sale of goods unless there was something to indicate that it should not apply.[35]

---

[33] *Cunliffe-Owen v Teather & Greenwood* [1967] 1 WLR 1421, 1438–9.
[34] (1836) 1 M & W 466.
[35] See now the Sale of Goods Act 1979, s 12(1) and (3).

Many other such terms were implied into contracts for the sale of goods at **common law**, and in 1893 the law was codified in the Sale of Goods Act of that year. The Act was re-enacted with some amendments in 1979. The general principle of the Act remains that the terms will be implied unless there is something which indicates that the parties intended otherwise.[36] As a result of this legislation, it is clear that it will generally be implied into contracts for the sale of goods that the goods will be of a satisfactory quality and fit for purpose;[37] that where goods are sold by description the goods must match that description;[38] that goods sold by sample will correspond with the sample in quality;[39] and, of course, that the seller has **title** to sell the goods.[40] These are perhaps the most important terms which are implied into contracts for the sale of goods as a result of the 1979 Act. Indeed, there are now similar provisions in the context of contracts of sale between a trader and a consumer in the Consumer Rights Act 2015,[41] and consumers are generally now better protected under the 2015 Act, since such implied terms (or, in the language of the 2015 Act, terms 'to be treated as included' in the contract) cannot be excluded by a trader against a consumer.[42] There are many other types of contract of common occurrence where terms will be implied, often by virtue of a statute which codifies, modifies, or adds to the common law terms.[43]

Implying a term 'in law' into a type of contract by virtue of a statute is relatively straightforward. It is slightly trickier when the term is implied by judges, relying upon the common law. This is partly because judges are not elected so do not have the democratic legitimacy of Parliament when deciding that all contracts of a certain type should include a particular implied term. After all, implying a term in this manner might be seen to interfere with the parties' freedom of contract, so courts tend to be somewhat cautious in their approach. Indeed, the approach of the common law in this area is similar to that adopted as regards terms implied in fact: the implied term must be necessary. But the term need not be necessary to give effect to the intentions of the parties; instead, the courts must be willing to imply the relevant term as a necessary incident of every contract of the type which the term was being implied into. A wider range of policy considerations can be taken into account when determining whether a term is necessary in this wider sense.

The leading case on terms implied in law is *Liverpool City Council v Irwin*.[44] The contracts in that case were tenancy agreements for flats in a tower block. The agreement imposed obligations on the tenant but said nothing whatsoever about the obligations of the landlord council. The conditions of the block deteriorated seriously because of the activities of vandals and the behaviour of some of the tenants. The defendants refused to pay rent and, in the ensuing litigation, one of the questions was whether the council was in

---

[36] However, as we shall see in Chapter 15, in the interests of protecting purchasers, certain terms may not invariably be excluded.

[37] Sale of Goods Act 1979, s 14.

[38] Ibid, s 13.

[39] Ibid, s 15.

[40] Ibid, s 12.

[41] See the Consumer Rights Act 2015, ss 9–17. See too similar terms in the context of 'services contracts' where the trader provides a service to a consumer: ss 51–52, and within contracts for digital content: ss 34–40.

[42] Ibid, s 31. See further Chapter 15, Section 4. However, it should be noted that some terms of the 1979 Act do continue to apply to consumer contracts, such as s 6 on perised goods (discussed in Chapter 22, Section 1).

[43] See eg the Supply of Goods and Services Act 1982, Part II.

[44] [1977] AC 239.

breach of contract. Any breach must be a breach of an implied term, since the council had not expressly undertaken any obligations. It was held that it was necessary to imply a term that the council take reasonable care to keep the block in reasonable repair and utility. Lord Edmund-Davies said that:[45]

> ... an obligation is placed on the landlords in all such lettings of multi-storey premises as are involved in this appeal by the general law, as a legal incident of this kind of contract, which the landlords must be assumed to know about as well as anyone else.

It is important to note that the court would imply such a term as was necessary, no more and no less. Thus, as in *The Moorcock*, the court would not imply an absolute obligation to keep in repair, only an obligation to use reasonable care to do so. On the particular facts of *Liverpool City Council v Irwin* the House of Lords held that the council had satisfied that obligation and so were not in breach of contract.

Implied terms in law offer the courts the chance to develop the law in certain areas. For example, in *Malik v Bank of Credit and Commerce International SA (in liquidation)*,[46] the House of Lords affirmed that in a contract of employment there is an implied term that the employer will not, without reasonable cause, conduct itself in a manner likely to destroy or seriously damage the relationship of trust and confidence between itself and its employee. BCCI broke this term by carrying on a massive and notorious fraud resulting in the collapse of the company and the redundancy of the employee who was entitled to damages for any disadvantage incurred in the employment market through his association with BCCI.

Whether or not a term should be implied may be influenced by statute. So a statute requiring an employer to provide his employee with a written statement of the terms of his employment, including a note of how to apply for redress of grievances, led to the finding that it is an implied term that the employer will provide an opportunity for the prompt and reasonable redress of employees' grievances.[47] On the other hand, in the important case of *Johnson v Unisys Ltd*,[48] it was held that legislation precluded the court from implying a term that it might otherwise have considered necessary. An employer exercised its express contractual right to dismiss the claimant, J, with four weeks' notice, but did so unfairly. J contended that there was an implied term that the employer would not exercise its right except for good cause and after giving J the opportunity to show that there was no such good cause. It was held that the statutory introduction of elaborate machinery for compensation for unfair dismissal precluded the court from implying that term. J's claim for damages for breach of contract, far in excess of the statutory compensation he received, failed.[49]

---

[45] Ibid, 266.

[46] [1998] AC 20.

[47] *Goold (WA) (Pearmak) Ltd v McConnell* [1995] IRLR 516 (Morison J).

[48] [2001] 2 All ER 801, HL (Lord Steyn dissenting).

[49] This remains a controversial decision for labour lawyers. For further discussion, see A Bogg and H Collins, 'Lord Hoffmann and the Law of Employment: The Notorious Episode of *Johnson v Unisys Ltd*' in PS Davies and J Pila (eds), *The Jurisprudence of Lord Hoffmann* (Hart, 2015).

4 Distinguishing terms implied in fact from terms implied in law

It might be thought that there is no sharp dividing line between the various categories of implied terms; Lord Wilberforce said that they are 'shades on a continuous spectrum'.[50] Indeed, in *Irwin*, Lord Salmon thought that unless there was an obligation on the council 'at least to use reasonable care to keep the lifts working properly and the staircase lit, the whole transaction becomes inefficacious, futile and absurd'.[51] This comes close to a 'business efficacy' test. Nevertheless, the House of Lords clearly thought it an inappropriate case for the application of either *The Moorcock* or *Shirlaw*: if the council had been asked whether it would agree to the proposed term it may well have responded 'Certainly not!' rather than 'Oh, of course!'

The House of Lords therefore looked to the *kind* of contract, namely leases of flats in high-rise blocks generally, rather than the particular, individual contract at issue. The judges appear to have thought that this approach enabled them to take into account a wider range of considerations; yet the considerations actually taken into account by the House all seem to have been aspects of this particular case, as well as, no doubt, of many similar tenancies. The effect is to lay down a rule that the term is to be imported into tenancies of this type generally, in the absence of a contrary intention. Yet the difference, if it exists at all, may be thought to be marginal. Did not *The Moorcock* establish a rule for a class of contract—contracts for the berthing of ships at wharves where the river bed is owned by a third party?

Nevertheless, subsequent cases have shown that the courts are willing to take into account much wider policy considerations when considering implication in law as opposed to implication in fact. For example, in *Crossley v Faithful & Gould Ltd*, Dyson LJ thought that implied terms in law 'raise questions of reasonableness, fairness and the balancing of competing policy considerations'.[52] Such factors are not relevant to terms implied in fact. However, the issue of reasonableness should not be pushed too far: the House of Lords in *Irwin* firmly rejected the view expressed by Lord Denning MR in the Court of Appeal that a term should be implied when it is reasonable to do so; the House of Lords insisted upon a touchstone of necessity. This might be explained on the basis that a term implied in law must be necessary to give effect to broader policy considerations and fairness.

The distinction drawn between 'individualised implied terms' (terms implied in fact) and 'standardised implied terms' (terms implied in law) still represents good law.[53] However, the dividing line between a particular contract and a particular type of contract may sometimes seem very fine. In *Scally v Southern Health and Social Services Board*,[54] a doctor sued his employer for not bringing to his attention new rules regarding pension benefits. These rules had been agreed during negotiations between his employer and the doctor's

---

[50] *Liverpool City Council v Irwin* [1977] AC 239, 254.
[51] Ibid, 262.
[52] [2004] EWCA Civ 293, [2004] 4 All ER 447 [36].
[53] *Equitable Life Assurance Society v Hyman* [2002] 1 AC 408, [2000] 3 WLR 529 (Lord Steyn).
[54] [1992] 1 AC 294.

representative body. The claimant argued that there should be an implied term in the contract of employment that the employer will take reasonable steps to bring the employee's rights to his attention. The House of Lords agreed. The doctor had a valuable right which was useless unless he knew about it, but he could not be expected to know about it unless it was brought to his attention. As Lord Bridge put it:[55]

> A clear distinction is drawn … between the search for an implied term necessary to give business efficacy to a particular contract and the search, based on wider considerations, for a term which the law will imply as a necessary incident of a definable category of contractual relationship.

This is entirely orthodox. But the 'definable category' was defined very restrictively by the House of Lords. The type of contract was not thought to be simply contracts of employment generally, but rather contracts of employment negotiated between employers and a representative body which contain a particular term that confers on the employee, if the employee takes a certain course of action, a benefit which he could not be expected to know about unless the term is brought to his attention. This is a somewhat particular type of contract. Whilst it is understandable that courts may feel cautious about whether it is legitimate for them—as opposed to Parliament[56]—sweepingly to imply terms into contracts of a very general type, it seems obvious that the more narrowly the type of contract at issue is defined, the thinner the boundary between terms implied in law and terms implied in fact may become.

5 Exclusion of terms usually implied

The general principle is that any term which would otherwise be implied must give way to an inconsistent express term.[57] So, in *Les Affréteurs Réunis Société Anonyme v Leopold Walford (London) Ltd*,[58] an express term in the contract that the **broker**'s commission should be payable 'on signing this **charter**' excluded a custom in the shipping trade that the commission was payable only in respect of hire duly earned under the **charterparty**. The express term showed beyond doubt that the parties did not intend the customary term to apply. This principle seems to have been misunderstood in *Lynch v Thorne*.[59]

The claimant agreed to buy from the defendant, a builder, a plot of land with a partially erected house on it. The defendant agreed to complete the house in accordance with the specification he produced. This provided that the walls were to be nine-inch brick walls. The house was built precisely in accordance with the specification, with sound materials and good workmanship. Unfortunately, it turned out to be unfit for human habitation because rain penetrated the walls. Now, there is generally no implied term on the sale of

---

[55] Ibid, 305.

[56] There is therefore an important difference between terms implied in law under the common law and under statute: the latter clearly has the force of Parliament, whereas the former depends upon unelected judges.

[57] For consideration of some implied terms that are non-excludable, see Chapter 15.

[58] [1919] AC 801, HL, discussed at Chapter 10, Section 8.

[59] [1956] 1 All ER 744, CA.

land (including houses and other buildings) that it is fit for any particular purpose; but in a contract to build a house, or to complete a partially built house, a term is implied at common law that the house, when completed, will be reasonably fit for habitation. The claimant relied on this term. The court accepted, for the purposes of the case, that such a term is usually implied but it must 'yield to the express letter of the bargain'.[60]

In order to build a house on that site that would keep the rain out, the builder would have had to depart from the express letter of the bargain—to break his contract. Nine-inch brick walls would, inevitably, let in the rain. In order to build a habitable house, the builder would have had to erect cavity walls. Thus the court held that the alleged implied term was inconsistent with the express term and could not be imported. But was not the buyer, as a reasonable man, entitled to suppose that the builder was promising him *both* (a) that he would build the house in accordance with the specification which he produced *and* (b) that the house, when so built, would be habitable? In fact, it was impossible to fulfil both promises but the buyer certainly did not know that; nor, presumably, did the builder. At the very least, the buyer might be entitled to suppose that the builder would inform him if walls built according to the specification would be defective, and that the builder would then give him the chance to vary the specification. The 'inconsistency' in *Lynch v Thorne* is entirely different from that in *Walford*'s case. No sane person could possibly suppose that the ship-owner was promising to pay the commission on the signing of the charter and promising to pay it only after the ship had sailed on the voyage.

In fact, there is clear authority that *Lynch v Thorne* applied the inconsistency principle incorrectly. In *Harbutt's Plasticine Ltd v Wayne Tank and Pump Co Ltd*,[61] the defendants contracted to supply to the claimants machinery in accordance with a specification prepared by the defendants. The defendants carried out the work in accordance with the specification, using 'durapipe' as the specification required. Durapipe proved to be unsuitable and the results were disastrous. The factory was burned down. The court held that the defendants promised both (a) to do the work according to a particular specification and (b), impliedly, that the work so done would be reasonably fit for its purpose. It was impossible to fulfil both promises—to satisfy the second the defendants would have had to use stainless steel pipes, which would have been a breach of the first—yet the court, rightly, had no difficulty in finding that both promises were made.[62] Similarly, a contract for the sale of a Bugatti car, 'fully equipped and finished to standard specification as per the car inspected', was held to be breached even though the car delivered complied exactly with the specification. There was an implied term that it would be reasonably fit for the purpose for which the buyer had told the seller he wanted it—touring purposes. It was impossible to supply a car that both complied with the specification and was fit for touring purposes; but it was not impossible to promise to do so; and the court rightly found that this was what the seller had done.[63]

---

[60] Ibid, 746 (Lord Evershed MR).

[61] [1970] 1 QB 447, CA. Note that Lord Denning's adherence in this case to a rule of 'fundamental breach' has since been overruled: see Chapter 15, Section 1(c).

[62] Although damages for breach of the first promise would be only nominal since the claimants would suffer no loss: see Chapter 28, Section 6.

[63] *Baldry v Marshall* [1925] 1 KB 260, CA.

Further Reading

A Phang, 'Implied Terms Revisited' [1990] JBL 394 and 'Implied Terms in English Law—Some
    Recent Developments' [1993] JBL 242.
Critical of the distinction between terms implied in fact and terms implied in law, and of the scope
of the latter category. The second article revisits this theme, making great use of the *Scally* decision.

A Phang, 'Implied Terms, Business Efficacy and the Officious Bystander—A Modern History'
    [1998] JBL 1.
Considers the development of the traditional tests for implied terms in fact and the relationship
between them.

E Peden, 'Policy Concerns Behind Implication of Terms in Law' (2001) 117 LQR 459.
Supports the distinction between terms implied in fact and in law, and identifies a number of relevant factors. This article was cited with approval by Dyson LJ in *Crossley*.

A Kramer, 'Implication in Fact as an Instance of Contractual Interpretation' (2004) 63 CLJ 384.
Argues that implication is a special instance of contractual interpretation. This article predates
Belize, but supports a similar approach.

PS Davies, 'Recent Developments in the Law of Implied Terms' [2010] LMCLQ 140.
Sceptical about the approach taken by *Belize*, and considers its initial reception in English law.

R Hooley, 'Implied Terms after *Belize Telecom*' (2014) 73 CLJ 315.
Offers support for Lord Hoffmann's approach in *Belize*, and suggests that the traditional tests should
be discarded. (This, and all the other articles, were obviously written before the decision of the
Supreme Court in *Marks & Spencer plc v BNP Paribas Securities Services Trust Co (Jersey) Ltd* [2015]
UKSC 72.)

Question

'I accept that both (i) construing the words which the parties have used in their contract and (ii) implying terms into the contract, involve determining the scope and meaning of the contract. However,
Lord Hoffmann's analysis in *Belize Telecom* could obscure the fact that construing the words used and
implying additional words are different processes governed by different rules.' (Lord Neuberger in
Marks and Spencer plc v BNP Paribas Securities Services Trust Company (Jersey) Ltd)
    What is the basis for the implication of terms in contract law?

14 Rectification

🔑 Key Points

- Rectification is an equitable remedy that can correct a mistake in a written contract.

- There is no limit to the range of evidence that might be introduced in order to establish that a mistake has been made. This includes the content of pre-contractual negotiations.

- A party seeking rectification will need convincing proof that a mistake has been made before the court will contemplate altering the language chosen in a formal, written document.

- Rectification might be granted because both parties share a common mistake that the written document reflects their prior continuing agreement when it does not.

- For 'common mistake' rectification, the actual, subjective intentions of the parties have traditionally been crucial. However, more recent developments suggest that the parties' intentions should be objectively assessed.

- Rectification may also be granted where only one party has made a mistake, provided that the other party actually knew of the mistake, or at least recklessly turned a blind eye to the mistake, such that it would be unconscionable for that party to deny that the contract should be rectified.

- Rectification is a discretionary remedy. Rectification may not be granted if to do so would prejudice third parties, for instance.

Rectification is an equitable remedy[1] through which the court can rectify, or correct, a mistake in a written instrument. For example, where both parties have orally agreed to a deal and then set down the terms of their deal in writing, rectification may be available to correct a mistake made when recording the agreement in writing. It is important to appreciate that the court has no power to correct a mistake in the contract itself, but can only correct mistakes made in the way in which the contract has been recorded in writing. There are two principal forms of rectification that need to be examined in this chapter. Rectification for common mistake arises where both parties make the same mistake. This is the better-established form of rectification. However, it is now also clear that in some circumstances rectification for unilateral mistake will be granted in situations where only one party is mistaken but the other party has acted unconscionably or dishonestly.

---

[1] See Chapter 1, Section 6(e).

1 The scope of rectification: limited by the common law

Being an equitable remedy, rectification should be considered after the **common law** doctrines of interpretation and implication. The expanding scope of interpretation and implication[2] means that many mistakes might be corrected through those common law doctrines. A more liberal approach to interpretation and implication correspondingly restricts the scope of rectification.

However, rectification remains significant and is necessary in circumstances where the common law is unable to establish and consider the import of a party's mistake. For example, the **parol evidence** rule[3] does not restrict the range of evidence that can be used in support of a rectification claim, and both pre-contractual negotiations and evidence of the parties' subjective intentions are admissible for the purposes of rectification, unlike at common law.[4] Indeed, such evidence can be used even where there is an entire agreement clause that would operate at common law.[5] Any evidence that might establish a relevant mistake can be taken into account by a judge when deciding whether to grant the discretionary equitable remedy of rectification. Rectification is also able to insert entire missing pages into a document, which could be beyond the outer limits of interpretation or implication.

The broader approach to interpretation favoured in *Investors Compensation Scheme*[6] and subsequent decisions might be thought to be satisfactory and sufficient to ensure that mistakes are corrected where necessary. However, there remain important differences between interpretation and rectification. As Lord Neuberger recently commented in the decision of the Supreme Court in *Marley v Rawlings*:[7]

> At first sight, it might seem to be a rather dry question whether a particular approach is one of interpretation or rectification. However, it is by no means simply an academic issue of categorisation. If it is a question of interpretation, then the document in question has, and has always had, the meaning and effect as determined by the court, and that is the end of the matter. On the other hand, if it is a question of rectification, then the document, as rectified, has a different meaning from that which it appears to have on its face, and the court would have jurisdiction to refuse rectification or to grant it on terms (eg if there had been delay, change of position, or third party reliance).

It might be added that whether or not rectification should be ordered is a question of fact, whilst questions of interpretation are a matter of law. There are therefore fewer appeals regarding rectification than there are concerning interpretation; this might be thought to be advantageous in reducing the cost and time involved in obtaining final judgment. Moreover, 'convincing proof'[8] is required to contradict the inherent probability that the

---

[2] Seen in decisions such as *ICS* and *Chartbrook* (Chapter 12) and *Belize* (Chapter 13).
[3] See Chapter 11, Section 4.
[4] *Chartbrook Ltd v Persimmon Homes Ltd* [2009] UKHL 38, [2009] 1 AC 1101.
[5] *Surgicraft Ltd v Paradigm Biodevices Inc* [2010] EWHC 1291 (Ch).
[6] See Chapter 12, Section 3.
[7] *Marley v Rawlings* [2014] UKSC 2, [2014] 2 WLR 213 [40].
[8] *Joscelyne v Nissen* [1970] 2 QB 86.

written instrument truly represents the parties' intention because it is a document signed by them. The burden of proof on the claimant is particularly 'formidable' if the formal written instrument is detailed and recorded with the benefit of expert legal advice,[9] such that rectification is generally viewed as more difficult to establish than a particular interpretation of the contract.[10] But most significantly, perhaps, rectification is much better equipped to protect third party rights than the common law.

2 Common mistake rectification

In general, a claim for rectification on the basis of a common mistake will only succeed if four criteria are established. First, that there was some prior agreement between the parties. Secondly, that this was still effective when the contract was **executed**. Thirdly, that by mistake the instrument fails to reflect that agreement. Fourthly, that the instrument would carry out the agreement if rectified as claimed.[11] These four elements will now be examined in turn.

(a) Prior agreement

It used to be assumed that rectification would only be available to correct a written instrument so that it could accurately reflect a prior, specifically enforceable agreement,[12] but the prior accord no longer needs to be specifically enforceable. If there is a common intention with regard to the particular provisions of the agreement in question, and that common intention continues up to the date of the written instrument, then rectification is possible even if that common intention did not create a specifically enforceable contract. This was established most clearly in *Joscelyne v Nissen*.[13] A man ran a car hire business, and when his wife fell ill he decided to hand the running of the business over to his daughter. In return, his daughter was to pay all the household bills. This was agreed between them, but in the final, written agreement there was no mention of the need for the daughter to pay gas and electricity bills. The daughter later sought to stop paying such bills, and relied upon the fact that the written contract did not require her to do so. However, the Court of Appeal rectified the agreement so that it included the daughter's obligation to pay the bills. This reflected the parties' prior accord; and despite the fact that the prior accord was not specifically enforceable, this did not prevent rectification.

---

[9] See eg *James Hay Pension Trustees Ltd v Kean Hird et al* [2005] EWHC 1093 (Ch) [81].

[10] Although the courts have said that they will not easily accept that something has gone wrong with the contractual language in the context of interpretation as well: see eg *ICS* Principle 5.

[11] See generally *The Olympic Pride* [1980] 2 Lloyd's Rep 67, 72–3 (Mustill J).

[12] See eg **dicta** in *Lovell and Christmas Ltd v Wall* (1911) 104 LT 85 and *Frederick E Rose (London) Ltd v William H Pim Jnr & Co Ltd* [1953] 2 QB 450.

[13] [1970] 2 QB 86.

(b) **Continuing common intention**

Rectification will only be granted to reflect a prior accord if that accord continued up until the time the written contract was signed. Of course, the fact that the document does not mirror the prior accord may be explained on the basis that the parties decided to depart from terms previously agreed. A court will therefore need to be convinced that the discord between the written document and prior accord is the result of a mistake shared by the parties rather than simply a change in the agreement.

Traditionally, the parties' actual, or subjective, intentions needed to be established: the court could only rectify a written instrument if it failed to reflect the actual intentions of the parties.[14] This approach is consistent with the equitable roots of rectification: **equity** intervened because it would not allow the parties to act unconscionably, and such unconscionability only arose where the parties' consciences would actually be affected. It would be unconscionable for a party to insist upon the written terms of the agreement if he knows that there has been a mistake made in recording the agreement. Rectification could therefore be seen as a 'safety valve' that allows the parties' subjective intentions to be taken into account in order to avoid holding parties to a document which, because of a mistake, fails accurately to record their bargain but would nevertheless be given effect by the rigorously objective approach of the common law of interpretation.

However, there has been a drift away from a 'pure' subjective approach. The first signs of this may have been in *Joscelyne v Nissen*,[15] in which the Court of Appeal insisted that there needed to be 'some outward expression of accord'. This was controversial,[16] but might be explained on the basis that, although the courts should really be concerned with the parties' subjective intentions, in practice there has to be some outward expression of those intentions for the court to be in a position to infer, from the evidence presented, that there was such an intention.[17]

This analysis may have been undermined by recent decisions. In *Chartbrook Ltd v Persimmon Homes Ltd*, Lord Hoffmann somewhat provocatively said that 'the authorities suggest that ... the question is what an objective observer would have thought the intentions of the parties to be'.[18] Such comments were *obiter* since the case was resolved through interpreting the contract at common law,[19] but the comments of Lord Hoffmann will no doubt be influential. His Lordship appears to suggest that what is important is whether or not the reasonable person would consider the parties to be mistaken. On this basis, rectification may be ordered even if one or both of the parties were not actually mistaken. This is a controversial decision.

It is suggested that the reasoning of Lord Hoffmann on this point is unsatisfactory for reasons of principle, policy, and its use of precedent. On the point of principle, equity should only interfere where the consciences of the parties are actually affected.[20] This requires

---

[14] *The Commissioners of Inland Revenue v Rafael* [1935] AC 96, 143 (Lord Wright).
[15] See Section 2(a).
[16] It was immediately criticised: see eg L Bromley, 'Rectification in Equity' (1971) 87 LQR 532.
[17] *Cambridge Antibody Technology v Abbott Biotechnology Ltd* [2004] EWHC 2974 (Pat), [2005] FSR 27.
[18] *Chartbrook* [60].
[19] Chapter 13.
[20] As is the approach in Australia: *Ryledar Pty Ltd v Euphoric Pty Ltd* [2007] NSWCA 65, (2007) 69 NSWLR 603.

both parties actually to be mistaken, yet nevertheless one party seeks to take advantage of the mistake. The equitable exercise is distinct from that undertaken by the common law when considering interpretation, in that subjective intention is relevant in equity but not at common law.

On the issue of policy, the objective approach means that an earlier, objective accord between the parties might trump the later formal, written contract. This seems particularly inappropriate where the parties understand that anything provisionally agreed is 'subject to' signing a formal document. It would be preferable for the later agreement to take priority over earlier, less formal agreements in the absence of an actual mistake. By contrast, the approach in *Chartbrook* reaches the opposite result. Indeed, in *Chartbrook* itself, the judge at first instance found as a matter of fact that the directors of Chartbrook honestly believed that there was no mistake in the written document.[21] This meant that the directors of Chartbrook, in good faith, relied upon the plain meaning[22] language of a written agreement which Persimmon (a significantly larger commercial entity) had drafted and checked. Yet Lord Hoffmann's objective approach to rectification would circumvent such subjective beliefs, and impose upon Chartbrook a contract to which it did not actually agree, thereby allowing Persimmon to escape a bad bargain. It is a distortion of language to say that there was a *common* mistake shared between Chartbrook and Persimmon. Indeed, doing so blurs the boundary between common mistake and unilateral mistake rectification, which should remain distinct.[23]

The use of precedent in *Chartbrook* might also be questioned. Of course, being the highest **appellate court** the House of Lords was not bound by previous decisions, but the approach taken towards rectification represents a significant departure from orthodoxy without the benefit of the opinions of the lower courts, which seems unfortunate,[24] particularly since the discussion of the rectification point was *obiter*. Moreover, Lord Hoffmann thought that the majority judgment of the Court of Appeal in *Britoil plc v Hunt Overseas Oil Inc*[25] lends no support to the view that a party must be mistaken as to whether the document reflects what he subjectively believes the agreement to have been. This seems to underplay much of the reasoning of Hobhouse LJ: the majority insisted that the parties should actually be mistaken.[26]

Nevertheless, *Chartbrook* has been applied to a rectification claim by the Court of Appeal in *Daventry District Council v Daventry & District Housing Ltd*.[27] The case concerned a term of a contract relating to which party was to bear responsibility for a deficit in an employee's pension fund:

---

[21] Admittedly, this finding in itself was perhaps dubious: see eg [2008] EWCA Civ 183, [2008] 2 All ER (Comm) 387, [163]–[169] (Lawrence Collins LJ) and [55] (Lord Hoffmann).

[22] If the interpretation issue in *Chartbrook* had been decided differently: see Chapter 12, Section 5(a)(ii).

[23] See Section 3.

[24] See eg C Nugee, 'Rectification After *Chartbrook v Persimmon*: Where Are We Now?' (2012) 26 Trust Law International 76.

[25] [1994] CLC 561 (Hobhouse and Glidewell LJJ; Hoffmann LJ dissenting).

[26] Lord Toulson, 'Does Rectification Require Rectifying?' (TECBAR Annual Lecture, 31 October 2013) https://www.supremecourt.uk/docs/speech-131031.pdf.

[27] [2011] EWCA Civ 1153, [2012] 1 WLR 1333.

In relation to the Transferring Employees the Council shall make a payment of £2.4 million pounds (being an amount representing the deficit in the funding of the Transferring Employees pension benefits up until the Completion Date) within five business days of the Completion Date.

The plain meaning of this clause (which was part of a much larger commercial arrangement) was that the council should pay the money. The judge at first instance refused to rectify the contract to make the defendant, Daventry & District Housing Ltd, pay instead.[28] Both sides had been advised by lawyers, understood the importance of the final, written contract, and the judge found as a matter of fact that the defendant was not mistaken about the plain meaning of the provision. Nevertheless, the Court of Appeal, by a majority, allowed the appeal.

The decision is very difficult, with three full and thoughtful speeches. However, it seems to be clear that the defendant in *Daventry*—like the defendant in *Chartbrook*—was not actually making any mistake in thinking that the contractual language meant what it did. There was therefore no mistake in the recording of the contract. This is perhaps emphasised by the fact that the contract was negotiated by third parties who had no authority to enter into a contract for either side—the board of directors of the defendant company therefore decided to sign the contract based upon the plain meaning of the contractual language chosen rather than any prior assumptions. Yet it does not seem to have been seriously argued that an actual, common mistake needed to be established for rectification to be granted: instead, the parties appear to have assumed that Lord Hoffmann's approach in *Chartbrook* should be followed and that it was sufficient for a reasonable person to think that both parties were mistaken. Etherton LJ summarised the requirements for rectification as follows:

(1) the parties had a common continuing intention, whether or not amounting to an agreement, in respect of a particular matter in the instrument to be rectified; (2) which existed at the time of execution of the instrument sought to be rectified; (3) such common continuing intention to be established objectively, that is to say by reference to what an objective observer would have thought the intentions of the parties to be; and (4) by mistake, the instrument did not reflect that common intention.[29]

The majority of the Court of Appeal held that a reasonable person would think that the parties made a mistake because the written document did not accord with what had been initially agreed by the negotiators for both sides (that the council would not have to pay for the pension deficit).[30] Just as in *Chartbrook*, this had the unfortunate effect of imposing upon the defendant a contract to which it did not agree, and would not have agreed: the board of directors would not have signed the contract had it known that it would bear responsibility for the deficit in the pension fund. Etherton LJ, dissenting, agreed with the trial judge that rectification was inappropriate in such circumstances: a reasonable person would have

---

[28] [2010] EWHC 1935 (Ch).

[29] [2011] EWCA Civ 1153, [2012] 1 WLR 1333 [80]. This test appears to have been supported by all three judges in the Court of Appeal.

[30] eg [17] (Toulson LJ), [213] (Lord Neuberger MR).

thought that, once the clause was inserted into the draft agreement and accepted by the council and its lawyers, any prior objective accord was replaced by the later agreement encapsulated in the contract.

The difference in approach between the majority and minority shows how malleable the objective test of mistake may be. The advantage of an objective approach is supposed to be an increased level of certainty,[31] but this is clearly undermined if the objective test of common intention can be readily manipulated to reach any result the court desires.[32] Indeed, it now seems very difficult for a non-mistaken party to ensure that the court will accept that the concluded written document represents the bargain made and is not afflicted by mistake. Uncertainty ensues from the court's ability to *deem* that the parties have made a mistake in situations where one party has not actually made a mistake at all.

It is hard to be sure in what direction the law will continue to develop in this area. Dissatisfaction has been expressed with the objective approach taken in *Chartbrook*, and it is not impossible that a subjective approach will continue to be invoked. This is because the *obiter* comments of the House of Lords in *Chartbrook* do not obviously trump the **ratio** of earlier decisions of the Court of Appeal, such as *Britoil*. Since the latter decision was not cited to the Court of Appeal in *Daventry*, the law is currently in a messy state. It is to be hoped that an appellate court will soon provide clarity in this area. In the meantime, however, it would be a 'bold course'[33] for a court not to follow *Chartbrook*.

(c) Failure to represent agreement

Rectification is available where the 'wording does not reflect what the parties agreed not merely what they or one of them thought it meant'.[34] What is required is a literal disparity between the language of the agreement and that of the instrument, and not merely a misunderstanding of the meaning of that language. This is well illustrated by the famous decision in *Frederick E Rose Ltd v William H Pim & Co Ltd*.[35]

In this case, a customer placed an order for 'Moroccan horsebeans known here as feveroles'. This order was accepted by Frederick E Rose, who set about trying to acquire such goods. Rose then asked its suppliers, Pim, what feveroles were, and was told that feveroles were just horsebeans. Rose was apparently satisfied by this, and the parties orally agreed to the sale of horsebeans. Subsequently, in the written contract, the goods were described as 'horsebeans'.

The problem was that there is in fact a difference between 'feveroles' and 'horsebeans'. 'Horsebeans' is only a generic term for a wide range of beans. And the horsebeans that Pim supplied to Rose were not feveroles. Rose's customer refused to accept horsebeans

---

[31] eg [2011] EWCA Civ 1153, [2012] 1 WLR 1333 [111] (Etherton LJ).

[32] Etherton LJ commented, at [104], that 'Our different judgments and conclusions in the present case reflect significant differences of view about the way the objective test should be applied on the facts of this case.'

[33] *Daventry* [180] (Toulson LJ); see too *Tartsinis v Navona Management Co* [2015] EWHC 57 (Comm) [90]–[99] (Leggatt J).

[34] *Ted Baker Plc v AXA Insurance Plc* [2012] EWHC 1406 (Comm) (Eder J).

[35] [1953] 2 QB 450.

which were not feveroles, which obviously left Rose with a load of horsebeans which he did not want.

Rose therefore sought to sue Pim. But such an action faced the serious obstacle that the contract provided for the sale of horsebeans, and that is precisely what happened. Rose therefore argued that the contract should be rectified to say feveroles. The claim for rectification failed. This was because the oral contract, which the written document was meant to reduce to writing, was also for horsebeans. There had been no mistake in the recording of the agreement, so there was no reason to rectify the contract.

(d) Rectification to carry out the agreement

Rectification ensures that the instrument contains the provisions which the parties intended it to contain, and not those which it would have contained had they been better informed.[36] Rectification should only be granted if the contract would then accurately represent the true agreement of the parties at the time when it was executed; if there is doubt as to this, then rectification should be withheld.[37]

3 Unilateral mistake rectification

A good example of unilateral mistake rectification is to be found in *Thomas Bates v Wyndham's*.[38] The contract in question was a **lease**, which contained a provision for a rent review clause every five years. The parties agreed that if they could not agree on the rent, then the rate could be fixed by an arbitrator. Unfortunately, the **landlords**, by mistake, did not include the arbitration clause in the final, written document. This mistake was spotted by the **tenants**, who knew that the landlords had made this error, but nevertheless the tenants did not inform the landlords. As a result, there was no common mistake: only the landlords were mistaken. The tenants were not mistaken at all, but nevertheless rectification was granted because the tenants had tried to take advantage of the landlords' unilateral mistake. The Court of Appeal held that the tenants had acted unconscionably in failing to draw the landlords' attention to the mistake.

An unhappy side effect of the objective approach to common mistake rectification is that it threatens to sideline rectification for unilateral mistake. Although '[t]hey sound like two varieties of mistake about the same thing, they are actually the expression of quite different principles.'[39] The preferable view is that where only one party is mistaken, then unilateral mistake rectification is still the more appropriate doctrine to rely upon. Indeed, *Chartbrook* and *Daventry* may both preferably have been considered as potential cases for rectification

---

[36] *Khan v Khan* [2013] EWHC 4065 (Ch) [17].
[37] *Allnutt v Wilding* [2007] EWCA Civ 412, [2007] WTLR 941.
[38] [1981] 1 All ER 1077.
[39] *Kowloon Development Finance Ltd v Pendex Industries Ltd* [2013] HKCFA 35 [19] (Lord Hoffmann NPJ).

on the basis of unilateral mistake, since in both cases the trial judge had found as a matter of fact that one party to the contract was not actually mistaken about the meaning of the contract at all. This was recognised by Toulson LJ[40] and Lord Neuberger[41] in *Daventry*,[42] but the broad scope of rectification on the basis of an objectively-ascertained common mistake engulfed the unilateral mistake analysis and proved sufficient in *Daventry* itself. But it is unsatisfactory to corrupt the language used in this area—where only one party and not both parties were mistaken, it is appropriate to use the language and principles of unilateral mistake rather than common mistake.

Unilateral mistake rectification was not considered by the House of Lords in *Chartbrook*, so it seems unlikely that Lord Hoffmann's objective approach was intended to apply to cases of unilateral mistake as well. His Lordship subsequently made this clear in *Kowloon Development Finance Ltd v Pendex Industries Ltd*,[43] a decision of the Hong Kong Court of Final Appeal. Lord Hoffmann insisted that rectification for unilateral mistake is distinct from rectification for common mistake and that the former 'is very much concerned with the subjective states of mind of the parties'.[44] Such a subjective approach is consistent with equitable principles—especially the need for the non-mistaken party's conscience actually to be affected.

Rectification on the basis of a unilateral mistake should not lightly be granted. After all, it 'has the result of imposing on the defendant a contract which he did not, and did not intend to, make and relieving the claimant from a contract which he did, albeit did not intend to, make'.[45] As such, it is a 'drastic' remedy.[46] It is for this reason that the English Court of Appeal has consistently demanded that the defendant must actually know of the mistake, or at least recklessly turn a blind eye to the mistake, in order for his conscience to be affected and equitable relief justified.[47] Such unconscionable conduct generally involves sharp practice.

In *Daventry*, all the discussion regarding unilateral mistake rectification was *obiter* since the decision was reached on the basis of there being a common mistake. Nevertheless, interesting comments were made. Etherton LJ considered 'the critical broad distinction being between honesty and dishonesty',[48] which is consistent with orthodoxy. Etherton LJ was prepared to accept that the defendant's knowledge of the claimant's mistake must fall within one of the first three categories set out by Peter Gibson J in *Baden v Société Générale pour Favoriser le Développement du Commerce et de l'Industrie en France SA*:[49] (a) actual knowledge; (b) wilfully shutting one's eyes to the

---

[40] Ibid, [185].

[41] Ibid, [225].

[42] See too eg *Tartsinis v Navona Management Co* [2015] EWHC 57 (Comm) [97].

[43] *Kowloon Development Finance Ltd v Pendex Industries Ltd* [2013] HKCFA 35.

[44] Ibid, [20].

[45] *George Wimpey UK Ltd v VI Construction Ltd* [2005] EWCA Civ 77, [2005] BLR 135 [75] (Blackburne J).

[46] *Agip SpA v Navigazione Alta Italia SpA, 'The Nai Genova'* [1984] 1 Lloyd's Rep 353, 365 (Slade LJ).

[47] *A Roberts & Co Ltd v Leicestershire County Council* [1961] Ch 555; *Thomas Bates v Wyndham's* [1981] 1 All ER 1077; *Commission for New Towns v Cooper* [1995] Ch 259.

[48] [2011] EWCA Civ 1153, [2012] 1 WLR 1333 [97].

[49] [1993] 1 WLR 509.

obvious; and (c) wilfully and recklessly failing to make such inquiries as an honest and reasonable man would make.[50]

On the other hand, Toulson LJ expressed sympathy[51] for a different, broader approach put forward by Professor McLauchlan: unilateral mistake rectification should be awarded where the defendant *ought* to have been aware of the claimant's mistake, and the claimant was led reasonably to believe that the defendant was agreeing to the claimant's interpretation of the bargain.[52] This again places great emphasis on an objective prior accord which should be given effect. But it undermines the primacy of the final, written document. It is suggested that this is inappropriate. It would be unfortunate for the law to recognise that a party can properly read and understand the terms of the document without making a mistake or acting dishonestly, and yet still be saddled with a contract to which he did not actually agree simply because that person *ought* to have known that the other party was making a mistake. A more subjective approach should be preferred.

4 Discretion to refuse relief

Rectification is a discretionary remedy. A court may refuse to grant such equitable relief if to do so would prejudice third parties who are **bona fide purchasers** for value without notice, or if the party seeking rectification has acted unconscionably in some way. Rectification will only be granted if necessary: if the party can obtain satisfaction through the common law doctrines of interpretation or implication, for example, there will be no need for equity to intervene and actually alter the words of the written document.

 Further Reading

A Burrows, 'Construction and Rectification' in A Burrows and E Peel (eds), *Contract Terms* (OUP, 2007).
Argues that rectification is almost redundant as a result of the broad, modern approach to interpretation at common law.

D McLauchlan, 'The "Drastic" Remedy of Rectification for Unilateral Mistake' (2008) 124 LQR 608.
Argues that rectification for unilateral mistake should be granted where one party has reasonably led the other to believe that he is assenting to the other party's terms.

PS Davies, 'Rectifying the Course of Rectification' (2012) 75 MLR 387.
Criticises the objective approach to common mistake in *Chartbrook* and *Daventry*, arguing instead that the courts should focus upon the subjective intentions of the parties.

---

[50] *Daventry* [95]. Cf [184] (Toulson LJ).
[51] *Daventry* [173]–[178].
[52] See D McLauchlan, 'The "Drastic" Remedy of Rectification for Unilateral Mistake' (2008) 124 LQR 608.

D McLauchlan, 'Refining Rectification' (2014) 130 LQR 83.
Contrasts the more 'subjective' approach of the Australian courts with *Daventry*, and concludes that rectification ought to be available where a written contract fails to record *either* (a) the *actual* common intention of the parties, whether or not evidenced by communications 'crossing the line' *or* (b) their *objective* consensus.

Question

'Does the remedy of rectification serve any useful purpose, or has it been subsumed into the modern approach to the interpretation of contracts?' (Lewison LJ in *Cherry Tree Investments Ltd v Landmain Ltd*)

15 The control of exclusion clauses and unfair terms

🔑 Key Points

- Exclusion clauses are terms which exclude or limit a defendant's liability.
- At common law, the court is unable to interfere with the substantive terms of the parties' bargain, since a court should respect the parties' freedom to enter into a contract on agreed terms. This meant that the courts developed various techniques to avoid weaker parties being bound by exclusion cases and unfair terms, notably concerning incorporation and interpretation.
- The common law techniques for avoiding the worst effects of exclusion clauses are now of reduced importance after the enactment of the Unfair Contract Terms Act 1977 and the Consumer Rights Act 2015. Both statutes enable the courts to control the substance of the contract.
- The Unfair Contract Terms Act 1977 only applies to non-consumer contracts. This statute empowers a court not to enforce exclusion clauses where they are unreasonable. Reasonableness is assessed at the time the contract was made, and can take into account any relevant factor. One very significant factor is the relative strength of the parties' bargaining positions. If both parties are well-advised commercial entities, the court will be unwilling to interfere with their contract and find a clause unreasonable. Where one party is much stronger than the other, the court may find a clause unreasonable in order to protect the weaker party.
- The Consumer Rights Act 2015 applies to consumer contracts. Unlike the Unfair Contract Terms Act 1977, it is not limited to exclusion clauses; all terms can be subject to a test of fairness. A term will be unfair if, 'contrary to the requirement of good faith, it causes a significant imbalance in the parties' rights and obligations under the contract to the detriment of the consumer'. Only some terms are exempt from this test of fairness: such terms generally specify the main subject matter of the contract or set the core price, and must be transparent, prominent, legible, and expressed in plain and intelligible language.

If a term is incorporated into a contract,[1] the general rule is that a court should simply give effect to that term. At **common law**, the courts had no power to strike down terms of a contract just because they were unfair. Although various techniques were developed to try not to give effect to the most outrageous terms, these were inevitably somewhat haphazard

---

[1] See Chapter 11.

and limited. As a result, Parliament passed the Unfair Contract Terms Act 1977 (commonly known as UCTA 1977) which allowed the courts not to enforce exclusion clauses in some instances. However, that statute is largely restricted to exclusion clauses, and does not cover all terms. UCTA 1977 now only applies to non-consumer contracts. A more recent development has been the Consumer Rights Act 2015.[2] This Act is not limited to exclusion clauses, and covers a wider range of terms which the courts might not enforce. As the title of the 2015 Act suggests, it only affords protection to consumers. Each statutory regime will be analysed in turn, but first it is helpful to consider the state of the common law, which must be considered before turning to the legislative provisions.

1 The common law

'Exclusion' or 'exemption' or 'exceptions' clauses are terms in a contract which exclude or limit, or purport to exclude or limit, a liability which would otherwise arise. The liability which such clauses seek to exclude or limit may be a contractual liability, but it may also be a liability arising under the common law independently of contract, or it may even be a statutory liability.[3] For example, potential tortious liability may be excluded by a contractual term, and the same is true for a liability arising under the common law of **bailment** and other common law rules. A statutory liability may be excluded unless the terms of the statute itself preclude exclusion. Section 2(1) of the Occupiers' Liability Act 1957 imposes on the occupier of premises 'a common duty of care' to all his visitors but does not prevent him from excluding this duty 'by agreement or otherwise'.

Suppliers of goods and services often seek to exclude or limit their possible legal liability by the insertion of exclusion clauses into their standard forms of contract. This is unsurprising. However, sometimes these clauses are very far-reaching. The courts have long been hostile to such clauses. Usually, they are not freely negotiated but are, in effect, imposed by one party on the other. The supplier declares that he will contract on his standard terms and no other, and the customer frequently has to accept those terms or go without the service he wants. There is no 'equality of bargaining power'. Because of their sympathy with the weaker party, the courts have frequently sought to avoid such clauses operating to the detriment of the weaker party by applying the rules concerning the interpretation and formation of contracts strictly in favour of the weaker party, resolving any doubts against the stronger party. Indeed, the courts developed various techniques to find certain exclusion clauses to be inoperative. The three most significant techniques at common law are:

(a) holding the clause not to be part of the contract because notice of it was insufficient or too late;

---

[2] There are also other, more particular, statutes that offer protection against unfair terms (eg the Consumer Credit Act 1974) which are beyond the scope of most undergraduate contract courses and will not be examined further here.

[3] The courts almost invariably consider exclusion clauses as a defence to breach of contract. For a different view that exclusion clauses simply define the parties' obligations, see B Coote, *Exception Clauses* (Sweet & Maxwell, 1964).

(b) interpreting the clause strictly against the party relying on it (*contra proferentem*) and holding it to be inapplicable to the events which occurred; and

(c) invoking the 'doctrine of fundamental breach'. The essence of this (now discredited) doctrine was that a person who has committed a breach of a fundamental term or a fundamental breach of an **innominate term**[4] should be precluded from relying on any exclusion clause, at least if the contract was terminated as a result of the breach.

Each of these techniques must be examined in turn in order to understand the development of the common law in this area. However, it is important to appreciate that one major impact of UCTA 1977 (and the Consumer Rights Act 2015) is that the common law principles are not applied with the same degree of strictness as they were before. This is because, in many instances, the legislative regimes have diminished or removed the need for the special protection which these rules afforded. For example, there may no longer be any need to strain the common law rules to say that an exclusion clause has not been incorporated into a contract, or that an exclusion clause should be strictly interpreted not to cover the events in question, because even if the clause is incorporated into the agreement and covers the relevant events, that clause will have no effect if it is unreasonable under UCTA 1977 (or unfair under the Consumer Rights Act 2015). And if the clause is not considered to be unenforceable under the relevant statutory regimes, perhaps there are good reasons why the clause should take effect.

Nevertheless, an understanding of the common law principles is still both necessary and relevant. The common law continues to be of significance because some very important classes of contract are outside the scope of the legislative regimes. Moreover, where UCTA 1977 provides that an exclusion clause is valid if reasonable, for example, the claimant may argue (a) that the clause is not part of the contract at all or (b) that, on its true construction, it does not apply to the situation which has arisen. If either argument (a) or (b) is successful, the exclusion clause is ineffective, even if it is a reasonable clause. It is therefore sensible first to analyse the common law principles before examining the statutes.

(a) **The incorporation of the clause**

There are no special rules relating to the incorporation of exclusion clauses in contracts. The relevant principles apply to all terms generally. This issue was analysed in Chapter 11, Section 2. It is true that courts have traditionally been particularly sensitive about holding that an exclusion clause has been incorporated into a contract because this might well enable a business to rely upon its own exclusion clause in order to escape liability where this would be unfair. However, this does not warrant special treatment for exclusion clauses—especially now that unfair clauses should not be enforceable given the legislative protection in place (both UCTA 1977 for non-consumer contracts and the Consumer Rights Act 2015 for consumer contracts).

---

[4] See Chapter 24, Section 2.

(b) **The interpretation of the clause**

When it has been decided that the clause is part of the contract, the next question is whether it applies to the state of affairs which exists, or the events which have occurred. This is a question of interpretation. The principles of interpretation were considered in detail in Chapter 12. However, some particular considerations in the context of exclusion clauses should be raised here. But caution should be exercised when dealing with some of the older authorities in this area: under the modern, contextual approach to interpretation favoured in the wake of *Investors Compensation Scheme Ltd v West Bromwich Building Society*,[5] it may now be the case that the usual contextual approach should be adopted without much further inquiry.

In any event, it is important to distinguish between two classes of exclusion clause. First, there are clauses which seek to exclude or qualify *obligations* which would otherwise arise under the contract or by virtue of some rule of law. Secondly, there are clauses which seek to exclude or qualify the *remedies* which would otherwise be available for breach of those obligations. The importance of the distinction is that only in the first category is there a direct conflict between the obligation and exclusion clause. If the obligation exists, the exclusion clause is invalid to the extent to which it conflicts with the obligation. If the exclusion clause is valid, the obligation does not exist to the extent that it is excluded. However, this conflict does not arise in the second class of case, since here the obligation exists even if the exclusion clause is valid. For example, if a contractual obligation is broken, the injured party may sue for breach of contract and the relevant clause might limit, or purport to limit, the amount of damages recoverable, or the time within which the action must be brought, or the right to **rescind** or terminate the contract. But such a clause does not seek to deny that an obligation exists.

A good illustration of the problem which faces the court in the first class of case is *Andrews Bros Ltd v Singer & Co Ltd*.[6] That case concerned a written contract for the sale of 'new Singer cars'. One of the cars delivered was not 'new'. That looks like a clear case of a breach of an express obligation to deliver a new car. However, there was an exclusion clause in the contract which stated that 'All **conditions**, warranties and liabilities implied by statute common law or otherwise are excluded.' Section 13 of the Sale of Goods Act 1893 (now 1979) provided that 'where there is a contract for the sale of goods by description, there is an implied condition that the goods shall correspond with the description'. The seller argued that he had excluded all implied conditions, including this one, and so he was not liable. The court held that the promise that the car would be new was an express and not an implied term of the contract, and as a result (notwithstanding the wording of s 13) the exclusion clause did not apply to it. The buyer was therefore entitled to recover damages for breach of contract.

However, Scrutton LJ did say that if a seller wanted to avoid liability in such a case, 'he must do so by much clearer language than this'. Too much importance should not be attached to this *dictum*. It has been sensibly criticised on the ground that it confusingly suggests that it is possible to exclude liability for breach of an express term. After all,

> A man cannot in one and the same contract expressly include a term (whether condition or warranty) and also exclude it ... Once the court has decided that the sale was a sale by

---

[5] [1998] 1 WLR 896.
[6] [1934] 1 KB 17, CA.

description of 'new Singer cars' then nothing else could satisfy the contract and by no artifice could the seller avoid the obligation to provide 'new Singer cars'.[7]

This is surely right. But if the seller had said, 'I promise to deliver Singer cars which, to the best of my knowledge, are new', the situation would be very different, and it is perhaps that situation which Scrutton LJ had in mind. In short, the seller may make it clear that he is giving no promise; but the seller cannot logically both promise and not promise the same thing.

An aspect of this rule is often called the 'main purpose' rule. Once the court has answered the question, 'What is the main purpose of the contract?' anything that is inconsistent with the main purpose of the contract must give way to that purpose. If the parties intended the fulfilment of their main purpose—and, *ex hypothesi*, they did—they cannot have intended the exclusion clause to apply where the clause is incompatible with the main purpose of the contract. In the *Rambler Cycle* case,[8] a **bill of lading** required delivery 'unto order or his or their assigns'. The main purpose of the contract was that the carrier should carry the goods to their destination and deliver them to the holder of the bill of lading. The bill also provided that the liability of the carrier should 'cease absolutely' after the goods had been discharged from the ship. After the goods had been discharged, the carrier delivered them to the **consignee** who did not produce the bill of lading and never paid for the goods. The Privy Council held the carrier liable. He could not contract to deliver to the holder of the bill of lading (the main purpose) and also contract that he was to be at liberty to deliver to someone who did not hold the bill. This was logically impossible.

Another way of looking at such cases is to say that the clause must be sensibly interpreted in the light of what reasonable men must have intended. Lord Denning suggested that, if the carrier's argument in *Rambler Cycle* was right, 'by parity of reasoning they would have been absolved if they had given the goods away to some passer-by or had burnt them or had thrown them into the sea'. If the officious bystander had suggested to the parties at the time they made their contract that it meant that the carrier was to be at liberty to do such things, it may safely be assumed that, as reasonable men, they would have 'testily suppressed him':[9] of course, the clause did not mean that. And the actual facts of the *Rambler Cycle* case were not so different, because the carrier had given the goods to someone he knew was not entitled to have them. It was not necessary to determine what effect, if any, the clause had. It did not apply to this event.

An example of the construction of a clause of the second class of case is *Alderslade v Hendon Laundry Ltd*.[10] The claimant was suing the defendant for damages for the loss of articles sent for laundering. The contract contained the clause, 'The maximum amount allowed for lost or damaged articles is 20 times the charge made for laundering.' The claim was in negligence and there was nothing in the clause which was inconsistent with the duty of care owed by the laundry. The question was whether the clause was effective to limit liability for negligence. If the clause was intended to do anything at all, it must have been intended to limit liability for negligence because the laundry company could not have been

---

[7] D Finnemore and A James, *Benjamin on Sale* (8th edn, Sweet & Maxwell, 1950) 622.
[8] *Sze Hai Tong Bank Ltd v Rambler Cycle Co Ltd* [1959] AC 576, PC.
[9] See Chapter 13, Section 1(a).
[10] [1945] 1 KB 189, CA.

held liable for the loss of the articles otherwise than through its negligence. It was therefore held that the clause was effective to limit the defendant's liability.

It may be different where the defendant, in the absence of any exclusion clause, might be subject to strict liability—in other words, liability without any negligence on his part. In such a case, if the clause did not expressly apply to negligence, the court might hold it effective only to exclude the strict liability. This would leave the defendant liable in negligence. Such an exclusion clause was clearly intended to do something, but, construing it strictly *contra proferentem* ('against the person relying upon it'), the court might decide that sufficient effect is given to the clause by finding that it operates to exclude the strict liability only. Courts tend to be more willing to accept that a clause will exclude liability for a no-fault breach of contract, for example, rather than allow a party to rely upon a clause to escape liability for his own negligence.

This approach appears to derive from *Canada Steamship Lines Ltd v The King*.[11] In that case, the Privy Council said that if an exclusion clause expressly covers negligence, this must be given effect (as occurred in *Alderslade v Hendon Laundry Ltd*). However, if the clause does not expressly cover negligence, it is then necessary to consider whether the clause is wide enough to cover negligence. But even if it is, the court will not hold that liability for negligence is excluded by the clause if the clause is sufficiently wide to cover strict liability as well: the court will decide that the exclusion clause only covers the strict liability claim rather than the negligence claim. This might be illustrated by *White v John Warwick & Co*.[12] The claimant hired a bicycle from the defendants under a written agreement which provided that 'nothing in this agreement shall render the owners liable for any personal injuries'. While the claimant was riding the bicycle, the saddle tilted forward and he was injured. In the absence of the exclusion clause, the defendants might have been held liable (a) for negligence and (b) for breach of their contractual undertaking that the bicycle was reasonably fit for its purpose. As the clause did not expressly apply to negligence, the court held that it operated only to exclude the second, strict liability. Since negligence was established on the facts of the case, the court held that the defendants were liable and could not rely upon the exclusion clause.[13]

However, it is suggested that the more liberal approach to interpretation adopted in the *Investors Compensation Scheme* case[14] means that the courts should now interpret exclusion clauses in the same manner as all other clauses. As a result, courts should interpret exclusion clauses in the context of the whole instrument, taking into account the admis-sible background and 'matrix of fact'. A strict adherence to the *Canada Steamship* guidelines therefore seems inappropriate. Indeed, in *HIH Casualty and General Insurance Ltd v Chase Manhattan Bank*,[15] the House of Lords, whilst politely saying that *Canada Steamship* remains 'helpful', strongly cautioned against a 'mechanistic' application of those principles. This has since been endorsed by the decision of the Court of Appeal in *Mir Steel UK*

---

[11] [1952] AC 192.

[12] [1953] 2 All ER 1021, CA.

[13] The defendants would now inevitably be liable for negligence causing personal injury under the Unfair Contract Terms Act 1977, s 2(1); but the case remains a useful authority on the general principle.

[14] See Chapter 12.

[15] [2003] UKHL 6, [2003] 1 All ER (Comm) 349.

Ltd v Morris,[16] which emphasised that *Canada Steamship* provides no more than guidance, and does not provide an automatic solution in any particular case. The courts cannot avoid the usual task of interpretation by applying rigid rules.

Nevertheless, the general principle that all exclusion clauses are interpreted *contra proferentem* does appear to survive. In other words, any ambiguity in the clause will be resolved against the party relying on that clause. Although the *contra proferentem* rule has been described as 'a rule of, if not last, then very late resort',[17] it is still applied by the courts[18] and has been referred to as 'a principle not only of law but of justice'.[19] Yet the courts must not strive to create an ambiguity where there is none,[20] and often the courts do not need to rely upon the *contra proferentem* rule anyway:[21] the flexible approach to interpretation favoured in the *Investors Compensation Scheme* case means that courts have some scope to reach the same, desired outcome simply by relying upon the 'factual matrix'.

(i) Distinctions between exclusion and limitation clauses

It has been suggested that the *contra proferentem* rule is applied more stringently to a clause which excludes liability altogether than to one which merely limits liability. The reason is said to be that there is a higher degree of improbability that a party would agree to a complete exclusion than to a limitation. This is thought to follow from *Ailsa Craig Shipping Co Ltd v Malvern Fishing Co Ltd*,[22] where the contract contained both an exclusion clause and a limitation clause. It was held that liability was limited but not excluded.

Another possible distinction between exclusion clauses and limitation clauses is that only an 'exclusion' clause can possibly be held to be merely declaratory of the common law. In *Hollier v Rambler Motors*,[23] a clause stating that a garage proprietor was not responsible for damage by fire to customers' cars was held to be intended to inform the customers of the common law position—that the proprietor was not responsible for damage caused by accidental fires—and therefore meant that the garage proprietor was liable for a fire caused by his negligence. By contrast, a limitation clause cannot be declaratory because the common law has no rules limiting liability. As a result, a limitation clause must necessarily have been intended to limit an existing liability.

However, it is important not to overstate the difference between limitation and exclusion clauses. A clause which limits liability to one penny may strictly limit but not exclude liability, yet in substance the effect of the clause is virtually the same.

---

[16] [2012] EWCA Civ 1397, [2013] 2 All ER (Comm) 54. See too *Greenwich Millennium Village Ltd v Essex Services Group Plc (formerly Essex Electrical Group Ltd)* [2014] EWCA Civ 960, [2014] 1 WLR 3517.

[17] *The Olympic Brilliance* [1982] 2 Lloyd's Rep 205, 208 (Eveleigh LJ).

[18] See eg *William Hare Ltd v Shepherd Construction Ltd* [2010] EWCA Civ 283, [2010] BLR 358.

[19] *Association of British Travel Agents v British Airways plc* [2000] 2 All ER (Comm) 204 [75] (Sedley LJ).

[20] *Direct Travel v McGeown* [2003] EWCA Civ 1606, [2004] Lloyd's Rep IR 599 [13].

[21] See eg *K/S Victoria Street (a Danish Partnership) v House of Fraser (Stores Management) Ltd* [2011] EWCA Civ 904, [2012] Ch 497 [68].

[22] [1983] 1 WLR 458, HL.

[23] [1972] 2 QB 71.

(c) 'Fundamental terms,' 'fundamental breaches', and exclusion clauses

Over a period of about 15 years before 1966, the courts held in a series of cases that a person who had committed a breach of a 'fundamental term' of a contract, or 'a fundamental breach' of the contract, was not entitled to rely upon any exclusion clause in the contract. The proposition was often stated and applied as if it were a rule of law which operated without regard to the intention of the parties as expressed in the contract. Thus, even though the exclusion clause might, on its true construction, apply to the event which had occurred, the defaulting party could not rely on it if that event constituted a breach of a fundamental term or a fundamental breach. However, this 'fundamental breach' rule was always the subject of much controversy, and it should now be considered to be defunct.

A major difficulty inherent in this doctrine was that of determining whether a term, or a breach of a term, was 'fundamental'. Devlin J said that a fundamental term must be:

> something narrower than a condition of the contract for it would be limiting the exceptions too much to say that they applied only to breaches of warranty. It is … something which underlies the whole contract so that, if it is not complied with, the performance becomes something totally different from that which the contract contemplates.[24]

This attempt to describe a fundamental term is problematic because it is precisely the same as the classic definition of a condition by Fletcher Moulton LJ in *Wallis v Pratt*.[25] A condition is, by definition, a fundamental term. Nevertheless, Devlin J was undoubtedly right when he said that the effect of exclusion clauses could not be confined to breaches of warranty—or, indeed, breaches of the then undiscovered innominate term. The very nature of the doctrine of 'fundamental breach' thus made it impossible to construct a rational theory. This was grossly inconvenient, not only for academic exponents of the law, but also for practitioners. If no rational theory underlies the law, it becomes impossible to predict the decisions of the courts and to give reliable advice. Not only did the doctrine of fundamental breach contain a fundamental flaw but it also contradicted a basic principle of the law of contract: it is for the parties, not the court, to make the bargain. If the parties have clearly agreed that there should be no, or limited, liability on one of them in certain circumstances, it is not for the court to overrule that agreement. Accordingly, in the *Suisse Atlantique* case,[26] the House of Lords held that there is no such doctrine and '[t]hat the question whether an exceptions clause was applicable where there was a fundamental breach of contract was one of the true construction of the contract'.[27]

However, Lord Denning and others were reluctant to see a doctrine which they had carefully nurtured (and which, no doubt, had achieved fairness in many cases) die so easily. In *Harbutt's Plasticine Ltd v Wayne Tank and Pump Co Ltd*,[28] the Court of Appeal held that the doctrine was excluded only where, as in the *Suisse Atlantique* case itself, the contract was affirmed after the fundamental breach was committed. The court decided that

---

[24] *Smeaton Hanscomb & Co Ltd v Sassoon I Setty, Son & Co* [1953] 2 All ER 1471, QBD.

[25] [1910] 2 KB 1003.

[26] *Suisse Atlantique Société d'Armement Maritime SA v NV Rotterdamsche Kolen Centrale* [1967] 1 AC 361, HL.

[27] This is quoted from the headnote to the case, and was approved in the *Photo Production* case.

[28] [1970] 1 QB 447, CA.

if the contract came to an end as a result of the breach, the effect of that was to avoid the exclusion clause *ab initio*, leaving the defendant liable even for breaches which, on its true construction, the clause was intended to cover. It took a second decision of the House of Lords, *Photo Production Ltd v Securicor Transport Ltd*,[29] to reaffirm the true position as stated in the headnote to *Suisse Atlantique* quoted above. Whether the contract is affirmed or not, the question of whether the exclusion applies is always one of interpretation: was the clause intended to apply to the breach which has occurred, regardless of whether or not that breach was fundamental?

The only proper use now for the expression 'fundamental term' is as the equivalent of 'condition'. The only proper use of 'fundamental breach' is to designate such a breach of an innominate term as entitles the injured party to put an end to the contract.[30] But the importance of the term broken, or of the breach, will still tend to be of some relevance in answering the question of construction. For example, in the *Rambler Cycle* case,[31] the court envisaged hypothetical breaches analogous to the one before the court, and concluded that they were of such a nature that the parties, as reasonable men, could not have intended the clause to apply to them.

If the clause is clearly expressed to exclude negligence then it will also exclude strict liability; but it does not follow that such a clause will always be effective. The defendant may have been guilty of something worse than negligence which the parties, as reasonable persons, could not have intended to be excluded. If, in the *Rambler Cycle* case, the goods had been negligently lost after they were unloaded it may well be that the clause would have been effective to protect the carrier; but that would have been quite different from deliberately throwing them into the sea or burning them, which the court equated with the event which had actually occurred. It is the deliberate character of the breach which takes it out of the protection of the clause.[32] In some of the fundamental breach cases, the breach was said to be fundamental because it was deliberate; but in *Suisse Atlantique* it was pointed out that the mere fact that a breach is deliberate does not mean that it is also 'fundamental'. After all, a deliberate delay of one day in loading a ship might have little or no effect on the substantial performance of the contract. However, the question of whether the breach was fundamental is a different question from whether it was intended to be covered by the clause. In answering the latter question, deliberateness may well be an important factor.

Where a clause is wide enough to exclude a negligent but not a deliberate breach of contract, it becomes vitally important to know what sort of breach occurred. The burden of proof is placed upon the defendant: if the defendant can show that the breach occurred through his negligence, he will escape liability, because such liability is excluded; but, if he cannot show negligence, the court may infer that there was a deliberate breach, leaving the defendant liable. It has been held that when goods in the possession of a **bailee** are lost or damaged and there is an exclusion clause covering negligence, the onus is on the bailee to prove that the loss occurred either without his fault, or through negligence, and

---

[29] [1980] AC 827.

[30] See Chapter 24, Section 2.

[31] See Section 1(b).

[32] See eg *Kudos Catering (UK) Ltd v Manchester Central Convention Complex Ltd* [2013] EWCA Civ 38, [2013] 2 Lloyd's Rep 270.

not through something worse. In *Levison v Patent Steam Carpet Cleaning Co Ltd*,[33] the defendants lost the claimant's carpet in some unexplained way. The agreement between the parties exempted the defendants from liability for negligence, but this did not assist the defendants, who were nonetheless held liable. The defendants were the ones who should know what happened to the carpet and the onus was on them to prove that the loss was not due to what the court called a 'fundamental breach' going beyond mere negligence. Because the defendants could not establish that the carpet was lost due to negligence, the court proceeded on the basis that the carpet had been deliberately lost, and the defendants were therefore unable to rely upon the exemption clause.

This principle is easily understandable where the fundamental or deliberate breach is committed by the contracting party personally. So, if I personally undertake to clean your designer dress and then give it away to my girlfriend, there is unlikely to be any difficulty in deciding that no exclusion clause, however widely drawn, could reasonably have been supposed to have been intended to cover that.[34] On the other hand, imagine that the designer dress has been stolen by one of my employees. Here, I personally may not even have been negligent, because I may have taken all proper care in employing that employee. But it seems that the courts will regard this as worse than a negligent breach, such that I will not be able to rely upon an exclusion clause to limit my liability. My employee is committing the tort of **conversion** and I am vicariously liable for torts committed by him in the course of his employment. In *Levison*'s case, Lord Denning said that the clause would be ineffective if 'the goods were stolen by one of his servants; or delivered by a servant to the wrong address; or damaged by reckless or wilful misconduct; all of which the offending servant will conceal and not make known to his employer'. The burden on the employer of proving that none of these things happened therefore seems rather formidable.

In the *Photo Production* case, Securicor agreed to provide security services, including night patrols, at the claimants' factory. Their employee, Musgrove, while carrying out a night patrol, deliberately started a small fire (in order to keep warm!) which spiralled out of control and destroyed the factory, valued at £615,000. Securicor successfully relied on a clause which provided that under no circumstances should they be 'responsible for any injurious act or default by any employee of the company unless such act or default could have been foreseen and avoided by the exercise of due diligence on the part of the company as his employer …' In the Court of Appeal, the doctrine of fundamental breach made what should be positively its last appearance. The Court of Appeal held that there had been a fundamental breach which brought the contract to an end, and, following *Harbutt's Plasticine*, the clause could therefore no longer be relied upon. However, the House of Lords held that the question was simply one of construction, and overturned the decision of the Court of Appeal. Their Lordships held that, on its true construction, the clause applied to the event which had occurred. In commercial transactions, as distinct from consumer contracts, there was everything to be said for leaving the parties free to apportion the risks as they thought fit, and the decisions of commercial parties should be respected. The House of Lords was clearly influenced by Securicor's very modest charge for the services provided—it

---

[33] [1978] QB 69, CA.
[34] cf *Morris v CW Martin & Sons Ltd* [1966] 1 QB 716, which concerned a mink stole.

worked out at 26p a visit—and the relative means of knowledge of the parties: Securicor could know nothing of the value of the factory and efficacy of the fire precautions. It was not reasonable in these circumstances to suppose that the parties could have intended Securicor to assume responsibility for the substantial risk of damage to the premises.

Deliberately starting a small fire is one thing and deliberately burning down the factory is another. It does not necessarily follow that the latter act would have been protected by the clause. Still less does it follow that a deliberate act done personally by the contracting party (as distinct from an employee for whom he is vicariously liable) would be protected. If Securicor's board of directors had resolved to burn the factory down, clearly Securicor would not have been able to rely on the clause. It may also be the case that Securicor would not have been able to rely upon the clause had the board of directors, or someone who could be identified with the company, authorised employees to light small fires on the premises to keep warm. The question would be whether the parties, as reasonable commercial men, could have intended the clause to apply in that situation.

(i) Deviation

It is reasonable to suppose that an exemption clause is intended to protect a party only when he is performing the contract, and to leave him subject to his usual liability when he is doing something completely outside its terms and deviating from the envisaged performance of the contract. For example, if A contracts with B to store B's goods in warehouse X and then proceeds to store them in warehouse Y, where they are destroyed, it may well be that an exclusion clause which would have been effective to protect A against the loss had it occurred in warehouse X will be ineffective.[35] The clause protected A while he was performing the contract, but he was not doing so when the loss occurred. Similarly, when a shipowner deviates from the contractually agreed voyage he may be disabled from relying on exemption clauses in the contract of carriage.[36] In the *Photo Production* case, Lord Wilberforce suggested that it may be preferable to regard the deviation cases as a body of authority *sui generis* with special rules derived from historical and commercial reasons, but the general principle seems relatively straightforward: an exclusion clause will only protect a party whilst he is performing his contractual obligations, but not whilst he is deviating from performance of the contract.

(d) Misrepresentation

At common law, the only usual effect of misrepresentation is to create a right to rescind.[37] Misrepresentation requires special mention in this context because it may also limit or exclude reliance on an exclusion clause. In *Curtis v Chemical Cleaning and Dyeing Co*,[38] the defendant's employee misrepresented the effect of an exclusion clause. The claimant took

---

[35] cf *Lilley v Doubleday* (1881) 7 QBD 510 (although there was no exclusion clause in that case).
[36] cf *Daewoo Heavy Industries Ltd v Klipriver Shipping Ltd (The Kapitan Petko Voivoda)* [2003] EWCA Civ 451, [2003] 1 All ER (Comm) 801.
[37] See Chapter 16, Section 4.
[38] [1951] 1 KB 805, CA.

her wedding dress to be cleaned, and was asked to sign a form. When the claimant asked why she needed to sign the form, she was told that it was because the company would not accept liability for certain specified risks, including damage to the beads and sequins on the trimming of the dress. In fact, the clause provided that the company was not to be liable for 'any damage, however arising'. When the dress came back, the beads and sequins were all right, but the dress had a stain on it. It was held that the employee had unwittingly created a false impression. The effect of this misrepresentation was to disentitle the company from relying on the clause, except with regard to the beads and sequins.

2 UCTA 1977

The title of the Unfair Contract Terms Act 1977 may be misleading in two respects. First, it is not concerned with all contract terms which might be thought to be 'unfair' but with only two types of term: exclusion clauses and indemnity clauses.[39] Secondly, the Act is not confined to contractual terms. It applies to cases where there is no contractual relationship between the parties but an attempt is made to exclude tortious or other liability by means of a notice or other disclaimer.

It is important to appreciate that the scope of UCTA 1977 has been significantly narrowed by the Consumer Rights Act 2015. It is the latter statute, rather than the former, which applies to consumer contracts. As a result, UCTA 1977 now only applies to non-consumer contracts, which is different from the previous law.[40] Decisions reached prior to the coming into force of the 2015 Act need to be read with this in mind.

(a) Clauses affected by the Act

UCTA 1977 does not provide a definition of an exclusion clause but section 13(1) provides that:

> To the extent that [Part I of the Act] prevents the exclusion or restriction of any liability it also prevents—
>
> (a) making the liability or its enforcement subject to restrictive or onerous conditions;
> (b) excluding or restricting any right or remedy in respect of the liability, or subjecting any person to any prejudice in consequence of his pursuing any such right or remedy;
> (c) excluding or restricting rules of evidence or procedure;
>
> and (to that extent) sections 2, 6 and 7 also prevent excluding or restricting liability by reference to terms and notices which exclude or restrict the relevant obligation or duty.

An agreement in writing to submit disputes to arbitration is not to be treated as excluding or restricting liability and so is unaffected by the Act (s 13(2)). However, UCTA 1977 does apply to clauses requiring claims or complaints to be made within a specified time or in a

---

[39] Admittedly, s 3 might be considered to be a little broader: see Section 2(c)(ii).
[40] See eg UCTA 1977, s 12; *R & B Customs Brokers v UDT* [1988] 1 All ER 847. Section 12 has been repealed as a result of the Consumer Rights Act 2015, Sch 4, para 11.

specified form (para (a)). The Act also covers clauses which purport to exclude the right to rescind or avoid a contract, and to clauses which preclude a buyer of goods or services from withholding part of the price by reason of defects in the goods or services supplied[41] (para (b)). Clauses which provide that a customer's signature should be conclusive proof that goods comply with a contract or have a certain value are also within the ambit of UCTA 1977 (para (c)). Whereas a clause which *limits* the amount of damages payable on breach of contract is plainly covered by the statutory regime, a clause which *fixes* the amount is probably not within the ambit of the Act:[42] such a clause is valid if it is a **liquidated damages** clause but void if it is a penalty clause.[43] There may be difficult questions of interpret-ation about whether a clause fixes or limits the amount payable, but the usual principles of interpretation must be applied: what would a reasonable observer understand the parties to have intended?

An agreement to settle an action for damages is an agreement to exclude or restrict liability, but UCTA 1977 will not affect such agreements. That is because settlement agreements are concerned with an existing liability, whereas UCTA 1977 is concerned with prospective liability. In other words, the focus of the Act is upon liabilities which the parties contemplate might arise (for example, under a contract which they are about to enter into). Although section 15 provides that the Act does not affect the validity of settlement agreements in Scotland and there is no corresponding provision for England, it has been held that the Act is not intended, and does not apply, to such a settlement.[44]

(b) **Contracts affected by the Act**

Sections 2–7 of the Act apply:[45]

> (except where the contrary is stated in section 6(4)) only to business liability, that is liability for breach of obligations or duties arising—
>
> (a) from things done or to be done by a person in the course of a business (whether his own business or another's); or
>
> (b) from the occupation of premises used for business purposes of the occupier ...

'Business' includes a profession and the activities of any government department or local or public authority.[46] The Act therefore applies to the obligations of a solicitor, a doctor, the proprietor of a private school operated for profit, a local authority in respect of its swimming baths, and so on. But the Act does not apply to a university or a private school which is a charitable foundation, and any person not carrying on business may continue to exclude liability to the same extent as before the Act. In such circumstances, the common law rules remain crucial. However, it is nearly always in respect of business liability that the issue of unfair terms arises.

---

[41] *Stewart Gill Ltd v Horatio Meyer & Co Ltd* [1992] 2 All ER 257.
[42] cf *Suisse Atlantique* [1967] 1 AC 361.
[43] See Chapter 27.
[44] *Tudor Grange Holdings Ltd v Citibank NA* [1991] 4 All ER 1, ChD (Browne-Wilkinson V-C).
[45] s 1(3).
[46] s 14.

There are other limitations to the scope of the Act. Sections 2–7 do not extend to the contracts listed in Schedule 1, paragraph 1, which include any contract of insurance, any contract relating to the creation, transfer, or termination of an interest in land, or in any patent, trade mark, copyright, or other intellectual property, and any contract relating to the formation or dissolution of any company.

The Act does not apply to 'international supply contracts', which are contracts for the sale of goods, or contracts under which the ownership or possession of goods passes, made by parties whose places of business (or, if they have none, habitual residences) are in different states *and* either:[47]

(a) when the contract is made, the goods are in the course of carriage, or will be carried, from one state to another; or

(b) the acts of offer and acceptance are done in different states; or

(c) the contract provides for the goods to be delivered in a state other than that in which the offer and acceptance took place.

The Act does not apply to contracts which are governed by English law only because the parties have so provided, and the substantial connection of the contract is with the law of a country outside the UK.[48] But UCTA 1977 does apply where a term purporting to apply the law of some other country appears to the court or arbitrator to have been imposed wholly or mainly for the purpose of enabling the party imposing it to evade the operation of the Act.[49]

(c) **The effect of the Act**

(i) **Avoidance of liability for negligence**

Negligence is defined by section 1(1) to include the breach of any duty to take reasonable care or exercise reasonable skill; this duty can arise out of a contract, or be imposed by the common law or the Occupiers' Liability Act 1957. No term of any contract or notice to which section 2(1) applies can exclude or restrict liability for negligence causing death or personal injury,[50] and liability for other loss or damage can be excluded or restricted only insofar as the term or notice satisfies the requirement of reasonableness laid down by the Act.[51] A notice may be relevant evidence that a defendant has satisfied a duty of care by giving warning of a danger; however, section 13(1) makes it clear that a term or notice may not negative a duty which would otherwise give rise to a liability which could not be excluded.[52] So simply adding the words 'without responsibility, on our part'[53] may no

---

[47] s 26.
[48] s 27(1).
[49] s 27(2).
[50] *Johnstone v Bloomsbury Health Authority* [1991] 2 All ER 293; see too *Ashdown v Samuel William & Sons Ltd* [1957] 1 QB 409.
[51] See Section 2(d).
[52] *Smith v Eric S Bush (a firm)* [1990] 1 AC 831, HL.
[53] See eg *Hedley Byrne & Co Ltd v Heller & Partners Ltd* [1964] AC 465.

longer be effective to exclude a duty in tort that would otherwise arise, unless the defendants persuade the court that the disclaimer satisfied the requirement of reasonableness.[54]

Under section 2(2) of UCTA 1977, an exclusion clause will only operate to exclude or restrict liability for negligence that does not cause death or personal injury if the clause satisfies the requirement of reasonableness. The scope of section 2(2) was discussed in *Phillips
Products Ltd v Hyland*.[55] *A* hired an excavator, together with a driver and operator of the
machine, *B*, to *C*. Whilst operating the machine, *B* negligently caused damage to *C*'s building. *C* sued both *A* and *B* in negligence. One question was whether *A* could rely upon a
clause that purported to transfer from *A* to *C* responsibility for damage caused by *B* whilst
being hired by *A*. The Court of Appeal held that, in essence, this clause did seek to exclude
A's liability to *C* in negligence, and therefore fell within the scope of section 2(2) (and was
in fact unreasonable under s 11). By contrast, in *Thompson v T Lohan (Plant Hire) Ltd*,[56]
there was a similar accident with an excavator, but the relevant clause in the contract provided that, effectively, the hirer was to indemnify the owner of the excavator in respect of
all claims to third parties arising out of the use of the machine. The Court of Appeal held
that this clause did not fall within section 2. This is because the clause did not seek to exclude or limit liability towards the victim of the negligence. Rather, the clause was simply
concerned with the allocation of responsibility for compensating the victim. This is not an
exclusion clause, so is outside the scope of section 2.

(ii) Avoidance of liability, otherwise than for negligence, in contract

This is provided for by section 3 of the Act which now only operates where a party is dealing on the other's written standard terms of business. The party proffering such terms is, *ex
hypothesi*, making the contract in the course of a business. In order to fall within section 3,
the terms must be written (although not necessarily signed) and 'standard'. Importantly,
terms will not fail to qualify as 'standard' just because some particular matters are negotiated, such as the price and time of performance, or if some minor alterations are made that
are 'immaterial' and 'insubstantial'.[57] However, if the whole of the written terms have been
written for this particular contract, clearly they are not 'standard'.

The written standard terms may be prepared by the individual contractor or by a trade or
professional organisation, for example. But if the terms used have been prepared by a trade
organisation, those terms must also be the usual terms of the party using them if they are
to constitute that party's written standard terms of business.[58] Such terms must be terms of
business. This was highlighted in *Keen v Commerzbank AG*.[59] A term in a bank employee's
contract of employment did not fall within the scope of section 3 of UCTA 1977 because it
was not concerned with the bank's standard terms of business: the bank's business was not
entering into contracts with its employees but rather banking.

---

[54] See eg *Titan Steel Wheels Ltd v Royal Bank of Scotland Plc* [2010] EWHC 211 (Comm), [2010] 2 Lloyd's Rep
92 [98]–[108] (Steel J).

[55] [1987] 1 WLR 659, CA.

[56] [1987] 1 WLR 649.

[57] *Watford Electronics Ltd v Sanderson CFL Ltd* [2001] 2 All ER (Comm) 696.

[58] *British Fermentation Products v Compair Reavell* [1999] BLR 352.

[59] [2006] EWCA Civ 1536, [2006] 2 CLC 844.

The effect of section 3 is that the party proffering the standard terms cannot:

(a) when in breach of contract, exclude or restrict liability, except insofar as the contract term satisfies the requirement of reasonableness; or

(b) claim to be entitled to render a contractual performance substantially different from that which was reasonably expected of him, or to tender no performance at all, except insofar as the contract term authorising him to do so satisfies the requirement of reasonableness.

Paragraph (a) applies only when the defendant is in breach. If a term purports to exclude or restrict liability for breach of the promise, it is caught by paragraph (a) and is ineffective unless it satisfies the requirement of reasonableness. However, a term may exclude an alleged promise, in which case there is no breach.[60] Section 13, which prevents the exclusion or restriction of duties, does not apply to section 3.

The importance of this limitation on the effect of paragraph (a) is greatly reduced by paragraph (b). This is because paragraph (b) covers situations which do not involve a breach of contract. The different performance, or non-performance, contemplated by (b) is not a breach of contract. If it were, it would be covered by (a). Paragraph (b) therefore assumes that there are (at least) two ways of performing the contract. Each is a 'contractual performance' but only one is 'reasonably expected'. Performing the contract in the other way will effectively be a statutory breach of contract, unless the term authorising that performance satisfies the requirement of reasonableness. An example may make this clearer. Suppose that standard terms provide:

(i)   Accommodation will be provided in the Majestic Hotel

. . .

(ix) If accommodation in the Majestic Hotel is not available it will be provided in another hotel of comparable quality.

If clause (ix) is held to be an attempt to exclude liability for breach of a promise to provide accommodation in the Majestic, it is caught by paragraph (a) and is ineffective unless it satisfies the requirement of reasonableness. But if clause (ix) is held to provide for an alternative mode of performance of the contract, and the claimant reasonably expected to be accommodated in the Majestic, it is caught by paragraph (b) and there is effectively a statutory breach of contract unless the defendant shows that the term satisfies the requirement of reasonableness. In *Timeload Ltd v British Telecommunications Plc*,[61] it was suggested that a clause entitling BT to terminate a customer's telephone line without reason might be caught by paragraph (b), because that may be a different performance from what the customer expected. But in *Paragon Finance plc v Nash*,[62] a clause in a **mortgage** contract giving a lender the power to vary interest rates did not fall within paragraph (b) since the exercise of that power was not a 'contractual performance'—by altering the interest rate, the lender was not affecting its own obligation of performance.

---

[60] See Section 1(b) of this chapter.
[61] [1995] EMLR 459.
[62] [2002] 2 All ER 248.

(iii) Contracts under which possession or ownership of goods passes

By section 6, the seller or supplier of goods cannot, by any contract term, exclude or restrict his undertaking as to **title** implied by section 12 of the Sale of Goods Act 1979 or section 8 of the Supply of Goods (Implied Terms) Act 1973—although he may still contract to give only such title as he has. However, the seller may be able to exclude or restrict liability for the implied undertakings as to conformity of goods with description, or sample, or as to their quality or fitness for a particular purpose, but only insofar as the relevant clause satisfies the requirement of reasonableness. It is worth highlighting here that such terms cannot be excluded as against a consumer.[63] Section 7 makes similar provision for other contracts under which ownership or possession of goods passes.

(d) **The requirement of reasonableness**

Although the title of UCTA 1977 indicates that it is concerned with 'unfair' terms, many exclusion or limitation clauses will only be considered 'unfair' if they fail the statutory test of 'reasonableness' in section 11. In relation to a contractual term which excludes or limits liability, the requirement is that the term shall have been a fair and reasonable one to be included in the contract, having regard to the circumstances which were, or ought reasonably to have been, known to, or in the contemplation of, the parties when the contract was made.[64] This last point should be emphasised: reasonableness should be assessed at the time the contract was made, rather than with the benefit of hindsight which takes into account the nature of the breach. In determining whether a term satisfies the requirement of reasonableness for the purposes of sections 6 and 7 (sale, **hire-purchase**, and miscellaneous contracts under which goods pass), a court or arbitrator must have regard to the matters specified in Schedule 2. These include the relative bargaining power of the parties; whether there was an inducement to agree to the term or an opportunity to enter into a similar contract without such a term; whether the customer knew, or ought reasonably to have known, of the term; whether the goods were manufactured, processed, or adapted to the special order of the customer; and, where the term applies if some condition is not complied with, whether it was reasonable to expect that compliance with the condition would be practicable.

In determining whether the requirement of reasonableness is satisfied for the purpose of other sections, there are no statutory guidelines. However, a court will naturally take account of the matters mentioned in Schedule 2 where they are relevant. Whatever section is in issue, the list of factors to be considered is neither exclusive nor exhaustive.

Essentially, reasonableness is a question of fact particular to any individual contract. For this reason, it is difficult to rely too much upon decided cases as precedents for future disputes: a range of factors will always be taken into account by the court. Indeed, **appellate courts** have consistently said that they will be reluctant to interfere with decisions made by a trial judge who has heard all the evidence on whether or not an exemption clause is

---

[63] Consumer Rights Act 2015, s 31.
[64] s 11.

reasonable,[65] and it is impossible to state all factors that might be relevant to deciding on the issue of reasonableness. Nevertheless, it is instructive to consider some leading cases.

In *George Mitchell (Chesterhall) Ltd v Finney Lock Seeds Ltd*,[66] the parties entered into a contract for the sale of Dutch winter white cabbage seeds. The sale price was about £200, and there was a clause in the contract which limited the sellers' liability for defective seeds to the price of the seeds themselves. Unfortunately, the seeds were the wrong type of cabbage seeds and worthless to the claimant farmers. The claimants sought damages for breach of contract of over £60,000. The House of Lords held that the limitation clause was unreasonable and could not be relied upon by the sellers. Their Lordships gave a range of factors that should be taken into account when determining reasonableness. These included the fact that the price of the seeds was very cheap[67] and the clause was very clear. Such factors pointed towards a conclusion that the clause was unreasonable. However, those considerations were outweighed by the fact that the sellers might be expected to be insured for the events that occurred,[68] the sellers were in a much stronger position than the purchasers, the term had not been negotiated, and, perhaps most importantly, even though the clause appeared to be standard in the relevant industry, it was rarely invoked. This was thought to indicate that the clause itself was considered to be unreasonable in the trade.[69] Indeed, the sellers had initially sought to negotiate a settlement with the purchasers, without trying to hold the farmers to the limitation clause, which perhaps confirmed the view that the clause was unreasonable.

The discussion in *George Mitchell* of the factors to be weighed against each other when considering reasonableness remains useful. Nevertheless, it is important not to place too much emphasis on the decision. It is famous for being Lord Denning's last case in the Court of Appeal, and the House of Lords reached the same conclusion as Lord Denning, but the case concerned transitional provisions which were in effect pending the coming into force of UCTA 1977. The case does not, therefore, consider section 11 of UCTA 1977 as it is currently enacted. Whilst the House of Lords discussed whether it was fair and reasonable to rely on the limitation clause, the discussion now should focus on whether it was fair and reasonable to include the term in the contract. The nature and circumstances of the breach should not be taken into account when assessing the reasonableness of a term under UCTA 1977, whereas this was relevant in *George Mitchell*. A further difference is that, under the 1977 Act, the burden of proof is squarely placed on the person claiming that the clause is reasonable to prove that it is,[70] but the burden of proof in *George Mitchell* was placed upon the claimants.

One factor that courts often seem to find telling is the relative strength of the bargaining powers of the parties. Where both parties are well-advised commercial entities, a court may generally be more reluctant to interfere with the parties' bargain and hold that

---

[65] See eg *George Mitchell (Chesterhall) Ltd v Finney Lock Seeds Ltd* [1983] 2 AC 803; *Cleaver v Schyde Investments Ltd* [2011] EWCA Civ 929, [2011] 2 P & CR 21.

[66] [1983] 2 AC 803.

[67] cf *Photo Production*, discussed at Section 1(c).

[68] See now UCTA 1977, s 11(4)(b).

[69] A different conclusion may be reached on different facts: cf *Schenkers Ltd v Overland Shoes Ltd* [1998] 1 Lloyd's Rep 498.

[70] s 11(5).

an exemption clause is unreasonable. This is well illustrated by the decision in *Watford Electronics Ltd v Sanderson CFL Ltd*.[71] The claimant company, which sold computers by mail order, contracted with the defendant company for the supply of a software system to deal with its affairs. The software system was defective, and the claimant sought damages of over £5.5 million. The defendant sought to rely on two exclusion clauses. The first excluded liability for any 'claims for indirect or consequential losses whether arising from negligence or otherwise', and the second limited liability to the contract price (just over £100,000). The Court of Appeal held that both terms were reasonable under section 11 of UCTA 1977. In a robust decision, Chadwick LJ insisted upon the court's respecting the agreement reached by commercial parties who knew full well what they were doing. According to the view of Chadwick LJ, if the clause really was unfair then the parties would not have agreed to it, and each party enjoyed a sufficiently strong bargaining position to be able to renegotiate or walk away from the deal rather than accept an unfair term.[72] The court should not rewrite the parties' bargain.

Interestingly, in *Watford Electronics* the two exemption clauses were separate and could be examined separately. However, in *Stewart Gill Ltd v Horatio Myer & Co Ltd*[73] the Court of Appeal held that where one exclusion clause contains two elements—one of which may be reasonable and the other unreasonable—it is not possible to 'sever' the unreasonable part so that the clause is valid to the extent that it is reasonable: any particular term must be assessed for reasonableness as a whole. This should prompt those drafting contracts not to include all-encompassing exclusion clauses. However, the court may nonetheless be prepared to consider different elements of a single term separately where they are in substance 'independent'.[74]

It should be emphasised that the application of the considerations laid out in section 11 of and Schedule 2 to UCTA 1977 clearly depend on the particular facts of the case. In *St Alban's City and District Council v International Computers Ltd*,[75] the council purchased from the defendants software to be used to facilitate the council's collection of the poll tax. There were errors in the software which led to the council setting the rate of poll tax at too low a level. As a result, the council did not collect as much money as it should have, and also had to pay a large sum to the county council. The council sought damages for its losses of about £1.3 million. The defendants sought to limit their liability to £100,000 by virtue of a limitation clause. Both the judge at first instance and the Court of Appeal held that the limitation clause was unreasonable. The judge thought that the defendants were in a much stronger bargaining position than the council: the defendants were one of a small number of companies who could satisfy the council's requirements, and the council was governed by particular financial risks and found it impractical to insure against commercial risks. Admittedly, this was, perhaps, not an obvious conclusion. But the judge also pointed out that there was no objective justification for why the figure of £100,000 had been chosen in the limitation clause. This suggested that the clause was unreasonable. As a result of this

---

[71] [2001] EWCA Civ 317, [2001] All ER (Comm) 696.
[72] See too eg *Regus (UK) Ltd v Epcot Solutions Ltd* [2008] EWCA Civ 361, [2009] 1 All ER (Comm) 586.
[73] [1992] QB 600, CA.
[74] *Regus (UK) Ltd v Epcot Solutions Ltd* [2008] EWCA Civ 361, [2009] 1 All ER (Comm) 586.
[75] [1996] 4 All ER 481, CA; see also the first instance decision: [1995] FSR 686.

decision, parties would now be well advised to make sure that any limit chosen in a limitation clause can be both explained and defended. Otherwise, a court may conclude that the limitation is set at too low a level, and is unreasonable and ineffective.

It might further be suggested that the broader the interpretation of an exclusion clause, the less likely it is to be reasonable.[76] For instance, if an exclusion clause is interpreted broadly such that it can cover deliberate and reprehensible breaches of duty, then it is less likely to be found to be reasonable than an exclusion clause which does not cover such conduct. In any event, it is clear that when a clause purporting to exclude liability or a remedy for misrepresentation is assessed for reasonableness under section 3 of the Misrepresentation Act 1967, the same approach to section 11 of UCTA 1977 should be adopted.[77] It is worth now considering a little further the relationship between UCTA 1977 and the Misrepresentation Act 1967.

3 The Misrepresentation Act 1967

Section 3 of the Misrepresentation Act 1967,[78] as amended by the Unfair Contract Terms Act 1977, provides:

> 3. If a contract contains a term which would exclude or restrict—
>
> (a) any liability to which a party to a contract may be subject by reason of any misrepresentation made by him before the contract was made; or
>
> (b) any remedy available to another party to the contract by reason of such a misrepresentation,
>
> that term shall be of no effect except in so far as it satisfies the requirement of reasonableness as stated in section 11(1) of the Unfair Contract Terms Act 1977; and it is for those claiming that the term satisfies that requirement to show that it does.

So, if a person brings an action for rescission of the contract for innocent misrepresentation or for damages under section 2(1) of the 1967 Act, the defendant cannot rely on a clause purporting to exclude or restrict his liability for misrepresentation unless he can satisfy the court that the term was a fair and reasonable one to be included, having regard to the circumstances which were or ought reasonably to have been known to, or in the contemplation of, the parties when the contract was made. Under the 1967 Act as originally passed, the test was whether reliance on the term was fair and reasonable in the circumstances of the case. This allowed—and indeed required—the court to take into account relevant events occurring after the contract was made. But this is clearly no longer the case.[79] The court must decide whether the clause was a fair and reasonable one to include in the contract and, if it was, the clause is valid and must be applied.

---

[76] *Regus (UK) Ltd v Epcot Solutions Ltd* [2008] EWCA Civ 361, [2009] 1 All ER (Comm) 586.

[77] *Cleaver v Schyde Investments Ltd* [2011] EWCA Civ 929, [2011] 2 P & CR 21; *Lloyd v Browning* [2013] EWCA Civ 1637, [2014] 1 P & CR 11.

[78] See Chapter 16, Section 7.

[79] For further consideration of the Misrepresentation Act 1967, s 3, see Chapter 16, Section 7.

Section 3 would also apply if an action were brought for damages for a negligent misrepresentation under the doctrine of *Hedley Byrne*.[80] However, it is not so clear that the section is applicable to an action for breach of contract. This may pose some difficulties, since a misrepresentation may be incorporated into a contract.[81] Imagine that there is a clause excluding liability for both misrepresentation and breach of contract. If the **repre-sentee** claims damages under section 2(1) of the Misrepresentation Act 1967, or rescission for misrepresentation, the clause may be struck down under section 3 of the 1967 Act. But what if the representee claims damages for breach of contract, or to terminate the contract for breach of condition? In some cases, the corresponding provision of UCTA 1977 relating to breach of contract will apply and there will be no problem; indeed, the same 'fair and reasonable' test under section 11 of UCTA 1977 will apply. But whereas section 3 of the 1967 Act applies to all contracts (apart from consumer contracts[82]), UCTA 1977 does not apply to all contracts. If the contract is one of those excluded from the operation of UCTA 1977, it becomes very important to determine the scope of section 3 of the 1967 Act. One view is that section 3 invalidates the whole clause and that the representee is therefore unable to exclude liability for breach of contract to the extent that the relevant term is a misrepresentation for which he cannot exclude liability. But this is not completely clear. If there were two exclusion clauses, one excluding liability for misrepresentation and the other excluding liability for breach of contract, it would be clear that section 3 of the 1967 Act applied only to the first and not to the second. Why should it be different when the two provisions are put into one clause of a contract rather than into two clauses? The substance is the same. If this second view is right, section 3 of the 1967 Act does not limit the ability of a party to a contract to exclude liability for contractual undertakings as to matters of fact, whether or not they amounted to misrepresentations before the conclusion of the contract. Whether this view is right or wrong, it is of course clear that section 3 does not limit the ability to exclude liability for contractual undertakings as to the future, for that does not involve misrepresentation.

4 The Consumer Rights Act 2015

The Consumer Rights Act 2015 now governs the control of unfair terms in consumer contracts. This is a welcome development. Before the enactment of this Act, there was a messy overlap between UCTA 1977 and the Unfair Terms in Consumer Contracts Regulations 1994,[83] which were later replaced by the Unfair Terms in Consumer Contracts Regulations 1999.[84] These Regulations were enacted in the UK in order to implement Council Directive 93/13/EEC on Unfair Terms in Consumer Contracts. But they did not operate in harmony with UCTA 1977 and section 3 of the Misrepresentation Act 1967. The Consumer Rights

---

[80] For further consideration of this case, and indeed misrepresentation more generally, see Chapter 16.

[81] See Misrepresentation Act 1967, s 1; see further Chapter 16.

[82] See the Consumer Rights Act 2015, s 75 and Sch 4, para 1. In consumer contracts, the clause is subject to the general test of fairness under s 62: see Section 4(c) of this chapter.

[83] SI 1994 No 3159.

[84] SI 1999 No 2083.

Act 2015 resolves this problem: neither UCTA 1977 nor section 3 of the Misrepresentation Act 1967 applies to consumer contracts. Instead, the court must look exclusively to the Consumer Rights Act 2015. It is this statute which satisfies the UK's obligations to implement the European Directive, and the Act must be interpreted in accordance with the Directive.

The case law relevant to the Directive therefore remains useful when deciding how the 2015 Act should be interpreted. However, caution must be exercised when using cases decided in England and Wales under the old, now defunct, Regulations when applying the 2015 Act. Where the wording of the Regulations was the same as that found in the Directive and now the 2015 Act, decisions interpreting those provisions no doubt remain persuasive. But some authorities should no longer be followed. The decision of the Supreme Court in *Office of Fair Trading v Abbey National plc*,[85] which will be discussed further in Section 4(d) is a good example of one case which would probably now be decided differently. The *Abbey National* case is also a good example of a case being brought by the Office of Fair Trading to police unfair terms in consumer contracts for the benefit of individual consumers; it remains possible for the Competition and Markets Authority and other public organisations to bring such actions under the 2015 Act.[86]

(a) Scope of the Consumer Rights Act 2015

It is obviously important to determine the scope of the 2015 Act. Part 2 of the Act governs unfair terms. It applies to a contract between a trader and consumer,[87] which is known as a 'consumer contract'. A trader is a person acting for purposes relating to that person's trade, business, craft, or profession,[88] and a consumer is 'an individual acting for purposes that are wholly or mainly outside that individual's trade, business, craft or profession'.[89] The burden is placed on the trader to prove that an individual is not dealing as a consumer:[90] in effect, it is presumed that individuals entering into contracts with businesses are dealing as consumers. However, it is important that the consumer is an individual: a business cannot be dealing as a consumer under the 2015 Act. The same approach is now taken in UCTA 1977 in order to achieve some consistency about what 'consumer' means.[91] The Law Commission had originally proposed to extend the protection against unfair terms to small businesses,[92] but this has not been implemented in the 2015 Act. As a result, small businesses can only rely upon UCTA 1977 to protect them from unfair terms.

A possible example of an individual acting as a consumer is provided by the facts of *Evans v Cherry Tree Finance Ltd*.[93] Mr Evans took out a mortgage on a property where he

---

[85] [2009] UKSC 6, [2009] 3 WLR 1215.

[86] s 70.

[87] s 61.

[88] s 2(2).

[89] s 2(3).

[90] s 2(4).

[91] UCTA 1977, s 12 has now been repealed, meaning that *R & B Custom Brokers v United Dominions Trust* [1988] 1 All ER 847 would be decided differently today: a company cannot be dealing as a consumer.

[92] Law Commission, *Unfair Terms in Contracts* (Law Com No 292, 2005) Part 5.

[93] [2008] EWCA Civ 331.

both lived and carried out his business. It was conceded by the lender that if Mr Evans was acting for any purpose which was outside his trade, business, or profession, then he would be a consumer. This was perhaps a generous concession under the old Regulations, but the same result should surely be reached under the 2015 Act if Mr Evans was *mainly* acting for non-business reasons. On the facts of the case, the mortgage appears to have been necessary primarily for Mr Evans's personal purposes, so the outcome seems correct.

Part 2 of the 2015 Act applies not only to consumer contracts, but also to 'consumer notices'[94] that relate to rights or obligations as between a trader and consumer which purport to exclude or restrict a trader's liability to a consumer.[95] Such notices include announcements made entirely orally.[96] For the sake of clarity, the rest of the analysis in this chapter will focus upon terms in consumer contracts rather than consumer notices, but it should be remembered that the same principles apply to consumer notices as well.

(b) Liability which cannot be excluded or restricted

Most terms in a consumer contract are subject to a test of fairness, and the scope and nature of this test is discussed in the following section. However, it is important to note that in some instances a trader's liability cannot be excluded or restricted in any event— regardless of any test of fairness. For instance, in the context of the sale of goods,[97] a trader cannot exclude or restrict his liability to a consumer that the goods are of satisfactory quality, fit for a particular purpose, or as described.[98] Similar provisions apply to contracts to supply digital content.[99] And in the context of contracts to provide services, a trader cannot exclude or restrict his liability to a consumer with respect to the trader's obligation to provide his services with reasonable care and skill, for instance.[100] Such terms are fundamental to the nature of the contracts entered into, and traders must not exclude or limit the effect of such terms. Consumers are well protected against any attempts by traders to do so, since under the 2015 Act the terms simply cannot be enforced, and a consumer does not have to prove that the terms are unfair. Similarly, it is not possible for a trader to exclude in consumer contracts liability for death or personal injury which results from negligence.[101]

(c) The test of fairness

Most terms in a consumer contract will be subject to a test of fairness. If a term is unfair, it will not bind a consumer.[102] The court now has a duty to consider whether a term is fair

---

[94] s 61(7).
[95] s 61(4).
[96] s 61(8).
[97] For consideration of the terms implied into contracts for the sale of goods, see Chapter 13, Section 3.
[98] s 31.
[99] s 47.
[100] s 57.
[101] s 65.
[102] s 62(2).

in a consumer contract even if neither party argues that the term is unfair.[103] The test for fairness is laid out in section 62:

> (4) A term is unfair if, contrary to the requirement of good faith, it causes a significant imbalance in the parties' rights and obligations under the contract to the detriment of the consumer.
> (5) Whether a term is fair is to be determined—
>   (a) taking into account the nature of the subject matter of the contract, and
>   (b) by reference to all the circumstances existing when the term was agreed and to all of the other terms of the contract or of any other contract on which it depends.

This is very similar to the language of the Directive and thus the old Regulations, but is broader in one important respect: the test of fairness is no longer limited to terms which have not been individually negotiated. As a result, the scope of the protection for unfair terms is expanded beyond merely standard terms. This is somewhat controversial, as it is difficult to see how a consumer could be 'surprised' by a term that has been individually negotiated,[104] but at least the approach under the 2015 Act avoids arguments about whether or not a particular term was individually negotiated. That issue is no longer important.

In any event, the substance of the test for fairness remains the same as it was under the Regulations. The leading English decision on the meaning of 'fairness' is that of the House of Lords in *Director General of Fair Trading v First National Bank plc*.[105] That case concerned the standard terms of a lending agreement used by First National Bank. The bank was worried about what would happen if a borrower defaulted on the payment of an instalment. The bank therefore added a term to its standard terms that if the borrower did default, then the bank would be able to demand repayment of the principal sum owed, as well as accrued interest, whether or not judgment had already been obtained against the borrower. This was important, since the bank was worried that some borrowers who were unable to make all the repayments might be repaying by instalments under a court order: if the borrowers were just repaying the instalments under a court order, then there was a danger that, without the additional clause, the borrowers would not be liable for the contractual rate of interest, because only a relatively low, statutory rate of interest would generally be awarded on judgment debts.

The House of Lords held that the relevant term was not unfair under what is now section 62(4). Their Lordships emphasised that the term was clear and that there was no 'significant imbalance' on the facts—it was not unfair to ask the customer to pay the agreed rate of interest on a debt the customer owes. In fact, Lord Bingham said that the 'absence of such a term would unbalance the contract to the detriment of the lender'. It is clear from the judgments in *First National Bank* that the test of 'significant imbalance' requires an assessment of the substantive terms of the contract. This is logical. As is the conclusion

---

[103] s 71.

[104] For further discussion of 'consumer surprise', see Section 4(c).

[105] [2002] 1 AC 481. In both this case and the Supreme Court decision in *Abbey National*, discussed at Section 4(d), the highest appellate court in this jurisdiction refused to refer any question to the Court of Justice of the European Union, which might perhaps be criticised since there may be a risk of undermining any attempts to establish consistency across the European Union.

that the imbalance must not be 'slight' but actually 'significant'.[106] However, it is not so clear to what the requirement of 'good faith' refers. It could be taken to refer to procedural considerations—in other words, the way the contract was formed—or to substantive considerations—essentially, the substance and performance of the contract. If the latter, it is perhaps unclear what 'good faith' adds to 'significant imbalance'. In the House of Lords, Lord Bingham appeared to think that good faith referred to essentially procedural concerns, whilst Lord Steyn insisted that good faith must not be restricted to purely procedural matters, and that this meant 'that there is a large area of overlap between the concepts of good faith and significant imbalance'. It is suggested that the latter view is preferable.[107] As Lord Millett pointed out, it is important to decide 'whether if [the term] were drawn to his attention the consumer would be likely to be surprised by it'. This idea of 'unfair surprise' seems crucial, and offers a good explanation for why some terms may not be considered for fairness if they are concerned with the main subject matter of the contract, and are transparent, prominent, legible, and expressed in plain and intelligible language.[108] A consumer would not be surprised by such terms, and so should not be able to argue that they are unfair: instead, the consumer should not have entered into what has turned out to be a bad bargain.

The 'leading case'[109] on the test of fairness in the Court of Justice of the European Union is *Aziz v Caixa d'Estalvis de Catalunya, Tarragona i Manresa*.[110] That decision concerned three particular terms in a loan agreement. The first provided for the acceleration of repayments in the event of the borrower's default. The second concerned the charging of default interest. And the third provided for the unilateral certification by the lender of the amount due for the purpose of legal proceedings. The Court of Justice emphasised that a significant element of judgement is left to the national court, and that the issue of 'significant imbalance' requires the court to consider whether the consumer is deprived of an advantage which he would normally have under national law. The significance, purpose, and practical effect of the term are all obviously important, and the term must be proportionate to the reasonable objectives which the particular term seeks to protect. Most significantly, perhaps, the Court of Justice held that whether or not a term is unfair and contrary to the requirement of good faith will depend on 'whether the seller or supplier, dealing fairly and equitably with the consumer, could reasonably assume that the consumer would have agreed to such a term in individual contract negotiations'.[111] The court should try to determine whether the reasonable consumer in that particular consumer's position would have agreed to the term if the contract had been individually negotiated. In the opinion of Advocate General Kokott, upon which the Court of Justice heavily relied, it is important to consider whether the contract terms are common, or surprising, or objectively justified.

---

[106] See too *Office of Fair Trading v Ashbourne Management Services Ltd* [2011] EWHC 1237 (Ch), [2011] ECC 31 [174] (Kitchin J).

[107] See too *West v Ian Finlay and Associates* [2014] EWCA Civ 316, [2014] BLR 324.

[108] s 64: see Section 4(c). Indeed, a trader must ensure that a term is transparent: s 68.

[109] According to Lord Neuberger and Lord Sumption in *Makdessi v Cavendish Square Holdings BV* [2015] UKSC 67 [105].

[110] Case C-26/13, 14 March 2013 [2013] 3 CMLR 89.

[111] Ibid, [69].

Terms might be unfair if they are excessive in relation to what is necessary to achieve a reasonable aim.

The guidance in the *Aziz* case is helpful and was endorsed by all members of the Supreme Court in *ParkingEye Ltd v Beavis*.[112] It clearly leaves some scope for national courts to use their own judgement, and is a flexible test. But such flexibility can lead to differences in opinion. Indeed, the Supreme Court Justices did not agree on whether the relevant term in *ParkingEye Ltd v Beavis* was unfair. ParkingEye ran a car park at a retail park. Customers who parked at the car park had a contract with ParkingEye. The terms of the contract stated that there was a '2 hour max stay', and that parking was free during that two-hour period. However, staying longer than two hours would lead to a 'Parking Charge' of £85. The defendant, Mr Beavis, left his car in the car park for nearly three hours, and ParkingEye sued for the Parking Charge of £85. This case is considered in detail in Chapter 27 in the context of penalty clauses, but Mr Beavis did not only contend that the clause was unenforceable as a penalty, but also that the clause was unfair under the consumer protection regime. The majority of the Supreme Court held that the Parking Charge was not unfair. Their Lordships recognised that a negotiated agreement to park a car is somewhat artificial, but highlighted the objective nature of the exercise and thought that a reasonable motorist would have agreed to a term imposing the £85 charge given that he could park for two hours for free.

However, Lord Toulson dissented on this point. Lord Toulson emphasised that 'the starting point of the Directive is that the consumer needs special protection', and that this is very different from the rule against penalties at common law, which is an exception to the principle that parties should be held to their bargains.[113] His Lordship thought that the burden was on ParkingEye to show that the consumer would have agreed to the term, and that it had not done so. This turns on the particular circumstances at issue and is of little wider import. More fundamentally, though, Lord Toulson thought that the approach of the majority 'waters down the test adopted' in the *Aziz* case, since the majority 'substituted their judgment of reasonableness of the clause for the question whether the supplier could reasonably have assumed that the customer would have agreed with the term'.[114] If correct, that would be very unfortunate indeed: it would be unsatisfactory for English law to protect consumers less well than the Court of Justice expects. But given the objective nature of the hypothetical negotiations, it is not at all clear that the majority did weaken the protection afforded to consumers. The Court of Justice recognises that there may be good reasons for parties to regulate their contractual affairs in various ways, and that the impact of a term alleged to be unfair must be examined broadly and from both sides.[115] On balance, it is suggested that the majority was correct to hold that the Parking Charge was not unfair.

In any event, it is very important to appreciate that a consumer will not be able to rely upon the legislative protection against unfair terms just because he has made a bad bargain. In *Bankers Insurance Co Ltd v South*,[116] a group of young men booked a holiday to

---

[112] [2015] UKSC 67, [2015] 3 WLR 1373.
[113] Ibid, [309]. See further Chapter 27.
[114] Ibid, [315].
[115] *Aziz* [AG94].
[116] [2003] EWHC 380 (QB).

Ayia Napa. Whilst riding a jet ski, one of the group, Mr South, was involved in a serious accident which injured Mr Gardner. Mr Gardner sought damages from Mr South, and Mr South relied upon his travel insurance to pay out compensation to Mr Gardner. The case itself was a dispute between Mr South and his insurance company. There was a term in the contract of insurance which said that the insurers would not pay compensation for accidents involving 'motorised waterborne craft'. The court held that this term was clear and covered jet skis. The court further insisted that the term was not unfair: there was no significant imbalance to the detriment of the consumer, since Mr South had paid a very low price for the insurance. In essence, Mr South got what he paid for: he paid a low sum, so did not receive total protection. However, the relevant term at issue may well have been unfair if Mr South had paid a much larger premium for the insurance policy.

Some provisions of the 2015 Act essentially mirror the pre-existing law. For instance, although an unfair term cannot be enforced against the consumer, the rest of the contract will continue to be binding.[117] Similarly, the *contra proferentem* rule[118] is incorporated into the Act.[119] Part 1 of Schedule 2 to the 2015 Act[120] provides a long 'indicative and non-exhaustive list of terms of consumer contract which may be regarded as unfair'. This 'grey list' includes exclusion clauses, **forfeiture** clauses, and automatic renewal clauses. Three new terms which might be unfair have been added to the 'grey list' by the 2015 Act: allowing the trader to decide the characteristics of the subject matter after the consumer is bound; allowing disproportionate charges or requiring the consumer to pay for services which have not been supplied when the consumer ends the contract; allowing the trader discretion over the price after the consumer is bound.

(d) Terms subject to the test of fairness

In principle, any term in any consumer contract can be assessed for fairness.[121] The test of fairness may therefore be applied to an arbitration clause or a liquidated damages clause, but it is suggested that it could not be applied in the context of a contract for the settlement of a dispute, because that could hardly be called a consumer contract. In any event, some terms in consumer contracts are excluded from an assessment of fairness as a result of section 64, which provides that:

(1) A term of a consumer contract may not be assessed for fairness under section 62 to the extent that—
  (a) it specifies the main subject matter of the contract, or
  (b) the assessment is of the appropriateness of the price payable under the contract by comparison with the goods, digital content or services supplied under it.
(2) Subsection (1) excludes a term from an assessment under section 62 only if it is transparent and prominent.

---

[117] s 67.
[118] See Section 1(b) of this chapter.
[119] s 69.
[120] See s 63(1) and (2).
[121] Although a trader is unable to exclude or restrict some types of liability in a consumer contract, eg liability for goods not being of a satisfactory quality: see ss 31, 47, and 57.

(3) A term is transparent for the purposes of this Part if it is expressed in plain and intelligible language and (in the case of a written term) is legible.

(4) A term is prominent for the purposes of this section if it is brought to the consumer's attention in such a way that an average consumer would be aware of the term.

(5) In subsection (4) 'average consumer' means a consumer who is reasonably well-informed, observant and circumspect.

This is a departure from the Regulations and the old law. Under the old law, there was no provision that stated that the term needed to be transparent and prominent such that the average consumer would be aware of the term. This led to the controversial decision in *Office of Fair Trading v Abbey National plc*.[122] That case concerned 'bank charges' that banks levied on their customers for unauthorised overdrafts. The Office of Fair Trading argued that such terms were unfair. The Supreme Court held that those terms could not even be assessed for fairness, as they concerned part of the price customers paid for their current accounts (especially where the current account was free to operate if in credit), and the fact that it was not an 'essential' or 'core' part of the price was irrelevant. However, by not even allowing such terms to be assessed for fairness, the Supreme Court greatly reduced the scope of protection afforded to consumers. This approach meant that consumer protection in England was less extensive than elsewhere in Europe,[123] and arguably did not accord with the thrust of the underlying Directive.[124]

However, *OFT v Abbey National* would most probably be decided differently under the Consumer Rights Act 2015: indeed, dissatisfaction with the outcome in that case was a major impetus for law reform. Terms imposing bank charges should now be subject to a test of fairness where they are not prominent in the contract between banks and customers such that a reasonably well-informed, observant, and circumspect consumer would not be aware of the term. In other words, if a consumer would be surprised by the term upon being told of it after entering into the contract, it will generally be subject to the test of fairness under the 2015 Act.

Further Reading

H Beale, 'Exclusion and Limitation Clauses in Business Contracts: Transparency' in A Burrows and E Peel (eds), *Contract Terms* (OUP, 2007).
Considers the test of 'reasonableness' under UCTA 1977 and ultimately concludes that it cannot easily be improved upon, given the difficulties of formulating a statutory test of 'unfair surprise'.

---

[122] [2009] UKSC 6, [2009] 3 WLR 1215.

[123] See eg the decisions of the Court of Justice of the European Union in Case C-415/11 *Aziz v Caixa d'Estalvis de Catalunya, Tarragona i Manresa*, 14 March 2013; Case C-26/13 *Kásler v OTP Jelzálogbank Zrt*, 30 April 2014; Case C-143/13 *Matei v SC Volksbank România SA*, 26 February 2015.

[124] See eg H-W Micklitz and N Reich, 'The Court and Sleeping Beauty: The Revival of the Unfair Contract Terms Directive (UCTD)' (2014) 51 CMLR 771.

Law Commission, *Unfair Terms in Consumer Contracts: A New Approach?* (Issues Paper, 2012) http://www.lawcom.gov.uk/wp-content/uploads/2015/06/unfair_terms_in_consumer_contracts_issues.pdf and Law Commission, *Unfair Terms in Consumer Contracts: Advice to the Department for Business, Innovation and Skills* (2013) http://www.lawcom.gov.uk/wp-content/uploads/2015/06/unfair_terms_in_consumer_contracts_advice_summary-web.pdf.

These Law Commission reports led to the Consumer Rights Act 2015, and explain the need for a more coherent approach to consumer protection, which includes departing from the approach found in the *Abbey National* case.

H-W Micklitz and N Reich, 'The Court and Sleeping Beauty: The Revival of the Unfair Contract Terms Directive (UCTD)' (2014) 51 CMLR 771.

Considers the jurisprudence of the Court of Justice of the European Union in interpreting the Unfair Contract Terms Directive and its utility in protecting consumers.

Question

Jemaine runs a business providing karaoke machines for office parties. Bret runs a company selling karaoke machines. Jemaine purchases from Bret two karaoke machines for £400 each, and tells Bret that he needs a new machine for a particularly lucrative agreement he has with a City firm of solicitors.

There is a notice in Bret's shop which states that liability for any loss caused by a faulty machine is limited to the contract price, and this is repeated on a sticker found on each machine.

Jemaine uses the first machine at an office party of the City firm of solicitors he mentioned to Bret. Unfortunately, the karaoke machine does not work properly, meaning that there is no music at the party. As a result, the solicitors refuse to pay Jemaine the contract price of £1,000 which they had agreed for the evening's entertainment. The solicitors also tell Jemaine that they will not hire him in the future (which they had intended to do).

Jemaine uses the second machine at his daughter's 10th birthday party. Again, the karaoke machine does not work properly, which prompts Jemaine to pay each of his daughter's 100 guests £5 as an apology for the lack of entertainment. When Jemaine tries to fix the karaoke machine at the end of the party, faulty wiring in the machine causes it to burst into flames, destroying the machine and causing damage to his home which costs £15,000 to repair.

Advise Jemaine.

16   Misrepresentation

Key Points

- A statement of fact or law which is false can be a misrepresentation if it induces a party to enter into the contract.
- A mispresentation may be made by words or by conduct.
- The time at which the truth of the statement is assessed is the time at which the contract was made.
- All misrepresentations entitle the misrepresentee to rescind the contract. This means that the whole transaction will be set aside and both parties restored to the position they were in before the contract was entered into.
- Rescission will be barred where it is impossible to put the parties back into their original position; or where the misrepresentee has affirmed the contract; or, perhaps, where a long period of time has elapsed; or where a third party who has acquired rights for value in good faith would be disadvantaged by rescission.
- Damages are available at common law for the tort of deceit or for negligent misrepresentation.
- Most claims for damages are now made under section 2(1) of the Misrepresentation Act 1967. The misrepresentor can only escape this provision if he is able to prove that he had reasonable grounds to believe and did believe up to the time the contract was made that the facts represented were true. This is a heavy burden to discharge. The remedy available under section 2(1) is the same as for fraud or deceit, although contributory negligence may be a defence.
- Under section 2(2) of the Misrepresentation Act 1967, the court has a discretion to award damages in lieu of an injunction.
- A consumer may be able to seek redress for unfair commercial practices under section 2(4) of the Misrepresentation Act 1967, which gives effect to the Consumer Protection from Unfair Trading Regulations 2008.
- Terms which restrict a liability or remedy in misrepresentation may not be enforced if they are unreasonable (or, if the victim of the misrepresentation is a consumer, unfair).

1 What is a misrepresentation?

A misrepresentation is a statement of fact or law which is false. It was previously thought that incorrect statements of law could not ground a claim in misrepresentation, but this is clearly no longer the case.[1] A typical case arises where *A* makes a statement to *B* before

---

[1] *Pankhania v Hackney London Borough Council* [2002] EWHC 2441 (Ch); *Brennan v Bolt Burdon* [2004] EWCA Civ 1017, [2005] QB 303 [10], [25].

they enter into a contract, which induces *B* to enter into that contract. For example, during negotiations for the sale of a house, *A* tells *B* that the drains are in good order. In due course, *B* signs a formal, written contract to buy the house for £250,000. The contract says nothing about the drains. In fact, the drains are in a bad state and *B* would not have entered into that contract had he known the truth. If *B* relied on the truth of *A*'s statement when he entered into the contract, *B* may have a remedy for misrepresentation.

Of course, *B* might also have a remedy for breach of contract: if *B* can prove that he made it clear that he was not going to sign the contract, or exchange the signed contracts, unless he had an assurance from *A* about the drains, and that assurance was then given, there is a collateral contract[2] which, once proved, is as good as if it were written down in the main contract. Such a collateral contract may be difficult to prove, however. A claim in misrepresentation may therefore be easier to establish, especially since it does not matter whether or not the representation became a term of the contract.

2 Establishing a misrepresentation

Although it is clear that a misrepresentation is a statement of fact or law which is false, it is not always easy to determine whether there has truly been a statement of fact or law, and some of the most troublesome areas must now be considered.

(a) Statements of opinion

The representation must be a statement of fact, not merely of opinion. This must be decided objectively: would a reasonable person have supposed that the **representor** was asserting a fact, or merely expressing an opinion? In *Bisset v Wilkinson*,[3] a seller of land in New Zealand said that the land, if properly worked, would carry 2,000 sheep. This proved to be wrong. Nevertheless, it was held that the seller had not made a misrepresentation and that **rescission** should not be granted. The buyer knew that the land had never been used for sheep farming, and that the seller's statement could not have been anything other than a matter of opinion. The seller had no special information or skills that would have reasonably led the buyer to believe that what the seller was saying was true. As a result, the buyer was not justified in treating it as a statement of fact.

In *Bissett v Wilkinson*, the Privy Council distinguished an earlier decision of the English Court of Appeal, *Smith v Land and House Property Corp.*[4] In that case, the vendors represented to the purchasers of a hotel that the current occupant was 'a most desirable **tenant**'. This was false: the tenant was overdue with his rent and on the verge of **bankruptcy**. The vendors argued that there had been no misrepresentation as they had only expressed an opinion. Bowen LJ rejected that argument since the vendors' statements were 'on a subject as to which **prima facie** the vendors know everything and the purchasers nothing'. The imbalance in knowledge between the parties meant that it was reasonable for the purchasers

---

[2] See Chapter 11, Section 3.
[3] [1927] AC 177, PC.
[4] (1884) 28 ChD 7, CA.

to think that the vendors knew whether or not the tenant was desirable. The vendors had therefore made a false representation about the desirability of the tenant.

Bissett v Wilkinson was different from *Smith v Land and House* because the purchaser of the land in *Bissett* could not reasonably have thought that the owner of land knew whether or not it could support 2,000 sheep, whereas in *Smith* the purchaser was entitled reasonably to think that the owners of the hotel knew whether or not the tenant was desirable, paid the rent on time, and so on. This explanation has since been supported by the Court of Appeal in *Esso Petroleum Co Ltd v Mardon*.[5] Mr Mardon was induced to take a **lease** of a petrol station owned by Esso by the latter's representation that the annual throughput of petrol was around 200,000 gallons. The true figure was less than half this. Lord Denning MR rejected the argument that Esso had merely expressed an opinion (like in *Bissett*) and held that Esso had made an actionable misrepresentation (like in *Smith*). Given Esso's expertise in the area, and the fact that it was in a much better position than Mr Mardon to make such a forecast, there was at the very least a representation that the figure was arrived at with reasonable care and skill. However, Esso had been thoroughly negligent in giving the inflated figure, and the claim in misrepresentation succeeded.

It is important to note that, in an insurance contract, a statement of belief does not import a representation that there are reasonable grounds for the belief. This is clearly shown by *Economides v Commercial Union*.[6] Mr Economides's statement that, 'to the best of his knowledge and belief', his parents' valuables were worth £4,000 was a gross underestimate, but it did not entitle the insurer to **repudiate** liability. Mr Economides had simply relied on his father's statement of the value. As a result, his representation was made in good faith and was true:[7] he *did* believe the valuables were worth only £4,000. In other circumstances, such as in *Esso v Mardon*, a statement of opinion might imply that the maker has reasonable grounds on which to base his opinion and that he has exercised reasonable care and skill in doing so—these are then implied statements of fact. An implied misstatement is just as effective as an express one, if it is relied on. But there was no misstatement on the facts of the *Economides* case.

(b) Representation by conduct

A representation may not only be made through words. Representations can be made by conduct as well. A good illustration of this is *Spice Girls Ltd v Aprilla World Service BV*.[8] The Spice Girls—through their company, Spice Girls Ltd—entered into a contract with Aprilla World Service (AWS) to sponsor the European leg of their Spice Girls World Tour. AWS organised a television commercial and advertising campaign featuring all five Spice Girls and Aprilla's scooters. One of the scooters advertised was orange, which was the colour associated with Geri Halliwell, otherwise known as Ginger Spice. By the time the contract was concluded, however, Geri Halliwell had told the other Spice Girls that she intended to leave the group. The Court of Appeal held that AWS's claim in misrepresentation should

---

[5] [1976] QB 801, CA.
[6] [1997] 3 All ER 636.
[7] Marine Insurance Act 1906, s 20(5).
[8] [2002] EWCA Civ 15, [2002] EMLR 27.

succeed. The Spice Girls had represented through their conduct in the negotiations, and through their participation in the photography for the advertising campaign, that they did not know that any member of the group intended to leave in the near future. This was a false representation—even though it was made through their conduct rather than orally—so the claim for damages succeeded.

(c) Half-truths

It is not enough to say something that is superficially true if there is also an underlying representation which is false. For instance, in *Dimmock v Hallett*,[9] the vendor of land said that two of the farms on the land were fully let. This was not false, but failed to disclose that both tenants had already given **notice to quit**. Since the vendor had stated that the tenants of some other farms had given notice to quit, the vendor had created the impression that the two farms had continuing tenants. This was false and therefore the purchasers were the victims of a misrepresentation.

A similar example is *Nottingham Patent Brick and Tile Co v Butler*.[10] The contract concerned the sale of land. The purchaser's solicitor asked the vendor's solicitor whether there were any restrictive **covenants** which would prevent the land from being used as a brickfield, and the vendor's solicitor replied that he was not aware of any restrictions. When challenged again by the purchaser, the vendor's solicitor repeated that he was not aware of any restrictive covenants. This was, taken literally, true. However, it was only true because the solicitor had not read the **title** deeds and had not checked whether or not there were any restrictive covenants. The solicitor had told a half-truth, and the purchaser could reasonably have expected the solicitor to be representing that he had taken reasonable care to check whether or not there were any restrictive covenants affecting the land. The purchaser therefore had a valid claim in misrepresentation.

(d) Silence

Mere silence, however, is generally not sufficient for misrepresentation. In *Smith v Hughes*,[11] it was held that 'the passive acquiescence of the seller in the self-deception of the buyer will not entitle the latter to avoid the contract'. That is a very strong case, because it is assumed that the seller knows that the buyer is making a mistake of fact about the seller's goods and does not tell the buyer of his mistake. A good example of the application of this principle is *Turner v Green*.[12] The claimant, having heard the result of a case which was crucial to his own prospects of success, negotiated a settlement with the defendant. The claimant knew that the defendant had not heard the result of that case and would not have entered into that settlement agreement if he had known of that result. It was held that, while this was not the sort of conduct to be expected of solicitors—Chitty J called it 'a shabby trick'—it did not invalidate the agreement.

---

[9] (1866–67) LR 2 Ch App 21.
[10] (1866) 16 QBD 778.
[11] (1871) LR 6 QB 597; see Chapter 2, Section 4.
[12] [1895] 2 Ch 205, ChD.

(i) Insurance contracts

There are certain classes of contract, which are said to require *uberrima fides*, which means 'the utmost good faith'. Such contracts impose a duty to disclose material facts. The most common and important of these has traditionally been the contract of insurance. The law used to demand that the consumer disclose every circumstance which he knew or was deemed to know and which a prudent insurer would consider to be material when fixing the insurance premium or determining whether the insurer would take on the risk.[13] This was applied strictly. Thus in *Pan Atlantic Insurance Co Ltd v Pine Top Insurance Co Ltd*,[14] the House of Lords held that a circumstance was material if a prudent insurer would consider it in deciding whether to accept the risk and, if so, on what terms. This was the case even though, after proper consideration, that circumstance would not affect the insurer's decision on either of these matters. This could lead to harsh decisions. For instance, in *Lambert v Co-operative Insurance Society Ltd*,[15] a woman, renewing an insurance policy covering her own and her husband's jewellery, did not disclose that the husband had recently been convicted of conspiracy to steal and theft and sentenced to 15 months' imprisonment. It was held that the insurance company was entitled to repudiate the policy on the ground that she had failed to disclose a material fact. Mrs Lambert may well not have realised that the conviction was a material fact, but that was irrelevant—a prudent insurer would have regarded it as material and there was evidence that the company would not in fact have renewed the insurance if they had known of it. Nor would it have mattered had Mrs Lambert believed that the full extent of her duty was to answer the specific questions asked of her: she had a positive duty to disclose any material fact. The reason for the rule was stated by Lord Mansfield in *Carter v Boehm*:[16]

> Insurance is a contract upon speculation. The special facts, upon which the contingent chance is to be computed, lie most commonly in the knowledge of the *insured* only: the under-writer trusts to his representation, and proceeds upon confidence that he does not keep back any circumstance in his knowledge, to mislead the under-writer into a belief that the circumstance does not exist ...

However, it has long been recognised that the law operated in a very harsh manner,[17] and has now been changed. The Law Commission's work[18] has led to two important pieces of legislation: the Consumer Insurance (Disclosure and Representations) Act 2012 and the Insurance Act 2015. Section 2 of the 2012 Act makes it clear that consumers do not have to volunteer material facts, but must take reasonable care[19] not to make a misrepresentation to the insurer. Section 4 of and Schedule 1 to the Act govern the remedies available for misrepresentation. If the misrepresentation was deliberate or reckless, the insurer may

---

[13] Marine Insurance Act 1906, s 18, repealed by Insurance Act 2015, s 21(2).

[14] [1994] 3 All ER 581, HL (Lords Templeman and Lloyd dissenting on this point).

[15] [1975] 2 Lloyd's Rep 485.

[16] (1766) 3 Burr 1905, 1909.

[17] See eg the recent comments of Leggatt J in *Involnert Management Inc v Aprilgrange Ltd* [2015] EWHC 2225 (Comm), [2015] 2 Lloyd's Rep 289 [186].

[18] See the papers and discussion at http://www.lawcom.gov.uk/project/insurance-contract-law/.

[19] See the Consumer Insurance (Disclosure and Representations) Act 2012, s 3.

avoid the contract and refuse all claims, and need not return the premiums already paid unless that would be unfair to the consumer. If the misrepresentation was simply careless, the insurer's remedies are based on what it would have done if the consumer had not acted carelessly. Thus, if the insurer would not have entered into the contract at all, the insurer can avoid the contract and return the premiums paid to the consumer. However, if the insurer would still have entered into the contract but on different terms, then the contract will be treated as if it had been concluded on those terms and the consumer may have to pay the insurer compensation. If the consumer's misrepresentation was honest and reasonable, then the insurer will not have any remedy against the insurer and must comply with the contract agreed.[20]

The Insurance Act 2015 principally affects the law concerning non-consumer insurance contracts. The duty of disclosure to which businesses were previously subject has been replaced by a duty to make a fair presentation of the risk to the insurer.[21] Effectively, businesses must disclose every material circumstance which they know or ought to know, or, failing that, give the insurer sufficient information to know that it needs to make further inquiries.[22] The remedies for breach are proportionate to the insured's breach.[23] If the breach was deliberate or reckless, the insurer may avoid the contract and refuse all claims, and need not return the premiums already paid. But if the breach was not deliberate or reckless, then the contract will be treated as being made on the terms which would have been agreed had there been no breach, and a proportionate amount of compensation may be payable.

As a result of the Consumer Insurance (Disclosure and Representations) Act 2012 and the Insurance Act 2015 it may well be that insurance contracts will no longer be considered to be contracts 'of the utmost good faith'. That is not to say that other relationships will not give rise to an obligation to disclose since they do require *uberrima fides*—such as between partners in a partnership[24] and where there is a **fiduciary** relationship[25]—but it is crucial to appreciate that the **common law** regarding insurance contracts has been significantly altered as a result of recent legislation.

(e) The statement must be true at the time the contract is made

The representor does come under a duty to speak out, even in contracts which do not require the utmost good faith, where he makes a statement which is true at the time it is made but, because of a change of circumstances, becomes untrue before the contract is entered into. The crucial moment is that at which the **representee** enters into the contract and, when that moment arrives, the representation is false. If the representor has not undeceived the representee, the representee may rescind for misrepresentation. If the representor knows that the statement has become false and that the representee is acting in reliance

---

[20] See ss 2(2) and 4.
[21] Insurance Act 2015, s 3.
[22] s 3(4).
[23] s 8 and Sch 1.
[24] *Conlon v Simms* [2008] 1 WLR 484 [127] (Jonathan Parker LJ).
[25] *Tate v Williamson* (1866) LR 2 Ch App 55.

on its truth, he may even be guilty of the tort of **deceit**. Damages may therefore be recoverable, since a misrepresentation has been made.[26]

In *With v O'Flanagan*,[27] a doctor represented to the claimant, a potential purchaser of his practice, that the practice was worth £2,000 a year. This was true in January 1934—the time at which the representation was made—but by the time the contract was entered into in May 1934, the statement had become untrue. The doctor's practice had diminished and was bringing in not more than £5 a week. The court held that the representation was to be treated as continuing until the contract was signed. The claimant had entered into the contract in reliance on the representation and was entitled to rescission. Presumably the converse therefore applies, and a statement which is false when made but true when the representee acts on it by entering into a contract is not an operative misrepresentation.

(f) Statements of intention

As Bowen LJ observed in *Edgington v Fitzmaurice*, 'the state of a man's mind is as much a fact as the state of his digestion'.[28] A false statement of a person's intention could therefore constitute a misrepresentation. It is instructive to consider *Wales v Wadham* in this regard,[29] where the court seems to have failed properly to apply the principle of *With v O'Flanagan*. In an agreement made in contemplation of divorce on the breakdown of their marriage, Wales agreed to pay his wife £13,000 out of his share of the proceeds of the sale of the matrimonial home if she would not make any further claim for maintenance. She had stated on several occasions that she would never remarry but, by the time the agreement was signed, she had decided to marry Wadham. She did not reveal her intention to Wales, because she did not wish Wadham to become involved in the divorce proceedings. Wales sought rescission of the agreement on the ground that he would never have entered into it had he known of his wife's intention to remarry: the agreement was intended to commute his liability for periodical payments after the divorce, and this was a liability which, under the circumstances, he would never have had since his wife remarried. Tudor Evans J distinguished *With v O'Flanagan* on the ground that there was no representation of fact in the present case:

> A statement of intention is not a representation of existing fact, unless the person making it does not honestly hold the intention he is expressing, in which case there is a misrepresentation of fact in relation to the state of that person's mind.

This is surely wrong.

A statement of intention is a representation of existing fact—the present state of that person's mind—whether the speaker holds the intention or not. If he does not hold it, the statement is a misrepresentation; if he does hold it, it is no less a representation, but it is

---

[26] This is therefore not simply an instance of non-disclosure, which (in the insurance context at least) leads only to rescission but not to damages: *Banque Keyser v Skandia* [1989] 3 WLR 25.

[27] [1936] Ch 575, CA.

[28] (1885) 29 ChD 459, 483, CA.

[29] [1977] 1 WLR 199.

then a true one. In *Wales v Wadham*, the statement, 'I will never remarry' truly represented the wife's state of mind—a fact—when it was made, but it became untrue before the husband signed the agreement in reliance on it. It is suggested that the case proceeded on a false premise and that, following *With v O'Flanagan*, the husband's action should have succeeded.

3 Reliance on the misrepresentation

The representee must have entered into the contract in reliance on the truth of the false statement. If he was unaware that it had been made, or he was aware of it but did not believe it to be true, or attached no importance to it whatsoever, his claim in misrepresentation will fail. If a company prospectus, with a view to enhancing the attractiveness of the company, falsely states that Mr X has agreed to be a director, then a person who buys **shares** without reading the prospectus, or who reads it and knows the statement is false, or who is wholly uninfluenced by it because he has no idea who Mr X is, may not rescind the contract. Although there was a misrepresentation, it was not an operative one.

The misrepresentation need only be *a* reason for the claimant's entering into the contract; it need not be the decisive reason or even the main reason. As Arden LJ put it in *Dadourian Group International Inc v Simms (Damages)*, 'the misrepresentation does not have to be the sole inducement for the representee to be able to rely on it: it is enough if the misrepresentation plays a real and substantial part, albeit not a decisive part, in inducing the representee to act'.[30] So, in *Edgington v Fitzmaurice*,[31] the claim for misrepresentation succeeded since the claimant relied upon the defendants' misrepresentation about what the money raised from the claimant would be used for. It did not matter that the claimant also relied upon his own mistaken beliefs about what he would receive under the terms of the contract. The misrepresentation had some influence upon the mind of the claimant, and the claim therefore succeeded.

If the misrepresentation would have influenced a reasonable person to enter into a contract, then the court will generally be prepared to infer that the misrepresentation did influence the mind of that particular representee and was therefore 'material'.[32] It is difficult, but not impossible, for the representor to persuade the court otherwise.[33] For example, in *Attwood v Small*,[34] the vendor made various misrepresentations about the property to be sold, but the claimants' claim in misrepresentation failed because it was found that the claimants relied upon the advice of their own agents and solicitors rather than what the vendor had told them. Similarly, in *JEB Fasteners v Marks Bloom & Co*,[35] the purchasers of a company sought to rescind a contract on the basis that there had been misrepresentations made in the accounts of the company. However, the claim failed: the purchasers honestly

---

[30] [2009] EWCA Civ 169, [2009] 1 Lloyd's Rep 601 [99].
[31] (1885) 29 ChD 459, CA.
[32] *Smith v Chadwick* (1884) 9 App Cas 187.
[33] *Dadourian Group International Inc v Simms* [2009] EWCA Civ 169 [99]–[101] (Arden LJ).
[34] (1838) 6 Cl & F 232.
[35] [1983] 1 All ER 583.

admitted that their real motivation was to acquire the directors of the company through the acquisition, regardless of the misrepresentation, and as a result the misrepresentation did not play a 'real and substantial' part in their decision to enter into the contract.

(a) Failure to check the truth of the representation

If the representee does enter into the contract in reliance on the misrepresentation, it is no answer to his claim to rescission that he would have known that it was false if he had taken reasonable care. In *Redgrave v Hurd*,[36] the defendant agreed to buy the claimant's house. This contract was associated with an agreement that the defendant would join the claimant's practice as a solicitor and as a partner. The claimant had represented that the practice was bringing in £300–£400 a year. He produced papers which, if carefully read, showed that the practice was practically worthless. However, the defendant did not read the papers and contracted to buy the house in reliance on the truth of the claimant's representation as to the value of the practice. On discovering the true state of affairs, he declined to complete and the claimant's action for **specific performance** failed. The defendant had in fact relied on the misrepresentation, and it was immaterial that a prudent buyer would have discovered the truth.[37]

4 Rescission of the contract

Any actionable misrepresentation, whether fraudulent, negligent, or innocent, makes the contract voidable, which means that the representee might seek the equitable remedy of rescission. If the representee does rescind the contract, this means that the whole transaction will be set aside and both parties restored to the position they were in before the contract was entered into. The equity of the matter is that a person should not be allowed to retain a benefit obtained by a statement which, it is now admitted or proved, was false. It is morally wrong of the representor to seek to retain that which he had obtained by a falsehood, even if it is an innocent one.

The Misrepresentation Act 1967 clarifies the law in two respects. First, even in circumstances where the misrepresentation is incorporated as a term in the concluded contract, the representee is still able to sue the defendant for misrepresentation (as well as for the breach of a term of the contract). Even if the term of the contract only has the status of a warranty, and the buyer cannot avoid the contract for breach of warranty,[38] he may nevertheless rescind the contract for misrepresentation. The second important clarification of the 1967 Act concerns situations where, after the misrepresentation has been made, the contract is concluded and completely **executed**. For example, the contract may be to grant a lease, and the lease might then be executed. There was some authority before the Act

---

[36] (1881) 20 ChD 1, CA.

[37] As to whether this failure to check would constitute contributory negligence and therefore a defence to a claim for damages, see Section 5(b)(i).

[38] See Chapter 24.

in favour of the view that the right to rescind was now lost,[39] but Lord Denning strongly resisted that conclusion.[40] As a result of the 1967 Act, it is now clear that the representee may rescind the executed contract.

These clarifications appear in section 1 of the 1967 Act:

1. Where a person has entered into a contract after a misrepresentation has been made to him, and—

   (a) the misrepresentation has become a term of the contract; or
   (b) the contract has been performed;

   or both, then, if otherwise he would be entitled to rescind the contract without alleging fraud, he shall be so entitled, subject to the provisions of this Act, notwithstanding the matters mentioned in paragraphs (a) and (b) of this section.

(a) Rescission and avoidance of contracts for breach

Rescission for misrepresentation and avoidance of a contract for breach of contract are different. When a contract is rescinded for misrepresentation, it is wiped out from the start. The parties must be put back into the position in which they were before the contract was made. If that cannot be done, the contract may not be rescinded. The same is not true for avoidance for breach. In the case of a contract which continues over a period of time, avoidance for breach terminates the contract only from the moment of avoidance. It is immaterial that the parties cannot be put back into the position in which they were before the contract was made, and rights and duties which accrued before the moment of avoidance remain good.[41] Where A has entered into a contract to employ B for five years and, after two years, B commits a fundamental breach of contract and A dismisses him, the contract for the final three years is avoided, but everything that was done during the first two years was validly done and stands unimpaired. The parties cannot be restored to the position in which they were before the contract was made—A cannot give back the services which B has rendered to him—but that is immaterial. It follows that B is entitled to retain the salary which he has received during those two years.

The two remedies were considered in *Leaf v International Galleries.*[42] The claimant bought a picture from the defendants who represented that it was by Constable. Five years later, the claimant discovered that it was not by Constable and claimed rescission of the contract in equity for misrepresentation. The Court of Appeal held that it was too late to rescind the contract,[43] not simply (as the county court judge held) because the contract had been executed, but because the claimant had accepted the picture in performance of the contract. This precluded rejection of the picture for breach of condition under section 11(1) (c) of the Sale of Goods Act 1893 (now the Sale of Goods Act 1979, s 11(4)) and, according to the Court of Appeal, it followed that he could not rescind for misrepresentation. Denning

[39] *Angel v Jay* [1911] 1 KB 666, DC.
[40] In eg *Leaf v International Galleries* [1950] 2 KB 86, CA.
[41] *Johnson v Agnew* [1980] AC 367, HL.
[42] [1950] 2 KB 86.
[43] See Section 5.

LJ was prepared to assume in the buyer's favour that the statement that the picture was by Constable was a condition. He said:

> Although rescission may in some cases be a proper remedy, it is to be remembered that an innocent misrepresentation is much less potent than a breach of condition; and a claim to rescission for innocent misrepresentation must at any rate be barred when a right to reject for breach of condition is barred. A condition is a term of the contract of a most material character, and if a claim to reject on that account is barred, it seems to me *a fortiori* that a claim to rescission on the ground of innocent misrepresentation is also barred.

This reasoning is controversial: rescission for misrepresentation and termination for breach of contract might legitimately be kept distinct.[44] This will be discussed further in Section 5 of this chapter.

(b) Indemnity

If a contract is rescinded, that means that the contract is wiped out from the start, so it is logically impossible also to recover damages for breach of contract (which assume that the contract was fully performed). However, a representee may be able to rescind a contract and be paid an indemnity to cover expenses which would necessarily have been incurred by the representor anyway. Otherwise, the representor would be unjustly enriched by the representee's expenditure.[45] This is illustrated by *Whittington v Seale-Hayne*.[46] The claimants were induced to take a lease of a farm used for breeding prize poultry by the defendant's misrepresentation that the premises were in a sanitary condition and a good state of repair. The claimants paid various rates and carried out repairs under the covenants in the lease before rescinding the agreement. Farwell J held that they were entitled to an indemnity for such expenses, since they would have had to be paid anyway by whoever had the farm at the time. However, the scope of the indemnity was limited to expenses incurred which benefited the defendant: the claimant received no indemnity for the loss of poultry, nor for lost profits.

(c) How does a party rescind a contract?

A person with a right to rescind a contract normally does so simply by informing the other party of his election to rescind the contract. The contract is then wiped out. There is often no need to go to court to rescind a contract, although it may be necessary to do so to compel a recalcitrant party to return what he has received under the contract. Rescission is generally a self-help remedy.[47]

---

[44] The confusing *obiter dicta* on this point from Lord Toulson in *Bunge SA v Nidera BV* [2015] UKSC 43, [2015] 3 All ER 1082 [76] should not be followed: the aim of damages is not to effect *restitutio in integrum* since damages are not backward-looking but are forward-looking.

[45] See Chapter 28, Section 4.

[46] (1900) 82 LT 49.

[47] For further critical discussion, see J O'Sullivan, 'Rescission as a Self-Help Remedy: A Critical Analysis' (2000) 59 CLJ 509.

Where a person does have the right to rescind, he must, normally, actually communicate his decision to do so to the other party. One exception appears to be where the contract is one to transfer property and he retakes possession. The contract, it seems, will be rescinded by that act, even before the other party knows of it. Another case where actual communication is not necessary is where the party at fault has deliberately put it out of the power of the other to communicate his decision to rescind the contract, knowing that the other will almost certainly want to do so. Here the contract may be rescinded by an overt act, clearly evincing an intention to rescind. In *Car and Universal Finance Co Ltd v Caldwell*,[48] the owner of a car sold his car to a rogue. The rogue convinced the owner to sell by making fraudulent misrepresentations. As soon as the owner realised that he had been deceived, he informed the police and the Automobile Association of the fraudulent transaction. The rogue, of course, was keeping well out of the way and had disappeared. It was held that the claimant could not have done more to make his position plain and that the contract was effectively rescinded before the car came into the hands of the **bona fide purchaser** who, accordingly, acquired no title.[49]

(d) **Bars to rescission**

(i) *Restitutio in integrum* **impossible**

Since rescission involves putting the parties back in the position in which they were before the contract was made—usually called *restitutio in integrum*—it follows that, if this is no longer possible, there can be no rescission. Thus, in *Clarke v Dickson*,[50] the claimant, who was induced to take shares in a partnership by a misrepresentation, sued unsuccessfully to get his money back after the partnership business had, with his assent, been registered as a company with limited liability. The nature of the thing he bought had changed and he could not return it. A partnership is very different from a company with limited liability. The court likened the case to that of a butcher who buys cattle and, after killing them, seeks to get his money back because of a misrepresentation by the seller. It would be similarly impossible to make restitution: returning a dead cow is very different from returning a cow which is alive.

It is important that the parties be put back into the position they were in before the contract was made 'in integrum', or 'in entirety'. However, in *Erlanger v New Sombrero Phosphate Co*,[51] Lord Blackburn held that 'the practice has always been for a Court of Equity to give this relief whenever, by the exercise of its powers, it can do what is practically just, though it cannot restore the parties precisely to the state they were in before the contract'.[52] In *Salt v Stratstone Specialist Ltd*,[53] the Court of Appeal recently emphasised the need for 'practical justice'. In that case, A purchased from B a car in September 2007. B told A that the car was 'brand new'. In fact, it was two years old and had had various

---

[48] [1965] 1 QB 525, CA.
[49] See Section 4(d)(iv).
[50] (1858) El Bl & Bl 148.
[51] (1878) 3 App Cas 1218.
[52] Ibid, 1279.
[53] [2015] EWCA Civ 745.

repairs after being involved in a collision. In 2009, *A* realised that he had been the victim of a misrepresentation, and sought to rescind the contract. The Court of Appeal held that *A* could rescind the contract, even though the car had depreciated in value and *A* had the benefit of the car for a period of time. Longmore LJ insisted that 'neither depreciation nor intermittent enjoyment should ... be regarded as reasons for saying restitution is impossible'.[54] After all, *A* never wanted a car which was not brand new, so should not be unduly disadvantaged by only discovering the misrepresentation after a period of time. However, if *B* had presented evidence about the depreciation of the car or the benefit received by *A*, then the court may have ordered an account to determine the terms on which restitution should be made.

Nevertheless, it is not possible to have 'partial rescission' of a contract which leaves some of the obligations under the contract in place. In *TSB Bank plc v Camfield*,[55] a wife agreed with a bank to guarantee the repayment of loans made to her husband's business venture. The husband had told his wife that their maximum liability under the guarantee was £15,000. This was a misrepresentation. Their liability was in fact unlimited. The Court of Appeal held that, as a result, the wife could rescind the contract with the bank.[56] The judges rejected the argument that the contract should be only partly rescinded, such that the bank could enforce the guarantee up to a value of £15,000. A misrepresentee can rescind the entire contract or not rescind the contract. It is not possible to pick and choose which bits of a contract to rescind, nor for the court to allow a misrepresentee to rescind only part of the contract.

However, where the parties are in a **fiduciary** relationship, this rule may be relaxed and rescission allowed even though it is impossible to put the parties back into precisely the same position as they were before. But the court must be satisfied that it can achieve what is practically just between the parties. A good example of this is the decision of *O'Sullivan v Management Agency*[57] (an instance not of misrepresentation but undue influence). In that case, it was impossible for the claimant to restore the benefit of the work done on his behalf by the defendant, but the court could achieve what was practically just by obliging the defendant to give up the profits and advantages he had obtained, while compensating him for the work he had done under the contract.

(ii) Affirmation

The representee loses his right to rescind if, knowing of the facts which give rise to that right, and also knowing that he has the right to rescind, the representee affirms the contract. It was decided in *Peyman v Lanjani*[58] that the representee will only lose the right to rescind if he knows not only the relevant facts, but also that he has a right to rescind. The claimant, who had entered into a contract to purchase the lease of a restaurant,

---

[54] Ibid, [22].
[55] [1995] 1 WLR 430, CA.
[56] For consideration of how the bank could have protected its position, see Chapter 18, Section 4.
[57] [1985] QB 428, CA.
[58] [1985] Ch 457, CA.

discovered that he had been induced to do so by misrepresentation. The solicitor who was acting for both parties urged him to continue with the contract, and he agreed to do so. A month later, on the advice of new solicitors, he rescinded the agreement and it was held that he was entitled to do so. He was an Iranian who spoke very little English, and when he agreed to continue with the contract he was not aware that he had a right to rescind the agreement. The supposed 'affirmation' was therefore ineffective and the contract was rescinded.

In *Payman v Lanjani*, the court distinguished an election to affirm from an **estoppel**. Where there is an operative election to affirm, it is effective as soon as it is made. Once it is communicated to the representor, the right to rescind is gone. It is not necessary to show that the representor acted on the affirmation. As in *Peyman v Lanjani* itself, the affirmation may be ineffective when made because the affirmer is not aware of his right to rescind. However, if it appears to the representor to be a good affirmation, since there is nothing to indicate to him that the affirmer is unaware of his right to rescind, and the representor acts to his detriment in reliance on that affirmation, the affirmer will be estopped from denying the validity of his affirmation.

Where a person has, and knows he has, the right to rescind, he must exercise it within a reasonable time. If he does not do so, he will be taken to have affirmed the contract.

(iii) Lapse of time

It has traditionally been thought that a right to rescind may be lost through the lapse of time.[59] This is because of the judgment of Lord Denning MR in *Leaf v International Galleries*,[60] considered in Section 4(a). In *Leaf*, it was considered 'unreasonable' to seek to rescind the contract five years after it was entered into. However, Lord Denning MR's reasoning that if the different remedies for breach of contract were barred due to lapse of time the remedy of rescission for misrepresentation should also be barred is controversial. After all, claims for breach of contract will be time-barred after six years have elapsed,[61] and only five years had elapsed in *Leaf*. On balance, this aspect of the decision in *Leaf* seems unsatisfactory. Equitable remedies might be barred by the equitable defence of laches, which requires the lapse of time, but laches was not made out in *Leaf* because, for laches, time only begins to run from the moment when the claimant knows (or ought reasonably to have known) of his right to rescind the contract. The claimant in *Leaf* acted promptly upon learning that the painting was not in fact by Constable.

In many situations, rescission will not be an available remedy after the lapse of a long period of time because it will be impossible to put the parties back into their original positions, but this was not an obstacle to rescission in *Leaf*. It is suggested that the Court of Appeal in *Leaf* were unduly influenced by the fact that rescission would have been hard on the defendant. In principle, it is suggested that rescission ought to have been possible.

---

[59] Unless the misrepresentation was fraudulent.
[60] [1950] 2 KB 86. See Section 4(a).
[61] Limitation Act 1980, s 5.

Indeed, in *Salt v Stratstone Specialist Ltd*,[62] the Court of Appeal doubted whether *Leaf* could still be good law. Longmore LJ said:[63]

> It must, moreover, be remembered that Leaf was decided well before the Misrepresentation Act was passed. It must be doubtful whether since the enactment of section 1 it is still good law that a representor should be in no worse position than if the representation had become a term of the contract, particularly if the representor takes no steps to prove that he was not negligent.
>
> In all the circumstances, it does not seem to me that lapse of time on its own can be a bar to rescission in this case.

It is to be hoped that the judgment in *Salt* will be followed. Of course, *Leaf* and *Salt* are distinguishable on their facts, and both are decisions of the Court of Appeal, neither having higher precedential value than the other. But the more recent decision considers *Leaf* carefully and concludes that there is no reason why lapse of time should, by itself, bar rescission. It is only if the lapse of time means that the parties cannot be put back into their original positions that rescission should be barred.

(iv) Third party rights

A bona fide purchaser for value without notice (*BFP*) is sometimes as known as 'Equity's Darling', since such a purchaser will take legal title to the goods bought free from any equitable claims. The importance of the *BFP* was examined in detail in Chapter 6.[64] A right to rescind is a mere equity, and it cannot be asserted against a *BFP*. The timing of events is therefore often important. Imagine that *A* sells a car to *B* as a result of *B*'s misrepresentation. The contract is voidable, which means that it is valid unless and until it is rescinded. This means that *B* does get good title to the car (prior to rescission) and, if he sells the car to *C* before *A* rescinds the *A*–*B* contract, then *C* will be a *BFP* and rescission will be barred. However, if *A* rescinds the *A*–*B* contract before *B* sells the car to *C*, then this means that *B* no longer has good title to the car, since title to the car is revested in *A*. As a result, *B* cannot give good title to the car to *C* because of the ***nemo dat*** principle.[65] *A* will therefore be able to sue *C* in the tort of **conversion**—this is a common law claim, not an equitable claim, and is not subject to the defence that *C* is a bona fide purchaser for value without notice. This explains why in *Car and Universal Finance Co Ltd v Caldwell* it was crucial to determine whether or not the owner had rescinded his contract with the rogue. If he had rescinded the contract before the rogue sold on the car, then that would mean that the rogue no longer had title to the car and the *nemo dat* principle would apply; as a result, the owner would be able to sue any third party purchaser in the tort of conversion. But if the owner had not succeeded in rescinding the contract, the owner would no longer have had legal title to the car and only a mere equity to rescind the contract, which could not be asserted against any BFP.

---

[62] [2015] EWCA Civ 745; see Section 4(d)(i).

[63] Ibid, [34]–[35]. See too at [42]–[50] (Roth J).

[64] Chapter 6, Section 2.

[65] See Chapter 6, Section 2.

5 Damages for misrepresentation

Whereas the equitable remedy of rescission is available for all types of misrepresentation, the remedy of damages varies depending upon what sort of misrepresentation is at issue. In essence, damages are available at common law if all the requirements for the tort of deceit or negligence are established. Damages are not available at common law for innocent misrepresentation, or in equity. However, the Misrepresentation Act 1967 has greatly expanded the range of situations where damages can be awarded. The existence of the 1967 Act means that the common law remedies are of much reduced importance.

(a) Common law

The common law distinguishes between fraudulent and innocent misrepresentations. A misrepresentation is fraudulent if the maker knows that it is false or he is reckless whether it is true or false.[66] He is reckless if he is aware that he does not know whether the statement is true or false, and yet he makes it anyway. So, if A asserts that the drains are in good order, but is actually thinking to himself, 'I really have no idea whether the drains are in good order or not', A will have made a fraudulent misrepresentation if the drains are not in fact in good order. If, on the other hand, A believes what he says to be true because he thinks the drains are in good order, he is making an innocent misrepresentation, even though he ought to have known that it was false. He is an honest man, even if, perhaps, a negligent one. In short, a misrepresentation is innocent if the representor believes it to be true, but fraudulent if he does not believe it to be true.

The significance of the distinction is that if a representee acted on a fraudulent misrepresentation (for instance, by entering into a contract with the representor) and thereby incurred a detriment, this amounts to a tort known as deceit. The representee could sue in tort for damages and, if he had entered into a contract with the representor, he could rescind it. But if the misrepresentation was innocent, no action in deceit would lie. Indeed, before 1963 the common law afforded the representee no remedy at all. But in *Hedley Byrne & Co v Heller & Partners*,[67] the House of Lords held that, in certain limited circumstances, an action would lie in tort for merely negligent misrepresentation. However, the duty of care on which such an action is founded is confined to cases where there is a 'special relationship' between the parties—normally 'a business or professional transaction whose nature makes clear the gravity of the inquiry and the importance and influence attached to the answer'.[68]

Details of the law relating to deceit and negligent misrepresentation are better covered in books on tort law. Nevertheless, it is important to note that a defendant who has committed the tort of deceit will be liable for all losses directly flowing from the fraudulent misrepresentation, regardless of whether or not such losses were reasonably foreseeable.[69] This is significant because, as will be seen, under section 2(1) of the Misrepresentation Act 1967

---

[66] *Derry v Peek* (1889) 14 App Cas 337.
[67] [1964] AC 465.
[68] Ibid, 539 (Lord Pearce).
[69] *Doyle v Olby* [1969] 2 QB 158.

damages are awarded on the same basis as the tort of deceit. Under the tort of negligence, by contrast, the defendant will only be liable to compensate for losses which were a reasonably foreseeable consequence of the misrepresentation.[70]

One leading case on the remedies available for deceit is *Smith New Court Ltd v Scrimgeour Vickers (Asset Management) Ltd*.[71] Smith New Court contracted to buy shares in a company, Ferranti, from Citibank. Prior to entering into the contract, Citibank represented to Smith New Court that there were also two other potential buyers who were bidding for shares. This was a fraudulent misrepresentation. As a result, Smith New Court bid approximately £23.2 million for the shares, which was accepted. But for the fraudulent misrepresentation, Smith New Court would have bid £22.02 million. Smith New Court therefore paid about £1 million more than it would have done had it not been the victim of deceit. However, after entering into the contract, a separate fraud was perpetrated on Ferranti, which meant that the value of the shares Smith New Court had purchased plummeted. Smith New Court eventually sold the shares for just under £12 million. The House of Lords held that Smith New Court was entitled to recover around £11 million—the difference between the price bought and sold—and was not restricted to £1 million—the difference between the price actually paid and the price that would have been paid had there been no fraudulent misrepresentation. Their Lordships emphasised that the victim of the tort of deceit can recover all losses directly flowing from the wrong. The date at which losses are assessed is not fixed at the date of the tort, but can be flexible in order to achieve full compensation for the claimant. On the facts of the case, Smith New Court's acquisition of the shares was taken as a 'market-making risk'; Smith New Court was therefore 'in a special sense locked into the shares having bought them for a purpose and a price which precluded them from sensibly disposing of them'.[72] Furthermore, it was not alleged or found that Smith New Court acted unreasonably in retaining the shares for such a period of time. As a result, Smith New Court was permitted to recover the losses suffered as a result of the significant drop in value of the Ferranti shares that had occurred subsequent to contract, even though it might be thought that the subsequent drop was not 'caused' by the original fraudulent misrepresentation, because Smith New Court was 'locked in' to the shares.[73]

Indeed, in an action for deceit a claimant may be able to recover for loss of profits where the deceit prevented the claimant from making profits from the same, or a similar, enterprise. *East v Maurer*[74] involved the sale of a hair salon from Mr Maurer to Mr East. Maurer also owned another salon in the area, called Canford Cliffs, but he told East that 'he had no intention of working at the Canford Cliffs salon unless, for example, a staff emergency arose due to illness or for some other reason' and that 'he intended to open a salon abroad'. These statements were false, but relied upon by East, who thought that the salon he purchased would not have much competition. However, Maurer continued to work at Canford Cliffs, and East's salon failed to make a profit. East then sued Maurer in deceit. He recovered

---

[70] *Overseas Tankship (UK) Ltd v Morts Dock & Engineering Co (The Wagon Mound)* [1961] AC 388.

[71] *Smith New Court Ltd v Scrimgeour Vickers (Asset Management) Ltd* [1997] AC 254, HL.

[72] Ibid, 268.

[73] See too *Parabola Investments Ltd v Browallia Cal Ltd (formerly Union Cal Ltd)* [2010] EWCA Civ 486, [2011] QB 477.

[74] *East v Maurer* [1991] 1 WLR 461.

damages for the losses he had suffered in purchasing the salon, attempting to run it as a business, and non-pecuniary losses for disappointment, and inconvenience. East also recovered damages for profits which he lost by not operating an alternative business. After all, if Maurer had not lied, East would not have entered the contract of sale, but would have purchased a different business, and operated that business to turn a profit. The loss of these profits was directly consequent on Maurer's wrong, and recoverable in deceit.[75]

It is unlikely that there will be much advantage in bringing a claim in the tort of negligence when a claimant can instead rely upon the Misrepresentation Act 1967, since under the Act there is no need to establish any 'special relationship' and the remedies available are also much more generous. However, it is conceivable that a claimant may still wish to sue in the tort of deceit, even though deceit is very difficult to prove. There are two main reasons for this. First, contributory negligence is no defence to the tort of deceit, whereas it is a defence under section 2(1) of the 1967 Act.[76] Secondly, liability for deceit cannot be excluded by a contractual term, whereas contract terms may be effective to exclude liability for negligent or innocent misrepresentations.[77] Nonetheless, in the vast majority of cases, claimants will be able to seek satisfactory monetary remedies by relying upon the 1967 Act.

(b) **Misrepresentation Act 1967**

At common law, apart from the *Hedley Byrne* principle, damages were not recoverable for a non-fraudulent misrepresentation. The Act creates two new rights to damages under section 2(1) and section 2(2).

(i) **Section 2(1)**

Section 2(1) provides:

> Where a person has entered into a contract after a misrepresentation has been made to him by another party thereto and as a result thereof he has suffered loss, then, if the person making the misrepresentation would be liable to damages in respect thereof had the misrepresentation been made fraudulently, that person shall be so liable notwithstanding that the misrepresentation was not made fraudulently, unless he proves that he had reasonable ground to believe and did believe up to the time the contract was made that the facts represented were true.

Suppose the defendant has said to a potential buyer of his house that the drains are in good order, honestly believing this to be true. However, it is false since the drains are in a very bad state of repair. If this misrepresentation causes the claimant to enter into the contract to buy the property and he suffers loss (because the property with bad drains is worth less or because he has to spend money having the drains repaired), the Act requires us to ask: 'Would the claimant have been entitled to damages if the defendant had known all along that the drains were not in good order?' This sends us to the law of the tort of deceit

---

[75] See too *Clef Aquitaine v Laporte Materials (Barrow) Ltd* [2001] QB 488.
[76] See Section 5(b)(i).
[77] See Section 7 below.

which is therefore incorporated by reference into the Act. The answer appears to be: Yes. The claimant is therefore prima facie entitled to his damages, even though the misrepresentation was not fraudulent.

Jurisdiction

However, the defendant might be able to escape the clutches of, and not have to pay damages under, section 2(1) if he can prove two things: (a) he had reasonable ground to believe and (b) he did believe, up to the time the contract was entered into, that the drains were in good order. Note that it is not enough that he had reasonable grounds to believe and did believe his representation to be true at the time he made it. As with the principle in *With v O'Flanagan*,[78] the crucial time is when the contract is entered into. For the purposes of section 2(1), it seems clear that 'misrepresentation' must mean such misrepresentation as would give rise to a right to rescind the contract in equity. The term 'misrepresentation' is not defined in the Act.

Where a person has entered into a contract after a misrepresentation has been made to him by another party and he has suffered loss, that person might, in some circumstances, be able to sue in tort.[79] However, it would seem that he would now, generally, be ill-advised to do so.[80] If he sues in deceit, he has the heavy burden of proving fraud. And if he sues in negligence, he has to satisfy the court that the defendant owed him a duty of care and was in breach of it. Under section 2(1), by contrast, he need only prove that there has been a misrepresentation, and then he is entitled to his damages unless the defendant can prove that he had reasonable grounds to believe and did believe the representation to be true.

The misrepresentation which grounds a remedy under section 2(1) is sometimes referred to as 'negligent' misrepresentation, but this is slightly misleading because it does not need to be proved that the misrepresentation was negligent. In *Howard Marine & Dredging Co Ltd v A Ogden & Sons (Excavations) Ltd*,[81] Bridge LJ said:

> . . . the liability of the representor does not depend on his being under a duty of care the extent of which may vary according to the circumstances in which the representation is made. In the course of negotiations leading to a contract the 1967 Act imposes an absolute obligation not to state facts which he cannot prove he had reasonable ground to believe.

In that case the owner of two barges told the hirer that their capacity was about 1,600 tonnes. This answer was based on the Lloyd's register 'deadweight' figure of 1,800 tonnes. Although the Lloyd's register was known as 'the Bible' in shipping circles, the figure it gave was wrong. The true capacity was only 1,195 tonnes. The misrepresentation induced, but was not incorporated in, the contract. The owner had in fact seen the correct figure in the shipping documents but had forgotten it. The Court of Appeal held, by a majority, that the owner had failed to prove that he had reasonable grounds for his belief in the truth of his representation and was liable under section 2(1). Lord Denning dissented, since he believed

---

[78] See Section 2(e).

[79] See Section 5(a).

[80] However, suing in deceit may be advantageous in order to circumvent any defence of contributory negligence (see Section 5(b)(i)) or if there is an exclusion clause (see Section 7).

[81] [1978] QB 574, CA.

that relying on the figures given by 'the Bible' of that industry did constitute reasonable grounds for the owner's representation. Nevertheless, the result in *Howard Marine* clearly shows that the burden placed on the representor to show that he had reasonable grounds to believe and did believe up to the time the contract was made that the facts represented were true is a heavy one that will not easily be discharged.

Quantum

It has now been conclusively held that the wording of section 2(1) means that the defendant will be liable as if the misrepresentation had been fraudulent, so the remedies under section 2(1) mirror those available for the tort of deceit.[82] This is very harsh on defendants and has been strongly criticised.[83] It means that an innocent defendant might be liable as if he had committed fraud, and therefore liable for even unforeseeable losses. This is particularly unfortunate given the onerous burden placed on a defendant to prove that he had reasonable grounds to believe and did believe up to the time the contract was made that the facts represented were true. So, in *Howard Marine*,[84] the defendant checked the industry's 'Bible' in good faith, yet under section 2(1) was liable as if he had committed fraud. This seems very unsatisfactory.

However, the remedies under section 2(1) do not appear to replicate precisely those available for the tort of deceit in one important respect. Contributory negligence[85] is not a defence to deceit,[86] but nevertheless seems to be a defence under section 2(1),[87] at least where the defendant owed a concurrent duty of care at common law.[88] If correct, this raises a subsequent question of what constitutes contributory negligence for the purposes of section 2(1). Most interestingly, would a failure to check the veracity of a representation constitute contributory negligence? *Redgrave v Hurd*[89] held that a failure to check did not mean that there was no actionable misrepresentation, nor that the remedy of rescission was unavailable, but the decision is silent on the issue of damages. This is entirely understandable: *Redgrave* was decided over 80 years before the Misrepresentation Act 1967 came into force. But if the facts of *Redgrave* were to arise today, it would be necessary for the courts to decide whether the claimant's damages should be reduced by his failure to take reasonable care to check the information provided. On one view, it might be thought that it would be inappropriate to allow a misrepresentor to reduce the amount of damages he has to pay by complaining of contributory negligence when the misrepresentor intended that his representation be relied upon.[90] However, where the claimant has himself failed to take

---

[82] *Royscot Trust Ltd v Rogerson* [1991] 2 QB 297. There is a potential difference as regards contributory negligence: see Section 5(b)(i).

[83] See eg R Hooley, 'Damages and the Misrepresentation Act 1967' (1991) 107 LQR 547; *Smith New Court Ltd v Scrimgeour Vickers (Asset Management) Ltd* [1997] AC 254, 283 (Lord Steyn), HL.

[84] See Section 5(b)(i).

[85] See Chapter 26, Section 2(d).

[86] *Standard Chartered Bank v Pakistan National Shipping Corp (No 2)* [2002] UKHL 43, [2003] 1 AC 959.

[87] *Gran Gelato Ltd v Richcliff (Group) Ltd* [1992] Ch 560.

[88] *Taberna Europe CDO II Plc v Selskabet (Formerly Roskilde Bank A/S) (In Bankruptcy)* [2015] EWHC 871 (Comm) [109] (Eder J).

[89] See Section 3(a).

[90] *Taberna Europe CDO II Plc v Selskabet (Formerly Roskilde Bank A/S) (In Bankruptcy)* [2015] EWHC 871 (Comm) [111] (Eder J).

reasonable care to look after his own interests, it is suggested that it would be sensible for his damages to be reduced, and this would lead to the conclusion that contributory negligence is no defence to rescission and only a defence to a claim for damages.

Representation by a third party

Taberna Europe CDO II Plc v Selskabet (formerly Roskilde Bank A/S) (In Bankruptcy)[91] raises the difficult issue of what should happen when the misrepresentation is made not by the other contracting party but by a third party. The facts of this case are very complicated, but essentially Roskilde, a Danish bank, issued loan notes. Deutsche Bank acquired some €27 million of notes. Taberna then purchased these notes for €26.5 million. Roskilde made various misrepresentations to Deutsche Bank. But Deutsche Bank had sold the notes and did not wish to sue Roskilde. However, Taberna did sue Roskilde for misrepresentation. Eder J held that this claim could succeed even though the contract which Taberna was really concerned with was between itself and Deutsche Bank, and Deutsche Bank did not make any misrepresentations. The judge held that Taberna's claim against Roskilde fell within section 2(1). With respect, this is somewhat surprising (and, at the time of writing, an appeal of this decision is pending). After all, that provision begins with the words: 'Where a person has entered into a contract after a misrepresentation has been made *to him by another party thereto*'.[92] Roskilde was not a party to that contract, so the claim should not have been held to fall within the scope of section 2(1).

In some situations, a misrepresentation made by a third party will clearly be relevant. For instance, a wife might agree to guarantee her husband's business debts as a result of the husband's misrepresentation. The contract of guarantee will be between the wife and the bank, and not the wife and the husband. The bank does not make any misrepresentation. Nevertheless, the wife may be able to rescind the contract if the bank has actual or constructive notice of the misrepresentation. This is because the bank is assumed to have taken conscious advantage of the husband's misrepresentation.[93] This is exactly the same analysis as applies in the context of undue influence, and is examined further in Chapter 18.[94] However, it is clearly distinguishable from the *Taberna* case. The third party's misrepresentation may still provide a basis for the rescission of the contract. But it should not allow the innocent party to claim damages under section 2(1).

(ii) Section 2(2)

Section 2(2) provides:

> Where a person has entered into a contract after a misrepresentation has been made to him otherwise than fraudulently, and he would be entitled, by reason of the misrepresentation, to rescind the contract, then, if it is claimed, in any proceedings arising out of the contract, that the contract ought to be or has been rescinded, the court or arbitrator may declare the contract subsisting and award damages in lieu of rescission, if of opinion that it would be equitable to do so, having regard to the nature of the misrepresentation and the loss that would

---

[91] [2015] EWHC 871 (Comm).
[92] Emphasis added.
[93] See eg *Royal Bank of Scotland plc v Etridge (No 2)* [2001] UKHL 44, [2002] 2 AC 773 [144] (Lord Scott).
[94] See Chapter 18, Section 4.

be caused by it if the contract were upheld, as well as to the loss that rescission would cause to the other party.

This subsection empowers the court to refuse rescission when it would otherwise be available, or to reconstitute a rescinded contract (which is a new concept) and to award damages in lieu. Suppose that an innocent misrepresentation that the drains are in good order has led to a contract for the sale of a house for £100,000. The purchaser either rescinds, or asks the court to rescind the contract. The cost of repairing the drains would be only £1,000. The court might well think it inequitable that the purchaser should be able to get out of the contract altogether when the sum involved is relatively trivial. In that case, it would declare the contract subsisting or refuse rescission, as the case may be, and award damages of, presumably, £1,000.

The leading discussion of this issue is to be found in *William Sindall plc v Cambridgeshire County Council*.[95] The claimants agreed to purchase land for development from the defendants for around £5 million. The claimants argued that the defendants made a misrepresentation in saying that there were no **easements** over the land, when in fact there was a private sewer under the site. The Court of Appeal held that there was in fact no misrepresentation, so the discussion of section 2(2) is therefore strictly *obiter*, but given that the issue was fully argued and the judgments deal with the point in some detail it remains a useful authority. The Court of Appeal would have refused to allow the contract to be rescinded and exercised its discretion to grant damages in lieu. The misrepresentation would only have cost £18,000 to put right. The claimants were essentially trying to escape a bad bargain which they had made, and the court would not allow them to do that when the cost of making good the misrepresentation was relatively trivial in the context of the contract as a whole. The court suggested that before exercising its discretion the court must consider:

(a) the importance of the representation in relation to the subject matter of the contract;

(b) the loss which would be caused to the misrepresentee by the misrepresentation if rescission were refused; and

(c) the loss which would be caused to the representor by rescission.

If damages are awarded, they should not exceed that which would have been awarded if the representation had been a warranty.[96]

Damages where the right to rescind has been lost

In *Witter (Thomas) Ltd v TBP Industries Ltd*,[97] Jacob J held that damages may be awarded under section 2(2) even though the right to rescind has been lost because it has become impossible to restore the parties to the position they were in before the contract was made. However, subsequent decisions have rejected this view. In *Government of Zanzibar v British Aerospace (Lancaster House) Ltd*,[98] Judge Jack QC decided that, where the contract could

[95] [1994] 3 All ER 932.
[96] See Chapter 24.
[97] [1996] 2 All ER 573, 590.
[98] [2000] 1 WLR 2333.

not be rescinded, section 2(2) damages were unavailable. Jacob J relied upon the view of the Solicitor-General at the time of the passing of the Act, whereas Judge Jack QC thought greater weight should be placed upon what was said by the Lord Chancellor.

In any event, the debate on this point now seems to have been resolved by the decision of the Court of Appeal in *Salt v Stratstone Specialist Ltd*,[99] in which Longmore LJ said:

> the words 'in lieu of rescission' must, in my view, carry with them the implication that rescission is available (or was available at the time the contract was rescinded). If it is not (or was not available in law) because e.g. the contract has been affirmed, third party rights have intervened, an excessive time has elapsed or restitution has become impossible, rescission is not available and damages cannot be said to be awarded 'in lieu of rescission'.

Such clear guidance is welcome. It highlights that there is no need to examine how government lawyers understood the Act in 1967. The wording of section 2(2) seems clear: damages may be awarded as an alternative to rescission. But this depends upon there being a right to rescind; if this has been lost, then it is not possible to award an alternative in its place. Section 2(2) was not designed to give claimants an extra remedy for damages, but rather to give courts the discretion to restrict instances of rescission by giving the courts the ability to award damages instead of rescission.

6 Consumer Protection from Unfair Trading Regulations 2008

The Consumer Protection from Unfair Trading Regulations 2008, as amended by the Consumer Protection (Amendment) Regulations 2014, has led to section 2(4) being inserted into the 1967 Act. This provides that section 2 'does not entitle a person to be paid damages in respect of a misrepresentation if the person has a right to redress under Part 4A of the Consumer Protection from Unfair Trading Regulations 2008 in respect of the conduct constituting the misrepresentation'. Regulation 5 of those 2008 Regulations covers what might generally be considered to be misrepresentations. The representation must be a 'commercial practice',[100] and regulation 5(2)(a) provides that a commercial practice will be misleading if:

(a) if it contains false information and is therefore untruthful in relation to any of the matters in paragraph (4) or if it or its overall presentation in any way deceives or is likely to deceive the average consumer in relation to any of the matters in that paragraph, even if the information is factually correct; and

(b) it causes or is likely to cause the average consumer to take a transactional decision he would not have taken otherwise.

---

[99] [2015] EWCA Civ 745 [17].

[100] This is defined in reg 2(1) as follows:

'commercial practice' means any act, omission, course of conduct, representation or commercial communication (including advertising and marketing) by a trader, which is directly connected with the promotion, sale or supply of a product to or from consumers, whether occurring before, during or after a commercial transaction (if any) in relation to a product.

Paragraph (4) refers to matters such as the existence and main characteristics of the product. If there has been a 'misleading action', then the consumer is entitled to unwind the transaction within a limited period of time,[101] or perhaps to a discount,[102] and also to claim damages not only for his financial loss, but also for any alarm, distress, or physical inconvenience suffered.[103] This may be broader in scope than the damages available under the 1967 Act. However, recoverable losses are expressly limited to those which were reasonably foreseeable at the time of the prohibited practice.[104] This is more limited than section 2(1) of the 1967 Act. Moreover, the consumer will not recover damages if the trader can prove that he 'took all reasonable precautions and exercised all due diligence to avoid the occurrence of the prohibited practice', or if the trader proves that the prohibited practice was due to a mistake, an accident, information supplied to the trader by a third party, or another cause beyond the trader's control.[105]

These Regulations offer a further form of protection from fraudulent practices for consumers. They operate alongside the common law. However, where the Regulations offer a means of redress, section 2 of the 1967 Act is disapplied, which means that the consumer cannot choose to rely upon section 2(1) even if that were to be the more advantageous remedy. The consumer might prefer a remedy under section 2(1) due to the favourable remoteness rules which result from the 'fiction of fraud', but will be unable to do so. Indeed, the consumer might wish to invoke section 2(1) of the 1967 Act in order to recover damages when compensation is not available under the 2008 Regulations, yet will be unable to do so. This seems odd: the purpose of the Regulations was clearly not to reduce consumer protection, yet a business claimant may recover more under section 2(1) than a consumer who is prevented from exploiting section 2(1). Perhaps, given the problems with section 2(1) generally,[106] it is no bad thing to limit its operation, but the law is now in a somewhat unsatisfactory state. In any event, there can clearly be no double recovery under both the Regulations and the common law.[107]

7 Excluding liability for misrepresentation

Section 3 of the Misrepresentation Act provides:

> **Avoidance of provision excluding liability for misrepresentation.**
> If a contract contains a term which would exclude or restrict—
>
> (a) any liability to which a party to a contract may be subject by reason of any misrepresentation made by him before the contract was made; or
> (b) any remedy available to another party to the contract by reason of such a misrepresentation,

---

[101] Regs 27E–27H.
[102] Reg 27I.
[103] Reg 27J.
[104] Reg 27J(4).
[105] Reg 27J(5)(b).
[106] See Section 5(b)(i).
[107] Reg 27L.

> that term shall be of no effect except in so far as it satisfies the requirement of reasonableness as stated in section 11(1) of the Unfair Contract Terms Act 1977; and it is for those claiming that the term satisfies that requirement to show that it does.

It is important to note that this provision only applies to non-fraudulent misrepresentations; it is a rule of the common law that a person cannot exclude liability for his own fraud.[108] Where the representation is not fraudulent, it is nevertheless sensible to restrict the ability of parties to sidestep the law of misrepresentation through unfair terms, which section 3 seeks to achieve.

Care needs to be taken when examining any particular clause and deciding whether or not it falls within the scope of section 3. An entire agreement clause which states that the only terms of the agreement are to be found in the written contract would not fall within the ambit of the provision. This is because such a clause prevents a party from asserting collateral contract terms, but does not restrict any claim in misrepresentation. A good recent example of such a clause was found in *AXA Sun Life Services v Campbell Martin*.[109] A contractual clause stated:

> This Agreement and the Schedules and documents referred to herein constitute the entire agreement and understanding between you and us in relation to the subject matter thereof. Without prejudice to any variation as provided in clause 1.1, this Agreement shall supersede any prior promises, agreements, representations, undertakings or implications whether made orally or in writing between you and us relating to the subject matter of this Agreement but this will not affect any obligations in any such prior agreement which are expressed to continue after termination.

Rix LJ was clear that section 3 does not apply to such clauses, since the clause only defined the contractual obligations, and there was no language to suggest that the parties were agreed that no representations had been made or relied upon.

On the other hand, a clause which seeks to deny that any representations have been made, or deny that any liability should result from a misrepresentation, clearly would fall within section 3. Thus in *Cremdean Properties Ltd v Nash*,[110] section 3 did catch a clause that stated that 'any error, omission or misdescription shall not annul the sale or be grounds on which compensation may be claimed and neither do they constitute any part of an offer of a contract'. Similarly, it is suggested that a clause which asserts that neither party has relied upon any representation should also fall within section 3, since reliance is a necessary element of a claim in misrepresentation. In substance, the clause will exclude or restrict liability in misrepresentation and so the courts should err towards finding that such clauses do fall within the scope of section 3, which means that they would therefore be subjected to a test of reasonableness.[111]

---

[108] See eg *HIH Casualty and General Insurance Ltd v Chase Manhattan Bank* [2003] UKHL 6, [2003] 1 All ER (Comm) 349.

[109] [2011] EWCA Civ 133, [2011] 2 Lloyd's Rep 1.

[110] [1977] 1 EGLR 58, CA.

[111] *JP Morgan v Springwell* [2010] EWCA Civ 1221, [2010] 2 CLC 705 [179]–[182] (Aikens LJ).

Admittedly, this analysis has sometimes been doubted. For example, in *Watford Electronics Ltd v Sanderson CFL Ltd*,[112] Chadwick LJ thought that a non-reliance clause fell outside the ambit of section 3. A similar clause was at issue in *Peekay Intermark Ltd v Australia and New Zealand Banking Group Ltd*.[113] Peekay entered into a contract with ANZ Bank under which Peekay invested in complex financial products. ANZ Bank had told Peekay that Peekay would be granted a proprietary interest in certain bonds. This was false. The Court of Appeal actually held that Peekay had not relied upon this term, so the claim in misrepresentation necessarily failed. Nevertheless, Moore-Bick LJ went on to suggest that there may be a 'contractual estoppel': the parties who signed such a clause should be 'estopped' from denying its effect.

This idea of 'contractual estoppel' is very controversial. It has received some support,[114] although it has since also been made clear that a clause in an agreement seeking to deny that a representation has occurred prior to contract must state so very clearly before a claim of 'contractual estoppel' will succeed.[115] Nevertheless, it is suggested that 'contractual estoppel' is a strange species of estoppel which should really be discarded. It is little more than an enhanced version of the rule in *L'Estrange v Graucob* that a person is bound by a clause that he signs.[116] 'Contractual estoppel' does not require a representation, or reliance, or unconscionability, despite these being the usual requirements of estoppel. It would be preferable to allow section 3 to apply and afford the protection against unreasonable terms that is envisaged by the 1967 Act. After all, as Christopher Clarke J pointed out in *Raiffeisen Zentralbank Österreich AG v Royal Bank of Scotland Plc*: 'to tell the man in the street that the car you are selling him is perfect and then agree that the basis of your contract is that no representations have been made or relied on, may be nothing more than an attempt retrospectively to alter the character and effect of what has gone before, and in substance an attempt to exclude or restrict liability'.[117]

In *Lloyd v Browning*,[118] the Court of Appeal recently held that the following clause did fall within the scope of section 3 of the 1967 Act:

> The buyer hereby admits that he has inspected the property and he enters into this contract solely as a result of such inspection and upon the basis of the terms of this contract, and that in making this contract no statement made by the seller or his agent has induced him to enter except written statements, if any, made by the seller's conveyancers in replies to enquiries raised by the buyer's conveyancers or in correspondence between the parties' conveyancers.

This outcome is sensible and should be supported. In substance, this clause restricts the remedy in misrepresentation as it purports to 'knock out' the element of reliance which is essential for a claim in misrepresentation. It is quite appropriate to subject such terms to

---

[112] [2001] EWCA Civ 317, [2001] 1 All ER (Comm) 696.

[113] *Peekay Intermark Ltd v Australia and New Zealand Banking Group Ltd* [2006] EWCA Civ 386, [2006] 2 Lloyd's Rep 511 [56]–[57] (Moore-Bick LJ).

[114] See eg *JP Morgan v Springwell* [2010] EWCA Civ 1221, [2010] 2 CLC 705 [165]–[177] (Aikens LJ).

[115] *AXA Sun Life Services v Campbell Martin* [2011] EWCA Civ 133, [2012] Bus LR 203.

[116] See Chapter 11, Section 2(a).

[117] [2010] EWHC 1392 (Comm), [2011] 1 Lloyd's Rep 123 [315].

[118] [2013] EWCA Civ 1637 [2014] 1 P&CR 11.

an assessment of reasonableness under section 3 of the 1967 Act. After all, if a clause is reasonable it will be upheld and given its full effect. The requirement of reasonableness under the Unfair Contract Terms Act 1977 is considered in Chapter 15.[119] However, it should be noted here that if the contract is between two commercial parties of equal bargaining power then it is very likely that the clause will be held to be reasonable. After all, it is readily understandable why commercial parties should seek to avoid the uncertainty of litigation based on allegations as to the content of oral discussions at pre-contractual meetings; such parties are generally in a position to protect themselves and consider the risks involved in signing such clauses (weighed against the price of the transaction).

It is also important to note that section 3 of the 1967 Act no longer applies to consumer contracts as a result of the Consumer Rights Act 2015.[120] Instead, such a clause in a consumer context would be subject to a test of fairness, examined in Chapter 15.[121]

Further Reading

P Atiyah and G Treitel, 'Misrepresentation Act 1967' (1967) 30 MLR 369.
A detailed consideration of the 1967 Act, in particular section 2. (The discussion of section 3 does not take into account the changes effected by UCTA 1977.)

I Brown and A Chandler, 'Deceit, Damages and the Misrepresentation Act 1967, s 2(1)' [1992] LMCLQ 40.
Critical of the 'fiction of fraud' measure of damages under section 2(1), arguing that the 'normal' tortious measure of damages should be awarded.

J Cartwright, 'Excluding Liability for Misrepresentation' in A Burrows and E Peel (eds), *Contract Terms* (OUP, 2007).
Considers the scope of section 3 of the 1967 Act, and concludes that whilst 'entire agreement' clauses are outside the ambit of the provision, the same is not true of non-reliance clauses.

Question

Oxfield Town FC is looking to relocate in order to increase the size and capacity of its football stadium. Oxfield Town FC enters into negotiations with Easybuck Ltd, which owns a large plot of land. Easybuck Ltd currently runs a not very successful casino on the site. Oxfield Town FC tells Easybuck Ltd that the site is particularly attractive since Oxfield Town FC want to incorporate a casino into the stadium plans, and the site must already have a licence to be used for the purposes of gambling.

During the course of negotiations, Oxfield Town FC asks Easybuck Ltd whether there are any rights of way over the land. Easybuck Ltd checks with its solicitor, Martha, and on the basis of her advice tells Oxfield Town FC that there are no such rights.

Oxfield Town FC and Easybuck Ltd later sign a formal contract for the sale of the land for £2 million. One of the terms of the contract provides that:

---

[119] Chapter 15, Section 2(d).
[120] Misrepresentation Act 1967, s 3(2); see too Consumer Rights Act 2015, s 75 and Sch 4, para 1.
[121] Consumer Rights Act 2015, s 62; see Chapter 15, Section 4.

'This contract constitutes the entire agreement of the parties, and supersedes all prior agreements and negotiations. The basis of the parties' agreement can be found exclusively in this contract.'

Some months later, Oxfield Town FC realises that there are in fact footpaths which run across the land, and that various neighbours do have rights of way over the land. This makes redevelopment impossible. At the same time, Oxfield Town FC finds out that just before the contract was signed, Easybuck Ltd received a letter from the council to inform it that gambling was not permitted on the land.

The land would only have been valued at £1.2 million at the time of contracting, if the rights of way over it had been known. But since the contract was entered into, the property market has crashed, and the land is now only worth £750,000.

Advise Oxfield Town FC.

17   Duress

🔒 Key Points

- Where *B* exerts illegitimate pressure upon *A* to enter into a contract, leaving *A* with no reasonable practical alternative but to enter into that contract, then a claim in duress is likely to succeed.

- Duress is not a tort, and *A* cannot recover damages for duress itself. However, duress does render a contract voidable.

- The two principal forms of illegitimate pressure concern threats of physical harm (physical act duress) and threats to *A*'s economic interests (economic act duress).

- Particularly in the context of economic duress, it is important that the threats caused *A* to enter into the agreement, and that *A* had no reasonable alternative but to succumb to the threat.

- As a general rule, any threatened breach of contract can constitute illegitimate pressure. In some instances, even a threat to carry out a lawful act may ground a claim in duress.

Duress will be made out where *B* exerts illegitimate pressure upon *A* to enter into a contract, leaving *A* with no reasonable practical alternative but to enter into that contract. Duress is founded upon a threat made by *B* to *A*, but there is no tort of duress. However, duress will render a contract voidable. There are two principal forms of duress that must be considered in this chapter.[1] The first is physical act duress, where *A*'s physical integrity is threatened. The second is economic duress, where *A*'s economic interests are threatened. The first is of very long standing, whereas the second has only been recognised relatively recently.

1 Physical act duress

It is not surprising that *A* is not bound by a contract with *B* if he entered into it only because *B* was holding a gun to his head and threatening to blow his brains out if he did not. What is surprising is that it is always said that duress does not make the contract

---

[1] There is also a type of duress known as 'duress to goods', where the threat is to damage *A*'s goods: see eg *Occidental Worldwide Investment Corp v Skibs A/S Avanti (The Siboen and The Sibotre)* [1976] 1 Lloyd's Rep 293; *Dimskal Shipping Co SA v International Transport Workers' Federation (The Evia Luck) (No 2)* [1992] 2 AC 152. This is far more straightforward than 'economic duress': the same issues arise, but are more readily resolved. For that reason the focus here is on physical act duress and economic duress.

void but merely voidable. The logical consequence would seem to be that, if it is a contract for the sale of *A*'s car and *B* leaves *A* beaten up while he finds a **bona fide purchaser** (*BFP*) to whom he sells the car, the *BFP* would get a good **title**, since *A* has done nothing to **rescind** the contract. Yet it seems nonsensical to require *A* to notify *B* that he does not wish to be bound by the contract in circumstances such as these. After all, *B* surely knows that *A* does not wish to be bound right from the start—otherwise, why produce the gun? In those circumstances, perhaps all that is meant is that although *A* is not bound by the contract, *B* would be bound if *A* decided he wished to hold him to it. In other words, *A* should have the option of holding *B* to the contract. Obviously, if *B* tries to escape the contract it should not be a good defence for him to say, 'But *A* only agreed to the contract because I threatened to shoot him.' In any event, the fact that *B* cannot be heard to say that the contract is void does not mean that it should not be regarded as void for all other purposes. To take the facts of *Cundy v Lindsay*,[2] even Blenkarn would surely have been liable on the contract to buy the linen if Lindsay had chosen to sue him for it, yet the contract was certainly a nullity otherwise.

Contracts at gunpoint may sound fanciful but this is what happened in the Australian case of *Barton v Armstrong*.[3] Even more remarkably, the Australian courts and a minority in the Privy Council held that the contract was binding as Barton had not entered into the contract because he was coerced by the threat of being shot, but rather for reasons of commercial necessity. However, all the judges agreed on the point of principle: just as a misrepresentation does not make a contract voidable if it has no effect on the mind of the **representee**, so too a threat which does not affect the judgement of the person threatened does not vitiate the contract. The onus is squarely placed on the threatener to prove that his threats made no contribution to the decision of the other to enter into the contract. This is a difficult burden to discharge. If the threat was one reason among others for entering into the contract, the person threatened is entitled to relief, even though it may be that he would have entered into the contract in the absence of any threat. The threat therefore has to be a reason, although not necessarily a 'but for' reason, why the person being threatened entered into the contract. In *Barton v Armstrong*, the majority of the Privy Council held that, on the facts, Armstrong had not satisfied the onus which lay on him to prove that the threat did not influence Barton, whereas the minority thought there was no justification for interfering with the finding of fact by the courts below.

Some of the older cases talk of *A*'s will being 'overborne' by the threat of *B*, and this language lingers on even in some recent cases. But it is clearly not right to say that *A* is not exercising any form of choice when entering into the contract. In fact, the opposite is true: *A* sensibly chooses to sell his car to *B*, rather than have his brains blown out. *A* is exercising a choice, or his will, when entering into the contract. The point is that he has been coerced into doing so by the illegitimate pressure exerted upon him by *B*. It is therefore more satisfactory to say that there has been 'coercion' of *A*'s will by *B*, and this explains why the contract should be voidable: *A* has not been able to give his *free* consent to the contract.

---

[2] See Chapter 6, Section 3.
[3] [1976] AC 104.

2 Economic duress

Duress is not limited in the law of contract to physical threats of this kind. The most significant other category of duress is 'economic duress'. This also makes a contract voidable. A threat to break a contract may ground economic duress.[4] In *North Ocean Shipping Co v Hyundai Construction Co*,[5] shipbuilders demanded an additional 10 per cent on the contract price of a ship they were building for the claimants. There was no justification for this demand. The claimants reluctantly gave in to the demand because a delay in delivery of the tanker might have had very serious consequences for them. Mocatta J, with some hesitation, found that there was consideration for the promise to pay the additional 10 per cent because in return the builders had complied with the claimants' request to increase by 10 per cent the letter of credit which they had opened to provide **security** for repayment of instalments in the event of their default in the performance of the contract. But he held that the builders' threat to break their contract unless they were paid the additional money constituted economic duress which rendered the contract voidable. However, since the owners had waited for eight months after delivery of the tanker before making any claim, the judge held that they must be taken to have affirmed the contract and therefore lost their right to rescind.[6] In the *North Ocean* case, the builders were not merely taking advantage of a strong bargaining position but were threatening to commit a legal wrong—to break their contract—unless their demand was met.

Economic duress was the principal ***ratio decidendi*** in *Atlas Express Ltd v Kafco*.[7] Kafco (*K*), a small company, secured and was ready to fulfil a large contract to supply goods to Woolworths, a prominent national chain of high-street shops. *K* made a contract with Atlas (*A*), a national road carrier, to distribute the goods to Woolworths' shops at an agreed price per carton. Because *A* had underestimated the size of the cartons, the price they had quoted and which had been agreed was uneconomically low. After the first delivery, *A* realised this. *A* then sent an empty vehicle to *K*'s premises. The driver carried a document amending the contract so as to provide better terms for *A*. The driver's instructions were to take the vehicle away unloaded unless the amended agreement was signed. It was essential to *K*'s commercial survival that it should meet delivery dates for Woolworths. If *K* had not done so, Woolworths would have cancelled the contract and sued for loss of profit. This would have been catastrophic for *K*, given the value of its contract with Woolworths. *K* therefore signed the amendment.

Tucker J held that *K* was not bound by the amendment to the agreement. He gave two reasons for his decision. First, *K*'s signature was procured by economic duress, which meant that *K* could rescind the agreement. Secondly, there was no consideration to support the amendment, since *A* was already obliged to deliver *K*'s goods at the originally agreed rate. It is useful to remember that the decision in *Atlas Express Ltd v Kafco* was reached before the decision of the Court of Appeal in *Williams v Roffey Bros*.[8] Yet the facts of the two

---

[4] *Occidental Worldwide Investment Corp v Skibs A/S Avanti (The Siboen and The Sibotre)* [1976] 1 Lloyd's Rep 293.

[5] [1979] QB 705.

[6] See Chapter 16, Section 4(d)(ii).

[7] [1989] QB 833, QBD.

[8] See Chapter 7, Section 1(e)(iii).

cases may be thought to be similar. In both cases, the party who had made a bad bargain was seeking better terms. It was an enormous benefit to *K* to have *A* carry out their contract rather than break it, so it is hard to see that there is any difference regarding consideration. If there was a 'practical benefit' which constituted consideration in *Williams v Roffey Bros*, then there was surely a similar 'practical benefit' in *Atlas v Kafco*.

However, that does not mean that the *Atlas* case would be decided any differently today on the issue of economic duress. *Atlas* and *Williams v Roffey Bros* are distinguishable on this point. *K* (the little company) was in a hopeless bargaining position, whereas the bargaining position of Roffey (the larger concern) was by no means so desperate (although it was difficult). Moreover, *A* gave an ultimatum to *K*, whereas Williams negotiated an agreement with Roffey and, so far as appears from the report of the case, made no threats. This point is crucial: without any threat, there cannot be any duress. Admittedly, one difficulty with the *Williams v Roffey Bros* decision is that there may well have been an implied threat made by Williams. By working slowly such that it was obvious to Roffey that the work would not be completed on time without more money and resources, it is possible that in some circumstances the court could find that an implied threat was made by Williams that the work would not be finished on time without more money. It will clearly be difficult to determine whether an implied threat has been made; on the facts of *Williams v Roffey Bros*, the Court of Appeal was satisfied that no such threat was made and that duress was therefore not established.

3 Reasonable practical alternative

The limits of economic duress are uncertain. It is said that there must be some factor 'which could in law be regarded as a coercion of his will so as to vitiate consent';[9] but such propositions are of very limited assistance. In the *North Ocean* case the owners did consent, albeit reluctantly; and they knew exactly what they were consenting to. In such circumstances—and they will be the usual circumstances—a phrase like 'vitiate consent' does not tells us very much. The key point is that the person threatened could not reasonably do otherwise than succumb to the threat. If there was a reasonable practical alternative open to the person threatened, then he should take advantage of that alternative and not accede to the threat. It is only if there was no reasonable practical alternative that consent can be said not to have been freely given, but only given under duress or coercion. If there was a reasonable practical alternative, then a claim in economic duress will fail, even if the person threatened complies with the threat: in such circumstances, the person threatened makes a (commercial) choice not to pursue the reasonable practical alternative but to give in to the threat.

For example, imagine that *C* enters into a contract with *D*, under which *D* will supply 1,000 mince pies for *C*'s Christmas party on 24 December for £500. On 1 May, *D* tells *C* that he will not supply any mince pies unless *C* pays *D* an extra £500. If *C* agrees to the extra

---

[9] *Occidental Worldwide Investment Corporation v Skibs A/S Avanti* [1976] 1 Lloyd's Rep 293, 336 (Kerr J), approved in *Pao On v Lau Yiu Long* [1980] AC 614.

payment, surely he cannot claim duress. Even though there was a threat of an unlawful act (the breach of contract) and the threat was a reason why *C* agreed to pay the extra £500, there were plenty of reasonable practical alternatives open to *C*. For instance, *C* could have contracted with another party for the supply of the mince pies. If the facts of this hypothetical example were altered such that on 23 December—the day before the party—*D* threatened not to supply the mince pies unless *C* paid more money, then duress is more likely to be established. It may no longer be reasonably practical for *C* to make alternative arrangements for the supply of mince pies.

Admittedly, this requirement of 'reasonable practical alternative' is not always made clear in judicial reasoning.[10] But it is clear that, for economic duress, the claimant bears the onus of proof to show a causal link between the pressure and his entering into the contract.[11] It is less clear precisely what causal link needs to be shown. There is some authority that a 'but for' cause is required,[12] but also that the pressure should be a 'significant cause'.[13] In any event, it would be unsurprising for a more demanding approach to causation to be taken in the context of economic duress than is recognised in physical act duress: after all, a threat to breach a contract is (in the vast majority of cases) less serious than a threat to cause physical harm to somebody. It is suggested that if the claimant can show that the threat was a reason why he entered into the contract, and that he had no reasonable practical alternative but to succumb to the threat, then the requirement of causation will invariably be satisfied.

In several cases[14] Lord Denning repeatedly stressed the importance of 'inequality of bargaining power', but it is quite clear that mere inequality of bargaining power, even where the stronger party takes advantage of his position, is not, in itself, sufficient to make the contract voidable. A person wanting to borrow money in order to meet urgent liabilities will have virtually no bargaining power and will have to accept the terms on which the bank or building society is willing to deal with him, or to do without the money. That person's contract with the bank will not be voidable as the result of duress. The courts will interfere only in exceptional cases due to inequality of bargaining power where the conduct of the stronger party has been 'oppressive or unconscionable'.[15]

4 The scope of illegitimate pressure

(a) All breaches of contract?

The basis of duress lies in the illegitimate pressure exerted by one of the parties to the contract.[16] But what is the scope of 'illegitimate pressure'? This is not an easy question to

---

[10]   cf *Huyton v Peter Cremer* [1999] 1 Lloyd's Rep 620, 635–9 (Mance J).

[11]   Ibid.

[12]   *Kolmar Group AG v Traxpo Enterprises Pvt Ltd* [2010] EWHC 113 (Comm), [2011] 1 All ER (Comm) 46 [92] (Christopher Clarke J).

[13]   *Dimskal Shipping Co SA v International Transport Workers' Federation (The Evia Luck) (No 2)* [1992] 2 AC 152, 165 (Lord Goff).

[14]   See notably *Lloyds Bank v Bundy* [1975] QB 326.

[15]   *Alec Lobb (Garages) Ltd v Oil GB Ltd* [1985] 1 WLR 173, CA; see Chapter 19, Sections 1 and 2.

[16]   *Universe Tankships Inc of Monrovia v International Transport Workers' Federation* [1983] 1 AC 366, 400 (Lord Scarman); *R v Attorney-General of England and Wales* [2003] UKPC 22, [15] (Lord Hoffmann).

answer. It is worth remembering that 'economic duress' itself is relatively new, such that only 50 years ago it was not the case that threatening to breach a contract was sufficient for illegitimate pressure. After all, the threatened person always had the alternative of refusing to succumb to the pressure and simply suing for breach of contract. This was invariably viewed as a reasonable and practical alternative. Indeed, such an approach remains particularly popular with those who believe that contract law is primarily concerned with ensuring efficient outcomes, and that breaches of contract are not invariably to be discouraged.[17] However, whilst there are some doctrines concerned with minimising waste,[18] it has now been clearly recognised that a breach of contract is an unlawful act. Thus, a breach of contract is an unlawful act that can ground the tort of intimidation.[19] Moreover, the unlawful nature of a breach of contract helps to explain why breaches of contract may be deterred through restitutionary damages[20] and the tort of inducing a breach of contract.[21]

Given the clear recognition that a breach of contract is an unlawful act, it might reasonably be supposed that any threatened breach of contract constitutes illegitimate pressure exercised upon the claimant. Although there is strong support for this view,[22] a contrary suggestion has been raised: only threats made in bad faith should be sufficient to ground duress.[23] In *DSND Subsea Ltd (formerly DSND Oceantech Ltd) v Petroleum Geo Services ASA*, Dyson J said:[24]

> In determining whether there has been illegitimate pressure, the court takes into account a range of factors. These include whether there has been an actual or threatened breach of contract; whether the person allegedly exerting the pressure has acted in good or bad faith; whether the victim had any realistic practical alternative but to submit to the pressure; whether the victim protested at the time; and whether he affirmed and sought to rely on the contract. These are all relevant factors. Illegitimate pressure must be distinguished from the rough and tumble of the pressures of normal commercial bargaining.

Significantly, Dyson J was concerned to distinguish 'illegitimate pressure' from what may be considered 'normal' contractual (re-)negotiations. This may be achieved through considering whether or not the threat was made in bad faith. However, not all the factors given by Dyson J seem relevant to whether or not the pressure was 'illegitimate'. After all, the existence of a 'realistic practical alternative' is really concerned with causation rather than legitimacy.

If the defendant has acted in bad faith that is particularly reprehensible. Nevertheless, bad faith seems more relevant to lawful act duress[25] rather than unlawful act duress. In the vast majority of cases, there is no real need to consider the somewhat nebulous requirement

---

[17] See Chapter 1, Section 6(c).

[18] See eg Chapter 26, Section 2(c).

[19] *Rookes v Barnard* [1964] AC 1129.

[20] *Attorney-General v Blake* [2000] 1 AC 268; see Chapter 28, Section 2.

[21] eg *Lumley v Gye* (1853) 2 E & B 216; see Chapter 10, Section 11.

[22] E McKendrick, 'The Further Travails of Duress' in A Burrows and A Rodger (eds), *Mapping the Law: Essays in Memory of Peter Birks* (OUP, 2006).

[23] *Huyton v Peter Cremer* [1999] 1 Lloyd's Rep 620.

[24] [2000] BLR 530 [131].

[25] Considered in the next section.

of 'bad faith' when a defendant has threatened to commit a breach of contract, since that is an unlawful act which the defendant is not entitled to do. Indeed, even if all threatened breaches of contract were sufficient for illegitimate pressure, the contract would only be rendered voidable for duress if the threatened person had no reasonable practical alternative. However, the decision in *Payzu v Saunders*[26] does perhaps illustrate that a threat to break a contract will not invariably amount to economic duress. The refusal of the seller to deliver further instalments of the goods unless he was paid cash on delivery was a threat to break his contract to deliver on credit terms. Nevertheless, the court held that the buyer was under a 'duty' to mitigate the damage by agreeing to a contract for cash sales. In other words, the buyer had to yield to the threat. But in that case, the buyer had committed a breach of contract by failing to pay within one month of the delivery of the first instalment and the seller may well have believed, albeit wrongly, that this entitled him to insist on cash in future. The prior breach of contract by the buyer may well have been important.

(b) Beyond breach of contract?

Now that it has been recognised that threats to breach a contract can ground duress, the next frontier is whether threats to commit lawful acts can similarly suffice. So, if D threatens C that he will not enter into a contract with C unless C agrees to something else, could that ever constitute duress? It may seem unlikely that a threat to do something lawful could ever constitute duress. But it is not inconceivable. After all, this is the basis of the crime of blackmail. If I tell you that I will report the murder you committed to the police unless you pay me £1,000, then I have not threatened to do anything unlawful. Indeed, I am under some sort of public duty to tell the police about your crime. Nonetheless, I have committed the crime of blackmail. So if I tell you that I will report your crime unless you sell me your car, then there is an argument that you might be able to rescind the contract on the basis of duress. This seems plausible, although it should be pointed out that in most instances you will have a reasonable practical alternative to acceding to the threat (for example, by confessing).

In *CTN Cash and Carry Ltd v Gallagher Ltd*,[27] G, who had a monopoly in respect of the distribution of popular brands of cigarettes, demanded payment of £17,000. This was the price of a stolen consignment which G believed, wrongly but in good faith, to be at C's risk. C refused to pay. G then threatened to withdraw credit facilities it offered to C, unless C paid the price of the consignment. G did not threaten to do anything unlawful: G had only extended credit facilities to C as a favour. C had no contractual entitlement to the credit facilities, and it would have been very damaging to C had the credit facilities been withdrawn. C therefore decided to pay the price of the consignment as the lesser of two evils. C's action to recover the money on grounds of economic duress failed: C had made a commercial decision, and did have a reasonable, practical alternative to acceding to the threat, since C could have dealt with G otherwise than on credit terms. The court recognised that the result

---

[26] [1919] 2 KB 581.
[27] [1994] 4 All ER 714.

was 'unattractive'—*G* was allowed to retain £17,000 which was not due to *G*—but found that the law compelled this result.

However, the Court of Appeal left open the possibility of 'lawful act duress' being established on other facts. Similarly, in *R v Attorney-General*,[28] the Privy Council recognised the same possibility. That case concerned a lawful threat that was held to be insufficient for duress. The UK Special Forces had experienced problems when a previous officer left the SAS and wrote a book detailing his experience in the SAS. Wishing to avoid a similar situation in the future, the Special Forces asked their existing officers to sign confidentiality agreements undertaking not to disclose details of their experiences within the Forces both during and after their employment. This request was coupled with a threat that, if an officer refused to complete an agreement, he would be 'returned to unit'. This was a process usually imposed upon officers as a penalty for professional unsuitability, involving exclusion from the social life of the forces, and a cut in remuneration for the officer's services. *R* was an officer in the SAS, who signed the agreement.

After leaving the Forces, *R* sought to publish an account of his time in the SAS, and the Attorney-General obtained an **injunction**[29] to enforce the confidentiality agreement. *R* pleaded duress in order to rescind the confidentiality agreement. The Privy Council held that duress was not established on the facts.[30] Lord Hoffmann, giving the leading judgment, emphasised that the pressure—in the form of a threat to 'return *R* to unit'—was lawful. However, his Lordship did accept that some lawful threats could ground a claim in duress. Lord Hoffmann pointed out that blackmail was grounded upon lawful threats, and thought that if *R* had been required to sign the confidentiality agreement as a matter of military law, then a claim in duress could have succeeded. The pressure to sign the agreement may still have been lawful, but could have been illegitimate.

It is arguable that the decision of the Privy Council in *Akai Holdings Ltd (Liquidators) v Ting*[31] is an instance where lawful act duress was successfully pleaded. However, this case concerned both lawful and unlawful acts. Mr Ting was the chairman and CEO of Akai. Mr Ting was corrupt and ran the company badly. Ultimately, Akai collapsed and its liquidators proposed a scheme of arrangement in order to realise some of the company's assets. This scheme required shareholder approval. Mr Ting controlled companies with a shareholding in Akai, and sought to oppose the scheme. In order to proceed with their plans, the liquidators entered into a compromise agreement with Mr Ting. The agreement stated that Akai would not pursue any claims against Mr Ting, and in exchange Mr Ting promised to cease opposition to the scheme. The liquidators subsequently sought to rescind this compromise agreement on the ground of duress. Their claim was successful. The Privy Council held that Mr Ting's threat to oppose the scheme of arrangement was illegitimate. In itself, Mr Ting's opposition was not unlawful so this may be viewed as an example of lawful act duress. However, the Privy Council found the pressure to be illegitimate not only because Mr Ting had no good reason for such opposition, but also

---

[28] [2003] UKPC 22.
[29] See Chapter 28, Section 8.
[30] Lord Scott dissented on the issue of undue influence: see Chapter 18, Section 3.
[31] [2010] UKPC 21.

because he had used forgery and false evidence to support the opposition, and his sole reason for opposing the scheme was to try to prevent an investigation into his own behaviour. Such fraudulent undertones were clearly relevant in deciding that the threat of lawful action was nonetheless illegitimate, and suggest that Mr Ting's actions were not after all entirely lawful.

Similarly, in *Progress Bulk Carriers Ltd v Tube City IMS LLC (The Cenk Kaptanoglu)*,[32] Cooke J allowed a claim in duress to succeed, but this was based partly on lawful acts and partly on unlawful acts. In that case, the illegitimate pressure took the form of prior unlawful conduct, in combination with the threat of future conduct. Tube City chartered a ship. The ship's owners committed a **repudiatory** breach of contract by withdrawing the ship and seeking to replace it under the **charterparty**. This created problems for Tube City, which suffered hardship as a result of the ensuing delays. The parties reached a settlement agreement whereby Tube City would accept a replacement ship, in exchange for a reduction in the price under the charterparty. However, the settlement contained a term that required Tube City to waive any claims for loss or damage following the owner's repudiatory breach in withdrawing the ship. This was included by the owners on a 'take-it-or-leave-it' basis. The owner later brought a claim under the settlement agreement, and Tube City argued that the settlement was voidable for duress. Tube City was successful. The judge reasoned that if threats to carry out unlawful acts in the future are illegitimate, it would be inconsistent to deny that unlawful actions that had already occurred could be illegitimate for the purpose of duress. These unlawful acts were taken into account when deciding that the pressure applied by the owners was illegitimate: the threat not to enter into a settlement agreement was itself lawful, but not viewed in isolation.

5 Consumer protection

Regulation 7 of the Consumer Protection from Unfair Trading Regulations 2008[33] prohibits aggressive commercial practices by a trader against a consumer. A practice is aggressive if it 'significantly impairs or is likely significantly to impair the average consumer's freedom of choice or conduct in relation to the product concerned through the use of harassment, coercion or undue influence'[34] and 'it thereby causes or is likely to cause him to take a transactional decision he would not have taken otherwise'.[35] A consumer has a right to redress under Part 4A of the Regulations if he is the victim of an aggressive commercial practice. Remedies under Part 4A were examined in Chapter 16.[36]

---

[32] [2012] EWHC 273 (Comm), [2012] 2 All ER (Comm) 855.
[33] SI 2008 No 1277.
[34] Reg 7(1)(a).
[35] Reg 7(1)(b).
[36] Chapter 16, Section 6.

Ⓘ Further Reading

P Atiyah, 'Economic Duress and the Overborne Will' (1982) 98 LQR 197.
Clearly rejects the 'overborne will' theory of duress, since the victim does choose and intend to submit to the threat.

D Tiplady, 'Concepts of Duress' (1983) 99 LQR 188.
Responds to the above article of Atiyah, arguing that the language of 'overborne will' is a useful shorthand to denote that the victim has succumbed to the threat, and that attention should really be focused on whether or not the pressure exerted was legitimate.

E McKendrick, 'The Further Travails of Duress' in A Burrows and A Rodger (eds), *Mapping the Law: Essays in Memory of Peter Birks* (OUP, 2006).
A broad examination of duress, making the important argument that threatening to breach a contract is always illegitimate and can ground a claim in economic duress.

❓ Question

Mike agrees to do decorating work for Harvey. Harvey tells Mike that it is important that the work is finished on time, because on 1 June Harvey will officially launch his new business from the premises. When Mike is about halfway through the work, he realises that he will not be able to finish on time unless Harvey pays him an extra £3,000. Mike informs Harvey of the situation. Harvey reluctantly agrees to pay the extra money in order to make sure that the official launch of his business is a success.

Mike finishes the work on time, but Harvey now refuses to pay the extra £3,000.

Advise Mike.

18   Undue influence

🔑 Key Points

- Where C places trust and confidence in D, and D exerts his influence upon C in a way which is 'undue', then C may have a claim for undue influence.

- The effect of undue influence is to render a contract voidable such that it can be rescinded.

- The basis of undue influence is controversial: it has been argued both that undue influence is based upon D's exploitation of the relationship, and that the focus is solely upon C's impaired consent.

- There is only one claim in undue influence, but there are two ways of proving undue influence. This explains the traditional categories of actual undue influence and presumed undue influence.

- Actual undue influence comprises overt acts of improper pressure or coercion such as unlawful threats. There is a significant overlap between actual undue influence and duress.

- Presumed undue influence requires C to prove that C placed trust and confidence in D and that the transaction calls for explanation. Some relationships are automatically regarded by the law as being ones of trust and confidence. In any event, D may be able to rebut the presumption by showing that C entered into the transaction voluntarily and fully aware of what he was doing. This can often be achieved by ensuring that C receives impartial legal advice.

- Undue influence may also affect a contract between C and a third party. A common problem arises when C agrees to act as a surety or guarantor of D's debts as a result of the undue influence of D. This often leads to an agreement between C and a bank. If the bank has actual or constructive notice of the undue influence, then it may be unable to enforce its contract with C because C is able to set aside the transaction, even though the bank itself did not exert any undue influence. A bank is put on inquiry whenever a surety guarantees the obligations of a debtor and the relationship between the two is non-commercial. A bank will then need to take reasonable steps to ensure that C was not entering into the transaction as a result of the undue influence of D.

Alongside the **common law** relating to duress there exists an equitable doctrine of 'undue influence'. Undue influence primarily developed in relation to **gifts**, but the doctrine is equally applicable to contracts. In a typical case of undue influence, C claims that a transaction should be set aside because he reposed trust and confidence in D, and the influence that D had upon C was exerted in a way which was 'undue'. It is for C to prove that this occurred. Undue influence renders a contract voidable.

Undue influence has been the subject of a number of relatively recent decisions of the House of Lords. In the most important of these, *Royal Bank of Scotland v Etridge*,[1] their Lordships considered eight appeals, and thoroughly reviewed and clarified the law. Indeed, although it is traditional to split the cases into those of actual undue influence and presumed undue influence,[2] in *Etridge* Lord Nicholls was keen to stress that actual undue influence and presumed undue influence are not different claims. They are both claims for undue influence. The difference lies only in the way the claim is proved. In actual undue influence, C proves that a relationship of undue influence existed at the time of his entering into the relevant transaction. In presumed undue influence, C proves primary facts that lead to a rebuttable presumption of the facts necessary to ground an undue influence claim.

Before considering further the elements of undue influence that need to be satisfied, it is helpful to discuss the basis of undue influence. This is a controversial issue.

1 The basis of undue influence

There is a divide between those who believe that undue influence is defendant-focused, and those who consider it to be claimant-focused. The former view contends that undue influence is the equitable counterpart of duress, such that the focus is upon the defendant's bad conduct.[3] The latter view claims that the basis of relief is simply that the claimant did not provide his free, fully informed consent to the transaction because his intention, or consent, was vitiated by the undue influence.[4] On this approach, the defendant does not need to have acted reprehensibly.

A key case that seems to support such reasoning is *Allcard v Skinner*.[5] Miss Allcard (C) wanted to join a convent, but had to take vows of poverty, chastity, and obedience. C therefore made gifts of money and shares to Miss Skinner (D), the Mother Superior of the convent. Some time later, C left the sisterhood and sought to recover the property she had given away. The Court of Appeal held that there had been undue influence: the Mother Superior clearly had influence over the young woman who intended to be a nun, and C had not received any independent advice to ensure that her consent to the gifts was free and fully informed, rather than unduly influenced by her relationship with D. However, although there had been undue influence, on the particular facts of the case C could not rescind the gifts due to her delay in bringing the claim (laches).[6]

It is difficult to criticise the conduct of the Mother Superior. *Allcard v Skinner* is not a case of duress: there was no threat or oppressive conduct. Although the Mother Superior could feasibly have ensured that C took independent advice before giving away her property, it does not appear to be the case that the Mother Superior was exploiting C. The basis of the relief granted focused on the intentions of C, rather than the conduct of D. C's

---

[1] [2001] 4 All ER 449, HL.

[2] *Allcard v Skinner* (1887) 36 ChD 145.

[3] eg R Bigwood, 'Undue Influence: "Impaired Consent" or "Wicked Exploitation"?' (1996) 16 OJLS 503.

[4] eg P Birks and NY Chin, 'On the Nature of Undue Influence' in J Beatson and D Friedmann (eds), *Good Faith and Fault in Contract Law* (OUP, 1995).

[5] (1887) 36 ChD 145.

[6] See Chapter 16.

intention had been vitiated by the undue influence exercised by *D*. In other words, *C*'s consent was not free and fully informed as a result of the undue influence. This view continues to receive some judicial support. For instance, in *Pesticcio v Huet*, Mummery LJ insisted that 'the basis of the court's intervention is not the commission of a dishonest or wrongful act by the defendant, but that, as a matter of public policy, the presumed influence arising from the relationship of trust and confidence should not operate to the disadvantage of the victim, if the transaction is not satisfactorily explained by ordinary motives'.[7]

However, there has been something of a shift away from viewing undue influence as claimant-focused, instead concentrating upon *D*'s exploitation of a relationship of influence over *C*. This is consistent with the view that the influence must be 'undue' in the sense of 'improper'. Thus, in *R v Attorney-General*, Lord Hoffmann said:[8]

> Like duress at common law, undue influence is based upon the principle that a transaction to which consent has been obtained by unacceptable means should not be allowed to stand. Undue influence has concentrated in particular upon the unfair exploitation by one party of a relationship which gives him ascendancy or influence over the other.

There is a tension between the defendant-focused and claimant-focused views. This tension is difficult to resolve, and the truth may lie somewhere in between.[9] In the *Etridge* case the House of Lords pointed out that there are many different forms of undue influence, and it may even be that some forms of undue influence are claimant-focused and others defendant-focused. In any event, it is important that undue influence is not too wide: gifts and (perhaps especially) contracts should not easily be set aside.

2 Actual undue influence

Actual undue influence 'comprises overt acts of improper pressure or coercion such as unlawful threats'.[10] Actual undue influence was perhaps more important when duress was limited to threats of physical harm; now that a threat to commit a breach of contract has been recognised as sufficient for 'economic duress',[11] there is, as Lord Nicholls has pointed out, 'much overlap'[12] between duress and actual undue influence. Lord Hobhouse has described actual undue influence as an 'equitable wrong committed by the dominant party against the other which makes it unconscionable for the dominant party to enforce his legal rights against the other'.[13]

A famous example of actual undue influence is *Williams v Bayley*.[14] Bayley's son had fraudulently forged his father's signature on some **promissory notes** and presented them to

---

[7] [2004] EWCA Civ 372, [2004] WTLR 699 [20]. See too *Macklin v Dowsett* [2004] EWCA Civ 904, [2004] 2 EGLR 75 [10] (Auld LJ).

[8] [2003] UKPC 22.

[9] M Chen-Wishart, 'Undue Influence: Beyond Impaired Consent and Wrong-Doing Towards a Relational Analysis' in A Burrows and A Rodger (eds), *Mapping the Law: Essays in Memory of Peter Birks* (OUP, 2006).

[10] *Etridge* [8] (Lord Nicholls).

[11] See Chapter 17, Section 2.

[12] *Etridge* [8].

[13] *Etridge* [103]. See too *Desir v Alcide* [2015] UKPC 24 [54].

[14] (1866) LR 1 HL 200.

a bank. The bank discovered the fraud, and at a meeting with Bayley said that it could press criminal charges. The bank then asked Bayley to meet his son's debts, and Bayley agreed to do so. The bank subsequently sought to sue Bayley under this agreement, and Bayley successfully argued that the agreement was voidable on the ground of undue influence.[15] In the House of Lords, Lord Westbury emphasised that Bayley had not acted as a free and voluntary agent, since his judgement was affected by the bank's threats relating to his son's criminal acts.

The facts of *Williams v Bayley* might today give rise to a claim in duress. However, not all cases of actual undue influence will involve illegitimate pressure and therefore will not always parallel the common law of duress. *D* may be able to abuse a relationship of influence he has over *C* without ever exerting illegitimate pressure. It is therefore not the case that actual undue influence is entirely without purpose. But 'he who alleges actual undue influence must prove it'.[16] Although it used to be thought that in cases of actual undue influence (as opposed to presumed undue influence) the court could find a contract voidable even if there was no 'manifest disadvantage' to the person pleading undue influence,[17] in *Etridge* Lord Nicholls pointed out that undue influence is only ever likely to arise where the transaction was disadvantageous to a party.[18]

3 Presumed undue influence

The leading analysis of presumed undue influence is to be found in the decision of the House of Lords in *Etridge*, which helps to resolve most of the difficulties in this area. However, it remains somewhat unclear precisely what is presumed. As Lord Clyde said in *Etridge*,

> Thus on the face of it a division into cases of 'actual' and 'presumed' undue influence appears illogical. It appears to confuse definition and proof. There is also room for uncertainty whether the presumption is of the existence of an influence or of its quality as being undue. I would also dispute the utility of the further sophistication of subdividing 'presumed undue influence' into further categories. All these classifications to my mind add mystery rather than illumination.

It is unfortunate that it is not clear whether it is the 'influence' or the 'undue' element of the claim that is presumed. In practice, however, courts do not seem to have been troubled by this. In *Etridge*, Lord Nicholls said that all *C* was required to do was prove that she placed trust and confidence in *D* and that the transaction calls for explanation: 'proof of these two facts is **prima facie** evidence that the defendant abused the influence he acquired in the parties' relationship'.[19] However, it is only prima facie evidence and the presumption of undue influence that is raised can be rebutted by *D*.

---

[15] Lord Cranworth LC and Lord Westbury also placed emphasis on a different reason for not upholding the contract: the consideration from the bank was an undertaking not to prosecute the son, and this was unenforceable on the grounds of public policy.

[16] *Etridge* [103].

[17] *CIBC Mortgages plc v Pitt* [1994] 1 AC 200.

[18] *Etridge* [12].

[19] *Etridge* [14].

The first fact that *C* must therefore prove is a relationship of trust and confidence. Certain relationships are automatically treated by the law as being ones of trust and confidence. These relationships include parent and child, guardian and ward, **trustee** and beneficiary, solicitor and client, medical adviser and patient. Where the relationship between the parties is not one which is presumed by the law to involve trust and confidence, *C* must prove that a relationship of trust and confidence did in fact exist. Although Lord Clyde in the passage quoted above doubted whether further categories within presumed undue influence are useful,[20] the language of 'Class 2A' is sometimes used to refer to the former category of case where the relationship is automatically treated as being one of trust and confidence, and 'Class 2B' to the latter category of case.[21]

In *National Westminster Bank v Morgan*,[22] *C* entered into a transaction, acting on the advice of her bank manager (*D*). The House of Lords was not satisfied that the relationship between *C* and *D* ever went beyond the normal business relationship of banker and customer (or that the transaction was disadvantageous to *C*). Their Lordships therefore held that no relationship of trust and confidence arose, and refused to set the transaction aside. However, the relationship that undoubtedly gives rise to the most litigation is the relationship between spouses. Spouses are not irrebuttably held to be in a relationship of trust and confidence, and a spouse pleading undue influence must therefore prove that he or she actually placed trust and confidence in his or her partner. (The reported cases tend to involve situations where a wife is subject to the undue influence of her husband, but there is no reason why a husband could not be subject to the undue influence of his wife, or why a relationship of influence could not arise within a homosexual marriage, for example.)

The second fact that *C* must establish is that the transaction 'calls for explanation'. This is an important requirement. As Lord Nicholls insisted in *Etridge*, it would be absurd if every gift by a child to his parent, or every fee paid by a client to his solicitor, were presumed to have been obtained by the exercise of undue influence. If a transaction is one that is readily explicable by the relationship, there are no grounds for an inference that something untoward has occurred. After all, there is nothing unusual or strange in a wife conferring substantial benefits on her husband, for instance. Such gifts may simply be motivated by love and affection. Nevertheless, a wife (to use the stereotypical example) may have trust and confidence in her husband, especially in financial matters, which is open to abuse.

Before the *Etridge* case, it was thought essential for *C* to prove that the transaction was 'manifestly disadvantageous' to him.[23] This language was criticised in *Etridge* as leading to unnecessary confusion and difficulties. It now appears that manifest disadvantage is only evidence (albeit important evidence) that undue influence has been exercised. Where there is no manifest disadvantage, the exercise of undue influence might be proved by other evidence. The key question is whether 'the gift is so large as not to be reasonably accounted for on the ground of friendship, relationship, charity, or other ordinary motives on which ordinary men act, the burden is upon the donee to support the gift'.[24]

[20] As did Lord Hobhouse [107] and Lord Scott [161].

[21] See eg *Bank of Credit and Commerce International SA v Aboody* [1990] 1 QB 923, 953; *National Westminster Bank plc v Morgan* [1985] AC 686, 703; *Barclays Bank v O'Brien* [1994] 1 AC 180, 190.

[22] [1985] AC 686.

[23] See eg *National Westminster Bank plc v Morgan* [1985] AC 686.

[24] *Allcard v Skinner* (1887) 36 ChD 145, 185.

If the transaction is not so readily explicable, then an evidential burden is placed on the defendant to show that the transaction was not carried out as a result of undue influence. The greater the disadvantage to the claimant, the more cogent must be the evidence to rebut the presumption. If the defendant does not offer such evidence, he loses—the transaction will be set aside. If he does offer such evidence, then the court must determine whether there has been undue influence as a question of fact: the court will only set aside a transaction on the basis of undue influence if it is satisfied on the balance of probabilities that the defendant did abuse his relationship of trust and confidence.

The defendant can offer a wide range of evidence to show the transaction was not tainted by undue influence. Any evidence that the claimant entered into the transaction voluntarily and fully aware of what she[25] was doing is admissible. However, it is not enough for the defendant to show that a reasonable explanation for the transaction existed: he must prove on the balance of probabilities that the claimant entered into the transaction of her own free will and not as a result of the defendant's influence.[26] Perhaps the easiest way to achieve this is to ensure that the claimant had independent legal advice to ensure that she understood exactly what she was doing at the time she entered into the transaction. This was clearly discussed in *Etridge*, and will be analysed further in the next section.

The relevance of legal advice was raised in *R v Attorney-General*.[27] This case was considered in the previous chapter.[28] The Privy Council was unanimous in concluding that when the Special Forces asked *R* to sign a confidentiality agreement that was not duress. The majority also held that there was no undue influence. Their Lordships were prepared to accept that there was a relationship of influence, and that *R* placed trust and confidence in his superiors and the Army as an institution. But this relationship was not abused and any influence present was not undue. There was nothing suspicious about asking *R* to sign the agreement, and it was reasonable for the Special Forces to expect *R* to do so if he wished to continue to serve in the SAS. However, Lord Scott dissented because he thought that undue influence was established on the facts. His Lordship was particularly concerned by the fact that legal advice was not made available to *R*. As a result, Lord Scott thought that the presumption of undue influence had not been rebutted. The majority admitted that they were 'troubled' by the lack of legal advice, but ultimately held that this should not affect the outcome of the case. It is suggested that the majority was correct in its approach. Since there was nothing to call into question the agreement in the first place, the presumption of undue influence did not arise so did not need to be rebutted. The lack of legal advice was therefore irrelevant, since it would only have been relevant to rebutting a presumption of undue influence, and the presumption simply did not arise.

---

[25] The female pronoun is used here to correspond with the typical example of a wife being under the undue influence of her husband, and for the sake of clarity: the female claimant can be distinguished from the male defendant. However, the roles can readily be reversed depending on the facts of any case.

[26] *Smith v Cooper* [2010] EWCA Civ 722, [2010] 2 FLR 1521 [65]–[66] (Lloyd LJ).

[27] [2003] UKPC 22.

[28] See Chapter 17, Section 4(b).

4 Three-party cases

In the typical case that troubled the House of Lords in a series of decisions,[29] a husband (D) sought to raise money, usually for the purpose of assisting his business. However, the bank would only lend money in return for a **charge**, or **security**, over the family home, which D jointly owned with his wife (C). C therefore had to agree to the bank's charge over her property, and in effect act as a guarantor, or surety, for her husband's debts. This posed difficulties when D's business subsequently failed, and the bank sought to sell the family home in order to recover the money it had advanced to D. Upon realising that she was about to be evicted from her home, C sought to set aside the transaction on the ground of undue influence (or misrepresentation[30]) by either D or the bank. As already noted, neither husband and wife nor banker and customer is a relationship in which trust and confidence is presumed. And claims based on the bank's own undue influence are notoriously difficult to prove, since rarely will the relationship go beyond the usual banker–customer relationship.[31] But the major area of dispute concerned that the question of whether the bank was a third party to the undue influence exerted by D, such that the transaction should still be set aside. This was the focus of the litigation in *Etridge*.

The judgments in *Etridge* are long and difficult. Lord Nicholls and Lord Scott gave the leading speeches. Since all their Lordships agreed with Lord Nicholls's judgment on the law, and Lord Nicholls and Lord Bingham saw no significant difference between Lord Nicholls's judgment and Lord Scott's judgment, it is sensible to focus on the speech of Lord Nicholls. Lord Nicholls explained that the contract between C and the bank may be set aside, even though the undue influence was exerted by D rather than the bank, if the bank had actual or constructive notice of the undue influence. If the bank actually knows of the undue influence, then the bank cannot really complain about the transaction being voidable. The nature and scope of constructive notice, however, is more difficult.

Lord Nicholls held that the bank has constructive notice if it is put on inquiry about the undue influence. This language can be confusing. His Lordship admitted that the phrase 'on inquiry' is, strictly speaking, a misnomer, since the bank does not need to inquire into more facts. Instead, all the phrase 'on inquiry' means is that the bank has (constructive) notice of certain matters which means that the bank should take certain steps to ensure that C is not acting subject to undue influence. However, Lord Nicholls considered the phrase 'on inquiry' to be too entrenched in legal discourse to be departed from.

Lord Nicholls considered that a bank would be put on inquiry whenever a surety (C) guarantees the obligations of a debtor (D) where the relationship between C and D is non-commercial. Significantly, this means that a bank is not just on inquiry because the surety and **debtor** are in a sexual relationship, or because the surety and debtor are in a relationship that the law automatically treats as one of trust and confidence. Lord Nicholls cited the decision of the Court of Appeal in *Credit Lyonnais Bank Nederland NV v Burch* in support of

---

[29] Perhaps most notably beginning with *Barclays Bank plc v O'Brien* [1994] 1 AC 180, HL and culminating with *Etridge*.

[30] Similar principles apply to misrepresentation and undue influence as regards the voidability of the transaction: *Barclays Bank plc v O'Brien* [1994] 1 AC 180, HL.

[31] *National Westminster Bank plc v Morgan* [1985] AC 686.

this proposition.[32] In that case, Ms Burch (C) was employed by Mr Pelosi (D). D asked C to permit a charge to be entered over her property in order to secure loans made by a bank to D's company. C agreed. This was obviously not to C's apparent advantage, so the bank wrote to C and advised her to seek legal advice, since her liability was unlimited in both time and amount. C did not take legal advice, and assured the bank that she understood the nature of the transaction. However, C also made it clear that D had been involved in preparing her response. Subsequently, D's company defaulted on its loans, and the bank sought to enforce its charge and sell C's property. C successfully argued that the transaction should be set aside on the basis of undue influence, even though the relationship between C and D was that of employer and employee and there was no sexual relationship between them. On the facts, the Court of Appeal held that it was a relationship of trust and confidence. Moreover, the transaction was not readily explicable on the basis of the relationship of employer and employee, and the bank was aware of the manifestly disadvantageous terms of the agreement from C's perspective. A presumption of undue influence therefore arose, and it was necessary for the bank to take reasonable steps to ensure that C provided her free and fully informed consent to the transaction. The bank had failed to take such steps: the bank knew that D was involved in the response given by C, and so its suspicions had not been allayed.

Credit Lyonnais v Burch highlights that a bank might be put on inquiry in a wide range of circumstances. However, the most common examples are when a wife secures her husband's debts, or when a wife secures her husband's company's debts. In both situations, the wife who acts as a surety or guarantor gains no obvious advantage from entering into the transaction, and often puts the family home at risk as security. A bank may be put on inquiry even when the guaranteeing spouse has interests in her spouse's company by way of shareholding, or is an officer of the company.[33] By contrast, a bank would not be on inquiry where a loan was advanced to a husband and wife jointly. This is because then the transaction would not call for explanation, since the wife would benefit from the money advanced. In such circumstances, the bank will only be put on inquiry if the bank was aware that the loan was really only being made for the husband's purposes, as distinct from their joint purposes.[34]

The burden is on the wife to prove that the bank had constructive notice, but this burden is easily discharged by showing that the bank knew that she was a wife living with her husband and that the transaction was not to her financial advantage. The burden is then on the bank to show that it took reasonable steps to satisfy itself that her consent was properly obtained.[35] In *Etridge*, the House of Lords held that if the bank is put on inquiry, then it should take steps to ensure that the surety receives advice from a solicitor who can explain the practical implications of the transaction to the wife. The bank must obtain the surety's direct agreement to the engagement of a particular solicitor. However, the solicitor does not necessarily need to act exclusively for the surety; for example, it may be reasonable for the solicitor also to act for the surety's spouse or for the bank. The court is generally

[32] [1997] 1 All ER 144.
[33] *Etridge* [49].
[34] *CIBC Mortgages plc v Pitt* [1994] AC 200.
[35] *Barclays Bank plc v Boulter* [1999] 4 All ER 513, HL.

prepared to place great faith in the integrity of solicitors and their advice. The bank must ensure the solicitor has full details of the transaction, and inform the solicitor of any of the bank's beliefs relating to the relationship between husband and wife. The bank must then receive written confirmation from the solicitor that the solicitor has explained to the surety the full implications of the transaction.

If the bank undertakes these steps, then the bank will not be fixed with constructive notice of, and its contract will not be voidable for, any undue influence. This strikes an important balance. Whilst it is important that spouses (often, but not exclusively, wives) are not tied to transactions entered into as a result of undue influence, it is also important that banks can feel confident that they will be able to enforce the security they receive in return for lending money. Otherwise, banks will refuse to lend money, and this could have very damaging effects on the economy as a whole. It is suggested that the House of Lords in *Etridge* reached a sensible position. If the bank is put on inquiry and nonetheless fails to take any steps to ensure that the surety is not acting under undue influence, then the bank cannot complain about not being able to enforce its security. But if the bank does take the reasonable steps suggested in *Etridge*, such that the surety has received impartial legal advice about the effect of the transaction, then it is fair for the bank to be able to rely upon its rights under the transaction. After all, the bank has not exerted any undue influence itself. Nevertheless, it should be noted that independent and impartial legal advice does not necessarily establish that the surety was not acting under undue influence, even when it shows that the surety fully understood the situation. All the evidence must be taken into account, and the court must decide the matter on the balance of probabilities.

In *Etridge*, Lord Nicholls also provided guidance for solicitors advising the surety in such transactions. The solicitor's primary duties are contained within the solicitor's contract with his client. But in all events, the solicitor must explain the nature of the transaction, and make it clear that the surety has a choice whether or not to proceed with the transaction. If it is obvious that the surety is acting as a result of undue influence, the solicitor should decline to act any further and not provide the confirmation sought by the bank. It is important to emphasise that although the advice in *Etridge* was focused upon wives who act as a result of their husbands' undue influence, the guidance is generally applicable in a wider range of situations; indeed, the guidance applies whenever a third party is put on inquiry as to the effects of any relationship on the surety's process of practical reasoning in entering into the relevant transaction (such as where a husband guarantees his wife's debts).

5 Remedy

There is no tort of undue influence. As a result, C cannot recover damages from D if a claim in undue influence is successful. This is sometimes criticised, and it may be that in time undue influence will evolve to be recognised as a wrong which triggers compensation,[36] but the traditional and orthodox view is that the only remedy for undue influence

---

[36] See eg L Ho, 'Undue Influence and Equitable Compensation' in P Birks and F Rose (eds), *Restitution and Equity* (Mansfield Press, 2000) vol 1.

is **rescission**.[37] It is worth highlighting that the usual bars of rescission apply.[38] As a result, in the three-party scenarios discussed in the previous section, if the bank is not put on inquiry and purchases its rights in good faith without notice of the undue influence, C will not be able to rescind the transaction since that would unfairly prejudice the bank. But if the bank is put on inquiry, then it will have notice of the undue influence, and as a result the rights it acquires will not be sufficient to prevent rescission unless that bank has taken reasonable steps to ensure that C has not entered into the transaction as a result of undue influence.

In *Etridge*, Lord Scott said:[39]

> If contractual consent has been procured by undue influence or misrepresentation for which a party to the contract is responsible, the other party, the victim, is entitled, subject to the usual defences of change of position, affirmation, delay etc, to avoid the contract.

There have indeed been cases where rescission has been shown to be a flexible remedy that has been granted on terms.[40] For example, in *Cheese v Thomas*,[41] the agreement was between C, aged 85, and his great-nephew, D, to buy a house to live in together. They purchased a house for £83,000; C contributed £43,000 in cash, and D contributed the rest of the money by way of a **mortgage**. D defaulted on the mortgage payments, and the house was sold for £55,000. The court held that the relationship between C and D was one of trust and confidence, and that the transaction was manifestly disadvantageous to C, since he paid a substantial sum of money for a 'seriously insecure' right that tied him to that particular house. However, the court did not order D to repay the £43,000 in full. Instead, the court held that the fall in the property market should be borne proportionately by the parties, since they were parties to a 'joint venture', such that D only had to pay C just under £29,000. The Court of Appeal thought that this outcome achieved 'practical justice', but it is a difficult result to justify.[42] However, it may be an example of the change of position defence raised by Lord Scott. It may be that D received a benefit of £43,000, but he was not a wrongdoer and this instance of presumed undue influence was thought by the Court of Appeal to be 'innocent'. It could be thought that the fall in the property market meant that there was a 'change of position' of D, such that it would be unfair to require him to give back the entirety of the £43,000. Change of position is an important defence to claims in unjust enrichment, which is discussed further in Chapter 28.[43]

It should also be noted that undue influence might constitute an aggressive commercial practice under the Consumer Protection from Unfair Trading Regulations 2008, in a similar manner to duress. As a result, a consumer might be able to seek a remedy under Part 4A of the Regulations. For further discussion of this point, see Chapters 16[44] and 17.[45]

---

[37] For general discussion of rescission, see Chapter 16.
[38] See Chapter 16, Section 4(d).
[39] *Etridge* [144].
[40] Although partial rescission is impossible: see Chapter 16, Section 4(d)(i).
[41] [1994] 1 WLR 129.
[42] See eg M Dixon, 'Looking Up a Remedy for Inequitable Conduct' (1994) 53 CLJ 232.
[43] Chapter 28, Section 4.
[44] Chapter 16, Section 6.
[45] Chapter 7, Section 5.

It should be noted that 'undue influence' as defined in the Regulations is broader in scope than undue influence at common law, since there only needs to be 'the exploitation of a position of power', and is not restricted to relationships of trust and confidence.[46]

Further Reading

P Birks and NY Chin, 'On the Nature of Undue Influence' in J Beatson and D Friedmann (eds), *Good Faith and Fault in Contract Law* **(OUP, 1995).**
Argues that undue influence should be clearly distinguished from duress; the former is concerned with the claimant's impaired consent and the latter with the defendant's wrongful exploitation of the claimant.

R Bigwood, 'Undue Influence: "Impaired Consent" or "Wicked Exploitation"?' (1996) 16 OJLS 503.
Rejects the Birks and Chin approach, arguing that the focus should really be upon the misconduct of the stronger party, and that impaired consent and exploitation are inextricably linked.

M Chen-Wishart, 'Undue Influence: Beyond Impaired Consent and Wrong-Doing Towards a Relational Analysis' in A Burrows and A Rodger (eds), *Mapping the Law: Essays in Memory of Peter Birks* **(OUP, 2006).**
Argues that undue influence cannot be explained solely by reference to the claimant's impaired consent or the defendant's conduct. Instead, a relational theory of undue influence is required; the nature and context of the relationship is crucial, and the defendant should ensure that the claimant is able to protect herself.

Question

Josh is infatuated with his new wife, Donna. Donna wishes to launch a start-up business and applies to Quickbuck Bank for a loan. The bank tells Donna that she must have a guarantor for the loan as her start-up business is a risky proposition. Donna asks Josh to be her guarantor, and Josh immediately agrees.

Quickbuck Bank asks Josh to obtain independent legal advice before signing the contract of guarantee. Josh goes to see Will, the solicitor who is also acting for Donna. Will tells Josh that start-ups are invariably risky propositions, and that Donna has no experience in the field. However, Josh disregards Will's advice, and tells Will that he is prepared to do whatever Donna asks him to do because: 'A happy wife means a happy life.'

Will tells Quickbuck Bank that he has met with Josh, and that Josh understands what a contract of guarantee means. Will also tells the bank that Josh is hopelessly infatuated with Donna and would do absolutely anything for her.

On the basis of this information, Quickbuck Bank agrees to lend Donna the money, with Josh as her guarantor. Donna's business fails within three months and she is unable to repay the loan.

Advise Quickbuck Bank.

---

[46] Regulation 7(3)(b).

19 Unconscionable bargains and good faith

Key Points

- English law is traditionally cautious about adopting overriding principles such as 'good faith', preferring instead to avoid unfair outcomes through particular doctrines (for example, misrepresentation, duress, and undue influence).

- Some contracts may be set aside if they are considered to be an 'unconscionable bargain'. A contract may be unconscionable if the claimant is 'poor and ignorant', the terms of the contract are substantially disadvantageous to the claimant, and the claimant had no independent advice. Moreover, the defendant must have exploited the claimant's weakness in a morally culpable manner.

- There is no general principle in English law that a contract can be set aside due to inequality of bargaining power (despite the best efforts of Lord Denning MR).

- English law continues not to recognise a general principle of good faith. However, the law in this area is developing. It appears that agreements to negotiate in good faith are not enforceable where no contract is yet in place, but, where the parties have already made an agreement, a term (whether express or implied) that the contract should be performed in good faith is enforceable. Good faith has a range of meanings, and its particular meaning in any given case will depend upon the precise facts of that case.

This chapter will consider some broader concepts and their impact on the law in England and Wales. However, English law has traditionally been cautious about wholeheartedly adopting such sweeping principles as 'unconscionability' and 'good faith'. As Bingham LJ pointed out in *Interfoto Picture Library Ltd v Stiletto Visual Programmes Ltd*,[1] 'English law has, characteristically, committed itself to no such overriding principle but has developed piecemeal solutions in response to demonstrated problems of unfairness'. Such piecemeal solutions fit well with the usual approach of the **common law**: incremental development on a case-by-case basis, gradually building up a corpus of law.

The law of contract is traditionally thought to be based upon liberal principles and freedom of contract. In general, courts will simply seek to give effect to what the parties have agreed. Judges are acutely aware of the fact that they do not have the power to improve the parties' bargain. As a result, ideas such as good faith are often looked upon with

---

[1] [1989] QB 433, 439. See Chapter 11, Section 2(b)(i).

suspicion. After all, it is often said that consideration must be adequate but need not be suf-ficient,[2] and that if a person voluntarily enters into a bad bargain that is simply his lookout. There is a fear amongst some lawyers that broader concepts such as good faith might be invoked in order to allow a court to interfere with the substance of the parties' bargain. This could make the interpretation of contracts and the outcome of disputes more unpredict-able, thereby undermining commercial certainty, which is widely considered to be a strong attraction of English contract law. When will a court interfere with the contract concluded between the parties? How will a court interfere?

Of course, there may be good reasons why the court should set aside a contract. If the bar-gain really is truly 'unconscionable' or concluded in total 'bad faith' then it is possible to be sympathetic to the view that the court should not simply passively give effect to the agree-ment. The law should obviously strive to be just and fair, and such considerations might trump concerns over certainty. After all, certainty is a 'second-order' principle, and a law could be certain but unfair (to give a silly example, that all men who are taller than two metres must be shot). It might even be thought that the parties could not have intended for the con-tract to be unconscionable, or to be made or performed in bad faith, and that this would further justify relying on these principles vigorously.

However, there is little doubt that certainty is an important consideration; commercial certainty is a significant reason why parties in other jurisdictions choose English law to govern their contracts. It would be unacceptable for the law to become too vague and un-certain. This means that if broad concepts such as unconscionability and good faith are to be used, their scope must be clearly defined and their content certain. It should be possible to invoke such ideas in a predictable way. At the moment, neither unconscionability nor good faith have unlimited scope, but this is an area where further developments are likely (especially as regards good faith).

When considering the potential role of broad notions which generally are used to ensure 'fair' outcomes, it is useful to bear in mind that ideas of fairness are usually invoked in order to protect weaker parties against exploitation by a stronger party, and that Parliament has periodically chosen to regulate in this area. For example, the Consumer Credit Act 1974, the Unfair Terms in Consumer Contracts Act 1977, and the Consumer Rights Act 2015 may all be thought to address this problem, even if this is, again, in a somewhat piecemeal fashion. Similarly, European influences—such as the Consumer Protection from Unfair Trading Regulations 2008—cover ground that could perhaps otherwise be dealt with by concepts such as unconscionability and good faith. Where there is legislation to govern a particular situation, then the matter is relatively straightforward for the courts, since they are bound to give effect to the legislation. It may well be thought more difficult for courts to develop sweeping notions of good faith by themselves, given that judges are not elected and may not be best placed to implement broad ideas that could have such substantial effects on the common law. That probably explains why judges are happier to develop the law on a smaller, incremental basis, and why judges tend to concentrate upon the manner in which the contract was formed, rather than take it upon themselves to regulate the contents of a contract in an area in which they are not expert and which may have a broader impact. Of

---

[2] Chapter 7, Section 1(c) and (d).

course, to some extent this depends on the temperament of certain judges, and the cases in this area are not always entirely consistent.

1 Unconscionable bargains

Unconscionability is a difficult term which is used in a variety of different ways. It is often said to be the touchstone of equitable relief. Indeed, we have already seen that it is an important element in claims of **estoppel**,[3] rectification,[4] and undue influence.[5] It is also invoked in the context of penalty clauses,[6] **injunctions**,[7] and **specific performance**,[8] for example. Unlike in some other jurisdictions, such as Australia,[9] in England and Wales judges are more cautious about using unconscionability as an overarching principle to justify the intervention of **equity**. This is probably motivated by fears of uncertainty; unconscionability has been criticised as 'the most slippery of words'.[10] This section will concentrate on the particular context of contracts which are held to be voidable because they are 'unconscionable bargains'. Further principles and guidance as to what constitutes an unconscionable bargain have evolved through the decided cases.

The jurisprudence regarding unconscionable bargains developed from old cases concerning the protection of 'expectant heirs' against exploitation, and the protection of the 'poor and ignorant'. This latter category is well illustrated by the famous case of *Fry v Lane*, decided in 1888.[11] Fry contracted to sell his reversionary interest under a will to Lane. Fry was a laundryman who earned £1 a week, and his interest had a market value of £475. However, he sold his interest for only £170. Kay J held that the contract of sale was voidable since Lane took undue advantage of the ignorance of Fry. The judge said:[12]

> where a purchase is made from a poor and ignorant man at a considerable undervalue, the vendor having no independent advice, a court of equity will set aside the transaction ... The circumstances of poverty and ignorance of the vendor, and absence of independent advice, throw upon the purchaser when the transaction is impeached, the onus of proving ... that the purchase was 'fair, just, and reasonable'.

Fry was poor and ignorant, the sale was at a considerable undervalue, and Fry had received no independent advice. Moreover, Lane could not show that the transaction was fair, just, and reasonable. The contract was therefore set aside.

Fry v Lane highlights the crucial elements of a claim that the contract is an unconscionable bargain. However, the three factors set out in *Fry v Lane* have since been slightly

---

[3] See Chapter 7, Section 2.
[4] See Chapter 14.
[5] See Chapter 18.
[6] See Chapter 27.
[7] See Chapter 28, Section 8.
[8] See Chapter 28, Section 7.
[9] *Commercial Bank of Australia Ltd v Amadio* (1983) 151 CLR 447.
[10] A Burrows, 'Construction and Rectification' in A Burrows and E Peel (eds), *Contract Terms* (OUP, 2007) 88.
[11] (1888) 40 ChD 312.
[12] Ibid, 322.

modified and updated. An important decision in this regard is *Cresswell v Potter*.[13] Ms Cresswell and Mr Potter entered into a financial settlement upon their divorce. This settlement greatly favoured Mr Potter to the substantial detriment of Ms Cresswell. Later, Ms Cresswell argued that it was an unconscionable bargain which should be set aside. Megarry J applied the three requirements from *Fry v Lane*, but also emphasised that these did not prescribe exhaustive circumstances under which unfair dealing could be made out. Indeed, his Lordship thought that 'poor and ignorant' needed to be interpreted in a more modern way. Megarry J considered that 'poor' meant a member of the lower income group, and did not require destitution, whilst 'ignorant' simply required someone who was less highly educated, in particular in relation to the relevant transaction. On the facts, Ms Cresswell satisfied these requirements: she was a telephonist who had little savings, and was considered to be poor (although her earnings were similar to those of Mr Potter). And since she had no advanced understanding of property transactions, she was considered to be ignorant. She had not received independent advice, and Mr Potter could not show that the transaction was fair, just, and reasonable. The settlement was therefore set aside.

It now appears that there is an additional requirement for a plea of unconscionable bargain to be successful: the wrongful exploitation of the claimant by the defendant. This was first raised in *Alec Lobb (Garages) Ltd v Total Oil (GB) Ltd*.[14] A garage was tied to source petrol exclusively from Total Oil for four years. The garage was in financial difficulties, and so it entered into a new contract with Total Oil. Under this agreement, the garage received funds immediately which allowed it to pay off its debts. In return, Total Oil obtained a new tie-in agreement on better terms. The garage later sought to set the contract aside on 'equitable grounds'. The Court of Appeal rejected the garage's claim.[15] Their Lordships emphasised that no unconscionability, coercion, or oppression had been illustrated. This suggests that there is a requirement of oppressive conduct additional to those requirements outlined in *Fry v Lane*. However, on the facts of the case, the garage had received independent legal advice, but deliberately chose to ignore it and enter into the contract anyway. The emphasis on Total Oil's lack of oppressive conduct was therefore unnecessary to the decision and strictly *obiter*.

More helpful on this point, perhaps, are two decisions of the Privy Council which provide persuasive guidance. In *Hart v O'Connor*,[16] an 83-year-old vendor of unsound mind contracted to sell farming land to Hart. Hart did not know of, and had no reason to suspect, the vendor's mental incapacities.[17] The vendor died, and his relative, O'Connor, claimed that the contract of sale was voidable since it was an unconscionable bargain. The Privy Council disagreed. Lord Brightman, giving the judgment of the Board, emphasised that Hart had not committed any unconscionable conduct. Hart had not been aware of the vendor's unsound mind, and the terms of the transaction had been suggested by the vendor's independent solicitor.

---

[13] [1978] 1 WLR 255.
[14] [1985] 1 WLR 173.
[15] See too Section 2.
[16] [1985] AC 1000.
[17] For further discussion of capacity, see Chapter 20.

In *Boustany v Pigott*,[18] Ms Pigott was Mrs Boustany's **landlord**. The **lease** contained a provision for renewal providing for the parties to reach agreement on the new rent amounts. Ms Piggott was said to be 'quite slow', and her affairs were generally dealt with by her cousin. Mrs Boustany knew this, but managed to get Ms Pigott to agree to a lease renewal on very disadvantageous terms. Ms Pigott subsequently granted her cousin a power of attorney, and the cousin immediately claimed that the rent renewal contract should be set aside by virtue of its being an unconscionable bargain. The Privy Council agreed. The Privy Council held that Mrs Boustany's behaviour had been unconscionable; Mrs Boustany knew that Ms Pigott's affairs were managed by her cousin, but purposefully chose to deal with Ms Pigott in order to secure a lease renewal upon better terms. This amounted to taking advantage of Ms Pigott.

It therefore seems that there is some focus on whether the conduct of the defendant was unconscionable, rather than simply whether the contract itself is unconscionable. In *R v Attorney-General*, Lord Hoffmann even thought that '[i]f the transaction was not such as to give rise to an inference that it had been unfairly obtained by a party in a position to influence the other, it must follow that the transaction cannot be independently attacked as unconscionable'.[19] In *Portman Building Society v Dusangh*,[20] Simon Brown LJ thought that the conduct of the defendant should be 'morally reprehensible'. This appears to be judged subjectively, such that the defendant must actually realise that his conduct is reprehensible, with a narrow extension in situations where the defendant deliberately turned a blind-eye[21] to facts he knew which would indicate that entering into the contract would be unconscionable.

This approach has the advantage of restricting the scope of the doctrine of unconscionable bargains, and thereby limiting the intervention of courts by reference to the substance of the parties' bargain. It also indicates that there is very much a focus on the manner or procedure in which the contract is concluded, rather than solely upon the substance of the contract itself, which is consistent with the way other **vitiating factors** operate (such as misrepresentation, duress, and undue influence). However, it does mean that a person who unwittingly enters into a tremendously advantageous contract with someone who is 'poor and ignorant' and acting without legal advice may be able to enforce the contract—since he has not acted in a 'morally reprehensible' manner—even though the contract may be considered to be substantively unfair.[22] But if the defendant manages to convince the court that this is the case (which may not be easy), and the claimant had capacity to enter into the contract,[23] then perhaps the common law is justified in taking a robust approach in holding people to bad bargains since some hard cases might be tolerated in order to achieve greater certainty more generally, and particularly in the commercial context. It might legitimately

---

[18] (1995) 65 P & CR 298.

[19] [2003] UKPC 22 [29].

[20] [2000] 2 All ER (Comm) 221.

[21] Sometimes called 'Nelsonian knowledge' after the story that Admiral Nelson explained his refusal to follow orders to withdraw prior to the Battle of Copenhagen on the basis that he did not know about them—but this was only because he held a telescope to his blind eye, rather than his good eye, when 'looking' at the signals being given! Such wilful conduct in seeking to avoid 'actual' knowledge can sensibly be equated with 'knowledge'.

[22] D Capper, 'The Unconscionable Bargain in the Common Law World' (2010) 126 LQR 403.

[23] See Chapter 20.

be thought important that those who do not act badly are able to rely upon agreements which they believe, in all good faith, to be binding.

Unconscionability is sometimes favoured as a broad umbrella concept that can also encompass duress and undue influence in this area.[24] But since there are different principles and considerations that apply to each vitiating factor, this does not seem a very useful approach on a practical level. Indeed, it is possible for the defendant to be innocent in some cases of undue influence[25] and misrepresentation,[26] but not as regards unconscionable bargains. Any theoretical advantages that may follow from endorsing a broadly applicable concept of unconscionability may be outweighed by the uncertainty it would provoke in (probably) expanding the grounds on which a court will set a contract aside, when the general principle is that contracts should be upheld and given effect.

However, the doctrine of unconscionable bargains appears to be welcomed by the judiciary as a useful tool in order to avoid giving effect to the most outrageous contracts. Moreover, in *Multiservice Bookbinding Ltd v Marden*,[27] Browne-Wilkinson J said: 'I do not think the categories of unconscionable bargains are limited: the court can and should intervene where a bargain has been procured by unfair means.' Indeed, an unconscionable bargain might be invoked against a third party applying the same principles as those in *Etridge*.[28] Nevertheless, it should be remembered that an argument that a contract should be voidable as an unconscionable bargain very rarely succeeds, and is something of a last resort. It is most unlikely ever to be countenanced between two large commercial entities, and often operates in order to protect private individuals who may well now be protected by legislative provisions anyway.[29] Be that as it may, the recent summary of the law by Blair J in *Strydom v Vendside Ltd* is helpful:[30]

> before the court will consider setting a contract aside as an unconscionable bargain, one party has to have been disadvantaged in some relevant way as regards the other party, that other party must have exploited that disadvantage in some morally culpable manner, and the resulting transaction must be overreaching and oppressive. No single one of these factors is sufficient—all three elements must be proved, otherwise the enforceability of contracts is undermined ... Where all these requirements are met, the burden then passes to the other party to satisfy the court that the transaction was fair, just and reasonable.

2 Inequality of bargaining power

Somewhat linked to the general concept of unconscionability is the notion that the court should be prepared to step in and hold that a contract can be set aside wherever there is

---

[24] eg D Capper, 'Undue Influence and Unconscionability: A Rationalisation' (1998) 114 LQR 479 and 'The Unconscionable Bargain in the Common Law World' (2010) 126 LQR 403.

[25] See Chapter 18.

[26] See Chapter 16.

[27] [1979] Ch 84.

[28] See generally Chapter 18, Section 4 and the discussion there of *Credit Lyonnais Bank Nederland NV v Burch* [1997] 1 All ER 144.

[29] See Section 3.

[30] [2009] EWHC 2130 (QB) [36].

a substantial inequality of bargaining power between the parties. This idea was strongly championed by Lord Denning. For example, in *Lloyds Bank Ltd v Bundy*,[31] Bundy's son's business owed a bank large sums of money. Bundy had entered into two contracts of guarantee in relation to those debts. Bundy then contracted to provide a third guarantee, and to allow a **charge** to be entered over his land, in exchange for the bank continuing to permit the son's company to draw upon its overdraft facility; the bank was considering removing this permission as the son's company was in financial difficulties. Bundy, his son, and the son's company all held accounts with the bank. The father trusted that his bank manager was loyal to his son. Unfortunately, the son's company failed, and the bank sought possession of the father's land through enforcing the charge. The Court of Appeal held that the contract of guarantee was voidable for undue influence.

However, the primary reason why Lord Denning MR (although not the other judges) held that the contract was voidable was based upon a general principle of inequality of bargaining power. Lord Denning MR relied upon five principles of contract law, from which he felt able to abstract an overriding principle of inequality of bargaining power. These principles were: duress to goods; unconscionable transactions, such as the transaction in *Fry v Lane*; undue influence; undue pressure, such as in *Williams v Bayley*;[32] and salvage agreements.[33] The general principle was that where a party entered into an unfair contract without receiving independent advice, and his bargaining power relative to the counterparty was unequal, the contract was voidable. Lord Denning considered that *Bundy* fell within this general principle, highlighting four particular reasons for this conclusion. First, the consideration provided by the bank was grossly inadequate relative to the risks the father was undertaking by guaranteeing the son's company's liability and allowing a charge to be entered upon his land. Secondly, the bank and the father were in a relationship of confidence. Thirdly, the father trusted the son, for whom he had great affection. Fourthly, the bank had a conflict of interest between the bank's interests and the father's interests.

A general principle of 'inequality of bargaining power' would give the courts greater freedom to interfere with the parties' contract. Lord Denning generally favoured allowing judges wide discretion to achieve fair results, but this obviously comes at the expense of certainty and predictability, both of which are highly prized in the contractual context. It is therefore unsurprising that this approach of Lord Denning has been roundly rejected. For instance, in the *Alec Lobb* case, the Court of Appeal rejected a general principle of inequality of bargaining power on the basis that it lacked authority. Similarly, in *Hart v O'Connor*, Lord Brightman said that where the purchaser neither knew, nor ought reasonably to have known, of the vendor's incapacity, no special principles applied to the case beyond the well-recognised law of duress, misrepresentation, undue influence, and other established vitiating factors. The law does not recognise a general principle of inequality of bargaining power.

Perhaps the most unequivocal rejection of a general principle of inequality of bargaining power is to be found in the decision of the House of Lords in *National Westminster*

---

[31] [1975] 1 QB 326.

[32] (1866) LR 1 HL 200; see Chapter 18, Section 2.

[33] See eg *Akerblom v Price* (1881) 7 QBD 129, 133 (Brett LJ); *The Port Caledonia and The Anna* [1903] P 184.

Bank v Morgan.[34] A married couple faced financial difficulties and contracted with a bank to refinance their debt. The bank agreed to provide the couple with a bridging loan in return for a charge over their property. The couple failed to meet the repayments on the bridging loan, and the bank sought to sell the property. The wife unsuccessfully argued that she only entered into the contract as a result of undue influence. Lord Scarman, with whom all their Lordships agreed, also discussed the wider principle espoused by Lord Denning MR in *Lloyd's Bank Ltd v Bundy.* Although this discussion was strictly *obiter,* as the wife had not sought to rely on a wider principle of inequality of bargaining power, the dismissal of this principle was compelling and has been followed. Lord Scarman doubted both whether there was a need for a general doctrine of inequality of bargaining power, and whether the court was the correct institution to be developing such a doctrine:[35]

> I question whether there is any need in the modern law to erect a general principle of relief against inequality of bargaining power. Parliament has undertaken the task—and it is essentially a legislative task—of enacting such restrictions upon freedom of contract as are in its judgment necessary to relieve against the mischief: for example, the **hire-purchase** and consumer protection legislation ... I doubt whether the courts should assume the burden of formulating further restrictions.

This was fully supported by Steyn LJ in *CTN Cash and Carry Ltd v Gallaher Ltd,*[36] who insisted that '[t]he control of monopolies is, however, a matter for Parliament. Moreover, the common law does not recognise the doctrine of inequality of bargaining power in commercial dealings'. In any given case it is likely that there is some inequality of bargaining power between the parties. It is unsatisfactory for the court to inquire into precise degrees of inequality and strike down contracts on that basis. The rejection of the suggestion of Lord Denning MR that there should be a wider principle of inequality of bargaining that allows a contract to be set aside is very welcome.

3 Consumer protection

Any push towards a general principle of inequality of bargaining power has also been stalled by consumer protection regimes. Examples include the Consumer Protection from Unfair Trading Regulations 2008[37] and the Consumer Rights Act 2015.[38] Beyond the context of consumers, the Unfair Contract Terms Act 1977 offers some protection where there is an imbalance between the parties.[39] It is clearly legitimate for Parliament to legislate in this way to govern common scenarios where there is an imbalance. And the fact that Parliament has chosen to regulate certain relationships or situations but not others could perhaps indicate that in those other circumstances the common law is thought to be satisfactory.

---

[34] [1985] 1 AC 686.
[35] Ibid, 708.
[36] [1994] 4 All ER 714; see Chapter 18, Section 4(b).
[37] See eg Chapter 16, Section 6 and Chapter 17, Section 5.
[38] Chapter 15, Section 4.
[39] Chapter 15, Section 2.

In *Plevin v Paragon Personal Finance Ltd*,[40] the Supreme Court recently discussed the protection afforded by section 140A of the Consumer Credit Act 1974 which provides that:

140A Unfair relationships between creditors and debtors

(1) The court may make an order under section 140B in connection with a credit agreement if it determines that the relationship between the **creditor** and the **debtor** arising out of the agreement (or the agreement taken with any related agreement) is unfair to the debtor because of one or more of the following—

   (a) any of the terms of the agreement or of any related agreement;
   (b) the way in which the creditor has exercised or enforced any of his rights under the agreement or any related agreement;
   (c) any other thing done (or not done) by, or on behalf of, the creditor (either before or after the making of the agreement or any related agreement).

(2) In deciding whether to make a determination under this section the court shall have regard to all matters it thinks relevant (including matters relating to the creditor and matters relating to the debtor).

Lord Sumption explicitly noted that this provision is 'deliberately framed in wide terms',[41] and depends on the court's judgment on the basis of all material facts. Although this is very broad, it is the expressed will of Parliament that courts should have wide discretion, and therefore must be applied. It would be far more awkward for judges to give themselves such sweeping powers. However, even under the Act, Lord Sumption emphasised some important points. First, what must be unfair is the relationship between the debtor and the creditor. Often this will be because the relationship is so one-sided that it limits the debtor's ability to choose. Secondly, not only hardship to the debtor but other matters relating to both the creditor and debtor can be taken into account. Thirdly, the unfairness must arise from one of the categories (a), (b), or (c) stated in section 140A. 'Fourthly, the great majority of relationships between commercial lenders and private borrowers are probably characterised by large differences of financial knowledge and expertise. It is an inherently unequal relationship. But it cannot have been Parliament's intention that the generality of such relationships should be liable to be reopened for that reason alone.'[42] Courts should be cautious about exercising their powers too freely.

4 Good faith

Another concept which is sometimes invoked as an overriding idea that runs throughout contract law is that of 'good faith'. This is a difficult notion. It is unclear precisely what good faith means, and what its scope and application might be. The orthodox approach is to insist that English law knows no general doctrine of good faith. As Lord Hope has observed, 'a general obligation to conform to good faith is not recognised... The preferred approach

---

[40] [2014] UKSC 61, [2014] 1 WLR 4222.
[41] Ibid, [10].
[42] Ibid.

in England is to avoid any commitment to over-arching principle, in favour of piecemeal solutions in response to demonstrated problems of unfairness.'[43]

The preference for piecemeal solutions was made clear by Bingham LJ in *Interfoto*.[44] But a failure explicitly to recognise an underlying principle of good faith is somewhat unusual. For example, in Roman law, the '*obligatio ex bona fide*' (or obligation to act in good faith) required parties to act in good conscience in fulfilling their obligations.[45] In civil law jurisdictions, the importance of good faith is well established; for instance, both the German[46] and Italian[47] civil codes impose general obligations on parties to act in good faith. Even within the common law world, the US Restatement (Second) of Contracts provides that 'every contract imposes upon each party a duty of good faith and fair dealing in its performance and enforcement'.[48] And, as was explained in Chapter 15, European consumer-protection legislation regulates unfair terms, with a test for unfairness incorporating a requirement of good faith.[49] The influence of European law in particular[50] ensures that debates about good faith remain prominent in England and Wales. Indeed, in *Yam Seng Pte Ltd v International Trade Corporation Ltd*,[51] Leggatt J thought that 'in refusing … to recognise any such general obligation of good faith, this jurisdiction would appear to be swimming against the tide'.

In *Yam Seng*,[52] Leggatt J noted a 'traditional English hostility' towards a doctrine of good faith, and identified three main reasons for this.[53] First, English law proceeds 'incrementally by fashioning particular solutions in response to particular problems rather than by enforcing broad overarching principles'.[54] English law tends to be wary about 'top-down' reasoning from an abstract principle to particular cases. Rather, the common law (but not always legislation) develops 'bottom-up', on the basis of particular facts of particular cases. Secondly, 'English law is said to embody an ethos of individualism, whereby the parties are free to pursue their own self-interest not only in negotiating but also in performing contracts provided they do not act in breach of a term of the contract'.[55] Commercial parties are characteristically viewed as adversaries, each seeking to conclude the best bargain possible for himself, without any need to worry about the position of the other party. On this approach, once the contract is agreed, any limits to the contractual rights need to be found in the contract itself.

---

[43] *R (European Roma Rights Centre and Others) v Immigration Officer at Prague Airport* [2004] UKHL 55, [2005] 2 AC 1 [59].

[44] See text to n 1.

[45] L Trakman and K Sharma, 'The Binding Force of Agreements to Negotiate in Good Faith' (2014) 73 CLJ 598, 607.

[46] German Civil Code, para 242.

[47] Italian Civil Code, Art 1137.

[48] Restatement (Second) of Contracts, para 205.

[49] See Chapter 15, Section 4.

[50] See too Principles of European Contract Law, Art 1:201: (1) 'Each party must act in accordance with good faith and fair dealing', and this duty cannot be excluded.

[51] [2013] EWHC 111 (QB), [2013] 1 All ER (Comm) 1321 [124].

[52] Ibid, [123], relying upon Bingham LJ in *Interfoto*.

[53] Although his Lordship thought that all could be overstated: see Section 4(b).

[54] [2013] EWHC 111 (QB), [2013] 1 All ER (Comm) 1321 [123].

[55] Ibid.

Thirdly, Leggatt J noted 'a fear that recognising a general requirement of good faith in the performance of contracts would create too much uncertainty. There is concern that the content of the obligation would be vague and subjective and that its adoption would undermine the goal of contractual certainty to which English law has always attached great weight.'[56] This is an important point. Introducing a general requirement of good faith could cause much consternation in the City of London, which is a major centre of commercial law. Much litigation and uncertainty would follow as the limits of good faith would need to be worked out through decided cases. It is unclear whether the effort and trouble would really be worth it. English law has already developed a number of distinct doctrines in order to reach the same results that would be achieved in other jurisdictions by way of good faith. Indeed, in *Interfoto* itself, where Bingham LJ strongly put forward the piecemeal approach of English law, there may well have been a lack of good faith and fair dealing, but the same outcome was reached by means of the law on incorporation of terms. It would be unsatisfactory if a general principle of good faith were to undermine the principles of interpretation, rectification, implication, and so on which have been well worked out (but continue to evolve incrementally) with the benefit of decided cases and experience.

However, this is not to say that arguments in favour of general principles of good faith are entirely without merit. But it does emphasise that the current position of the common law is not indefensible and may suit the particular legal tradition of England and Wales more easily. Yet it has also been argued that the purpose of contract law is to fulfil the reasonable expectations of honest men,[57] and that reasonable men do expect to deal with one another in good faith. On this view, it is unfortunate that a general doctrine of good faith is not recognised.

It is perhaps helpful to distinguish between situations where a contract has not yet been concluded and situations where a contract has been formed. Of course, good faith might be relevant to both. But it is suggested that if general principles of good faith do come to be recognised in English law, then they will be more readily accepted in the latter circumstances than the former.

(a) Good faith when negotiating an agreement

It has already been seen in Chapter 5[58] that there is no requirement for parties to negotiate in good faith. This proposition derives from the decision of the House of Lords in *Walford v Miles*.[59] Lord Ackner, who gave the leading speech, said:[60]

> the concept of a duty to carry on negotiations in good faith is inherently repugnant to the adversarial position of the parties when involved in negotiations. Each party to the negotiations is entitled to pursue his (or her) own interest, so long as he avoids making misrepresentations. To advance that interest he must be entitled, if he thinks it appropriate, to threaten to withdraw from further negotiations or to withdraw in fact, in the hope that the opposite party may seek to reopen negotiations by offering him improved terms.

---

[56] Ibid.
[57] eg Lord Steyn, 'Contract Law: Fulfilling the Expectations of Honest Men' (1997) 113 LQR 433.
[58] Chapter 5, Section 3.
[59] [1992] 2 AC 128.
[60] Ibid, 138.

This view continues to underpin the current approach of the law. A person cannot be forced to enter into a contract, and nor can he be forced to negotiate in good faith. Since there is not yet any contract between them, neither party is bound at all and each party is entitled to concentrate upon his own respective interests exclusively. Moreover, there are further reasons why courts are reluctant to impose a duty to negotiate in good faith. For example, it may be very difficult, if not impossible, to decide whether negotiations are brought to an end in bad faith. And it is unclear what remedy would be appropriate if a duty of good faith has been breached: how can the court decide whether any agreement would have been reached anyway, and what loss the claimant suffered? Perhaps the claimant could still recover his reliance loss,[61] but the appropriate remedy would obviously be difficult to assess. Ultimately, there are significant uncertainties that arise with a requirement of good faith.

However, there are also good reasons why parties may desire an enforceable principle of good faith. A party may not wish to commit time and resources to a negotiation if the other party can simply walk away from the negotiations arbitrarily and without any recriminations. That party may deserve sympathy, but it is not clear that he deserves legal protection. After all, the law is currently clear: there is no contractual protection for a party who has not yet agreed a contract and is only negotiating for a contract. That clarity and certainty may be especially welcome in a commercial context. Indeed, it is not even clear how important the law is in motivating commercial parties' approach to contract negotiations: such parties may be reluctant to withdraw arbitrarily from negotiations primarily as a result of the damage that might do to their business reputation, regardless of the legal position.

However, the view that a principle of good faith should be recognised even in the context of negotiations is not without support. Some support might be drawn from the judgment in *Emirates Trading Agency LLC v Prime Mineral Exports Private Ltd*,[62] in which Teare J held that a clause that disputes should be settled 'by friendly discussion' was enforceable (and had been complied with). The judge distinguished *Walford v Miles* by narrowing the application of that case to negotiations, suggesting that it was not binding when considering clauses concerning the resolution of disputes. This is understandable: the parties had entered into contractual relations, and had voluntarily agreed to the requirement that they try to settle disputes 'by friendly discussion'. As a result, this case might be sidelined as having little to do with contract negotiations. Yet much of the reasoning of Lord Ackner in *Walford v Miles* appears to be equally applicable to settlement disputes, since both have an adversarial nature. However, on balance the reasoning of Teare J should be supported: it was important that the main contract had already been concluded. Indeed, the reasoning of Teare J is consistent with that of Longmore LJ in *Petromec Inc v Petroleo Brasileiro SA*,[63] in which it was stressed that *Walford v Miles* concerned negotiations to agree the substantial agreement, rather than ancillary negotiations that were simply added to the main, valid agreement. Such ancillary negotiations—including those to resolve disputes—would be valid if they are sufficiently certain. It is worth noting that clauses requiring 'reasonable endeavours' or 'best endeavours' have been held to provide clear objective guidance and

---

[61] See Chapter 26, Section 7.
[62] [2014] EWHC 2104 (Comm), [2015] 1 WLR 1145.
[63] [2005] EWCA Civ 891, [2006] 1 Lloyd's Rep 121 [115]–[121].

are regularly upheld.[64] They provide an objective yardstick (judges are very used to dealing with concepts such as 'reasonable', for example) and are therefore sufficiently certain.

(b) Good faith within a binding contract

The analysis of good faith might therefore differ between situations where no contract has yet been agreed and circumstances where an agreement between the parties has already been concluded. If there is a contract in place, and the parties have agreed to perform in 'good faith', then this obligation will be given effect.[65] Courts will be very reluctant not to give effect to a term which has been expressly agreed between the parties, and will strive to give the term an objectively certain interpretation.[66] And if the court will give effect to an express term imposing a duty of good faith, then there is no reason why the court should not give effect to an implied term with similar content. This was recognised in *Yam Seng Pte Ltd v International Trade Corp Ltd*.

Yam Seng concerned a distributorship deal whereby Yam Seng agreed to market, and ITC agreed to supply, Manchester United-related products in various territories around the world. Yam Seng was constrained from selling, or authorising for sale, products below a 'particular price'. Leggatt J held that a general duty of good faith in the performance of the contract should be implied into the agreement. His Lordship thought that the usual techniques of construction led to this conclusion.[67] This general duty of good faith gave rise to two more specific duties. First, a duty for ITC to not 'knowingly provide false information' on which Yam Seng was likely to rely.[68] This term was breached on the facts, and the breach was considered **repudiatory**, justifying termination of the contract.[69] Secondly, there was a duty on ITC not to authorise the sale of relevant products in the contractual territories below the 'particular price' that constrained Yam Seng. There was, however, insufficient evidence to establish breach of this duty on the facts. *Yam Seng* has been much discussed and given rise to renewed interest in the idea of a general principle of good faith, but it might be wondered whether Leggatt J really needed to rely upon good faith at all: it appears that he could have implied the two duties on the basis of the normal principles of implication, without invoking good faith.[70]

In *Mid Essex Hospital Services NHS Trust v Compass Group UK and Ireland Ltd (t/a Medirest)*,[71] a clause of the contract provided that 'The Trust and the Contractor will co-operate with each other in good faith'. A question arose as to whether this applied to the general performance of the contract, or whether it applied more narrowly to two particular

---

[64] *Walford* 139–40; *Little v Courage* (1995) 70 P & CR 469, 476, CA.

[65] See eg *Mid Essex Hospital Services NHS Trust v Compass Group UK and Ireland Ltd (t/a Medirest)* [2013] EWCA Civ 200.

[66] See eg *Berkeley Community Villages Ltd v Pullen* [2007] EWHC 1330 (Ch) (Morgan J); *CPC Group Ltd v Qatari Diar Real Estate Investment Co* [2010] EWHC 1535 (Ch) (Vos J).

[67] Note that the term itself was not implied on the basis of good faith; rather an implied term of good faith was implied on the usual principles. Cf H Collins, 'Implied Terms: The Foundation in Good Faith and Fair Dealing' (2014) 67 Current Legal Problems 297.

[68] *Yam Seng* [156].

[69] Ibid, [173]–[174].

[70] S Whittaker, 'Good Faith, Implied Terms and Commercial Contracts' (2013) 129 LQR 463.

[71] [2013] EWCA Civ 200.

purposes, namely the 'transmission of information and instructions' and to enable the contracting party 'to derive the full benefit of the contract'. The latter interpretation was favoured.[72] Beatson LJ insisted that a broad obligation to cooperate in good faith should not cut across other, more specific provisions,[73] and that a narrower interpretation should be preferred.[74] Indeed, the principle of good faith should develop in an incremental and objective manner. However, Andrews J has stressed that 'there is no general doctrine of good faith in English contract law and such a term is unlikely to arise by way of necessary implication in a contract between two sophisticated commercial parties negotiating at arms' length',[75] concluding that the implication of such a term in *Yam Seng* was heavily dependent upon the particular facts of that case.

It now seems that good faith might be required when exercising contractual powers and making decisions that affect the interests of the counter-party.[76] In *Braganza v BP Shipping Ltd*, an employee died whilst in the service of the defendant employee.[77] This entitled the employee's widow, the claimant, to compensation unless, in the employer's opinion, the employee's death had been caused by suicide. The employer decided the death had been caused by suicide, and so refused to make the compensation payment.

The claimant brought an action seeking to quash the decision of the employer. The Supreme Court, by a 3:2 majority, held that the claim should succeed. All the judges agreed on the law. Lord Neuberger said that 'a decision-maker's discretion will be limited, as a matter of necessary implication, by concepts of honesty, good faith, and genuineness, and the need for the absence of arbitrariness, capriciousness, perversity and irrationality'. The disagreement between the judges was purely on the facts: the majority thought that the employer's decision had not conformed with the required standards, whereas the minority thought that it had. Significantly, the Supreme Court appeared to consider good faith to play a role alongside other concepts, such as non-arbitrariness and non-capriciousness.[78]

(c) Meanings of good faith

There is therefore clearly some role for good faith to play in English law. But for it to be really useful it must be clearly defined, since there are obvious dangers in invoking a vague and abstract concept. In *Interfoto*, Bingham LJ said that 'good faith':[79]

> does not simply mean that they should not deceive each other, a principle which any legal system must recognise; its effect is perhaps most aptly conveyed by such metaphorical colloquialisms as 'playing fair,' 'coming clean' or 'putting one's cards face upwards on the table.' It is in essence a principle of fair and open dealing.

---

[72] Ibid, [97]–[121], [148], and [149].

[73] Ibid, [154].

[74] See too *Portsmouth City Council v Ensign Highways Ltd* [2015] EWHC 1969 (TCC).

[75] *Greenclose Ltd v National Westminster Bank Plc* [2014] EWHC 1156 (Ch), [2014] 2 Lloyd's Rep 169 [150].

[76] cf J Morgan, 'Against Judicial Review of Discretionary Contractual Powers' [2008] LMCLQ 230.

[77] *Braganza v BP Shipping Ltd* [2015] UKSC 17.

[78] See too *MSC Mediterranean Shipping Co SA v Cottonex Anstalt* [2015] EWHC 283 (Comm), [2015] 2 All ER (Comm) 614 [97] (Leggatt J).

[79] *Interfoto* 439.

Indeed, even in the consumer context, there is some lack of clarity about whether good faith is concerned with purely procedural or also substantive concerns.[80]

In any event, it appears that good faith may have a range of meanings. As Leggatt J remarked in *Yam Seng*, 'what good faith requires is sensitive to context';[81] his Lordship made it clear that the content of any term of good faith is determined by a process of construction of the contract.[82] Similarly, in *Mid Essex* Lewison LJ observed that 'It is clear from the authorities that the content of a duty of good faith is heavily conditioned by its context.'[83] Good faith might simply require a party to take relevant considerations, and not take irrelevant considerations, into account when making a decision. Or good faith could demand rationality, in the sense of balancing reasons in an appropriate way.[84] But good faith could also require a party to communicate relevant facts,[85] or not knowingly to communicate falsehoods.[86] Good faith might also mean that a party must not act dishonestly, and must act in a commercially acceptable and not unconscionable way.[87] Or, as in *Yam Seng*, good faith might require a party to act or not act in a particular way, depending on the context in which the duty arises.

Significantly, 'the test of good faith is objective in the sense that it depends not on either party's perception of whether particular conduct is improper but on whether in the particular context the conduct would be regarded as commercially unacceptable by reasonable and honest people'.[88] Although the test is objective, it must take into account what the party actually knew. However, good faith is inevitably difficult to define with certainty. As Collins has observed:[89]

> The standard of good faith and fair dealing should be understood as comprising a spectrum of norms. At its narrowest end, good faith merely requires honesty in fact . . . At the other end of the spectrum of good faith, it edges close to fiduciary duties by requiring performance of the contract that takes the interests of the other party into account.

The key point seems to be that good faith must be understood in context. This is a normal aspect of contractual interpretation. This further explains why good faith is more readily accepted if it is a term in an already-agreed contract: good faith is then moulded by the parties' agreement and can be given an objective meaning. But where there is no contract in place at all, and the parties are still negotiating for a contract, then good faith is an unhelpful and uncertain yardstick which should not be relied upon.

---

[80] See Chapter 15, Section 4(c).
[81] *Yam Seng* [141].
[82] Ibid, [131]–[142] and [147]–[149].
[83] *Mid Essex Hospital NHS Trust v Compass Group* [2013] EWCA Civ 200 [105].
[84] *Braganza*.
[85] *Carter v Boehm* (1766) 3 Burr 1905.
[86] *Yam Seng*.
[87] *Bristol Groundschool Ltd v Intelligent Data Capture Ltd* [2014] EWHC 2145 (Ch) [196] (Richard Spearman QC). See too *The Federal Mogul Asbestos Personal Injury Trust v Federal-Mogul* [2014] EWHC 2002 (Comm) [119]–[120] (Eder J).
[88] *Yam Seng* [144].
[89] H Collins, 'Implied Terms: The Foundation in Good Faith and Fair Dealing' (2014) 67 CLP 297, 314.

In *Yam Seng*, Leggatt J said:

> I doubt that English law has reached the stage, however, where it is ready to recognise a
> requirement of good faith as a duty implied by law, even as a default rule, into all commercial
> contracts.[90]

This should reassure commercial parties. It ensures that any scope and role of good faith
is within the control of the parties, rather than externally imposed by the courts. There
remain piecemeal instances where good faith might, in effect, be required—possible
examples include the 'legitimate interest' exception in *White & Carter (Councils) Ltd v
McGregor*[91] and insurance contracts[92]—but these are justified by their own particular context. There is no overarching principle of good faith in English contract law.

Further Reading

S Thal, 'The Inequality of Bargaining Power Doctrine: The Power of Defining Contractual
   Unfairness' (1988) 8 OJLS 17.
Considers when contracts are set aside on grounds of 'unfairness', and argues that it is preferable to
focus upon procedural unfairness than substantive unfairness.

N Bamforth, 'Unconscionability as a Vitiating Factor' [1995] LMCLQ 538.
Argues that unconscionability is a distinct vitiating factor where there is a serious disadvantage, actual or constructive fraud, a lack of independent advice, and disadvantageous terms.

D Capper, 'Undue Influence and Unconscionability: A Rationalisation' (1998) 114 LQR 479; and
   'The Unconscionable Bargain in the Common Law World' (2010) 126 LQR 403.
Argues that unconscionability plays an important role, and can usefully encompass undue
influence.

E Peel, 'Agreements to Negotiate in Good Faith' in A Burrows and E Peel (eds), *Contract
   Formation and Parties* (OUP, 2010).
Analyses the limits to the enforceability of agreements to negotiate and suggests how the law might
be reformed.

H Hoskins, 'Contractual Obligations to Negotiate in Good Faith: Faithfulness to the Agreed
   Common Purpose' (2014) 130 LQR 131.
Discusses the circumstances in which contractual obligations to negotiate in good faith are
enforceable.

H Collins, 'Implied Terms: The Foundation in Good Faith and Fair Dealing' (2014) 67 Current
   Legal Problems 297.
Controversially argues that ideas of good faith and fair dealing should be central to the implication
of terms.

---

[90] *Yam Seng* [131].
[91] [1962] AC 413; see Chapter 25, Section 4.
[92] Marine Insurance Act 1906, s 17. See Chapter 15.

? Questions

1. Should a general duty of good faith be recognised in English law?

2. Adam wanted to purchase Bob's farm for development. Bob promised to negotiate with nobody other than Adam for a period of three months. Bob and Adam agreed that they will negotiate in good faith and use their best endeavours to reach an agreement. After three weeks and a series of increasingly unreasonable demands, Bob ended the negotiations. He never really intended to sell his farm, and just wanted to waste Adam's time.

    Adam was upset by this, and immediately sought to purchase other land on which he could build a house for him and his family. He noticed that Sainsco plc, a massive supermarket chain, was selling an unwanted property. Adam therefore contacted Sainsco plc, whose chief negotiator thought that Adam was probably drunk and definitely very angry throughout the whole process of concluding the agreement. Nevertheless, Sainsco plc and Adam quickly agreed that Adam would purchase the land for £200,000. Adam has subsequently discovered that the land is only worth £50,000.

    Advise Adam.

20 Capacity

🔐 Key Points

- The general rule is that contracts are not binding on minors (persons under 18 years of age). However, they are binding on adults. A minor can ratify a contract upon attaining the age of majority so that the contract is binding on both parties.

- Minors do have to pay a reasonable sum for 'necessaries' sold to the minor. 'Necessaries' are those things without which the minor cannot reasonably exist, taking into account the particular circumstances of the minor.

- A minor can enter into binding agreements of service, apprenticeship, or education, provided that the contract, taken as a whole, is manifestly for his benefit.

- At common law, mental incapacity is not by itself a reason to set aside a contract. But if the other party knows, or ought to know, of the mental incapacity, then the contract can be set aside. The Mental Capacity Act 2005 now operates in this area as well; the 2005 Act makes it clear that a person who lacks capacity must still pay a reasonable price for necessary goods and services

It is generally assumed that a person has the capacity to enter into a contract. It would make contracting a much more difficult and onerous process if each party had to prove the capacity to contract before entering into a transaction. Yet some persons do lack the capacity to contract, most notably because they are too young or lack the mental capacity to contract. There is a natural desire to protect such vulnerable persons. But strongly protecting those who lack capacity can have harsh consequences on innocent third parties who contract, in good faith, with those who lack capacity. There is a tension between protecting those who lack capacity and protecting innocent third parties. This is a tension that is difficult to resolve, and the law in this area is not always straightforward.

1 Minors

At **common law** persons under the age of 21 were categorised as 'infants' and had only a limited capacity to contract. Section 1 of the Family Law Reform Act 1969 reduced the age to 18 and authorised the use of the term 'minor' as an alternative to 'infant'. 'Minor' is now the preferred term. The capacity of a minor to contract is still regulated by the common law, but is now modified by the Minors' Contracts Act 1987, which repealed the troublesome Infants Relief Act 1874.

(a) **Contracts generally not binding on minors**

The general principle is that contracts made by a minor with an adult are binding on the adult but not on the minor. The contract becomes binding on the minor only if, after attaining the age of majority (which is 18), he ratifies it. Ratification is an act confirming the minor's earlier promise. It requires no fresh consideration from the adult[1] and makes the contract fully binding on the party who was a minor.

Although the contract is not binding on the minor, it is not void. Moreover, money paid or property transferred under the contract can only be recovered by the minor if he can show that there has been unjust enrichment on the basis of a total failure of 'consideration', or total failure of basis.[2] So, a minor who bought and enjoyed the use of furniture for several months was not allowed to recover the price,[3] and a minor who exchanged his motorcycle for a car could not get the cycle back when the car broke down.[4] This is because the minor received some benefit in return for the money paid or property transferred, so the basis of the transfer of the benefit did not wholly fail. These decisions were reached even though there was a provision of the Infants Relief Act that contracts for such non-necessary goods were 'absolutely void', which was unnecessarily confusing. Now that that Act has been repealed, it is clear that the same results would follow, and that the crucial issue is whether there has been a total failure of consideration.

(b) **Contracts 'voidable' by the minor**

In *North Western Railway v M'Michael*,[5] Parke B held that where a minor acquires an interest in 'a subject of a permanent nature ... with certain obligations attached to it'—such as a **leasehold** or **shares** in a company—he is bound by the obligations so long as he retains the 'subject'. In that case, the defendant was held liable to pay **calls** on shares even though he was a minor at the time he bought the shares and when the calls were made. It did not matter that he had never ratified the purchase, and the court stressed that he had also never **repudiated** the contract. The defendant was able to avoid the contract during his minority, or within a reasonable time after attaining the age of majority, but he had not done so. It was also irrelevant that the transaction was a disadvantageous one—after all, in such circumstances there are even stronger reasons to expect the infant to try to avoid the purchase, and thereby rid himself of the obligation. 'Avoid', as we have seen,[6] is an ambiguous word and the court in *M'Michael*'s case used it in the sense of **rescind**—the minor might avoid the contract *ab initio*, ridding himself not only of his liability to pay future calls but also of his liability to pay calls already due, but unpaid. However, the view that obligations are avoided only for the future and that the minor, or former minor, remains liable to meet obligations already accrued at the time of avoidance seems equally plausible.

---

[1] The position was different under the Infants Relief Act.
[2] See Chapter 28, Section 4.
[3] *Valentini v Canali* (1889) 24 QBD 166.
[4] *Pearce v Brain* [1929] 2 KB 310.
[5] (1850) 5 Ex 114, 123.
[6] See eg Chapter 16, Section 4(a).

The observations in *M'Michael* were *obiter*, and since there is no modern authority on this point the matter remains open.

If the right to repudiate is not exercised within a reasonable time after majority, it lapses. What is a reasonable time depends on all the circumstances of the case, and it is impossible to give clear guidance. In *Edwards v Carter*,[7] the House of Lords had no doubt that a party to a marriage settlement made a month before his majority had lost the right to repudiate the contract when he tried to do so four-and-a-half years later. That was much too late.

Whether avoidance is retrospective or not, it again seems clear that the minor cannot recover money which he has already paid, unless he can show that there has been a total failure of consideration. In *Steinberg v Scala Ltd*,[8] a minor's action to have her name removed from the register of shareholders succeeded, but she was not allowed to recover money paid by way of calls. She had received the very thing she bargained for, and it was immaterial whether she had derived any real advantage from the contract. In an action to recover money for a total failure of consideration there was no difference between a minor and an adult claimant: the claim for total failure of consideration is not a contractual claim but a claim in unjust enrichment, which is based upon different concerns.[9]

(c) Contracts for necessaries

The principal exception to the common law rule of the immunity of the minor is that he is liable to pay for 'necessaries' supplied to him. Since 1893, liability for necessary goods supplied to a minor has been regulated by the Sale of Goods Acts. Section 3 of the Sale of Goods Act 1979, which re-enacts the 1893 Act, provides that:

> ... where necessaries are sold and delivered to a minor ... he must pay a reasonable price therefor.
> ... 'necessaries' means goods suitable to the condition in life of the minor ... and to his actual requirements at the time of the sale and delivery.

'Necessaries' are those things without which a person cannot reasonably exist and obviously include food, clothing, lodging, and essential services. In *Chapple v Cooper*,[10] a widow who was a minor was held liable to an undertaker for his work in connection with the funeral of her late husband. The law allowed minors to marry, and a minor who did so might unhappily find it necessary to bury her spouse. The minor must therefore pay for it. Education or training in a trade has also always been regarded as 'necessary'.

The nature of the necessary thing was held to depend to some extent on the 'station in life' of the minor. As Alderson B said in *Chapple v Cooper*,[11] 'His clothes may be fine or coarse according to his rank; his education may vary according to the station he is to fill; and the medicines will depend on the illness with which he is afflicted, and the extent of his probable means when of age.' The application of the principle regarding necessaries must

---

[7] [1893] AC 360.
[8] [1923] 2 Ch 452, CA.
[9] See Chapter 28, Section 4.
[10] (1844) 13 M & W 252.
[11] Ibid, 258.

vary with changing social conditions. A servant in livery may have been a necessary for a rich minor in 1844 but it is impossible that this would be similarly true today. Alderson B said that 'articles of mere luxury are always excluded, though luxurious articles of necessity are sometimes allowed'. A well-to-do minor would have to pay for his Savile Row suits but a poor boy would not. The High Street shop would be good enough for him. The Savile Row tailor would therefore supply a minor at his peril, since he would only be entitled to be paid if the minor were rich. On the other hand, the High Street shop would not run the same degree of risk, since both rich and poor minors would have to pay for their suits.

As the Sale of Goods Act makes clear, the necessary goods supplied must be suitable, not only to the condition in life of the minor but also 'to his actual requirements at the time of sale and delivery'. If the minor has enough of the articles in question, more cannot be necessary to him. So, in *Nash v Inman*,[12] an undergraduate at Trinity College, Cambridge, was not liable to pay for clothing, including 11 fancy waistcoats, when his father gave evidence that his son was already amply supplied with clothes. The onus of proof was on the claimant to prove that the defendant minor was not adequately supplied. This was a very difficult burden for the claimant supplier of the clothes to discharge.

(i) Nature of the minor's liability for necessaries

The Sale of Goods Act declares the minor to be liable only where the goods are 'sold and delivered'. In such circumstances, the minor is only to pay a reasonable price, rather than any agreed price. In *Nash v Inman*,[13] Fletcher Moulton LJ said that this was a codification of the common law and that the basis of the action is 'hardly contract. Its real foundation is an obligation which the law imposes on the infant to make a fair repayment in respect of needs satisfied. In other words the obligation arises *re* [by virtue of something done] and not *consensu* [by virtue of agreement].'

The practical significance of this (apart from any difference between an agreed and a reasonable price) is that the minor would not be liable on an executory contract in damages. The seller would have no claim if the minor, in breach of the agreement, refused to accept delivery. This principle would apply regardless of whether the contract concerned necessary goods. Fletcher Moulton LJ's opinion is supported by the language of the Sale of Goods Act and by other eminent judges.[14] On the other hand, however, Buckley LJ in *Nash v Inman* nevertheless thought that it would be possible for there to be an action 'in contract on the footing that the contract was such as the infant, notwithstanding infancy, could make. The defendant, though he was an infant, had a limited capacity to contract'. More troubling than such *dicta* is the decision of the Court of Appeal in *Roberts v Gray*.[15] The claimant recovered damages from the defendant, a minor, for breach of a contract to join him in a world tour playing billiards. The claimant had expended time and trouble and incurred liabilities in making the arrangements, but this nonetheless seems to be a

---

[12] [1908] 2 KB 1, CA.

[13] Ibid, 8.

[14] In *Re Rhodes* (1890) 44 ChD 94, 105 (Cotton LJ) and *Pontypridd Union v Drew* [1927] 1 KB 214, 220 (Scrutton LJ).

[15] [1913] 1 KB 520, CA.

plain case of a minor being held liable for breach of an executory contract for necessaries. It was not a contract of employment but one for the teaching and instruction of the minor (the claimant was a noted billiards player). Hamilton LJ rejected the argument that the defendant would have become liable only on actually receiving the claimant's instruction, and held that the contract was binding on the minor from its formation. This decision is unsatisfactory. It does not seem possible to justify a distinction between necessary goods and necessary services on either a historical or a logical basis. The claim should have failed. It may be that the outcome in *Roberts v Gray* could have been justified as concerning a contract belonging to the next category of case to be considered—beneficial contracts of service—but the court specifically held that it was not a contract of employment but a contract for necessary instruction.

A contract is not binding on a minor merely because it is proved that it is for the minor's benefit. On the other hand, a contract which would normally be considered to be for necessaries will not be treated as a contract for necessaries if it contains harsh or onerous terms. A contract by a minor for the hire of a taxi to go five or six miles to collect his bag might be a contract for a necessary; but if it contains a term purporting to impose liability on him for any damage to the car, whether due to his negligence or not, it is not a contract for a necessary.[16]

(d) Beneficial contracts of service

The law sensibly allows minors to enter into contracts which are beneficial to the minor. This is obviously desirable. For instance, it is for the minor's benefit that he should be able to obtain employment and earn money. The minor could clearly not do this if he could not make a binding contract. The law therefore allows the minor to enter into binding agreements of service, apprenticeship, or education, provided that the contract, taken as a whole, is manifestly for his benefit. Whatever the position regarding necessaries, here any liability that arises from the agreement is plainly contractual.

In *Clements v London & North Western Railway*,[17] the claimant, a minor, was employed as a porter. The claimant had agreed to join an insurance scheme to which his employers contributed, and to forego any claims he might have against his employers under the Employers' Liability Act 1880. On sustaining an injury, he claimed under that Act. His action failed. The court emphasised that the contract must be looked at as a whole. The term by which he agreed to forego his rights was obviously not to the minor's advantage; but once a broader view was taken, the court found that the contract was, overall, for the minor's advantage and that the contract was therefore binding.

Many examples of beneficial contracts of service could be given. For instance, a minor pursuing a career as a professional boxer was held to be bound by his contract to observe the rules relating to that sport, especially since the rules were not particularly harsh or onerous to the minor. The contract enabled him to earn his living and so was for his benefit.[18] The same principle was applied to a contract with a young author to publish his

---

[16] *Fawcett v Smethurst* (1914) 84 LJKB 473.
[17] [1894] 2 QB 482.
[18] *Doyle v White City Stadium Ltd* (1929) [1935] 1 KB 110, note, CA.

book and to take an assignment of the copyright. The contract, judged at the date when it was made, was for the author's benefit. It was immaterial that it later turned out to be less beneficial than had been thought.[19] However, in *Proform Sports Management Ltd v Proactive Sports Management Ltd*,[20] it was held that a contract under which a 15-year-old footballer—Wayne Rooney—hired someone to act as his agent was voidable and could be set aside. Such a contract was not 'necessary'—Rooney could have played football without an agent—and was not analogous to a contract of service, apprenticeship, or education since the agent did not provide any training or advance Rooney's skills as a footballer.

(e) **Restitution by the minor**

The law is capable of producing injustice where a minor has obtained property under a contract which is not enforceable against him. He may acquire the property for nothing and the adult party, who may be in no way at fault, is the loser. This may be so even where the minor has lied about his age. It was held that the minor was not **estopped** from denying that he was an adult, so as to avoid the effect of the Infants Relief Act 1874,[21] and it is likely that the court today would similarly refuse to allow the policy of the common law against the imposition of liability on minors to be defeated by estoppel. It has also been decided that an action in **deceit** will not lie against the minor because that too would enable the contract to be indirectly enforced against him. However, the Minors' Contracts Act 1987 now affords a limited measure of redress to the adult party. Where a contract, made after the commencement of the Act, is unenforceable against a defendant because he was a minor when it was made, then section 3 of the Act provides that:[22]

> the court may, if it is just and equitable to do so, require the defendant to transfer to the claimant any property acquired by the defendant under the contract, or any property representing it.

Suppose *A*, a minor, has bought from *B* some non-necessary thing, such as a racehorse, for £10,000. He refuses to pay or to return the horse. The court now has a discretion to order *A* to return the horse. If *A* has exchanged the racehorse for a car, or he has sold it and paid the proceeds into his bank account, the court may require him to hand over the car or an appropriate part of the bank balance. However, if the proceeds of the sale have been dissipated and can no longer be identified in *A*'s possession, *B* has no redress under the 1987 Act.

If *B* lends money to *A*, a minor, then *B* will be unable to sue *A* to recover the money lent unless *B* is able to prove that he made the loan for the express purpose of enabling *A* to buy necessaries and that *A* in fact did so.[23] **Equity** gives relief on the ground that the money has in fact been expended on necessaries. If the money lent is identifiable in *A*'s hands—for example, because it is part of *A*'s credit balance at his bank—the lender might be able to

---

[19] *Chaplin v Leslie Frewin (Publishers) Ltd* [1966] Ch 71, CA, Lord Denning MR dissenting on the question whether the contract was beneficial.

[20] [2006] EWHC 2903 (Ch), [2007] 1 All ER 542 (Judge Hodge QC).

[21] *Levene v Brougham* (1909) 25 TLR 265.

[22] Minors' Contracts Act 1987, s 3(1).

[23] *Earle v Peale* (1711) 1 Salk 386; *Lewis v Alleyne* (1888) 4 TLR 560.

invoke section 3, for instance where the minor had fraudulently misrepresented that he was of full age.

(i) Restitution in equity

By section 3(2) of the 1987 Act, 'nothing in this section shall be taken to prejudice any other remedy available to the claimant.' Accordingly, B might still rely on the equitable doctrine which required a fraudulent minor to disgorge property which he had obtained by deception and which was still identifiable in his possession.[24] Clearly, there is an overlap between the statutory and equitable remedies and the former is wider in that it does not depend on proof of fraud. It is not clear that there would be any advantage in invoking the equitable remedy since that too is discretionary. And with equity, as with the statute, 'restitution stopped where repayment began'.[25]

(f) Guarantees of minors' contracts

C promises B that, if he will enter into a contract with A, a minor, then C will guarantee performance by A. B enters into the contract with A, who fails to perform or repudiates the contract. B then calls on C to honour his guarantee. Before the 1987 Act came into operation, C might have argued that, since A's promise was a nullity in law, there was nothing to guarantee and C's own promise was therefore equally void. However, section 2 of the 1987 Act clearly rules out any such argument: a guarantee of a minor's contract is not unenforceable merely because the contract with the minor is not enforceable against him on the basis that he is a minor. That provision is restricted to contracts which are unenforceable because of minority; the section does not apply if A's promise is not enforceable against him for some reason other than the fact that he is a minor, such as that he was induced to enter into the contract by misrepresentation or duress. In those circumstances, C would not be liable either.

2 Mental incapacity

At common law, mental incapacity is not by itself a reason for setting aside the contract. However, if the defendant knows of the claimant's incapacity,[26] or the other party ought to have known of the incapacity,[27] then the contract can be set aside. This was emphasised by the Privy Council in *Hart v O'Connor*;[28] Lord Brightman said that a person could not rely upon his incapacity as a free-standing reason to escape the contract, but that he might be able to set the contract aside on the more usual bases of duress, misrepresentation, undue influence, and unconscionability, for example. The position at common law as regards incapacity obviously differs from that concerning minors, where knowledge of the minor's

---

[24] *Leslie (R) Ltd v Sheill* [1914] 3 KB 607, CA.

[25] [1914] 3 KB 607, 618 (Lord Sumner).

[26] *Imperial Loan Co v Stone* [1892] 1 QB 599.

[27] *Dunhill v Burgin* [2014] UKSC 18, [2014] 1 WLR 933 [25] (Lady Hale).

[28] [1985] AC 1000; see Chapter 19, Section 1.

actual age is irrelevant.[29] It is also worth noting that the effect of incapacity, even when known, is only to make the contract voidable rather than void, which sits uncomfortably with the fact the doctrine of *non est factum* renders a contract void.[30]

However, the Mental Capacity Act 2005 has now had an important impact upon the common law. The Act makes it clear that a person is presumed to be of full capacity, unless it is established that he lacks capacity.[31] Merely making an unwise decision does not mean that a person lacks the capacity to make a decision.[32] Rather, 'a person lacks capacity in relation to a matter if at the material time he is unable to make a decision for himself in relation to the matter because of an impairment of, or a disturbance in the functioning of, the mind or brain'.[33] The impairment or disturbance may be only temporary.[34] A person is unable to make a decision for himself if he is unable:[35]

(a) to understand the information relevant to the decision;

(b) to retain that information;

(c) to use or weigh that information as part of the process of making the decision; or

(d) to communicate his decision (whether by talking, using sign language, or any other means).

A person must not be treated as unable to make a decision unless all reasonable practical attempts have been made to help him to understand the decision, and such attempts have been unsuccessful.[36] And incapacity cannot be established simply by age, appearance, or unjustified assumptions.[37] Significantly, even if a person lacks the capacity to contract, under section 7 of the 2005 Act he must pay a reasonable price for necessary goods and services. 'Necessary' in this context means suitable to a person's condition in life and to his actual requirements at the time when the goods or services are supplied. In the explanatory notes to the Act, an illustrative example is given: a person lacking capacity may have to pay the milkman for delivering milk as that is likely to be 'necessary', but a roofer who puts an unnecessary new roof on a house when only minor repairs were required will not be paid.

Beyond the scope of the Mental Capacity Act 2005, the common law principles continue to apply. Indeed, judges can adopt the new definition of incapacity in the 2005 Act 'if they think it appropriate',[38] which indicates that the common law rules continue to be relevant. So, if under the influence of drugs or alcohol, for example, a person did not understand what they were doing, and his impairment was known to the other party, then the contract might still be set aside at common law.[39]

---

[29] In Scotland, knowledge of the incapacity is not required: *John Loudon & Co v Elder's Curator Bonis* 1923 SLT 226.

[30] See Chapter 11, Section 2(a)(i).

[31] Section 1(1).

[32] Section 1(4).

[33] Section 2(1).

[34] Section 2(2).

[35] Section 3(1).

[36] Section 1(3).

[37] Section 2(3).

[38] See eg *Local Authority X v M* [2007] EWHC 2003 (Fam), [2009] 1 FLR 443 [80] (Munby J).

[39] See eg *Matthews v Baxter* (1872–73) LR 8 Ex 132.

3 Companies

Companies are legal persons and therefore are capable of entering into contracts. However, it used to be the case that a company could only act in ways authorised by the company's memorandum of association. A company which entered into a contract which did not fall within the scope of the company's objects and powers was said to act *ultra vires* (beyond its powers) and the contract was therefore void. This *ultra vires* rule was thought to provide important protection to shareholders who could be sure that the company would only act within certain parameters. However, the rule was very tough on third parties who entered into a contract with a company in all good faith, unaware that the company was acting *ultra vires*. As a result, the law has now been changed by the Companies Act 2006, which protects such third parties. Section 39(1) of the 2006 Act provides that 'The validity of an act done by a company shall not be called into question on the ground of lack of capacity by reason of anything in the company's constitution'; the *ultra vires* rule has effectively been abolished when a third party contracts with a company in good faith.[40]

4 Public authorities

Like a company, public authorities have legal personalities. But the *ultra vires* rule continues to limit the capacity of public authorities to contract.[41] Public authorities must act within the scope of their statutory powers. If a public authority enters into a contract by acting beyond its powers, then the contract will be void. This operates to protect the public taxpayers who pay for public authorities to fulfil certain functions (and not exceed their powers), but can operate harshly on third parties. However, if the contract is void as a result of a public authority acting *ultra vires*, then each contracting party should be able to recover any benefits it transferred to the other party through an action in unjust enrichment.[42]

Further Reading

A Hudson, 'Mental Incapacity Revisited' [1986] Conv 178.
Considers the law on mental incapacity, and suggests that it should not matter whether or not the defendant knows of the claimant's mental incapacity.

---

[40] See generally ss 39–41. See too s 31(1): the objects of a company are unrestricted unless specifically restricted by the company's articles of association, meaning that the company will **prima facie** have unlimited capacity.

[41] There has been a slight modification as regards services contracts which have been certified by a local authority, which are valid and enforceable: see Local Government (Contracts) Act 1997.

[42] See eg *Westdeutsche Landesbank Girozentrale v Islington London Borough Council* [1996] AC 669; *Haugesund Kommune v Depfa ACS Bank* [2010] EWCA Civ 579, [2012] QB 549.

P Watts, 'Contracts Made by Agents on Behalf of Principals with Latent Mental Incapacity: The Common Law Position' (2015) 74 CLJ 140.
Discusses the role of incapacity in the particular context of the agent–principal relationship.

B Häcker, 'Minority and Unjust Enrichment Defences' in A Dyson, J Goudkamp, and F Wilmot-Smith (eds), *Defences in Unjust Enrichment* (Hart, 2016).
Analyses the claims that arise where a minor seeks to recover benefits transferred, and when a party seeks to recover benefits transferred to a minor, in situations where the contract can be set aside.

? Question

'The rules on incapacity are confusing, unsatisfactory, and should be reformed.' Do you agree?

21 Illegality and restraint of trade

Key Points

- The law on illegality is very complicated. Often the existence of illegal conduct operates as a defence to a claim.

- Two Latin maxims are very important in this area. The first is *ex turpi causa non oritur actio*, often shortened to *ex turpi causa*, which might be translated as 'no cause of action will arise from an illegal act'. This means that a person cannot sue on the basis of his own illegal conduct.

- The second maxim is '*in pari delicto, potior est conditio defendentis*', often shortened to the '*in pari delicto*' principle, which might be translated as 'where the parties are equally culpable, the defendant is in the stronger position'. If both parties are tainted by the illegality at issue, then the claim will fail since the defendant is in the stronger position.

- The test of illegality is very controversial. The weight of authority seems to favour a 'reliance test', under which a claim will fail if the claimant has to rely upon evidence of illegal conduct. Otherwise the claim will succeed (unless there is a competing public policy which outweighs the public policy underpinning the illegality defence).

- The principal alternative to a 'reliance test' involves balancing a range of factors and deciding whether it is appropriate to bar a claim due to illegality. This has powerful support and is more flexible, but it is suggested that, on the authorities as they stand, this discretionary approach does not (yet?) represent the law.

- Illegality might arise in a wide range of circumstances. For example, the contract might be prohibited by statute or only concluded in order to achieve an illegal purpose.

- The illegality doctrine might apply to conduct which is not strictly illegal but contravenes public policy.

- An illegal contract is void, but property may pass under an illegal contract. However, a claimant cannot simply relabel his claim as one in tort or unjust enrichment in order to circumvent the illegality defence.

- A related doctrine concerns restraint of trade. Restraint of trade is concerned with balancing the competing rights of private parties, notably the employer's right to expect a certain degree of loyalty as regards his business against the employee's freedom to leave his employment and to undertake new business activities. The key consideration tends to be whether restraint of trade clauses are reasonable.

The law on illegality is very complicated. But it must obviously play some role in contract law: after all, a contract to kill somebody should not be enforced by the courts. But it is not even clear what 'illegality' means; the Law Commission considered this to be 'a surprisingly difficult question to answer'.[1] Illegal acts vary greatly in range and severity. Nor is it clear how a court should determine whether a contract is tainted by illegality such that a claimant should be unable to enforce it. These important questions will be analysed in this chapter. However, it is worth stating at the outset that 'illegality and the law of contract is notoriously knotty territory'.[2]

The House of Lords and Supreme Court have adopted different approaches to the issue of illegality, which makes the law especially confusing. In *Tinsley v Milligan*,[3] the House of Lords rejected the view that the court had a broad discretion whether or not to enforce the contract on the basis of asking whether enforcing the contract would be 'an affront to the public conscience'. Rather, the House of Lords insisted that the claim should succeed if the claimant does not need to rely upon any illegality, and fail otherwise. This tension between a discretionary approach taking into account a range of facts, and a more rigid approach based upon the 'reliance principle', continues to cause problems. For instance, in 2014 the Supreme Court in *Hounga v Allen*[4] favoured a discretionary approach, but soon after preferred the 'reliance principle' in *Les Laboratoires Servier v Apotex Inc*.[5] This is confusing. In 2015, the Supreme Court revisited the illegality defence in *Jetivia SA v Bilta (UK) Ltd (In Liquidation)*[6] and conflicting views were again expressed by different judges. Lord Neuberger PSC recognised that 'the proper approach to the defence of illegality needs to be addressed by this court (certainly with a panel of seven and conceivably with a panel of nine Justices) as soon as appropriately possible'.[7] At the time of writing, the appeal in *Patel v Mirza*[8] is expected to be heard by a panel of nine Justices of the Supreme Court in 2016. It is to be hoped that some clarity will be brought to this area of the law.

In the meantime, it is very difficult to know how to approach this topic. Different courts and commentators do not analyse the subject in the same ways. In this chapter, various different types of scenario will be discussed, but it should be recognised that not all judges adopt a similar classification and that the boundaries between each category of case are not watertight.

This chapter will also consider restraint of trade. Restraint of trade and illegality are often considered together in books on contract law. However, it is suggested that a distinction should be drawn between the two. Restraint of trade is concerned with balancing the competing rights of private parties, notably the employer's right to expect a certain degree of loyalty as regards his business against the employee's freedom to leave his employment and to undertake new business activities. This is different from the illegality doctrine, which is really concerned with the claimant's relationship with the court, and the question

---

[1] *Illegal Transactions* (Law Com CP No 154, 1999) para 1.54.
[2] *ParkingEye Ltd v Somerfield Stores Ltd* [2012] EWCA Civ 1338, [2013] QB 840 [28] (Sir Robin Jacob).
[3] [1994] 1 AC 340, HL. Another aspect of the case is considered in Section 7.
[4] [2014] UKSC 47, [2014] 1 WLR 2889.
[5] [2014] UKSC 55, [2015] AC 430.
[6] [2015] UKSC 23, [2015] 2 WLR 1168.
[7] Ibid, [15].
[8] [2014] EWCA Civ 1047, [2015] Ch 271.

of whether the claimant's illegal conduct should bar him from obtaining relief. For this reason, restraint of trade will be considered after illegality at the end of this chapter.

1 Illegality in contract law: an overview

Even though a contract is complete in every respect, a party may be unable to enforce it because of illegality in the making, or in the performance, of the contract. The decision of Lord Mansfield in *Holman v Johnson* has been very influential:[9]

> The objection that a contract is immoral or illegal as between **plaintiff** and defendant, sounds at all times very ill in the mouth of the defendant. It is not for his sake, however, that the objection is ever allowed; but it is founded in general principles of policy, which the defendant has the advantage of, contrary to the real justice as between him and the plaintiff, by accident, if I may say so. The principle of public policy is this; *ex dolo malo non oritur actio*. No court will lend its aid to a man who founds his cause of action upon an immoral or an illegal act. If, from the plaintiff's own stating or otherwise, the cause of action appears to arise *ex turpi causa*, or the transgression of the positive law of this country, there the court says he has no right to be assisted. It is upon that ground the Court goes; not for the sake of the defendant, but because they will not lend their aid to such a plaintiff. So if the plaintiff and defendant were to change sides, and the defendant was to bring his action against the plaintiff, the latter would then have the advantage of it; for where both sides are equally in fault, *potior est conditio defendentis*.

It is important to note that there are two Latin maxims that are particularly prominent in this area. The first is *ex turpi causa non oritur actio*, often shorted to 'ex turpi' or 'ex turpi causa'. This might be translated as 'no cause of action will arise from an illegal act'. So, a person cannot sue on the basis of his own illegal conduct. The second maxim is '*in pari delicto, potior est conditio defendentis*', often shortened to the '*in pari delicto*' principle. This might be translated as 'where the parties are equally culpable, the defendant is in the stronger position'. Thus, if both parties are tainted by the illegality at issue, then the claim will fail since the defendant is in the stronger position.

It is important to recognise at the outset that the application of these maxims can be very blunt. They do not seek to achieve justice as between the parties on the particular facts of a dispute. As Lord Goff recognised in *Tinsley v Milligan*,[10] 'It is important to observe that, as Lord Mansfield made clear, the principle is not a principle of justice; it is a principle of policy, whose application is indiscriminate and so can lead to unfair consequences as between parties to litigation. Moreover the principle allows no room for the exercise of any discretion by the court in favour of one party or the other.'

Tinsley v Milligan concerned a dispute over trusts, and *Apotex* a tort, but it is generally thought that the 'defence'[11] of illegality should apply in a consistent manner throughout the private law. Cases on trusts and tort may therefore be useful when considering how

---

[9] (1775) 1 Cowp 341, 343.

[10] [1994] 1 AC 340, 355.

[11] Since the fact of illegality operates to the advantage of the defendant on the basis of the *in pari delicto* principle.

the illegality defence should operate in contract. The view that *Tinsley* is a House of Lords decision that has not been departed from, and should govern all voluntary transactions including contracts, has been supported by, amongst others, Lord Walker and Lord Brown in *Moore Stephens v Stone & Rolls Ltd*,[12] and consistently by Lord Sumption in *Apotex*[13] and *Jetivia*; in *Jetivia*, Lord Sumption insisted that '*Tinsley v Milligan* is binding authority, subject to review in this court, and in the 20 years since it was decided, the highest court has never been invited to overrule it'.[14] This suggests that the 'reliance principle' should apply in contract law as well: if the claimant needs to rely upon illegality in order to establish his claim he should fail. However, if the claimant does not need to rely upon illegality his claim should succeed.

The reliance principle has been criticised as arbitrary and can lead to capricious results. After a very long review of the law—lasting almost 20 years—the Law Commission concluded that a discretionary approach would be preferable. This would allow the court to balance a range of competing factors in order to achieve justice on the facts of any given case. This approach has been supported by, amongst others, Lord Wilson in *Hounga v Allen* and Lord Toulson in *Jetivia*. It has the advantage of flexibility, but the consequent drawback is that its application can be unpredictable. Moreover, it is not clear how comfortably it sits with the decision of the House of Lords in *Tinsley*. As Lord Neuberger pointed out in *Jetivia*, 'Lord Toulson ... and Lord Hodge favour the approach adopted by the majority of the Court of Appeal in *Tinsley* and treat that of Lord Wilson in ... *Hounga* as supporting that approach.'[15] This might well be desirable, but it is surely difficult to prefer the decision of the Court of Appeal in *Tinsley* to that of the House of Lords in *Tinsley* when the House of Lords expressly overruled the Court of Appeal. If this is to be done, then the decision of the House of Lords in *Tinsley* must be clearly departed from, or legislation is required.

(a) Factors underpinning the illegality defence

Before considering the cases and their application, it is helpful to consider the reasons why a claim might fail due to illegality. These are not clearly articulated in the cases. However, a better understanding of the basis of the law might lead to clarity of thought when seeking to apply the principles underpinning illegality, and further inform what factors should be taken into account if a discretionary approach were to be adopted.

The illegality defence might be applied in order to further the purpose of the rule infringed.[16] This makes sense, but it can obviously be very difficult to decide what the purpose of the rule is. Similarly, the illegality principle is sometimes justified on the basis that it deters illegal conduct.[17] But as Treitel has said, '[d]eterrence by contractual principles is, it is suggested, a hit or miss affair'.[18] Of course, where both parties participate in the illegality,

---

[12] [2009] UKHL 39, [2009] 1 AC 1391 [128]–[131].

[13] *Apotex* [11]–[20].

[14] *Jetivia* [62].

[15] Ibid, [14].

[16] See eg G Treitel, 'Contract and Crime' in C Tapper (ed), *Essays for Sir Rupert Cross* (Butterworths, 1981).

[17] *K/S Lincoln v CB Richard Ellis Hotels Ltd* [2009] EWHC 2344 (TCC) (Coulson J).

[18] G Treitel, 'Contract and Crime' in C Tapper (ed), *Essays for Sir Rupert Cross* (Butterworths, 1981).

then the operation of the illegality defence is likely to deter the claimant but not the defendant, on the basis of the *in pari delicto* principle. The illegality defence might also operate to ensure that a person does not profit from his own wrongdoing,[19] or to ensure that the law is consistent: the criminal law and civil law should not contradict one another.[20] A weaker explanation sometimes given for the illegality defence is that it would offend the dignity of the court to hear cases concerning illegality; this is outdated and should not be given much weight.[21]

The Law Commission drew upon such factors and originally recommended[22] a 'structure discretion' under which the courts should have regard to:

(a) the seriousness of the illegality;

(b) the knowledge and intention of the claimant;

(c) whether refusing to allow standard rights and remedies would deter illegality;

(d) whether refusing to allow standard rights and remedies would further the purpose of the relevant rule;

(e) whether refusing to allow standard rights and remedies is a proportionate response to the claimant's participation.

However, the Law Commission ultimately concluded that legislative reform was not necessary in the area of contract law, and that the courts could develop a discretionary approach by themselves, emphasising that a proportionate, balancing approach was desirable.[23] By contrast, the Law Commission did recommend statutory reform to govern the area of trusts, because the decision of the House of Lords in *Tinsley v Milligan* was an otherwise insurmountable obstacle to judges developing a discretionary approach in that area (unless the Supreme Court departed from *Tinsley*).

Taking into account a wide range of factors allows judges to achieve the result they think fair. But it is difficult to predict, and undermines certainty. It is sometimes argued that those who participate in illegal conduct do not deserve certainty anyway, but it appears unsatisfactory for disputes to continue to escalate to the highest courts and for the leading judgments to be inconsistent. On the basis of *Tinsley v Milligan*, it seems that illegality operates in a blunt, arbitrary manner as a rule of public policy: a person who relies upon illegality should not succeed. (Although there may be a narrow exception where there is a competing public policy (not legal interest) that requires the imposition of civil liability even though the claim is founded on illegal acts.[24])

Often, the different approaches will not lead to different conclusions; in *Jetivia*, for example, both the rule-based and discretionary approaches led to the same result. But it is important to be clear as to what the law is. It is to be hoped that the Supreme Court in *Patel v Mirza* will bring some much-needed clarity and certainty to this topic. For the time

---

[19] eg *Moore Stephens* [226] (Lord Mance).

[20] *Hall v Herbert* [1993] 2 SCR 159; *Gray v Thames Trains Ltd and others* [2009] UKHL 33, [2009] 3 WLR 167.

[21] See eg *Saunders v Edwards* [1987] 1 WLR 1116, 1134 (Bingham LJ).

[22] *Illegal Transactions* (Law Com CP No 154, 1999)

[23] Law Commission, *The Illegality Defence* (Law Com No 32, 2010).

[24] *Jetivia* [101].

being, perhaps the best summary of the law of illegality in the contractual realm remains that of Lord Phillips in *Stone & Rolls Ltd v Moore Stephens Ltd*.[25]

> The policy underlying *ex turpi causa* … can be sub-divided into two principles in relation to contractual obligations:
> i) The court will not enforce a contract which is expressly or impliedly forbidden by statute or that is entered into with the intention of committing an illegal act.
> ii) The court will not assist a claimant to recover a benefit from his own wrongdoing.

2 Where the making of the contract is prohibited

Where the making of the contract is unlawful, neither party can sue on it. As Romer LJ commented in *Alexander v Rayson*, 'It is settled law that an agreement to do an act that is illegal or immoral or contrary to public policy, or to do any act for a consideration that is illegal, immoral or contrary to public policy, is unlawful and therefore void.'[26] Even a party who is unaware of the facts which make the contract illegal, and has been deceived by the other party, is unable to sue upon the contract. This proposition derives from the decision of the Court of Appeal in *Re Mahmoud and Ispahani*.[27] A sale of linseed oil was prohibited by legislation unless both the seller and the buyer had a licence. The claimant, who had a licence to sell, asked the defendant whether he had a licence to buy. The defendant replied that he did. This was untrue, but the claimant believed the defendant and, relying on the defendant's misrepresentation, the claimant agreed to sell linseed oil to the defendant. The defendant subsequently refused to accept delivery and, when sued for damages for non-acceptance, successfully pleaded the illegality of the contract. The contract was expressly forbidden and the court would do nothing to enforce it. Bankes LJ insisted that 'as the language of the Order clearly prohibits the making of this contract, it is open to a party, however shabby it may appear to be, to say that the Legislature has prohibited this contract, and therefore it is a case in which the Court will not lend its aid to the enforcement of the contract'.[28] This was obviously very tough on the claimant, who was clearly the victim of very bad conduct by the defendant. But the court held that it had no discretion about how to apply the statute or illegality defence, and as a question of statutory interpretation the decision might be supported.[29]

In *Mohamed v Alaga & Co*,[30] M, a Somali, contracted with the defendant solicitors that he would introduce Somali asylum-seekers to the firm and assist in the preparation of their cases by translating documents and so on in return for half the fees received by the solicitors from legal aid. Such a fee-sharing agreement is unlawful under rules made by the Law Society. M was unaware of this, but nevertheless he could not recover under the illegal contract. It was held,

---

[25] [2009] UKHL 39, [2009] 3 WLR 455 [26].
[26] [1936] 1 KB 169, 182.
[27] [1921] 2 KB 716.
[28] Ibid, 724.
[29] See too *Phoenix General Insurance Co of Greece SA v Halvanon Insurance Co Ltd* [1988] QB 216. Cf *Hughes v Asset Managers* [1995] 3 All ER 669 where a more purposive approach to statutory interpretation was taken.
[30] [1999] 3 All ER 699.

however, that he could recover a reasonable sum for the professional services of translation he provided. The court, somewhat generously, held that payment for these services was not part of the consideration payable under the unlawful contract, and it was only the payment of the 'introduction fees' that was unlawful. The court was very much influenced by the fact that M was less blameworthy than the solicitors, who either knew, or certainly ought to have known, of the illegal nature of the agreement. Nevertheless, it is not entirely clear whether it is appropriate for the court to sever the payment for translation from payment for introduction. The court held that it was not giving effect to the contract, and that payment for the translation services was only possible through a claim in unjust enrichment rather than contract,[31] but it is possible to think that in substance the court was giving effect to an illegal contract.

It follows that an agreement to commit a crime is not enforceable. Every agreement to commit a crime, even an offence triable only summarily, is indictable as a conspiracy. In other words, the agreement itself is an offence.[32] An agreement to defraud, even where the fraud contemplated does not amount to a crime, is also sufficient for the crime of conspiracy. In *Miller v Karlinski*,[33] an employer agreed to pay his employee £10 a week plus expenses. It was agreed that his 'expenses' should include the amount of income tax payable on his salary. The parties were effectively agreeing to defraud the Revenue. As a result, the employee's action to recover the **arrears** of his salary payments failed. The fraudulent term was not severable from the rest of the agreement, and invalidated the whole contract.

Moreover, an agreement to deceive is not saved from the taint of illegality because it is shown to be a common practice in trade or business. In *Brown Jenkinson & Co Ltd v Percy Dalton (London) Ltd*,[34] shippers of orange juice were advised by the shipowner that the barrels were old and leaking. The shipowner advised that a 'claused' **bill of lading**[35] should be issued but the shipper wanted a 'clean' bill and agreed to indemnify the shipowner if he would issue a bill stating that the barrels were 'shipped in apparent good order and condition'. The shipowner did so. When the barrels arrived, they were leaking and the shipowner had to compensate the holder of the bill. His action under the indemnity failed. As Morris LJ said, 'the promise upon which the claimants rely is in effect this: if you will make a false representation, which will deceive indorsees or bankers, we will indemnify you against any loss that may result to you'. The majority were unimpressed by the claim that such practice was common. By contrast, the dissenting judge, Lord Evershed MR, accepted the trial judge's view that the shipowners did not intend anyone to suffer any loss (presumably because any holder of the bill would be compensated) and that, though they may have been thoughtless and misguided, they were not dishonest.

---

[31] See Chapter 28, Section 4.
[32] Criminal Law Act 1977, s 1(1).
[33] (1945) 62 TLR 85.
[34] [1957] 2 QB 621, CA.
[35] Which is a bill of lading that shows a shortfall or damage to the delivered goods.

(a) **Implied prohibition of contracts**

In *St John Shipping Corp v Joseph Rank Ltd*,[36] and in *Archbolds (Freightage) Ltd v S Spanglett Ltd*,[37] there was much discussion of the question of the implied prohibition by Parliament of contracts. In the former case, Devlin J said, *obiter*, that since statute forbids the use of an unlicensed vehicle on a highway, 'there may well be' an implied prohibition of all contracts for the use of unlicensed vehicles. Such comments seem unnecessarily hesitant. It is surely possible to answer the question more categorically, at least on the assumption (which Devlin J appears to have made) that both parties know the vehicle to be unlicensed. Of course, the contract is prohibited because it is a conspiracy—it was a common law conspiracy when Devlin J decided the *St John Shipping* case and it is now a statutory conspiracy contrary to section 1 of the Criminal Law Act 1977. But if the hirer does not know that the vehicle is unlicensed then surely the contract is not prohibited because, as Devlin LJ said in the *Archbolds* case, there is probably an implied warranty that the vehicle is licensed. The hirer could sue on the contract for breach of the implied warranty. Of course, the letter of the vehicle would not be able to sue on the contract since he committed an illegal act in letting an unlicensed vehicle.

In the *St John* case, Devlin J said that contracts for the carriage of goods by unlicensed vehicles and contracts for the repairing or the garaging of unlicensed vehicles may well be different. Repairing and garaging would not in themselves involve any illegality and the agreements to repair or garage would not constitute criminal conspiracies. Devlin J, in a passage approved by Pearce LJ in *Archbolds'* case, said: 'The answer might be that collateral contracts of this sort are not within the ambit of the statute.' This is because the statute concerns the use of unlicensed vehicles on the road. As a result, not only could the repairer or garager sue on the contract, but the owner of the vehicle might also be able to enforce it. However, the owner would not be able to invoke the illegal use, or proposed illegal use, of the vehicle in support of his claim; indeed, the owner might be unable to advance his claim by showing that it had broken down, or that he had been prevented from using it, on a road. Furthermore, it is arguable that, if the repairer or garager knew of the intention to use the vehicle on the road, he would be guilty of aiding and abetting that use if it occurred;[38] and if the repairer or garager was an accessory to a crime, he could hardly be allowed to enforce the contract.

In *Archbolds v Spanglett*, the contract was for the carriage of a load of whisky from Leeds to London. The carrier performed the contract illegally since he used a vehicle for which he did not hold the requisite 'A' licence, and without that licence he was not entitled to carry the goods of others for reward. Unfortunately, the load of whisky was lost through the negligence of the driver. The claimants' action for the loss of their whisky succeeded. They neither knew, nor ought to have known, that the defendants did not have an 'A' licence. The contract of carriage was not prohibited, expressly or impliedly, and the claimants were guilty of no illegality. However, if they had known that the defendants had no 'A' licence,

---

[36] [1957] 1 QB 267.

[37] [1961] 1 QB 374, CA.

[38] D Ormerod and K Laird, *Smith and Hogan's Criminal Law* (14th edn, OUP, 2015) ch 8.4.

they would have been aiding and abetting the offence and presumably the claim would have failed.

3 Where the purpose of the parties is contrary to public policy

We have already seen that where the very making of a contract is illegal, or the performance of the contract necessarily involved the commission of a crime (or at least fraud), the doctrine of illegality can apply to prevent a party from suing upon the contract. However, the scope of 'illegality' in the law of contract appears to go beyond this. Adultery, fornication, and prostitution are not crimes in England, but contracts made with the purpose of promoting them have been regarded as 'illegal' and invalid. For instance, in *Pearce v Brooks*,[39] the contract was one of **hire-purchase** of a carriage, a miniature brougham, which in isolation seems harmless enough. But when the defendant returned the brougham in a damaged condition after paying only the second instalment, the claimant's action for breach of contract failed. The defendant pleaded successfully that the purpose of hiring the carriage, as the claimant well knew, was to enable her to pursue her calling as a prostitute. The claimant knew that he was assisting the defendant in her immoral purpose and that was enough for the court to hold that he could not enforce the contract. It was immaterial that it was not part of the contract that she should use it for the purposes of prostitution, and that it was not proved that he was to be paid out of the proceeds of the prostitution. It is therefore clear that the supplier of goods and services which he knows to be required solely for the purpose of prostitution cannot sue for the price; indeed, a supplier who receives such monies is probably guilty of the crime of living, in part, on the earnings of prostitution.[40]

However, the supplier of the ordinary necessities of life[41] can recover the price, notwithstanding his awareness of the fact that his customer is a prostitute who could not carry on without them. Bramwell B, in the course of argument in *Pearce v Brooks*, gave the example of shoes sold to a streetwalker. The shoes will certainly assist her in the practice of her profession, but she must have shoes regardless of her profession, so she may be required to pay for them. There is an exception to this principle where an excessive charge is made for the very reason that the other party is a prostitute, such as where a landlord charges an exorbitant rent because the property will be used for prostitution. In such circumstances, the landlord is probably guilty of the offence of living on the earnings of prostitution and, if so, it is clear that he cannot sue on the contract.

Public policy is a changing concept. At one time a contract by a man to take a flat for his mistress was treated as illegal;[42] but changing attitudes to sexual morality are such that the decision is unlikely to be followed today. Indeed, the Law Commission has recognised that

---

[39] (1866) LR 1 Ex 213.
[40] See Sexual Offences Act 2003, s 53.
[41] See Chapter 20, Section 1(c).
[42] *Upfill v Wright* [1911] 1 KB 506, not followed in *Heglibiston Establishment v Heyman* (1977) 36 P & CR 351.

the changing approaches to public policy mean that deciding what constitutes illegality 'is a surprisingly difficult question to answer'.[43]

4 Where the contract is lawfully made but carried out in an unlawful manner

In the cases considered so far, the contract was in some way tainted with illegality at the moment it was made. But even if a contract was perfectly lawful when made, and made for a lawful purpose, it may nonetheless be carried out in an illegal manner. If it is, the party or parties responsible for the illegal performance may be debarred from enforcing the contract. Whether a party is so debarred depends on whether the illegal act is central to the performance of the contract or merely incidental.[44]

In *Anderson v Daniel*,[45] the contract was for the sale of fertiliser. There is nothing wrong with that; but statute required the seller to deliver, along with the goods, an invoice stating their composition. It was an offence to fail to do so. The seller delivered 10 tons of artificial manure but no invoice. The buyer refused to pay, and the seller's claim for the contract price failed. This is a somewhat harsh result. The seller is liable to such punishment in a criminal court as is appropriate to his offence. But in addition to that, the seller also loses the value of the goods, even though there may be nothing wrong with them. The buyer, on the other hand, appears to be unjustly enriched. He can keep the goods without paying anything. Moreover, if the goods are defective, the seller's illegal performance of the contract does not debar the buyer from suing on it, unless the buyer has aided and abetted the seller's offence.

However, not every illegality committed in the course of performing a contract has this drastic effect. It would be absurd if a carrier were to be debarred from recovering the cost of carrying goods from London to Newcastle because his driver exceeded the speed limit at one point on the journey; or that a manufacturer should be unable to recover the cost of goods made in his factory because one of his machines was not fenced as required by law. Such circumstances are readily distinguishable from *Anderson v Daniel*: the offence in *Anderson v Daniel* existed for the protection of the buyer, whereas speed limits exist for the protection of the public and factory legislation for the protection of the workers in the factory.

In *St John Shipping Corp v Joseph Rank Ltd*,[46] the contract was for the **charter** of a ship to carry grain. In the course of the voyage, the master put into port and took on an additional load which submerged the ship's loadline. That was an offence under the Merchant Shipping Act 1932, for which the master was fined £1,200. The consignee withheld part of the freight due under the contract, and argued that the shipowner could not recover it due to his illegality. Devlin J held that the shipowner was entitled to recover the entire freight, since the illegal act was merely incidental to the performance of the contract. In *Shaw v Groom*,[47] a **landlord** failed to provide a **tenant** with a rent book as required by the

---

[43] Law Commission Consultation Paper, *Illegal Transactions* (Law Com No 154, 1999) para 1.54.
[44] *ParkingEye Ltd v Somerfield Stores Ltd* [2012] EWCA Civ 1338, [2013] QB 840.
[45] [1924] 1 KB 138.
[46] [1957] 1 QB 267.
[47] [1970] 2 QB 504, CA.

Landlord and Tenant Act 1962. Though this was an offence on his part, he was entitled to recover arrears of rent. This was not an obvious conclusion: the rent book is clearly for the protection of the tenant, and the case is not easily distinguishable from *Anderson v Daniel*. The court thought that the rent book was not essential to the contract of letting (even though it had been provided). That may have been true; but, then, was the invoice specifying composition any more essential to the contract of sale of fertiliser? The court attributed the result to the intention of the legislature: Parliament intended the landlord to be subjected to the prescribed penalty but did not intend that he should be precluded from recovering unpaid rent. This is really a fiction. The only intention expressed by Parliament in any of these cases is to impose the criminal penalty. The effect on a contract, if any, is invented by the court. Different courts take different views, and that explains why some cases (such as *Anderson v Daniel* and *Shaw v Groom*) are very difficult to reconcile.

In a series of employment law cases, it has recently been questioned whether the 'reliance principle' from *Tinsley v Milligan* should be applied. For example, in *Colen v Cebrian (UK) Ltd*[48] Waller LJ said: 'If the person seeking to enforce the contract has to rely on his illegal action in order to succeed then the court will not assist him. But if he does not have to do so, then in my view the question is whether the method of performance chosen and the degree of participation in that illegal performance is such as to "turn the contract into an illegal contract".' But if the person seeking to enforce the contract has to show that he has performed his side of the bargain in order to be able to enforce the other party's obligations, this may invariably involve relying upon illegality during the course of performance. As a result, in *Hall v Woolston Hall*[49] a different Court of Appeal took a different approach. Peter Gibson LJ said: 'In cases where the contract of employment is neither entered into for an illegal purpose nor prohibited by statute, the illegal performance of the contract will not render the contract unenforceable unless in addition to knowledge of the facts which make the performance illegal the employee actively participates in the illegal performance. It is a question of fact in each case whether there has been a sufficient degree of participation by the employee.'

This issue resurfaced in the decision of the Supreme Court in *Hounga v Allen*.[50] Miss Hounga worked as an au pair for the Allens. The Allens had fraudulently procured a visitor's visa for Miss Hounga, and knew she had no right to work in the UK. Some time later, the Allens dismissed Miss Hounga, and Miss Hounga sought relief in the statutory tort of discrimination. The Supreme Court, allowing the appeal, held that Miss Hounga's illegal conduct in working illegally did not bar her from obtaining relief. The Supreme Court recognised the force of the reliance test in *Tinsley*, but emphasised that all the policy factors needed to be taken into account when deciding whether the illegality should operate as a defence. After all, if Miss Hounga had to show that she worked in the UK in order to make good her claim, she would have had to introduce evidence of illegal activity. The Supreme Court held that such an approach was inappropriate. Their Lordships were influenced by the fact that the Allens were at greater fault than Miss Hounga, that employers should not be allowed to discriminate against workers—even illegal workers—with impunity, and

---

[48] [2003] EWCA Civ 1676, [2004] ICR 568 [23].
[49] [2001] ICR 99 [38].
[50] [2014] UKSC 47, [2014] 1 WLR 2889.

that the need to combat illegal trafficking of workers meant that illegal workers should not be prevented from bringing civil law claims. The Supreme Court suggested that there should be an 'inextricable link' between the illegality and the claim, which was lacking on the facts. The 'inextricable link' test is notoriously difficult and should probably be jettisoned,[51] but the result of *Hounga* must be correct. The illegal conduct of Miss Hounga must be trumped by wider considerations of public policy relating to the need to prevent human trafficking and discrimination.

5 Where the contract is so devised as to enable one party to perpetrate a fraud

Even though neither the contract nor the performance of it involves any illegality, if a party has deliberately devised it in such a form as to enable him to perpetrate a fraud then that party may be debarred from enforcing the contract on the basis of the illegality principle. In *Alexander v Rayson*,[52] the claimant let a serviced flat to the defendant. In one document he leased the premises at a rent of £450 a year; in another, he agreed to provide certain services for £750 a year. This looks somewhat eccentric, since the flat was substantially undervalued and the services grossly overvalued. However, the court is not interested in the adequacy of the consideration and there is nothing inherently wrong with such an arrangement. But when the claimant sued for unpaid rent, it was alleged that his purpose, unknown to the defendant at the time, was to produce the **lease** to the rating authority as evidence that the premises were worth only £450 a year in order to obtain a reduction in the rates he would have to pay for the premises. The Court of Appeal held that, if that were so, the claimant could not sue on either agreement. And if the defendant had been a party to the fraud, it would have been a conspiracy to defraud.[53] As the defendant was innocent, the agreement was not an offence but, at most, an act preparatory to the commission of an offence by the claimant. In effect, the defendant therefore could not be sued for the rent, and so lived in the flat rent-free.

6 Where one party to the contract has an illegal purpose

Where only one party has an illegal purpose, the agreement does not amount to a conspiracy and is not prohibited as such. Nevertheless, if the performance of the contract by A would assist B in the commission of an offence, A cannot be liable for breach of contract in refusing to perform when he learns of the illegal purpose. The law as a whole must be consistent: the law cannot hold both that A is criminally liable as an aider and abettor if he performs the contract and also that A is liable for breach of contract if he does not. The

---

[51] *Gray v Thames Trains Ltd* [2009] UKHL 33, [2009] 1 AC 1339.
[52] [1936] 1 KB 169, CA.
[53] cf *R v Hollinshead* [1985] AC 975, HL.

law is clear: not only may *A* properly refuse to perform, he must refuse to perform. If *A* has contracted to sell weedkiller to *B*—a contract perfectly lawful in itself—and only later discovers that *B*'s purpose is to administer the substance not to the weeds but to his wife, then not only is *A* entitled to refuse to deliver the weedkiller, but he is bound to refuse to do so. In *Cowan v Milbourn*,[54] the defendant agreed to let a room to the claimant for a series of lectures. He then discovered that the lectures were of a blasphemous character (which at the time was a crime) and refused the claimant the room. It was held that he was not only entitled but bound to do so.

However, there is a point at which the court will conclude that *B*'s intention to commit an illegal act is too remote from the contract itself such that the contract should not be held to be unenforceable by *B*. An illustration of this is to be found in the decision of Field J in *21st Century Logistic Solutions Ltd v Madysen Ltd*.[55] *B* intended to perpetrate a 'carousel fraud', by which he would buy goods from abroad without paying VAT, then sell those goods in the UK with VAT added, and keep the added VAT without paying customs. One of *B*'s buyers, *A*, alerted the authorities, and *B* entered into **liquidation**. However, the judge held that *B* was able to enforce the contract of sale with *A*, even though *B* had entered into the contract with an illegal purpose in mind: *B*'s illegal purpose was too remote to have an effect on its contract with *A*. Admittedly, this is not entirely easy to reconcile with cases such as *Alexander v Rayson*, apart from by concluding that issues of remoteness will depend on the particular facts of a particular case.

7 The effect of an illegal contract

It is important to appreciate that property may pass under an illegal contract. It has been seen in Chapter 6 that, where a contract is void because of a mistake of identity, whether of the subject matter of the contract or of a party to it, ownership does not pass to the buyer, even by delivery.[56] Yet even though contracts tainted by illegality are commonly described as 'void', it seems clear that property in the subject matter may pass from one party to the other (whether that be full ownership (described as 'the general property') or some lesser proprietary interest (designated 'a special property')). Illegality therefore seems to have an unusual effect upon a contract, since the contract is not without any effect at all, which is normally what is understood by the term 'void'.

Thus in *Singh v Ali*,[57] the Privy Council very clearly held that the property in a lorry passed when it was sold and delivered under an illegal contract. Lord Denning said:[58]

> Although the transaction between the plaintiff and the defendant was illegal, nevertheless it was fully executed and carried out: and on that account it was effective to pass the property in the lorry to the plaintiff ... The reason is because the transferor, having fully achieved his

---

[54] (1867) 2 Ex 230.
[55] [2004] EWHC 231 (QB), [2004] 2 Lloyd's Rep 92. See too *Anglo Petroleum Ltd v TFB (Mortgages) Ltd* [2007] EWCA Civ 456, [2007] BCC 407.
[56] See Chapter 6, Section 2.
[57] [1960] AC 167, PC.
[58] Ibid, 176.

unworthy end, cannot be allowed to turn round and **repudiate** the means by which he did it—he cannot throw over the transfer, and the transferee, having obtained the property, can assert his **title** to it against all the world, not because he has any merit of his own, but because there is no one who can assert a better title to it. The court does not confiscate the property because of the illegality—it has no power to do so—so it says, in the words of Lord Eldon: 'Let the estate lie where it falls'; see *Muckleston v. Brown*.

This clearly states the position in English law. So, in *Belvoir Finance Co v Stapleton*,[59] the Court of Appeal held that the claimants acquired a good title to cars under a contract of sale which amounted to a criminal conspiracy, even though the cars were never actually delivered to the claimants but rather to the car-hire firm which hired the cars from the claimants on hire-purchase terms.

(a) Circumventing the problems of illegal contracts

A contract may be illegal and therefore unenforceable, but it is clear that a claimant may seek to bring a different claim in order to obtain redress from a defendant. One major example concerns property rights: we have just seen that even though a contract may be unenforceable, a claimant may rely upon property rights that have passed under that contract. And by simply relying upon his property rights, a claimant does not need to rely upon any illegality.

Judges have also sometimes been quite creative in finding alternative ways to avoid applying the harsh rules of illegality to concluded contracts. For example, in *Strongman (1945) LD v Sincock*,[60] an architect owner contracted with builders to supply materials and carry out work at his premises. The architect gave an oral promise that he would obtain all the **licences** necessary for the work. Unfortunately, the work carried out was considerably in excess of the licences granted. The builders claimed the balance of the price of the work done over the licensed amount, but were unable to sue upon the contract because it was illegal under the regulations governing the licences.

However, the Court of Appeal held that the assurance from the architect that he would obtain the licences amounted to a warranty or a collateral contract that he would obtain the licences necessary for all the work, including the excess, and that he would stop the work if he could not obtain them. The architect had breached this obligation, and the builders succeeded in an action for damages for this breach. Denning LJ held that there was an important difference between enforcing the illegal contract and enforcing the collateral promise which was not tainted by illegality, but this distinction seems thin. Denning LJ emphasised that the builders were not wrongdoers, but the builders were professionals who should have understood the importance of the regulations and of written contracts. It is suggested that *Strongman (1945) LD v Sincock* was a generous decision, and that a court might be slow to find that a collateral agreement has been concluded.

Similarly, a court will be reluctant to find that a claim can succeed simply by relabelling it. So, if the contract is void for illegality, the claimant should not be able to succeed simply

---

[59] [1971] 1 QB 210.
[60] [1955] 2 QB 525.

by pleading the same facts as the basis for an **estoppel**[61] or a tort,[62] for instance. A good example is the case of *Parkinson v College of Ambulance Ltd and Harrison*.[63] The secretary of a charity fraudulently misrepresented to the claimant that, if the claimant made a large donation to the charity, he or the charity was in a position to ensure that the claimant would receive a knighthood. After making the donation but not receiving the knighthood, the claimant brought an action against the charity and its secretary. The claim failed. Lush J was clear that the contract was void for illegality: buying and selling honours is a crime. Equally, reframing the claim in tort (for **deceit**) or unjust enrichment must fail in the same way: *in pari delicto potior est conditio defendentis*. Both parties had acted badly, and the robust application of the illegality defence meant that the defendant was in a stronger position. Of course, if the claimant and defendant are not equally guilty, then the *in pari delicto* principle may not apply, such that the (more) innocent party could recover benefits transferred in an action in unjust enrichment.[64]

Another interesting illustration of this principle is the decision of the Court of Appeal in *Taylor v Bhail*.[65] The defendant headmaster agreed to employ the claimant builder to repair the roof of a school if the builder falsely inflated his estimate of the cost of the work in order to enable the headmaster to defraud the school's insurance company. The actual cost of the work was £12,480. Having paid £7,400, the headmaster refused to pay any more. The contract was unenforceable due to the illegality, and the Court of Appeal rejected the builder's attempt to claim instead in unjust enrichment. Millett LJ commented that '[t]he refusal of the court to enforce illegal contracts often leads to injustice and the unjust enrichment of a defendant', but, on the peculiar facts of the case, his Lordship felt 'some satisfaction' with the outcome:[66] the application of the illegality defence actually had the effect of roughly splitting the losses between the claimant and defendant, both of whom were willing parties to the same fraud. The builder was left about £5,000 out of pocket, and the headmaster £7,400 out of pocket (since he was unable to claim on the insurance). But this loss-splitting effect was entirely fortuitous, and it should be noted that the courts remain powerless to shape the outcome of a case in this way. This is because the illegality defence is not a principle of justice but of policy, designed to be uniformly applied rather than tailored to the particular facts of a case.

(b) Recovery of property transferred under an illegal contract

Cases concerning the recovery of property transferred under an illegal contract tend to focus upon the reliance principle. A leading case is *Taylor v Chester*.[67] The claimant claimed the return of half of a £50 banknote, which he alleged had been delivered to the defendant but was to be returned on request. The defendant pleaded that the half note had been deposited with her by way of a **pledge** to secure the repayment of money due from the claimant

---

[61] *Actionstrength Ltd v International Glass Engineering and St Gobain* [2003] UKHL 17, [2003] 2 AC 541.
[62] *Shelley v Paddock* [1980] QB 348.
[63] [1925] 2 KB 1.
[64] See eg *Oom v Bruce* (1810) 12 East 225.
[65] [1996] CLC 377.
[66] Ibid, 383.
[67] (1869) LR 4 QB 309.

to the defendant and not paid. The claimant's reply was that the money due was to be used for the purposes of debauchery in a disorderly house kept by the defendant. The claimant's action failed. This is often said to be because he had to disclose his own iniquity. However, the true reason why the claim failed was because, following *Scarfe v Morgan*,[68] the special property in the half note had passed to the defendant. Although the court referred to the *in pari delicto* maxim, and to the fact that the claimant was relying on the illegal nature of the transaction to recover his property, it seems that the principal reason why the defendant succeeded was that she had a special property in the note which entitled her to retain it until the money due was tendered. If the money due had been tendered, then the question would have arisen whether the claimant was debarred by the illegality from recovering his own property, because the tender of the amount for which the note was pledged would have freed the property from the defendant's special property in it. *Bowmakers Ltd v Barnet Instruments Ltd*[69] suggests that Taylor could then have sued successfully for the **conversion** of the half note.

In the *Bowmakers* case, there were three agreements under which Bowmakers let machine tools to the defendants on hire-purchase. All were assumed to be illegal, since they contravened a statutory instrument regulating hire-purchase transactions. The defendants, having fallen behind with the instalments, sold the machines which were the subjects of agreements 1 and 3 and refused to deliver up the one which was the subject of agreement 2. The defendants thereby committed breaches of contract. The claimants sued successfully in conversion. The ownership in the tools had passed from the original owner, Smith, to the claimants, notwithstanding the illegality of the transaction. And the claimants were not debarred from asserting their proprietary rights against the defendants merely because the goods had come into the possession of the defendants in the course of an illegal transaction. *Taylor v Chester* was distinguished on the ground that there the defendant had a right in possession of the half note since she was holding it as a pledge for money which remained due. Now, if Bowmakers had acquired the general property in the tools from Smith, notwithstanding the illegality of the whole transaction, it followed that the defendants had acquired a special property by reason of the **bailment**; but, in the case of agreements 1 and 3, this had been terminated by the sale of the tools. In respect of agreement 2, however, the defendants were still in possession of the tool. The claimants could show that they were entitled to possession of it only by proving that the defendants were in breach of the illegal agreement. To that extent, they appear to have been allowed to rely on it; but the case is still different from *Taylor v Chester* for there the claimant was relying not on a breach of the agreement but on the illegality of the agreement.

These cases were followed in *Tinsley v Milligan*,[70] in which the House of Lords held that the principles applicable to legal property rights in the *Bowmakers* case are equally applicable to equitable property. *T* and *M* jointly bought a house for use as a lodging house, but registered the property in the sole name of *T*, so that *M* could make false claims to the Department of Social Security for benefits. *T* and *M* later fell out, and *T* claimed that the house belonged to her alone. A bare majority of the House of Lords held that, since *M*

---

[68] (1838) 4 M & W 270.
[69] [1945] KB 65.
[70] [1994] 1 AC 340, HL.

had contributed to the purchase price, the presumption of a resulting trust applied so that she could establish an equitable interest in the property without relying in any way on the underlying illegality.[71] She was not seeking to enforce an illegal contract, but instead founding her case on a right of property acquired under the contract.

(i) *Locus poenitentiae*—'time for repentance'

One of the difficulties with the reliance principle is that, in a case like *Tinsley v Milligan*, the relationship between the parties is of paramount importance. In *Tinsley* itself, *T* and *M* were in a lesbian relationship, such that when *M* gave property to *T* a presumption of resulting trust applied.[72] However, if *M* and *T* had been husband and wife respectively, then a presumption of **gift** (not trust) would have arisen, and *M* would not have been able to assert any equitable interest in the property, since in order to do so he would have had to rely upon the illegal scheme, and reliance on illegality is forbidden. This highlights the arbitrariness of the reliance principle.

The courts have therefore sought to work around this problem. One doctrine that has been invoked is that of withdrawal. If a party seeks to withdraw from an illegal transaction within the '*locus poenitentiae*' or 'time for repentance', then that party can rely upon evidence of the illegal scheme in order to recover property transferred pursuant to that scheme. However, it is important that none of the illegal conduct has yet been carried out; otherwise it is too late to withdraw from the illegality. In *Tribe v Tribe*,[73] a father transferred **shares** to his son, on the understanding that the son would return the shares to the father on the father's request. The father's purpose was to defraud his **creditors** by hiding his assets. However, the creditors never made any demands from the father. When the father asked for the shares back from his son, the son refused. The Court of Appeal allowed the father's claim. A presumption of advancement, or gift, arose between the father and son, but the father was able to rebut that presumption by relying on the illegal purpose, since the father had withdrawn from the illegality within the *locus poenitentiae*. This decision is difficult to explain: after all, the father's purpose of hiding his assets from his creditors while there was a danger was fulfilled,[74] so it is not obvious that the father withdrew from the illegality before any part of the illegal purpose was carried into effect.[75] However, *Tribe* does make it clear that genuine, or moral, repentance is not required,[76] and it may well be that withdrawal may be effective even if it was not truly 'voluntary' but the claimant was left with no other choice.[77]

---

[71] The presumption of advancement may soon be abolished: see the Equality Act 2010, s 199; PS Davies and G Virgo, *Equity & Trusts: Text, Cases, and Materials* (OUP, 2013) ch 8.

[72] Although it may now be that in the context of family homes the focus should really be on constructive trusts not resulting trusts following *Stack v Dowden*: PS Davies and G Virgo, *Equity & Trusts: Text, Cases, and Materials* (OUP, 2013) ch 9.

[73] [1996] Ch 107.

[74] See eg F Rose, 'Gratuitous Transfers and Illegal Purposes' (1996) 112 LQR 386, 389–90.

[75] Indeed, the withdrawal appears to lie simply in the fact that the father brought a claim for restitution.

[76] cf *Bigos v Bousted* [1951] 1 All ER 92.

[77] *Patel v Mirza* [2014] EWCA Civ 1047, [2015] Ch 271; an appeal will be heard by the Supreme Court in 2016.

8 Void contracts

Occasionally Parliament declares a particular type of contract to be not illegal or an offence but to be void. The most conspicuous examples were of betting contracts, which used to be void under section 18 of the Gaming Act 1845, but under the Gambling Act 2005 betting contracts are no longer necessarily void.

However, public policy also attributes the effect of voidness rather than illegality to certain agreements. The difference appears to be that an illegal term in an agreement is said to taint the whole contract, generally including collateral transactions (unless it is possible to sever the offending term whilst still maintaining the agreement intended by the parties and not offending considerations of public policy). A term which is merely void does not have this effect. In appropriate circumstances, such a term may be severed from the rest of the contract which remains valid. The most important examples are contracts in restraint of trade and contracts to oust the jurisdiction of the courts. Only the former category is discussed in this chapter.

9 Contracts in restraint of trade

There are three principal categories of such agreements:[78]

(a) the vendor of a business covenants that he will not compete with the purchaser;

(b) an employee covenants with his employer that he will not compete with him on leaving his employment;

(c) a group of traders contract to regulate their prices, or output, and so on.

The third type of agreement is now regulated by the Competition Act 1998 and is not examined here.[79] The first two types are governed by the principles stated by Lord Macnaghten in *Nordenfelt's Case*[80] and Lord Parker in *Herbert Morris & Co v Saxelby*.[81] Since it is in the public interest that people should follow their calling and pursue their trades, all **covenants** in restraint of trade are **prima facie** contrary to public policy and void. However, a covenant may be upheld if:

(i) the covenantee shows that it is reasonable as between the parties to it; and

(ii) the covenantor does not show that it is unreasonable in the public interest.

The courts take a less strict view of covenants between vendor and purchaser than of similar covenants between employer and employee. If the vendor of a business were free immediately to set up in competition next door, the purchaser would not get what he had

---

[78] However, the categories are not closed: see eg *Proactive Sports Management Ltd v Rooney* [2011] EWCA Civ 1444, [2012] 2 All ER (Comm) 815 [93] (Arden LJ): 'a person's ancillary activity of exploiting his image rights is just as capable of protection under the doctrine of restraint of trade as any other occupation'.

[79] See R Whish and D Bailey, *Competition Law* (8th edn, OUP, 2015) ch 9.

[80] [1894] AC 535.

[81] [1916] AC 688.

paid for, so it will usually be fairly easy to establish that it is reasonable that some degree of restraint be imposed on the vendor. The restraint must, however, be no wider in terms of time and area than is necessary to protect the proprietary interest acquired by the purchaser. So, a covenant by the vendor of the goodwill of a brewer's licence that he will not brew beer is invalid if the vendor has never brewed beer; this is because there is no goodwill, in respect of beer, to protect.[82] If the vendor's business is worldwide, then a worldwide covenant may be upheld; but if the business has only a limited area of operation, a covenant precluding the vendor from carrying on business outside that area will be invalid. In *Ronbar Enterprises Ltd v Green*,[83] an agreement between partners in a weekly paper provided that if one bought the other out, the vendor should not 'carry on or be engaged in any business similar to or competing with the business of the partnership' for five years. The words 'similar to' were too wide because a 'similar' business might be anywhere in the world, which would be far wider than was necessary to protect the purchaser's interest in a paper with a very limited circulation. However, the court held that the offending words could be severed; and a covenant against joining a 'competing' business was valid because the purchaser was entitled to be protected against competition from the vendor for a reasonable period of time. If the words 'or competing with' had not been included in the covenant it would have failed altogether.

A restraint upon an employee will be upheld only where it is reasonably necessary to protect a proprietary right of the employer in the nature of a trade connection or trade secrets. The employer is not entitled to protect himself against mere competition by his former employees. But, if he can show that his former employee has acquired knowledge of a secret process or method of manufacture, he is entitled to enforce such restraint on the employee as will afford reasonable protection to that interest. A similar approach is adopted where the nature of the employment is such that the employee may acquire the trust of, or influence over, the customers, such that the customers may well take their business away with the employee if he sets up in competition. In *Fitch v Dewes*,[84] it was held that a contract by a solicitor's clerk that he would not practise within seven miles of Tamworth Town Hall was valid, even though it was unlimited in time.[85] Of course, the wider the covenant in terms of time and place, the heavier the onus on the covenantee to prove that it is reasonable.

The courts will not allow an employer to achieve indirectly what he cannot do directly. In *Kores Manufacturing Co Ltd v Kolok Manufacturing Co Ltd*,[86] two companies agreed that neither would, without the consent of the other, employ any person who had been an employee of the other within the previous five years. Although the agreement was made between two employers, its effect was to restrain employees and so was subject to the same tests. Both companies had trade secrets which they were entitled to protect. But the agreement applied to all employees, some of whom would have no access to secret information of any kind. As a result, the agreement was far wider than necessary and it was impossible

---

[82] *Vancouver Malt and Sake Brewing Co Ltd v Vancouver Breweries Ltd* [1934] AC 181, PC.

[83] [1954] 2 All ER 266.

[84] [1921] 2 AC 158, HL.

[85] It would now be generally expected that a restrictive covenant would be limited to a reasonable period of time.

[86] [1959] Ch 108, CA.

to sever it so as to render it applicable only to employees who were likely to learn the company's secrets. The agreement was therefore invalid.

In *Bull v Pitney-Bowes Ltd*,[87] the offending provision was in the company's pension scheme. The clause provided that any retired member who became employed in any activity in competition with the company, and who failed to discontinue the activity when required to do so, would be liable to forfeit his pension rights. Thesiger J held that the pension scheme was part of the contract of employment and the provision was void as an unreasonable restraint of trade.

The doctrine of restraint of trade affords no protection to a person who buys or leases land subject to a restrictive covenant. He has no right to be on the land, let alone trade there, before he obtains possession under the contract. Even though his right to trade on the land is limited, or non-existent, he is deprived of no right which he previously enjoyed; instead, he acquires some new rights.[88] However, the doctrine of restraint of trade does apply where a person already trading on a particular site accepts some restriction on his freedom to do so in future. In *Esso Petroleum Co Ltd v Harper's Garage (Stourport) Ltd*,[89] the owner of two garages entered into contracts (known as 'solus agreements') with Esso that he would buy only their fuel and sell it at their retail prices and comply with various other conditions. This agreement was subject to the restraint of trade doctrine. It restricted the right previously enjoyed by the owner to buy petrol from whomsoever he pleased. But, since the application of the solus system in this case was for the benefit of both parties, the restraint was reasonable and enforceable.

In the *Alec Lobb*[90] case, Alec Lobb Ltd, in order to solve its financial difficulties, leased the site of its garage to Total Oil Ltd for 51 years at a peppercorn rent in consideration of the payment by Total of a premium of £25,000 and a sub-lease of the garage to Mr and Mrs Lobb. This also included a solus agreement. Mr and Mrs Lobb had no previous legal interest in the site, because it had belonged to their company; but the court would not allow the doctrine to be evaded by a device of this kind. Mr and Mrs Lobb were granted the sub-lease only because they were the proprietors of the company previously in occupation. The court has 'ample power to pierce the corporate veil' and recognise a continuing identity of occupation. But, again, the restraints were reasonable and valid.

Similar principles apply to contracts for the entire services of another person. In *Schroeder Music Publishing Co Ltd v Macaulay*,[91] the claimant was a young and then unknown songwriter who signed the defendant company's standard form assigning to the company the copyright in anything produced by the claimant for five years and, if the royalties reached a total of £5,000, for a further five years. The defendant did not undertake to exploit his work, though the company did agree to pay royalties on any work in fact exploited. The company could terminate the agreement at any time but there was no provision for determination by the claimant. The House of Lords held that this was an agreement in restraint of trade and unenforceable against the claimant because it was unreasonable.

---

[87] [1967] 1 WLR 273, QBD.
[88] *Esso Petroleum Co Ltd v Harper's Garage (Stourport) Ltd* [1968] AC 269.
[89] Ibid.
[90] *Alec Lobb (Garages) Ltd v Total Oil GB Ltd* [1985] 1 WLR 173, CA. See Chapter 19, Section 1.
[91] [1974] 3 All ER 616, HL.

Of course, questions of reasonableness are necessarily fact-sensitive; this perhaps explains why Arden LJ has commented that 'the boundary between contracts that are contrary to public policy as being in restraint of trade and that will not be enforced, and contracts that contain acceptable restrictions is an uncertain and porous one'.[92]

Further Reading

PS Davies, 'The Illegality Defence: Turning Back the Clock' [2010] Conv 282.
Discusses the recommendations in the final Law Commission report, and whether and how a statutory discretion might operate.

Lord Sumption, 'Reflections on the Law of Illegality' (2012) 20 Restitution Law Review 1.
Examines the difficulties inherent within the law of illegality, and the importance of maintaining a predictable rule of public policy.

Lord Mance, 'Ex Turpi Causa—When Latin Avoids Liability' (2014) 18 Edinburgh Law Review 175.
Explores the scope, application, and effect of the maxim *ex turpi causa oritur non actio*, noting inconsistencies in, and qualifications to, its use.

Questions

1. Walter hires Jesse to kill Gus. The contract price is £100,000. Walter pays Jesse £50,000 as a deposit, the balance to be paid once Jesse has killed Gus. Jesse then changes his mind and decides not to go through with the assassination.
   Advise Walter.
   Do you think the law you have discussed is satisfactory? If not, what reforms would you suggest?

2. 'The illegality defence should be abolished. It creates more problems than it solves.' Do you agree?

---

[92] *Proactive Sports Management Ltd v Rooney* [2011] EWCA Civ 1444, [2012] 2 All ER (Comm) 815 [55].

22 Common mistake: contracts void for failure of a basic contractual assumption

 Key Points

- If a contract has been concluded on the basis of a particular contractual assumption, then the failure of that assumption before the contract has been concluded will mean that the contract is void. This is because both parties have made a fundamental mistake about a basic assumption.

- A contract cannot be void due to a common mistake where the risk of an assumption failing has been allocated to one of the parties under the contract, or where the failure is attributable to the fault of one of the parties.

- Very few assumptions are held to be 'basic'; the threshold is set at a very high level. The failure of the assumption must, at the very least, render performance of the contract fundamentally different from what was reasonably envisaged.

- Where the common error of the parties is not as to the existence or ownership of the thing but as to some quality of it, the courts will not regard the contract as void.

- Mistake may render a contract void, but can no longer render a contract voidable in England and Wales.

If there is a failure of a basic contractual assumption, then the contract may be invalid from the start; or, having been initially valid, the contract may be discharged as a result of the failure. The contract may be invalid even though the parties appear to be in perfect agreement. Where a basic contractual assumption fails, it seems entirely sensible to conclude that the parties, as reasonable people, do not intend the contract to operate. Indeed, in the leading case of *Bell v Lever Bros*, Lord Atkin approved the following proposition which had been formulated by Sir John Simon for the assistance of the House of Lords in that case:

> Whenever it is to be inferred from the terms of a contract or its surrounding circumstances that the consensus has been reached upon the basis of a particular contractual assumption, and that assumption is not true, the contract is avoided: *i.e.*, it is void *ab initio* if the assumption is of present fact and it ceases to bind if the assumption is of future fact.

Lord Atkin was confident that few people would disagree with this passage. However, his Lordship also recognised that its value admittedly depended upon the meaning of 'contractual assumption' and 'basis'. These terms will be analysed further below.

When the failure of the basic contractual assumption occurs before the contract is made, the case is traditionally treated in the books under the rubric, 'Mistake'. But where the failure occurs after the contract is made, it is a case of frustration and usually treated either under the rubric, 'Frustration', or under the general heading of 'Discharge of contract'. Historically, the frustration of a contract was based on an implied term and the same explanation has been offered to account for the initial invalidity of a contract through 'mistake'. The implied term theory is generally regarded sceptically by modern writers and judges,[1] but nevertheless continues to be invoked,[2] and it is suggested that this is the best explanation for the outcomes of the leading cases. The implied term theory also has the virtue of being equally applicable to initial invalidity (mistake) and subsequent invalidity (frustration). Implied terms in the form of promises are an established part of the law and there is no reason why conditions other than promises should not also be able to be implied. The implied term theory enables a consistency of approach and is followed in this book.

The most common alleged failure of a basic assumption arises where the subject matter of the contract has ceased to exist, either before the contract was made or before it was fully performed. In this chapter, we will focus on 'mistake' and consider first situations where the thing ceased to exist before the contract was made.[3] An approach based upon the implication of a term might lead to three possible conclusions in this situation:

(a) A impliedly promised B that the thing existed or would continue to exist;

(b) A impliedly promised B that he had taken reasonable care to find out whether the thing existed;

(c) A and B proceeded on a common assumption that the thing existed. Neither A nor B was more responsible than the other for this common assumption.

In determining whether (a) or (b) applies, the court must necessarily decide whether it is appropriate to imply a promissory term in accordance with the principles already discussed.[4] If the court decides that it is not appropriate to imply a promissory term and proceeds to solution (c), it is suggested that the natural and rational conclusion is that solution (c) depends upon an implied condition precedent. If that condition precedent fails, the contract is void. In other words, if the existence of the thing is the basic assumption on which the parties have relied in making their agreement, then the contract is void if that thing does not exist. A similar analysis may apply to cases where the subject matter of the

---

[1] See notably *Great Peace Shipping Ltd v Tsavliris Salvage (International) Ltd (The Great Peace)* [2002] EWCA Civ 1407, [2003] QB 679 [73] (Lord Phillips MR), discussed in Section 3.

[2] See eg *Graves v Graves* [2007] EWCA Civ 660, [2007] 3 FCR 26 [38]–[41] (Thomas LJ).

[3] For frustration, see Chapter 23.

[4] See Chapter 13.

contract ceases to exist after the contract is made, and this underpins the law of frustration. The law of frustration will be considered in the next chapter.[5]

1 Initial failure of a condition

Determining the right sort of term to imply will depend upon the precise circumstances of the case. In particular, the relative means of knowledge of the parties will be relevant, and it may be significant whether one party was relying on the other. Where *A* has all the means of knowledge and *B* has none, and *A* asserts that the thing exists when he knows, or ought to know, that *B* will act on this assertion in entering into and performing the contract, it will probably be held that *A* has promised *B* that the thing exists. As a result, if it later transpires that the thing does not exist, then *A* will be in breach of contract. On the other hand, if *A* and *B* have, and know they have, equal knowledge about the existence of the thing, and contract on the basis of their common assumption that the thing exists, then the contract is likely to be held to be void if the thing does not actually exist. In the first scenario, it is likely to be found that *A* has accepted responsibility for the existence of the thing. In the second situation, by contrast, the existence of the thing is no more the responsibility of *A* than of *B*.

The best example of the first scenario is *McRae v Commonwealth Disposals Commission*.[6] The defendant Commission invited **tenders** for the purchase of an oil tanker together with its contents, which were stated to be oil. The oil tanker was described as lying on Jourmand Reef off Papua. The claimants made a tender of £285 which was accepted. They then incurred considerable expenses, notably in modifying a vessel for **salvage** work. Unfortunately, all the claimants' work was futile: there was in fact no such oil tanker, nor was there even a place known as Jourmand Reef. The claimants sued for damages. The defendant Commission resisted the claim, arguing that the contract was void because the subject matter did not exist. The High Court of Australia rejected that argument and held the Commission liable for breach of contract. The Commission had promised that the tanker existed. Since the tanker did not exist, the Commission was in breach of contract. There was no 'common assumption' here that the tanker existed. The Commission stated that it did exist and the claimants were relying entirely on that assertion. The Commission bore the risk of the tanker not actually existing.

Compare a case in which *A* and *B* travel together from Nottingham to London to view *A*'s theatre which *B* is thinking of hiring. *B* considers the theatre to be suitable for his needs, so in the course of the train journey back to Nottingham, the parties sign a contract under which *A* agrees to let the theatre, and *B* to hire it, for three months. Five minutes before they sign the agreement, the theatre is completely destroyed by an explosion. Neither *A* nor *B* is

---

[5] See Chapter 23. Of course, in those circumstances where the contract is frustrated, (b) is obviously inapplicable and it is much less probable that a person would promise that a thing would continue to exist (relevant to frustration) than that it does exist (relevant to mistake): see eg *Great Peace Shipping Ltd v Tsavliris Salvage (International) Ltd (The Great Peace)* [2002] EWCA Civ 1407, [2003] QB 679 [85].

[6] (1951) 84 CLR 377, High Court of Australia.

in any way responsible for the explosion. Obviously, *A* is now unable to perform his contract. *A* has contracted to provide a theatre to *B* and he cannot do so. Yet it would be very harsh for the law of contract to hold *A* liable for breach of contract in these circumstances, and that result is indeed very unlikely. The **common law** has consistently taken the view that reasonable men would not consider *A*'s promise to be binding in these circumstances. It is suggested that this is best explained on the basis that there is a common assumption that the theatre exists. *B* is not relying on *A* for his belief in its existence—after all, *B* has just seen the theatre with his own eyes. There is an unexpressed but implied **condition** in the contract that the theatre exists.

In *McRae v Commonwealth Disposals Commission*, the Australian courts were greatly troubled by the decision of the House of Lords in *Couturier v Hastie*.[7] That decision had long been believed to lay down a proposition of law that a contract of sale was void where the subject matter of the sale, without the knowledge or fault of the seller, had ceased to exist. However, the High Court demonstrated convincingly that *Couturier v Hastie* decided nothing of the sort.

Couturier v Hastie concerned the sale of a cargo of corn which had been shipped from Salonica. The parties believed that the cargo was at sea at the time of the sale. However, the cargo had already fermented and decayed so the captain had put into port and sold it. On the day that the contract was concluded, there was in fact no cargo in existence since it had already been sold. The question was whether the buyer was nonetheless liable to pay the contract price. The seller argued that the buyer was liable because, in truth, the contract was for the sale of 'the adventure'—the commercial enterprise which the seller had set in motion. The seller's obligation was therefore not to deliver a cargo of corn, but rather to deliver the shipping documents representing the adventure, which the seller was able to do. Those documents were the **bill of lading**, which would enable the buyer to take possession of the cargo if it arrived, and the policy of insurance, which would enable the buyer to claim the insurance monies if the cargo did not arrive. On the other hand, the buyer argued that what was at issue was simply a straightforward contract for the sale of a cargo of corn. The cargo had not been delivered, so the buyer did not have to pay for it. The Court of Exchequer decided that a contract for the sale of the adventure had been agreed, but both the Court of Exchequer Chamber and the House of Lords held that it was a contract for the sale of the cargo. The seller had not performed his contract and was therefore obviously not entitled to the price.

As a result, the question of whether or not the contract was void did not arise. It would have arisen if the buyer had sued the seller for failure to deliver the promised cargo, but that did not happen and it is impossible to be certain what the outcome would have been had the buyer brought such a claim. It seems quite likely that the right answer is that the contract was void, for it was made on the common assumption that a cargo was at sea in the course of a voyage from Salonica to England. The seller (in 1853) could know no more than the buyer about what might have happened to the cargo in the course of the voyage.

In any event, the case of *Couturier v Hastie* did not decide that the contract was void. The decision is therefore not authority for any general proposition that a contract of sale

[7] (1856) 5 HLC 673.

was void where the subject matter of the sale, without the knowledge or fault of the seller, had ceased to exist. Yet before *McRae*, this is what the case was commonly understood to have decided. Such a common understanding was incorrect. The High Court of Australia was therefore quite free to decide as it did, even though at the time of the case the High Court regarded itself to be bound by a decision of the House of Lords. Indeed, the decision in *McRae* has since been approved by the English Court of Appeal in *Great Peace Shipping Ltd v Tsavliris Salvage (International) Ltd (The Great Peace).*[8]

A more difficult matter concerns section 6 of the Sale of Goods Act 1979. This provision re-enacts section 6 of the Sale of Goods Act 1893:

> Where there is a contract for the sale of specific goods and the goods without the knowledge of the seller have perished at the time the contract is made, the contract is void.

This provision seems to have made it into the law because the draftsman of the 1893 Act misunderstood *Couturier v Hastie*. He thought that the case established the proposition discussed, and sought to reflect this in the legislation. However, *Couturier v Hastie* clearly did not decide any such thing. Nevertheless, section 6 now represents the law. The High Court in *McRae* managed neatly to sidestep section 6 by noting that the Australian equivalent of section 6, like section 6 itself, applied only to goods which have perished, whereas the tanker had never existed and therefore could not have perished. But that is not a rational basis for such an important distinction. If section 6 is taken to lay down a rule of law which applies in all circumstances, including those where a seller with all the means of knowledge asserts the existence of the thing to a buyer whom he knows to have no such means, then the common law, as described above, has been altered. But this is unlikely. For instance, imagine that a seller assures a buyer that a thing is in existence. The seller does this in order to persuade the buyer to buy that thing and alleviate the buyer's obvious doubts about the transaction. The seller may even give an undertaking as to the existence of the thing in the written contract. However, the thing does not exist at the time the contract is made. In those circumstances, the court surely would give effect to the express undertaking of the seller rather than to section 6. It seems more appropriate for the buyer to be able to sue the seller for damages than to conclude that the contract is void. This result can be reached by finding that section 6, like many of the provisions of the Sale of Goods Act, will be interpreted so that it gives way to a contrary intention of the parties. Indeed, if section 6 can be excluded by an express term, it must follow that it can also be excluded by an implied one, for there is no difference in principle.

2 When is a common assumption 'basic'?

Parties to a contract may make many assumptions which are unfounded. The vast majority of these assumptions will not impair the validity of the contract. For example, the parties may make a common assumption as to the value of the goods they are buying and selling, but even if the goods are in fact worth much more, or much less, than the parties have

---

[8] *The Great Peace* [77]–[80] (Lord Phillips MR).

assumed, both parties are bound by the contract they have made. The courts have taken a very strict and limited view of the 'basic' common assumption.[9]

In *Bell v Lever Bros*, Lord Atkin gave only two clear examples where a contract would be void for the failure of a basic common assumption. The first example was the case of non-existent subject matter. Lord Atkin, following the then prevailing view of *Couturier v Hastie*, thought that this necessarily invalidated the contract. We now know that this is not so. The existence of the subject matter may or may not be a basic common assumption, depending on the circumstances.

The second example given by Lord Atkin was the case of a contract of sale by A to B when it turns out that the property in question belongs not to A but to B. It certainly seems reasonable to suppose that a basic assumption of a contract of sale by A to B is that the property to be sold belongs to A and not to B. If the contrary is true, the basic assumption has failed.[10] However, it should be noted that this must be subject to the same qualification as *McRae* makes to *Couturier v Hastie*: if the correct interpretation of the agreement is that A is promising B that he is the owner, then the contract is not void but is broken by A.

Of course, Lord Atkin only provided examples in *Bell v Lever Bros*, so it does not follow that initial voidness is confined to the two cases recognised by Lord Atkin. For instance, in *Griffith v Brymer*[11] the claimant entered into an oral agreement with the defendant at 11 am on 24 June 1902. The contract was for the hire of a room on 26 June to view the scheduled coronation procession of Edward VII. Unfortunately, the King had already fallen ill, and at 10 am on 24 June a decision had already been taken to operate on the King and perform an appendectomy. As a result, the coronation procession had to be postponed. Wright J held that the contract between the claimant and defendant was void and that the claimant was entitled to recover the money he had already paid to the defendant. The common assumption of both parties was that there was going to be a coronation procession. It was mistaken and it was basic to the agreement. Indeed, other cases recognised that the cancellation of the procession frustrated similar contracts which had already been made;[12] and it seems right that an event which will frustrate a contract if it occurs after the making of the contract should render the contract void from the start if it occurs before the contract is concluded.

The test for common mistake has been restated by the Court of Appeal in *The Great Peace*:[13]

> the following elements must be present if common mistake is to avoid a contract. (i) there must be a common assumption as to the existence of a state of affairs; (ii) there must be no warranty

---

[9] In *Rose v Pim* [1953] 2 QB 450, discussed in Chapter 14, Section 2(c), the common assumption that the feveroles were horsebeans, though regarded by Lord Denning as 'fundamental', did not avoid the contract.

[10] Admittedly, in *Cooper v Phibbs* (1867) LR 2 HL 149, where such a situation arose in relation to the lease of a fishery, the House of Lords treated the contract as voidable. But several distinguished judges—including, in *Bell v Lever Bros*, Scrutton LJ in the Court of Appeal ([1931] 1 KB 557, 585), Lord Atkin in the House of Lords ([1932] AC 161, 218), and Lord Wright in the decision of the Privy Council in *Norwich Union Fire Insurance Society Ltd v Wm H Price Ltd* [1934] AC 455, 463—have since said that such an agreement is more properly regarded as void, and this view was supported by the Court of Appeal in *The Great Peace*, especially at [100]–[108] (Lord Phillips MR), which is discussed further at Section 3.

[11] (1903) 19 TLR 434.

[12] See Chapter 23, Section 2(c).

[13] *The Great Peace* [76].

by either party that that state of affairs exists; (iii) the non-existence of the state of affairs must not be attributable to the fault of either party; (iv) the non-existence of the state of affairs must render performance of the contract impossible; (v) the state of affairs may be the existence, or a vital attribute, of the consideration to be provided or circumstances which must subsist if performance of the contractual adventure is to be possible.

This test is not confined to particular instances of mistake, but it is undoubtedly very narrow indeed. The Court of Appeal explicitly recognised that 'cases where contracts have been found to be void in consequence of common mistake are few and far between'.[14] This is entirely appropriate: it should not easily be concluded that a contract is void for mistake. However, the formulation of the test proposed in *The Great Peace* might itself be criticised as too narrow. In particular, the fourth requirement of 'impossibility' may be too severe. In *Brennan v Bolt Burden*,[15] the Court of Appeal rightly held that common mistakes of law might be sufficient to render a contract void, although on the facts of the case the compromise agreement was not vitiated by mistake. In the course of his judgment, Sedley LJ considered that a test of 'impossibility' was too narrow—particularly where the relevant mistake concerned a rule of law—and that it would be preferable to ask whether, absent the mistake, 'there would still have been an intelligible basis for their agreement' or whether the common mistake renders the performance of the contract quite different from that which the parties contemplated.[16] In a similar vein, in *Kyle Bay v Underwriters*,[17] Neuberger LJ thought that in the context of the decision as a whole, the Court of Appeal in *The Great Peace* meant 'impossibility' to mean much the same thing as a test of whether the mistake rendered the contract essentially and radically different from what the parties had assumed to be the state of affairs. This is clearly not as narrow as 'impossibility', and seems more consistent with what was said by the House of Lords in *Bell v Lever Bros*. This approach should be followed. After all, *The Great Peace* strongly endorsed *Bell v Lever Bros*, and since *The Great Peace* is a decision of the Court of Appeal and *Bell v Lever Bros* a decision of the House of Lords, the latter must trump the former if there really is a conflict between the cases. As Lord Thankerton put it in *Bell v Lever Bros*, the common assumption of the parties which fails must 'relate to something which both must necessarily have accepted in their minds as an essential and integral element of the subject-matter'.[18]

(a) Mistake as to quality

Where the common error of the parties is not as to the existence or ownership of the thing but as to some quality of it, it seems that the courts will not regard the contract as void. Thus, in *Bell v Lever Bros* the House of Lords made it clear that, under a contract for the sale of a horse, the contract would still be valid if the horse was actually unsound (in other words, in ill-health) yet the parties both mistakenly assumed that the horse was sound (in

---

[14] Ibid, [85].
[15] [2004] EWCA Civ 1017, [2005] QB 303.
[16] Ibid, [60].
[17] [2007] EWCA Civ 57, [2007] 1 CLC 164 [24].
[18] [1932] AC 161, 235, HL.

other words, healthy). In such circumstances, there would be a valid contract for the sale of a horse, and the mistake as to quality would not render that contract void. Admittedly, it is true that in *Bell v Lever Bros* Lord Atkin did also say that a mistake would have the effect of rendering the contract void where it is 'as to the existence of some quality which makes the thing without that quality essentially different from the thing as it was believed to be'.[19] However, it is suggested that this *dictum* is difficult, and perhaps even impossible, to reconcile with the decision of the House of Lords in *Bell v Lever Bros* itself.

Bell was employed by Lever Bros at a salary of £8,000 a year for a certain period of time. Before the end of that time period, Bell was made redundant. Lever Bros offered Bell £30,000 as compensation for terminating his services. Bell accepted this offer. Lever Bros then discovered that Bell had committed breaches of his contract of service during his employment, and that as a result Lever Bros could have dismissed Bell for breach of contract without paying him even a penny. Lever Bros therefore sued to get their £30,000 back, claiming **rescission** of the contract on the ground of fraud.[20] At trial, a jury found that Lever Bros would have dismissed Bell without paying him anything if Lever Bros had known of Bell's breaches of contract. However, the jury also found that there had been no fraud. Bell did not fraudulently conceal the breaches of his contract of service. Bell simply did not have those breaches in his mind when entering into the agreement for £30,000 compensation, and he did not appreciate their effect.

Nevertheless, Wright J and the Court of Appeal held that Lever Bros should succeed on the ground that the compensation agreement was void, having been made under a common mistake. The House of Lords, by a bare majority, allowed the appeal. The contract was not void due to a common mistake. This outcome is puzzling. The subject matter of the contract was Bell's contract of service. It definitely existed, but both parties were making a mistake about a fundamental quality of it: both parties thought that it was not terminable **at will** by Lever Bros, whereas it was in fact terminable at will by Lever Bros because of Bell's breaches of contract. It might reasonably be thought that the terminability of the contract of service was the quality which mattered above all else. Negotiations would never even have started if Lever Bros had known the true quality of Bell's contract of service: Lever Bros would simply have dismissed Bell. That Bell was not dismissible at will was certainly the basic assumption made by Lever Bros, and it does not seem unreasonable to say that Bell's basic assumption was similarly that he had something to sell. That something was his right to continue in Lever Bros' employment. Yet because he had no right to continue in their employment, since he was dismissible at will, in reality Bell had nothing to sell. Bell therefore received £30,000 for nothing. The thing (namely, the contract) with the quality it was believed to have (namely, that it was not terminable at will) was worth £30,000; but without that quality it was worth nothing. The two dissenting judges in the House of Lords—Lords Warrington and Hailsham—were surely right to say that the erroneous assumption made by both parties was as fundamental to the bargain as any that could be imagined. Contrary to their view, however, the majority of their Lordships held that the compensation agreement was not void. If Bell's contract of service had been void—that is, non-existent from the outset—and not merely voidable or terminable at will, presumably

[19] *Bell* 218.
[20] See Chapter 16.

the decision of the majority would have been different. But this just emphasises how odd the decision in the case really is, since there would have been no difference in substance—the fundamental point is that it was still £30,000 to nothing at all. It is suggested that, in effect, Bell was selling to Lever Bros the right to put an end to his contract—and this was something that, unknown to them, Lever Bros already owned. Thus, the compensation agreement should have been held to be void.

As it is impossible to envisage a mistake as to quality which is more fundamental than that in *Bell v Lever Bros*, it appears that, while that decision of the House of Lords stands, no common assumption as to the quality of the subject matter of the contract will be regarded as sufficiently basic to render the contract void. That this is the practical effect of the decision seems to have been implicitly recognised by the Court of Appeal in *The Great Peace*:[21]

> Lord Atkin himself gave no examples of cases where a contract was rendered void because of a mistake as to quality which made 'the thing without the quality essentially different from the thing as it was believed to be'. He gave a number of examples of mistakes which did not satisfy this test, which served to demonstrate just how narrow he considered the test to be. Indeed this is further demonstrated by the result reached on the facts of *Bell v Lever Brothers* itself.

In *Associated Japanese Bank (International) Ltd v Credit du Nord SA*,[22] Steyn J condemned as 'too simplistic' an analysis of *Bell v Lever Bros* similar to that made above. Admittedly, it is true that the analysis is inconsistent with a passage in Lord Atkin's speech in which he said:

> Mistake as to the quality of the thing contracted for … will not affect assent unless it is the mistake of both parties, and is as to the existence of some quality which makes the thing without the quality essentially different from the thing as it was believed to be.

Steyn J suggested that there was some doubt about whether or not Lever Bros' decision to enter into the compensation agreement would have been affected if it had known that the service agreement was voidable, and that therefore this quality did not necessarily make the service agreement essentially different from what it was believed to be. But this contradicts the finding of the jury that Lever Bros would have dismissed Bell without compensation if Lever Bros had known the truth.

In no case since *Bell v Lever Bros* has it been held that a mistake as to quality rendered a contract void. Notwithstanding the above *dictum* cited by Steyn J, it seems that there can be no such case. Steyn J also suggested that in *Bell v Lever Bros* the compensation was intended to be: (a) a tangible recognition of Bell's outstanding services to the company and (b) an inducement to him to cooperate in the reorganisation of the company. But the former would be a past consideration, which is not good consideration in the eyes of the law.[23] The latter suggestion is also unconvincing: a letter to Bell stated plainly that the payment was made in consideration of his retirement and made no mention of future collaboration.

In the *Japanese Bank* case, Steyn J held that a guarantee of a lessor's performance of his agreement to lease four machines was void because there was an implied condition

---

[21] *The Great Peace* [86].
[22] [1988] 3 All ER 902, QBD.
[23] See Chapter 7, Section 1(b).

precedent that the machines existed and they did not. That accords with the theory relating to implied terms advanced in this chapter. However, in case he was wrong in so deciding, Steyn J went on to consider whether the guarantee was void 'for mistake'. It is submitted that there is no room for such an inquiry. Once it is found that there was no unsatisfied express or implied condition precedent to the existence of a contract, it is established that the parties intended the contract to exist. Admittedly, in *The Great Peace* the Court of Appeal criticised 'the theory of the implied term ... as unrealistic'. This appears to be because the parties have not considered what should happen in the event of a mistake at all. As a result, the Court of Appeal thought that '[t]he avoidance of a contract on the ground of common mistake results from a rule of law under which, if it transpires that one or both of the parties have agreed to do something which it is impossible to perform, no obligation arises out of that agreement.'[24] This 'rule of law approach' may be itself somewhat uncertain. And criticism of the implied terms theory is often misplaced. After all, it is clear that terms may be implied even where the parties have not actually considered the matter in question,[25] and the implied terms approach has continued to be invoked by the Court of Appeal even after *The Great Peace*.[26] For the reasons given in this chapter, it is a sound approach that is best equipped to explain the leading cases. Nevertheless, it is probably true that the 'rule of law approach' and 'implied terms approach' are likely to lead to the same results in practice, and given the very narrow ambit of common mistake, it is to be expected that instances of mistake being successfully pleaded will remain rare.

3 Effect of mistake

In *Bell v Lever Bros*, Lord Atkin said, 'If mistake operates at all it operates so as to negative or in some cases to nullify consent.' In other words, mistake prevents any agreement from arising (as, for example in *Raffles v Wichelhaus*[27]) so there is no contract; or it nullifies the agreement which has been arrived at, so there is no contract; or it has no effect at all. Lord Atkin did not allow for the possibility of mistake rendering a contract voidable. Although Lord Denning tried to establish that a mistake could render a contract voidable, starting with his influential decision in *Solle v Butcher*,[28] orthodoxy has now been restored after the decision of *The Great Peace* and it is clear that, in this jurisdiction at least, mistake cannot make a contract voidable. However, it is important to explain the nature of the jurisdiction under *Solle v Butcher* and the importance of *The Great Peace*.

(a) Void but not voidable

Despite what was said in *Bell v Lever Bros*, in *Solle v Butcher*[29] the Court of Appeal held that a common mistake as to the quality of the subject matter may render the contract

---

[24] *The Great Peace* [73].
[25] See Chapter 13.
[26] *Graves v Graves* [2007] EWCA Civ 660, [2007] 3 FCR 26 [38]–[41] (Thomas LJ).
[27] See Chapter 2, Section 3.
[28] [1950] 1 KB 671.
[29] Ibid.

not void but voidable. In *Solle v Butcher*, the defendant leased a flat to the claimant for seven years at a rent of £250 per year. Both parties believed that the flat was not bound by the Rent Restriction Acts and that they were free to negotiate whatever rent they thought appropriate. In fact, the flat was bound by the Acts and therefore was subject to rent control. This meant that it was not supposed to be leased at more than the standard rent of £140 per year, notwithstanding the parties' agreement to the contrary. The claimant, having paid rent at £250 per year for some time, sued for a declaration that the standard rent was £140 and to recover the amount overpaid. The majority of the Court of Appeal held that the contract was voidable for mistake, and could be set aside on terms laid down by the court. The court found that the agreed rent of £250 was in fact fair. Indeed, if the defendant had given notice of his intention to raise the rent in accordance with the Acts before granting the lease, he could properly have done so; but, once the lease was granted, it was too late. Taking these factors into account, the terms imposed by the court were that the lease would only be rescinded if the defendant gave the following undertakings: first, to permit the claimant to remain as a **licensee** pending the grant of a new lease; secondly, to serve the proper notice to raise the standard rent; and, thirdly, to grant a new lease to the claimant (if requested to do so within one month) at the full permitted rent, which was not to exceed £250 per year.

This was a case where, in Denning LJ's words, the parties 'were agreed in the same terms on the same subject-matter'.[30] There was no question of the **lease** being void, or of consent being negatived or nullified. But the parties were mistaken as to a quality of the subject matter, namely whether or not the flat was bound by the Rent Restriction Acts. That was important, but not by any means as fundamental as the mistake at issue in *Bell v Lever Bros*. Looked at in economic terms, the difference in *Solle v Butcher* was between £250 per year and £140 per year, compared with £30,000 and nothing in *Bell v Lever Bros*. The landlord in *Solle v Butcher* was getting a substantial rent for his flat, even though it fell well short of what he had bargained for and of what the flat was really worth. So, if the contract was voidable in *Solle v Butcher*, it should, *a fortiori*, have been voidable in *Bell v Lever Bros*—yet none of the Law Lords in the latter case even considered this possibility. In *Solle v Butcher*, Denning LJ's explanation of this was that the House of Lords was, once again,[31] overlooking equity. Denning LJ, assisted by Bucknill LJ, invented a new principle, namely:

> A contract is … liable in equity to be set aside if the parties were under a common misapprehension either as to the facts or as to their relative and respective rights, provided that the misapprehension was fundamental and the party seeking to set it aside was not himself at fault.[32]

Denning LJ remarked that 'there was a good deal to be said for the view that the lease was induced by an innocent material misrepresentation by the claimant'.[33] The parties had been in partnership as estate agents. The claimant was a surveyor, and knew at least as

---

[30] *Leaf v International Galleries* [1950] 2 KB 86, 89, referring to *Solle v Butcher*.
[31] See too his Lordship's treatment of *Foakes v Beer* in the *High Trees* case, discussed in Chapter 7, Section 2.
[32] *Solle* 693.
[33] Ibid, 695.

much about the flat as the defendant. The claimant had told the defendant that he could charge a rent of £250 per year. This may have been a misrepresentation, but the court did not find it necessary to reach a conclusion on that point, deciding the case instead on the ground of mistake. Had the decision been reached on the ground of misrepresentation, it would have been uncontroversial. But that was not the basis of the decision. The Court of Appeal clearly based its analysis on mistake. *Solle v Butcher* must therefore be taken to be a decision on a case where the parties were making a common assumption for which neither party was more responsible than the other.

Denning LJ expressed the view that although a material misrepresentation need not be 'fundamental' to ground rescission, the common misapprehension must be 'fundamental' for mistake to justify rescission. However, it is not clear what 'fundamental' means. The mistake need not be so fundamental as to render the contract void because then the question of rescission would simply not arise. Yet 'fundamental' here apparently means something more than 'material', since Denning LJ drew a distinction between the two terms. Perhaps 'fundamental' in the context of mistake in **equity** is used only to mean that the mistake is sufficiently important to satisfy the court that it is fair to rescind the contract. This is obviously somewhat vague and uncertain.

The principle of Denning LJ can be supported only by recognising that *Bell v Lever Bros* was based on an incomplete statement of the law. It was followed by some subsequent cases,[34] but was heavily criticised in *The Great Peace*. In that case, the Court of Appeal reviewed the law of common mistake in great detail and concluded that *Solle v Butcher* rested on shaky foundations[35] and should be overruled as inconsistent with the decision of the House of Lords in *Bell v Lever Bros*. The test for common mistake at common law is essentially whether or not the mistake was 'fundamental'. There is no room for a test for common mistake in equity based upon whether or not the common mistake was 'fundamental'. If the contrary were true, their Lordships would have alerted us to that possibility in *Bell v Lever Bros*. But they did not. It is unrealistic to think that the House of Lords in *Bell v Lever Bros* were unaware of the existence of equitable doctrine.

In *Solle v Butcher*, Denning LJ rode roughshod over the authority of the House of Lords in *Bell v Lever Bros*, and this was corrected by the Court of Appeal in *The Great Peace*. As a result, the law in this area is now easier to reconcile with fundamental principles of common law, such as the principle of **caveat emptor** (which can be translated as 'buyer beware' or 'let the buyer look out for himself').[36] If A sells to B an old picture which both believe to be worth only a small sum, is the contract to be voidable if it turns out to be a painting by an old master?[37] If A contracts to sell to B land which both believe to be of no great value, is the contract voidable if it is discovered to be sited over a great oil well? The answer to these questions is now clearly 'No'. This must be right: if these contracts were voidable, it would follow that they would still be voidable even if B is aware of A's mistake of fact before the contract is concluded (for instance, where B has realised that the picture is an old master, or that the land is oil-bearing). This would be inappropriate, and would also mean that

---

[34] See eg *Grist v Bailey* [1967] Ch 532, ChD; *Magee v Pennine Insurance Co Ltd* [1969] 2 QB 507.

[35] Including the reliance placed on *Cooper v Phibbs*: see n 10.

[36] cf *William Sindall plc v Cambridgeshire County Council* [1994] 1 WLR 1016, 1035 (Hoffmann LJ).

[37] cf *Leaf v International Galleries* [1950] 2 KB 86, discussed in Chapter 16, Section 4(a).

the contract in *Smith v Hughes*[38] must have been voidable if the seller knew the buyer was making a mistake as to the age of the oats. But this is not what *Smith v Hughes* stands for, and that decision is generally regarded (though not by Lord Denning!) as a pillar of the law of contract.

The Great Peace effectively rids English law of *Solle v Butcher*. But it should be noted that the decision is somewhat controversial. This is for three main reasons. First, it is not clear that the facts of *The Great Peace* really lent themselves to overruling *Solle v Butcher*. The case concerned a ship, *The Cape Providence*, which suffered serious structural damage in the south Indian Ocean. The defendants offered salvage services, and then contracted to hire *The Great Peace* from the claimants to assist the salvage operation. The defendants thought *The Great Peace* was only 35 miles away from *The Cape Providence* but in fact it was 410 miles away. Upon realising this mistake, the defendants cancelled the contract and refused to pay the hire price. Both the first instance judge and the Court of Appeal held that the mistake was not fundamental and that the defendants could not escape the contract. However, it would appear that the mistake would not have been considered to be fundamental even under the doctrine of *Solle v Butcher*, particularly since the risk of the ship being further away than thought seemed to have been allocated between the parties in the contract through a cancellation clause.[39] The overruling of *Solle v Butcher* was therefore not necessary for the decision.

Secondly, there is a question of precedent. The Court of Appeal is bound by its own decisions, yet *The Great Peace* departed from *Solle v Butcher* and the subsequent Court of Appeal decisions that followed the approach of Denning LJ. The Court of Appeal should only depart from an earlier decision of the Court of Appeal in three different types of situation: (a) where there are two conflicting decisions of the Court of Appeal and the court must choose which to follow; (b) where a decision of the Court of Appeal is inconsistent with a subsequent decision of the House of Lords; and (c) where a decision of the Court of Appeal was **per incuriam**. None of these criteria appear to justify the decision of the Court of Appeal in *The Great Peace*. It might therefore be open to a subsequent Court of Appeal to favour *Solle v Butcher* over *The Great Peace*.[40] But to do so would be highly surprising and rest upon an extremely technical basis. The strong Court of Appeal in *The Great Peace* considered this area of the law thoroughly and reached an eminently sensible conclusion. Indeed, this seems to have been recognised by the Supreme Court: in *Pitt v Holt*,[41] Lord Walker said, albeit **obiter**, that *The Great Peace* has 'effectively overruled' *Solle v Butcher*.[42]

Thirdly, as a matter of policy, it has been suggested that *Solle v Butcher* was a desirable development since it introduced a welcome element of remedial flexibility. This was because, in Denning LJ's view, rescission could be granted 'on terms' in equity. This has been given as a reason why the Canadian courts, for example, have not followed *The Great Peace*.[43] Indeed, the lack of flexibility in the realm of mistake might be thought to contrast

---

[38] See Chapter 2, Section 4.
[39] F Reynolds, 'Reconsider the Contract Textbooks' (2003) 119 LQR 177.
[40] S Midwinter, '*The Great Peace* and Precedent' (2003) 119 LQR 80.
[41] [2013] UKSC 26, [2013] 2 AC 108 [115].
[42] See too *Statoil v Louis Dreyfus Energy Services* [2008] EWHC 2257 (Comm) [102]–[105] (Aikens J).
[43] *Miller Paving Ltd v B Gottardo Construction Ltd* (2007) 285 DLR (4th) 568 (Ontario CA) [26] (Goudge JA).

unfavourably with the consequences of frustration, examined in the next chapter.[44] In *The Great Peace*, the Court of Appeal was conscious of this factor when it suggested that legislative reform might be needed to give the courts greater flexibility.[45] However, this suggestion is a little strange. Not only is it highly unlikely that legislative time will be spent on this somewhat narrow area of the law, but the effect of *The Great Peace* is to remove the remedial flexibility the Court of Appeal itself recognises might be required. Of course, the decision in *The Great Peace* can nonetheless be defended on the basis that it is for Parliament to depart from the decision of the House of Lords in *Bell v Lever Bros*, not Denning LJ in the Court of Appeal in *Solle v Butcher*. Moreover, given that it will only be in extremely rare cases that a contact will be vitiated for the failure of a basic contractual assumption, it might be thought desirable to have a clear rule that such a failure will render the contract void.

Further Reading

JC Smith, 'Contract, Mistake, Frustration and Implied Terms' (1994) 110 LQR 400.
Further explains the utility of the implied terms approach which leaves no room for a distinct doctrine of mistake.

C Macmillan, 'How Temptation Led to Mistake: An Explanation of *Bell v Lever Brothers Ltd*' (2003) 119 LQR 625.
Considers the background to *Bell v Lever Bros* and suggests that the case was unfortunately influenced by Lever Bros' desire to sanction Bell for unacceptable conduct.

A Tettenborn, 'Agreements, Common Mistake and the Purpose of Contract' (2011) 27 JCL 91.
Argues that the law on mistake is now too narrow after *The Great Peace* and that equity should be more willing to grant relief from a common mistake.

Questions

1. 'The Great Peace case has restored coherence to the law of common mistake.'
   Discuss. What, if any, reforms of the law do you consider to be desirable in relation to common mistake?

2. Jake owns an antique shop. Amy enters the shop and inspects a rare Chinese vase, which is in excellent condition, and a table thought to be from the Victorian period. Jake gives Amy his telephone number and tells her that she can pay over the telephone if she wants to buy either or both items.
   The following day, Amy rings Jakes and pays £100,000 for the vase and £15,000 for the table. Unfortunately, the vase had been severely damaged by an accident overnight. Jake only learns of the accident and damage to the vase when Amy arrives later that afternoon in order to collect the vase. Amy is very upset. However, the table is not damaged at all. In fact, the next week Amy discovers that the table is not from the Victorian period but is instead from the Georgian period and is worth £80,000.
   Advise Amy.

---

[44] Notably under the Law Reform (Frustrated Contracts) Act 1943. See Chapter 23.
[45] *The Great Peace* [161].

23 Frustration: contracts discharged for failure of a basic contractual assumption

 Key Points

- If the failure of a basic contractual assumption occurs after the contract has been concluded, the contract may be frustrated.
- A frustrating event kills off the contract automatically. However, everything that was done from the making of the contract up to its frustration was, and remains, validly done in pursuance of that contract.
- A contract cannot be frustrated where the risk of an assumption failing has been allocated to one of the parties under the contract (for example by a *force majeure* clause), or where the failure is attributable to the fault of one of the parties
- A frustrating event should render performance of the contract radically different from that which was undertaken by the contract. This is restrictively defined. For example, the contract may be frustrated where performance becomes impossible or illegal, or depended upon the existence of a thing which no longer exists.
- At common law, a party may be able to claim restitution of benefits transferred prior to the frustrating event through an action in unjust enrichment if there has been a 'total failure of consideration'. However, it is now more likely that the Law Reform (Frustrated Contracts) Act 1943 will determine the consequences of frustration. This legislation provides a statutory mechanism for adjusting the rights of parties after a contract has been frustrated.

Chapter 22 examined contracts which were avoided because of the failure of a basic contractual assumption *before* the contract was entered into. This chapter focuses on instances where the failure occurs *after* the contract has been concluded. The question of timing—whether the failure occurs before or after the contract is made—is crucial to the difference between mistake and frustration.[1] There are some good reasons for keeping these two areas distinct: after all, the parties might be expected to know of things that currently exist (thus restricting the ambit of mistake), but cannot be expected to know what will happen in the

---

[1] See eg *Amalgamated Investment & Property Co v John Walker* [1976] 3 All ER 509.

future to the same extent (meaning that frustration might not be as restrictive as mistake). However, the differences between mistake and frustration can also be exaggerated. The failure of the basic contractual assumption might occur a second before or a second after a contract is signed, yet that will be crucial when deciding whether the law discussed in Chapter 22 or this chapter should apply.

Judges have often recognised that the boundary between mistake and frustration can be very fine. In *The Great Peace*, Lord Phillips MR explicitly said that 'consideration of the de-velopment of the law of frustration assists with the analysis of the law of common mistake'.[2] In *The Great Peace*, the Court of Appeal thought that the law on common mistake and frus-tration both rested upon a similar basis. As a result, current orthodoxy appears to favour an approach that explains frustration as a doctrine which is imposed by law where there is a change of circumstance which would, in the words of Lord Radcliffe in *Davis Contractors Ltd v Fareham Urban District Council*, make performance 'a thing radically different from that which was undertaken by the contract. *Non haec in foedera veni*. It was not this that I promised to do'.[3] In *The Sea Angel*, Rix LJ said:[4]

> the application of the doctrine of frustration requires a multi-factorial approach. Among the factors which have to be considered are the terms of the contract itself, its matrix or context, the parties' knowledge, expectations, assumptions and contemplations, in particular as to risk, as at the time of contract, at any rate so far as these can be ascribed mutually and objectively, and then the nature of the supervening event, and the parties' reasonable and objectively ascertainable calculations as to the possibilities of future performance in the new circumstances. Since the subject matter of the doctrine of frustration is contract, and contracts are about the allocation of risk, and since the allocation and assumption of risk is not simply a matter of express or implied provision but may also depend on less easily defined matters such as 'the contemplation of the parties', the application of the doctrine can often be a difficult one. In such circumstances, the test of 'radically different' is important: it tells us that the doctrine is not to be lightly invoked; that mere incidence of expense or delay or onerousness is not sufficient; and that there has to be as it were a break in identity between the contract as provided for and contemplated and its performance in the new circumstances.

The modern approach appears largely to reject an explanation of the law in this area which is based upon implied terms. But it is difficult to know what the rationale of the doctrine is understood to be. Perhaps frustration is justified because the parties would not have consented to the radical change in the nature of the obligation, so the contract should be killed off.[5] Or perhaps frustration is simply explained on the grounds of fairness. In *The Super Servant Two*, Bingham LJ said that frustration developed in order 'to mitigate the rigour of the **common law**'s insistence on literal performance of absolute promises ... The object of the doctrine was to give effect to the demands of justice, to achieve a just and rea-sonable result, to do what is reasonable and fair ...' This might have some intuitive appeal,

---

[2] *Great Peace Shipping Ltd v Tsavliris Salvage (International) Ltd (The Great Peace)* [2002] EWCA Civ 1407, [2003] QB 679 [61]. See Chapter 22.

[3] *Davis Contractors Ltd v Fareham Urban District Council* [1956] AC 696, 728 (Lord Radcliffe).

[4] *Edwinton Commercial Corp v Tsavliris Russ (Worldwide Salvage & Towage) Ltd (The Sea Angel)* [2007] EWCA Civ 547, [2007] 2 All ER (Comm) 634 [111].

[5] eg *Davis Contractors Ltd v Fareham Urban District Council* [1956] AC 696, 728 (Lord Radcliffe).

but it does not really explain why any losses suffered should not simply lie where they fall (which is the default approach of English law). It is suggested that the best explanation for why some contracts are killed off is that there is an implied term that if a common basic assumption should fail, the contract will be killed off. This is for very similar reasons as those presented in Chapter 22 the context of common mistake. Although not a fashionable view, some courts do still invoke the implied terms theory in the context of frustration.[6] In any event, the theoretical basis of frustration—whether, for example, frustration should be explained by 'a rule of law' approach or 'an implied terms theory'—is unlikely to lead to different results on the facts of any given case, since the law on frustration is now well established.

For the purposes of illustrating how frustration operates, some of the key types of implied conditions that may fail such that a contract is frustrated will be examined. However, it is important to emphasise that the examples given are not exhaustive, and there is, in principle, no restriction on the types of conditions that may be implied. The usual techniques of implication of terms into a contract should be employed.[7] All that is required is that a term can be implied into the contract that if a particular condition fails the contract will be killed off. But before examining that issue in further detail, it is useful first to say something about the scope of frustration.

1 Scope of frustration

As the previous quotation from *The Sea Angel* illustrates,[8] frustration is a very narrow doctrine. Two main reasons might be given for this. First, it is not a 'radical change in the nature of the obligation' if a contract simply becomes more difficult to perform; establishing that a contract has been frustrated is very demanding indeed. Secondly, the parties themselves might expressly allocate the risk of an event occurring to one of the parties, which would preclude the operation of frustration.

(a) Performance becomes difficult

The starting point must be that a party is not excused from performing his contract merely on the ground that performance turns out to be unexpectedly burdensome or difficult. This was highlighted by a series of cases that arose from the Suez Crisis and closure of the Suez Canal in 1956. One such case was *Tsakiroglou & Co Ltd v Noblee Thorl GmbH*.[9] Sellers in Port Sudan had agreed to ship goods to various European ports for a fixed price. The sellers had expected to be able to send the goods through the Suez Canal. However, because this was impossible, the sellers had to send the goods round the Cape of Good Hope. This route was more than four times as far. The cost to the sellers was obviously far greater than they had expected, but their argument that the contract of sale was frustrated nevertheless

---

[6] See eg *Graves v Graves* [2007] EWCA Civ 660, [2007] 3 FCR 26 [38]–[41] (Thomas LJ).
[7] See Chapter 13.
[8] See n 4.
[9] *Tsakiroglou & Co Ltd v Noblee Thorl GmbH* [1962] AC 93, HL.

failed. The contract was still capable of performance, since the goods were not so perishable that they would not survive the journey round the Cape of Good Hope. The bargain had turned out to be a very bad one for the sellers, but it was still capable of being performed. The sellers had to perform it or pay damages.

Similarly, in *Davis Contractors Ltd v Fareham Urban District Council*,[10] a contract to build houses for £92,000 within a period of eight months ran into significant difficulties due to an unexpected shortage of skilled labour and building materials. The project ultimately took 22 months to complete and cost £17,000 more than estimated. That was very bad luck for the contractor, but it was clear that the contract was not frustrated. The contract had simply become more difficult to perform.

Another illustration of this principle is to be found in the famous old case of *Paradine v Jane*.[11] A **landlord** sued his **tenant** for three years' **arrears** of rent. The tenant argued that he should not have to pay because throughout that period of time the tenant had been expelled from the premises by a German prince called Prince Rupert (described by the court as 'an alien born, enemy to the King') and his army. Despite this state of affairs, the court insisted that the tenant was bound to pay his landlord the rent which was in arrears. The rule stated by the court was hard and uncompromising: 'though the land be surrounded, or gained by the sea, or made barren by wildfire, yet the **lessor** shall have his whole rent'. The court distinguished between duties imposed by law and duties undertaken by contract. Whereas performance of duties imposed by law might be excused by circumstances, performance of duties undertaken by contract would not be excused unless the contract provided for this possibility. So, on the facts of *Paradine v Jane*, the tenant could have qualified his undertaking to pay rent when he gave it. But, since this had not been done in the contract, the obligation to pay was taken to be absolute. The court pointed out that the tenant would have taken the benefit of 'casual profits' during the relevant period of time. For example, if Rupert had, uncharacteristically, offered gold for the privilege of camping on the land, the tenant would have been entitled to keep the gold. And because the tenant had the potential advantage of casual profits, he also had to bear the corresponding burden of 'casual losses'. Nevertheless, it should be noted that the decision in *Paradine v Jane* is very hard and may not be followed today. In *Paradine v Jane*, the court suggested that if the '**lessee covenant** to repair a house, though it be burnt by lightning, or thrown down by enemies, yet he ought to repair it', but this seems to be inconsistent with subsequent decisions such as *Taylor v Caldwell*.[12]

(b) Risk allocated by the contract

There is no scope for frustration to operate if the risk of the relevant event occurring is allocated to one of the parties in the contract itself.[13] Whether the risk of the event occurring lies with one of the parties is a question of contractual interpretation.[14] Parties often expressly state what should happen if unexpected events should occur by including a '*force*

---

[10] [1956] AC 696.

[11] (1647) Aleyn 26, KB.

[12] See Section 2(a).

[13] cf *McRae v Commonwealth Disposals Commission* (1951) 84 CLR 377, considered in Chapter 22, Section 1.

[14] See Chapter 12.

majeure' clause. A good example of a *force majeure* clause is found in the contract at issue in *The Super Servant Two*:[15]

> [The party] has the right to cancel its performance under this Contract whether the loading has been completed or not, in the event of force majeur [*sic*], Acts of God, perils or danger and accidents of the sea, acts of war, warlike-operations, acts of public enemies, restraint of princes, rulers or people or seizure under legal process, quarantine restrictions, civil commotions, blockade, strikes, lockout, closure of the Suez or Panama Canal, congestion of harbours or any other circumstances whatsoever, causing extraordinary periods of delay and similar events and/or circumstances, abnormal increases in prices and wages, scarcity of fuel and similar events, which reasonably may impede, prevent or delay the performance of this contract.

If one of these events should occur, then the court should give effect to the parties' intentions and allow the party to cancel its performance under the contract. Frustration can only operate where there is a gap in the contractual allocation of risk. There is simply no scope to imply a term that the contract will be killed off on the occurrence of a certain event if that event is already provided for in the contract. After all, it is impossible to imply a term that is contrary to the express terms of the agreement.[16]

Force majeure clauses, and 'hardship clauses', which provide what should happen in the event of unexpected hardship occurring, are very useful. They provide the parties with a greater degree of certainty about their affairs. Such clauses enable contracting parties to avoid the difficult and uncertain law on frustration, particularly concerning the consequences of frustration.[17] This may be considered to be desirable. However, the courts will sometimes be slow to interpret a clause such that it excludes the doctrine of frustration. This is well illustrated by the decision in *Metropolitan Water Board v Dick Kerr and Co Ltd*.[18] The defendant contracted with the claimant to build a reservoir in six years, beginning in July 1914. In 1916, the Ministry of Munitions exercised its wartime powers to force the defendant to stop the work and to sell its plant. There was a clause in the contract that said that, in the event of any difficulties 'whatsoever and howsoever occasioned', the defendant should apply for an extension of time. This very broad clause may reasonably be thought to have covered the situation in which the defendant found itself, but the House of Lords interpreted the clause in a narrow manner. Their Lordships held that the clause was only intended to cover temporary obstacles in the construction of the reservoir. On the facts of the case, the delay was substantial and more than temporary, and was not covered by the clause. The House of Lords held that the contract was frustrated.

---

[15] *J Lauritzen AS v Wijsmuller BV (The Super Servant Two)* [1990] 1 Lloyd's Rep 1, CA. This case is considered further in Section 3; on the facts, the defendants could only partially rely upon this clause as giving them a right to cancel the contract.

[16] See Chapter 13, Section 5.

[17] See Section 4.

[18] [1918] AC 119, HL.

(i) Foreseeable events

A somewhat related issue concerns foreseeable events: should the fact that the event in question was foreseeable preclude frustration? There is some suggestion in the cases that an event foreseeable at the time of entering into the contract should not be able to constitute a frustrating event.[19] However, despite this, the better view is that an event might frustrate a contract despite being foreseeable at the time of the conclusion of the contract, provided that the risk of that event occurring was not allocated to one of the parties in the contract.[20] Of course, where only one party could have foreseen the occurrence of the event, that might suggest that that party bore the risk of the event happening. But where both parties foresaw the possibility of the event (such as the closure of the Suez Canal) but failed to state what should happen if the event actually occurred, there appears to be room for the doctrine of frustration to operate. As Rix LJ noted in *The Sea Angel*, 'most events are to a greater or lesser degree foreseeable. That does not mean that they cannot lead to frustration.'[21] It is nevertheless true that the less foreseeable an event is, the more likely it is that the occurrence of that event will mean that the contract is frustrated (although it must be remembered that frustration will always only operate within very narrow confines).

2 Implied conditions

Although there can be no exhaustive list of the types of implied conditions that may fail such that a contract is frustrated, the most important cases concern implied conditions relating to the existence of a person or thing; the impossibility of an 'adventure'; and the occurrence of a particular event. These instances will now be examined in turn, before considering some general issues relating to the sale of goods and **leases**.

(a) The existence of a person or thing

In the leading case of *Taylor v Caldwell*,[22] Blackburn J stated the general rule that the contractor must perform a contract which had become unexpectedly burdensome 'or even impossible', but then went on to say:

> But this rule is only applicable when the contract is positive and absolute, and not subject to any condition either express or implied: and there are authorities which, as we think, establish the principle that where, from the nature of the contract, it appears that the parties must from the beginning have known that it could not be fulfilled unless when the time for the fulfilment of the contract arrived some particular specified thing continued to exist, so that, when entering into the contract, they must have contemplated such continuing existence as the foundation of what was to be done; there, in the absence of any express or implied warranty that the

---

[19] *Walton Harvey Ltd v Walker & Homfrays Ltd* [1931] 1 Ch 274.
[20] *The Eugenia* [1964] 2 QB 226.
[21] *The Sea Angel* [127].
[22] (1863) 3 B & S 826, QB.

thing shall exist, the contract is not to be construed as a positive contract, but as subject to an implied condition that the parties shall be excused in case, before breach, performance becomes impossible from the perishing of the thing without default of the contractor.

The defendant had agreed to let a music hall and gardens to the claimant for a period of four days for the purpose of concerts and fêtes. The price of hire was £100 a day. Before the beginning of the hire period, the hall was destroyed by fire. Neither party was at fault for the fire. The claimant sued for damages for breach of contract in failing to provide the hall. Applying the principle stated above, the court held that the contract was frustrated. It had come to an abrupt end and each party was discharged from liability to perform.

Exceptionally, Blackburn J relied heavily on Roman law for the proposition that the contract was subject to a condition that its subject matter should continue to exist. However, Blackburn J did not invent the English doctrine of frustration in *Taylor v Caldwell*. There was ancient authority to show that contracts requiring personal performance, including contracts to marry, were terminated by the death of the **promisor** before the time for the fulfilment of the promise, even though there was no express provision for this in the contract. Indeed, this was generally understood to be the law at the time, since it was something that went without saying,[23] as every reasonable man would agree.

In *Cutter v Powell*,[24] the second mate of a ship, Mr Cutter, agreed to be paid 30 guineas if he fulfilled his duties on a voyage from Jamaica to Liverpool. Mr Cutter died before the ship reached Liverpool. It was famously held that Mrs Cutter could not recover any part of her late husband's wages.[25] However, it should also be noted that at least Mrs Cutter was not liable as Mr Cutter's personal representative for any breach of contract in failing to serve as the second mate for the whole voyage. Mr Cutter was, of course, discharged from his obligation by death.

In *Taylor v Caldwell*, Blackburn J recognised that it had long been established that if a painter who had contracted to paint a picture went blind, the contract came to an end. And in other situations, a contract might be conditional on the continuing life of a third party. For instance, a father who had covenanted that his son would serve as an apprentice for seven years was not liable for breach of contract if the son died within that period. By the time of *Taylor v Caldwell*, it was also already settled that a seller of goods was discharged from his duty to deliver the goods and bound to refund the price paid if, before the ownership (and, with it, the risk) had passed to the buyer, the goods were destroyed without his fault. Moreover, a borrower or **bailee** of goods was discharged from his duty to return the goods if they were destroyed without his fault. Blackburn J was able to rely upon all these examples to find authority for a general principle that:[26]

in contracts in which the performance depends on the continued existence of a given person or thing, a condition is implied that the impossibility of performance arising from the perishing of the person or thing shall excuse the performance.

---

[23] See Chapter 13, Section 1(a).
[24] (1795) 6 TR 320.
[25] See Chapter 24, Section 8.
[26] (1863) 3 B & S 826, 839.

It should be noted, however, that Blackburn J did not treat this as an absolute rule of law. It applied only 'in the absence of any express or implied warranty that the thing shall exist'.[27] His Lordship recognised that just as in the case of initial impossibility of performance,[28] the implied condition precedent would give way to an implied promise if that was the correct construction of the contract. Although it is less likely that a person will promise that a thing will continue to exist (relevant in the context of frustration) than that he will promise that a thing does exist (relevant in the context of mistake), this possibility cannot simply be discounted.

(b) The impossibility of 'an adventure'

In *Taylor v Caldwell*, Blackburn J concentrated on impossibility arising from the non-existence of a person or thing because that was the nature of the case before him. But frustration is not confined to such cases. For example, older cases refer to the impossibility of 'an adventure' as leading to frustration. In the commercial context, businesses may contract with a particular 'adventure', or a particular commercial enterprise, in mind. That adventure may, without their fault, become impossible to perform. The impossibility will usually arise from some factor which causes inordinate delay. As a result, even though all the physical features required for performance remain in existence (such as the ship, the goods, and the ports of loading and discharge) the 'adventure' can no longer be performed. So, if there were a contract for 'a spring voyage' by a particular vessel, and an accident postponed the availability of the vessel until the autumn, the spring voyage contemplated by the parties will have become impossible. In the absence of an absolute promise that the vessel would be available come what may, the contract is likely to be regarded as frustrated.

In effect, that was the situation which Bramwell B thought had arisen in *Jackson v Union Marine Insurance Co Ltd*.[29] A ship was chartered to proceed with 'all possible dispatch' (dangers and accidents of navigation excepted) from Liverpool to Newport, and then to load a cargo of iron rails for San Francisco. The ship sailed on 2 January 1872, but ran aground on 3 January. The ship was refloated on 8 February but required repairs which took until the end of August. In the meantime, on 15 February, the charterers had given up on the **charter** and chartered another ship. The court held that the charterers were entitled to do so. A voyage after the repairs had taken place would have been a different adventure from that contemplated by the parties, even though the same ship would be carrying the same rails between the same ports. As Bramwell B remarked, 'If this **charterparty** be read as a charter for a definite voyage or adventure, then it follows that there is necessarily an implied condition that the ship shall arrive at Newport in time for it.'[30] The identity of the 'adventure' in such circumstances is, of course, difficult to define with precision (and perhaps more vague than in the example of 'a spring voyage'). Basically, whether the delay is such as to destroy the identity of the 'adventure' or commercial enterprise is a question of degree and one for the judgement of the court.[31] In order to resolve this issue, the court

[27] See text to n 21.
[28] See Chapter 22.
[29] (1874) LR 10 CP 125, Exchequer Chamber.
[30] Ibid, 142.
[31] *Pioneer Shipping Ltd v BTP Tioxide Ltd (The Nema)* [1982] AC 724, 752, HL (Lord Roskill).

must try to put itself into the position of commercial parties at the relevant time. So, in the *Jackson* case, the court had to decide whether the reasonable charterer, on 15 February, would have believed that the adventure as originally envisaged was now impossible.

A more recent example was provided in *The Sea Angel*.[32] There was a contract for the hire of a vessel for up to 20 days in order to assist with a '**salvage** adventure'. Having completed the salvage work, and with three days left of the charter agreement, the vessel was detained by the Pakistani port authority. The port authority said that all port charges had not been paid, and that compensation needed to be paid for the pollution caused by leaking oil. It took three months to resolve this issue, during which time the vessel remained in the Pakistani port and was not redelivered on time. The Court of Appeal held that the contract had not been frustrated. Although the delay was significant, the identity of the 'adventure' had not been destroyed: the salvage adventure was a success. Their Lordships pointed out that the risk of something happening which would prevent the vessel from being returned on time should generally fall upon the charterer, and as a result the charterer was liable for breach of contract in failing to redeliver the vessel in accordance with the contract.

This principle is not confined to commercial contracts. A contract for a four-year apprenticeship as a plumber was frustrated when, after about 21 months, the apprentice was convicted of conspiracy to commit assault and affray, and consequently sentenced to borstal training which would probably last 39 weeks and possibly more.[33] And a contract by which the claimant, a music hall artiste (professionally known as 'Charlie Chester'), appointed the defendant to be his agent for a term of ten years was held to be frustrated when, in 1940, the claimant was called up for service in the army for the duration of the war. 'The original contract was so fundamentally invaded by the calling up of Mr. Chester that it must be held to have been frustrated by reason of that event.'[34]

(c) **The occurrence of a particular event**

The fundamental common assumption of the parties may be that a particular event is going to occur. In those circumstances, it may well be that, if that event is cancelled, the contract is frustrated. In *Krell v Henry*,[35] that event was to be the coronation procession of King Edward VII. The defendant saw an announcement in the windows of the claimant's flat in Pall Mall. The announcement made it clear that the claimant was willing to hire out his flat on the days of the coronation procession, namely 26 and 27 June. The claimant's housekeeper pointed out to the defendant that he would have an excellent view of the procession from the flat. The defendant then entered into a contract with the claimant on 20 June. The defendant agreed in writing to take the flat for the days (but not the nights) of 26 and 27 June. The contract price was £75. Of that, £25 was paid immediately and £50 was to be paid on 24 June. The written contract did not mention the procession. Unfortunately, early in the morning of 24 June, the procession was cancelled due to the King's illness. The

---

[32] *Edwinton Commercial Corp v Tsavliris Russ (Worldwide Salvage & Towage) Ltd (The Sea Angel)* [2007] EWCA Civ 547, [2007] 2 All ER (Comm) 634.

[33] *Shepherd FC & Co Ltd v Jerrom* [1986] 3 All ER 589, CA.

[34] *Morgan v Manser* [1948] 1 KB 184, 195 (Streatfeild J).

[35] [1903] 2 KB 740, CA.

defendant then refused to pay the further £50, and the claimant sued for that £50. The defendant counterclaimed for the return of the £25 he had already paid.

If the court had been confined to considering only the written contract, the claimant would most likely have succeeded. He had agreed to provide the defendant with the use of the rooms on two days, no more and no less, and he was ready and willing to do so. There would be no question of frustration. But when the surrounding circumstances are looked at, it is apparent that the claimant was not simply selling the use of two rooms. The claimant was selling a view of the coronation procession, and he was unable to provide that (albeit through no fault of his own). The **parol evidence** rule[36] did not apply so as to prevent the court from learning the true purpose of both parties to the contract. The common and fundamental assumption was not merely that the rooms at 56A Pall Mall would exist on 26 and 27 June, but also that a procession would be passing.

Krell v Henry was distinguished in another case which was under consideration at the same time by the same court and which reached a different result—*Herne Bay Steam Boat Co v Hutton*.[37] The contract was for the hire of a steamboat on 28 and 29 June, following a public announcement that there was to be a Royal Naval Review at Spithead on those days. On each day, the steamboat was to be at the disposal of the defendant 'for the purpose of viewing the naval review and for a day's cruise round the fleet'. The review was cancelled because of the king's illness, but the fleet was still there. The court held that the contract was not frustrated. Whereas no one in his right mind would want to spend two days looking out of the windows of 56A Pall Mall at the ordinary traffic, back in the days when 'Britannia ruled the waves', the fleet was well worth seeing. In the court's opinion, the happening of the naval review was not the foundation of the contract in *Herne Bay Steam Boat Co v Hutton*.

It is not obvious what principle distinguishes the *Herne Bay* case from *Krell v Henry*. Although exactly the same judges decided both cases only a few days apart, neither decision refers to the other. This is unfortunate. It may be significant that the defendant in *Krell v Henry* was a consumer, whereas the defendant in the *Herne Bay* case was acting in the course of business. Or perhaps that there was more than one purpose of the contract in the *Herne Bay* case (to see the fleet and to view the naval review), whereas there was only one possible purpose of hiring the flat in *Krell v Henry* (the viewing of the procession).

Another potential distinction is that *Krell v Henry* concerned a very unusual sort of contract, which could only be explained by a desire to watch the procession, whereas the contract in *Herne Bay* was not at all unusual. This explanation might gain some support from the difficult example, discussed in both *Herne Bay* and *Krell v Henry*, of a cabman (a driver of a horse-drawn hackney carriage) who has contracted to take someone to Epsom on Derby Day, and the Derby is later cancelled. The cabman is simply selling a ride to Epsom. The ride is a valuable service which he offers every day, so the contract would not be frustrated by the cancellation of the Derby. On the other hand, we may be sure that the claimant in *Krell v Henry* was not in the habit of letting out the view from his windows—there was no market for it. The happening of the Derby might be the foundation of the contract

---

[36] See Chapter 11, Section 4.
[37] [1903] 2 KB 683.

from the point of view of the hirer, but it is not clear that it would be the foundation of the contract from the point of view of the cabman. The cabman is not generally concerned with his customer's reasons for wishing to go to a particular destination—and, for all he knows, the customer may be going to Epsom to visit his aunt whose birthday happens to be on Derby Day. However, if a bus company were to advertise 'an excursion to Epsom on Derby Day', the cancellation of the Derby might frustrate the contract for the company now appears to be offering to sell a visit to the Derby. The fact that a particular customer hated horse-racing and bought a ticket in order to visit his aunt should not make any difference, because the intentions of the parties should be judged objectively. One party's secret intention should be irrelevant.

The difficulty with this analysis, however, is that the hypothetical cabman in the example used by the Court of Appeal was charging an 'enhanced rate' for his services, presumably because the trip was on Derby Day. This surely suggests that a reasonable person would think that the occurrence of the Derby was important not only to the hirer but also to the cabman, since it must objectively be concluded that what leads to the cabman asking for an 'enhanced rate' is the event of the Derby. A more modern example can be given. Imagine that I book a taxi on the day of the FA Cup Final from Liverpool to Wembley. The contract price is £1,000. On any other day, the contract price would be £250. The reason why the taxi driver quadrupled the price is, presumably, because he knows that it is the day of the FA Cup Final and that transport to Wembley will be at a premium. If the FA Cup Final is cancelled, should the contract be frustrated? The taxi service is a normal service, and there could be a variety of reasons why I may want to travel to Wembley. As a result, it might be thought that this example is closer to *Herne Bay* than *Krell v Henry* and that the contract should not be frustrated. Indeed, that would be consistent with what the Court of Appeal said of the cabman example in both cases: the contract would not be frustrated. But presumably the reason for the inflated price is the fact that travel is on the day of the FA Cup Final—an event which is cancelled. It is arguable that this is actually similar to *Krell* in that the purpose of paying such a high price was to go to Wembley on the day of the FA Cup Final. The example of the cabman is therefore very difficult to reconcile with *Krell* (although it would be easy if the cabman were not asking for an 'enhanced rate'). Of course, the cabman example is only a hypothetical case and not part of the *ratio* of either *Krell* or *Herne Bay*, so perhaps too much attention should not be given to it. Yet because the cabman example is one of the few aspects of the judges' reasoning that is common to both *Krell* and *Herne Bay*, there is an understandable reluctance simply to discard this hypothetical case. It is suggested that *Krell v Henry* may simply be an unsatisfactory decision which should not be followed: the hirer of the flat simply made a bad bargain, and should have included a *force majeure* clause. As Lord Wright remarked in *Maritime National Fish Ltd v Ocean Trawlers Ltd*, the authority of *Krell v Henry* is 'certainly not one to be extended'.[38]

---

[38] [1935] AC 524, 529, PC. See too *North Shore Ventures Ltd v Anstead Holdings Inc* [2010] EWHC 1485 (Ch), [2011] 1 All ER (Comm) 81 [310] (Newey J) (reversed, but not on this point: [2011] EWCA Civ 230, [2012] Ch 31).

(d) **Sale of goods**

A contract for the sale of specific goods is generally frustrated if, without the fault of either party, the goods are destroyed before ownership passes to the buyer. Section 7 of the Sale of Goods Act 1979 provides:

> Where there is an agreement to sell specific goods and subsequently the goods, without any fault on the part of the seller or buyer, perish before the risk passes to the buyer, the agreement is avoided.

If the ownership has passed to the buyer (in other words, the agreement to sell has become a sale) before the goods perish, the contract has not been frustrated. This is because the main purpose of the contract has been accomplished: ownership has been transferred. Unless the parties have agreed otherwise, the risk passes with the ownership of the goods, so the buyer must bear the loss when the goods perish after he has acquired ownership. Just as section 6 may be capable of exclusion by a promise that the thing exists,[39] so might section 7 be capable of exclusion by a promise that the thing will continue to exist. However, for obvious reasons, the latter type of promise is less likely than the former.

Where the contract is to sell goods of a particular description rather than specific goods, the contract will not be frustrated just because the particular goods which the seller had in mind are destroyed. The contract can still be performed, since the contract does not re-quire the sale of specific goods. The seller must simply acquire other goods answering the description. A fundamental assumption of the seller may have failed, but this is not true of the buyer; a contract will only be frustrated where a fundamental assumption that is com-mon to both parties has failed.

In *Blackburn Bobbin Co Ltd v TW Allen & Sons Ltd*,[40] timber merchants entered into a contract for the sale of Finnish birch timber. The outbreak of the First World War then essentially prevented the sellers from importing timber from Finland as they had contem-plated, and meant that the sellers could not perform their contract with the purchasers of the timber. The sellers argued that the contract was frustrated. This was rejected by the Court of Appeal. The seller was liable for a breach of contract to sell Finnish birch timber. Even though the custom of English timber merchants was to import Finnish timber as required, and not to hold stocks of such timber, the buyer neither knew nor had reason to know of this custom. As a result, the existence of this custom was wholly immaterial. The buyer might reasonably have thought that the sellers had such timber in stock. In any event, it was not a shared, common assumption by both the buyer and the seller that the timber would need to be imported from Finland. However, if the buyer had been a timber mer-chant, the result may well have been different since then the buyer would also have known and assumed that the timber could and would be imported from Finland.

Of course, a contract for the sale of goods by description may be frustrated in many other ways. A straightforward example would be the enactment of legislation prohibiting

---

[39] See Chapter 22, Section 1.
[40] [1918] 2 KB 467. See too *CTI Group Inc v Transclear SA (The Mary Nour)* [2008] EWCA Civ 856, [2009] 2 All ER (Comm) 25.

dealing in the goods in question. Legislation rendering the performance of a contract illegal necessarily frustrates it.[41]

(e) Leases

It was once thought that a **lease** can never be frustrated because a lease is something more than a contract: a lease conveys an estate in land, which continues regardless of fundamental changes in the circumstances.[42] Indeed, the hard line taken by the court in the old case of *Paradine v Jane*[43] was in the context of a lease. However, a lease may be terminated prematurely by reason of an express term, so it seems equally possible that it might be terminated by an implied term, if such a term should properly be implied.

The circumstances in which such a term is necessarily implied in a lease are likely to be rare. Indeed, in neither of the two leading cases in which the House of Lords has considered the matter was the lease held by any of their Lordships to be frustrated. In *Cricklewood Property and Investment Trust Ltd v Leighton's Investment Trust Ltd*,[44] the lease was granted in 1936 for a term of 99 years. The land was to be used as sites for shops which the lessee covenanted to erect within a certain time limit. When war broke out in 1939, no building had been done, and it then became impossible to do so because of government restrictions. The lessee's claim that the lease was frustrated failed. This is clearly right under the principles already discussed. Although prospects seemed very bleak in the early days of the war, it was still assumed that there would be plenty of time before the year 2035 during which the shops could be built and enjoyed. The invasion of the contract period—whether actual or contemplated—was not sufficiently extensive to prevent substantial performance. Two of their Lordships thought, *obiter*, that a lease could never be frustrated, but two others took the opposite view. The latter approach should be preferred. Suppose that legislation had permanently prohibited building, declaring the area an open space forever. If the common purpose of the lease were the erection of buildings, that common purpose would have failed. Surely the lease would be frustrated.

In *National Carriers Ltd v Panalpina (Northern) Ltd*,[45] four out of five members of the House of Lords agreed that a lease might be frustrated, although they also recognised that it would rarely happen and had certainly not happened in that case. The case concerned the lease of a warehouse for ten years. After a little more than five years had elapsed, the local authority closed the street giving the only access to the warehouse because of the dangerous condition of a listed building opposite. It seemed likely that the closure would last just over 18 months, leaving the lease with three more years to run. The closure of the street would obviously cause a severe interruption of the lessee's business and force the lessee to incur considerable expense and inconvenience, but this is not enough to frustrate a

---

[41] cf *Metropolitan Water Board v Dick Kerr and Co Ltd* [1918] AC 119, HL, considered at Section 1(b).
[42] See eg K Gray and S Gray, *Land Law* (7th edn, OUP, 2011) ch 4.
[43] Section 1(a).
[44] [1945] AC 221.
[45] [1981] AC 675.

contract.[46] The interruption was for one-sixth of the total term and (perhaps more to the point) one-third of the remainder of the term. The interruption had not:[47]

> so significantly changed the nature of the outstanding contractual rights and obligations under the lease from what the parties could reasonably have contemplated at the time of its execution that it would be unjust to hold them to the literal sense of its stipulations.

Clearly, the result might have been different if it had appeared that the road would be closed for the whole, or substantially the whole, of the remainder of the term.

It appears that where a lease has a particular purpose (such as building, warehousing, dwelling, and so on) an event which prevents the fulfilment of that purpose may frustrate the lease. If property is let as a warehouse, it certainly seems reasonable to conclude that the basic common assumption of the parties is that the property is, and will remain, capable of use as a warehouse. Lord Russell, dissenting in *Panalpina* on the issue of principle, thought that the purchaser of a **leasehold** interest, like the purchaser of a **freehold**, takes the risk that the property may become quite unsuitable for the purpose he has in mind, but this view was not shared by the other members of the House of Lords.

3 Self-induced frustration

The essence of frustration is that performance has been rendered impossible without the fault of either party, and so it is said that 'reliance cannot be placed on a self-induced frustration'. On the contrary, a party who causes a 'frustrating' event will usually be in breach of contract. If the father who had contracted that his son would serve as an apprentice for seven years had, during that time, killed or incapacitated his son, he could not have relied on frustration. If Caldwell had deliberately burnt down the music hall, he would clearly have been liable to Taylor for the failure to provide it.[48]

In *The Eugenia*,[49] a charterparty prohibited the charterers from bringing the vessel into a dangerous zone. In breach of contract, the charterers sailed the vessel to Port Said at a time when it was a dangerous zone. The ship was then trapped in the Suez Canal and it became impossible to carry out the charterparty. The charterers argued that the contract was therefore frustrated. However, the Court of Appeal held that the charterers could not rely on their own 'self-induced frustration' to say that the contract was at an end. The charterers were liable for breach of contract.

In *Maritime National Fish Ltd v Ocean Trawlers Ltd*,[50] the appellants chartered the respondents' trawler, the *St Cuthbert*, for 12 months. The trawler was to be used in the fishing industry only. Both parties knew that the vessel could only be used with an otter trawl and that it was an offence to use a vessel with an otter trawl without a **licence** from the appropriate Canadian minister. The appellants, who were operating five trawlers, applied

---

[46] See Section 1(a).
[47] [1981] AC 675, 707 (Lord Simon of Glaisdale).
[48] cf *Taylor v Caldwell*, considered at Section 1(a).
[49] [1964] 2 QB 226, CA.
[50] [1935] AC 524, PC.

for five licences but were granted only three. The appellants were asked to name the three trawlers to be licensed. They named three of their trawlers, but not the *St Cuthbert*. The appellants sought to escape from their contractual obligation to charter the *St Cuthbert* by arguing that the contract was frustrated since the *St Cuthbert* was not licensed and could not be used with an otter trawl for fishing. The Privy Council held that the appellants could not rely on the lack of a licence as the basis of frustration, because the lack of a licence for the *St Cuthbert* and consequent inability to use that vessel with an otter trawl for fishing was due to the appellants' own actions: the appellants could have named the *St Cuthbert* for a licence, but chose not to do so. Presumably, the case would have been decided differently if the minister (and not the appellants) had named the trawlers to be licensed and had excluded the *St Cuthbert*. That would have been beyond the control of the appellants.

The *Ocean Trawlers* case was followed by the Court of Appeal in *The Super Servant Two*.[51] The defendants contracted to carry the claimants' rig from Japan to Rotterdam on either the *Super Servant One* or the *Super Servant Two*. The defendants intended to use *Two*, but that vessel sank. However, by that time the defendants had already also entered into other contracts and needed to use *One* to perform those. The defendants argued that their contract with the claimants was frustrated because it was no longer possible to perform that contract: *Two* had sunk and *One* was tied up as a result of other contracts. The Court of Appeal held that the defendants' contract with the claimants was not frustrated. Admittedly, the defendants could not perform all their contracts and may have acted reasonably in the circumstances; but the fact that their inability to perform their contract with the claimants was the result of the defendants' own choice to perform other contracts instead was fatal to the plea of frustration. Although this might seem to be a hard decision, it is important to note that the contract afforded the defendants a choice whether to use *One* or *Two* to fulfil its obligations with the claimants.[52] The price of this choice is that it makes frustration harder to establish. If the contract had stated that *Two* was the only vessel that could be used, and *Two* then sank, then it is much more likely that the contract would have been frustrated.

Where it is uncertain whether or not the alleged frustrating event was due to the 'fault' of one of the parties, and neither party is able to establish what happened, it is crucial to determine which party bears the burden of proof. If it is for the party claiming that the 'frustration' was self-induced to prove that it was self-induced, the claim will fail. But if it is for the other party to prove that it was not self-induced, the contract will be frustrated. This issue arose in *Joseph Constantine Steamship Line Ltd v Imperial Smelting Corp Ltd*.[53] In that case, the relevant event was an explosion in a ship which prevented the shipowner from delivering the ship in accordance with the terms of a charterparty. The charterer claimed damages, and the shipowner argued that the contract had been frustrated. The explosion may or may not have been due to the fault of the shipowner. It was impossible to say. The House of Lords held that the onus of proof lay on the charterer to show that the shipowner was at fault. The charterer's action therefore failed. Some of their Lordships explained the

---

[51] *J Lauritzen AS v Wijsmuller BV (The Super Servant Two)* [1990] 1 Lloyd's Rep 1, CA.

[52] This also explains why the *force majeure* clause, set out at Section 1(b), did not give the defendant the right to cancel the contract.

[53] [1942] AC 154, HL.

decision on the basis of a general principle that the party who brings a matter into issue must prove it. Since it was the charterers who were saying that the shipowner was at fault, the charterers should have to prove that. But, equally, it might be said that the shipowner, simply by raising the defence of frustration, was asserting that he was not at fault, because the whole essence of a frustrating event is that it is one which occurs without the fault of either party. On this view, the shipowner should have to prove a lack of fault. Nevertheless, the outcome of the case does seem satisfactory, although it should be noted that the House of Lords was perhaps influenced by the context of the dispute. It was a wartime case, and Viscount Simon envisaged the case of a ship being torpedoed and sinking immediately. Is the shipowner to be liable because he cannot prove affirmatively that the crew were behaving with all proper care, keeping a good lookout, obscuring lights, and so on? It would seem unreasonable that he should bear that burden of proof.

4 The effect of frustration

The occurrence of the frustrating event brings the contract to an end. It 'kills the contract'.[54] The contract is not, however, invalidated from the start. Everything that was done from the making of the contract up to its frustration was, and remains, validly done in pursuance of the contract. The consequences of frustration differ at common law and under the Law Reform (Frustrated Contracts) Act 1943. Both will now be examined in turn.

(a) Common law

At one time, the courts held that money paid in pursuance of the contract before the frustrating event was necessarily irrecoverable, and that promises to pay which were made before the frustrating event remained enforceable. In *Chandler v Webster*,[55] the claimant made a contract for the hire of a room to view the coronation procession for £141 15s, payable immediately. He paid £100. Subsequently, the procession was cancelled. The court held that the claimant was not entitled to recover the £100. Moreover, the court insisted that the claimant was bound to pay the additional £41 15s. This was a valid obligation incurred by virtue of a promise made by the claimant while the contract was still alive.

The decision in *Chandler v Webster* was overruled by the House of Lords in *Fibrosa Spolka Akcyjna v Fairbairn Lawson Combe Barbour Ltd*.[56] The House of Lords insisted that benefits transferred from the claimant to the defendant prior to the frustrating event could be recovered by the claimant if there had been a 'total failure of consideration'. It is now important to distinguish between two meanings of 'consideration'.[57] When we are discussing the formation of contracts, 'consideration' means the promise. But when we are concerned with the action in unjust enrichment based on total failure of consideration, 'consideration' means the performance of the promise. In *Fibrosa*, an English company contracted to sell

---

[54] *The Super Servant Two* (Bingham LJ).
[55] [1904] 1 KB 493.
[56] [1943] AC 32.
[57] See further Chapter 28, Section 4.

machinery to a Polish company. The contract price was £4,800, one-third of which was payable immediately. In fact only £1,000 was paid. The contract was then frustrated by the outbreak of war. The House of Lords, reversing the Court of Appeal which had followed *Chandler v Webster*, held that the Polish company was entitled to recover the £1,000. The Polish company's cause of action was what we would now call unjust enrichment, and the relevant unjust factor was total failure of consideration. Although the English company had done a considerable amount of work on the machinery before the frustrating event, none had been delivered and the House of Lords treated this as a total failure of consideration. This outcome achieves better justice than *Chandler v Webster*, which should be decided differently today: the promise to provide a view of the procession, even though a perfectly good promise and consideration for the claimant's promise to pay, was wholly unperformed. As a result, there had been a total failure of the basis upon which the claimant had enriched the defendant, so the claimant ought to have recovered his £100 and been discharged from his obligation to pay the £41 15s.

In *Fibrosa*, the House of Lords recognised that the law was still not entirely satisfactory. This was for two main reasons. First, money was recoverable only where the failure of consideration was total; the performance of even a small part of the consideration would defeat the claim.[58] Secondly, it might be unfair if a party who had prudently requested payment in advance in order to be able to meet expenses would then have to repay that payment after the frustrating event. Indeed, it may be that the English company in *Fibrosa* was left with a considerable amount of useless half-built machinery on its hands.

(b) Law Reform (Frustrated Contracts) Act 1943

Parliament acted swiftly after *Fibrosa* by passing the Law Reform (Frustrated Contracts) Act 1943. The 1943 Act has nothing to say about when a contract is frustrated; that remains a matter of common law. The legislation is instead concerned with adjusting the rights of parties as fairly as possible after frustration has occurred.

Nevertheless, the common law—where recovery will only be possible in unjust enrichment on the basis of a total failure of consideration following the *Fibrosa* case—is not entirely redundant. This is because there are some important contracts to which the Act does not apply at all, namely: charterparties, except time charterparties or charterparties by way of demise;[59] contracts of insurance;[60] contracts for the sale of specific goods which are frustrated by the perishing of the goods, where section 7 of the Sale of Goods Act 1979 applies;[61] and any other contract for the sale of specific goods which is frustrated by the perishing of the goods.[62]

The Act applies only in the absence of any provision to the contrary.[63] If the parties agree on some different solution to the problems that arise on the occurrence of a frustrating

---

[58] *Whincup v Hughes* (1871) LR 6 CP 78; see Chapter 28, Section 4.
[59] s 2(5)(a).
[60] s 2(5)(b).
[61] s 2(5)(c).
[62] s 2(5)(c).
[63] s 2(3).

event, then the parties' agreement, and not the Act, should prevail. This raises a serious doubt about whether the Act would apply at all to the contract in *Cutter v Powell*, at least as it was interpreted by the King's Bench.[64] Lord Kenyon CJ said that Mr Cutter 'stipulated to receive the larger sum if the whole duty were performed, and nothing unless the whole of that duty were performed: it was a kind of insurance'. If that is the right interpretation of the contract, the parties had provided for the event which occurred and their provision must prevail. However, in *BP Exploration Co (Libya) v Hunt (No 2)*, Robert Goff J thought that the fact that a contract is 'entire'[65] should not automatically preclude an award under section 1(3).[66]

(i) Section 1(2)

Section 1(2) provides that all money paid or payable before the frustrating event shall be recoverable or cease to be payable. It is not necessary to show that the consideration has totally failed. But there is a proviso that, if the party to whom money was paid or payable under the contract has incurred expenses for the purpose of the performance of the contract, the court may, if it thinks it just to do so, allow that party to retain or recover a sum not exceeding that payable under the contract and not exceeding the amount of expenses incurred. So, if *Fibrosa* occurred today and the English company had incurred expenses amounting to £1,200, the court might, in its discretion, allow the English company to retain the £1,000 paid and to recover a further £200. But if the expenses incurred amounted to £1,800, the maximum sum which the court could require the Polish company to pay would be £600 (and not £800), because only £1,600 was payable before the frustrating event (one-third of the contract price).

In *Gamerco SA v ICM/Fair Warning (Agency) Ltd*,[67] the claimants were concert promoters who entered into a contract with the defendants (the company behind Guns N' Roses) to organise a concert at the Vicente Calderon stadium (the home of Atlético Madrid Football Club). The claimants paid the defendants $412,500 in advance, but a few days before the concert the public authorities banned all use of the stadium and the concert was cancelled. A further $362,500 was due to be paid to the defendants. Both parties had incurred expenses—the claimants around $450,000 and the defendants around $50,000. Garland J accepted that the contract had been frustrated, and applied section 1(2) such that the defendants had to pay back to the claimants the $412,500 already paid. The judge did not think it just to allow the defendants to retain any of the money to cover their expenses already incurred. Garland J held that the statute conferred upon the court a 'very broad discretion' to achieve a just result in all the circumstances of the case through suitable loss apportionment. This is consistent with the language of the legislation, but the provision itself seems unnecessarily restrictive. Why limit the court's discretion to apportion losses by first demanding that the party who incurred expenses had already been paid, or was entitled to be paid, in advance? The removal of this restriction would be welcome.

---

[64] See Section 2(a).
[65] See Chapter 24, Section 8.
[66] See Section 4(b)(ii).
[67] [1995] 1 WLR 1226.

(ii) Section 1(3)

Whereas section 1(2) is concerned with the payment of money prior to the frustrating event, section 1(3) deals with situations where one party confers a non-monetary benefit upon the other party. Section 1(3) provides that where one party (A), in performing the contract, has conferred a valuable benefit on the other (B), the court may allow A to recover from B such sum, if any, as the court considers just, not exceeding the value of the benefit to B. In estimating the just sum, the court must take into account expenses incurred by B, including any money which he has paid, or is required to pay, to A under section 1(2), and the effect of the circumstances giving rise to the frustration of the contract. It is important to note that the value of a benefit conferred may be recovered even though there is no provision for an advance payment in the contract.

If, in a case like *Fibrosa*, the English company had delivered machinery which was worth £3,000 to the Polish company, the court could, if it thought it just to do so, allow the English company to retain the £1,000 paid and to recover not more than a further £2,000 from the Polish company under section 1(3). And if there had been no provision for payment, and no payment was made before the frustrating event, the court could have allowed recovery of up to £3,000.

Where the Act applies to a contract like that in *Cutter v Powell*,[68] the effect would be that the widow might recover from the master the value to him of the mate's services up to the time of the mate's death, assessed on an objective basis. If the mate had served for about three-quarters of the voyage, this may have amounted to something like £6, which would be a proportion of the usual, objectively reasonable wage, rather than the exceptionally large sum which the master had agreed to pay.

In *BP Exploration Co Libya v Hunt (No 2)*,[69] the defendant was the owner of an oil concession in Libya. He entered into a contract with BP under which BP would explore the concession for oil, in return for a large share of the profits if an oilfield were found. The exploration was successful, but the Libyan government then expropriated the concession, which meant that the contract was frustrated. Robert Goff J had to decide how section 1(3) should operate. His Lordship thought that the first stage of the inquiry required the valuable benefit to be identified and valued. The judge drew a distinction between the provision of services which had an end product, and those which did not. So, if A transports goods for B, B receives a benefit which is the value of the transport. There is no further end product. But on the facts of *BP v Hunt* there was an end product: the services provided by BP led to the discovery of oil, and Robert Goff J held that the oil was the end product of the services. As a result, the judge held that the value of the oil was the 'ceiling' amount which Hunt might have to pay to BP. Robert Goff J himself recognised that this conclusion was somewhat awkward, but thought that it was required by the language of section 1(3). This reasoning is controversial and does not seem to be necessary. It would be preferable to value the benefit Hunt received as the market value of BP's services, regardless of the value of the ultimate end product. In *Cobbe v Yeoman's Row Management Ltd*,[70] Lord Scott gave the example of a locksmith who makes a

---

[68] See Section 2(a).

[69] [1979] 1 WLR 783.

[70] [2008] UKHL 55, [2008] 1 WLR 1752 [41]. This case did not concern frustration, but the discussion concerning the valuation of a benefit is of general importance.

key which is used to open a cabinet with valuable treasure inside. The benefit the locksmith confers on the owner of the cabinet is the value of the locksmith's services in making the key. After all, the owner of the cabinet already owned the treasure, so it would be artificial to say that the benefit conferred on the owner of the cabinet by the locksmith is the treasure. The same analysis should have been applied in *BP v Hunt*: Hunt already owned the oil, so the value of the oil was not conferred on Hunt by BP.

The second stage of section 1(3) under Robert Goff J's analysis requires the court to establish the 'just sum' to be paid by *B* to *A*. This might be less, but cannot be more, than the value of the benefit conferred upon *B* by *A*. The judge thought that the aim of the court was to prevent the unjust enrichment of *A* at *B*'s expense, so the principles involved should be similar to those involved in an action for *quantum meruit*.[71] This analysis of Robert Goff J therefore rested upon the idea that section 1(3) is concerned with unjust enrichment. This is controversial. On appeal, neither the Court of Appeal nor the House of Lords offered much further guidance as to the operation of the 1943 Act, deciding that an **appellate court** should be slow to interfere with the assessment of the just sum by a trial judge. However, Lawton LJ in the Court of Appeal did not endorse Robert Goff J's reasoning based upon unjust enrichment,[72] pointing out that the language of unjust enrichment was not to be found in the statute and the statute should not be so constrained by the requirements of unjust enrichment. Lawton LJ said that '[w]hat is just is what the trial judge thinks is just'. Indeed, Robert Goff J's further suggestion that section 1(2) could also be explained by reference to unjust enrichment and not loss apportionment was clearly rejected by Garland J in *Gamerco*.

Nevertheless, the first instance decision in *BP v Hunt* remains the leading case on section 1(3) of the 1943 Act. This is unsatisfactory, but does highlight how difficult the provision is. One effect of section 1(3) as understood in *BP v Hunt* seems to be that *Appleby v Myers*[73] would still be decided in the same way. In that case, there was a contract to install machinery in the defendant's premises. The bulk of the work had already been done when the premises were burnt down and the machinery destroyed. Neither party was at fault. The contract price was only to be paid once the work was completed. Because all the work had not been completed, the court held that the claimant could not recover anything. It appears that this result would be unaffected by section 1(3) as interpreted in *BP v Hunt*. The night before the fire, the claimant had indeed conferred a benefit upon the defendant—the premises with the machinery were worth more than the premises without it—but the benefit was destroyed by the frustrating event. The court is required to take into account 'the effect, in relation to the said benefit, of the circumstances giving rise to the frustration of the contract' and because the end product of the services was destroyed it would appear that the defendant received no benefit at all from the claimant's work. This focus upon the 'end product' seems somewhat unsatisfactory, and it is perhaps not unlikely that an appellate court would depart from this aspect of the decision in *BP v Hunt* if presented with a suitable opportunity.

Indeed, it might reasonably be thought that the 1943 Act is not very clear or well drafted and could easily be improved. Some of the difficulties with the 1943 Act might be attributable to the fact that the Act was passed very soon after the decision of the House of Lords in

---

[71] See Chapter 28, Section 4.
[72] [1981] 1 WLR 232.
[73] (1867) LR 2 CP 651; see Chapter 24, Section 8.

the *Fibrosa* case. Parliament was no doubt motivated by the number of pleas of frustration facing the courts due to the outbreak of war. However, it would be helpful to be clear about whether the focus is and should really be upon the prevention of unjust enrichment or the apportionment of losses after a frustrating event. At the moment, this is still somewhat unclear. The lack of clarity has perhaps prompted many commercial parties to choose either to settle disputes before going to court, or to include *force majeure* and hardship clauses in their contracts at the outset, thereby circumventing any need to test current doctrine. As a result, the best guidance on the interpretation of section 1(2) remains the *Gamerco* case, and the best guidance on the interpretation of section 1(3) remains *BP v Hunt*.

Further Reading

E McKendrick, 'Frustration, Restitution and Loss Apportionment' in A Burrows (ed), *Essays on the Law of Restitution* (OUP, 1991).
Criticises the drafting of the 1943 Act, concluding that the Act is essentially concerned with restitution (the giving back of benefits) rather than loss apportionment, although it would be preferable to favour the latter. (Note that this article was written before the decision in *Gamerco* which does approach the statute as a matter of loss apportionment.)

JC Smith, 'Contract, Mistake, Frustration and Implied Terms' (1994) 110 LQR 400.
Further explains the utility of the implied terms approach which leaves no room for a distinct doctrine of frustration (see too Chapter 22).

P Mitchell, '*Fibrosa spolka Akcyjna v. Fairbairn Lawson Combe Barbour Limited* (1942)' in C Mitchell and P Mitchell (eds), *Landmark Cases in the Law of Restitution* (Hart, 2006).
A detailed examination of the decision and circumstances of the decision in *Fibrosa*.

E McKendrick, '*Force Majeure* Clauses: the Gap between Doctrine and Practice' in A Burrows and E Peel (eds), *Contract Terms* (OUP, 2007).
Examines the advantages of including *force majeure* clauses in a contract and how they operate in practice.

Question

Ray wanted to organise an exhibition chess match between Garry and Nigel on 9 April. Ray hired the conference facilities at the Reuben Hotel in London for this purpose. The contract price was £30,000, and Ray paid the full amount to the Reuben Hotel upon entering into the agreement.

Ray also entered into separate contracts with Garry and Nigel. Both Garry and Nigel were to receive £20,000 for taking part in the match, and each player received £5,000 upon signing the contract. Ray agreed to pay the winner a further £10,000.

On 6 April, Garry is due to catch his aeroplane to fly from Croatia to London to prepare for the event, but his visa is revoked due to a criminal conviction in Croatia for protesting against the government. As a result, Ray has to cancel the event.

Advise Ray.

24 Conditions, warranties, and innominate terms

🔑 Key Points

- The victim of a breach of contract can always sue for damages for the breach. However, he will not always be able to terminate the contract. Termination of the contract for breach means that the contract no longer needs to be performed, but that everything done in pursuance of the contract up to the point of breach remains valid.

- An injured party will be entitled to choose to terminate the contract for breach of condition, or for a sufficiently serious breach of an innominate term. An injured party may never terminate a contract for breach of warranty.

- Some terms are explicitly characterised as conditions or warranties by statute (see, for example, Sale of Goods Act 1979, ss 12–15A). Otherwise, whether a term is a condition, innominate term, or warranty is a question of construction. Parties are able expressly to make a term a condition or warranty, for instance. Some terms are regularly recognised as conditions as a result of consistent and regular usage in a particular context.

- Parties may expressly agree that the contract will terminate on the occurrence of a certain event. Such express termination clauses may be triggered by an event which is not a breach of contract, and therefore the party invoking the clause may not be entitled to damages. However, where the triggering event is a repudiatory breach of contract, the innocent party will generally be entitled to damages.

- In the context of an 'entire obligation', the complete performance of the obligation is a condition of the liability of the other party. If that obligation is not fulfilled, the other party does not have to pay the defaulting party unless there has been 'substantial performance'. In this context, the failure to satisfy a condition does not entitle the innocent party to terminate the contract, but instead to refuse to perform his side of the bargain unless and until the condition is fulfilled.

All promises in a contract have to be performed. If any one of them is not performed, the party in breach is liable to pay damages. But not all promises in a contract have the same significance. Some breaches of contract not only entitle the injured party to claim damages, but also entitle him to put an end to the contract. It is in connection with the right to terminate the contract on breach that the nature of the term becomes important.[1]

---

[1] The innocent party is obviously not compelled to exercise his right to terminate: for further discussion of election, see Chapter 25.

It is important at the outset to make it clear that when a party terminates a contract that does not mean that the contract is wiped out from the beginning.[2] Termination in this context needs to be clearly distinguished from **rescission**. Breach operates prospectively but not retrospectively. This explains why, in *Photo Production Ltd v Securicor*[3], Lord Diplock distinguished between primary obligations and secondary obligations. Primary obligations are the obligations of performance demanded under the contract. Secondary obligations are obligations which arise upon breach of contract and replace the primary obligations of performance—typically, secondary obligations are obligations to pay damages. This is what Lord Diplock meant when he said that 'breaches of primary obligations give rise to substituted or secondary obligations on the part of the party in default'.

It has always been clear that a party may terminate a contract for breach of **condition**, but never for breach of warranty. It has now been recognised that some terms are neither conditions nor warranties; such terms are often called 'intermediate' or **innominate terms**. It may be possible to terminate a contract for breach of an innominate term if the breach is sufficiently serious. Breaches which justify termination are often called 'repudiatory breaches'. It will be important to clarify the meaning and scope of conditions, warranties, and innominate terms. This chapter will also consider express termination clauses and another difficult sense in which the term 'condition' is used, namely to denote an 'entire obligation'.

1 Old orthodoxy: conditions and warranties

For many years, writers on the law of contract assumed that there were only two classes of contractual promise: every promise was either a condition or a warranty. If it was a condition, any breach of it entitled the injured party to terminate the contract as well as to claim damages. Hence, the language of 'condition'—*A*'s liability to perform is conditional on *B*'s fulfilling his promise.[4] A breach of a warranty, on the other hand, entitled the injured party to damages only. He was not entitled to terminate the contract for breach of a warranty, and his liability to perform his part of the contract continued unimpaired. Whether a party had a right to terminate the contract depended on the nature of the term broken—in other words, whether the term was a condition or a warranty. The nature of the term was determined in the light of the state of affairs when the contract was made. The nature of the breach was immaterial.

However, even this explanation of the law perhaps worked better in theory than in practice. In practice, courts often seem to have had regard to the effect of the breach in deciding whether the injured party could treat the contract as at an end. Stock examples of a warranty and a condition that were often cited in the textbooks are the cases of *Bettini v Gye*[5] and *Poussard v Spiers*.[6] These cases are not easy to reconcile. The claimant in each case was

---

[2] See Chapter 16, Section 4(a).
[3] [1980] 1 All ER 556.
[4] For further uses of the word 'condition' which have caused some confusion in contract law, see Section 8.
[5] (1876) 1 QBD 183.
[6] (1876) 1 QBD 410.

a singer who, because of illness, was unable to be present on the day on which the singer's presence was first required. In each case, the defendant purported to terminate the contract and the claimant sued for damages. But in *Bettini* it was held that the defendant could not terminate the contract, whilst the opposite result was reached in *Poussard*.

Bettini was required by his contract to be present six days before the first performance for rehearsals and he arrived three days late. Bettini had been hired to sing in theatres, halls, and drawing rooms from 30 March to 13 July 1875. His failure to arrive on time clearly did not prevent the contract from being substantially carried out. The court held that Bettini's failure to arrive on time did not go to the root of the contract and the defendant was not entitled to dismiss him (although the defendant was still entitled to claim damages). On the other hand, in *Poussard*, the court held that the defendant was justified in terminating the singer's contract and engaging another artiste. Poussard was taken ill five days before the first performance, and her illness appeared to be a serious one of uncertain duration.

The difference between *Bettini* and *Poussard* was explained by many writers on the basis that Bettini committed a breach of warranty only, whereas Poussard committed a breach of condition. In neither case, however, did the court scrutinise the contract at the time it was made and identify a term as a condition or a warranty. Rather, the court looked at the effect of the failure to perform in the circumstances existing at the time of the failure. So, if a temporary substitute for Poussard could have been obtained on reasonable terms, the defendant would not have been justified in dismissing her. Because no such substitute was available, the claimant's 'breach' went to the root of the matter. And if Bettini's contract had been for a very short duration, perhaps the outcome in that case would have been different. In any event, however, the term at issue in both *Bettini* and *Poussard* seems to have been the same—the promise to be available on a certain day. The difference between them was in the nature and effect of the breach.[7] But such considerations ought not to be relevant when deciding whether a term is a condition or warranty at the time the contract is made.

However, although *Bettini* and *Poussard* are difficult to reconcile under the 'old' law, it has since been explicitly recognised that the court can now take into account the nature and effect of a breach of contract when considering a third category of terms, often called 'innominate terms', which are to be placed between conditions and warranties on a possible 'scale' of terms.

2 The modern approach: recognition of innominate terms

The courts have now recognised that the classification of promises into conditions and warranties is not exhaustive. There is a third class of term, a breach of which may or may not entitle the injured party to put an end to the contract. Whether or not the injured party is entitled to terminate the contract depends on the nature and effect of the breach. Such

---

[7] It should also be observed that it is doubtful if there was a true breach by the singer in either case. The contract in *Poussard* was surely frustrated and therefore at an end; and a failure to perform through illness is surely excused, even if it does not amount to a frustrating event. See further Chapter 23.

terms, being a relatively recent discovery of the courts, have no accepted name and in this book are called 'innominate terms'. Sometimes the courts and writers refer to them as 'intermediate terms', because they lie between a condition (any breach of which entitles the injured party to end the contract) and a warranty (no breach of which entitles him to do so). See Table 24.1.

Table 24.1

Breach of condition:	damages + right to terminate
Breach of innominate term:	damages + maybe a right to terminate, depending on the nature and effect of breach
Breach of warranty:	damages only

Some breaches of an innominate term may have only a slight effect on the subsequent performance of the contract, whereas other breaches will render the contract substantially incapable of performance. If the breach is of the former type, the injured party has his remedy in damages but remains bound to perform his side of the contract. If it is of the latter type, he is entitled to damages and to put an end to the contract.

The leading case recognising the existence of innominate terms is the *Hongkong Fir* case.[8] The contract was the **charter** of a ship, the *Hongkong Fir*, for a period of 24 months. The term in issue was the shipowner's express promise that the ship was seaworthy, 'being in every way fitted for ordinary cargo service'. Previous authorities showed that such a term was broken by the slightest failure to be fitted 'in every way' for service. A wooden vessel was therefore considered to be unfit if a nail was missing from one of the timbers, or if proper medical supplies, or two anchors, were not on board at the time of sailing. In the *Hongkong Fir*, the court thought that it would be contrary to common sense that a party should be entitled to put an end to a large contract because of such trivial and easily re-mediable breaches. On the other hand, however, there might be other serious breaches of the same term which should obviously entitle the charterer to decline to proceed with the contract. For example, the ship may not be 'in every way fitted for ordinary cargo service' because the bottom of the ship is so rotten that it is likely to fall out as soon as the ship puts to sea. Because of the wide range of possible breaches of that same innominate term, it is necessary to consider the particular breach which has occurred and estimate its effect on the further performance of the contract when deciding whether the breach is sufficiently serious to allow the injured party to terminate the contract. If the party in default is still able to do substantially what he has promised to do, then the injured party has no right to put an end to the contract; but if the breach would deprive him of substantially the whole benefit he expected to receive from the contract, then he may refuse to proceed with the contract.

In the *Hongkong Fir* itself, the unseaworthiness was the defective state of the ship's engines and the inefficiency of the engine room staff. This resulted in five weeks' delay

---

[8] *Hongkong Fir Shipping Co Ltd v Kawasaki Kisen Kaisha Ltd* [1962] 2 QB 26.

and a further 15 weeks to do repairs. However, even at the end of that period of time, the **charterparty** still had 20 months to run. As a result, the breach did not deprive the charterers of substantially the whole benefit of the contract and they were not entitled to terminate the charter.

Where an innominate term is at issue, it is crucial to determine the effect of the particular breach when deciding whether the innocent party is able to terminate the contract. In *Maple Flock Co Ltd v Universal Furniture Products (Wembley) Ltd*,[9] Lord Hewart CJ said that, in the context of a contract for the sale of goods by instalments, it was important to consider 'the ratio quantitatively which the breach bears to the contract as a whole, and secondly the degree of probability or improbability that such a breach will be repeated'. In that case, the contract was for the sale of 100 tons of rag flock. This was to be delivered in three loads of 1.5 tons per week until the full 100 tons had been delivered. It was a term of the contract that all rag flock supplied should conform to government standards, but the sixteenth delivery contained too much chlorine. The buyers then refused to take further deliveries of the rag flock, claiming that there had been a **repudiatory**[10] breach of contract and that they were entitled to terminate the agreement. The Court of Appeal disagreed. The breach concerned a very small proportion of the total amount to be delivered—1.5 tons out of 100 tons—and was unlikely to be repeated, since all the previous (and three subsequent) deliveries were in compliance with the contractual terms. The buyers were therefore themselves in breach of contract by refusing to accept the deliveries.

Whether or not an innocent party is entitled to terminate the contract for breach of an innominate term depends heavily upon the particular facts of a case. But general formulations of principle by judges continue to be made and may be helpful. For instance, in *Telford Homes (Creekside) Ltd v Ampurius Nu Homes Holdings Ltd*, Lewison LJ said that it was important to consider:[11]

> the effect of the breach on the injured party. What financial loss has it caused? How much of the intended benefit under the contract has the injured party already received? Can the injured party be adequately compensated by an award of damages? Is the breach likely to be repeated? Will the guilty party resume compliance with his obligations? Has the breach fundamentally changed the value of future performance of the guilty party's outstanding obligations?

Lewison LJ also criticised the language of deciding whether the breach 'goes to the root of contract', since speaking in such metaphors is opaque.[12] But although there will be difficulties on particular facts when determining whether a breach of contract deprives the innocent party of substantially the whole benefit of the contract, it is difficult to formulate the test in a more transparent way. As Arden LJ has since said, 'I do not myself criticise the vagueness of these expressions of the principle since I do not consider that any satisfactory fixed rule could be formulated in this field.'[13]

---

[9] [1934] 1 KB 148, 157, CA.
[10] A repudiation, or renunciation, is where one of the parties evinces an intention not to continue with the contract.
[11] [2013] EWCA Civ 577, [2013] 4 All ER 377 [52].
[12] Ibid [50].
[13] *Valilas v Januzaj* [2014] EWCA Civ 436 [59].

It often appears to be the case that courts are generally reluctant to allow the innocent party to terminate a contract where there has been a breach of an innominate term; indeed, there seems to be some desire to keep contracts alive where possible, and limit the innocent party to a claim in damages. For instance, in *Telford Homes* itself the innocent party was not entitled to terminate the contract to take leases in four mixed-use blocks when the construction company was late in building two of the blocks. The innocent party was to take the commercial units in the blocks under 999-year leases, and the delay of nine months was not sufficient to entitle the innocent party to repudiate the contract: the innocent party was not deprived of substantially the whole benefit of the contract and was limited to a claim for damages.

Similarly, in *Valilas v Januzaj*,[14] the Court of Appeal, by a majority,[15] held that the owner of a dental practice was not entitled to terminate a contract with a dentist when the dentist's periodic payments under the contract (for use of the owner's facilities) were made late. The owner of the practice knew that the money would eventually be paid, and was not deprived of substantially the whole benefit of the contract. As Floyd LJ put it, 'Whether a breach or threatened breach does give rise to a right to terminate involves a multi-factorial assessment involving the nature of the contract and the relationship it creates, the nature of the term, the kind and degree of the breach and the consequences of the breach for the injured party'.[16] In *Valilas v Januzaj*, the Court of Appeal was content for the contractual relationship to continue; all the owner of the practice had lost was the use value of the money whilst waiting for the delayed payments. This could easily be compensated, and was not sufficiently serious for the owner of the practice to terminate the contract.

3 The survival of conditions and warranties

One view is that the law ought to treat all terms like innominate terms—that the right to terminate the contract for breach should always depend on the nature and effect of the breach. However, it is clear that this view does not represent the current state of the law, and that conditions and warranties continue to exist. For instance, it is established law that certain classes of term have the status of conditions unless, in a particular case, the parties have made it clear that the term is not to have that status. This is so even in respect of many terms which bear the same characteristic as the shipowner's promise that the vessel is seaworthy, in that some breaches of the term may be extremely trivial, others extremely serious.

Some examples of common terms will now be considered. However, it is important to appreciate that whether a term is a condition or an innominate term, for example, is simply a question of interpretation.[17] It may nevertheless be true that courts are increasingly willing to interpret a term as an innominate term, as this then allows the courts to

---

[14] [2014] EWCA Civ 436, [2015] 1 All ER (Comm) 1047.

[15] Floyd LJ and Arden LJ; Underhill LJ dissented.

[16] Ibid [53].

[17] See eg the different judgments in *BS&N Ltd (BVI) v Micado Shipping Ltd (Malta) (The Seaflower)* [2001] 1 All ER (Comm) 240. On interpretation generally, see Chapter 12.

take into account the effect of breach when deciding whether or not the innocent party is entitled to terminate the contract. This might explain why in *The Hansa Nord* the term 'shipment in good condition' was not considered to be a condition but rather an innominate term.[18]

(a) Conditions in the Sale of Goods Act

When Chalmers drafted the Sale of Goods Act 1893, he assumed that every term must be either a condition or a warranty and categorised the implied terms in a contract for the sale of goods accordingly. For example, section 13 of the 1979 Act, as amended, provides that, in a contract for the sale of goods by description, there is an implied term that the goods will correspond with the description;[19] and that that term is a condition. The description may be a very detailed specification. Nevertheless, a failure to comply with that specification in some respect, however trivial, is a breach of condition which, in principle, entitles any buyer to reject the goods. This can lead to harsh results.

For example, in *Arcos Ltd v EA Ronaasen & Son*,[20] the buyers entered into a contract to purchase timber to be used in making cement barrels. The timber was described in the contract as being half an inch thick. In breach of contract, the sellers delivered timber which was nine-sixteenths of an inch thick. The House of Lords held that the purchasers were entitled to reject the timber for breach of a condition, even though such timber was just as good for making cement barrels, and the purchasers' actions were really only motivated by a desire to take advantage of a falling market.

If the facts of the *Arcos* case were to arise today it is unclear whether the same result would be reached. This is because a new section was inserted into the Sale of Goods Act in 1994: section 15A provides that, where the buyer is not a consumer[21] and 'the breach is so slight that it would be unreasonable for him to reject [the goods]', the breach is not to be treated as a breach of condition but may be treated as if it were a breach of warranty. This means that the buyer would not invariably be able to terminate the contract for breach of the term. Section 15A applies to terms implied by sections 14 (quality and fitness) and 15 (sale by sample) as well as section 13. These terms, although described as conditions, are effectively now innominate terms in non-consumer contracts. However, whether or not section 15A would cover situations such as that in the *Arcos* case will depend upon how courts interpret the requirement that the breach be 'so slight'. It is, perhaps, not entirely obvious that the difference between half an inch and nine-sixteenths of an inch is 'so slight' given the proportions involved. Given such uncertainty, it is unclear whether the insertion of section 15A was in fact desirable: section 15A appears to undermine certainty in the context of contracts concluded by commercial parties, despite the commercial context being one area where certainty is very highly prized.

---

[18] *Cehave NV v Bremer Handelsgesellschaft mbH (The Hansa Nord)* [1976] QB 44.
[19] For further discussion of implied terms, see Chapter 13.
[20] [1933] AC 470, HL.
[21] For consideration of the position as regards consumers, see Section 6.

(b) Particular terms expressly made conditions by the parties

The parties themselves are able to stipulate that any particular term of the contract should have the status of a condition. This is important. It respects the parties' freedom to make it clear which terms are considered to be crucial, and it also enhances commercial certainty, since any breach of a term which has been given the status of a condition will allow the injured party to terminate the contract.

However, whether a term has the status of a condition is a question of interpretation of the contract. The fact that a term is given the label of 'condition' is therefore not conclusive. In *Schuler (L) AG v Wickman Machine Tool Sales Ltd*,[22] a contract granting *W* sole selling rights of presses manufactured by *S* provided that '[i]t shall be a condition of this agreement' that *W* should send its representative to visit the six largest UK motor manufacturers at least once in each week. No other term in the 20 clauses of the agreement used the word 'condition'. This would normally indicate that the clause was in fact intended to have the status of 'condition'. Yet the majority of the House of Lords held that the term was not a condition and that *S* was not entitled to put an end to the contract on the particular breaches which had occurred when *W* failed to make the required visits. This conclusion was reached by looking at the contract as a whole, and finding that there was some ambiguity about whether or not the parties truly intended that any breach of the term should entitle *S* to terminate the contract. This ambiguity was then resolved in favour of *W*, since the majority thought that it was unlikely that the parties really intended that *S* should invariably be entitled to terminate the contract if this term was breached.

It is important to note the decision in *Schuler* depends very much on its facts. Within the particular contract, there were clauses which might be thought to have been inconsistent and to have created some ambiguity, such that the term in issue could not confidently be said to be intended to have the status of a 'condition'. Yet the majority decision was greatly influenced by the view that it was wholly unreasonable that *S* should be able to put an end to the contract merely because, in one week, *W* failed to send its representative to one manufacturer. Their Lordships were not prepared to put such a construction on the contract unless they had to.

Where two parties to a contract do not understand the legal importance of the language of 'condition', an approach similar to that adopted by the majority in *Schuler* is understandable. This is because the parties may not really intend the breach of that term inevitably to give rise to a right to terminate the contract. But *Schuler* itself concerned commercial parties who deliberately chose to use the word 'condition' and might reasonably be expected to understand the significance of such language. Indeed, Lord Wilberforce, dissenting in *Schuler*, was not prepared to assume 'that both parties to this contract adopted a standard of easygoing tolerance rather than one of aggressive, insistent punctuality and efficiency'.[23] This more robust approach is generally to be favoured in commercial agreements.[24] Indeed, it is perhaps telling that it was Lord Wilberforce who insisted upon such a strict

---

[22] [1974] AC 235, HL.

[23] Ibid 263.

[24] In *Tullow Uganda Ltd v Heritage Oil and Gas Ltd*, Beatson LJ described *Schuler* as a 'high-water mark': [2014] EWCA Civ 1048, [2014] 2 CLC 61 [33].

approach, given that Lord Wilberforce was generally prepared to look at background factors and helped to coin the phrase 'matrix of fact'.[25] If even Lord Wilberforce thought that the chosen language of 'condition' should be given effect, great caution should be exercised before deciding otherwise. In any event, it is important to note that the decision in *Schuler* is something of an outlier; in most commercial contracts, the language of 'condition' is understood to afford the particular term the status of 'condition' without much dispute.

(c) **Conditions as to time**

In mercantile contracts, case law has established that many stipulations as to time are conditions.[26] Obviously, the breach of such a stipulation may vary greatly in its effect. For instance, the seller's tendering of goods one day late may be vastly different from his tendering them one month late. However, both breaches are breaches of the same term and, if that term is a condition, either breach entitles the buyer to put an end to the contract. It has sometimes been said that a condition is a term, any breach of which 'may fairly be considered by the other party as a substantial failure to perform the contract at all';[27] but this clearly needs qualification. If a term is of such a nature that any breach of it will have that effect, then it can hardly fail to be a condition. But the examples already given show that some recognised conditions do not have that characteristic. As Blackburn J said, 'Parties may think some matter, apparently of very little importance, essential; and if they sufficiently express an intention to make the literal fulfilment of such a thing a condition precedent, it will be one.'[28] This principle is not confined to expressed intention; it may be inferred from commercial custom and precedent. This has been established for stipulations as to time in mercantile contracts. In *Bunge Corp New York v Tradax Export SA, Panama*,[29] a contract for the sale of goods required the buyers to give the sellers at least 15 consecutive days' notice of probable readiness of the vessel to be loaded. The buyer gave only 13 days' notice and the seller repudiated the contract. It was held that he was entitled to do so. The term was a condition and it was not necessary to consider what the effect of the particular breach might be.

Obligations as to time are of vital importance in the shipping industry. But it would seem that the same might not be said of stipulations as to time in other contexts; whether such a term is generally considered to be a condition will depend upon both custom and practice. Thus in *Valilas v Januzaj*, considered in Section 2 of this chapter,[30] the stipulation that payment be on time was considered by all the judges to be an innominate term rather than a condition. Underhill LJ even said that '[t]ime of payment is not generally of the essence of a commercial contract unless the parties have agreed (either expressly or by necessary implication) that it should be'.[31] The breach of the time condition was insufficiently serious

---

[25] See eg *Prenn v Simmonds* [1971] 1 WLR 1381, discussed further in Chapter 12, Section 5.

[26] See eg *Lombard North Central plc v Butterworth* [1987] QB 527.

[27] See eg *Wallis v Pratt* [1910] 2 KB 1003, 1012 (Fletcher Moulton LJ, whose dissenting judgment in the Court of Appeal received the support of the House of Lords: [1911] AC 394).

[28] *Bettini v Gye* (1876) 1 QBD 183, 187.

[29] [1981] 1 WLR 711, HL.

[30] *Valilas v Januzaj* [2014] EWCA Civ 436, considered at Section 2.

[31] Ibid [29].

in *Valilas* since the owner of the dental practice had other sources of income and was not dependent upon prompt payment to run his affairs.[32] A similar approach was taken by the Court of Appeal in *Decro-Wall International SA v Practitioners in Marketing*.[33] In that case, there was a series of late payments by purchasers to their suppliers. But the delays were very short, had caused only minimal (and recoverable) losses, and had only occurred for reasons which were forgivable, which the suppliers well understood and which gave no reason to doubt that they would soon receive payment in full, even though that would be a few days late.

In any event, it obviously remains possible for the parties themselves expressly to make it clear that an obligation as to time is to be treated as a condition. Moreover, following a breach of contract, the innocent party might then serve a notice on the defaulting party that time is 'of the essence', even if it was not 'of the essence' in the original contract. Provided that the notice allows the defaulting party a reasonable time within which to remedy the breach, then failure to comply should allow the innocent party to terminate the contract.[34] Admittedly, however, the Court of Appeal has recently expressed the contrary view that the innocent party should only be entitled to terminate if the defaulting party's failure to comply with the notice was itself a sufficiently serious breach,[35] but this approach undermines commercial certainty and should be rejected.[36]

(d) The survival of warranties

The recognition of innominate terms might reasonably be thought to render warranties redundant. After all, why specify that a breach of a particular term can *never* entitle the injured party to terminate the agreement? Why not retain a greater degree of flexibility by saying that that term is an innominate term, such that termination remains an option? In practice, courts are now reluctant to find that a term is a warranty such that the injured party is only ever entitled to claim damages. But some terms continue to be classified as warranties. Indeed, some statutory provisions mean that certain terms are inevitably warranties.[37] There seems to be no good reason to restrict the parties' freedom expressly to designate certain terms to be 'warranties', even if this freedom is perhaps rarely exploited.

4 Express termination clauses

The parties may expressly agree that the contract will terminate on the occurrence of a certain event. Of course, this may be by making a term a condition, but the parties may also include an express termination clause in their contract. An express termination clause might be widely drafted such that it will apply in situations where there would have been

---

[32] cf *Alan Auld Associates v Rick Pollard Associates* [2008] EWCA Civ 655.
[33] [1971] 1 WLR 361.
[34] *Behzadi v Shaftesbury Hotels Ltd* [1992] Ch 1.
[35] *Samarenko v Dawn Hill House Ltd* [2011] EWCA Civ 1445, [2013] Ch 36; see too *Urban I (Blonk Street) Ltd v Ayres* [2013] EWCA Civ 816, [2014] 1 WLR 756.
[36] J Carter, 'Deposits and "Time of the Essence"' (2013) 129 LQR 149.
[37] See eg Sale of Goods Act 1979, s 12(2), (4), (5), (5A).

no right to terminate at **common law** because the breach was, perhaps, insignificant. There is no reason why parties should not be able to include such clauses in their agreements, and the courts are clearly prepared to give effect to them.

However, sometimes the courts have been unwilling to give such terms their natural meaning. For instance, in *Rice v Great Yarmouth Borough Council*,[38] the express termination clause provided that 'If the contractor ... commits a breach of any of its obligations under the Contract ... the Council may ... terminate the Contractor's employment under the Contract by notice in writing having immediate effect.' The contractor was in breach, and the council sought to terminate the agreement by invoking this express termination clause. Yet the Court of Appeal held that the council had not been entitled to terminate the contractor's employment because the clause only covered a repudiatory breach—in other words, a sufficiently serious breach to justify termination—and the contractor had not committed such a breach. This decision involves a strained interpretation of the express termination clause, since the clause expressly covered 'a breach of any of [the Contractor's] obligations'. It is therefore suggested that this aspect of the decision in *Rice* should not be followed: it undermines commercial certainty and the freedom of parties to create their own bargains.

A separate issue concerns the overlap which occurs between a party's right to terminate a contract for breach of a condition or the fundamental breach of an innominate term, and a party's right to terminate a contract under an express termination clause. This is important: a party has no right to damages if it terminates a contract by exercising a right under an express termination clause,[39] but if there has been a breach which entitles a party to terminate the agreement at common law, then the innocent party is entitled to damages.[40] Although it has sometimes been suggested that damages will be available even in the former situation,[41] the better view is that when terminating a contract under an express termination clause, the party is affirming the contract and relying upon its provisions, rather than asserting that the contract has been breached. Indeed, an express termination clause may be triggered by an event that is not a breach of contract. So, in *Financings Ltd v Baldock*,[42] a **hire-purchase** agreement was terminated by the owner for non-payment of hire under an express contractual power. The Court of Appeal held that the owner was only entitled to damages for the two instalments of hire which had not been paid at the time of termination, and that he could not recover for future payments which would have been made until the end of the agreement. This was because the owner was not relying upon a repudiatory breach of contract, but rather enforcing the contract through the express termination clause.

However, where a contract is terminated pursuant to a breach of a condition, then it is clear that the contract comes to an end at the point of termination, and that the primary obligations that should have been performed under the remaining period of the contract

---

[38] (2001) 3 LGLR 4, CA.

[39] *Financings Ltd v Baldock* [1963] 2 QB 104, CA.

[40] *Lombard North Central plc v Butterworth* [1987] QB 527, CA.

[41] See eg *Afovos Shipping Co SA v R Pagnan & Fratelli (The Afovos)* [1983] 1 WLR 195, 203 (Lord Diplock); *Stocznia Gdynia SA v Gearbulk Holdings* [2009] EWCA Civ 75, [2009] 1 Lloyd's Rep 461 (Moore-Bick LJ).

[42] [1963] 2 QB 104, CA.

are replaced by a secondary obligation to pay damages.[43] So, in *Lombard North Central plc v Butterworth*,[44] a hire agreement was terminated for non-payment of hire, just as in *Financings Ltd v Baldock*. But unlike in *Financings Ltd v Baldock*, the owner in the *Lombard* case was able to recover damages for loss of bargain because the parties had expressly agreed that punctual payment was to be 'of the essence': by breaching that term, the hirer had breached a condition of the contract, which entitled the innocent owner both to terminate the agreement and to recover damages for loss of bargain.

Given the fact that an innocent party would be deprived of loss of bargain damages by exclusively relying upon an express termination clause, the courts will be slow to find that an express termination clause excludes a party's concurrent right to terminate a contract at common law and recover damages as well.[45] After all, it is highly unlikely that the insertion of an express termination clause into a contract was intended to exclude a party's common law rights.

5 Election

An innocent party does not have to terminate the contract following a repudiatory breach of contract. Nor does the repudiatory breach automatically bring a contract to an end.[46] The innocent party has a right to elect whether to terminate or to affirm the contract.

Affirmation was considered generally with regards to the right to rescind for misrepresentation in Chapter 16.[47] Similar principles apply in this context. The innocent party must know of the facts giving rise to his right to terminate, and of the right to terminate itself, before he will be considered to have affirmed the contract.[48] And he will only be taken to have affirmed the contract if he does something unequivocal to show that he intends to keep the contract on foot.[49] The decision whether to terminate or to affirm the contract is irrevocable: the innocent party cannot later change his mind. However, the innocent party is entitled to take some time to decide whether or not to terminate the contract. How long the party will have to make such a decision will depend upon the precise facts of a case, but the court will allow a party a reasonable period of time to reach a decision, taking into account the complexity of the case and whether there is any urgency.[50] In practice, however, if the innocent party waits too long he may be taken to have affirmed the contract.[51]

---

[43] See eg *Photo Production v Securicor* [1980] 1 All ER 566; *Johnson v Agnew* [1980] AC 367.

[44] [1987] QB 527, CA.

[45] *Dalkia Utilities Services Plc v Celtech International Ltd* [2006] EWHC Civ 63 (Comm); *Stocznia Gdynia SA v Gearbulk Holdings* [2009] EWCA Civ 75, [2009] 1 Lloyd's Rep 461.

[46] *Geys v Société Générale London Branch* [2012] UKSC 63, [2013] 1 AC 523 (although cf the dissenting judgment of Lord Sumption).

[47] See Chapter 16, Section 4(d)(ii).

[48] *Peyman v Lanjani* [1985] Ch 457.

[49] *The Kanchenjunga* [1990] 1 Lloyd's Rep 391.

[50] *Force India Formula One Team Ltd v Etihad Airways PJSC* [2010] EWCA Civ 1051 [2011] ETMR 10.

[51] *Stocznia Gdanska SA v Latvian Shipping Co* [2002] EWCA Civ 889, [2002] 2 Lloyd's Rep 436.

It is also important to note that a party's termination of a contract will be valid even if he puts forward a bad or invalid reason for terminating the contract, provided that there was in fact a good reason for terminating the contract at the time of termination.[52]

6 Consumer's right to reject

It should here also be noted that under the Consumer Rights Act 2015 none of the terms 'to be treated as included' (in other words, implied terms) are considered to be 'conditions'. This means that the consumer is not able both to sue for damages and also to reject the goods for breach of a term that the goods be of satisfactory quality, for example.[53] This is different from the situation that arises under section 14 of the Sale of Goods Act 1979, where a similar term is characterised as a condition. This seems unfortunate, since it offers weaker protection to a consumer than to a commercial party. Of course, a consumer can still insist upon a term expressly being made a condition, in which case the remedies available under the general law will still be available to the consumer.[54]

However, a consumer may be entitled to reject goods under a 'goods contract',[55] which essentially means a contract to sell or transfer goods; or a contract to hire goods; or a hire-purchase agreement.[56] If the goods fail to conform to the contract in certain specified ways[57]—such as by not being of satisfactory quality[58] or being fit for purpose[59]—then a consumer may well be entitled simply to reject the goods and 'treat the contract as at an end'. Under this statutory protection afforded to consumers, the consumer must indicate to the trader that he is rejecting the goods,[60] and this must be clear.[61] Once a consumer has exercised his right to reject, then the trader has a duty to give the consumer a refund.[62] A consumer may also be able to reject some of the goods if they do not conform to the contract, without rejecting all the goods.[63] Such 'partial rejection' will not be possible if dividing up the conforming and non-conforming goods would have an impact upon the price of the goods which might be seen as one 'commercial unit'.[64]

The 2015 Act provides for a consumer's 'short-term right to reject'[65] and 'final right to reject'.[66] As regards the former, the consumer must exercise his right to reject within 30 days

[52] *The Mihalis Angelos* [1971] 1 QB 164; see too *Force India Formula One Team Ltd v Etihad Airways PJSC* [2010] EWCA Civ 1051, [2011] ETMR 10 [116] (Rix LJ).
[53] See eg s 20(21).
[54] s 19(10)–(13).
[55] Similar provisions also apply to digital content contracts (ss 42–46) and contracts of services (ss 54–57) under the Consumer Rights Act 2015.
[56] s 3.
[57] s 19.
[58] s 9.
[59] s 10.
[60] s 20(5).
[61] s 20(6).
[62] s 20(7).
[63] s 21.
[64] s 21(3)–(4).
[65] ss 20 and 22.
[66] s 24.

from when ownership is transferred to him, or from when the goods have been delivered, or from when the trader has notified the consumer that goods have been installed and can be used by the consumer.[67] However, this period will be shorter if the goods can reasonably be expected to perish in a shorter time frame.[68] Once the time limit for the short-term right to reject has expired, the consumer may exercise his right to repair or replacement.[69] Moreover, the consumer will be entitled to either a price reduction or a final right to reject where, after one repair or one replacement, the goods do not conform to the contract;[70] or where both repair and replacement are impossible;[71] or where the consumer has required the trader to repair or replace the goods, but the trader is in breach of the requirement[72] to do so within a reasonable time and without significant inconvenience to the consumer.[73] The consumer must clearly choose between rejecting the goods and asking for a price reduction.[74]

7 No evaluation of terms in unilateral contracts

Unilateral contracts are much easier to analyse in this context, since, by definition, there is a promise on one side only. This means that either the **offeree** does the act requested, in which case the **promisor** must perform his promise, or he does not, in which case there is no contract. There is therefore no need to engage with difficult questions of whether a particular term is a condition, or a warranty, or an implied term.

A similar analysis applies where the offer to enter into a bilateral contract requires the offeree, if he wishes to accept, to perform some defined act. This act will usually be to give notice of acceptance within some defined period, or within a reasonable period of time. Of course, a failure to do that act within the stipulated period is not a breach of contract because the offeree is not bound to accept. In *United Dominion Trust (Commercial) Ltd v Eagle Aircraft Services Ltd*,[75] Eagle Aircraft wished to sell an aircraft to Orion Airways. The transaction was financed by Eagle selling the aircraft to a finance company, UDT, which then let it on hire-purchase to Orion. UDT agreed to buy the aircraft only on condition that Eagle agreed to buy it back again if Orion defaulted on their payments and UDT then called on Eagle to do so. The agreement required UDT to notify Eagle of any default by Orion within seven days of its occurrence. Orion defaulted, but UDT (a) did not notify Eagle within seven days and (b) did not call upon Eagle to repurchase within a reasonable time. Widgery J held that these were two breaches of contract by UDT but that they did not go to the root of the contract and therefore did not allow Eagle to repudiate its obligation to repurchase. This decision was overturned on appeal. The Court of Appeal thought that the judge might have been right regarding (a), but it was unnecessary to decide the point since

---

[67] s 22(3).
[68] s 22(4).
[69] s 23.
[70] s 24(5)(a).
[71] s 24(5)(b).
[72] s 23(2)(a).
[73] s 24(5)(c).
[74] s 24(5).
[75] [1968] 1 WLR 74, CA.

(b) could not have been a breach of contract. The failure to call upon Eagle to repurchase within a reasonable time was clearly not a breach of contract at all—there was no obligation on UDT to call upon Eagle to repurchase the aircraft. Instead, there had simply been a failure to accept within the time implicitly stipulated in Eagle's offer. It was immaterial whether this failure was great or small. The offer had come to an end before the purported acceptance, and that was that.

8 Conditions and 'entire obligations'

Where the contract is bilateral but stipulates for one entire piece of work to be done by one party, the complete performance of that work is a condition of the liability of the other, unless the parties have stipulated otherwise. This is a different meaning of 'condition' from that examined earlier, but it is nevertheless useful to consider here. For example, imagine that O says to A, 'If you will undertake to walk to York, I promise to pay you £100 for doing so.' A gives the undertaking, but fails to walk to York. He is in breach of contract. Suppose he gave up within 100 yards of the city boundary. It was only a slight failure, but that will make no difference. He can recover nothing because complete performance of his obligation will be regarded as a condition of O's liability.

This was, in effect, what happened in the leading case of *Cutter v Powell*.[76] The defendant was the master of a ship. The defendant gave Cutter a note promising to pay him 30 guineas, 'provided he proceeds, continues and does his duty as second mate in the said ship from [Kingston, Jamaica] to the port of Liverpool'. The ship sailed on 2 August and Cutter served as second mate until 20 September when he died before the ship reached Liverpool. It seems clear that this was a bilateral contract, since Cutter undoubtedly had a contractual obligation to do his duty as second mate. It also seems clear that Cutter was not guilty of any breach of contract, since the contract was frustrated by his death.[77] Nevertheless, his widow's claim to recover 30 guineas failed because the condition precedent to Cutter's right to recover payment had not been fulfilled, since Cutter had not fulfilled his duty all the way through to Liverpool. Furthermore, the widow's argument that she was entitled to recover a proportionate part of the wages on a *quantum meruit*[78] basis for work done also failed. The court held that Cutter had contracted to receive 30 guineas if the whole voyage were performed and nothing if it was not. In reaching this conclusion, the court was greatly influenced by the fact that 30 guineas was very high pay—the voyage normally lasted two months and the usual rate of pay was £4 per month. (Since the contract was frustrated by Cutter's death, it would be necessary to consider the effect of the Law Reform (Frustrated Contracts) Act 1943 if a similar case arose today.[79])

The same principles were applied in *Appleby v Myers*[80] to a contract to install machinery in the defendant's premises. The bulk of the work was done when, without the fault of either

---

[76] (1795) 6 TR 320.
[77] See Chapter 23, Section 2(a).
[78] See Chapter 28, Section 4.
[79] See Chapter 23, Section 4.
[80] (1867) LR 2 CP 651.

party, the premises were burnt down and the machinery destroyed. The claimant could not recover anything. Blackburn J stated that 'there is nothing to render it either illegal or absurd in the workman to agree to complete the whole, and to be paid when the whole is complete and not till then; and we think that the claimants in the present case had entered into such a contract'. It is the same where the claimant does complete the job, but the work done is substantially different from that required by the contract. In *The Liddesdale*,[81] repairers undertook to do specified repairs to the defendant's ship, and then did good work which added value to the ship, but they could still recover nothing under the contract where the work done was not the stipulated work: for example, the repairers had used iron girders where the contract required steel. It was irrelevant that the work was as good as, or indeed better than, the work contracted for—it was not what the defendants had contracted to pay for.

It is different where the defendant has an option to accept or reject the claimant's incomplete or different performance. If the defendant chooses to accept it, the court will infer a new contract to pay what it is worth. This contract is not inconsistent with the first contract because it is made later in time; there is no difficulty in holding that both contracts have been made. The application of the principle to contracts for the sale of goods is neatly summed up in section 30(1) of the Sale of Goods Act 1979:

> Where the seller delivers to the buyer a quantity of goods less than he contracted to sell, the buyer may reject them, but if the buyer accepts the goods so delivered he must pay for them at the contract rate.

So, if there is a contract to deliver 144 bottles, but instead the claimant delivers 143, in principle the buyer is entitled to reject the delivery. However, section 30(2A) (inserted by the Sale and Supply of Goods Act 1994), provides that a non-consumer may not reject if the shortfall is so slight that it would be unreasonable for him to do so. This is equally so where the excess is slight (for example 145 bottles).[82]

In *Cutter v Powell* and *Appleby v Myers*, the defendant had no option to accept or reject the incomplete work. Similarly, in *The Liddesdale* the Privy Council took the view that the shipowner's acceptance of the ship did not found a contract to pay for the work that had been done. Short of abandoning his ship, the shipowner had no option but to accept it with the iron girders and any other extra-contractual work.

The entire obligations rule works harshly in these cases. It is impossible not to feel sympathy with the claimants in *Cutter v Powell* and *Appleby v Myers*; but these were cases of frustrated contracts and there is now the Law Reform (Frustrated Contracts) Act 1943, one of the objects of which is to do justice in this sort of case. To what extent it does so is considered in Chapter 23.[83] But there are other cases where the claimant failed to render entire

---

[81] *Forman & Co Proprietary Ltd v The Ship 'Liddesdale'* [1900] AC 190, PC.
[82] cf s 15A, considered at Section 3(a).
[83] Chapter 23, Section 4.

performance because of some event not amounting to frustration but still due to misfortune rather than his fault.[84] In such circumstances, the 1943 Act will not help.

In *Sumpter v Hedges*,[85] the claimant had entered into an entire contract to erect buildings for £565. When he had done work to the value of £333 he ran into financial difficulties and had to abandon the job. He had received part of the price but his action to recover the balance of the value of the work he had done failed. The entire obligation had not been satisfied so he was not entitled to payment. The defendant then in fact completed the work, using materials left by the claimant on the site. The defendant was held liable to pay for the materials, because he certainly had an option whether to use them. This was different from the work done by the claimant. The court held that the defendant had no option to accept or reject an unfinished building on his land, so was not liable to pay anything for the work done. The unfinished building was simply there on the land and could not be rejected. Moreover, the defendant was bound not to leave it in an incomplete state.

Because of the harsh effects of the 'entire obligations' rule, courts might be expected to be slow to construe an obligation as entire where it is possible to regard it as severable into distinct parts. But *Bolton v Mahadeva*[86] shows that the rule is still a live one. The claimant contracted to install a combined heating and domestic hot-water system for £560. The installation was defective, providing inadequate heat and emitting fumes. The deficiencies were assessed at £174, but the claimant had refused to rectify them. It was held that the claimant could recover nothing.

(a) Substantial performance

There is one principle which may mitigate the defaulter's liability. This is the doctrine of substantial performance. If the performance falls short of the standard required by the contract only in some relatively trivial respect, that failure may be treated like a breach of warranty. As a result, the defaulter may recover the price for the entire work, but the defendant may counterclaim for the loss he has suffered by reason of the defective performance. In *Bolton v Mahadeva*, the court declined to apply this principle because the defect in performance was not a trivial one but rather went to the root of the contract. On the other hand, in *Hoenig v Isaacs*[87] the Court of Appeal declined to interfere with an official referee's finding that a contract to decorate and fit out a one-roomed flat had been substantially performed when the work had been completed but with defects which would cost £56 to rectify, the contract price for the whole being £750. The case was a borderline one and, if the official referee's decision had gone the other way, it is likely that it would have been upheld. The fact that the whole job was done (albeit defectively) was material. The court thought that if the second mate in *Cutter v Powell* had completed the voyage, his widow would not have failed to recover the sum agreed in the note merely because he had committed some minor breach of contract in the course of the voyage. In that case, the master's remedy

---

[84] A personal financial failure, though rendering performance impossible in fact, is not a frustrating event: see Chapter 23, Section 1(a).

[85] [1898] 1 QB 673.

[86] [1972] 1 WLR 1009, CA.

[87] [1952] 2 All ER 176.

would have been a counterclaim for damages for that breach. But, as *Bolton v Mahadeva* shows, the claimant will not necessarily succeed on the ground that he has done the whole job if the performance is defective. It appears that the essential question is whether the breach goes to the root of the contract.

The plight of the party who has failed to complete, or substantially complete, performance of an entire contract for some reason other than frustration has been considered by the Law Commission.[88] The Law Commission recommended that he should be entitled to recover from the other party to the contract a sum representing the value of what he has done under the contract to that person who has had the benefit of it, whether he is a party to the contract or not. The court would have no discretion to reduce or disallow the claim on the ground of the conduct of the party in breach, but the sum awarded would not exceed the proportion of the work done to the whole of the work promised. The party not in breach would be able to counterclaim for damages and the normal rules relating to remoteness and mitigation would apply. This report has not yet been implemented, and, despite the harsh nature of the current law, it is suggested that the report should not be adopted. Indeed, there was a strong dissent to the report by one of the Law Commissioners, Brian Davenport QC. The basis of his dissent is that it can often be important to demand that an entire obligation actually be fulfilled before payment can be ordered, and that this would be undermined by the Law Commission's proposal. For instance, if *A* contracts with *B* to build a house for *A*, and that obligation is entire, then it is very useful for *A* to be able to insist upon *B*'s finishing the building since *A* does not want an unfinished building. A major incentive for the builder to finish the work, and one of the few 'tools' that *A* can use in order to achieve that result, is for *A* to refuse to pay anything to *B* until the work is finished. This is the result achieved by the 'entire obligations' rule. A corollary of this is that there is no need for *A* to pay anything to *B* to reverse an 'unjust enrichment' since *A*'s enrichment is not 'unjust'; rather, it is justified on the basis of the contract between the parties.

Further Reading

B McFarlane and R Stevens, 'In Defence of *Sumpter v Hedges*' (2002) 111 LQR 569.
Defends the decision in *Sumpter v Hedges* and the importance of 'entire obligations'.

JW Carter, 'Discharge as the Basis for Termination for Breach of Contract' (2012) 128 LQR 283.
Examines the law on termination on the grounds of discharge, and the availability of damages.

E Peel, 'The Termination Paradox' [2013] LMCLQ 519.
Discusses how express contractual powers of termination differ from the power to terminate for repudiatory breach and may be affected by the principle of affirmation of the contract.

---

[88] *Pecuniary Restitution on Breach of Contract* (Law Com No 121, 1983).

? Question

Carrie runs a jam factory. Brody is a sugar manufacturer. They enter into a contract under which Brody promises to supply Carrie with 100 tonnes of sugar every month for two years. The contract provides that:

It is a condition of this contract that each delivery will be made on the first Monday of every month, no later than 3 pm.

The first six deliveries are all made on time, but the seventh delivery arrives at 4 pm. The eighth delivery is only made on the first Wednesday of the month (two days late). Carrie refuses to accept delivery, and tells Brody that she will accept no further instalments. Carrie later learns that the eighth instalment of sugar contained small stones in it, which would have made the sugar unusable in her jam factory.

Advise Brody.

25 Anticipatory breach of contract

Key Points

- An anticipatory breach occurs where, before the time comes for one party to perform his part of the contract, he declares that he is not going to do so.
- The innocent party can choose whether or not to accept an anticipatory breach. If he accepts the breach, the contract is terminated and the innocent party can sue for damages immediately, but if the anticipatory breach is not accepted, then the contract remains on foot.
- If the innocent party elects not to accept the breach and to keep the contract alive, then he may proceed to perform his side of the bargain (assuming that the other party's cooperation is not required) and sue for the contract price. However, it appears that this action for the agreed sum, or action in debt, may not succeed if the innocent party had no 'legitimate interest' in taking such steps. The scope and nature of this exception to the ability to sue for the agreed sum is very controversial.

1 The nature of anticipatory breach

It is clear that one party cannot, by his wrongful act, bring a contract to an end without the consent of the other party. If *A* commits a breach of a **condition**, or a fundamental breach of an **innominate term** of his contract with *B*, it is for *B* to decide whether to terminate the contract or not. This was explained in Chapter 24, and is just as true of 'anticipatory breach' as of any other breach of contract.

An anticipatory breach occurs where, before the time comes for *A* to perform his part of the contract, he declares that he is not going to do so. This **repudiation** (which should perhaps properly be called a 'renunciation'[1]) of the contractual obligation is itself a breach of contract. There are competing justifications for the doctrine of anticipatory breach. One popular explanation rests upon there being a breach of an implied promise to maintain the contractual obligation intact from the making of the contract until it is performed. Another considers that anticipatory breach is a breach of the contractual obligations yet to fall due: anticipatory breach is established by an objectively reasonable inference that the contractual obligation will not be properly performed when due. Current orthodoxy favours the latter approach, since the remedies awarded are for the breach of the

---

[1] *Bunge SA v Nidera BV* [2015] UKSC 43, [2015] 3 All ER 1082 [12] (Lord Sumption).

contractual obligation yet to fall due, rather than for the breach of any distinct implied term. In any event, however, it is clear that the repudiation by A gives B a right, which he previously lacked, to terminate the contract and sue for damages. This is pragmatically very useful: there is no point in B waiting around for the date of performance to pass before he is able to take steps to mitigate any loss he might suffer, and bring a claim against A. It is this pragmatic utility that underpins anticipatory breach. As Lord Mustill has commented, 'The concept of anticipatory breach cannot be rationalised, but must be seen as a piece of positive law, firmly established but not anchored in or deducible from the ordinary course of the law of contract.'[2] This has recently been endorsed by Lord Sumption in *Bunge SA v Nidera BV,* who noted that anticipatory breach 'is a response to the pragmatic concern of Victorian judges to avoid the waste of economic resources implicit in any inflexible rule which required the parties to go through the motions of performing a contract which was for practical purposes dead'.[3]

Of course, B may choose to ignore A's anticipatory breach. It is nevertheless important to note that an unaccepted anticipatory breach is still a breach,[4] similar to any other breach of condition which the injured party chooses to ignore. If the anticipatory breach is ignored, the contract remains on foot; after all, 'an unaccepted repudiation is a thing writ in water and of no value to anybody'.[5] If B chooses to ignore A's anticipatory breach and, when the time for performance comes, A has changed his mind and carries out the contract, so much the better—all obligations under the contract are satisfied. But if A fails to perform, then B may sue A for that breach of contract.

It is important to appreciate that B does not have to wait to see if A will change his mind and perform his obligations. As soon as A repudiates the contract, B may sue him for damages. The peculiarity of anticipatory breach is that, if B does so, he is said to 'accept' the breach, and this brings the contract to an end. This seems to mean that B accepts the fact that A is not going to perform the contract and that B is accordingly free from his own obligations and able to sue for the injury he will incur through A's non-performance. With an ordinary breach of condition or fundamental breach of an innominate term, the injured party may sue for damages, *and* keep the contract alive or terminate it, as he thinks fit. But the same does not apply to anticipatory breach. B's claim for damages terminates the contract. When B recovers his damages he is compensated in advance for A's anticipated failure to perform. It follows that A's duty to perform must now be abrogated.

In the leading case of *Hochster v De la Tour,*[6] the defendant had agreed to employ the claimant as a courier on 1 June 1852. On 11 May 1852, the defendant told the claimant that he had changed his mind and did not require the claimant's services on 1 June. The claimant began an action on 22 May. The defendant's objection that there could be no breach before 1 June was rejected. Lord Campbell CJ said that the contract constituted a relationship

---

[2] Lord Mustill, 'The *Golden Victory*—Some Reflections' (2008) 124 LQR 569, 584.
[3] [2015] UKSC 43, [2015] 3 All ER 1082 [12].
[4] *Tilcon Ltd v Land and Real Estate Investments Ltd* [1987] 1 All ER 615, CA.
[5] *Howard v Pickford Tool Co* [1951] 1 KB 417, 420.
[6] (1853) 2 E & B 678.

between the parties and each impliedly promised the other that he would not do anything inconsistent with that relationship.

In *Frost v Knight*,[7] A promised B that he would marry her when his father died. During his father's lifetime, A broke off the engagement. It was held that A had committed an anticipatory breach of contract (since the father had not died), and B was entitled to her damages. The court held that there was no difference between a case where the time for performance was a certain day and a case where the time for performance depended on a contingency, such as the death of the father.

It should be pointed out that this procedure relating to anticipatory breach may be for the benefit of both parties. Not only is A able to escape his contractual obligations in advance, but B may then take steps to mitigate his losses.[8] Indeed, by accepting an anticipatory breach, B may be able to reduce his losses to a far greater extent than he would be able to if it were necessary to wait until the time for performance. This may be of great commercial importance. Imagine that, in January, Company A contracts with Company B to provide entertainment at an event on Christmas Eve. In February, A tells B that it cannot perform the contract. If there were no doctrine of anticipatory breach, then B may be forced to wait another ten months before being able to sue A, and B would also be likely to suffer substantial problems at an event which could damage its reputation. This would be highly unsatisfactory. Far better for B to accept A's anticipatory breach and contract with Company C to provide the required services on Christmas Eve. This will allow B's event to go smoothly, and will also reduce the amount A will have to pay in damages, since B will have mitigated its losses such that A only has to compensate B for any extra money B has to pay C.

If B elects not to sue for the anticipatory breach but to keep the contract alive, the contract continues to subsist for the benefit of both parties. So, if B chooses to keep the contract alive but subsequently commits a breach of contract himself, A can sue B for damages.[9] Similarly, if a frustrating event occurs before the time for performance arrives, the contract is 'killed off' by frustration and B's right to 'accept the breach' and claim damages disappears. In *Avery v Bowden*,[10] the defendant **chartered** the claimant's ship to load a cargo at Odessa within 45 days. The ship proceeded to Odessa and remained there for a great part of the 45 days, during which time the defendant repeatedly told the captain he had no cargo for him and advised him to go away. Before the 45 days elapsed, the Crimean War broke out and frustrated the contract. The court held that the claimant no longer had any rights to damages. No breach, other than the anticipatory breach, had occurred, or could occur, before the end of the 45 days. The defendant's declaration that he would not be able to provide a cargo may have been an anticipatory breach but, even if it was, the claimant had not accepted it. The contract therefore remained on foot and was frustrated by the outbreak of war.

---

[7] (1872) LR 7 Exch 111.
[8] See Chapter 26, Section 2(c).
[9] *Fercometal Sarl v MSC Mediterranean Shipping Co SA (The Simona)* [1989] AC 788.
[10] (1855) 5 E & B 714.

2 Mistaken repudiation

In most of the cases, there could be no doubt that *A* knew very well that he was announcing his intention to commit a breach of contract. However, in some cases this will not be so clear. For example, *A* might mistakenly believe that he has a right to repudiate the contract, when in fact he has no such right. Nevertheless, by acting on his mistaken belief, *A* is announcing his intention to commit a breach of contract—after all, if he puts his intention into effect, he will commit such a breach.[11] Is this an anticipatory breach which entitles *B* to treat the contract as repudiated and claim damages? Lord Denning thought so. In *Federal Commerce Navigation Co Ltd v Molena Alpha Inc*, he said: 'I have yet to learn that a party who breaks a contract can excuse himself by saying that he did it on the advice of his lawyers; or that he was under an honest misapprehension. Nor can he excuse himself on those grounds from the consequences of a repudiation.'[12]

However, in *Woodar Investment Development Ltd v Wimpey Construction UK Ltd*,[13] a bare majority of the House of Lords took a different view. A clause in a contract for the sale of land provided that the buyer, Wimpey, should be entitled to **rescind** it in certain specified circumstances. Wimpey, because it misconstrued the contract, thought those circumstances had arisen and purported to rescind the agreement. Woodar alleged that this amounted to a repudiation and claimed damages. The view of the majority[14] was that Wimpey thought it was acting on the terms of the contract, and that it therefore followed that Wimpey was not repudiating it. This conclusion is a little surprising. After all, it did reasonably appear to Woodar that Wimpey was repudiating the contract.[15] It is suggested that the logic of Lord Denning in *Federal Commerce* is compelling, and that the approach of the minority in *Woodar* should be preferred. In any event, it is perhaps worth highlighting that the result in *Woodar* would not necessarily have been the same if Wimpey had purported to end the contract in the mistaken belief that some action of Woodar's amounted to a breach of condition or fundamental breach, since the facts of the case only concerned Wimpey's reliance on an express clause in a contract permitting rescission of the contract. Admittedly, however, it is difficult to see why there should be any difference in principle and why the scope of the decision in *Woodar* should be confined in that way. Ultimately, the decision in *Woodar* is unsatisfactory and the approach in *Federal Commerce Navigation Co Ltd v Molena Alpha Inc* should be preferred.

3 Communication of acceptance

Does 'acceptance of the breach' require communication? Where *B* has expressly renounced the contract, it must surely be terminated by *A* then acting in a way that makes performance

---

[11] This situation should be distinguished from that where the party gives a bad reason for terminating the contract, but actually had (an unknown at the time) good reason to do so; under such circumstances, the termination of the contract will be effective: *Bunge v Tradax* [1981] 2 All ER 513, HL.

[12] [1978] QB 927, 979.

[13] [1980] 1 WLR 277.

[14] Lords Wilberforce, Keith, and Scarman.

[15] See the dissenting judgments of Lords Salmon and Russell.

impossible. For instance, imagine that, in a case like *Frost v Knight,* A wrote to B to tell her that he would never marry her, and B did not reply to A but promptly married another man. If A's father had died the next day and A had then called on B to marry him under the terms of their contract, A could surely not have succeeded in an action for breach of contract. A could hardly complain that B had taken him at his word. It is different where A has not declared the contract to be at an end but has committed a 'repudiatory breach'—a breach entitling B to terminate the contract. Here A, far from intending to repudiate the contract, may be very anxious that it should continue. As with rescission for fraud or misrepresentation, if B wants to terminate the contract, B must tell A.

It is difficult to be sure whether B can 'accept the breach' simply by not performing his own obligations. The answer seems to be that where B's non-performance would make it clear to a reasonable person that B accepted that the contract was at an end, this may be sufficient. In *Vitol SA v Norelf Ltd*,[16] Lord Steyn discussed the hypothetical case of an employer telling a contractor that he is repudiating the contract and that the contractor need not return the next day. If the contractor does not return the next day, or at all, his failure to perform may convey a decision that the contract is at an end. However, as Lord Steyn recognised, this will be the case 'in the absence of any other explanation'. If the contractor did not return only because he was sick or otherwise detained, then it may be unreasonable to find that the contractor has accepted the breach.

4 Keeping the contract alive and suing for the agreed sum

In *Hochster v De la Tour, Avery v Bowden*, and *Frost v Knight* the courts were insistent that the respective claimants had an option: they could 'accept' the breach by suing for damages, or they could keep the contract alive and wait and see whether the defendant performed on the due date. There was, however, no question of the claimant in those cases going ahead and performing on his own: Hochster could not act as courier until he was given something to carry; Avery could not sail away with a cargo which had not been supplied; Frost could not marry without Knight's cooperation (and, anyway, the day for marriage had not yet come). Given the need for cooperation from the other party, the claimants could not simply perform their contractual obligations and sue for the agreed sum: an action for the agreed sum depends upon the claimant having fulfilled his side of the bargain.[17] Suppose, however, that the victim of an anticipatory breach is able to perform his part without the cooperation of the other—may he simply ignore the anticipatory breach, fulfil his own contractual obligation, and claim the consideration promised?

In *White & Carter (Councils) Ltd v McGregor*,[18] a Scottish case, the House of Lords answered this question in the affirmative. The defender's sales manager, acting within his ostensible authority, contracted with the pursuers that the pursuers would display

---

[16] [1996] AC 800, 811, HL.

[17] *Hounslow London Borough Council v Twickenham Garden Developments Ltd* [1971] Ch 233 (Megarry J).

[18] [1962] AC 413.

advertisements for the defender's business on litter bins for three years.[19] The defender immediately cancelled the contract—an anticipatory breach. The pursuers refused to accept the breach and proceeded to display the advertisements, which they were able to do without any further cooperation from the defender. A term of the contract provided that the first annual payment was due seven days after the first display and, if it remained unpaid for four weeks, the whole amount due for the three years became payable. The pursuers sued under this term for the full contract price.

The courts were faced with a potential conflict of two principles. First, that the victim of an anticipatory breach has an option to keep the contract alive. Secondly, that a party injured by breach of contract has a 'duty'[20] to mitigate the damage. If there is, in these circumstances, a duty to mitigate, there is no real option to keep the contract alive. The defender could mitigate the pursuer's loss only by abandoning his 'right' to perform the contract and claim his loss of profits.

A bare majority of the House of Lords held that the pursuers had no duty to mitigate and had a right to perform the contract. The pursuers were suing not for damages, but for the price of services rendered. Mitigation was therefore irrelevant, since mitigation only reduces the amount owed under the secondary obligation to pay damages which arises after a breach of contract.[21] The action in *White & Carter* sought to enforce the primary obligations arising under the terms of the contract, rather than rely upon there being any breach. This was advantageous to the pursuers not only because it avoided any duty to mitigate and consequent difficulties of assessment, but also because an action in debt for the agreed sum is procedurally much more straightforward than a claim in damages. For instance, there is no need for a judge to assess the quantum of damages if the claimant sues for an agreed sum.

However, Lord Reid, who was in the majority, thought that the ability of a claimant to ignore an anticipatory breach and perform his obligations in order to sue for the agreed sum should perhaps be subject to 'a general equitable principle, or element of public policy':[22]

> It may well be that if it can be shown that a person has no legitimate interest, financial or otherwise, in performing the contract rather than claiming damages, he ought not to be allowed to saddle the other party with an additional burden with no benefit to himself.

This *dictum* is difficult. It appears to have been an innovation of Lord Reid and was not addressed by counsel. It is not at all clear what 'legitimate interest' means. In *White & Carter* itself, the example was given of a person who contracts to go to Hong Kong at his own expense and write a report in return for £10,000. Before the expert sets out and before he has incurred any expense, he is informed by the other party that the report is no longer required. Is the expert entitled to go to Hong Kong and prepare a report which is no longer required, and then claim in debt for his fee? It seems that, even allowing for Lord

---

[19] Since this was a Scottish case, the language of 'defender' and 'pursuer' is used; the equivalents in English law are 'defendant' and 'claimant' respectively.

[20] This is not a 'duty' in the strict sense: see Chapter 26, Section 2(c).

[21] See Chapter 26, Section 2(c). See too *MSC Mediterranean Shipping Co SA v Cottonex Anstalt* [2015] EWHC 283 (Comm), [2015] 2 All ER (Comm) 614 [101] (Leggatt J).

[22] At 430–431 (Lord Reid).

Reid's qualification, he might be able to do so: the expert could have a legitimate interest in performing the contract, since this would keep him in work and perhaps enhance his reputation if he produces a good report.

It is fair to say that the decision in *White & Carter* has received some strong criticism. Indeed, Lords Morton and Keith, dissenting, thought that the pursuers' only claim should be in damages and that they had a duty to mitigate. The contract was not, in its nature, specifically enforceable; yet the pursuer, because he could do his part without the cooperation of the defender, was able to achieve the same effect, and this has sometimes been considered to be a sort of 'self-help specific performance'. However, it is clearly distinct from specific performance since an action in debt for the agreed sum does not require an order from a court exercising its equitable jurisdiction.

It is perhaps not entirely clear what the 'legitimate interest' restricts: is it the innocent party's right to keep the contract alive, or is it the ability to recover the agreed sum? In *Geys v Société Générale London Branch*,[23] Lord Sumption, dissenting, suggested the former. The majority of the Supreme Court insisted it was only the latter. In *Geys*, a bank summarily dismissed a banker in breach of his contract of employment in November 2007. If the contract was immediately terminated, then the banker's bonus would have been about €5.5 million less than if the banker was entitled to refuse to accept the repudiatory breach and the contract was only terminated in January 2008. Lord Wilson, for the majority, thought that restricting the banker's right to keep the contract alive would be tantamount to 'turning basic principles of the law of contract upon their head';[24] after all, a wrongdoer should not be entitled to choose when a contract ends at the expense of an innocent party. This is entirely orthodox and satisfactory. But the arguments by no means flow in one direction. Lord Sumption, dissenting, thought that the legitimate interest exception should be focused upon whether or not the innocent party is entitled to keep the contract alive. This would have the advantage of pushing cases where there is no legitimate interest into the realm of damages where the duty to mitigate clearly applies. This was thought to be desirable by Lord Sumption, who sought to avoid 'economically wasteful' outcomes.[25] But a breach of contract is an unlawful act, and it is inappropriate to allow wrongdoers to dictate to innocent parties when the contract should terminate.

Nevertheless, Lord Sumption's reluctance to allow actions for the agreed sum to proceed and therefore sidestep a duty to mitigate is clearly shared by other judges.[26] Megarry J has stated that 'the decision [in *White & Carter*] is one which I should be slow to apply to any category of case not fairly within the contemplation of their lordships',[27] while Lord Denning said that he would follow *White & Carter* only in a case which was precisely on all fours with it.[28] However, *Geys* makes it clear that the 'legitimate interest' exception is best

---

[23] [2012] UKSC 63, [2013] 1 AC 523.

[24] Ibid [66].

[25] See Chapter 1, Section 6(c).

[26] See, in a very different context, *AIB Group (UK) Plc v Mark Redler & Co Solicitors* [2014] UKSC 58, [2014] 3 WLR 1367 [64] (Lord Toulson).

[27] *Hounslow London Borough Council v Twickenham Garden Developments Ltd* [1971] Ch 233.

[28] *Attica Sea Carriers Corp v Ferrostaal Poseidon Bulk Deederei GmbH (The Puerto Buitrago)* [1976] 1 Lloyd's Rep 250.

understood to restrict the ability to claim the agreed sum, rather than keep the contract alive. In most circumstances, of course, the result will be the same: the claimant will not be able to recover more than compensation for his loss. In any event, it remains important to determine what 'legitimate interest' means.

The cases do not all speak with one voice on this issue. This is partly attributable to the fact that judges have different views on whether *White & Carter* is a sensible decision—which is unsurprising, given that in *White & Carter* itself the House of Lords was split 3:2. Courts have said that if the conduct of the claimant was 'perverse',[29] 'wholly unreasonable',[30] or even just 'unreasonable',[31] then the action for the agreed sum should fail. In *The Alaskan Trader*,[32] there was a time-charter of a ship. The charter was for a period of two years, but after about a year the engine needed to be repaired. The charterers said that they no longer required the ship, but the owners nevertheless went ahead with the repairs and kept the ship ready for the charterers until the end of the contract period. Lloyd J held that the owners had no legitimate interest in holding the contract open and claiming the agreed price of the hire of the ship.

This decision is not in absolute isolation, but it seems difficult to reconcile with *White & Carter* itself. After all, Lord Reid—from whom the 'legitimate interest' requirement derives—was in the majority in *White & Carter*. Lord Reid must therefore have thought that there was a 'legitimate interest' in *White & Carter* itself. But what was it? This is not an easy question to answer. The interest of the pursuers was essentially financial: they would obtain more money through the action for the agreed sum than they would have obtained had they been limited to a claim in damages, with the concomitant duty to mitigate their loss. It may be that the 'acceleration clause', which meant that the entire amount for the three-year contract period became payable at a much earlier date than the end of the contract, means that *White & Carter* might be distinguishable on its facts, but their Lordships did not seem to place much emphasis on the existence of this clause. But if the interest of the pursuers in *White & Carter* was purely financial, then any claimant will be able to point to a similar 'legitimate interest', and as a result it is difficult to conceive of cases where the action for the agreed sum should fail. After all, *White & Carter* itself may be thought to be an extreme case: it would not have been all that difficult for the defenders to find another company to pay to advertise on litter bins and thereby mitigate any loss that might be suffered. It is suggested that the 'legitimate interest' exception was not very well thought-through in *White & Carter* and should be very much restricted if it is to be maintained at all. In *The Aquafaith*,[33] Cooke J rightly thought that it would need to be 'an extreme or unusual case' before the exception would apply.

---

[29] *The Aquafaith* [2012] EWHC 1077 (Comm), [2012] 2 Lloyd's Rep 61 [56] (Cooke J).
[30] *The Odenfeld* [1978] 2 Lloyd's Rep 357, 374 (Kerr J).
[31] *The Dynamic* [2003] EWHC 1936 (Comm), [2003] 2 Lloyd's Rep 693 [23] (Simon J).
[32] [1983] 2 Lloyd's Rep 645, QBD (Lloyd J).
[33] [2012] EWHC 1077 (Comm), [2012] 2 Lloyd's Rep 61 [56].

📖 Further Reading

JC Smith, 'Anticipatory Breach of Contract' in E Lomnicka and C Morse (eds), *Contemporary Issues in Commercial Law: Essays in Honour of AG Guest* (Sweet & Maxwell, 1997).

Examines key areas of controversy concerning anticipatory breach, developing the analysis presented in this chapter.

Lord Mustill, *'The Golden Victory—Some Reflections'* (2008) 124 LQR 569.

Discusses the nature of anticipatory breach, and considers that it can only really be explained by reference to pragmatic considerations.

Q Liu, 'The *White & Carter* Principle: A Restatement' (2011) 74 MLR 171.

Considers the 'legitimate interest' exception in *White & Carter*, and argues that the principal focus should really be on whether the wastefulness of the victim's continuing performance outweighs its performance interest in earning the contract price.

❓ Question

Richard and Julia are engaged. They are due to get married on 14 July at Roberson Hall. On 18 February they enter into a contract with Sophie for her to make a large wedding cake, and 500 personalised cupcakes for their wedding. On each cupcake Sophie agrees to write 'Julia & Richard' in pink icing. The contract price is £3,000.

On 20 June, Julia calls off the wedding. She telephones Sophie and tells her that the contract is cancelled. Sophie refuses to accept this, as she has been looking forward to using her icing skills on all the cupcakes. Sophie is offered £4,000 to provide comparable services to Britney and Jason for their wedding on 14 July, but Sophie rejects this offer because she is so pleased with the designs that she has already made for Richard and Julia, and Sophie plans to use the finished products in advertising material for her business.

Sophie therefore makes the large wedding cake and cupcakes according to the terms of her contract with Richard and Julia. She takes them to Roberson Hall, where they are accepted by the receptionist.

Advise Sophie.

26 Compensatory damages

🔑 Key Points

- Damages can be awarded to compensate a claimant for his loss. The general principle is that damages should, so far as money can do it, put the party injured by a breach of contract in the same position as he would have been in had the contract been performed. This is sometimes known as the 'compensatory principle'.

- The most common measure of damages is the claimant's 'expectation loss', which is calculated by reference to the profits lost due to the contract not being performed as expected.

- The loss must be caused by the defendant's breach of contract and not be too remote from the breach.

- Traditionally, it has long been the case that losses will not be too remote if they arise naturally from the breach of contract, or are of a type that may reasonably be supposed to have been in the contemplation of both parties at the time the contract was made. It now also appears that losses will not be too remote if the parties 'assumed responsibility' for the loss.

- A claimant is under a 'duty' to mitigate his loss by taking reasonable steps to reduce the losses suffered. However, this is not a duty in the usual sense. The claimant commits no wrong by choosing not to mitigate. The point is that whether the claimant mitigates the damage or not, he will recover only those damages which would have been incurred had he done so.

- Damages are generally assessed at the date of breach. However, this general rule may be displaced in order to ensure that the compensatory principle is satisfied. It is now clear that the court can take into account events that occur after the date of breach when assessing damages.

- Damages are not generally recoverable for disappointment or injured feelings resulting from the breach. But, if an object of a contract is to provide pleasure, or the distress is a result of physical inconvenience caused by the breach of contract, then damages for non-economic loss may be recoverable.

- An injured party may sometimes seek to recover his 'reliance loss'. This can be quantified by calculating his expenditure wasted upon the expected performance of the contract. However, an injured party cannot recover his reliance loss where he has made a bad bargain and would have suffered such loss anyway.

Contracting parties are keen to know and understand what remedies are available for breach of contract. Indeed, the issue of what remedies are available is crucial to many contractual disputes. As we have seen,[1] in some instances a party may be able to terminate the contract, which is a sort of 'self-help' remedy in the sense that the party can choose to terminate the contract by itself. The remaining few chapters of the book will focus on remedies awarded by the courts. The most common remedy is damages, but a court may also make an equitable order to compel performance, for example.[2]

Damages are said to be available 'as of right' for a breach of contract. The innocent party will always be able to recover something—even if only a nominal sum[3]—if the defendant has committed the wrong of breach of contract. The principal types of damages are awarded either to compensate the claimant for his loss, or to strip a defendant of his gains. The former is loss-based and therefore compensatory. The latter is gain-based and therefore restitutionary. This chapter will focus on compensatory damages. The following chapters will discuss other remedies which are not concerned with compensation for loss.

The innocent party will often seek to recover damages to compensate him for his 'expectation loss'. Essentially, such loss corresponds to the profits the claimant hoped to make from the contract. Damages based upon 'expectation loss' protect the innocent party's 'expectation interest' in having the contract performed. Other interests may perhaps be identified, such as the 'reliance interest'.[4] Damages awarded to protect the claimant's reliance interest are assessed by reference to the claimant's wasted expenditure. However, the better view may be that the award of 'reliance damages' can also be justified on the basis of the reliance loss principle. This chapter will examine the first two of these interests, which are clearly compensatory since they are focused on the claimant's loss (either his expectation loss or reliance loss).

1 Compensatory damages

It is often said that the purpose of the law of contract is, as far as is possible, to fulfil the reasonable expectations of the contracting parties.[5] The corresponding object of damages is, so far as money can do, to put the party injured by a breach of contract in the same position as he would have been in had the contract been performed. This was famously made clear by Parke B in *Robinson v Harman*:[6]

the rule of the common law is, that where a party sustains loss by reason of a breach of contract, he is, so far as money can do it to be placed in the same situation, with respect to damages, as if the contract had been performed.

---

[1] See Chapters 24 and 25.
[2] See Chapter 28, Section 7.
[3] See Chapter 28, Section 6.
[4] L Fuller and R Perdue, 'The Reliance Interest in Contract Damages' (1936) 46 Yale LJ 52.
[5] Lord Steyn, 'Contract Law: Fulfilling the Reasonable Expectations of Honest Men' (1997) 113 LQR 433.
[6] (1848) 1 Exch 850, Court of Exchequer.

Two important questions need to be asked. First, how well off would the claimant have been if the contract had been performed? Secondly, how well off is the claimant now? The difference is the measure of damages.

This principle is well illustrated by the law of sale of goods. Imagine that the buyer, in breach of contract, refuses to accept and pay for the goods. If there is a market for the goods, the seller should be able to sell them to another party. In that case, the measure of damages is the difference between the market or current price of the goods at the time when they ought to have been accepted and the contract price.[7] But substantial damages will only need to be paid where the market price is lower than the contract price. If the market price is the same as, or even higher than, the contract price, then the seller has suffered no loss. In such circumstances, the seller will only be entitled to nominal damages (generally no more than £5).[8] The same analysis applies where the seller commits a breach of contract by refusing to deliver the goods. If there is a market for similar goods, the buyer can buy them and recover from the seller the difference between the contract price and (assuming it to be greater) the market or current price of the goods at the time when they ought to have been delivered.[9]

Where a seller of 'Vanguard' cars could sell all the Vanguards he could lay his hands on, he was entitled only to nominal damages from a buyer who, in breach of contract, refused to take delivery of a car. As there was a waiting list of buyers, the seller simply sold that car to someone else. If he could only acquire, say, 20 Vanguards a year, he could make 20 times the profit on a Vanguard, no more and no less, and it made no difference to whom he sold them.[10] But where there were more cars than buyers, the seller was entitled to the loss of profit from a defaulting buyer. So, where the seller sold, say, 20 'Hillman Minx' cars in the year, but would have sold 21 if the defendant buyer had not defaulted, the seller is entitled to be put into the position he would have been in if the contract had been performed; as a result, the seller can recover the loss of profit from the sale of that extra car.[11]

In *The Golden Victory*,[12] Lord Scott said that '[t]he lodestar is that the damages should represent the value of the contractual benefits of which the claimant had been deprived by the breach of contract, no less but also no more'.[13] In that decision, discussed further in Section 3,[14] the House of Lords strongly endorsed the 'compensatory principle'. However, working out exactly how much the claimant can recover can often lead to difficulties. The major factors to be considered will be analysed in this chapter.

[7] Sale of Goods Act 1979, s 50(2) and (3).
[8] For nominal damages, see Chapter 28, Section 6.
[9] Sale of Goods Act 1979, s 51(2) and (3).
[10] *WL Thompson v Robinson (Gunmakers) Ltd* [1955] Ch 177.
[11] cf *Charter v Sullivan* [1957] 2 QB 117.
[12] [2007] UKHL 12, [2007] 2 WLR 691.
[13] [36].
[14] Section 3.

2 Establishing a claim for loss

In a typical claim for breach of contract, the claimant seeks to recover his financial loss. This is generally equal to expected profits which the claimant has lost. Such financial loss will be the focus of the analysis in this chapter, although it is important to note that there are some types of loss which are not financial but are nonetheless recoverable following a breach of contract, and these will be examined later.[15]

(a) Causation

If the loss has not been caused by the breach of contract, then the defendant should not have to compensate the claimant for that loss. There must be a causal link between the defendant's wrong and the claimant's loss. In principle, this requires both 'factual causation' and 'legal causation'.[16] It should therefore first be established as a matter of fact that the loss would not have been suffered had there not been a breach of contract—in other words, the breach of contract must be a 'but for' cause of the loss. However, this factual issue alone is insufficient. It must also be shown that the law should hold the contract-breaker responsible for the innocent party's loss—for example, because there was no other intervening act to break the chain of causation between the defendant's wrong and the claimant's loss.

Both factual causation and legal causation are difficult. The 'but for' test of causation can be somewhat vague and malleable, and has been discussed in detail in numerous specialist works on causation.[17] Indeed, in *Galoo Ltd v Bright Grahame Murray*,[18] Glidewell LJ somewhat unhelpfully suggested that answers to questions of causation can be found through the exercise of 'common sense'. This is unfortunately unclear. Only a little more helpfully, *Galoo* establishes that a distinction should be drawn between a breach of contract which merely gave the claimant the opportunity to suffer a loss, and a breach of contract which actually causes loss.[19] This appears to be a question of fact that will depend upon the circumstances of any particular case. In *Galoo*, the claimants sued their auditors for failing to exercise due care when drawing up their accounts. This was a breach of contract. The claimants argued that if the accounts had been properly drawn up then they would have stopped trading and therefore stopped suffering losses. This argument was rejected by the Court of Appeal. The judges held that the auditors' breach of contract only provided the claimants with the opportunity of suffering losses. The real reason for the claimants' loss was the way in which they ran their business.

Perhaps the most important aspect of legal causation is the concept of a *novus actus interveniens*. A *novus actus interveniens* is a 'new intervening act' that will be considered to break the chain of causation from the defendant's breach of contract to the claimant's loss. This is because, in such circumstances, the real cause of the claimant's loss will be the

---

[15] Section 4.
[16] H Hart and T Honoré, *Causation in the Law* (2nd edn, OUP, 1985).
[17] Most notably, perhaps, ibid.
[18] [1994] 1 WLR 1360, CA.
[19] See similarly *Quinn v Burch Bros (Builders) Ltd* [1966] 2 QB 370.

new intervening act rather than the contract-breaker. As a result, the law will not allow the claimant to recover against the contract-breaker, even though he may be a factual 'but for' cause of the loss. Nevertheless, the contract-breaker will not escape liability if he had undertaken to prevent that very act from occurring. For instance, in *Stansbie v Troman*,[20] a decorator was left alone in the claimant's house which he was decorating. The decorator left the house to obtain materials for his work, and unfortunately left the door to the house unlocked. A thief entered the house and stole various items. Clearly, the decorator leaving the house unlocked was a factual, 'but-for' cause of the claimant's loss, but the decorator argued that the real cause of the claimant's loss was the conduct of the thief, and that this was a new intervening act such that he should not be held to be legally responsible for the loss. This was a plausible argument, but decisively rejected by the Court of Appeal. The judges held that even though the most immediate cause of the claimant's loss was the conduct of the third party (the thief), the decorator should be liable to compensate the claimant since it was as a direct result of the decorator's breach of contract that the claimant suffered loss: the reason why the decorator promised not to leave the house unlocked was in order to prevent thieves from entering the claimant's house.

In some situations, the claimant's own conduct may constitute a *novus actus interveniens*. For that to be the case, the conduct of the claimant 'must constitute an event of such impact that it "obliterates" the wrongdoing ... of the defendant'.[21] This is a high threshold. For example, in *Lambert v Lewis*[22] a farmer used a trailer which became detached from his car. The trailer then careered across the road and killed and injured other people. The coupling had been defectively designed and was dangerous, but the House of Lords held that the dealers and manufacturers were not liable for causing the loss claimed in the case (as a result of the personal injuries): by continuing to use the trailer after the coupling had broken, the farmer had acted entirely unreasonably, and this constituted a new intervening act. But *Lambert v Lewis* is perhaps an unusual case. Courts will generally be sympathetic to claimants who are themselves victims of a breach of contract, and slow to find that they have acted so unreasonably that the defendant should not bear responsibility for the loss.[23] Where the defendant's conduct remains an effective cause of the loss, the chain of causation will not usually be broken.

(b) Remoteness

There is a strong link between causation and remoteness. However, it is helpful to consider the two separately. Causation is to do with establishing a link between the breach of contract and loss. Remoteness is about limiting the amount of compensation the defendant has to pay, even though the losses might be said to have in fact been caused by the breach of contract. The law has long recognised that it would be too harsh to make a contracting party liable for all loss which results in fact, no matter how unpredictable or unforeseeable

---

[20] [1948] 2 KB 48, CA.
[21] *Borealis AB v Geogas Trading SA* [2010] EWHC 2789 (Comm), [2011] 1 Lloyd's Rep 482 [44] (Gross LJ), citing AM Jones and MA Dugdale (eds), *Clerk & Lindsell on Torts* (19th edn, Sweet & Maxwell, 2005) para 2-78.
[22] [1982] AC 225, HL.
[23] *Compania Naviera Maropan v Bowaters (The 'Stork')* [1955] 2 QB 68.

that loss might be. Some losses may therefore be considered to be too 'remote' from the breach of contract.

Remoteness is something of a 'hot topic' in contract law at the moment. This is because it remains slightly unclear what impact the relatively recent decision of the House of Lords in *The Achilleas*[24] will have upon the traditional approach under *Hadley v Baxendale*.[25] It is suggested that the two approaches exist alongside one another, and each will now be examined in turn before considering their relationship with one another.

(i) The traditional approach: *Hadley v Baxendale*

The classic statement of the remoteness rule in contract law is that of Alderson B in *Hadley v Baxendale*:[26]

> Where two parties have made a contract which one of them has broken, the damages which the other party ought to receive in respect of such breach of contract should be such as may fairly and reasonably be considered as either arising naturally, *i.e.* according to the usual course of things, from such breach of contract itself, or such as may reasonably be supposed to have been in the contemplation of both parties, at the time they made the contract, as the probable result of the breach of it.

This proposition has been customarily analysed as putting forward two 'rules', or 'limbs'. The first limb concerns loss 'arising naturally'. The second limb concerns loss which does not arise naturally from the breach of contract but 'which may reasonably be supposed to have been in the contemplation of both parties'. Analysis in later cases suggests that there might really only be a single principle at play—that of foreseeability as a likely result. But this is not, generally, very helpful, since what a person foresees depends on what he knows. Everyone is taken to know 'the ordinary course of things', whether or not he actually does so in fact. That is provided for by the first limb. But a person may have special knowledge at the time of entering into the contract, over and above that which every reasonable man is presumed to have. A person with that special knowledge may reasonably be expected to foresee as likely a loss which would not have been reasonably foreseeable without that knowledge. This is provided for by the second limb. The person with the special knowledge may be liable for the further loss.

The application of the two limbs is well illustrated by *Hadley v Baxendale* itself. The crankshaft of the steam engine used in a mill was broken. The owners of the mill therefore entered into a contract with carriers that the carriers would transport the broken crankshaft to engineers in Greenwich. The owners told the carriers that the crankshaft had to be sent immediately, and the carriers promised to deliver it to the engineers the next day. In breach of contract, the carriers delivered the crankshaft to the engineers five days too late. It transpired that the broken shaft was sent as a pattern for a new one, and that until the new shaft was received, the mill could not operate. The mill owners therefore sued the

---

[24] [2008] UKHL 48, [2009] 1 AC 61.

[25] (1854) 9 Exch 341.

[26] Ibid, 355.

carriers and claimed £300 loss of profit for the five days by which the resumption of work was delayed. The claim failed.

The only facts communicated to the carriers were that the article to be transported was the broken shaft of a mill and that the claimants were millers. In the opinion of the court, in the vast majority of cases this would not have meant that the operations of the mill would have to be stopped. Presumably, the judges considered that the great majority of millers were sufficiently prudent to own a spare shaft. As a result, the court held that this was not a loss occurring 'in the ordinary course of things', so the first limb did not apply. Nor did the second limb avail the mill owners. Had the carrier been told, 'The mill is stopped and cannot operate until we receive a new shaft, for which this broken one is a pattern', presumably the result would have been different.[27] The carrier would then have had special knowledge, outside the ordinary course of things, from which it would have been readily foreseeable that loss of profits was likely if there was a delay in delivery.

How likely must the loss be?

The question of how likely the loss must be was debated in the two modern leading cases on the subject. In *Victoria Laundry (Windsor) Ltd v Newman Industries Ltd*,[28] Asquith LJ said that it is enough that the loss is one foreseen as 'liable to result', but in *The Heron II*[29] Lord Reid criticised the word 'liable' both as too vague and as including possible but improbable loss. In *Hadley v Baxendale* itself it was certainly *possible* that the delay in delivery would result in closure of the mill. Lord Reid was also critical of Asquith LJ's use of the phrases 'a real danger', 'a serious possibility', or 'on the cards' to describe the necessary degree of likelihood. His own preference was for 'likely' or, better, 'not unlikely'. However, it should be noted that the other Law Lords in *The Heron II* were not so critical of Asquith LJ's formulation of the test generally, although they all deprecated the use of the phrase 'on the cards', since that was capable of denoting a most improbable and unlikely event. Drawing the ace of hearts out of a pack of cards may be 'on the cards', but it is highly unlikely.

In the *Victoria Laundry* case, damages for a business's loss of profits arising from the delay of five months in delivering a boiler were held to be recoverable. *Victoria Laundry* is distinguishable from *Hadley v Baxendale* since in *Victoria Laundry* the defendants were not carriers but the sellers of the boiler. In fact, the sellers were an engineering company who might be expected to know more about the use of boilers than the ordinary man, and the sellers knew that they were selling the boiler to a laundry company which obviously (according to the judgment of the court) wanted the boiler to heat water in order to wash clothes and thereby make profits. The sellers argued that this was not so obvious at all. The sellers contended that the laundry company might conceivably have wanted the boiler to replace another which was functioning satisfactorily in the meantime. In fact, the claimants wanted the boiler to expand their business. Although the sellers were not informed of this, there was at the time 'a famine in laundry facilities' and, in the court's opinion, reasonable persons in the defendants' shoes would have foreseen that a delay of five months

---

[27] The headnote to the case is misleading insofar as it suggests that this information was given.

[28] [1949] 2 KB 528, CA.

[29] [1969] 1 AC 350.

was 'likely' to result in financial loss—and certainly there was a 'real danger', 'a serious possibility', and it was 'liable' to happen.

With respect to these lost profits, *Victoria Laundry* was a case that fell within the 'first limb'. However, the decision perhaps illustrates the fact that there is no hard and fast line between the two so-called rules. In any event, the fact that the defendant was a seller rather than a carrier was significant, since a seller is likely to be much more aware of, and concerned with, the purposes to which an article is to be put than a carrier would be; and an engineering company might be expected to be more aware than some other seller. So we are looking at all the relevant circumstances in order to determine what is reasonably foreseeable as 'likely' or 'not unlikely'.

It is clear than an event may be 'not unlikely' even though there is substantially less than an even chance that it will occur. In *The Heron II*, the contract was to carry a cargo of sugar to Basrah or, at the option of the claimant (who was the owner of the sugar) to Jeddah. The option was not exercised and the ship arrived at Basrah. However, the ship arrived nine days late, because the carrier had made deviations in breach of contract. It was always the intention of the claimant to sell the sugar immediately upon arrival in Basrah. He did so, but the price had fallen substantially during the nine days in which the ship was delayed. The claimant therefore claimed the difference in damages. The defendant did not know of the claimant's intention to sell but he knew that there was a market for sugar in Basrah; if the defendant had thought about this issue, he must have realised that it was 'not unlikely' that the sugar would be sold on arrival. He must also have known that market prices fluctuate, even though he had no reason to suppose that the price would go down rather than up. If the price had gone up, the claimant would actually have made a profit as a result of the breach (and the defendant would not have had to pay substantial damages). Of course, the sugar might not have been intended for sale on arrival; and even if it was, the price might have gone up or down. Nevertheless, it was held that the loss which the claimant had actually incurred was 'not unlikely' and he was therefore entitled to the damages claimed.

The courts avoid laying down precise mathematical rules. But in *The Heron II* Lord Reid thought a one in four chance 'not unlikely'. It was not unlikely that the top card of a well-shuffled pack of playing cards would prove to be a diamond. A one in fifty-two chance, however, was unlikely—it was not likely that the top card would be the nine of diamonds (even though, in his Lordship's opinion, this could be described as 'on the cards', 'a serious possibility', or 'a real danger'). Somewhere in between a line is drawn. We cannot expect the courts to tell us precisely where. It is a matter for the judgement and the sense of fairness of the particular court in determining where the loss should lie.

What must be foreseen?

It seems that it is sufficient that the defendant should have foreseen a head or type of damage, and does not need to have foreseen its quantum. In *Wroth v Tyler*,[30] a defendant failed to complete his contract to sell a house for £6,050. When the contract was made, a rise in the price of houses was in the contemplation of the parties, so the defendant was held liable to pay damages to the claimant when the value of the house rose by the day of judgment.

---

[30] [1974] Ch 30 (Megarry J).

In fact, the value of the house rose to £11,500, so the defendant was liable to pay damages of £5,500. This was, of course, a huge rise—after all, the price of the house nearly doubled. But the court was clear that it was immaterial that the parties had not foreseen the scale of the increase in price. It was enough that the parties had contemplated the type of loss suffered by an increase in house prices. Similarly, in *Parson (Livestock) Ltd v Uttley Ingham & Co Ltd*,[31] it was held that the seller of a defective hopper must have foreseen, had he been aware of the defect, that it was not unlikely that the pig nuts to be stored in the hopper would deteriorate and cause the pigs to be ill. As a result, even though the very serious illness which in fact resulted to the pigs was not at all likely, the defendant was liable for its consequences.

These decisions seem irreconcilable with the holding in the *Victoria Laundry* case that, while the defendants were liable for the loss of 'normal' dyeing contracts which were reasonably to be expected, the defendants were not liable for the loss of certain particularly lucrative dyeing contracts which the claimants had entered into with the Ministry of Supply. Such contracts were unusually lucrative, and, according to the Court of Appeal, the damage suffered by losing those contracts could not be said to be 'arising naturally … according to the usual course of things'. As a result, such damage did not fall within the first limb of *Hadley v Baxendale*. Nor did it fall within the second limb, since the defendants had no knowledge of these contracts. This aspect of the decision in the *Victoria Laundry* case is very difficult to explain. It might sensibly be criticised since it draws a distinction between 'usual' contracts and 'lucrative' contracts. This distinction appears to be concerned with the quantum of loss rather than the type of loss, even though in principle only the type of loss needs to be foreseen. In *Victoria Laundry*, the better view may have been to conclude that the damages under the 'lucrative' contract were of the same type as the damages suffered under the 'usual' contracts and so should be recoverable. Nevertheless, *Victoria Laundry* appears to suggest that if the quantum of loss is to be unusually large, then that may mean that the loss is of a different type and will fall within the second limb of *Hadley v Baxendale*.[32] This issue will be explored further when considering *The Achilleas* below.

When must the loss be foreseen?

In *Jackson v Royal Bank of Scotland*,[33] a bank disclosed confidential information about a client's business to that client's customers. This disclosure was a breach of the contractual duty of confidence the bank owed to its client. The client therefore sued the bank for breach of contract, and the first instance judge found that the customers would have continued their relationship with the client for a further four years. The judge awarded damages on that basis. The Court of Appeal overturned the decision of the trial judge, saying that 'the cut-off point for the bank's liability was the end of such period as was within the reasonable contemplation of the bank at the time of breach', and this was held to be only one year rather than four. Significantly, the House of Lords overturned the decision of the Court of Appeal and was very critical of the reasoning employed in that court. Lord Hope insisted

---

[31] [1978] QB 791, CA.

[32] See too *Brown v KMR Services Ltd* [1995] 4 All ER 598.

[33] [2005] UKHL 3, [2005] 1 WLR 377, HL.

that the Court of Appeal had misunderstood *Hadley v Baxendale*. The key moment is the time at which the contract was made, not the time of breach. His Lordship explained that 'the assumption is that the defendant undertook to bear any special loss which was referable to those special circumstances. It is assumed too that he had the opportunity to seek to limit his liability under the contract for ordinary losses in the event that he was in breach of it.' This is crucial to a proper understanding of the second limb of *Hadley v Baxendale*. Unlike most tort claims,[34] in the contractual context the parties are in a position where one party can bring to the other's attention the risk of losses which would not naturally arise from a breach of contract. Upon doing this, the other party can choose whether or not to enter into the contract at all, or to demand a higher price, or the insertion of a limitation clause, or any other modification of the agreement. But all this happens at the point of contract formation. It is surprising that the Court of Appeal in *Jackson* departed from this orthodox approach, but welcome that the House of Lords restored clarity.

(ii) A new approach: *The Achilleas*

The preceding analysis may once have been sufficient to explain the law of remoteness, although it should be noted that there has always been a suggestion that mere knowledge of unusual losses will not always be sufficient to recover under the second limb of *Hadley v Baxendale*. For instance, in *British Columbia Sawmill Co Ltd v Nettleship*,[35] the defendant carrier lost a box which he knew to contain part of the machinery of a sawmill to be erected in Vancouver Island. Although the defendant knew that the box contained part of the machinery, he did not know that the part was essential to the working of the machinery. The mill could not operate without the missing part, and the claimant sued for his loss of profits. The court held that the defendant was not liable for the claimant's loss. Willes J said that knowledge of the use to which the article would be put was not enough, since

> there must have been knowledge under such circumstances as would raise the presumption that he intended to make himself liable for the special consequences and that the person contracting with him believed, and had reasonable grounds for believing, that he intended to undertake such liability and unless there was a special payment it would be very difficult to get a jury to come to such a conclusion.

This suggests that there has to be, in effect, a term in the contract imposing this exceptional liability. But subsequent cases, such as *The Heron II*, did not seem to insist on so strict a requirement. At the same time, it may be questioned whether a casual remark to the defendant's clerk—'The mill is stopped till we get the shaft back, you know'—should suffice to impose liability on the defendants in a case like *Hadley v Baxendale*.

This problem resurfaced in the difficult decision of the House of Lords in *The Achilleas*. Under a time **charter**, the defendant charterers should have redelivered the ship to the claimant owners by 2 May 2004. In breach of contract, they did not redeliver to the owners

---

[34] Although see Section 2(b)(iv).
[35] (1868) LR 3 CP 499.

until 11 May. This meant that the owners needed to renegotiate a follow-on charter, due to commence on 8 May, which they had already agreed with another charterer. Because the market rates had fallen, under the follow-on charter the owners were forced to reduce the rate of hire from $39,500 to $31,500 a day, which meant a loss of $8,000 a day. The owners sued the defendants for the losses suffered.

The defendants accepted that they were liable for the losses that arose as a result of the difference between the market rate and the charter rate for the nine-day overrun period between 2 and 11 May. This amounted to $158,301. However, the owners sought also to recover the losses it suffered ($8,000 a day) for the whole period of the follow-on charter. That amounted to $1,364,584. The House of Lords unanimously overturned the decision of the courts below and held that the losses suffered for the whole period of the follow-on charter were too remote.

It should be noted at the outset that the decision does not seem consistent with a traditional understanding of the principles in *Hadley v Baxendale*. It is entirely normal for the owner of a ship to enter into follow-on charters, and it would therefore be in the natural course of things that the late redelivery of the ship would cause the owner loss in respect of follow-on charters. It is suggested that the claim in *The Achilleas* should have fallen within the first limb of *Hadley v Baxendale* and should not have been considered to be too remote.

However, even Lord Rodger and Baroness Hale, who applied *Hadley v Baxendale* to the facts at hand, disagreed with this analysis. Lord Rodger held that 'this loss could not have been reasonably foreseen as being likely to arise out of the delay in question. It was, accordingly, too remote to give rise to a claim for damages for breach of contract'. But it is not clear why this is so. The basis appears to be that the change in market rates was so extreme that it could not have been foreseen and was highly unusual. Yet the *type* of loss—financial loss under the follow-on charter—was surely both foreseeable and natural. The approach of Lord Rodger and Baroness Hale is similar to that in *Victoria Laundry*—it is the extreme financial consequences that make this sort of loss of a different 'type'. But even this is unconvincing. Whereas in *Victoria Laundry* there were special sorts of contracts involved—the 'lucrative' contracts with the Ministry of Supply—in *The Achilleas* there was nothing special about the follow-on charters at all.

Lord Hoffmann and Lord Hope offered a different approach, and it is this approach with which *The Achilleas* is now best associated. Their Lordships based the principles of remoteness upon the parties' voluntary assumption of responsibility for the loss in question. Lord Hoffmann said:[36]

> Is the rule that a party may recover losses which were foreseeable ('not unlikely') an external rule of law, imposed upon the parties to every contract in default of express provision to the contrary, or is it a **prima facie** assumption about what the parties may be taken to have intended, no doubt applicable in the great majority of cases but capable of rebuttal in cases in which the context, surrounding circumstances or general understanding in the relevant market shows that a party would not reasonably have been regarded as assuming responsibility for such losses?

His Lordship favoured the latter option. Lord Hoffmann considered that whether or not a particular loss was too remote could be ascertained by looking at the parties' intentions at the time the contract was made, given the surrounding background and matrix of fact.

---

[36] Ibid [9].

This approach is entirely consistent with Lord Hoffmann's approach to interpretation[37] and implication,[38] under which all the answers can be found by looking at the parties' agreement. On the facts of *The Achilleas*, the settled understanding of those in the shipping industry appeared to be that damages for late redelivery were confined to the overrun period and not the whole period of the follow-on charter, which explains why the House of Lords concluded that the losses were too remote.

This 'assumption of responsibility' analysis helps to explain some difficult cases. One notorious example is where the claimant contracts with a taxi driver to take him to a meeting, telling the taxi driver that at the meeting the claimant will make a huge amount of money by signing a lucrative deal. In breach of contract, the taxi driver arrives late and takes the wrong route, which means that the claimant loses the opportunity to make the huge amount of money. It is generally thought that the claimant should not be able to sue the taxi driver for the huge amount of money, even though this was in the contemplation of the parties at the time the contract was made. Lord Hoffmann explains this on the basis of assumption of responsibility: interpreting the parties' agreement, the reasonable observer would not conclude that the taxi driver assumed responsibility for such losses. Prior to *The Achilleas*, courts had sometimes hinted at a similar approach,[39] but generally thought that the result rested on the fact that it was not 'reasonable'[40] or 'proper'[41] for the taxi driver to be so liable.

The approach of Lord Hoffmann and Lord Hope in *The Achilleas* might therefore be useful in unusual circumstances, and it is indeed in the difficult cases that it seems to be invoked.[42] However, it is suggested that it is ultimately somewhat unsatisfactory. After all, there will usually be very little evidence from which the court will be able to discern the intentions of the parties, since the parties will rarely have thought about who should bear the risk of certain types of loss. Lord Hoffmann suggested that it will be possible to imply a term into the contract to such effect, but it is unclear whether it is really necessary to do so to give effect to the parties' intentions. Moreover, Lord Hoffmann has since suggested that the term may be implied at law into all contracts of a particular type, such as all shipping contracts of the type that was at issue in *The Achilleas*.[43] Yet on this approach the rules of remoteness again become externally imposed, rather than being internal to the parties' agreement, which is the very essence of Lord Hoffmann's criticism of *Hadley v Baxendale*. In any event, the test of 'assumption of responsibility' seems very malleable and may not improve commercial certainty in this area. For example, it does not even seem certain how it should apply on the facts of *The Achilleas*. We are told by the House of Lords that the market expectation was such that the defendants would not be liable for losses suffered for the whole period of the follow-on charter, but this may perhaps only be the situation where the market suffered such a significant crash. On balance, it is suggested that the 'assumption

---

[37] See eg *Investors Compensation Scheme Ltd v West Bromwich Building Society* [1998] 1 WLR 896; *Chartbrook Ltd v Persimmon Homes Ltd* [2009] UKHL 38, [2009] 1 AC 1101.

[38] *Attorney General of Belize v Belize Telecom Ltd* [2009] UKPC 10, [2009] 2 All ER (Comm) 1.

[39] See eg *British Columbia Sawmill Co Ltd v Nettleship* (1868) LR 3 CP 499.

[40] *The Heron II*, 422.

[41] Ibid, 385.

[42] See Section 2(b)(iii).

[43] (2010) 14 Edinburgh Law Review 47, 60.

of responsibility' approach is unsatisfactory given its artificial nature and unclear scope. It would be preferable to focus upon policy concerns and external rules of law. Nevertheless, the House of Lords has endorsed the 'assumption of responsibility' view, and it is important now to understand its relationship with the traditional approach in *Hadley v Baxendale*.

(iii) The relationship between *Hadley v Baxendale* and *The Achilleas*

It is important to note that *Hadley v Baxendale* remains good law. Indeed, this is one of the *ratios* of *The Achilleas*. This is because Lord Walker supported both the approach based upon *Hadley v Baxendale* favoured by Lord Rodger and Baroness Hale, and also the new approach adopted by Lord Hoffmann and Lord Hope. As a result, a majority of the House of Lords endorsed *Hadley v Baxendale*. And a majority of the House of Lords also endorsed the 'assumption of responsibility' view. This is an unusual situation.

The courts seem to have reconciled these two approaches by saying that *Hadley v Baxendale* will apply in most cases, but in unusual circumstances the court might go on to consider whether the result would be any different under the 'assumption of responsibility' test. Thus in *Sylvia Shipping Co Ltd v Progress Bulk Carriers Ltd* Hamblen J said:[44]

> The orthodox [*Hadley v Baxendale*] approach remains the general test of remoteness applicable in the great majority of cases. However, there may be 'unusual' cases, such as *The Achilleas* itself, in which the context, surrounding circumstances or general understanding in the relevant market make it necessary specifically to consider whether there has been an assumption of responsibility. This is most likely to be in those relatively rare cases where the application of the general test leads or may lead to an unquantifiable, unpredictable, uncontrollable or disproportionate liability or where there is clear evidence that such a liability would be contrary to market understanding and expectations.

This is sensible. Courts should certainly start with the *Hadley v Baxendale* principles and then apply the 'assumption of responsibility' test in the 'relatively rare cases' identified by Hamblen J. In *SC Confectia SA v Miss Mania Wholesale Ltd*, Beatson LJ pointed out that *The Achilleas* only seems to apply to cases that fall within the second limb of *Hadley v Baxendale*, and not the first.[45] Moreover, *Hadley v Baxendale* 'remains the standard rule' which can only be displaced 'if, on examining the contract and the commercial background, it can be said that the loss in question is within or outside the scope of the contractual duties'.[46]

As this quotation from Beatson LJ suggests, the effect of *The Achilleas* may not always be to limit liability further than would be the case under *Hadley v Baxendale*. The assumption of responsibility test may also be thought to expand the range of recoverable losses: a wider range of losses may now fall within the scope of losses which are not too remote because the defendant assumed responsibility for them. A good example of this is *Supershield Ltd v Siemens Building Technologies FE Ltd*.[47] The owners of a building had entered into

---

[44] [2010] EWHC 542 (Comm), [2010] 2 Lloyd's Rep 81 [40].

[45] [2014] EWCA Civ 1484 [26]. Of course, whether or not *The Achilleas* itself should rightly be considered to fall within the first or second limb of *Hadley v Baxendale* is controversial: see Section 2(b)(ii).

[46] [2014] EWCA Civ 1484 [25].

[47] [2010] EWCA Civ 7, [2010] 2 All ER (Comm) 1185.

a contract with a contractor to supply and install a sprinkler system in such a way that the water used for the system was properly contained. The contractor subcontracted this work, and the dispute was actually between the contractor and subcontractor about liability. Nevertheless, the important issue of principle was whether the contractor was liable to the owners for losses that were suffered when a nut and bolt connection on a float valve failed, and water from a storage tank overflowed into the basement of the building causing extensive damage. This was because of a lack of sufficient tightening when the valve was installed. The contractors argued that it was very unlikely that this breach of contract would cause a flood: it would generally be expected that the water would be able to escape through the drains. But on the facts of the case, the drains also failed. It was improbable that both the valve would fail and the drains would fail, but this did not mean that the losses suffered by the claimants were too remote. As Toulson LJ said, 'drains do block, drain pumps malfunction, building management systems do not always operate and maintenance is not always effective. I would conclude that the flood which resulted from the escape of water from the sprinkler tank, even if it was unlikely, was within the scope of [the contractor's] contractual duty to prevent.'[48] This reasoning relied upon the assumption of responsibility approach, but might it not be thought that such losses were also within the scope of the second limb of *Hadley v Baxendale*? After all, if the valve failed, would it not be contemplated as 'not unlikely' that one of the consequences would be flooding? This was the conclusion of Ramsey J at first instance, and suggests that a similar result might still be reached through traditional reasoning.

Admittedly, it is currently still somewhat unclear what effect *The Achilleas* will come to have over time.[49] There are some cases that now base the whole law concerning remoteness on the parties' intentions, usually on the basis of an implied term.[50] But a wholesale shift in approach appears unlikely (even if it may be on the cards): *Hadley v Baxendale* remains the correct starting point when considering issues of remoteness.[51]

(iv) The relationship between contract and tort

In *The Achilleas*, Lord Hoffmann referred to his own earlier judgment in *Banque Bruxelles Lambert SA v Eagle Star Insurance Co Ltd (sub nom South Australia Asset Management Corp v York Montague Ltd)*.[52] The principle from this *SAAMCO* case has been generally applied in tort law to represent a need to establish the 'scope of duty' owed by the defendant: it must be determined for what types of loss the parties should fairly and reasonably be taken to bear responsibility. This is a difficult test that has been heavily criticised.[53] Its scope and

---

[48] [45].

[49] As Beatson LJ has said, 'As to *The Achilleas*, the effect of that case on the understanding of remoteness of damage in the law of contract has of course been profound. Law students up and down the country are probably set the task of identifying the ratio of that case': *SC Confectia SA v Miss Mania Wholesale Ltd* [2014] EWCA Civ 1484 [23].

[50] See eg *John Grimes Partnership Limited v Gubbins* [2013] EWCA Civ 37 [2013] BLR 126.

[51] The approach of Lord Hoffmann and Lord Hope in *The Achilleas* has been rejected in Singapore: *MFM Restaurants Pte Ltd v Fish & Co Restaurants Pte Ltd* [2010] SGCA 36, [2011] 1 SLR 150.

[52] [1997] AC 191.

[53] E Peel, '*SAAMCO* Revisited' in A Burrows and E Peel (eds), *Commercial Remedies: Current Issues and Problems* (OUP, 2003).

operation are uncertain. But *The Achilleas* seems to favour a similar approach. However, it is unclear whether *SAAMCO* should really be considered to be concerned with remoteness. The operation of *SAAMCO* is binary, in the sense that either a particular type of loss is within the scope of the defendant's duty or it is not. The rules of remoteness, on the other hand, are analogue, in the sense that even though some losses may be considered to be too remote, the claimant will still be able to recover losses that are not considered to be too remote.[54] In effect, *SAAMCO* is a gateway to a type of loss, but the extent of recoverability of that loss is a question of remoteness.[55]

Where the claims in contract and tort overlap because the tortious duty of care arises in parallel to a contractual relationship, there has been much discussion about whether to apply the tortious rules of remoteness or the contractual rules of remoteness. Given that the foundation of the principles in *Hadley v Baxendale* rests upon the fact that the parties had the opportunity to bring special risks to each other's attention, it might be thought that the contractual rules should trump the tortious rules, even where the claim is brought in tort. This was the approach favoured by the Court of Appeal in *Brown v KMR Services Ltd*.[56] The suggestion of Lord Denning in *Parsons v Utley Ingham*[57] that the rules on remoteness should depend upon whether the loss in question is loss of profit or physical damage has not been favoured in subsequent cases. This is understandable: it is unclear what the nature of the division between the two types of loss really is.[58]

(c) Mitigation

Following a breach of contract, the innocent party should act reasonably in order to mitigate, or reduce, his loss. The claimant is entitled only to such damages as would have been suffered by a person acting reasonably after the breach. If it is possible for the injured party to take steps which will result in no loss whatsoever occurring *and* if it is reasonable for him to take those steps, then he is entitled only to nominal damages. If taking those reasonable steps will reduce the loss which would otherwise occur, then he is entitled to damages only for that reduced loss. This principle is usually described in terms of the claimant's 'duty to mitigate' the damage. This derives from the classic statement of Viscount Haldane LC in *British Westinghouse Electric v Underground Electric Railways*, who spoke of a principle that[59]

> imposes on a plaintiff the duty of taking all reasonable steps to mitigate the loss consequent on the breach, and debars him from claiming any part of the damage which is due to his neglect to take such steps.

---

[54] *Cory v Thames Ironworks* (1867–68) LR 3 QB 181.

[55] See M Stiggelbout, 'Contractual Remoteness, "Scope of Duty" and Intention' [2012] LMCLQ 97, 114–17.

[56] [1995] 4 All ER 598. This was also recently endorsed in *Wellesley Partners LLP v Withers LLP* [2015] EWCA Civ 1146.

[57] [1978] QB 791.

[58] See generally J Cartwright, 'Remoteness of Damage in Contract and Tort: A Reconsideration' (1996) 55 CLJ 488.

[59] [1912] AC 673, 689.

However, it is important to note that the term 'duty' is loosely used. The claimant commits no wrong by choosing not to mitigate. The claimant is entitled to act as he thinks best in his own interest, and is under no 'duty' (in the usual sense) to minimise his loss. The point is that whether the claimant mitigates the damage or not, he will recover only those damages which would have been incurred had he done so.[60] This is sometimes explained on the ground that the defendant is only liable for those reduced damages because it is only those damages that were caused by his breach of contract; the additional damage arising from a failure to mitigate might be considered to have been caused by the claimant's own unreasonable behaviour. Lord Bingham has recently suggested that '[t]he rationale of the rule is one of simple commercial fairness. The injured party owes no duty to the repudiator, but fairness requires that he should not ordinarily be permitted to rely on his own unreasonable and uncommercial conduct to increase the loss falling on the repudiator'.[61]

Whether loss is avoidable by reasonable action by the claimant is a question of fact to be decided in the light of all the circumstances of a particular case. So, if an employee (the claimant) is dismissed immediately and in breach of a contractual duty to give him three months' notice, the claimant will lose out on three months' pay. But if the employee is then offered immediate re-employment in similar work at the same or a higher rate of pay, it is likely (although all the circumstances must be taken into account) that he will be entitled only to nominal damages, regardless of whether he accepts the offer or not. Thus in *Brace v Calder*,[62] where the dismissal was of a technical nature resulting from the dissolution of a partnership, and the continuing partners offered to re-employ the claimant, the claimant was only entitled to nominal damages against the original firm, even though he declined that offer. The 'duty' to mitigate meant that the court awarded damages on the basis of the loss the claimant would have suffered had he taken reasonable steps to mitigate his loss. Of course, *Brace v Calder* might have been decided differently if the continuing partners had acted in bad faith or had acted in a way that made it unreasonable to expect the claimant to enter into their employment.

In *Payzu Ltd v Saunders*,[63] there was a contract to deliver goods over a period of nine months, payment to be made within one month of delivery of each instalment. The seller declined to deliver any more goods after the first instalment. This was a breach of contract. However, the seller did offer to continue deliveries at the contract price if the buyers agreed to pay cash with each order. The buyers rejected the offer, and sued the sellers for the difference between the contract price and the market price, which had risen. The buyers' claim failed. The reasonable buyer would have accepted the seller's offer.

Similarly, in *The Solholt*[64] the sellers of a ship failed to deliver on the due date. The buyer properly cancelled the contract and claimed the difference between the contract price and the market price, which was $500,000 higher. However, the sellers' ship was available shortly after the due date, and they were still prepared to sell it to the buyers at the contract price. This was a very good deal for the buyers, and yet the buyers only offered to buy the

---

[60] *The Solholt* [1983] 1 Lloyd's Rep 605.
[61] *The Golden Victory* [2007] UKHL 12, [2007] 2 AC 353 [10].
[62] [1895] 2 QB 253.
[63] [1919] 2 KB 581, CA.
[64] [1983] 1 Lloyd's Rep 605.

ship at a lower price. The sellers refused this offer. The court held that the buyers were entitled to nominal damages only. Even though accepting the ship at the contract price would have, in effect, nullified the decision which the buyers were entitled to make to cancel the contract, it was still the reasonable thing to do. As a result, the buyers were entitled only to recover for the damage they would have incurred if they had acted reasonably. However, *The Solholt* was a tough decision; it will often not be reasonable to expect an injured party to take the initiative, and far more reasonable to expect the party in breach to put forward a properly formulated and documented proposal.[65]

It is important to remember that the burden of proof on the issue of mitigation is on the defendant.[66] It is not easy for the defendant to show that the claimant acted unreasonably, and a court's sympathy might reasonably lie with the innocent claimant rather than the wrongdoing defendant, such that considerable leeway might be granted to the claimant when deciding whether or not he took reasonable steps to mitigate his loss. As Lord Macmillan said in *Banco de Portugal v Waterlow*:[67]

> It is often easy after an emergency has passed to criticise the steps which have been taken to meet it, but such criticism does not come well from those who have themselves created the emergency. The law is satisfied if the party placed in a difficult situation by reason of the breach of a duty owed to him has acted reasonably in the adoption of remedial measures, and he will not be held disentitled to recover the cost of such measures merely because the party in breach can suggest that other measures less burdensome to him might have been taken.

(i) Mitigation and anticipatory breach

It will be recalled that in *White & Carter (Councils) Ltd v McGregor*[68] the House of Lords held that the victim of an anticipatory breach has a true option whether or not to accept the anticipatory breach: the innocent party is not precluded from deciding to perform the contract, where he can do so without the cooperation of the party in breach, merely because performing the contract will aggravate the loss which will be suffered by the party in breach. The fact that this effectively circumvents the duty to mitigate was a major reason why the minority judges dissented in *White & Carter* itself.

Of course, where the injured party 'accepts' the breach as putting an end to the contract, he is then under the so-called 'duty' to mitigate—he will only recover the damages which he would have incurred if he had taken reasonable steps. Where a person who has agreed to buy goods at a future date declares that he will not accept the goods when that date arrives, the seller who accepts the breach as putting an end to the contract will be treated, for the purpose of assessing damages, as if he had sold the goods at the first opportunity, if that is the course which a reasonable businessman who desired to mitigate the loss would take. If the price is falling dramatically, the seller cannot sit back and charge the buyer with the difference between the contract price and the much reduced market price at the time fixed

---

[65] *Manton Hire and Sales Ltd v Ash Manor Cheese Co Ltd* [2013] EWCA Civ 548.

[66] *Borealis AB v Geogas Trading SA* [2010] EWHC 2789 (Comm), (2011) 1 Lloyd's Rep 482 [50] (Gross LJ).

[67] [1932] AC 452, 506, cited with approval by Gross LJ in *Borealis AB v Geogas Trading SA* [2010] EWHC 2789 (Comm), [2011] 1 Lloyd's Rep 482 [50].

[68] See Chapter 25, Section 4.

for delivery.[69] But the standard required of the injured party is not a strict one. His 'duty' is only to act not unreasonably. The wrongdoer has no right to expect from the man whom he has wronged the utmost amount of diligence, the utmost amount of skill, and the most accurate conclusion in a matter of judgement.[70]

(d) **Contributory negligence**

Section 1(1) of the Law Reform (Contributory Negligence) Act 1945 states:

> Where any person suffers damage as the result partly of his own fault and partly of the fault of any other person or persons, a claim in respect of that damage shall not be defeated by reason of the fault of the person suffering the damage, but the damages recoverable in respect thereof shall be reduced to such extent as the court thinks just and equitable having regard to the claimant's share in the responsibility for the damage.

This is the essence of contributory negligence: a claimant should recover a reduced amount of damages if he is at fault and responsible for some of the loss suffered. However, for some time it was unclear whether contributory negligence is a defence to breach of contract or only to tortious claims. After all, section 4 of the Act provides that '"fault" means negligence, breach of statutory duty or other act or omission which gives rise to a liability in tort or would, apart from this Act, give rise to the defence of contributory negligence'.

It is now clear that in some cases contributory negligence will be a defence to breach of contract. In *Vesta v Butcher*,[71] Hobhouse J—whose judgment was subsequently endorsed on appeal—held that there are three categories of case. Category One arises where a defendant is in breach of a strict contractual duty. Category Two is where the defendant is in breach of a contractual duty of care. Category Three concerns situations where the defendant is in breach of a contractual duty of care and would also be liable in the tort of negligence. Contributory negligence is a defence only to Category Three. This is apparently because the defendant should not be deprived of the defence of contributory negligence simply because the claimant chooses to frame his claim in contract rather than tort, and this approach has since been supported by the Court of Appeal.[72]

Vesta v Butcher itself would have been a Category Three case had the defendant's breach of contract caused the claimants' loss. The claim failed because of a lack of causation, so the discussion of contributory negligence was, strictly, *obiter*. Nevertheless, it has been very influential and clearly represents the law in this jurisdiction today. But it does raise important questions about whether the state of the law is satisfactory. For instance, it means that there is an incentive for the *defendant* to argue that he did not just breach a strict contractual duty, but was also at fault and committed a tort. This is bizarre: surely it should be for the claimant to establish that a tort has been made out, and a defendant should not be in a better position if he is at fault than if he is not at fault. This criticism seems persuasive, but there are then two directions that the law could take in order to

---

[69] *Roth & Co v Taysen, Townsend & Co* [1895] 1 Com Cas 240.
[70] *Dunkirk Colliery Co v Lever* (1880) 41 LT 633 (James LJ).
[71] *Forsikringsaktieselskapet Vesta v Butcher* [1988] 2 All ER 43, CA.
[72] See eg *UCB Bank plc v Hepherd Winstanley and Pugh* [1999] Lloyd's Rep PN 963, CA.

be consistent. The first would allow contributory negligence to be a defence to all claims in breach of contract. This would have the advantage of 'fairness' in taking into account a claimant's faulty conduct. Such an approach might derive some support from the fact that contributory negligence applies to strict liability torts, so why not strict liability in contract as well? The other route to consistency is to abolish contributory negligence from the law of contract entirely. This would help to preserve certainty as to the remedies which might be awarded. In *Barclays Bank Ltd v Fairclough Building Ltd*,[73] the Court of Appeal robustly rejected any suggestion that contributory negligence could apply in Category One. Nourse LJ said:

> It ought to be a cause of general concern that the law should have got into such a state that a contractor who was in breach of two of the main obligations expressly undertaken by him in a standard form building contract was able to persuade the judge in the court below that the building owner's damages should be reduced by 40 per cent. because of its own negligence in not preventing the contractor from committing the breaches. In circumstances such as these release, waiver, forbearance or the like are the only defences available to a party to a contract who wishes to assert that the other party's right to recover damages for its breach has been lost or diminished. It ought to have been perfectly obvious that the Law Reform (Contributory Negligence) Act 1945 was never intended to obtrude the defence of contributory negligence into an area of the law where it has no business to be.

It should be noted that the Law Commission provisionally recommended that contributory negligence should apply to all three categories of case,[74] but ultimately proposed only an extension to Category Two.[75] This may be a pragmatic compromise, but it does not put the law on a satisfactory footing. Unsurprisingly, the proposals have not been implemented.

3 Date of assessment

The general rule is that damages are assessed at the date of breach.[76] This is desirable for reasons of commercial certainty. It enables the parties to assess at the date of breach how much is likely to be payable in damages, and then seek to settle their disputes accordingly. So, if A commits a **repudiatory** breach of contract, B can decide whether or not to terminate the contract and sue for damages. Part of B's calculation when deciding what to do will be the likely amount he will be able to recover in damages. This needs to be known, to some degree at least, at the moment of breach.

---

[73] [1994] 3 WLR 1057.

[74] Law Commission, *Contributory Negligence as a Defence in Contract* (Law Com Working Paper No 114, 1990).

[75] Law Commission, *Contributory Negligence as a Defence in Contract* (Law Com No 219, 1993).

[76] *The Golden Victory* [11] (Lord Bingham); *Johnson v Agnew* [1980] AC 367, 400–1; *SC Confectia SA v Miss Mania Wholesale Ltd* [2014] EWCA Civ 1484 [17] (Beatson LJ).

However, the breach-date rule is only a general rule and clearly subject to exceptions. This was explicitly recognised by Oliver J in *Radford v De Froberville*, who helpfully drew a link with mitigation:[77]

> It is sometimes said that the ordinary rule is that damages for breach of contract fall to be assessed at the date of the breach. That, however, is not a universal principle and the rationale behind it appears to me to lie in the inquiry—at what date could the **plaintiff** reasonably have been expected to mitigate the damages by seeking an alternative to performance of the contractual obligation?

For example, in *Hooper v Oates*,[78] a buyer failed to complete the purchase of a property in breach of contract. The Court of Appeal held that the damages that the buyer had to pay should not be calculated at the date of breach but rather at a later date, since it was unrealistic to expect the seller to be able to sell his property immediately. Real property is not a liquid market in the same manner as wheat, grain, or **shares**, for instance. As a result, the court held that the usual 'breach-date' rule should be displaced, and that the sellers should be afforded some time to take reasonable steps to sell the property again. The appropriate date to assess the seller's loss was when they sold the property or brought to an end their reasonable attempts to sell the property. The decision might be considered a little harsh on the defaulting purchaser, who found himself liable for a very substantial amount given a crash in the property market,[79] but does emphasise a strong link between the general 'breach-date' rule and the principles of mitigation.[80]

However, the breach-date rule may have been somewhat undermined by the decision of the House of Lords in *The Golden Victory*. In December 2001, the defendant charterers wrongfully repudiated a **charterparty**. The claimant shipowners accepted the repudiation, and argued that it should be able to recover damages for the remaining four years of the charter. The defendants argued that this would overcompensate the claimants, since in March 2003 war broke out in Iraq, and this would have entitled the charterers to terminate the contract lawfully. The defendants therefore argued that the claimants should only be able to recover damages up to the outbreak of war in 2003. A bare majority of the House of Lords agreed.

The majority in *The Golden Victory* emphasised that the compensatory principle required the claimant to be compensated for his loss, but no less and no more. Yet if the claimant were to be compensated for the period after the outbreak of war, he would be placed in a better position than if there had not been a breach of contract, and this was thought to be unsatisfactory. Moreover, the majority were clearly uncomfortable with disregarding known facts: why speculate artificially about what would happen for the remaining period of the charter when, at the time of trial, it was known that war broke out in 2003?

This approach might be considered to be both flexible and fair. But it is suggested that it is ultimately rather unsatisfactory. As Lord Bingham and Lord Walker observed in their

---

[77] [1977] 1 WLR 1262, 1285–6.

[78] [2013] EWCA Civ 91, [2014] Ch 287.

[79] For criticism see N Hopkins, 'Damages for Breach of Contract to Purchase Land: Getting the Principles Right' [2014] Conv 147.

[80] See further A Dyson and A Kramer, 'There is No "Date of Breach Rule"' (2014) 130 LQR 259.

strong dissents, commercial law requires clear rules and certainty. This was downplayed by Lord Scott, in the majority, who thought that, 'Certainty is a desideratum and a very important one, particularly in commercial contracts. But it is not a principle and must give way to principle.'[81] Yet concerns of certainty should not readily be sidelined. The parties' positions should be clear at the moment of breach—considerations of mitigation aside— and neither party should be encouraged to stall on any possible settlement of the dispute in the hope that subsequent events will occur which will improve his position. However, as a result of *The Golden Victory*, a defendant may now be encouraged not to pay up and settle a claim straight away, in the hope that the circumstances will evolve to reduce the amount he has to pay. This seems unfortunate.

Nevertheless, *The Golden Victory* is clearly good authority for the principle that the court will sometimes take into account events after the breach of contract when assessing a claimant's loss. Indeed, even though *The Golden Victory* might reasonably have been thought only to apply to post-termination events which are known to have occurred by the time of the trial, in *The Glory Wealth*,[82] Teare J held that the same principle applied to the claimant's inability to perform the contract post-breach. In that case, there was a contract between the disponent owners of a ship (who had commercial control over the ship without actually owning it) and her charterer. Under the contract, the disponent owners were obliged to carry six cargoes of coal in bulk in each of the years 2009, 2010, and 2011. The charterer failed to declare laycans[83] for the fifth and sixth shipments in 2009 and all six shipments in 2010. This was a repudiatory breach of contract, which was accepted by the disponent owners. Because of a crash in the freight markets in 2008, the disponent owners sought about $5.5 million in damages. The disponent owners were successful before an arbitration panel, but not Teare J. Teare J was heavily influenced by this crash in the market, and persuaded by the charterer's argument that the crash had placed the disponent owners in a much-weakened financial position such that the disponent owners would be unable to provide the required ships to perform the contract. Teare J held that the disponent owners had to prove that they would have been able to perform their obligations in order to recover substantial damages. This is difficult to reconcile with earlier authority,[84] although the thrust of the reasoning is perhaps consistent with that in *The Golden Victory*: why ignore post-breach facts which are known? The risk of 'overcompensating' the claimant again looms large if he would be in a better position if the contract is not performed.

Nevertheless, on balance, the approach of Teare J may also seem troubling.[85] To what extent should the court consider factors relating to the claimant's ability to perform? Indeed, the claimant might struggle to perform after a breach of contract precisely because the breach of contract adversely affects his financial situation. Nor is it clear how closely the court is to inquire into a claimant's circumstances and ability to perform. It may have been

---

[81] *Golden Victory* [38].

[82] [2013] EWHC 3153 (Comm), [2014] 2 WLR 1405.

[83] A 'laycan' is a period of time defined by Rix LJ in *Tidebrook Maritime Corp v Vitol SA of Geneva (The Front Commander)* [2006] EWCA Civ 944 [38] as 'the earliest day upon which an owner can expect his charterer to load and the latest day upon which the vessel can arrive at its appointed loading place without [the voyage] being at risk of being cancelled'.

[84] eg *Gill & Duffus v Berger* [1984] AC 382.

[85] See E Peel, '*Desideratum* or Principle: The "Compensatory Principle" Revisited' (2015) 131 LQR 29.

preferable to insist upon the principle that damages are assessed at the date of breach. After all, termination wipes out the primary obligation to perform the contract in the future, so the ability or otherwise of the claimant to perform his side of the bargain might be considered to be irrelevant. The outcome in *The Glory Wealth* effectively allowed the charterers to escape a contract which had become a bad bargain as a result of a falling market.

However, there is now little doubt that *The Golden Victory* and *The Glory Wealth* represent good law. Indeed, in *Bunge SA v Nidera BV*[86] the Supreme Court supported the majority in *The Golden Victory* and held that its reasoning applied to contracts of sale of a single cargo, and was not limited to instalment contracts. In *Bunge SA v Nidera BV*, the buyers entered into a contract with the sellers to buy a large quantity of Russian milling wheat crop. The contract was entered into in June 2010, and the wheat was to be shipped between 23–30 August 2010. On 5 August, Russia introduced a legislative embargo on exports of wheat between 15 August and 31 December. On 9 August the sellers notified the buyers of the embargo and purported to declare the contract cancelled. This was a wrongful repudiation of the contract, since the embargo might have been lifted. The buyers accepted this repudiation on 11 August. The sellers then offered to reinstate the contract on the same terms the following day, but the buyers did not agree. Instead, the buyers claimed damages of over $3 million. This was thought to be the difference between the contract and the market price on 11 August, the date on which the repudiation was accepted. However, the Supreme Court overturned the decisions of the lower courts and held that the buyers could not recover substantial damages. This was because the buyers had in fact suffered no damage, because the embargo was not lifted. The Supreme Court held that it was possible to take into account events that occurred after the breach of contract, and strongly supported *The Golden Victory*.

Lord Sumption offered a helpful explanation for the difference between the majority and minority in *The Golden Victory*:

> The real difference between the majority and the minority turned on the question what was being valued for the purpose of assessing damages. The majority were valuing the chartered service that would actually have been performed if the charterparty had not been wrongfully brought to a premature end. On that footing, the notional substitute contract, whenever it was made and at whatever market rate, would have made no difference because it would have been subject to the same war clause as the original contract ... The minority on the other hand considered that one should value not the chartered service which would actually have been performed, but the charterparty itself, assessed at the time that it was terminated, by reference to the terms of a notional substitute concluded as soon as possible after the termination of the original. That would vary, not according to the actual outcome, but according to the outcomes which were perceived as possible or probable at the time that the notional substitute contract was made. The possibility or probability of war would then be factored into the price agreed in the substitute contract ...

Lord Sumption favoured the former view, since sections 50 and 51 of the Sale of Goods Act[87] award damages by calculating the difference between the contract price and market price

---

[86] [2015] UKSC 43.
[87] See Section 4.

of the goods which should have been delivered under the contract, and are not concerned with the value of the contract as an article of commerce in itself. Lord Sumption was unimpressed by the argument that this might undermine commercial certainty. His Lordship noted that the degree of uncertainty that might be engendered by taking into account subsequent events is 'no greater than the uncertainty inherent in the contract itself'.[88] After all, there was always the possibility of the outbreak of war (in *The Golden Victory*) or the embargo not being lifted (in *Bunge SA v Nidera BV*). Lord Sumption observed that 'it can rarely be thought to justify an award of substantial damages to someone who has not suffered any'.[89] Lord Toulson supported the result, saying 'I see no virtue in such circumstances in the court attempting some form of retrospective assessment of prospective risk when the answer is known. To do so would run counter to the fundamental compensatory principle.' It is therefore the case that although a party may decide to terminate a contract expecting a certain amount of damages, he may in fact recover far less if subsequent events mean he would not actually have recovered as much had the contract remained on foot.

4 Recovery for non-economic loss

The cases considered so far have all related to economic loss of some kind. It is no longer the law, if it ever was, that damages are confined to such loss. Damages are generally not recoverable for disappointment or injured feelings resulting from the breach. But, if the purpose of a contract is to provide pleasure and, because of a breach, it fails to do so, damages are recoverable. In *Jarvis v Swan's Tours*,[90] travel agents were held liable to pay the claimant damages of £125 when a holiday costing £63.45 fell disastrously short of what was promised. The claimant would not be adequately compensated merely by giving him back his money. The only fortnight holiday he received, and to which he looked forward all the year, had been ruined.

Dicta of the court in *Jarvis* went further. Imagine that a man has a ticket for the opera festival at Glyndebourne. It is the only night he can attend the festival. He hires a car to take him there. The car does not turn up. It was said that he can recover from the car-hire firm damages for his disappointment and loss of entertainment. This is a difficult example. Presumably it would be necessary to show that the firm knew he was going to the performance at Glyndebourne. But even so, the firm's business is to provide a ride from A to B, not to provide entertainment. So, if the *dicta* in *Jarvis* are right, they go well beyond the actual decision in the case.

It is far from clear that such *dicta* are consistent with the approach of the House of Lords in *Farley v Skinner*.[91] A surveyor wrongly and negligently advised the buyer of a house in the country that it was unlikely to be affected by aircraft noise. This was a breach of contract. The surveyor was liable to pay £10,000 damages for the buyer's discomfort and inconvenience. The House of Lords held that non-pecuniary loss could be recoverable if a major

---

[88] *Bunge* [23].
[89] Ibid.
[90] [1973] 1 QB 233.
[91] [2001] UKHL 49, [2002] 2 AC 732.

or important part of the contract is to give pleasure, relaxation, or peace of mind. This broadens the scope of recovery. So does the alternative basis of the decision, which is that the award relates to physical inconvenience caused by the breach of contract.[92] Damages for physical inconvenience resulting from breach—such as having to walk five miles home on a wet night—have long been recoverable.[93] But the scope of 'physical inconvenience' was broadened in *Farley v Skinner* to cover sensory discomfort. As Lord Scott said:[94]

> the critical distinction to be drawn is not a distinction between the different types of inconvenience or discomfort of which complaint may be made but a distinction based on the cause of the inconvenience or discomfort. If the cause is no more than disappointment that the contractual obligation has been broken, damages are not recoverable even if the disappointment has led to a complete mental breakdown. But, if the cause of the inconvenience or discomfort is a sensory (sight, touch, hearing, smell etc) experience, damages can, subject to the remoteness rules, be recovered.

Further examples illustrate the same general point. If the purpose of the contract is to provide protection from harassment and, because the contract is broken, the claimant is harassed, damages for the resulting distress are recoverable. This follows from *Heywood v Wellers (A firm),*[95] where solicitors negligently failed to obtain and enforce an **injunction** to restrain a man from molesting the claimant. The court was prepared to assume that the injunction would be effective unless the defendants proved that it would not.

Dicta in *Cook v Swinfen*[96] go beyond this. Lord Denning MR said that a solicitor who conducted litigation negligently would be liable for the client's consequent breakdown in health if it could be proved that this was a reasonably foreseeable consequence of the breach of contract. In that case it was not reasonably foreseeable. The claimant was peculiarly liable to nervous shock but it was not proved that this was known to the defendants. If it had been so proved, damages for the breakdown might have been recoverable.

Where the contract is to supply a 'pleasurable amenity' which the supplier fails to deliver, the claimant is entitled to damages for the loss of the anticipated pleasure, however difficult it may be to assess and quantify that loss. But the claimant is not entitled to recover the cost of providing the amenity where to do so would be wholly disproportionate to the non-monetary loss he has suffered. In *Ruxley Electronics and Construction Ltd v Forsyth,*[97] F contracted with R to build a swimming pool in F's garden with a maximum depth of 7ft 6in. When it was complete, F discovered that it was only 6ft 9in deep. The pool was perfectly safe for diving and of no less financial value than if it had been in accordance with the contract. Nevertheless, the cost of rebuilding the pool in order to ensure that it complied with

---

[92] This decision builds on *Watts v Morrow* [1991] 1 WLR 1421, where Bingham LJ highlighted that there are two categories of case where damages for 'mental distress' may be awarded: where the object of the contract was to provide pleasure or peace of mind, and where mental suffering was directly caused by physical inconvenience caused by the breach.

[93] *Hobbs v L & SW Rly Co* (1875) LR 19 QB 111, QB (contract to carry family from Wimbledon to Hampton Court; the train terminated at Esher, which meant that the family had to walk home).

[94] *Farley* [85].

[95] [1976] QB 446, CA. The Protection from Harassment Act 1997 would also now be relevant.

[96] [1967] 1 WLR 457.

[97] [1995] 3 All ER 268, HL.

the contractual specifications would have been £21,500, and F claimed that sum. The judge refused to award that amount, and instead awarded £2,500 for loss of amenity. The House of Lords agreed. Although their Lordships considered that the sum awarded by the judge (£2,500) may have been on the high side, they were not invited to interfere with it. It was taken to represent the 'consumer surplus'[98] valued by F, and that figure may, possibly, now be reached by employing the hypothetical bargain measure of damages.[99]

It is different where the service provided has a commercial value lower than that contracted for. 'If A hired and paid in advance for a four-door saloon at £200 a day and received delivery of a two-door saloon available for £100 a day, he suffered loss.'[100] This is so even if A did not intend to carry any passengers and the car provided was just as good for all practical purposes as the car contracted for. A would be entitled to recover £100 per day—or more if the difference in market value was greater.

In *Addis v Gramophone Co Ltd*,[101] the House of Lords held that damages in contract are for pecuniary loss caused by the breach, and that nothing can be recovered for mental distress, anxiety, or injury to feelings. Although some exceptions have already been illustrated, this remains the general principle which should be applied. In *Addis* itself, the claimant was not entitled to compensation for the harsh and humiliating manner of his dismissal from employment by the defendants. The House of Lords insisted that the claimant could not, in an action for breach of contract, recover damages for non-pecuniary injury to his reputation.[102] Nearly 100 years later, in *Johnson v Unisys Ltd*,[103] the House of Lords (Lord Steyn dissenting) declined to reconsider *Addis*. As a result, *Addis* continues to represent the current orthodoxy. However, the possibility that injury to reputation resulting in damage to the claimant's employment prospects should be compensated if there has been a breach of contract continues to receive favour from some quarters; this is a controversial issue which is much discussed in the specialist context of employment law.[104] More broadly though, the principle stated by Bingham LJ in *Watts v Morrow* remains true: 'A contract-breaker is not in general liable for any distress, frustration, anxiety, displeasure, vexation, tension or aggravation which his breach of contract may cause to the innocent party. This rule is not, I think, founded on the assumption that such reactions are not foreseeable, which they surely are or may be, but on considerations of policy.'[105] The policy can operate harshly, and has led to some criticism of the rules surrounding awards of compensatory damages: a claimant will never be put in quite the same position as he would have been had the contract been performed, since he will not recover for the hassle and stress of having to find alternative means of performance, and so on. But in the commercial context, at least,

---

[98] Per Lord Millett, citing AI Ogus, D Harris and J Phillips, 'Contract Remedies and the Consumer Surplus' (1979) 95 LQR 581.

[99] See Chapter 28, Section 3.

[100] Per Bingham MR in *White Arrow Express Ltd v Lamey's Distribution Ltd* [1995] TLR 430.

[101] [1909] AC 488.

[102] Compare *Mahmud v BCCI SA* [1998] AC 20, HL (pecuniary loss of reputation is recoverable).

[103] [2001] 2 All ER 801.

[104] For a balanced discussion, see A Bogg and H Collins, 'Lord Hoffmann and the Law of Employment: The Notorious Episode of *Johnson v Unisys Ltd*' in PS Davies and J Pila (eds), *The Jurisprudence of Lord Hoffmann* (Hart, 2015).

[105] *Watts v Morrow* [1991] 1 WLR 1421, 1445.

it is thought that a commercial actor may be just as likely to be a contract-breaker as an innocent party, and that as a result such hassles are simply part of the 'commercial game'; by entering into contracts a party agrees to take the rough with the smooth. As Lord Cooke remarked in *Johnson v Gore Wood & Co*, '[c]ontract-breaking is treated as an incident of commercial life which players in the game are expected to meet with mental fortitude'.[106]

5 Cost of cure

Ruxley is an interesting, controversial, and important case. It highlights that in some circumstances there may be a difference between, on the one hand, awarding the claimant the difference in value between what he expected to receive and what he actually received, and, on the other hand, awarding the claimant the amount necessary to put himself into the position he would have been in had the contract been properly performed. In most situations—such as the sale of generic goods—the two measures will be the same. But they were not the same in *Ruxley*, and the decision of the House of Lords appears to limit the ability of the claimant to recover its full 'cost of cure'.[107] In *Ruxley*, it would have cost £21,500 to rebuild the pool so that it was in accordance with the contractual specifications, but there was no financial loss suffered by the claimant. Their Lordships held that there was no need to award the cost of cure measure of £21,500 in order to compensate the expectation loss suffered by the claimant. Two strands of reasoning appear from the judgment. The first concerns reasonableness: the cost of cure was wholly disproportionate to the diminution in value, and to *F*'s loss of the pleasure he would have taken in his deeper pool. The second concerns the claimant's intention. The judge was not satisfied that if *F* recovered the full £21,500 he would then spend it on rebuilding the pool.

Both strands of reasoning may be criticised. As regards the first, why should the defendant contract-breaker be in a better position if the cost of cure is huge than if it is small? It can also lead to uncertainty: how are 'reasonableness' and 'disproportionate' to be assessed? The High Court of Australia has been somewhat critical of the reasoning of the House of Lords in *Ruxley* on this issue, preferring instead to favour the cost of cure measure as the general measure of damages that best serves to protect a claimant's expectation, or performance, interest. In *Tabcorp Holdings Ltd v Bowen Investments Pty Ltd*,[108] a tenant of a commercial property destroyed the existing foyer and replaced it with a new one. This was a clear breach of the **tenant**'s contract with its **landlord**. The difference between the value of the property with the old foyer and the value with the new foyer was just over AUS$34,000, and this was the sum awarded by the trial judge. But both the Full Federal Court and the High Court of Australia awarded the full cost of cure: AUS$580,000 to restore the foyer to its original condition (and AUS$800,000 for loss of rent while the restoration was being carried out). The High Court was unconvinced of any need for

---

[106] [2001] 2 WLR 72, 108.

[107] It may be that if the facts of *Ruxley* were to arise today, Mr Forsyth would have the right to acquire repeat performance of the service under s 55 of the Consumer Rights Act 2015: see Chapter 28, Section 7(a).

[108] [2009] HCA 8, (2009) 236 CLR 272.

proportionality in order to recover this sum, and approved the earlier English decision in *Radford v De Froberville*.[109] In that case, the defendant failed to build a wall in accordance with her contractual obligations, and the claimant recovered the full cost of building the wall—£3,400—even though no financial loss at all was suffered as a result of the breach of contract in not having the wall built.

The second strand of reasoning in *Ruxley* relates to the intention of the parties, and this is also difficult. After all, the courts are not generally concerned with the uses to which claimants put an award of damages. If you steal my book, and I successfully sue you for the value of the book, I do not need to spend the £20 which I recover on replacing the book. I can spend it on anything I like. So why should the claimant ever need to show that he intends to spend the damages on curing the breach of contract? Nevertheless, the reasoning in *Ruxley* was foreshadowed in the decision of Megarry V-C in *Tito v Waddell (No 2)*.[110] A company failed to replant an island in the Pacific Ocean as it had promised to do. The judge held that the cost of cure measure of damages should not be awarded unless the claimants truly intended to cure the breach by replanting the island (which they did not) or had already done so (which they had not). This was repeated by Oliver J in *Radford v De Froberville*, but in both decisions the judges thought that if the claimant offered an undertaking that he would use the damages to cure the breach then the court should generally award a cost of cure measure of damages. Yet in *Ruxley*, before both the Court of Appeal and the House of Lords, *F* did offer such an undertaking, but the House of Lords was unimpressed by this offer. This is surprising: if *F* breached his undertaking, he would be in contempt of court and liable to fines and imprisonment. Surely, therefore, his undertaking to use the damages to cure the breach deserved greater consideration, and showed that *F* *did* intend to use the damages for the purpose of obtaining a pool of the 'correct' depth.

6 Loss of chance and minimum obligations

In *Chaplin v Hicks*,[111] the defendant organised a newspaper beauty competition. There were to be 12 winners. Thousands of women entered the competition, and the claimant was one of the final 50 to be interviewed. Unfortunately, the defendant breached its contract with the claimant by not informing her of the interview, so she was deprived of the opportunity to participate in the final selection process. Of course, it was not certain that the claimant would have won the competition, and purely based on the numbers it seems more likely than not that she would not have been successful. Nevertheless, the Court of Appeal held that substantial damages for loss of the chance to win should be awarded. Quantifying the chances is obviously a difficult exercise, but one that the court should not shrink away from.

In *Allied Maples Group Ltd v Simmons & Simmons*,[112] the Court of Appeal drew a distinction between situations where the loss of a chance arises because of the conduct of a third party and situations where the chance is lost because of the claimant's own conduct.

---

[109] [1977] 1 WLR 1262.
[110] [1977] Ch 106.
[111] [1911] 2 KB 786, CA.
[112] [1995] 1 WLR 1602.

In the latter situation, the usual 'balance of probabilities' approach applies: a claimant should be able to show that he would have acted in a particular way in order to recover his loss. But it is more difficult for a claimant to establish what a third party would have done, and thus the loss of chance approach more readily applies. In the *Allied Maples* case, a solicitor failed to warn his client about potential risks associated with acquiring a particular company. This was a breach of contract. The Court of Appeal held that the client could recover if it could show, on the balance of probabilities, that it would have acted on the solicitor's proper advice and would have had a substantial chance of persuading the company it was acquiring to renegotiate the deal.

When assessing the value of chances—and indeed of compensation generally—it should be borne in mind that the court should assess damages on the basis that the contract-breaker would have performed his obligations in a manner most advantageous to himself.[113] This is a sensible rule. It accords with the need for the defendant to protect its own position. However, in *Durham Tees Valley Airport v BMI Baby*,[114] the Court of Appeal held that where the defendant has a wide discretion about how to perform its obligations, the court should ascertain how the defendant would in fact have performed. On the facts of that case, this may have been a pragmatic decision given the difficulties involved in determining the minimum performance required (about operating flights from an airport). Nevertheless, it is suggested that this decision should be treated with some caution.

7 Recovery of wasted expenditure

There are some cases where it would be very difficult for the victim of a breach of contract to prove that he would have been better off if the contract had been performed, yet the victim can easily prove that he has, quite properly, incurred expenditure in, or for the purpose of, the performance of the contract. As a result of that breach of contract, the expenditure will be wasted. In such a case, the victim of the breach is permitted to claim his 'reliance' damages, and it is sometimes said that this is instead of 'expectation' damages. He has incurred expenditure in reliance on the other party's promise to perform and he claims compensation for that. In so doing, the claimant abandons his right to be compensated for the disappointment of his legitimate expectations that the contract would be performed. He cannot have both, because if his expectations had been fulfilled, he would have incurred the expenditure. It therefore follows that if he were put in the position in which he would have been had the contract been performed, he would have incurred that expenditure. So he cannot recover both.

In general, a claimant may choose between his 'reliance' damages and 'expectation' damages. However, this is not because there are two different principles at play. In *Omak Maritime Ltd v Mamola Challenger Shipping Co*,[115] Teare J held that there were not two different principles at issue, one concerning the reliance basis and the other the expectation basis. Rather, the judge concluded that the expectation loss principle can provide 'a rational

---

[113] *Lavarack v Woods of Colchester Ltd* [1967] 1 QB 278.
[114] [2010] EWCA Civ 485, [2011] 1 All ER (Comm) 731.
[115] [2010] EWHC 2026 (Comm), [2011] 2 All ER (Comm) 155.

and sensible explanation for the award of reliance losses'. A claimant will be presumed to have made a good bargain, and therefore the claimant is entitled to expect to make more money from the contract than the expenditure he incurred. So if he chooses to claim for his expenditure, this would go some way towards protecting his expectation loss, provided that the claimant did not make a bad bargain. The advantage of claiming reliance losses is that the burden of proof lies upon the defendant to show that the expenditure would not have been recouped and would have been wasted in any event.[116]

In *McRae v Commonwealth Disposals Commission*,[117] the facts of which are analysed in Chapter 22,[118] the claimant would have found it very difficult, if not impossible, to prove any 'expectation' loss: even if there had been a tanker at the latitude and longitude specified, this entirely mythical vessel might have been worthless, or not capable of profitable **salvage**, or even of salvage at all. The courts will award damages for loss of a chance to earn a reward and must not be deterred from doing so because of the difficulty of assessing the value of the chance;[119] but in the *McRae* case the court thought that the claimants could not show that the absence of a tanker caused them any 'expectation loss' at all. However, the claimants could show that they had incurred expenditure in reliance on a broken promise, and that the breach of promise made it *certain* that the expenditure would be wasted. This shifted the burden onto the Commission to prove that, if there had been a tanker there, the expenditure would equally have been wasted. Of course, the Commission was unable to prove this; it was just as impossible for the Commission to prove this as it was for McRae to prove the contrary.

A claimant's claim to recover his expenditure will fail to the extent that the defendant can prove that, even if he had performed his contract, the claimant would not have succeeded in recouping his outlay. If the claimant's outlay was £1,000 and the defendant proves that the claimant would have made nothing out of the transaction, the claimant can recover nothing; but if the claimant would have made £400 then he is entitled to £400 of wasted expenditure. Of course, the result in those circumstances is the same as if the claimant had been awarded 'expectation' damages; the difference is in the onus of proof.[120] If the claimant would not have recovered his expenditure even if the defendant had performed the contract,[121] the claimant has made a bad bargain and the law should not, and does not, shift the loss resulting from the claimant's bad bargain to the defendant.

In *C & P Haulage (A Firm) v Middleton*,[122] the defendant was ejected from premises, in breach of a contractual **licence** renewable on a six-monthly basis, ten weeks before the end of a six-month period. He claimed the cost of improvements he had made to the premises. But the contract provided that any fixtures he put in were not to be removed at the end of the licence. So, if the contract had not been broken but had been lawfully determined at

---

[116] *Yam Seng Pte Ltd v International Trade Corp Ltd* [2013] EWHC 111 (QB), [2013] 1 All ER (Comm) 1321 [186]–[187] (Leggatt J).

[117] (1951) 84 CLR 377.

[118] See Chapter 22, Section 1.

[119] *Chaplin v Hicks* [1911] 2 KB 786, CA, see Section 6.

[120] cf *Albert & Son v Armstrong Rubber Co*, 178 F2d 182 (1949), cited in *CCC Films Ltd v Impact Quadrant Films Ltd* [1984] 3 All ER 298.

[121] The focus is on whether the innocent party would have recovered his expenditure from his gross returns on the contract: *Grange v Quinn* [2013] EWCA Civ 24, [2013] 1 P & CR 18.

[122] [1983] 1 WLR 1461, CA.

the end of the six-month period, there could have been no question of his recovering his expenditure. As a result, the defendant's claim failed. The defendant appears to have made a bad bargain in agreeing that the fixtures should belong to the claimant, and it was not the function of the court to put him in a better position than he would have been in if the contract had been performed. A party must bear the risk of entering into a bad bargain.

The innocent party's expenditure will only be recoverable if it was reasonable for him to incur those expenses. In *Mason v Burningham*,[123] the buyer of a second-hand typewriter had to return it to the true owner because the seller had no **title** to it. The Court of Appeal held that the buyer was entitled to recover not only the price of the typewriter but also the cost of having it overhauled. The county court judge had dismissed the claim, saying that if the buyer had had the machine gold-plated, she could not recover the cost of that. Of course, she could not; but having the typewriter overhauled was 'the ordinary and natural thing' to do in the circumstances. The buyer had acted entirely reasonably; gold-plating the machine would not have been similarly reasonable.

More controversially, it has been held in *Anglia Television v Reed*[124] that damages may be recovered for costs incurred *before* the contract was made if they are:

(a) legal costs of approving and executing the contract; or

(b) costs of performing an act required to be done by the contract, notwithstanding that the act was done in anticipation of it; or

(c) such costs 'as would reasonably be in the contemplation of the parties as likely to be wasted if the contract was broken'.

In *Anglia Television Ltd v Reed*,[125] the claimants incurred expense in preparation for filming a television play. Subsequently, they entered into a contract with the defendant to play the lead role. Unfortunately, the defendant repudiated the contract and the claimants were unable to find a substitute. It was held that they were entitled to recover the whole of the wasted expenditure: the defendant must have known that the expenditure, whether incurred before or after the contract was made, would be wasted if he broke his contract. This is controversial because it is arguable that a person who incurs expenditure before a contract has been entered into does so at his own risk. The expenditure is not incurred in reliance on the contract-breaker's promise—after all, that promise has not yet been made. On the other hand, it may be said that the asset represented by the expenditure is put at risk in reliance on the promise and that this is enough. This appears to have been the view of the Court of Appeal in the *Reed* case.

8 Damages beyond loss: valuing rights

It should be recognised that the account of the law of compensatory damages presented in this chapter is a traditional and orthodox one. However, there is a powerful view that

---

[123] [1949] 2 KB 545, CA.
[124] [1972] 1 QB 60.
[125] Ibid.

damages are really awarded not to compensate for loss, but rather to vindicate the claimant's right that has been infringed.[126] In effect, damages are awarded as a substitute for the right of performance of which the claimant has been deprived due to the defendant's wrong. Such 'substitutive damages' are the next best thing to performance, and the best the law can do in remedying the infringement of the claimant's rights.

This approach has many attractive features. For example, it might explain the 'broad view' of the majority in *Panatown*, considered in Chapter 10:[127] the right to performance is itself valuable, and deserves to be compensated through a substantial award of damages. Moreover, it helps to explain some of the cases on damages awarded in the context of the sale of goods. So, in *Williams Bros v Ed T Agius Ltd*,[128] the claimant contracted to purchase coal from the defendant for 16s 3d per ton. The claimant then entered into a contract to re-sell the coal to a third party for 19s per ton. The defendant breached his contract by failing to deliver the coal. On the basis of a 'compensation for loss' approach, it would be expected that the claimant could recover (19s minus 16s 3d =) 2s 9d per ton. This is because that represents the loss of profits on the resale contract which the claimant was now unable to make. Yet the House of Lords awarded the claimant a much greater sum: 7s 3d per ton. This is because the market price at the time of the breach was 23s 6d. Their Lordships held that it did not matter that the claimant had not bought substitute goods at the higher market price and did not intend to do so. Moreover, the claimant was not sued by the sub-buyer. All this suggests that the remedy was not to compensate the claimant for financial loss actually suffered. It might be justified by reference to the need for commercial certainty as to remedy, and the particular language of section 53 of the Sale of Goods Act 1979. But the statute merely codifies the common law. It may be that the remedy reflects the value of the right of the claimant which has been infringed, and is awarded as a substitute for that.

A similar analysis may help to explain cases where the seller commits a breach of contract by delivering defective goods which are wanted for resale. For instance, in *Slater v Hoyle and Smith Ltd*[129] the claimant bought cotton from the defendant. The claimant had contracted to sell the cotton on to the third party. The cotton which was delivered was of inferior quality than warranted. This was a breach of contract. However, the claimant suffered no financial loss because the sub-purchasers paid the contract price in full. The defendant therefore argued that the claimant's damages should be nominal only. Yet the Court of Appeal applied the reasoning in *Williams Bros v Agius Ltd* and awarded that claimant a substantial sum based upon the difference in market value at the time of delivery between the defective cotton and cotton conforming to the quality requirements of the contract. Such a remedy might be considered to be a substitute for the right infringed.

Furthermore, the 'substitutive damages' thesis may best explain the 'hypothetical bargain' measure of damages awarded in cases such as *Wrotham Park Estate Co Ltd v Parkside Homes Ltd*[130] and *Experience Hendrix LLC v PPX Enterprises Inc.*[131] These cases are

---

[126] R Stevens, 'Damages and the Right to Performance: A Golden Victory or Not?' in J Neyers, R Bronaugh, and S Pitel (eds), *Exploring Contract Law* (Hart, 2009); see too R Stevens, *Torts and Rights* (OUP, 2007) ch 4.

[127] Chapter 10, Section 6(b)(i).

[128] [1914] AC 510, HL.

[129] [1920] 2 KB 11. See too *Clark v Macourt* [2013] HCA 56.

[130] [1974] 2 All ER 321.

[131] [2003] EWCA Civ 323, [2003] 1 All ER (Comm) 830.

discussed in Chapter 28, and difficult to fit within traditional concepts of gain and loss.[132] There is much to be said in favour of the substitutive damages view, since it helps to explain many decided cases.

Nevertheless, the language of 'substitutive damages' is not used by the courts, and some caution should be exercised before accepting it as the current law. Indeed, all the cases do not speak with one voice. For example, in *Bence Graphics International Ltd v Fasson UK Ltd*,[133] the Court of Appeal did not follow *Slater v Hoyle and Smith Ltd*. In that case, the claimant purchased vinyl from the defendant to make decals. The vinyl was defective. The claimant sold the decals on, and received some complaints. One minor claim was settled by the claimant, and the defendant reimbursed the claimant for this. The claimant sought the difference in market value between the defective vinyl and contracted-for vinyl. The trial judge granted the claimant such relief, following *Slater v Hoyle and Smith*. But the Court of Appeal allowed the appeal, awarding a small sum based on the financial loss actually suffered by the claimant due to its liability to subsequent purchasers. Admittedly, *Bence Graphics* is a difficult case to explain.[134] The Court of Appeal did not convincingly explain why *Slater v Hoyle and Smith* should be distinguished. The cases may perhaps be reconciled on the basis that in *Slater* the claimant knew the cotton was defective *before* it employed it in the sub-sale, whereas in *Bence* the defect was discovered only *after* the vinyl films had been delivered to the sub-buyers.[135] Only in the former case could the claimant have gone to the market before the sub-sale, which explains why the difference in market value was awarded. The fact that he did not do that and yet still managed to sell the cotton was '*res inter alios acta*: "circumstances peculiar to the plaintiff" which cannot affect his claim one way or the other'.[136] By contrast, in *Bence* the claimant had no choice whether to resort to the market, and it had not acted unreasonably or unforeseeably in selling on the goods in ignorance of the defect. Any difference in value was irrelevant. Admittedly, such a reconciliation of the cases is not to be found in the decisions themselves.

More tellingly, perhaps, Auld LJ in *Bence* simply refused to follow *Slater*. This has been welcomed by some commentators,[137] most significantly on the basis that there is no reason why a claimant should be able to recover more than his actual financial loss. Such a view continues to garner substantial support. For instance, this 'compensatory principle' was thought to be a 'lodestar' in *The Golden Victory*, and in *Bunge SA v Nidera BV* Lord Sumption thought that concerns of certainty 'can rarely be thought to justify an award of substantial damages to someone who has not suffered any'.[138] Moreover, there are some difficulties in valuing a claimant's right other than by loss suffered. How can this sensibly be done?[139] In *Panatown*, Lord Goff gave the example of a philanthropist (*B*) who undertakes to renovate the village hall, owned by trustees, at his own expense. He contracts with a

---

[132] See Chapter 28, Section 3.

[133] [1998] QB 87, CA.

[134] G Treitel, 'Damages for Breach of Warranty of Quality' (1997) 113 LQR 188.

[135] See A Dyson and A Kramer, 'There is No "Date of Breach Rule"' (2014) 130 LQR 259, 274–5.

[136] *Slater v Hoyle & Smith Ltd* [1920] 2 KB 11, 23 (Scrutton LJ).

[137] eg A Burrows, *Remedies for Torts and Breach of Contract* (3rd edn, OUP, 2004) 216.

[138] Ibid.

[139] For further discussion, see A Burrows, 'Damages and Rights' in D Nolan and A Robertson (eds), *Rights and Private Law* (Hart, 2012) 278–80.

builder (*A*) who does defective work. *B* recovers damages. But how can these be quantified? The natural response may be to suggest the 'cost of cure' measure, but why should *B* be able to pocket such a large sum, particularly if that would leave the village with defective premises and no remedy.[140] It may be preferable to maintain the orthodox approach whereby damages are only awarded on the basis of financial loss suffered, taking into account issues of mitigation.

 Further Reading

AI Ogus, D Harris, and J Phillips, 'Contract Remedies and the Consumer Surplus' (1979) 95 LQR 581.
Argues that the courts should be more willing to award damages to compensate the 'consumer surplus', which is the subjective value a consumer places upon the subject matter of a contract above its market value.

B Coote, 'Contract Damages, *Ruxley* and the Performance Interest' (1997) 56 CLJ 537.
Considers that the courts should protect the 'performance interest' more strongly by awarding the cost of cure measure of damages.

R Stevens, 'Damages and the Right to Performance: A Golden Victory or Not?' in J Neyers, R Bronaugh, and S Pitel (eds), *Exploring Contract Law* (Hart, 2009).
Argues that a distinction should be drawn between damages awarded as a substitute for the contractual right and those awarded to compensate for consequential losses suffered.

L Hoffmann, '*The Achilleas*: Custom and Practice or Foreseeability?' (2010) 14 Edinburgh Law Review 47.
Discussion of the judgment of the House of Lords in *The Achilleas* by the Law Lord who wrote arguably the leading speech, setting the decision and principles in their broader context.

A Dyson and A Kramer, 'There is No "Date of Breach Rule"' (2014) 130 LQR 259.
Argues that the use of the date of the breach for the assessment of damages is not an independent rule in its own right, should not be rigidly applied, and is best viewed as a function of the principles of mitigation.

A Burrows, 'Lord Hoffmann and Remoteness in Contract' in PS Davies and J Pila (eds), *The Jurisprudence of Lord Hoffmann* (Hart, 2015).
Critical of the decision in *The Achilleas* and the notion of 'assumption responsibility'. Argues instead that remoteness is based upon considerations of policy, and aims to achieve a fair and reasonable allocation of risk

? Question

Walter is a professional photographer. He stops at Jesse's petrol station, where he is met by Jesse himself. Jesse explains that customers are no longer allowed to fill their cars with petrol themselves, and that Jesse will do this for Walter. Walter tells Jesse that it is crucial that he fill up the car with unleaded

---

[140] See Chapter 10, Section 6(b)(i).

petrol quickly, since Walter is going to his son, Flynn's, wedding in Albuquerque; Walter explains that he will be the official photographer at the wedding. Jesse agrees, but mistakenly puts diesel rather than unleaded petrol into Walter's car.

Walter's car breaks down ten minutes after leaving the petrol station. Walter has to pay £500 in towage and repair costs. Walter also misses his flight to Albuquerque; that ticket cost £1,000. Walter then spends £2,000 on a flight to Albuquerque the following day, but arrives too late for his son's wedding. Walter was going to take photographs at the wedding for free; in order to replace Walter, Flynn hires a different photographer at a cost of £3,000. Walter is upset not to be at his son's wedding, and is angry to have missed the chance to impress Gus, a local businessman, who had promised to hire Walter as his official photographer for £1 million per year if Walter took good photographs of the wedding. Walter has a nervous breakdown as a result of all the stress.

Advise Walter.

27 Agreed remedies

Key Points

- Parties may choose to insert a clause into their agreement which stipulates what remedy should be awarded upon breach of contract.

- If the term states that a certain amount of damages should be paid upon breach, that term might be valid as a liquidated damages clause or unenforceable as a penalty. If the amount chosen is a genuine pre-estimate of loss, or is 'commercially justified', then it is likely to be valid. However, if the sum fixed is extravagant and unconscionable in amount in comparison with the greatest loss that could conceivably be proved to have flowed from the breach or the legitimate interest that the clause protects, then it is likely to be a penalty.

- If the defaulting party had already paid money to the innocent party as a deposit, the innocent party may be able to forfeit that deposit. This means that the innocent party can keep the deposit. However, courts have an equitable jurisdiction to grant relief against forfeiture if the deposit itself is extravagant and allowing forfeiture would be unconscionable.

- A term stipulating that specific performance or an injunction will be granted upon breach will not bind the court. However, the court may take into account such a term when deciding whether to exercise its equitable discretion.

This chapter is concerned with remedies agreed by the parties. There are good reasons why parties may wish to include a term in the contract which dictates what should happen in the event of breach of contract. For example, such a term can provide the parties with certainty about their rights and obligations, and avoid the need to negotiate a settlement after breach or for courts to have to assess damages. Parties may also wish to determine, at the time the contract is made, the amount of money payable by a defaulting party in the event of breach, in order to ensure that they are not under-compensated as a result of some of the perceived problems underpinning compensatory damages, such as the difficulty in recovering for general hassle and annoyance.[1]

General principles of freedom of contract suggest that if the parties choose to insert an agreed damages clause into their contract then this should be respected by the court and given effect.[2] Yet courts are wary about allowing an agreed damages clause to operate in a

---

[1] See Chapter 26.
[2] It should be remembered that if the term is unfair against a consumer then it might be challenged under the Consumer Rights Act 2015: Sch 2, para 6. See generally Chapter 15, Section 4.

manner that would punish a breach of contract.[3] If that is the purpose of the agreed damages clause then it is a 'penalty clause' and is not enforceable. However, if the purpose of the clause is not to punish the party in breach, then the clause is generally known as a **liquidated damages** clause and is enforceable (**unliquidated damages** are assessed by the judge).

The restriction on the parties' freedom of action which follows from the jurisdiction to strike out penalty clauses is controversial. In *Makdessi v Cavendish Square Holdings BV*,[4] Lord Neuberger and Lord Sumption recognised that '[t]he penalty rule in England is an ancient, haphazardly constructed edifice which has not weathered well'.[5] Similar difficulties surround the equitable jurisdiction to grant relief against **forfeiture**, which commonly arises where the court holds that it would be unconscionable for an innocent party to retain, or to forfeit, (all of) a deposit already paid by a party in breach. The relationship between forfeiture and penalty clauses will be considered further below.[6]

1 Liquidated damages and penalties

The parties to a contract may anticipate the possibility of a breach of contract and include a term that a certain sum shall be paid by the defaulting party in the event of a specified breach or breaches. That sum may be enforceable as a liquidated damages clause, or unenforceable as a penalty, depending on whether the test for penalty clauses is satisfied. However, it is important to note that although the vast majority of these clauses concern the payment of money, there is no reason why a clause which does not stipulate that a sum of money should be paid, but instead stipulates that certain assets should be transferred, should not be capable of constituting a penalty.[7] So, if a clause provides that, in the event of a breach of contract, the defaulting party shall transfer to the injured party property other than money, then that clause might be unenforceable as a penalty if the value of the property to be transferred is far greater than either the actual loss suffered by the injured party, or the value of the legitimate interest of the injured party which the clause seeks to protect. This concept of 'legitimate interest' is discussed further below.[8]

(a) The test for penalties

Whether a particular clause provides for liquidated damages or for a penalty is a question of interpretation. The fact that the parties have used the label 'liquidated damages' or 'penalty' is far from conclusive. The traditional approach has focused upon whether the predominant function of a clause was to deter a party from breaking the contract or to compensate the innocent party for breach. Although the Supreme Court recently held that this approach can be insufficient and even unhelpful in more complicated cases, their

---

[3] For further discussion of punishment see Chapter 28, Section 5.
[4] [2015] UKSC 67 [2015] 3 WLR 1373 [13].
[5] *Makdessi* [3].
[6] See Section 3(a).
[7] *Makdessi* [16] (Lord Neuberger and Lord Sumption); [170] (Lord Mance). See further the discussion of *Jobson v Johnson* at Section 2(c).
[8] See Section 2(a)(ii).

Lordships also recognised that the traditional approach leads to satisfactory results in the vast majority of relatively straightforward cases. As a result, it is to be expected that the traditional approach will continue to be invoked. This approach will therefore be outlined first, before dealing with the crucial criticisms of it and the more modern test for penalties.

(i) The traditional test: the *Dunlop* case

The test for whether a clause is a penalty clause has traditionally been taken from the speech of Lord Dunedin in *Dunlop Pneumatic Tyre Co Ltd v New Garage and Motor Co Ltd*.[9] Lord Dunedin laid out four tests:[10]

> They were (a) that the provision would be penal if 'the sum stipulated for is extravagant and unconscionable in amount in comparison with the greatest loss that could conceivably be proved to have followed from the breach'; (b) that the provision would be penal if the breach consisted only in the non-payment of money and it provided for the payment of a larger sum; (c) that there was 'a presumption (but no more)' that it would be penal if it was payable in a number of events of varying gravity; and (d) that it would not be treated as penal by reason only of the impossibility of precisely pre-estimating the true loss.

On the basis of this approach of Lord Dunedin, it has often been said that if the sum is a genuine estimate of the actual damages likely to be suffered in the event of breach, then the term is enforceable and is known as a 'liquidated damages clause'. This is still likely to be the case. On the other hand, if the sum fixed is not a genuine estimate of loss but is greater than any loss likely to be caused, and the term is intended to operate as a threat to keep a potential defaulter to his bargain, then the term has generally been described as a 'penalty clause' and has not been considered to be enforceable. This proposition will no longer invariably be true after the decision of the Supreme Court in *Makdessi* (since not all clauses aimed at deterring breach will be penal),[11] but will probably still prove to be a useful rule of thumb in many instances.

It has been said that 'when a single lump sum is made payable by way of compensation, on the occurrence of one or more or all of several events, some of which may occasion serious and others but trifling damage', there is a presumption that it is a penalty.[12] It should be emphasised that this is only a presumption which may be rebutted on an interpretation of the clause within the contract as a whole. However, if a clause demands that, following a breach of contract, an amount be paid periodically without an end in sight, then that is very likely to be considered penal. In *MSC Mediterranean Shipping Co SA v Cottonex Anstalt*,[13] Leggatt J considered what would have happened if a clause in the contract had the effect of allowing **demurrage**[14] to accrue indefinitely following a breach of contract. His Lordship

---

[9] [1915] AC 79, HL. See Chapter 10, Section 2.

[10] The following passage is quoted from *Makdessi* [21].

[11] For further explanation see the next section.

[12] Lord Watson in *Lord Elphinstone v Monkland Iron and Coal Co* (1886) 11 App Cas 332, HL (Sc), cited by Lord Dunedin in the *Dunlop* case.

[13] [2015] EWHC 283 (Comm), [2015] 2 All ER (Comm) 614.

[14] Effectively demurrage is a fee to be paid if a ship is delayed.

was clear that such a clause could be unenforceable as a penalty: 'Making every allowance for the advantages of certainty and avoiding disputes, it is impossible to justify on compensatory grounds a provision which can require payments without end for so long as the [innocent party] chooses to keep the contract in force. Such a clause could only be explained as serving the function of penalising breach of the contract.'[15]

Where damage from any particular breach would be difficult to predict, the courts may be more willing to find that a clause fixing the amount to be paid upon breach should properly be regarded as a liquidated damages clause rather than a penalty. So, in the *Suisse Atlantique* case,[16] the provision requiring the charterers to pay demurrage of $1,000 a day was held to be a liquidated damages clause, even though a delay of one day, or a few days, might cause the shipowners no loss of freight and only a small amount by way of increased overheads in port. This was what was agreed by the parties to provide some certainty as to what would happen in the event of breach. This decision might now be explained on the basis that such a clause was 'commercially justified', particularly since it was clear that the aim of the clause was not to punish a breach of contract, and this concept of commercial justification must now be considered.

(ii) The modern approach: commercial justification

In *Makdessi*, the approach of Lord Dunedin in *Dunlop* was said to be 'perfectly adequate' for the 'great majority of cases' regarding penalty clauses which concern 'more or less standard damages clauses in consumer contracts'.[17] But it is not the case that all clauses will be concerned with ensuring monetary compensation for breach of contract, and in those circumstances Lord Dunedin's scheme has been found wanting. Nevertheless, some courts have previously felt constrained by the strictures of Lord Dunedin's four tests and have held that Lord Dunedin's approach must invariably be rigorously applied; indeed, the Court of Appeal in *Makdessi* provides one such example.[18] This was criticised by the Supreme Court in allowing the appeal in *Makdessi*. Lord Neuberger and Lord Sumption deprecated the fact that 'Lord Dunedin's speech in *Dunlop* achieved the status of a quasi-statutory code'[19] and instead insisted that a broader approach should be taken.

Their Lordships pointed out that the seeds for a broader approach were sown both in *Dunlop* itself, and in the earlier decision of the House of Lords in *Clydebank Engineering & Shipbuilding Co Ltd v Don Jose Ramos Yzquierdo y Castaneda*.[20] In the *Clydebank* case, Lord Robertson thought that a key question when deciding whether or not a term of the contract was a penalty clause was: 'had the respondents no interest to protect by that clause, or was that interest palpably incommensurate with the sums agreed on?'[21] And in *Dunlop*, Lord Atkinson held that Dunlop 'had an obvious interest to prevent this undercutting, and on the evidence it would appear to me impossible to say that that interest was incommensurate

---

[15] *MSC Mediterranean Shipping* [115].
[16] See Chapter 15, Section 1(c).
[17] *Makdessi* [25]. See too *Makdessi* [32].
[18] See Section 2(a)(iii).
[19] *Makdessi* [22].
[20] [1905] AC 6.
[21] Ibid, 20.

with the sum agreed to be paid'.[22] Such passages suggest that courts have long been concerned with whether or not there was a 'legitimate interest'[23] for the clause at issue. More recent decisions have similarly emphasised the need for a 'commercial justification' of a clause. This test appears to be more flexible than that of Lord Dunedin in *Dunlop*, and has been invoked to justify an increase in the rate of interest payable on a defaulting loan in order to reflect an increased credit risk,[24] and to justify a higher sum payable in the event of wrongful dismissal.[25]

This test of 'commercial justification' was strongly endorsed by the Supreme Court in *Makdessi*. In their joint judgment, Lord Neuberger and Lord Sumption (with whom Lord Carnwath agreed) held that:[26]

> The true test is whether the impugned provision is a secondary obligation which imposes a detriment on the contract-breaker out of all proportion to any legitimate interest of the innocent party in the enforcement of the primary obligation. The innocent party can have no proper interest in simply punishing the defaulter.

Lord Hodge formulated the test for penalties in a slightly different way:[27]

> the correct test for a penalty is whether the sum or remedy stipulated as a consequence of a breach of contract is exorbitant or unconscionable when regard is had to the innocent party's interest in the performance of the contract. Where the test is to be applied to a clause fixing the level of damages to be paid on breach, an extravagant disproportion between the stipulated sum and the highest level of damages that could possibly arise from the breach would amount to a penalty and thus be unenforceable. In other circumstances the contractual provision that applies on breach is measured against the interest of the innocent party which is protected by the contract and the court asks whether the remedy is exorbitant or unconscionable.

This test of Lord Hodge was explicitly endorsed by Lord Toulson[28] and is very similar to the formulation of Lord Mance.[29] Since Lord Clarke agreed with both the speech of Lord Neuberger and Lord Sumption, and also the speeches of Lord Mance and Lord Hodge, it may reasonably be suggested that there is no substantial difference between these formulations. Nevertheless, it is regrettable that a clear test was not explicitly agreed upon by all their Lordships, especially if there is no meaningful difference between their respective wordings. In any event, however, it now seems to have been established that the emphasis is on whether the amount demanded is 'extravagant' or 'unconscionable' in the sense of being 'out of all proportion' with the legitimate interest being protected.

The Supreme Court made it clear that the emphasis should lie on 'unconscionability', in the sense of 'extravagant', rather than upon deterrence.[30] The previous emphasis on

---

[22] *Dunlop Pneumatic Tyre Co Ltd v New Garage and Motor Co Ltd* [1915] AC 79, 92, HL.

[23] cf Chapter 25, Section 4.

[24] *Lordsvale Finance Ltd v Bank of Zambia* [1996] QB 752.

[25] *Murray v Leisureplay Plc* [2005] EWCA Civ 963, [2005] IRLR 946.

[26] *Makdessi* [32].

[27] Ibid, [255].

[28] Ibid, [293].

[29] Ibid, [131]–[153].

[30] See eg ibid, [31].

deterrence was misguided. After all, '[m]any contractual provisions are coercive in nature, encouraging a contracting party to perform his or her obligations; the prospect of liability in **common law** damages itself is a spur to performance.'[31] Deterrence is not in itself penal, and the focus should be on whether a clause should be held to be a penalty.

It is also worth emphasising that the threshold for a clause being a penalty is set at a high level.[32] Lord Hodge thought that '[t]he criterion of exorbitance or unconscionableness should prevent the enforcement of only egregious contractual provisions',[33] and Lord Neuberger and Lord Sumption were careful to emphasise that, since the rule against penalties is a blatant interference with freedom of contract, courts will not easily hold that a clause is unenforceable as a penalty. Any other approach would undermine the important principle of certainty of contract. It is highly unlikely that in a commercial contract between two well-informed and well-advised parties, a court would interfere with the contract and decide that a term is unenforceable as a penalty.

In situations where the relevant clause will sometimes work to the advantage of one party, and sometimes to that of the other, then each side derives an advantage from having the figure fixed by the contract and from being able to know in advance what the consequences of a breach will be. So, if litigation later occurs, the liquidated damages clause eliminates what might have been the heavy costs of proving, or disproving, the amount of damages claimed. These are significant advantages and further explain why the courts should not be too quick to categorise clauses as penalties and thereby nullify their effect. However, where the clause is likely to benefit one party only, then it is more likely to be a penalty clause. In *Lamdon Trust Co v Hurrel*,[34] a **hire-purchase** agreement provided that if, as a result of a breach by the hirer, the owner terminated the agreement, the hirer should pay, as compensation for depreciation, 75 per cent of the total sum due under the agreement. The Court of Appeal held that this was a penalty and unenforceable. If the hirer had failed to pay the first instalment, then, according to the agreement, the owner could have recovered a car which had hardly depreciated at all *and* 75 per cent of its value. This amount would be 'unconscionable' or 'extravagant'.

(iii) Applying the modern approach in the Supreme Court

In November 2015, the Supreme Court handed down an important judgment in two conjoined appeals: *Makdessi v Cavendish Square Holdings BV* and *ParkingEye Ltd v Beavis*.[35] The rule against penalties had not been considered by this jurisdiction's highest **appellate court** for 100 years,[36] so the significance of the decision of the Supreme Court should be clear. The decision is very long, and will no doubt be much-discussed as the courts digest the approach endorsed by the Supreme Court. It is suggested that the facts of the appeals under consideration provide useful guidance as to how the rule against penalties will be

---

[31] Ibid, [248] (Lord Hodge).
[32] eg ibid, [248] (Lord Hodge).
[33] Ibid, [266].
[34] [1955] 1 WLR 391.
[35] [2015] UKSC 67 [2015] 3 WLR 1373.
[36] *Makdessi* [1].

applied. The decision in general is likely to be known as *'Makdessi'*, but when the facts of the two appeals need to be distinguished the fuller names of *Makdessi v Cavendish* and *ParkingEye v Beavis* will be used.

Makdessi v Cavendish Square Holdings BV

In *Makdessi v Cavendish*, M agreed to sell to C a majority interest in a company. A large part of the price reflected goodwill. There was a clause in the contract that stated that if M became a defaulting shareholder, he would not be able to receive any further payment in respect of the price (Clause 5.1). There were various restrictive **covenants** which set out when a shareholder would be in default. There was also a clause which granted C a right to buy M's remaining shareholding if M became a defaulting shareholder, and the price was to be calculated by reference to the net asset value of the company, without incorporating the goodwill value (Clause 5.6).

The Court of Appeal overturned the decision of Burton J and held that both Clause 5.1 and Clause 5.6 were penalty clauses. There was no genuine pre-estimate of loss, and neither was there a commercial justification for the clauses: the purpose of the clauses was to deter breach, which meant that the clauses were penal in nature according to the test of Lord Dunedin in the *Dunlop* case. However, the Court of Appeal did emphasise that the test of whether a term was a penalty really depended upon whether the term was 'unconscionable' or 'extravagant'.[37] As Christopher Clarke LJ put it: '"unconscionable" would, perhaps, more appropriately be used for a clause which provides for extravagant payment without sufficient commercial justification'.[38]

The Supreme Court overturned the decision of the Court of Appeal and held that the clauses were not penalties. Lord Sumption and Lord Neuberger held that the relevant clauses did not arise upon a breach of contract and restrict the secondary obligation to pay damages at all, and this aspect of the decision will be considered further in the next section.[39] However, all the judges agreed that if the rule against penalties was engaged then the test for penalties was not satisfied. It was accepted that Clause 5.1 had no relationship with the measure of loss attributable to the breach of contract. But this did not matter, and the contrary suggestion of Lord Dunedin in the *Dunlop* case was correspondingly criticised. Their Lordships found that C had a legitimate interest in ensuring that the restrictive covenants were respected, and the goodwill of the business was of critical value to C. The loyalty of M was crucial to the goodwill, and the clause was not extravagant or unconscionable in seeking to achieve the legitimate aim of ensuring that M's loyalty and the goodwill were properly maintained. As Lord Hodge put it, C 'had a very substantial and legitimate interest in protecting the value of the company's goodwill'.[40] It is worth noting as well that Lord Mance explicitly recognised that an important factor in reaching this conclusion

---

[37] Leggatt J has said that 'in assessing for the purpose of comparison with the sum payable under the contract the sum which the injured party could recover as compensation for its loss in the absence of the payment provision, it is clearly necessary to take into account the mitigation principle': *MSC Mediterranean Shipping Co SA v Cottonex Anstalt* [2015] EWHC 283 (Comm), [2015] 2 All ER (Comm) 614 [113].

[38] *Makdessi* [125].

[39] See Section 2(b).

[40] *Makdessi* [274].

was that the parties were well-advised commercial parties who understood fully what they were doing.[41]

Clause 5.6 was slightly more difficult, but the same conclusion was reached for similar reasons. The Supreme Court Justices pointed out that it was commercially legitimate for C to seek not to pay for the value of goodwill if M defaulted such that his efforts and connections were no longer available for the benefit of the company. Admittedly, the purpose of both Clauses 5.6 and 5.1 may have been to deter breach, but the Supreme Court held that this did not make the clauses penal (departing again from Lord Dunedin in *Dunlop*) since they were not extravagant or unconscionable. As regards Clause 5.6, it was not unconscionable to attribute a nil value to goodwill when there had been a breach of the restrictive covenants at issue. Lord Hodge explained that this was 'a legitimate means of encouraging [M] to comply with their ... obligations which were critical to [C's] investment'.[42]

ParkingEye Ltd v Beavis

In *ParkingEye v Beavis*, ParkingEye ran a car park at a retail park. Customers who parked at the car park had a contract with ParkingEye. The terms of the contract stated that there was a '2 hour max stay', and that parking was free during that two-hour period. However, staying longer than two hours would lead to a 'Parking Charge' of £85. The defendant, Mr Beavis, left his car in the car park for nearly three hours, and ParkingEye sued for the Parking Charge of £85. The Supreme Court upheld the decisions of the lower courts that this was not a penalty.

The court emphasised that the charge was justified by two reasonable objectives. The first was to manage the efficient use of the parking spaces by deterring commuters or other long-stay motorists from parking for long periods of time, which would reduce the space available to other members of the public. The second was to provide an income stream to ParkingEye. Both objectives meant that ParkingEye had a legitimate interest in charging motorists who stayed longer than two hours. Lord Neuberger and Lord Sumption emphasised that 'deterrence is not penal if there is a legitimate interest in influencing the conduct of the contracting party which is not satisfied by the mere right to recover damages for breach of contract'.[43] The decision is sensible: the business model on which ParkingEye ran the car park was perfectly justifiable, and customers needed to accept that in return for not paying for two hours of parking, they would have to pay thereafter. Of course, the court's finding on the facts of the case that the Parking Charge was justified, even though it was intended to deter breach, would not permit ParkingEye to charge however much it wanted: if the charge had been £850 rather than £85 then there can be little doubt that that would have been held to be 'unconscionable' and 'extravagant' and therefore a penalty.[44]

---

[41] Ibid, [181].

[42] Ibid, [282].

[43] Ibid, [99].

[44] The Supreme Court Justices noted that £85 was below the maximum charge above which members of the British Parking Association must justify their charges under their code of practice: see eg [100].

Conclusions

The outcome of the appeals in both *Makdessi v Cavendish* and *ParkingEye v Beavis* emphatically demonstrate that the law will not mechanistically apply the four tests of Lord Dunedin in the *Dunlop* case. After all, in *Makdessi v Cavendish* the relevant clauses would operate in a similar manner regardless of the severity of the breach, and were not a genuine pre-estimate of any loss, yet the Supreme Court overturned the decision of the Court of Appeal and held that they were not penalty clauses. And in *ParkingEye v Beavis*, the very purpose of the clause was to deter breach (and the same might be said about *Makdessi v Cavendish*) yet the deterrence itself provided a legitimate justification for the clause which meant that it was not a penalty. This is far removed from Lord Dunedin's warning that a clause which operated *in terrorem* would inevitably be penal.

The Supreme Court insisted upon a test of 'unconscionable' or 'extravagant' when deciding whether a clause is penal. This may be criticised as somewhat vague and uncertain, which is undesirable in a commercial context. However, if courts show proper restraint in finding a mutually agreed term in a contract 'unconscionable', then the test might be viewed as providing desirable flexibility whilst at the same time being very difficult to satisfy. The judgments in *Makdessi* show that the courts will not be quick to strike out a clause as penal, especially in the commercial context where parties are well informed and have been advised by lawyers. It is only in extreme cases that a clause should be unenforceable as a penalty.

Perhaps the most difficult aspect of the decision of the Supreme Court concerns the distinction between clauses which are triggered by a breach of contract and those which are not triggered by breach. This remains an important and difficult distinction to draw, and is considered further in the next section.

(b) **Money payable otherwise than on breach**

The orthodox approach is to say that penalties and liquidated damages have one clear thing in common: they both concern money, or other specified property, which, by the terms of a contract, is payable on breach of that contract. A term which provides that a sum of money shall be payable on some event other than a breach of contract cannot be either a penalty or a liquidated damages clause.[45] The £100 'reward' in the *Carbolic Smoke Ball* case was payable on the claimant catching flu; but that event was not a breach of contract, because the defendants had not undertaken that the users of the ball would not catch flu. If they had made such a promise, then the money would have been payable on a breach of contract and the question whether it was a penalty or liquidated damages clause would have arisen.

In *Alder v Moore*,[46] a professional footballer was insured by his union against permanent total disablement from playing professional football. He suffered an injury which the insurers were satisfied amounted to permanent total disablement. As required by the policy, he signed a declaration that he would take no part in any form of professional football as a

---

[45] Nor can an 'acceleration clause', which simply accelerates an existing liability, since no new liability to pay money arises: see *Protector Loan Co v Grice* (1880) 5 QBD 592; *BNP Paribas v Wockhardt EU Operations (Swiss) AG* [2009] EWHC 3116 (Comm) [38] (Christopher Clarke J).

[46] [1961] 2 QB 57, CA.

playing member, and that 'in the event of the infringement of this condition, [the footballer] will be subject to a penalty of the amount paid to him in settlement of his claim'. He started playing football again and the insurers sued to recover £500.

Devlin LJ, dissenting, upheld the decision of the trial judge and decided that, as the clause was described as 'a penalty', the onus was on the insurers to prove that it was not a penalty. Devlin LJ found that the insurers had in fact exacted a promise from the defendant that he would not play again. However, the majority of the Court of Appeal held that this was a contract for the payment of a sum upon a certain event which was not a breach of contract—according to Slade J, there was 'no *contractual* ban upon the defendant from playing professional football again'. But the defendant had promised that if he played football, under the contract he was obliged to pay £500 to his insurers. This was a primary obligation under the contract (rather than a secondary obligation arising upon breach) and was enforceable by the insurers.

These principles produce a strange anomaly: the defendant who has committed a breach of contract is better off than the defendant who has not. The former can say to the claimant, 'You are trying to enforce a penalty.' The latter cannot say the same. In *Bridge v Campbell Discount Co Ltd*,[47] the hirer of a car had a right under the hire-purchase agreement to return it at any time, but, if he did so, he was required by the agreement to pay 'by way of agreed compensation for depreciation' such sum as would make his payments up to two-thirds of the purchase price. He returned the car after paying only one monthly instalment. The Court of Appeal held that this was not a breach of contract and therefore the company's claim for the 'agreed compensation' was not a claim for a penalty: the defendant had to pay. Yet a majority of the House of Lords managed to find that the defendant was not exercising his contractual right to return the car, but was breaking his contract. As a result, their Lordships held that the claim was for a penalty and that the hirer was not liable to pay it. Lord Denning said that this meant that '**equity** commits itself to this absurd paradox: it will grant relief to a man who breaks his contract but will penalise the man who keeps it'. The defendant is therefore in a better position if he can show that he breached his contract, rather than if he adhered to it.

Nevertheless, Lord Denning's suggestion that 'equity commits itself to this absurd paradox' is unconvincing. In *Andrews v Australia and New Zealand Banking Group Ltd*,[48] the High Court of Australia examined the equitable foundations of the rule against penalties which did not require there to be any breach of contract. Until the nineteenth century, the operation of the rule against penalties usually applied to the non-fulfilment of conditions in penal bonds. The High Court held that the non-fulfilment of those conditions were not breaches of contract. So, if in exchange for certain services, A promises B that he will pay B £1 million, but it is also agreed that A will be released from his obligation to pay £1 million if A cleans B's windows by the end of the week, that is the essential structure of penal bonds. If A does not clean B's windows, there is no breach of contract and under the terms of the agreement B is entitled to £1 million. But in such circumstances, equity would intervene and find that the clause was penal if the amount asked for was unconscionable.

---

[47] [1962] AC 600, HL.
[48] [2012] HCA 30, (2012) 247 CLR 205.

As a result of extensive historical analysis, the High Court in *Andrews* therefore held that the rule against penalties can be invoked even where there has been no breach of contract. *Andrews* itself concerned 'bank charges'. Such charges were considered in Chapter 15;[49] the holder of a current account or a credit card may be charged up to £50 for overdrawing or exceeding a credit limit by £1 for a brief time, even though the bank's costs of processing the relevant payments and overdraft are minimal. These charges arise under the terms of the contract; going overdrawn or exceeding a credit limit is not a breach of the customer's contract with the bank. Nevertheless, the High Court of Australia held that such clauses *might* be penalties if they satisfied the substantial test for penalties. The High Court concluded that:

> a stipulation *prima facie* imposes a penalty on a party ('the first party') if, as a matter of substance, it is collateral (or accessory) to a primary stipulation in favour of a second party and this collateral stipulation, upon the failure of the primary stipulation, imposes upon the first party an additional detriment, the penalty, to the benefit of the second party.

So, if a primary stipulation that the customer should not make purchases beyond his credit card limit with Powerful Bank plc is subject to a further, collateral stipulation that the customer should pay Powerful Bank plc a sum equal to the value of Blenheim Palace upon failure of the primary stipulation (that is, exceeding his credit card limit), then prima facie the collateral stipulation is a penalty: it is 'in the nature of a security for and *in terrorem* of the satisfaction of the primary stipulation'.[50]

Andrews is a decision of the highest court in Australia. The Supreme Court in *Makdessi* recognised that it therefore had 'strong persuasive force'.[51] Nevertheless, their Lordships refused to follow the lead of the Australian judges. Lord Neuberger and Lord Sumption pointed out that *Export Credits Guarantee Department v Universal Oil Products Co* provided binding House of Lords authority that a breach of contract was required to engage the rule against penalties.[52] This is true, although it might also be observed that the reasoning in the *Universal Oil Products* case was brief, and that cases concerning penal bonds do not seem to have been cited to the court. More fundamentally, in *Makdessi* their Lordships considered that the jurisdiction not to enforce penalty clauses was concerned exclusively with the secondary obligations that arise following a breach of contract:[53]

> There is a fundamental difference between a jurisdiction to review the fairness of a contractual obligation and a jurisdiction to regulate the remedy for its breach. Leaving aside challenges going to the reality of consent, such as those based on fraud, duress or undue influence, the courts do not review the fairness of men's bargains either at law or in equity. The penalty rule regulates only the remedies available for breach of a party's primary obligations, not the primary obligations themselves.

---

[49] See Chapter 15, Section 4(d) for discussion of the parallel decision of the English courts in *Office of Fair Trading v Abbey National plc* [2009] UKSC 6, [2009] 3 WLR 1215.

[50] *Andrews* [10]; see P Davies and P Turner, 'Relief Against Penalties Without a Breach of Contract' (2013) 72 CLJ 20.

[51] *Makdessi* [42].

[52] *Export Credits Guarantee Department v Universal Oil Products Co* [1983] 1 WLR 399, HL.

[53] *Makdessi* [13].

Their Lordships thought that it would lead to unnecessary and undesirable uncertainty to extend the rule against penalties to obligations that arise other than on breach of contract. Indeed, to do so 'would represent the expansion of the courts' supervisory jurisdiction into a new territory of uncertain boundaries, which has hitherto been treated as wholly governed by mutual agreement'.[54]

More controversially, perhaps, Lord Neuberger and Lord Sumption thought that the historical analysis in *Andrews* was unpersuasive. They considered the equitable jurisdiction to relieve against penalties in the context of penal bonds which were defeasible in the event of the performance of a contractual obligation 'necessarily posited a breach of that obligation'. On the basis of the analysis outlined earlier, it is unclear whether this is convincing. It is suggested that one reason why Lord Neuberger and Lord Sumption were comfortable in reaching this conclusion was because of their insistence that 'the classification of terms for the purpose of the penalty rule depends on the substance of the term and not on its form or on the label which the parties have chosen to attach to it'.[55] Although their Lordships thought that the rule against penalties is now exclusively governed by the common law, which has departed decisively from its equitable roots, even at common law there remains an emphasis on 'substance over form'. This means that the court will be able to consider whether 'disguised' clauses fall within the scope of the rule against penalties. This chimes well with the comments of Bingham LJ in the *Interfoto* case, discussed in Chapter 11;[56] Bingham LJ was careful to say that it had not been argued that the relevant clause was a 'disguised penalty', and expressed his 'reluctance' at being unable to consider this point. More recently, in *Office of Fair Trading v Abbey National Plc* (the English equivalent of *Andrews* concerning bank charges), Lord Phillips in the Supreme Court said that counsel for the banks 'rightly conceded, however, that the Banks could not convert what were in effect penalties into "price" simply by wording their contracts so as to ensure that the contingencies that triggered liability to pay the charges did not constitute breaches of contract'.[57] This further supports the idea that a breach of contract cannot easily be disguised by simply drafting the clause in another way.

However, even though the emphasis in *Makdessi* on substance over form is both important and welcome, it nevertheless remains true that parties will be able to draft around the rule against penalties. Lord Neuberger and Lord Sumption explicitly said: 'We would accept that the application of the penalty rule can still turn on questions of drafting, even where a realistic approach is taken to the substance of the transaction and not just its form.'[58] This is unavoidable, and it is likely that a significant criticism of the rule against penalties will continue to focus upon the fact that it is so easily avoided by clever drafting. It might be thought more consistent for the law either to abolish the rule against penalties in its entirety, or for the rule against penalties to apply equally to extravagant sums demanded upon breach as to extravagant sums demanded on a certain other

---

[54] *Makdessi* [42].

[55] Ibid, [15].

[56] [1989] QB 433, 445–6. See Chapter 11, Section 2(b)(i).

[57] *Office of Fair Trading v Abbey National Plc* [2009] UKSC 6, [2010] 1 AC 696 [83]. See too Moore-Bick LJ in the Court of Appeal in the *ParkingEye* case: [2015] EWCA Civ 402 [42].

[58] *Makdessi* [43].

event whose only real purpose is to ensure performance of a major term of the contract. Understandably, however, the Supreme Court in *Makdessi* felt unable to take either step, especially since such significant reform should best be effected by Parliament after a thorough review of the impact and desirability of such reform (probably by the Law Commission).[59]

Lord Neuberger and Lord Sumption emphasised that the interference with freedom of contract made by the rule against penalties was somewhat anomalous, and that it should not be extended.[60] This is a pragmatic response to a well-established doctrine. As an exception to the principle of freedom of contract, the rule against penalties should be interpreted narrowly. The rule against penalties is indeed exceptional, since the court has no general jurisdiction to decline to enforce contractual terms just because they are onerous or unfair. Penalty clauses are unique, and to treat one class of term in a radically different way from any other cannot fail to produce anomalies. Nevertheless, Lord Mance was quite comfortable with a distinction between clauses which are triggered by a breach of contract, and clauses which are triggered by other events. His Lordship thought that the requirement of breach was not 'without rational or logical underpinning', since 'in most cases parties know and reflect in their contracts a real distinction, legal and psychological, between what, on the one hand, a party can permissibly do and what, on the other hand, constitutes a breach and may attract a liability to damages for—or even to an **injunction** to restrain—the breach'.[61]

However, the decision in *Makdessi* highlights that this distinction is not at all easy. After all, on the facts of *Makdessi v Cavendish* itself, Lord Neuberger and Lord Sumption, with whom Lord Carnwath agreed, thought that both Clause 5.1 and Clause 5.6[62] were not triggered by a breach of contract. Their Lordships considered Clause 5.1 to be in effect a price-adjustment clause, whilst Clause 5.6 also concerned the primary obligations under the contract. Admittedly, the judges said that some price-adjustment clauses could be unenforceable if they were a disguised punishment for a breach of contract, but in their opinion that was not the case on the facts of *Makdessi v Cavendish*. By contrast, Lord Mance, Lord Hodge, and Lord Toulson all thought that the rule against penalties was engaged because Clause 5.6 was triggered by a breach of the contractual covenants.[63] Lord Hodge[64] was equivocal about whether Clause 5.1 was also a secondary obligation, but Lord Mance appeared to think that Clause 5.1 was triggered by a breach of contract. Lord Clarke agreed generally with the reasoning of both Lord Neuberger and Lord Sumption, and Lord Mance and Lord Hodge, but favoured the judgment of Lord Hodge on this point. In any event, the different approaches shown by different Justices of the Supreme Court to this issue highlights that the distinction between primary and secondary obligations is not at all easy, and is likely to prove to be the subject of further discussion in subsequent cases.

---

[59] See generally Section 2(d).
[60] eg *Makdessi* [43].
[61] Ibid, [130].
[62] See Section 1(a)(iii).
[63] See eg *Makdessi* [280] (Lord Hodge).
[64] *Makdessi* [270].

(c) **The effect of a clause being a penalty**

If a clause is unenforceable because it is a penalty, then the injured party can still sue for damages at common law. However, he will generally recover no more than the loss actually sustained by him as a result of the breach, estimated in accordance with the usual principles discussed in Chapter 26. It is important to note that a penalty clause is unenforceable in its entirety. It is not possible for the court only partially to enforce a clause which is considered to be penal. This differs from the law regarding relief from forfeiture, and the relationship between these two areas is discussed further below.[65]

This 'all or nothing' approach towards penalty clauses led the Supreme Court in *Makdessi* to criticise the remedy awarded by the Court of Appeal in *Jobson v Johnson*.[66] That case concerned an agreement for the sale of **shares** in Southend Football Club for £350,000, which was payable by £40,000 immediately and then six half-yearly instalments. The agreement provided that, if the buyer defaulted on the second or a subsequent instalment, he must return the shares to the seller for £40,000. The seller was not required to refund instalments paid. After the buyer had paid £140,000, he defaulted and the seller claimed **specific performance** of the agreement to re-transfer the shares. It was held that the relevant term was a penalty clause and could not be enforced. On the facts of the case, however, the form of relief actually to be granted to the buyer was complicated by the fact that there was no evidence as to the value of the shares. The court therefore offered alternatives to the buyer, one involving the sale, and the other the valuation, of the shares. The object of the relief granted was clearly to compensate the seller for the loss actually caused by the buyer's breach and no more. But in so doing, the Court of Appeal held that a penalty was enforceable *pro tanto* or on a 'scaled down' basis, such that it could be enforced only to the extent of any actual loss suffered by the breach. In *Makdessi*, Lord Neuberger and Lord Sumption said that 'so far as it related to the form of relief, *Jobson* was wrongly decided'[67] and Lord Hodge similarly commented 'that the decision of the Court of Appeal in *Jobson v Johnson* was incorrect in so far as it modified a penalty clause'.[68] Such flexibility is possible in equity when granting relief against forfeiture.[69] But the rule against penalties now operates exclusively at common law. The common law is much more rigid: either the clause is enforceable or it is not.

A different issue arises where a claimant has suffered damages in excess of the sum stipulated in a penalty clause. In such circumstances, it is unclear whether the claimant can disregard the penalty clause and sue for damages in excess of the sum stipulated. This question has been left open by the House of Lords.[70] In principle, it might be contended that whether or not a penalty clause is valid should be assessed at the date of contracting, and if it is invalid as a penalty then the claimant should be able to ignore it and sue for the greater amount.[71] On the other hand, the claimant who is bringing the claim cannot sensibly argue

---

[65] Section 3(a).
[66] [1989] 1 All ER 621, CA.
[67] *Makdessi* [87].
[68] Ibid, [283]. Cf [186] (Lord Mance).
[69] See Section 3.
[70] *Cellulose Acetate Silk Co Ltd v Widnes Foundry (1925) Ltd* [1933] AC 20.
[71] *Wall v Rederiaktiebolaget Lugudde* [1915] 3 KB 66.

that he is being 'oppressed' by the penalty clause, and it remains arguable that as a result his claim should be capped by the limit which he imposed as a penalty.[72] It is suggested that it is somewhat unsatisfactory as a matter of policy for a party who inserts a penalty clause to later choose to ignore it if it operates to his detriment, and that as a result the second view should be preferred.

(d) Assessing the rule against penalties

In *Makdessi*, the Supreme Court considered the argument that the rule against penalties should be abolished. This was largely based on the contention that the penalty rule is an unwarranted intrusion into the general principle of freedom of contract;[73] as Christopher Clarke LJ recognised in the Court of Appeal in *Makdessi*, '[t]he law of penalties is a blatant interference with freedom of contract'.[74] However, the Supreme Court refused to jettison the rule against penalties. The judges emphasised that the penalty rule is common to all major systems of law. Moreover, the rule against penalties might be considered to be consistent with other areas where the court might decline to give full force to contractual provisions, such as the jurisdiction to grant relief from forfeiture and refusal to grant specific performance.

Lord Neuberger and Lord Sumption said:[75]

> We rather doubt that the courts would have invented the rule today if their predecessors had not done so three centuries ago. But this is not the way in which English law develops, and we do not consider that judicial abolition would be a proper course for this court to take.

It is suggested that the Supreme Court was quite right to take this approach. The rule against penalties is so well entrenched in English law that it would be unsatisfactory for it to be jettisoned by a court. If the rule is ever to be abolished, this should preferably be the result of legislation, which should only be passed following a thorough review of the law and the likely consequences of abolition, which would probably be carried out by the Law Commission. However, it is suggested that such a review is very unlikely to happen— the Supreme Court in *Makdessi* has probably settled this debate in the medium-term at least—and that even if it were to take place there are good reasons why the penalty rule should be maintained. After all, the rule against penalties at least means that one party is not hoping that the contract will be breached in order to receive an extravagant payment. It may be thought odd that terms can be included in the contract which lead one party to hope that the other party does not perform his obligations: the essence of the contract should be performance. It might even be suggested that since contract law does not award punitive damages,[76] it has set its face against punishment more generally, and that this should be reflected by not allowing penalty clauses either. This might, however, be partially

---

[72] *Elsley v JG Collins Ins Agencies* (1978) 3 DLR (3d) 1.

[73] See eg S Worthington, 'Common Law Values: The Role of Party Autonomy in Private Law' in A Robertson and M Tilbury (eds), *The Common Law of Obligations: Divergence and Unity* (Hart, 2015).

[74] *Makdessi* [44].

[75] Ibid, [36].

[76] See Chapter 28, Section 5.

undermined by the decision in *Attorney-General v Blake*[77] which suggests that deterrence does have some role to play in the law of contract.

The case against the penalty rule seems strongest when dealing with fully informed and well-advised commercial parties. Why should the courts interfere with such a contract? Indeed, it is generally thought that the role of the courts is not to interfere with the parties' bargain; this explains why the court will not examine the adequacy of the consideration,[78] or consider the fairness of terms of the contract in general,[79] so why single out penalty clauses for special treatment? Based on the decision of the Supreme Court in *Makdessi*, the answer to this second question appears to lie in the fact that the courts are happy to consider whether a clause relating to the *secondary* obligations that arise from breach are 'unconscionable', even though they remain reluctant to do the same for *primary* obligations.

The Supreme Court also refused to abolish the rule against penalties in the context of 'commercial' contracts. This is also to be welcomed. Had the Supreme Court decided otherwise, there would undoubtedly have been much litigation which would seek to define the boundaries of commercial contracts. It is not worth the effort and complications that would follow from creating such an unclear category of case: it is unclear what 'commercial contracts' precisely means. In principle, even a clause in a commercial contract might be penal,[80] although this now appears to be very unlikely. As Lord Neuberger and Lord Sumption said, 'In a negotiated contract between properly advised parties of comparable bargaining power, the strong initial presumption must be that the parties themselves are the best judges of what is legitimate in a provision dealing with the consequences of breach.'[81]

It is true that protection for consumers is provided for in the Consumer Rights Act 2015.[82] As a result, the rule against penalties is most important in non-consumer contracts. But there are many non-consumer cases which do not involve two substantial companies which are both legally advised and of strong bargaining power. For example, a very powerful company might contract with a small business or with an individual acting in the course of his trade or profession. In such circumstances, there is an inequality in the parties' bargaining positions, but the consumer protection regime does not apply. If the more powerful party insists on a penalty clause in the contract, what should the smaller party do? If there were no rule against penalties, then the smaller party should simply refuse to sign the contract. But, commercially, this may not be a viable option: the party might depend upon this contract in order to keep afloat, and be fearful of competitors taking lucrative business away from it. Lord Mance cited with approval a passage from *Robophone Facilities Ltd v Blank*[83] where Diplock LJ remarked that 'in these days when so often one party cannot satisfy his contractual hunger à la carte but only at the table d'hôte of a standard printed contract, [the rule against penalties] has certainly not outlived its usefulness'.

---

[77] See Chapter 28, Section 2.

[78] See Chapter 7, Section 1(c).

[79] See Chapter 19.

[80] eg *Makdessi* [35].

[81] *Makdessi* [35]. However, in principle a clause in a 'commercial contract' could be penal: see eg *Makdessi* [34]; *Imperial Tobacco Co (of Great Britain and Ireland) Ltd v Parslay* [1936] 2 All ER 515, 523, CA (Lord Wright MR).

[82] See Sch 2, para 6. See generally Chapter 15, Section 4.

[83] [1966] 1 WLR 1428, 1447.

Moreover, parties tend to be (overly) optimistic about performance, and simply work on the basis that they will not breach their obligations. This may be simply human nature, and consequently mean that the rule against penalties is a useful doctrine in saving parties from their own misguided optimism. It is also worth noting that the Law Commission originally recommended that similar protection be granted to small businesses as to consumers,[84] but this has not been enacted in the Consumer Rights Act 2015, and it is suggested that this bolsters the decision of the Supreme Court in *Makdessi* that the penalty rule should be maintained. Furthermore, when the rule against penalties has been considered by both the English and Scottish Law Commissions, they have not recommended abolition but rather expansion in that they have criticised the requirement that there needs to be a breach of contract before the penalty rule is engaged.[85]

2 Forfeiture

A clause which specifies that a certain sum is payable on breach may be a penalty clause. This means that the innocent party has to chase the money. However, if the money is paid in advance, and there is a clause in the contract that states that the money does not have to be returned in the event of the other party's breach of contract, then that clause might not engage the penalty rule but rather the equitable jurisdiction to grant relief from forfeiture. The innocent party may forfeit the money and keep it for himself. In some instances, however, equity will grant relief against forfeiture in order to prevent 'unconscionable' results. There is a similar tension here to that present in the context of penalty clauses: the parties' autonomy and freedom to set the terms of their own bargain is balanced against considerations of policy and 'unconscionability'.

In *Cukurova Finance International Ltd v Alfa Telecom Turkey Ltd*, Lord Neuberger said that '[t]he paradigm case for relief ... is where the primary object of the bargain is to secure a stated result which can be effectively attained when the matter comes before the court, and where the forfeiture provision is added by way of security for the production of that result'.[86] His Lordship noted the 'breadth and flexibility of the equitable discretion to give relief against forfeiture'[87] and that all the circumstances relevant at the time relief is sought can be taken into account. In particular, it is important to consider the conduct of the parties, how serious the breaches were, and the difference between the value of the property forfeited and the damages caused by the breach.[88]

The *Cukurova* case concerned a large commercial transaction between well-advised parties. *A* lent over $1 billion to *C* and took security over *C*'s shareholding. *C* defaulted, and *A* sought to forfeit the shares. The Privy Council granted relief against forfeiture. *C* had in fact tendered the amount due shortly after the contractually agreed date for repayment,

---

[84] Law Commission, *Unfair Terms in Contracts* (Law Com No 292, 2005).

[85] England: *Penalty Clauses and Forfeiture of Monies Paid* (Law Com Working Paper No 61, 1975); Scotland: *Discussion Paper on Penalty Clauses* (Scot Law Com Discussion Paper No 103, 1997),

[86] [2013] UKPC 2, [2015] 2 WLR 875 [90].

[87] Ibid, [124].

[88] Ibid, [116], citing Lord Wilberforce in *Shiloh Spinners Ltd v Harding* [1973] AC 691.

and this had been rejected by *A*. In the judgment of the Privy Council, this represented un-conscionable behaviour by *A*: *A* was seeking to abuse its position to put itself in a far better position that it would have been in had the primary obligations been performed.[89]

It is important to note that the law relating to forfeiture does not restrict the right of the innocent party to terminate an agreement for breach of contract. For example, in *Union Eagle Ltd v Golden Achievement Ltd*,[90] the purchaser of a property agreed to pay 10 per cent of the purchase price as a deposit. The purchaser then failed to complete by the spec-ified time, but did tender the purchase price ten minutes after the time for completion had passed. The Privy Council held that the vendors were entitled to forfeit the deposit. Lord Hoffmann gave the advice of the Board and emphasised that in commercial trans-actions, certainty is very important. Where the parties have stipulated that time is of the essence, this should be respected. Their Lordships did not consider it 'unconscionable' for the vendor to forfeit the deposit, especially since the 'reasonable' amount of 10 per cent had been paid.[91] This decision perhaps emphasises that only rarely will relief against forfeiture (or against a 'penalty clause') be granted, since courts are largely unwilling to interfere with and strike down provisions of the parties' bargain.[92]

(a) The relationship between forfeiture and penalty clauses

There is an interesting and uneasy relationship between forfeiture and penalty clauses. The roots of both doctrines appear to be shared, but according to the Supreme Court in *Makdessi* the penalty rule has now been developed at common law, whereas relief against forfeiture remains equitable. This has led to significant differences between the two areas.

An interesting practical illustration of the interplay between forfeiture and penalty clauses is provided by *Workers Trust and Merchant Bank Ltd v Dojap Investments Ltd*.[93] In order to understand this case, it is important to be able to distinguish part-payments of the contract price from deposits. The general principle is that money paid in advance of performance will generally be recoverable if it is a part-payment of the contract price,[94] but not if it is a deposit.[95] A deposit is taken by way of security in order to ensure performance. Whether a payment is a part-payment of the price or a deposit is a question of interpret-ation, and the usual principles of interpretation apply.[96]

However, even when the payment in advance is a deposit, the court may not allow the innocent party to keep the deposit. For example, in the *Dojap Investments* case,[97] the pur-chasers of a property paid a deposit of 25 per cent of the purchase price to the sellers. When the purchasers failed to complete the transaction, the sellers sought to forfeit the

---

[89] However, there was subsequent disagreement about the terms on which relief from forfeiture should be granted: see [2013] UKPC 20; noted by P Turner, 'Mending Men's Bargains' (2014) 130 LQR 188.

[90] [1997] AC 514.

[91] cf *Workers Trust and Merchant Bank Ltd v Dojap Investments Ltd* [1993] AC 573, PC.

[92] See generally *Philips Hong Kong Ltd v Attorney General of Hong Kong* (1993) 61 BLR 41, PC.

[93] [1993] AC 573, PC.

[94] *Dies v British and International Mining and Finance Co* [1939] 1 KB 715. The cause of action is unjust en-richment on the ground of total failure of consideration: see Chapter 28, Section 4.

[95] *Howe v Smith* (1884) 27 ChD 89.

[96] See generally Chapter 12.

[97] [1993] AC 573, PC.

deposit. The Privy Council held that the sellers could not keep the deposit. Lord Browne-Wilkinson, giving the advice of the Board, held that it is 'not possible for the parties to attach the incidents of a deposit to the payment of a sum of money unless such sum is reasonable as earnest money'. Their Lordships thought that a deposit of around 10 per cent was reasonable in the context of such property transactions, and that 25 per cent was excessive, particularly since the sellers had failed to show any 'special circumstances' which could justify such a deposit. The 25 per cent was considered to be extravagant.

The *Dojap* case is very significant. It seems like a straightforward case of forfeiture. However, the judgment itself suggests that relief was available at common law. This is somewhat unorthodox: forfeiture is an equitable doctrine. It was often thought that in order to obtain relief against forfeiture the innocent party had to be ready and willing to perform his obligations under the contract, given the equitable maxim of 'he who seeks equity must do equity'.[98] If correct, this would have made it difficult for the courts to grant equitable relief since the purchasers were no longer willing to go through with the transaction. Yet the House of Lords sidestepped this issue by applying the rules against penalties that had developed at common law. This is controversial. There are many similarities between penalty clauses and forfeiture clauses, and it might be thought that the basis of relief in both instances is that simply enforcing the contractual terms would be 'unconscionable'. But on an orthodox understanding of the law as it currently stands, there are important differences between penalty clauses and forfeiture clauses. For example, whether or not an agreed damages clause is a penalty is assessed at the date the contract is made, often considering whether the stipulated sum is a genuine pre-estimate of loss. Forfeiture clauses, on the other hand, are assessed at the date of breach, and the crucial factor tends to be whether or not the deposit is 'reasonable'. Moreover, forfeiture clauses do not only arise upon breach of contract, but can arise upon other events. In addition, a clause can be partially enforced when granting relief from forfeiture, but not when the penalty rule applies.[99] In that sense, the law concerning relief from forfeiture is broader than the law of penalties. On the other hand, however, the law regarding relief from forfeiture is more restricted than the rule against penalties, since—'at least on the current state of the authorities'[100]—only proprietary or possessory rights can be forfeited.[101]

In *Makdessi*, the Supreme Court noted that it is 'unclear'[102] precisely how the penalty rule should be distinguished from the jurisdiction to grant relief from forfeiture. There was understandably little argument on forfeiture in the Supreme Court, since forfeiture was not at issue in either *Makdessi v Cavendish* or *ParkingEye v Beavis*.[103] However, their Lordships appear to have recognised that a clause could be both a penalty clause and a forfeiture

---

[98] See Romer LJ in *Stockloser v Johnson* [1954] 1 QB 476, although Denning and Somervell LJJ disagreed.

[99] See the discussion of *Jobson v Johnson* in Section 1(c). See too *UK Housing Alliance (North West) Ltd v Francis* [2010] EWCA Civ 117, [2010] 3 All ER 519. C Conte, 'The Jurisdiction to Relieve Against Penalties and Forfeitures: Time for a Rethink' (2010) 126 LQR 529.

[100] *Makdessi* [69].

[101] *Scandinavian Trading Tanker Co AB v Flota Petrolera Ecuatoriana (The Scaptrade)* [1983] 2 AC 694; *On Demand Information Plc v Michael Gerson (Finance) Plc* [2001] 1 WLR 155.

[102] *Makdessi* [3].

[103] Ibid, [18].

clause and that both doctrines could be relevant.[104] A clause should first be assessed under the penalty rule, and then under the forfeiture rule. As Lord Hodge put it:[105]

> There is no reason in principle why a contractual provision, which involves forfeiture of sums otherwise due, should not be subjected to the rule against penalties, if the forfeiture is wholly disproportionate either to the loss suffered by the innocent party or to another justifiable commercial interest which that party has sought to protect by the clause. If the forfeiture is not so exorbitant and therefore is enforceable under the rule against penalties, the court can then consider whether under English law it should grant equitable relief from forfeiture, looking at the position of the parties after the breach and the circumstances in which the contract was broken. This was the approach which Dillon LJ adopted in *BICC plc v Burndy Corpn* [1985] Ch 232 and in which Ackner LJ concurred. The court risks no confusion if it asks first whether, as a matter of construction, the clause is a penalty and, if it answers that question in the negative, considers whether relief in equity should be granted having regard to the position of the parties after the breach.

3 Agreements concerning specific relief

Finally, it is worth noting that the parties might try to agree that equitable relief—such as specific performance[106] or an injunction[107]—will be granted following a breach of contract. However, courts will not consider themselves bound to respect such clauses.[108] This is because equitable relief is discretionary, and the discretion of the court should not be fettered. But it is conceivable that in some situations the court might have regard to the existence of a clause which stipulates that an injunction or specific performance will be awarded, although even then such a clause will only be one factor amongst a range of considerations that the court will take into account.[109]

Further Reading

T Downes, 'Rethinking Penalty Clauses' in P Birks (ed), *Wrongs and Remedies in the Twenty-First Century* (OUP, 1996).
Argues that the law on penalty clauses is simply an aspect of a broader, more general notion of 'unconscionability'. Importantly, this would mean that freely negotiated penalty clauses between commercial parties of equal bargaining power would be valid.

---

[104] Lord Neuberger and Lord Sumption (with whom Lord Carnwath agreed) could 'see the force' in this argument presented by Lord Mance [160] and Lord Hodge [227], and supported by Lord Clarke [291] and Lord Toulson [294], but did not wish to decide the matter since it was unnecessary to do so.

[105] *Makdessi* [227].

[106] See Chapter 28, Section 7.

[107] See Chapter 28, Section 8.

[108] *Quadrant Visual Communications Ltd v Hutchison Telephone UK Ltd* [1993] BCLC 442.

[109] *Warner Bros Pictures Inc v Nelson* [1937] 1 KB 209, 220–1 (Branson J).

L Smith, 'Relief against Forfeiture: A Restatement' (2001) 60 CLJ 178.
Examines the law on relief against forfeiture, building on its historical roots in the law of mortgages.

S Rowan, 'For the Recognition of Remedial Terms Agreed *Inter Partes*' (2010) 126 LQR 448.
Argues that contracting parties should be afforded greater liberty to supplement the default remedial regime by agreeing upon the remedies that ensue from a breach of their contract.

? Question

Melchester Wanderers FC purchases land on which the club intends to build a new stadium. In order for everything to be ready for the new season, the club calculates that the work needs to be completed by 30 June. This is to allow the Football League time to inspect and formally approve the stadium sufficiently far in advance of the first match of the season.

Melchester Wanderers FC enters into a contract with Elbury Ltd to carry out the building work. The price is fixed at £25 million, with completion said to be no later than 30 June. In order to ensure completion on time, Melchester Wanderers FC asks Elbury Ltd to pay a 'deposit' of £2 million in order to secure the contract. A term of the contract provides that the deposit will be returned in full if the work is completed by 30 June; that 50 per cent of the deposit will be returned if the work is completed after 30 June but before 15 July; and that if the work is completed after 15 July the deposit will be retained in full by Melchester Wanderers FC.

Elbury Ltd completes the work on 14 July. Advise Elbury Ltd. How, if at all, would your answer differ if the work was completed on 16 July?

28 Remedies beyond compensatory damages

 Key Points

- Damages may be awarded to strip a defendant of gains made from a breach of contract. Such 'restitutionary damages' are only awarded in 'exceptional circumstances' where the usual remedies for breach of contract are 'inadequate', and the claimant has a 'legitimate interest' in preventing the defendant's profit-making activity and depriving him of his profit. They are very rare.

- More common is the 'hypothetical bargain measure of damages'. The defendant may have to pay the claimant the sum he would have had to pay had he bargained for the right not to perform his contract immediately prior to breach. In constructing a hypothetical bargain, the court will assume that the parties were willing to act reasonably and make a deal, and will take into account both the claimant's expected loss and the defendant's expected gains.

- Gain-based damages must be distinguished from restitution of an unjust enrichment on the ground of total failure of consideration. A claimant who transfers a benefit to a defendant on a basis which totally fails may be able to recover the value of that benefit. This is not an action for breach of contract but in unjust enrichment. It is important that the contract has been discharged (or has not been concluded) for an action in unjust enrichment to succeed.

- Where damages are inadequate to achieve justice, the court may grant equitable relief. The most important equitable orders are for specific performance and injunctions. These are discretionary remedies.

- Specific performance compels a person to perform his contract. Specific performance is generally only granted where the subject matter of the contract is unique (such as land).

- Injunctions can either prevent a person from breaching his contract (called prohibitory injunctions) or force a person to comply with his contract (called mandatory injunctions). An injunction will not be granted if this would in effect compel a person to perform his contract in situations where specific performance would not be granted.

1 Introduction

In Chapter 26, we examined the most usual remedy for breach of contract: compensatory damages. In the language of Fuller and Perdue,[1] compensatory damages might protect an 'expectation interest' or 'reliance interest', and it was seen that the two should not be considered entirely distinct.[2] However, there are other interests that may be protected. The most important as regards damages is the 'restitution interest', under which the claimant can strip the defendant of a gain made at the claimant's expense. This chapter will consider such gain-based remedies, and also equitable remedies—in particular **specific performance** and **injunctions**—which can be awarded in situations where restricting the claimant to damages would be inadequate. However, it is important to remember that the remedies for breach of contract discussed in this chapter are less common than the compensatory awards discussed in Chapter 26 and, generally, will only be awarded where compensatory damages are considered to be insufficient to achieve adequate justice in a case.[3]

2 Accounting for profits obtained by breach of contract

There are cases in which D's breach of contract causes no loss to the other party, C, but the breach enables D to make a profit. In very limited and exceptional circumstances, the court may order D to account to C for the profits obtained from the breach of contract. This was recognised by the House of Lords in *Attorney-General v Blake*.[4] Blake had been a member of the secret service. In breach of the Official Secrets Act 1989, he divulged information to the Soviet Union and, in 1961, was sentenced to 42 years' imprisonment. In 1966, he escaped and took refuge in Russia, where he still lives today. In 1989, he entered into a contract with an English publisher to publish his book, which included an account of his activities in the secret service. The publisher was to pay Blake royalties amounting to £150,000. The Attorney-General, acting on behalf of the state, sued Blake for the profits he was expected to make.

It was difficult for the Attorney-General clearly to establish the basis of the claim. At first instance, Scott V-C rejected the argument that Blake was in breach of the **fiduciary** duties he owed to the state—for which an account of profits would readily have been available—because Blake's employment by the Crown had ceased a long time previously.[5] Nor were the contents of the book still confidential—they were widely known, which meant that Blake did not commit the wrong of breach of confidence. The only private law claim open to the Attorney-General was that of breach of contract: Blake had promised never to publish the material in the book. This cause of action initially looked very unpromising, since it was

---

[1] L Fuller and R Perdue, 'The Reliance Interest in Contract Damages' (1936) 46 Yale LJ 52.

[2] See Chapter 26, Section 7.

[3] A notable exception might concern the hypothetical bargain measure of damages, which may be best considered to be compensatory in any event: see Section 3.

[4] [2001] 1 AC 268.

[5] Nevertheless, this decision might be criticised since fiduciary obligations should not ordinarily come to an end so easily: see P Davies and G Virgo, *Equity & Trusts: Text, Cases, and Materials* (OUP, 2013) ch 14, section 2(e).

long-established that a person who breaches his contract does not need to disgorge his gains, but merely compensate the innocent party for his loss.[6] Nevertheless, the House of Lords held that the Attorney General was entitled to an account of profits and to be paid a sum equal to that owed by the publisher to Blake.

The decision of the House of Lords is controversial. Indeed, Lord Hobhouse forcefully dissented, insisting that compensation is the intellectually sound and just remedy for breach of contract. Lord Hobhouse warned that there are significant dangers in introducing new restitutionary rights into commercial law. For instance, disgorging the defendant's gains may be considered to be inconsistent with ideas of 'efficient breach', since a defendant might no longer be able to decide whether a breach of contract would be worthwhile by calculating the amount of compensation he would have to pay to the claimant versus his expected profit. After all, if the defendant would have to disgorge the profits he made by breaching his contract, there is no incentive for the defendant to breach: why bother if he has to give up his gains anyway? As a result, the defendant may persevere with an 'inefficient' contract, and the most 'efficient' outcome may be frustrated.[7] On the other hand, of course, the existence of a gain-based award strengthens the protection of contractual rights by deterring breach. But how strongly should contractual rights be protected? We would presumably not be comfortable with throwing contract-breakers into prison merely because they failed to comply with a private agreement. So there are limits to the protection we are happy to grant to contractual rights. The question of whether that should extend to stripping a defendant of profits made in breach is difficult to answer.

In *Blake*, Lord Nicholls made it clear that the gain-based remedy will be granted only in 'exceptional circumstances'. The usual remedies for breach of contract should be 'inadequate', and the claimant should have a legitimate interest in preventing the defendant's profit-making activity and depriving him of his profit. Lord Steyn said that '[e]xceptions to the general principle that there is no remedy for disgorgement of profits against a contract breaker are best hammered out on the anvil of concrete cases'.[8] That anvil has rarely been struck. Indeed, it now looks like the decision of the House of Lords in *Blake* is something of an outlier.

Admittedly, *Blake* was soon followed in one decision at first instance. In *Esso Petroleum Co Ltd v Niad*,[9] Sir Andrew-Morritt V-C awarded an account of profits against the contract-breaker. In that case, Niad received fuel from Esso at a discounted rate. In return, Niad promised to match the price at which it sold fuel to customers with what its competitors were paying in the area. In breach of contract, Niad charged its customers more than it should have done under the terms of the agreement. Esso repeatedly complained, and ultimately sued Niad for breach of contract. The judge held that Esso had a legitimate interest in the performance of the agreement, and stripped Niad of the gains it had made from its breach of contract. This was a bold judgment, no doubt influenced by the very recent, ground-breaking decision in *Blake*. Interestingly, Esso did not try very hard to

---

[6] *Teacher v Calder* [1899] AC 451; *Addis v Gramophone Co Ltd* [1909] AC 488.
[7] See Chapter 1, Section 6(c).
[8] *Blake*, 291.
[9] [2001] All ER (D) 324.

establish its loss, for fear that doing so would lead to the court only granting a compensatory remedy. This does not seem very satisfactory.

The decision in *Niad* has not been followed. Apart from *Blake* and *Niad*, there are no reported decisions where the court has ordered a defendant to disgorge all the profits made from a breach of contract.[10] It is suggested that *Niad* would probably be decided differently today. The judgment was made in the expectation that *Blake* would lead to a substantial expansion of the gain-based remedy, such that an account of profits would be granted much more readily. But this has not happened. The result in *Blake* may also seem odd, but is best justified on the specific facts of *Blake* itself: the case concerned a traitor, who used to be a fiduciary, and in the very unusual circumstances of the case it was considered unpalatable to allow the wrongdoer to retain the profits he made.

A good example of a case that stamped down on the prospect of a widening of the remedy of an account of profits is *The Sine Nomine*.[11] That was an arbitration about the withdrawal of a ship from the claimant's service. The arbitrators took the somewhat unusual step of making sure their decision was reported, such was their desire to emphasise that an account of profits is not a welcome remedy in the context of commercial contracts. The arbitrators were particularly hostile to disgorging the defendants of their gains when they said:[12]

> It is by no means uncommon for commercial contracts to be broken deliberately because a more profitable opportunity has arisen. Or the contract-breaker takes an over-generous view of his rights, knowing that the law may ultimately be against him. In such a case he may have little or nothing to lose by taking the chance; the downside at worst is that he will have to pay the costs of both sides. International commerce on a large scale is red in tooth and claw.

It is just about possible to reconcile the decisions in *Esso v Niad* and *The Sine Nomine*: the latter concerned a marketable commodity (a ship) whereas the former did not (the price-matching scheme was obviously not a marketable commodity).[13] But the tenor of the decisions is very different, and the approach in *The Sine Nomine* appears to have won out. However, that is not to suggest that *Blake* has not proved to be an important and influential decision. The contrary is true. It is just that the biggest impact of the decision in *Blake* has been to increase the availability of the 'hypothetical bargain' measure of damages, considered in the next section, rather than the remedy of an account of profits.

It should be noted that the terminology in this area can be confusing. In *Blake*, Lord Nicholls preferred to avoid the language of 'restitutionary damages', but it is not entirely clear why he was so concerned to do so.[14] After all, if 'restitution' is understood to mean 'gain-based', and 'damages' to indicate a monetary award for a wrong, then the award in *Blake* does appear to be one of 'restitutionary damages'—damages based upon the defendant's gain

---

[10] For calculation of what profits are caused by the breach of contract, the usual principles of causation (including *novus actus interveniens*) should apply: see Chapter 26, Section 2(a).

[11] [2002] 1 Lloyd's Rep 805.

[12] Ibid, [9].

[13] J Beatson, 'Courts, Arbitrators and Restitutionary Liability for Contract' (2002) 118 LQR 377.

[14] J Edelman, *Gain-Based Damages* (Hart, 2002). Indeed, the Law Commission preferred the term 'restitutionary damages': see Law Com No 247, *Aggravated, Exemplary and Restitutionary Damages* (1997).

rather than the claimant's loss. However, Lord Nicholls preferred the language of 'account of profits'. This is well established in the equitable sphere, and perhaps emphasises that this gain-based remedy is discretionary. Nevertheless, even the language of 'account of profits' may be misleading at times, since a defendant may have to account for expenses saved rather than extra profits made. Both are obviously 'gains' made by the defendant. In any event, the difference in terminology seems to be simply semantic: in this context, 'restitutionary damages' may be equated to 'account of profits'—the focus is on stripping the defendant of gains made, rather than compensating the claimant for losses suffered.

3 Hypothetical bargain measure of damages

Perhaps the greatest impact *Blake* has had upon the law of contractual remedies is to be found in the wider availability of the 'hypothetical bargain' measure of damages. This measure of damages is known by other names as well—such as 'user damages' or 'negotiating damages'—and reflects the fact that the defendant may have to pay the claimant the sum he would have had to pay had he bargained for the right not to perform his contract immediately prior to breach. The negotiations envisaged by the court are clearly hypothetical and treat both the claimant and defendant as reasonable parties who are prepared to reach an agreement, even if this contradicts reality.

In *Blake*, the House of Lords explicitly approved the decision of Brightman J in *Wrotham Park Estate Co Ltd v Parkside Homes Ltd*.[15] A vendor sold land subject to a restrictive **covenant** limiting building on the land to a particular layout. A purchaser built 14 houses in breach of this restrictive covenant. This caused no loss to the vendor, but Brightman J held that the vendor was entitled to recover a proportion (5 per cent) of the profits resulting from the development in breach of contract.

Wrotham Park is a very difficult decision to analyse. The remedy awarded may well be considered to be compensatory. What the claimant has lost is the opportunity to bargain with the defendant for the relaxation of his rights.[16] As Lord Hobhouse put it in *Blake*, 'What the claimant has lost is the sum which he could have exacted from the defendant as the price of his consent to the development.'[17]

However, Lord Hobhouse was the dissenting judge in *Blake*. The majority of the House of Lords appear to have regarded *Wrotham Park* as an example of the court stripping the defendant of some of his gains. As Lord Nicholls commented:[18]

> The *Wrotham Park* case, therefore, still shines, rather as a solitary beacon, showing that in contract as well as tort damages are not always narrowly confined to recoupment of financial loss. In a suitable case damages for breach of contract may be measured by the benefit gained by the wrongdoer from the breach. The defendant must make a reasonable payment in respect of the benefit he has gained.

---

[15] *Wrotham Park Estate Co Ltd v Parkside Homes Ltd* [1974] 2 All ER 321. The *Wrotham Park* case is preferred to *Surrey County Council v Bredero Homes Ltd* [1993] 3 All ER 705, CA.

[16] RJ Sharpe and SM Waddams, 'Damages for Lost Opportunity to Bargain' (1982) 2 OJLS 290.

[17] [2000] 4 All ER 385, 410.

[18] *Blake* 283–4.

This passage has proved influential. In *Experience Hendrix LLC v PPX Enterprises*,[19] Peter Gibson LJ recognised *Wrotham Park* to be an important 'stepping stone' in Lord Nicholls's reasoning towards the availability of a full account of profits remedy for breach of contract, and in *Devenish Nutrition Ltd v Sanofi-Aventis SA*,[20] Arden LJ observed that '[i]f user damages and *Wrotham Park* damages were purely compensatory, they would not have been stepping stones to the conclusion that the court could grant an account of profits for a breach of contract'.

However, prior to *Blake* it was commonly thought that the availability of the hypothetical bargain measure of damages was limited to contracts concerning land.[21] This is because such contracts are generally specifically enforceable,[22] and the damages are awarded in lieu of an injunction—and therefore reflect the loss of injunctive relief rather than any other loss. Yet Lord Nicholls invoked *Wrotham Park* as an example of the remedies available for breach of contract more generally, and it is not surprising to find that subsequent courts have followed the lead of the House of Lords in this regard. Indeed, in *Experience Hendrix*, Mance LJ observed that *Blake* 'marks a new start in this area of the law',[23] and expanded the scope of the hypothetical bargain measure of damages such that it now also covers breaches of contract that are not related to property.

In *Experience Hendrix LLC v PPX Enterprises Inc*, PPX exploited master recordings of Jimi Hendrix owned by the legendary artist's estate. This was a breach of a contract between PPX and the Hendrix estate, which had been concluded in settlement of an earlier dispute. The estate suffered no loss through the actions of PPX, but PPX made substantial gains. Mance LJ thought that 'any reasonable observer of the situation would conclude that, as a matter of practical justice, PPX should make (at the least) reasonable payment for its use of masters in breach of the settlement agreement'.[24] The fact that the estate suffered no loss did not mean that the claimant should be limited to nominal damages only. The decision in *Blake* allowed the Court of Appeal to award damages the purpose of which was not to compensate the claimant for its financial injury.

The decision in *Experience Hendrix* is very significant. It recognises the landmark decision in *Blake* but makes it clear that courts do not always have to disgorge the entirety of the defendant's gains. Instead, the court might only require a defendant to give up a proportion of his gains. On the facts of *Experience Hendrix*, the Court of Appeal suggested that this may be about one-third of the profits made by the defendant. This raises the important question of whether there is a 'sliding scale' of damages now, moving from 100 per cent of the defendant's profits all the way down to 0 per cent of the defendant's profits and up to 100 per cent of the claimant's loss.

It is important next to consider both the nature and quantification of this remedy, as well as its availability. Commercially, these are all now very significant and difficult issues. However, it should be emphasised that *Experience Hendrix* makes it abundantly clear that

---

[19] [2003] EWCA Civ 323, [2003] 1 All ER (Comm) 830 [56].
[20] [2008] EWCA Civ 1086, [2009] Ch 390 [49].
[21] See eg *Surrey County Council v Bredero Homes* [1993] 1 WLR 1361; *Jaggard v Sawyer* [1995] 1 WLR 269.
[22] See Section 7.
[23] *Experience Hendrix* [16].
[24] Ibid, [42].

this hypothetical bargain measure of damages is not restricted to contracts to do with property. The contract between Jimi Hendrix's estate and PPX concerned personal contractual rights. Yet the bargain measure of damages was nonetheless available.

So, how should the remedy in *Wrotham Park* be analysed? In both *Wrotham Park* itself and *Experience Hendrix*, the courts quantified the remedy by referring to the defendant's gain, and this is supported by the analysis of the majority of the House of Lords in *Blake*. The focus on the defendant's gain means that this remedy can feasibly be called 'restitutionary'; it might not appear to be compensatory because the focus is not on the claimant's loss. Indeed, in many situations the claimant's financial position will be no worse. It may be that *Blake* is to do with the defendant giving *up* gains, whereas *Wrotham Park* is concerned with the defendant giving *back* gains,[25] but on both analyses the focus is on the defendant's gains.

However, there are powerful alternatives to the 'gain-based' view of *Wrotham Park*. It may be that damages are awarded to reflect a lost opportunity to bargain with the defendant for the release of the claimant's rights,[26] or awarded as a substitute for the right infringed,[27] or to compensate for the loss of a power to prevent the infringement.[28] This would be consistent with the minority approach of Lord Hobhouse in *Blake*. However, it might be criticised as being somewhat artificial in situations where the claimant would simply not have bargained away its rights. For instance, in *Blake*, the claimant lost nothing as it would simply not have bargained for the relaxation of its contractual rights with the traitor George Blake. Similarly, in *Wrotham Park*, the claimants would not have agreed to relax the restrictive covenants and allow the development to proceed as the defendant intended. On the other hand, claimants are regularly compensated for losses they would not have wished to suffer (such as a broken leg) so this objection to a compensatory approach may not be insurmountable.

In any event, it now seems clear that the award in *Wrotham Park* must take into account both the claimant's loss and the defendant's gain. As Lord Lloyd put it in *Inverugie Investments v Hackett*,[29] 'The principle need not be characterised as exclusively compensatory, or exclusively restitutionary; it combines elements of both.' This is logical: when negotiating a bargain for the release of the claimant's rights, the claimant will generally seek to recover more than his loss, whilst the defendant will bear in mind his expected gains in the negotiations too. However, it is important to note that the court will assess the hypothetical bargain that would reasonably have been agreed immediately prior to the breach. If the parties at that moment in time would reasonably expect the defendant to make substantial profits which do not in the event materialise, this may mean that the amount the defendant has to pay under the hypothetical bargain is greater than the profits he actually made.

---

[25] What Edelman has described as the difference between disgorgement and restitutionary damages: J Edelman, *Gain-Based Damages* (Hart, 2002).

[26] RJ Sharpe and SM Waddams, 'Damages for Lost Opportunity to Bargain' (1982) 2 OJLS 290.

[27] R Stevens, *Torts and Rights* (OUP, 2007) ch 4.

[28] See K Barker, '"Damages Without Loss": Can Hohfeld Help?' (2014) 34 OJLS 1; N McBride, 'Restitution for Wrongs' in C Mitchell and W Swadling (eds), *The Restatement Third: Restitution and Unjust Enrichment: Critical and Comparative Essays* (Hart, 2013) 272–4.

[29] [1995] 1 WLR 713, 718 (admittedly, this case concerned the tort of trespass rather than contract, but this discussion of the remedy is equally applicable in the contractual context).

This occurred in *Pell Frischmann Engineering Ltd v Bow Valley Iran Ltd*.[30] The defendants breached a confidentiality agreement concerning the development of an offshore oil field. The most the defendants made from this breach of contract was around $1.8 million. Nevertheless, the Privy Council held that the defendants were liable to pay $2.5 million (plus interest) under the *Wrotham Park* measure of damages. This is because the court found that the defendants would have had to pay $2.5 million for the claimant to relax its contractual rights at the time of the breach of contract: the fact that the development proved to be less successful than anticipated was irrelevant. This is an instructive case that undermines the view that the *Wrotham Park* measure of damages is concerned with profit-stripping: how can it be when the remedy goes beyond the profits actually made? Moreover, *Pell Frischmann* is a good example of the Privy Council endorsing the view that the *Wrotham Park* remedy is available for breaches of non-proprietary contracts as well as contracts related to land.

The above analysis means that the earlier decision of the Court of Appeal in *WWF-World Wide Fund for Nature v World Wrestling Federation Entertainment Inc*[31] should be read with some caution. In that case, Chadwick LJ expressed the view that both *Blake* and *Wrotham Park* should 'each be seen as a flexible response to the need to compensate the claimant for the wrong which has been done to him'.[32] Whilst this may explain *Wrotham Park*, it is difficult to see how this can accurately describe *Blake*. After all, the state suffered no loss, and would clearly not have entered into any deal with the traitor. The remedy in *Blake* was squarely focused on the defendant's gain. To call such a remedy 'compensatory' runs the risk of losing all linguistic clarity. Compensation is concerned with loss. Restitution is concerned with gain. *Blake* is an example of a restitutionary measure. Of course, if Blake had not actually made any profits then a substantial remedy may still have been appropriate, and this might be explicable on the basis of a hypothetical bargain, or perhaps even a punitive measure. But that was not the case in *Blake*.

Regardless of the nature and scope of the hypothetical bargain measure of damages, it is difficult to be sure exactly how the monetary remedy is to be quantified. The award in *Wrotham Park* itself was only 5 per cent of the profits, in *Experience Hendrix* the suggested remedy was around 33 per cent of the profits, and in *Pell Frischmann* more than 100 per cent of the defendant's profits were awarded to the claimant. Helpful guidance has been provided by Gabriel Moss QC in *Tamares (Vincent Square) v Fairpoint Properties (No 2)*:[33]

(1) The overall principle is that the court must attempt to find what would be a 'fair' result of a hypothetical negotiation between the parties.
(2) The context, including the nature and seriousness of the breach, must be kept in mind.
(3) The right to prevent a development (or part) gives the owner of the right a significant bargaining position.
(4) The owner of the right with such a bargaining position will normally be expected to receive some part of the likely profit from the development (or relevant part).[34]

---

[30] [2009] UKPC 45, [2011] 1 WLR 2370.
[31] [2007] EWCA Civ 286, [2008] 1 All ER 74.
[32] [59].
[33] [2007] EWHC 212 (Ch), [2007] 1 WLR 2167 [22].
[34] In *Tamares*, the breach of contract was the development itself, but this will not be true in all cases.

(5) If there is no evidence of the likely size of the profit, the court can do its best by awarding a suitable multiple of the damages for loss of amenity.

(6) If there is evidence of the likely size of the profit, the court should normally award a sum which takes into account a fair percentage of the profit.

(7) The size of the award should not in any event be so large that the development (or relevant part) would not have taken place had such a sum been payable.

(8) After arriving at a figure which takes into consideration all the above and any other relevant factors, the court needs to consider whether the 'deal feels right' [cf *Amec Developments Ltd v Jury's Hotel Management (UK) Ltd* [2001] 1 EGLR 81, 87].

It is unlikely that this guidance can be greatly improved upon. There will inevitably be an element of uncertainty in the quantification of this remedy.

Given that uncertainty is seen as inimical in the commercial field, a pressing question concerns the scope of the *Wrotham Park* measure of damages. Is it available for any breach of contract? The answer to this question is unclear. In a thorough analysis in *Vercoe v Rutland Fund Management*,[35] Sales J concluded that '[i]t seems natural that the law governing the extent of the remedies available in these different contexts should reflect the strength of the interest which the law recognises in each case as deserving protection'. This flexible approach might suggest that the *Wrotham Park* measure of damages will only be employed when the interest of the claimant is sufficiently important to deserve protection through such a remedy. This could correspond with Mance LJ's desire to achieve 'practical justice' in *Experience Hendrix*.[36] Yet it might be argued that whenever a defendant commits a breach of contract, he should have to pay the claimant the amount he would have had to pay had they entered into a bargain for the relaxation of the claimant's rights. It is just that in most cases, the amount the parties would agree upon—being reasonable parties prepared to make a bargain—is simply the claimant's loss. So, even the 'ordinary' compensatory principle might be an example of the hypothetical bargain measure, and in those circumstances the defendant's gain is not taken into account as all the claimant reasonably seeks is compensation for his loss. Even if this approach were to be accepted, however, it is important that it does not undermine the clear principles of compensation examined in Chapter 26.

4 Unjust enrichment on the ground of total failure of consideration

If a claimant has paid money over to the defendant and received nothing in return, or provided services for nothing in return, then the claimant may sue the defendant for restitution of the money paid or of the services rendered. It is crucial to appreciate that the claimant's cause of action to recover the enrichment of money or services conferred upon the defendant is not breach of contract. Instead, it is unjust enrichment. It is imperative that

---

[35] [2010] EWHC 424 (Ch) [343].
[36] See text at n 24.

'restitutionary damages' are distinguished from 'restitution to reverse an unjust enrichment'. The former rests upon a breach of contract. The latter does not.

Unjust enrichment is subsidiary to contract.[37] So, if a contract is still subsisting, then no cause of action in unjust enrichment should lie.[38] The contract must be discharged—either as a result of frustration, or through termination due to a breach of contract, or alternatively the contract might be void or not have been formed.[39] In those situations, it is said that the contract is no longer subsisting and therefore there is scope for unjust enrichment to operate. However, it is worth noting that this reasoning is open to criticism in the context of contracts terminated for breach. After all, even after a contract has been discharged for breach, the secondary obligation to pay damages remains. And it might be argued that this secondary obligation to pay damages should 'trump' any cause of action in unjust enrichment.[40]

There are many reasons why an enrichment might be considered to be 'unjust' such that a claim in unjust enrichment might succeed. For instance, the claimant might have transferred a benefit to a defendant by mistake or because of undue pressure from the defendant. However, the most important ground of restitution when analysing the remedies available in the present context is 'total failure of consideration'. Where a claimant transfers a benefit to a defendant on a consideration, or basis, which totally fails, then restitution for unjust enrichment is possible. It should be noted that the language of 'failure of consideration' in this context may be confusing. It is not consideration in the contractual sense examined in Chapter 7 that is meant here. Rather, consideration in the context of unjust enrichment means simply the 'basis' or **condition** on which the benefit was transferred. It is the failure of this basis that makes the retention of the benefit by the defendant unjust. As Viscount Simon LC remarked in *Fibrosa Spolka Ackyjna v Fairbairn Lawson Combe Barbour Ltd*, 'it is, generally speaking, not the promise which is referred to as the consideration, but the performance of the promise'.[41] It may be better to speak of 'failure of basis'; in *Crown Prosecution Services v Eastenders Group*,[42] Lord Toulson said that '[t]he attraction of "failure of basis" is that it is more apt, but "failure of consideration" is more familiar'. Given the prevalence of 'failure of consideration' in the cases, it is this term which will be used here.

So, when will the cause of action for total failure of consideration be advantageous when the claimant also has a remedy for breach of contract? The answer is: when the claimant has made a bad bargain. Suppose that the claimant contracts to buy from the defendant 1,000 melons for £1,000 and pays the money in advance. The market for melons then crashes, and the defendant would be able to buy the melons for £500 today. If the defendant refuses to deliver the melons, then the claimant would only be able to recover £500 as compensatory damages. But if the claimant sues for unjust enrichment, he will be able to recover the full £1,000, thereby escaping from a bad bargain. The £1,000 was transferred on the basis that

---

[37] For fuller consideration of this cause of action, see generally A Burrows, *The Law of Restitution* (3rd edn, OUP, 2011) and G Virgo, *Principles of the Law of Restitution* (3rd edn, OUP, 2015).

[38] *Pan Ocean Shipping Co Ltd v Creditcorp Ltd, The Trident Beauty* [1994] 1 WLR 161. Cf *Roxborough v Rothmans of Pall Mall Australia Ltd* [2001] HCA 68, 208 CLR 516.

[39] See eg *British Steel Corp v Cleveland Bridge & Engineering Co Ltd* [1984] 1 All ER 504.

[40] See eg *Taylor v Motability Finance Ltd* [2004] EWHC 2619 (Comm).

[41] [1943] AC 32, 48.

[42] [2014] UKSC 26, [2015] AC 1 [105].

the claimant would receive melons, but he has received none at all. Although this might be thought unduly generous to a claimant—after all, the claimant cannot sue for reliance loss if that would allow him to escape from a bad bargain—it might be argued that if the defendant refuses to perform any part of the contract at all, then he is simply not participating in the contract at all, so cannot rely upon contractual remedies. This might explain why it is so important that the consideration fail totally and not partially.[43]

It should, however, be noted that some benefits that the claimant receives from the defendant may be characterised as 'collateral' benefits, such that a cause of action for total failure of consideration may still succeed.[44] But more significantly, the court might apportion the consideration to find that the consideration has totally failed as regards some of the benefit supplied. For example, if the claimant has agreed to buy 1,000 melons for £1,000, and the defendant supplies 10 melons, then the court might avoid finding that the consideration has only partially failed—which would prevent any remedy in unjust enrichment— and instead apportion the consideration such that the consideration for each melon is £1. On that basis, the defendant has provided nothing in return for £990, and in respect of that sum of money the consideration has totally failed.

This reasoning was accepted by the Privy Council in *Goss v Chilcott*,[45] and applied by the English court in *DO Ferguson & Associates v M Sohl*.[46] In that case, Sohl contracted with Ferguson for Ferguson to carry out building works on Sohl's property for just over £32,000. Ferguson did not finish the work, and after receiving over £26,000 repudiated the contract. Sohl actually managed to finish the work himself for less than what he would have paid to Ferguson. As a result, Sohl suffered no loss, which meant that his contractual claim was worthless. Sohl therefore sought a remedy in unjust enrichment. Sohl argued that the value of Ferguson's work was only about £22,000, so there was a difference of over £4,000 between what Sohl had paid to Ferguson and the benefit Ferguson conferred on Sohl. Sohl therefore argued that he could recover this 'overpayment' since there had been a total failure of consideration as regards this £4,000. The Court of Appeal agreed. This is an extreme example of apportionment. Indeed, it appears that the court was apportioning the consideration very minutely, such that it does not appear that there is a significant difference from saying that the consideration only partially failed. Nevertheless, orthodoxy insists that a claimant can only recover in unjust enrichment if the consideration has totally failed.

5 Punitive damages

English law has traditionally set its face against awarding punitive damages (also known as exemplary damages) for breach of contract.[47] The only remedy for breach of contract was traditionally said to be compensation for loss. But the decision of the House of Lords

---

[43] Although this has been criticised: see eg *Giedo van der Garde BV v Force India Formula One Team Ltd (formerly Spyker F1 Team Ltd (England))* [2010] EWHC 2373 (QB) [367] (Stadlen J).

[44] See eg *Rowland v Divall* [1923] 2 KB 500.

[45] [1996] AC 788.

[46] (1992) 62 BLR 95.

[47] See eg *Addis v Gramophone Co Ltd* [1909] AC 488.

in *Attorney-General v Blake* clearly opens the door for courts to strip a defendant of gains made, and this is obviously a departure from the view that remedies should be restricted to compensation for loss. So, now that English law is not solely confined to compensation for loss, should it extend to awarding punitive damages against those who commit a breach of contract?

The issues here are finely balanced. Punitive damages are now available, in principle, for all torts, as a result of the decision of the House of Lords in *Kuddus v Chief Constable of Leicestershire Constabulary*.[48] If both torts and breaches of contract are considered to be civil law wrongs, there is some argument for consistency of treatment. Indeed, it does seem odd that punitive damages can be awarded for the tort of intentionally inducing a breach of contract, and yet not for the breach of contract itself.[49] In the leading tort case of *Rookes v Barnard*, Lord Devlin said that '[e]xemplary damages can properly be awarded whenever it is necessary to teach a wrongdoer that tort does not pay'.[50] The same might be true of a contract-breaker. Punitive damages should only ever be an exceptional remedy of last resort, but may be appropriate where compensatory or restitutionary remedies are considered to be insufficient to sanction the wrongdoer's conduct.

On the other hand, there is a strong view that punishment should be the exclusive domain of the criminal law, and that the civil law is neither well suited nor well equipped to punish defendants. Moreover, a breach of contract may generally be considered to be 'less serious' than the commission of a tort, since the contractual obligation only arises through the parties' consent rather than by imposition of the general law. Punitive damages may also deter 'efficient breach';[51] yet the same may be said of restitutionary damages, and this argument did not persuade the House of Lords to decide *Attorney-General v Blake* differently. Clearly, the introduction of punitive damages would introduce uncertainty into the law of contractual remedies: there would be uncertainty surrounding both *when* punitive damages should be awarded, and about *how much* should be awarded. Quantifying the punitive element of an award is very difficult indeed: how much punishment is required of a contract-breaker? In addition, it might be thought that if the defendant should be punished, why should that punishment not go to the state (as is the case with most fines imposed by the criminal law)? The answer to this last question is perhaps the easiest: it is important to provide the claimant with an incentive to bring a claim against wrongdoing defendants, and this might best be achieved by providing the incentive of a punitive award.

As Longmore LJ observed in *Devenish Nutrition Ltd v Sanofi-Aventis SA*, 'In the current state of the law, exemplary damages are not available for breach of contract even if a contract-breaker has made a similarly cynical calculation that it will benefit him more to break a contract than to perform it.'[52] But it is possible that English law will evolve in the light of *Blake* (and *Kuddus*) and recognise punitive damages in certain, limited situations. Indeed, the example in this regard has been set by the decision of the Supreme Court of

---

[48] [2001] UKHL 29, [2002] 2 AC 122.

[49] N McBride, 'A Case for Awarding Punitive Damages in Response to Deliberate Breaches of Contract' (1995) 24 Anglo-American Law Review 369.

[50] [1964] AC 1129, 1227.

[51] See Chapter 1, Section 6(c).

[52] [2008] EWCA Civ 1086 [143], citing *The Siboen and Sibotre* [1976] 1 Lloyd's Rep 293.

Canada in *Whiten v Pilot Insurance Co.*[53] The claimant's house had burned down, and the defendant insurers refused to pay out under her insurance policy. The insurers continued to insist that the claimant had committed arson, despite there being no evidence to support this accusation at all: the chief of the fire brigade and the insurers' own independent expert had told the insurers that the fire was not as a result of arson. Yet the insurers' continuing refusal, in bad faith, to pay out the insurance monies which were due made life tremendously difficult for the claimant and her family, who were not on a sound financial footing. The claimant had to spend around $320,000 on an insurance claim worth $345,000. The Supreme Court of Canada made the defendant pay $1 million as punitive damages. Given the outrageous conduct of the defendant insurers, this result seems appropriate. For it to be followed in this jurisdiction, English law would have to recognise the availability of punitive damages for breach of contract.

In any event, it is important to appreciate that although the decision of the House of Lords in *Blake* recognises that English law can disgorge a defendant of the gains he makes from a breach of contract, this is not usually considered to be a punitive measure. After all, stripping the defendant of gains made puts the defendant back to the position he was in had he not committed a breach of contract: he is in no worse a position (apart, perhaps, from a lost opportunity to do other things).[54] However, if the traitor George Blake had had to give up all his gains *and* pay an extra amount as punitive damages, then he would have been in a worse position than he was in prior to the breach and would have been punished. Restitutionary damages deter breach. Punitive damages punish the breach.

6 Nominal damages

Even if the claimant has suffered no loss, he might recover nominal damages for breach of contract. This is a sum—generally no greater than £5—which reflects the fact that the claimant's rights have been infringed. For this reason, it is often said that damages are available 'as of right' for breach of contract: any breach of contract entitles the innocent party to recover damages, even if such damages are only nominal damages. The utility of nominal damages, however, is minimal, since a claimant could just as well seek and obtain a declaration that the claimant's rights have been infringed.[55] Nominal damages are rarely awarded.

7 Specific performance

A decree of specific performance is an order by the court directing a party to a contract to carry it out. Specific performance is an equitable remedy. Since **equity** acts *in personam*,

---

[53] [2002] 1 SCR 595.

[54] This assumes that the defendant is stripped of his net profits only; effectively, the defendant should be granted an allowance to recognise the impact of his skill and effort in making the gains. This is well discussed in the more developed area of account of profits in equity: see PS Davies and G Virgo, *Equity & Trusts: Text, Cases, and Materials* (OUP, 2013) ch 14, section 5.

[55] See eg *Cullen v Chief Constable of the Royal Ulster Constabulary* [2003] UKHL 39, [2003] 1 WLR 1763 [81] (Lord Millett).

the order takes effect upon a particular party. If that party fails to comply with the order, he will be in contempt of court. This will expose the person to fines and even imprisonment. The sanctions for failing to comply with an order for specific performance are therefore much more onerous than those for breaches of contract. This is one reason why specific performance is often considered to be an exceptional remedy in contract law: a defendant who breaches a contract would generally expect simply to have to pay damages, whereas a person who fails to comply with an order for specific performance might end up in prison. Courts are cautious about elevating the seriousness of a breach of contract, although it should be remembered that a person will never be fined or imprisoned for a breach of contract, but only for the distinct wrong of failing to comply with a court order.

It has already been seen that courts of equity intervened only when the **common law** was considered to be inadequate in some way. As a result, it is generally recognised that specific performance is available only when damages are not an adequate remedy. Specific performance is therefore rarely available in a contract for the sale of generic goods. The injured seller can obviously be fully compensated by money, and so too may an injured buyer if he can buy similar goods elsewhere. On the other hand, the contract might be specifically enforceable if it was for the sale of some unique thing. Thus, contracts for the sale of land are generally specifically enforceable because each piece of land is unique,[56] and damages would not be able to provide the innocent party with that particular parcel of land. The scope of this approach to 'unique' goods is somewhat unclear beyond the context of land transactions. On the unusual facts of *Sky Petroleum Ltd v VIP Petroleum Ltd*,[57] even diesel and petrol were considered to be unique. This was because, at the time of the dispute, there was an oil crisis and supplies of petrol and diesel were scarce. The market was very volatile, and the court could not hope sensibly to assess what losses the claimant would suffer from not being supplied with petroleum: it was unlikely that the claimant would be able to source petroleum from elsewhere, and even if he could the market was fluctuating so significantly that quantifying the claimant's loss would be extremely difficult. Goulding J therefore effectively ordered specific performance.[58] It should be noted, however, that the *Sky Petroleum* case is something of an outlier, decided in very extreme circumstances. Subsequent courts have shown themselves to be very reluctant to grant specific performance to enforce contracts for the sale of goods. Although section 52 of the Sale of Goods Act 1979 provides that a court *may* grant specific performance where there is a 'contract to deliver specific or ascertained goods', this remains very much a discretionary remedy. And where the goods are neither specific nor ascertained, the courts are most unwilling to grant specific performance.[59]

In any event, the idea of 'adequacy of damages' is unclear and prone to be manipulated. For what purpose must damages be adequate? It is suggested that it would be better to focus on whether specific performance is an appropriate remedy in all the circumstances of the

---

[56] Although compare the unorthodox decision of the Supreme Court of Canada on this point: *Southcott Estates Inc v Toronto Catholic District School Board*, 2012 SCC 51, [2012] 2 SCR 675.

[57] [1974] 1 WLR 576.

[58] Strictly the judge ordered a mandatory injunction because specific performance cannot be ordered at the interim stage: see Section 8.

[59] See eg *Société des Industries Metallurgiques SA v Bronx Engineering Co Ltd* [1975] 1 Lloyd's Rep 465.

case. Indeed, as Lord Hodson put it in *Beswick v Beswick*, 'The only question is, "What is the appropriate remedy?" '[60] This appears to be supported by modern decisions which focus on a wide range of considerations rather than merely the adequacy of damages.[61]

Nevertheless, equitable remedies are clearly discretionary. A party injured by a breach of contract is entitled to damages as a matter of right, but the court will grant specific performance only if it considers it just and equitable to do so. The discretion is, however, exercised in accordance with principles, so the decision is not an arbitrary one. The court should take into account a variety of considerations, although the weight to be given to any particular factor will depend upon the facts of a given case. Some of the most important elements will now be discussed.

'Mutuality' is said to be a condition of specific performance. In equity, it is thought that if one party to a contract is entitled to performance, then so too should the other party.[62] The vendor of land may perhaps be adequately compensated by damages; but since the purchaser would be entitled to specific performance, the vendor is entitled to it as well. But the principle of mutuality has another, apparently inconsistent, aspect. If one party could not have specific performance, then, in equity, neither should the other party. As a result, a minor will not be granted specific performance even of a contract which is in its nature specifically enforceable, because specific performance could not be ordered against him.[63]

Equity will not, generally, grant equitable relief to a person who has acted badly, since 'he who comes to equity must come with clean hands'. Specific performance may therefore not be granted in favour of a person who has acted badly.[64] Similarly, equity will not grant relief if to do so would cause severe hardship. Thus in *Patel v Ali*,[65] specific performance of a contract for the purchase of a house was refused where this would have caused severe hardship to one of the vendors: since agreeing to the contract, the vendor had suffered from cancer and had to have a leg amputated, her husband had been sent to prison, and she had had two more children. Forcing her to sell her house would have caused her significant hardship, particularly since she relied heavily on the help of her neighbours. The court therefore refused to grant specific performance, even though the hardship had not been caused by the claimant.

Contracts for personal services are also not, generally speaking, specifically enforceable. In *De Francesco v Barnum*, Fry LJ insisted that 'the Courts are bound to be jealous, lest they should turn contracts of service into contracts of slavery'.[66] The courts should clearly not force a person to work where that would be tantamount to slavery. Indeed, this has now been prohibited by statute in the context of contracts of employment.[67] However, where there still exists a relationship of trust and confidence between the employer and employee even after the breach of contract, the court may grant an order of specific performance

---

[60] [1968] AC 58, 78; see too at 88 (Lord Pearce). For further discussion of this case, see Chapter 10, Section 6(a).
[61] See eg *Rainbow Estates v Tokenhold* [1999] Ch 64.
[62] *Price v Strange* [1978] Ch 337.
[63] See Chapter 20, Section 1(a).
[64] *Shell UK Ltd v Lostock Garages Ltd* [1976] 1 WLR 1187. Other general bars to equitable relief may also apply, such as acquiescence and lapse of time.
[65] [1984] Ch 283.
[66] (1890) 45 ChD 430, 438.
[67] Trade Union and Labour Relations (Consolidation) Act 1992, s 236.

against the employer.[68] Given that many parties to contracts are large commercial entities, it might be expected that courts would now be more willing to grant specific enforcement since an order against a company does not run the risk of leading any individual to slavery—the employees of the company will simply do the work they are told to do by the company (which would be the subject of the order)—but even in this context the court seems reluctant to order specific performance.[69]

It has also been said that specific performance will not be granted if the order would require the constant supervision of the court.[70] This appears to be supported by the decision of the House of Lords in *Co-op Insurance Society Ltd v Argyll Stores Ltd*,[71] which is now the leading decision on specific performance. Hillsborough Shopping Centre (owned by the claimants) consisted of about 25 shops, of which Safeway (a supermarket owned by the defendants) was the 'magnet store'. It was crucial to the success of the shopping centre that the supermarket was a **tenant**, since shoppers who visited the shopping centre in order to go to the supermarket would necessarily go past other shops and that would have a beneficial effect on footfall. Unfortunately, the supermarket was not profitable and was making substantial losses. In 1995, the defendants decided to close the store. This was a breach of contract: the **lease**, which was entered into in 1979, included a covenant that the defendants would keep open a supermarket until 2014. The claimants sought specific enforcement of this term of the lease.

Leading up to the *Argyll Stores* case, there appeared to be a greater willingness to grant specific performance than had previously been shown by older decisions. Indeed, the majority of the Court of Appeal in *Argyll Stores* itself granted specific performance of the covenant in the lease, concluding that damages would not be an adequate remedy. This was partly because the departure of the defendants would have a serious effect on the claimant's other tenants of neighbouring shops. Moreover, the defendants' breach was cynical and equitable relief seemed to be appropriate. There is much to be said in favour of this view: it would be very difficult to calculate the loss the claimant might suffer as a result of the loss of visitors to the shopping centre more generally, but given the fact that the supermarket was the 'magnet store' designed to attract visitors, it might be expected that the losses would be substantial. Specific performance might therefore be considered to be appropriate.[72]

Nevertheless, the House of Lords overturned the decision of the Court of Appeal and refused to grant specific performance. This puts a significant brake on the previous expansion of specific performance and, in practice, restricts the award of such equitable relief in the medium term at least. Lord Hoffmann, giving the only reasoned judgment, highlighted that it is settled law that an order requiring the carrying on of a business will not be made. The traditional reason for this is that the enforcement of the order would require the constant supervision of the court, which is impracticable. The powerful weapon of contempt

---

[68] See eg *Hill v CA Parsons & Co* [1972] Ch 305; *Irani v Southampton and South West Hampshire Health Authority* [1985] ICR 590.

[69] See *The Scaptrade*, discussed at Section 8(a).

[70] *Ryan v Mutual Tontine Westminster Chambers Association* [1893] 1 Ch 116.

[71] [1998] AC 1, HL.

[72] Indeed this result was reached on essentially identical facts by the Scottish courts: *Highland & Universal Properties Ltd v Safeway Properties Ltd (No 2)*, 2000 SC 297, 2000 SLT 414.

of court is an unsuitable instrument for overseeing the carrying on of a business and there would be the possibility of repeated applications which would be costly to the parties and the judicial system. Lord Hoffmann suggested that there is a difference, however, between orders to carry on an activity, which will usually not be made, and orders to achieve a result, which may well be.

There is no doubt that the speech of Lord Hoffmann is very influential and has been followed. However, the problems of supervising the implementation of an equitable order should not be over-exaggerated. In the vast majority of cases, there will be no problem at all: a party will simply comply with the order, or bargain around it, since that party will not want to be in contempt of court. For similar reasons, a small degree of imprecision in the order made is unlikely to be fatal. As a result, even after the *Argyll Stores* case, some courts have shown themselves willing to grant specific performance where some degree of supervision or imprecision must be tolerated.[73]

Lord Hoffmann was also concerned that the loss which the defendant may suffer by running a business at a loss for a long time may be far greater than the loss which the claimant will suffer from the breach, for which he may recover damages. This argument rests upon ideas of 'economic efficiency',[74] as does the idea that the granting of an equitable order will allow the claimant to hold the defendant to ransom. For example, had specific performance been granted in the *Argyll Stores* case, then the claimants would have been entitled to demand any price they wished from the defendant in order to agree to relax the equitable order. Yet this does not necessarily seem inappropriate: the defendant had made a promise, and was simply being held to his promise. It is difficult to accept that this would be a punitive measure.

Nevertheless, it is suggested that it is right that specific performance only be granted in exceptional circumstances. This is because of the restrictions specific performance place on a party's liberty.[75] Whereas there are many things a party can do to pay damages—the money paid can come from anywhere—and his freedom of action is therefore largely preserved, if an order for specific performance is granted then that person's freedom of action is very much restricted to having to perform that specified task. Where there is a choice between a remedy which preserves a person's liberty and another which does not, the former should be preferred. This also explains why the order for specific performance needs to be drafted with sufficient certainty.

(a) Contracts with consumers

The general law on specific performance has, however, now been altered as regards consumer contracts[76] by the Consumer Rights Act 2015. A consumer has the right to enforce a term of the contract that the goods be of satisfactory quality, fit for a particular purpose, as described, and match a sample, for example.[77] We have already seen that breaches of such

---

[73] *Rainbow Estates v Tokenhold* [1999] Ch 64.
[74] See Chapter 1, Section 6(c).
[75] D Kimel, *From Promise to Contract* (Hart, 2003) 95–103.
[76] See Chapter 15, Section 4(a).
[77] Consumer Rights Act 2015, s 19.

terms give the consumer the right to reject,[78] and that a consumer can also ask for repair or replacement,[79] which may enforce the contract more effectively.[80] Similarly, under contracts for the provision of services, a consumer has a right of 'repeat performance' within a reasonable period of time.[81] This is potentially a very generous right, as it might allow consumers to obtain, in effect, specific performance more readily. Indeed, the general scheme of the Consumer Rights Act 2015 places the right to repeat performance as the primary remedy, and other remedies (such as a price reduction) as secondary. Moreover, it might appear at first that the only restriction on the consumer's right to repeat performance arises where such repeat performance is impossible.[82] This is obviously a very high threshold. However, it should also be noted that the 2015 Act grants the court the power to order specific performance[83] even where the consumer claims to exercise another right, and vice versa,[84] which perhaps allows the court a certain amount of discretion to refuse to order repeat performance where this would be wholly unreasonable, for example.[85] Specific relief may be granted by the court 'unconditionally or on such terms and conditions as to damages, payment of the price and otherwise as it thinks just'.[86]

8 Injunction

Injunctions are another equitable remedy that may be awarded when damages are an inadequate remedy. Injunctions may usefully be considered in two separate categories: prohibitory injunctions and mandatory injunctions. An injunction which prevents a person from doing something is known as a 'prohibitory injunction'. An injunction which obliges a person to do something is known as a 'mandatory injunction'. The former is negative in effect, the latter positive. Mandatory injunctions raise the same issues as specific performance, considered in Section 7 of this chapter, and need not be discussed further here. However, it should be noted that specific performance cannot be awarded at the interim stage (pending a full trial). This explains why the remedy granted in the *Sky Petroleum* case was actually a mandatory injunction rather than specific performance. There are no significant differences in the principles to be applied to mandatory injunctions and specific performance.

---

[78] See Chapter 24, Section 6.

[79] s 23. A similar provision applies to contracts for digital content: see s 43.

[80] However, a consumer cannot ask for repair or replacement if that is impossible (s 23(3)(a)) and he cannot insist on one of those remedies if it is disproportionate compared to the other (s 23(4)). The consumer must also give the trader a reasonable time to repair or replace, provided that would not cause significant inconvenience to the consumer: s 23(6)–(7).

[81] s 55.

[82] s 55(3).

[83] s 58(2).

[84] s 58(3) and (4).

[85] Otherwise, it is suggested that the result of *Ruxley Electronics and Construction Ltd v Forsyth* [1995] 3 All ER 268, HL, discussed in Chapter 26, Sections 4 and 5, may well be different, since the consumer (Mr Forsyth) could have the right to repeat performance.

[86] s 58(7).

(a) **Prohibitory injunctions**

In *Doherty v Allman*, Lord Cairns LC said:[87]

> If parties, for valuable consideration, with their eyes open, contract that a particular thing shall not be done, all that a Court of Equity has to do is to say, by way of injunction, that which the parties have already said by way of covenant, that the thing shall not be done; and in such case the injunction does nothing more than give the sanction of the process of the Court to that which already is the contract between the parties.

Prohibitory injunctions are not uncommon. For example, they are often awarded to enforce restrictive covenants against departing employees such that they cannot work for a competitor for a specified period.[88] However, the award of even a prohibitory injunction is always discretionary and never automatic.[89] It is therefore important to consider further the principles that guide the exercise of the court's discretion.

One particularly controversial issue concerns the granting of equitable relief in the context of contracts for services. This is because restraining a party from committing a breach of contract might have the practical effect of forcing that party to perform the contract. Yet in *Lumley v Wager*, Lord St Leonards LC said 'I disclaim doing indirectly what I cannot do directly'.[90] In that case, Johanna Wagner, an opera singer, had agreed with Mr Lumley not to sing at any theatre other than his without written permission, and this term was enforced by the court via an injunction. It is notable that the contract was of very short duration (only three months) and Miss Wagner was therefore not prevented from plying her trade for very long. More onerous was the decision in *Warner Bros Pictures Inc v Nelson*,[91] in which Branson J restrained the film star Bette Davis from making movies for anyone other than Warner Brothers for three years. It was perhaps unrealistic to expect Bette Davis to do anything other than work as an actress for Warner Brothers following that ruling.

There appeared to be some retreat from injunctive relief in *Page One Records Ltd v Britton*,[92] where Stamp J was not prepared to prevent the pop group 'The Troggs' from hiring another manager as he did not wish to force unwilling persons to have to work with another. However, injunctive relief clearly remains available to prevent a breach of contract, and was given something of a boost by the important decision of the Court of Appeal in *LauritzenCool AB v Lady Navigation Inc*.[93]

LauritzenCool concerned a time **charter**. The claimants managed two of the defendants' vessels as part of a shipping pool. The defendants sought to use their vessels outside the pool, but were restrained from doing so by a prohibitory injunction. The Court of Appeal accepted that the practical effect of this would be that the defendants would continue to provide the vessels to the pool and perform the charter.[94] A time charter is a contract for

---

[87] (1878) 3 App Cas 709, 720.

[88] See eg H Beale (ed), *Chitty on Contracts* (31st edn, Sweet & Maxwell, 2012) para 27-069.

[89] cf *Redland Bricks v Morris* [1970] AC 652 (Lord Upjohn).

[90] (1852) 1 De GM & G 604, 620.

[91] [1937] 1 KB 209.

[92] [1968] 1 WLR 157. Similar reasoning was employed in *Warren v Mendy* [1989] 1 WLR 853.

[93] [2005] EWCA Civ 579, [2005] 1 WLR 3686.

[94] Mance LJ (ibid [7]) accepted that there was 'no realistic alternative'.

services, but Mance LJ emphasised that there is no firm rule that an injunction cannot be granted where the contract is for services; injunctive relief remains a matter for the court's discretion.

The result in *LauritzenCool* is sensible: the vessels, as commercially valuable assets, were clearly going to be employed in some form, and whether they were hired out by the claimants or by another party did not affect any particular individual. There was therefore no 'human necessity' in the case,[95] so there was no fear of forcing an individual to perform work in anything resembling a modern form of slavery.[96] Indeed, on the facts of *LauritzenCool*, the claimants and defendants had managed to maintain a workable professional relationship,[97] and it was highly unlikely that the parties would be unable to make their contractual agreement function pursuant to the injunction. This will often be the case in the commercial environment: commercial parties tend to be able to manage difficult relationships, and it is unrealistic to suppose that they will deliberately fail to comply with equitable orders.

Mance LJ in *LauritzenCool* cited the pertinent comments of Ackner LJ in *Regent International Hotels (UK) Ltd v Pageguide Ltd*:[98]

> this action raises the further serious question, as yet unresolved by English authority, as to the extent to which a commercial arrangement of this kind between two independent companies, which does not provide for the employment of any named individuals and is part of a larger package ... can be properly treated as analogous to a contract of personal service.

The distinction between contracts where a particular individual is named as being bound to perform, and contracts between corporate entities who promise to ensure a service is provided, is significant. In the latter situation, no individual is forced to work against his will. For example, if Company *A* contracts with Company *B* to provide a venue and staff for an event, it is not unreasonable to assume that the staff of Company *A* would be happy (and possibly contractually bound) to work regardless of whether the event is for Company *B* or Company *Z*.

This issue remains important. In *Société Générale v Geys*, Lord Wilson noted that '[t]he big question whether nowadays the more impersonal, less hierarchical, relationship of many employers with their employees requires review of the usual unavailability of specific performance has been raised ... but is beyond the scope of this appeal.'[99] It is suggested that the thrust of the reasoning in *LauritzenCool* should be exploited such that, where damages would be an inadequate remedy, injunctions should be granted even in the context of services.[100] After all, injunctive relief has been granted to enforce contracts of personal service in some instances.

---

[95] cf *Warren v Mendy* [1989] 1 WLR 853, cited at [22] (Mance LJ).

[96] See eg R Stevens, 'Involuntary Servitude by Injunction' (1921) 6 Cornell Law Review 235.

[97] The trial judge was confident that this could be maintained even though 'the parties, in the course of their dispute, have been abusive about one another': [2004] EWHC 2607 (Comm), [2005] 1 All ER (Comm) 77 [26] (Cooke J).

[98] The Times, 13 May 1985.

[99] [2012] UKSC 63, [2013] 1 AC 523 [77].

[100] Compare the opening sentence of *Warren v Mendy* [1989] 1 WLR 853, 857 (Nourse LJ): 'It is well settled that an injunction to restrain a breach of contract for personal services ought not to be granted where its effect will be to decree performance of the contract.'

Nevertheless, in some situations the overall exercise of the court's discretion might lead to a refusal to grant equitable relief, even though damages may seem to be inadequate. This is most likely to be the case where "'the services are so linked to some special skill or talent whose continued display is essential to the psychological material or physical well being of the servant" so as to make negative injunctions restraining breach of the contracts of service impossible'.[101] Yet even here it is important to remember that injunctions may still be awarded where the 'servant' is only restrained from acting over a short period. Thus in *Araci v Fallon*[102] the Court of Appeal overturned the decision of the trial judge and granted an injunction to prevent the champion jockey Keiren Fallon from riding another's horse in breach of his contract with the claimant, even though this had the effect of preventing Fallon from riding in the Derby. Although a very prestigious event, Fallon was only prevented from competing on that one day. The result may have been different if the period of time during which Fallon could not exercise his trade had been one year and Fallon's skills could have gone stale.

It appears that the courts now consider whether or not there has been a loss of confidence between the parties such that, if an injunction were granted and the practical effect would be that the parties had to work together, that relationship would be impossible. This approach is preferable to a blanket rule[103] that injunctions will not be granted where contracts for services are concerned.[104] Courts should be sceptical about arguments that commercial actors will be unable to make a relationship work, and therefore more willing to grant injunctions.[105] It is generally only where close cooperation and trust between the parties is required that the balance will be tipped in favour of refusing injunctive relief.[106]

LauritzenCool is an important decision that indicates greater scope for injunctive relief where contracts for services are concerned. But the result was not obvious. The defendants relied upon the decision of the House of Lords in *The Scaptrade*.[107] In that case, Lord Diplock held that:[108]

> To grant an injunction restraining the ship owner from exercising his right of withdrawal of the vessel from the service of the charterer, though negative in form, is pregnant with an affirmative order to the shipowner to perform the contract; juristically it is indistinguishable from a decree for specific performance of a contract to render services; and in respect of that category of contracts, even in the event of breach, this is a remedy that English courts have always disclaimed jurisdiction to grant.

---

[101] *Isabella Shipowner SA v Shagang Shipping Co Ltd (The Aquafaith)* [2012] EWHC 1077 (Comm), [2012] 2 All ER (Comm) 461 [38] (Cooke J), citing the first instance decision in *LauritzenCool* [2004] EWHC 2607 (Comm), [2005] 1 All ER (Comm) 77 [27] (Cooke J).

[102] [2011] EWCA Civ 668.

[103] The idea that there was a 'jurisdictional bar' where contracts for services are concerned was again rejected in *Akai Holdings Ltd v RSM Robson Rhodes LLP* [2007] EWHC 1641 (Ch) [39] (Briggs J).

[104] *Ferrara Quay Ltd v Carillion Construction Ltd* [2009] BLR 367 [74]–[77]; *Vertex Data Science Ltd v Powergen Retail Ltd* [2006] EWHC 1340 (Comm), [2006] 2 Lloyd's Rep 591.

[105] Especially since the parties may bargain for the relaxation of an injunction if necessary: cf Section 3.

[106] A recent example is *Ashworth v Royal National Theatre*, which concerned the production of the play, 'War Horse', and an injunction sought by musicians: [2014] EWHC 1176 (QB), [2014] 4 All ER 238 [23]–[25] (Cranston J).

[107] [1983] 2 AC 694.

[108] Ibid, 701.

In *The Scaptrade*, equitable relief to restrain a party from exercising its contractual right of withdrawal was refused. It was distinguished in *LauritzenCool* on the facts: *The Scaptrade* did not consider the question of whether a party could be restrained from employing its vessel outside the charter. Nevertheless, there seems to be a tension between the two judgments. It is suggested that the House of Lords' insistence that contracts of services cannot be specifically performed is outdated and should be jettisoned; the fact that a contract is for personal services is simply another factor that informs the exercise of the court's discretion.[109] The approach in *LauritzenCool* should be preferred to that of *The Scaptrade*.[110]

(i) The relevance of limitation clauses

The recent decision in *AB v CD*[111] might also confirm a greater willingness to award injunctions than may previously have been supposed. The parties entered into a licensing agreement, under which *AB* obtained the right to market *CD*'s internet-based platform. A clause in the contract purported to exclude liability for loss of profits in the event of a breach, or of any cause of action, and also to cap the recoverable damages under any head of claim according to a prescribed formula. *AB* sought an **interim** injunction[112] to require *CD* not to terminate the agreement. At first instance, the judge refused to grant an injunction as he considered that *AB* would be adequately compensated by damages.[113] A unanimous Court of Appeal allowed *AB*'s appeal, insisting that the clause in the contract should be taken into account when deciding whether or not the remedies which would be available at common law were adequate to reflect the substantial justice of the situation.[114] This was consistent with previous guidance from the Court of Appeal[115] and was thought to be right in principle. As Underhill LJ put it:[116]

> The primary obligation of a party is to perform the contract. The requirement to pay damages in the event of a breach is a secondary obligation, and an agreement to restrict the recoverability of damages in the event of a breach cannot be treated as an agreement to excuse performance of that primary obligation.
>
> …
>
> The primary commercial expectation must be that the parties will perform their obligations. The expectations created (indeed given contractual force) by an exclusion or limitation clause are expectations about what damages will be recoverable in the event of breach; but that is not the same thing.

---

[109] I Spry, *Equitable Remedies* (9th edn, Sweet & Maxwell, 2013) 70.

[110] See too *Sunrise Brokers LLP v Rodgers* [2014] EWCA Civ 1373, [2015] ICR 272 [59] (Longmore LJ).

[111] [2014] EWCA Civ 229, [2015] 1 WLR 771.

[112] The thrust of the reasoning seems equally applicable to final injunctions: see eg [2014] EWCA Civ 229, [2015] 1 WLR 771 [32] (Ryder LJ).

[113] [2014] EWHC 1 (QB) (Stuart-Smith J).

[114] [2014] EWCA Civ 229, [2015] 1 WLR 771 [27]. See too P Turner, 'Inadequacy in Equity of Common Law Relief: The Relevance of Contractual Terms' (2014) 73 CLJ 493, 495–6.

[115] *Bath and North East Somerset District Council v Mowlem Plc* [2004] EWCA Civ 115, [2015] 1 WLR 785.

[116] [2014] EWCA Civ 229, [2015] 1 WLR 771 [27]–[28].

The logic of this reasoning is clear. Contracts should be performed, and clauses which limit the amount of damages payable do not undermine this point: such clauses restrict the secondary obligation to pay damages in the event of breach, but not the primary obligation to perform. Injunctive relief therefore remains available, and the court is entitled to consider wider losses which would be irrecoverable if an injunction were not granted. The court clearly did not think that such a result was 'uncommercial'. The decision does perhaps make it more difficult for a draftsman to know whether including a limitation clause in a contract would make injunctive relief more likely,[117] but this does not undermine the reasoning in *AB v CD*. Indeed, Underhill LJ was clear that even if it is established that damages are inadequate—perhaps in part because of a limitation clause—that 'only opens the door to the exercise of the court's discretion'.[118] It will still need to be established what the parties' liabilities would have been in the absence of a limitation clause, for example. Although parties cannot bind the courts to grant an injunction through their contractual arrangements,[119] *AB v CD* usefully highlights that equitable relief cannot easily be sidelined by a term in the contract. Injunction remains an important remedy in commercial disputes.

9 Damages in lieu of an injunction

Damages in lieu of an injunction can be awarded under Lord Cairns' Act.[120] They are quantified on the same basis as at common law.[121] The hypothetical bargain measure of damages is generally applied. Indeed, *Wrotham Park* itself was a case where damages were awarded in lieu of a mandatory injunction to demolish the properties which had been built in breach of the restrictive covenant. Importantly, because the remedy is awarded in lieu of an injunction, the cause of action does not yet have to have accrued; unlike at common law, damages in lieu of an injunction can be awarded for an anticipated wrong which has not yet happened.[122]

Further Reading

E McKendrick, 'Breach of Contract, Restitution for Wrongs and Punishment' in A Burrows and E Peel (eds), *Commercial Remedies* (OUP, 2003).

Analyses *Blake* and emphasises the exceptional nature of the remedy, whilst also arguing that punitive damages should be available for breach of contract in exceptional cases.

D Kimel, *From Promise to Contract: Towards a Liberal Theory of Contract* (Hart, 2003) 95–109.

Argues that coercive equitable orders should not be preferred to damages because they intrude upon the defendant's liberty of action to a much greater extent.

---

[117] See eg ibid, [33] (Laws LJ).
[118] Ibid, [30].
[119] *Warner Brothers Pictures, Inc v Nelson* [1937] 1 KB 209, 221 (Branson J).
[120] See now Senior Courts Act 1981, s 50.
[121] *Johnson v Agnew* [1980] AC 367, 400, HL.
[122] *Jaggard v Sawyer* [1995] 1 WLR 269, CA.

R Cunnington, 'Should Punitive Damages be Part of the Judicial Arsenal in Contract Cases?' (2006) 26 Legal Studies 369.

Argues that punitive damages should be available in order to deter outrageous breaches of contract.

A Burrows, 'Are "Damages on the *Wrotham Park* Basis" Compensatory, Restitutionary or Neither?' in R Cunnington and D Saidov (eds), *Contract Damages: Domestic and International Perspectives* (Hart, 2008).

Clear examination of whether the hypothetical bargain measure of damages is best understood as compensatory, restitutionary, or as a substitute for the right infringed.

? Question

Field Lane is a stadium that is normally used by Race Rovers FC to play football. However, the owner of the stadium, Fleetway plc, enters into a contract with Blackford RFC to play rugby at the stadium every summer for the next five years. Blackford RFC agrees to lay a new pitch at the stadium at the end of the five-year contract. Blackford RFC also agrees not to sell any stories about Race Rovers FC or Fleetway plc to any national newspaper.

At the end of the contract period, Blackford RFC refuses to lay a new pitch. This would cost £100,000 to do. Fleetway plc is currently in negotiations to sell the stadium, and with a new pitch Fleetway plc would be able to sell the stadium for £20,000 more than it can achieve with the old pitch still in place. Furthermore, Blackford RFC has started negotiations with a tabloid newspaper to divulge various stories about its time as a tenant of Field Lane.

Advise Fleetway plc.

Glossary

Ab initio 'from the beginning'.

Administrator/administratrix a court-appointed personal representative who manages a deceased's estate. To be distinguished from an **executor/executrix** who is chosen by the deceased to manage his estate. Administrator may refer to a male or female, whereas an administratrix is always female.

A fortiori 'all the more so', or 'for even greater reason'."

Ancillary orders/relief an order subsidiary to and supportive of a primary order. For example, a primary order may declare that a defendant owes a claimant a debt. An ancillary order may require a portion of the defendant's income to be paid directly to the claimant each month to satisfy that debt.

Appellate court any court hearing a claim, other than the first court that hears the claim. For example, if a contractual claim is brought in the High Court, then heard in the Court of Appeal, and then heard in the Supreme Court, the Court of Appeal and Supreme Court are the appellate courts.

Arrears money that is owed which should have already been paid. For example, we might say a **tenant** was in arrears with payment if, in March, he had not paid rent due in January and February.

Assignment/assign the transfer of a contractual right from one party to another. The party the contractual right is assigned *from* is referred to as the assignor, whilst the party the right is assigned *to* is referred to as the assignee.

At will as one wishes, or thinks fit. For example, a tenancy at will is a tenancy determinable by the landlord as he thinks fit.

Bailee (for reward) a party who takes goods into his custody, in return for a fee. For example, a warehouse-man who stores goods for a payment.

Bailee (gratuitous) a party who takes goods into his custody, for free. For example, an attendant of a free cloakroom in a restaurant who stores customers' coats.

Bailment a relationship where one party (the **bailee**) takes the goods of another (the **bailor**) into his custody. The relationship imposes certain obligations upon the bailee.

Bailor a party who transfers personal property to a **bailee** in a relationship of **bailment**.

Bankruptcy/bankrupt a status of an individual, where the individual's assets are managed by someone else. A person usually enters bankruptcy when his debts exceed the value of his assets. Bankruptcy is a form of **insolvency** that is inapplicable to companies.

Bill of lading a document used in shipping, generally issued by a carrier to a shipper. A bill of lading may contain or evidence the parties' contractual agreement under a contract of carriage, and it may be used as evidence that goods have been shipped. **Title** to goods may be transferred when the goods are at sea by transferring the bill of lading.

Bill of lading (claused) a bill of lading indicating that goods were shipped other than in good condition.

Bill of lading (clean) a bill of lading indicating that goods were shipped in good condition.

Bona fide purchaser a buyer of property who acts in good faith. Used in particular to indicate that a buyer did not know that the seller was not the true owner of the goods.

Broker a party who negotiates a contract between two other parties for a commission. For example, an insurance broker will negotiate with an insurer, and with the insured, in order to form a contract between the insurer and the insured.

Calls an option to buy some asset at a particular time and price. The buyer is under no obligation to exercise the option, but if he does the seller is under an obligation to sell.

Calls (on shares) a company usually issues **shares** for a price. It may be that the price for the issue of a particular share is not entirely paid. Such shares are called unpaid shares. The company may issue a 'call' for the unpaid amount, payable by the current holder of the share.

Caveat emptor Latin for 'buyer beware'. Refers to the idea that sellers, generally, need not inform the buyer of defects in the subject matter of a sale. It is the responsibility of the buyer to check the goods he is buying.

Charge a security interest over property. A lender can take a charge over the borrower's property in order to secure a debt; this does not give the lender ownership rights, but does give the lender a proprietary interest in the property such that he can sell the property if the borrower defaults. A common example is a **mortgage**.

Charter shortened version of charterparty.

Charterparty a contract for the hire of a ship.

Chattel tangible property that is not real property (in other words, property that is not related to land).

Chose (in action) this can be translated as 'thing in action'. It is an intangible right which is essentially a right to sue.

Common law (as distinct from equity) the system of judge-made law historically applied by the common law courts, as opposed to equity which was the system of judge-made law historically applied by the courts of Chancery. Equity often appears to 'soften' the common law, and where there is a conflict between equity and the common law, equity should prevail. Both common law (in this sense) and equity fall under the umbrella of common law (in the sense given next).

Common law (as distinct from statute) Judge-made law, as opposed to statutory provisions.

Composition a contract made between an insolvent party and its creditors, under which the creditors accept less than the full amounts they are owed in satisfaction for the whole debt.

Condition (as a particular fact) a particular fact upon which the due performance of a contractual obligation depends. For example, if a contractual obligation must be performed if it rains tomorrow, the fact of its raining tomorrow is referred to as a condition.

Condition (as contractual term) any term forming part of a contract.

Condition (as describing a term) a subset of contractual terms; the breach of a condition gives the innocent party the power to terminate the contract. To be distinguished from warranties and innominate terms.

Consensus ad idem this can be translated as 'agreement to the same thing', but is often used as synonymous with the expression 'meeting of the minds'. It refers to the reaching of an agreement, and in particular to the acceptance *matching* the offer.

Consideration of marriage (also marriage consideration) an undertaking to marry another person. It is effectively consideration in the form of marriage.

Consignee the party set to receive goods under a contract of carriage.

Consignor the party dispatching goods under a contract of carriage.

Conversion a tort committed through infringements of another party's property rights in goods. Examples include selling, buying, and destroying the goods of another person.

Covenant (as contractual term) a contractual obligation contained in a deed.

Covenant (as deed) another word for a deed.

Covenant (as proprietary right) an obligation that attaches to land and can bind future holders of the land, notwithstanding an absence of privity of contract. For example, a covenant limiting the building of structures above three storeys on a parcel of land will generally bind future owners of the land.

Creditor the party to whom a monetary sum is owed.

Debtor the party who owes a monetary sum.

Deceit a tort where a party knowingly or recklessly makes a false statement to another party, causing that other party harm. A fraudulent misrepresentation can lead to a claim in deceit.

Demurrage a fee to be paid if a ship is delayed.

Dicta/dictum a shortening of *obiter dicta/dictum*.

Dishonoured cheque a cheque that is not paid upon when handed to the payor's bank, usually because the payor has insufficient funds in his account.

Disposition the process of transferring a right.

Dividend money paid by a company to its shareholders, as an aspect of their entitlements as shareholders.

Easement a proprietary right to use land belonging to another person. Examples include a right of way, a right of support, and a right to run water.

Encumbrance A proprietary right which is attached to land belonging to another and may make the land less valuable. Includes leases, easements, and charges.

Equity the system of judge-made law that was originally enforceable in the courts of Chancery. All courts can now award equitable remedies and recognise equitable rights. To be distinguished from the system of judge-made law known as the common law.

Estoppel/estop estoppel in its simplest and most common form arises where one person (the representor) makes a statement of fact to another (the representee) in reliance on which the representee reasonably supposes he is intended to, and does, act to his detriment. In any litigation which later takes place between them, the representor will not be allowed to say that his representation was untrue, even if it is certain that it was in fact untrue. In other words, the representor will be estopped from going back on his representation.

Execute/executory to effect, or to make legally binding. An executory contract is one which has not yet been fully performed. An executed contract is one which has been fully performed.

Executor/executrix A person appointed by a testator to execute, or carry out, the testator's will. An executor is male, and executrix female.

Ex hypothesi 'by hypothesis' or 'as a consequence of assumptions made'.

Fiduciary a position held by a party, who is in a relationship with a principal. The fiduciary must act in the best interests of the principal, and the fiduciary must not profit from his position or allow his own interests to conflict with his principal's interests. Examples of fiduciary relationships include solicitor–client, agent–client, and trustee–beneficiary.

Forbearance/forbear the (non-)action of a party who has a legal claim, and does not exercise his claim.

Forfeiture/forfeit a process under which a party must give up some benefit. For example, the buyer of goods may forfeit any deposit already paid if he refuses to complete the contract.

Freehold another word for the fee simple, a property right in land, which exists for an indeterminate period of time. Colloquially, the freeholder would often be called the owner.

Fusion the effect of the Judicature Acts 1873 and 1875, which led to the systems of common law and equity both being administered in the same courts, rather than in the separate common law courts and court of Chancery. The 'fusion' effected by these Acts was purely procedural. There is a debate about whether there should also be fusion of the substantive common law and equity.

Gift the voluntary giving of a benefit to another party without receiving any consideration in return.

Hire-purchase a type of contract under which a party receives a right to use goods for a period, with either an obligation or power to purchase the goods at the end of that period. Commonly used for cars and expensive equipment.

Injunction a court order requiring a party to comply with an obligation.

Innominate term a type of contractual term, the breach of which may entitle the innocent party to terminate the contract, depending on the nature and effect of the breach. If the breach is sufficiently serious to deprive the non-breaching party of substantially the whole benefit under the contract, then the innocent party can terminate the contract. Innominate terms can be contrasted with conditions (as contract terms), and warranties.

Insolvency/insolvent an umbrella term covering the processes of bankruptcy, liquidation, and administration. The common theme to the processes is that a party's assets are put under the management of another

party. The processes are usually entered into when the party's debts exceed its assets.

Interim or interlocutory the description of an order or judgment which is given at an intermediate stage pending final trial. It is now more common to use the language of 'interim' rather than 'interlocutory', but both terms mean the same thing.

Landlord the party who grants a lease to a lessee or tenant.

Lease a right to exclusive possession of land for a defined period of time. A lease can have both proprietary and contractual consequences.

Leasehold the right to an estate in land held by lease.

Lessee the party who receives a lease granted by a landlord. An alternative term for a lessee is tenant.

Lessor the party who grants a lease; a landlord.

Licence a liberty or permission to do something. A licence to enter land is not a property right.

Licensee a party who holds a licence.

Licensor a party who grants a licence.

Lien a type of security interest, similar to a mortgage.

Liquidation a process under the umbrella of insolvency. The process involves the winding-up of a company and a redistribution of its assets. The process is managed by a liquidator.

Liquidated damages damages of a fixed amount set by the parties. Unliquidated damages are assessed by the court.

Mortgage a type of contract under which a lender advances a sum of money in return for a security right over land.

Mortgagee the party who lends money on the security of a mortgage. Banks are commonly mortgagees.

Mortgagor the party who receives money in return for a mortgage over his land.

Negotiable instrument a document detailing an obligation upon a debtor to pay a sum of money to the proper holder of the document. The obligation can be assigned through transferring the document. Examples include cheques and bills of exchange.

Nemo dat quod non habet Latin for 'no one can give what he does not have'. This illustrates the fact that parties can only transfer rights to goods that they have, and cannot transfer rights which they do not have.

Notice to quit a communication exercising a power to impose an obligation upon a party to leave land. Often used by landlords when a lease is terminated.

Novus actus interveniens Latin for 'a new interven-ing act'. A *novus actus interveniens* will be considered to break the chain of causation from the defendant's breach of contract to the claimant's loss.

Obiter dicta/dictum a judicial statement not form-ing part of the *ratio decidendi* of a decision.

Obligee a party to whom an obligation is owed.

Obligor a party who owes an obligation.

Offeree a party receiving an offer.

Offeror a party making an offer.

Parol evidence evidence which is extrinsic to a writ-ten document. The 'parol evidence rule' provides that extrinsic evidence should not be admissible if it would add to, vary, or contradict the written agreement. This rule is subject to many exceptions.

Pawn pledge of an item of personal property as **security** for a loan. For example. a person might pawn his watch in return for money from a pawnbroker. Until the money is repaid, the pawnbroker will have a security interest over the watch.

Per incuriam 'through lack of care'. A judgment decided *per incuriam* has been decided without refer-ence to an earlier judgment or statutory provision that would have been relevant.

Personal representative an umbrella term for **administrators** and **executors**.

Plaintiff the old word for claimant (the party bringing a claim).

Pledge a **bailment** that conveys possessory **title** to property owned by the pledgor (or **debtor**) to the pledgee (or **creditor**) in order to secure repayment of a debt.

Prima facie Latin for 'on the face of it'. Often used to indicate something which appears to be true, but is in fact false. For instance, prima facie we might conclude that the parties have formed a contract, but when we focus our attention, there was no acceptance of the offer.

Promisee a party to whom a promissory obligation is owed.

Promisor a party who owes a promissory obligation.

Promissory note a document containing an obligation payable by a **debtor** to the bearer of the document.

Ratio decidendi/ratio Latin for 'the reason for the decision'. It is the principle established by a case. In other words, this provides the aspect of judicial reason-ing that must be applied by future courts under the doctrine of precedent.

Receiver a person appointed to manage a company's assets, when the company is not operating as well as it could be (often in the event of **insolvency**).

Representee the person who receives a statement.

Representor the person who makes a statement.

Repudiation/repudiate a breach of a contract which entitles the innocent party to terminate the contract.

Rescission/rescind the process by which the whole transaction will be set aside and both parties restored to the position they were in before the contract was entered into. The innocent party may rescind a contract if a **vitiating factor** is present in the process of contract formation.

Salvage a concept in maritime law whereby a party who recovers another party's ship or cargo at sea becomes entitled to some monetary payment.

Security a property right over an obligor's asset, used to protect against non-compliance by the **obligor** with his obligation. Failure to comply with the obligation may result in the holder of the security selling the asset in question.

Shares units of stock in a company. Shareholders have certain rights, which vary according to the particular company in which shares are held. Common examples include an entitlement to receive dividends, and an entitlement to vote in meetings of the company.

Specific performance an order for an **obligor** to perform a positive obligation. Common examples include transferring a fee simple to land or **title** to goods.

Stay a ruling by the court which puts a hold on pro-ceedings. The hold may be granted indefinitely.

Stevedores parties who load and unload a ship's cargo.

Subpoena an official order requiring a party to pro-duce evidence or attend a hearing.

Sue on a cheque the action of enforcing a cheque against the party obligated by the cheque. The party obligated is usually a bank.

Sui generis 'of its own kind' or 'unique'.

Suit another word for an action brought in court.

Summary judgment a court order given when the defendant has no reasonable prospect of successfully defending the claimant's claim (or a particular aspect of the claim). Summary judgment is given without a full trial.

Telex an old form of communication similar to a fax machine.

Tenant the party who is granted a **lease**. Another word for **lessee**.

Tender an application to contract with the person issuing the invitation to tender. Invitations to tender are often used by public authorities who wish to contract-out various services.

Testator/testatrix a deceased person who has written a will. Testator may refer to a male or female, whereas a testatrix is always female.

Title a person who has title to goods can be considered to have a right to exclusive possession of the goods. The holder of such a right is colloquially known as the owner.

Trustee a person who has **title** to property, and manages that property for a beneficiary. A trustee often owes **fiduciary** duties.

Unliquidated damages damages which are assessed by the court, rather than fixed by the parties themselves.

Vitiating factors events which make a contract voidable and entitle the innocent party to **rescind** a contract. Such events include duress, undue influence, and misrepresentation.

Index